David Friedrich Strauss, George Eliot

The Life of Jesus

Critically Examined

David Friedrich Strauss, George Eliot

The Life of Jesus
Critically Examined

ISBN/EAN: 9783743314481

Hergestellt in Europa, USA, Kanada, Australien, Japan

Cover: Foto ©Lupo / pixelio.de

Manufactured and distributed by brebook publishing software
(www.brebook.com)

David Friedrich Strauss, George Eliot

The Life of Jesus

THE

LIFE OF JESUS,

CRITICALLY EXAMINED

BY

DR. DAVID FRIEDRICH STRAUSS.

Translated from the fourth German Edition

BY

MARIAN EVANS,

TRANSLATOR OF FEUERBACH'S "ESSENCE OF CHRISTIANITY."

VOL. I.

NEW YORK:

PUBLISHED BY CALVIN BLANCHARD,

76 NASSAU STREET.

1860.

CERTIOR factus ex Britannia, librum meum, quem da vita Jesu XI ab hinc annis composui, virorum ejusmodi studiis faventium cura in linguam Britannicam translatum, brevi illic in publicum prodiiturum esse, lætitia anxietate temperata commoveor.

Nam ut gratulari sibi æquum est auctorem, cujus operi contigit, patriæ terræ ac linguæ fines transgredi, ita sollicitudo eundem subeat necesse est, ne, qui domi placuit liber, foris displiceat, aut cujus inter populares vel adversariorum numero creverat auctoritas, apud exteros neglectus in obscuro maneat. Solum enim cœlumque vix minore libri quam plantæ periculo mutant. Et facilius quidem transtuleris opera in illis rebus versantia, de quibus inter diversas gentes communis quidam aut certe parum discrepans sensus obtinet : ut, quæ poetæ aut disciplinarum quas exactas dicunt periti proferunt, inter politiores hujus seculi nationes fere solent esse communia. Neque tamen vel hoc in librorum genere plane æquum Germano cum Britannis aut Gallis certamen. Peregrina enim cum facilius nostra quam illorum et lingua et indoles recipiat, longe frequentius poetæ quoque illorum in nostram quam nostri in illorum linguas transferuntur. At Germanicum opus in theologiæ et philosophiæ quasi confinio versans, si trajicere in Britanniam parat, ne illa quidem inter utramque gentem sensus et studiorum communione adjuvatur. Tam diversa enim utrimque via istæ disciplinæ processerunt, ut in theologia impii, in philosophia superstitiosi Britannis Germani iidem videamur. Cum iis, qui in Britannia ausi sunt, historias, Judæorum et Christianorum religione sacratas, examini ut ajunt critico subjicere, nihil agendum esset, nisi ut Lockii sui atque Humii principia philosophica, sicut at reliquas omnes historias, ita ad illas etiam, quas legibus istis hucusque superstitio subtraxerat, adhiberent : in Germania ad hoc monstri res degeneraverat, ut superstitioni a theologorum potissima parte derelictæ philosophia succurreret, critico ergo non simplex sanæ philosophiæ contra theologorum superstitionem, sed duplex et contra philosophorum ex sanioribus principiis deductas ineptas conclusiones, et contra theologorum propter philosophica ista auxilia ornamentaque inflatam atque induratam superstitionem, certamen ineundum esset. Ex hoc rei statu proprie Germanico natum opus meum, nominibus insuper atque opinionibus theologorum ac philosophorum nostratium refertum, nec scholarum etiam vocabula, quibus nostræ tantum aures

assuevere, satis evitans, a Britannorum usu ingenioque non posse
non abhorrere, tam probe scio, ut de translato in eorum linguam, li-
cet interpretatio, quantum quidem ejus inspicere potuerim, et accu-
rata et perspicua sit et librum, quantum in ipsa est, popularibus
commendet, num gaudendum mihi magnopere sit, mehercule nes-
ciam.

Accedit, quod a primo libri mei ortu duo lustra, et a recentis-
sima etiam editione unum jam lustrum intercessit. Ut tum, quum
opus inchoabam, via incedebam, quam pauci ingressi, totam emen-
sus nemo erat, ita per primum illud lustrum nullæ fere nisi adversariorum voces audiebantur, principia mea negantium et historiam
in Evangeliis vel meram, vel levissima tantum erroris rumorisve
adspersione tinctam contineri affirmantium, cum quibus non modo
non disputandum, sed a quibus ne discendum quidem quidquam
erat, quod ad rem et ad librum vere emendandum pertineret. Pro-
ximo demum lustro viri vestigia mea non refugientes neque evitan-
tes, sed persequentes, ubi egi substiteram longius progressi, rem re-
vera juverunt atque promoverunt. Narrationes in Evangeliis tra-
ditas, quas rerum vere gestarum esse persuadere mihi non potueram,
mythorum in modum, qui inter antiquas gentes inveniuntur, aut in
ore populi a minutis initiis coaluisse et eundo crevisse, aut a singu-
lis, sed qui vere ita evenisse superstitiose in animum induxerant,
fictas esse existimaveram. Quod ut sufficit explicandis plerisque
eorum, quæ dubitationem moventia tribus prioribus Evangeliis con-
tinentur : ita quarti Evangelii auctorem ad tuendas et illustrandas
sententias suas haud raro meras fabulas scientem confinxisse, a
Baurio, theologo Tubingensi doctissimo, nuper ita demonstratum
est, ut critici me judicii rigori me religiosius quam verius temperasse
intelligam. Dumque prima a Christo secula accuratius perscrutan-
tur, partes partiumque certamina, quibus nova ecclesia commoveba
tur, in apricum proverunt, narrationum haud paucarum, quas fabulas esse ego bene quidem perspexeram, sed unde ortæ essent de-
monstrare non valueram, veram in illis primæ ecclesiæ motibus ori-
ginem detegere theologis Tubingensibus contigit.

Imperfectum igitur opus meum, ut solent rerum initia, non ob
hoc tamen, quod sententiæ deest, timerem, ne a Britannis sperne-
tur, nisi formæ etiam illud quod supra dixi peregrinum atque inusi-
tatum accederet. Qui si suum Hennellium non audiverunt, de iisdem rebus cum Britannis Britannice agentem, quomodo audient, si
quis Germanus surget, cujus liber cum sua lingua non potuerit co-
gitandi quoque disputandique morem prorsus Germanicum exuere?
Sed absit omen verbis meis, atque ut pridem in Germania, ita mox
in Britannia jaceat liber hic εἰς πτῶσιν καὶ ἀνάστασιν πολλῶν καὶ εἰς
σημεῖον ἀντιλεγόμενον ὅπως ἂν ἀποκαλιφθῶσιν ἐκ πολλῶν καρδιῶν δια-
λογισμοί.

STRAUSS.

Scribebam Heilbronnæ,
Med. mens. April. a. 1846.

PREFACE.

IT appeared to the author of the work, the first half of which is herewith submitted to the public, that it was time to substitute a new mode of considering the life of Jesus, in the place of the antiquated systems of supranaturalism and naturalism. This application of the term antiquated will in the present day be more readily admitted in relation to the latter system than to the former. For while the interest excited by the explanations of the miracles and the conjectural facts of the rationalists has long ago cooled, the commentaries now most read are those which aim to adapt the supranatural interpretation of the sacred history to modern taste. Nevertheless, in point of fact, the orthodox view of this history became superannuated earlier than the rationalistic, since it was only because the former had ceased to satisfy an advanced state of culture, that the latter was developed, while the recent attempts to recover, by the aid of a mystical philosophy, the supranatural point of view held by our forefathers, betray themselves, by the exaggerating spirit in which they are conceived, to be final, desperate efforts to render the past present, the inconceivable conceivable.

The new point of view, which must take the place of the above, is the mythical. This theory is not brought to bear on the evangelical history for the first time in the present work: it has long been applied to particular parts of that history, and is here only extended to its entire tenor. It is not by any means meant that the whole history of Jesus is to be represented as mythical, but only that every part of it is to be subjected to a critical examination, to ascertain whether it have not some admixture of the mythical. The exegesis of the ancient church set out from the double presupposition: first, that the gospels contained a history, and secondly, that this history was a supernatural one. Rationalism rejected the latter of these presuppositions, but only to cling the more tenaciously to the former, maintaining that these books present unadulterated, though only natural, history. Science cannot rest satisfied with this half-measure: the other presupposition also must be relinquished, and the inquiry must first be made whether in fact, and to what extent, the ground on which we stand in the gospels is historical. This is the natural course of things, and thus far the appearance of a work like the present is not only justifiable, but even necessary.

It is certainly not therefore evident that the author is precisely the individual whose vocation it is to appear in this position. He has a very vivid consciousness that many others would have been able to execute such a work with incomparably superior erudition. Yet on the other hand he believes himself to be at least possessed of one qualification which especially fitted him to undertake this task. The majority of the most learned and acute theologians of the present day fail in the main requirement for such a work, a requirement without which no amount of learning will suffice to achieve anything in the domain of criticism, namely, the internal liberation of the feelings and intellect from certain religious and dogmatical presuppositions; and this the author early attained by means of philosophical studies. If theologians regard this absence of presupposition from his work, as unchristian: he regards the believing presuppositions of theirs as unscientific. Widely as in this respect the tone of the present work may be contrasted with the edifying devoutness and enthusiastic mysticism of recent books on similar subjects; still it will nowhere depart from the seriousness of science, or sink into frivolity; and it seems a just demand in return, that the judgments which are passed upon it should also confine themselves to the domain of science, and keep aloof from bigotry and fanaticism.

The author is aware that the essence of the Christian faith is perfectly independent of his criticism. The supernatural birth of Christ, his miracles, his resurrection and ascension, remain eternal truths, whatever doubts may be cast on their reality as historical facts. The certainty of this can alone give calmness and dignity to our criticism, and distinguish it from the naturalistic criticism of the last century, the design of which was, with the historical fact, to subvert also the religious truth, and which thus necessarily became frivolous. A dissertation at the close of the work will show that the dogmatic significance of the life of Jesus remains inviolate: in the mean time let the calmness and insensibility with which, in the course of it, criticism undertakes apparently dangerous operations, be explained solely by the security of the author's conviction that no injury is threatened to the Christian faith. Investigations of this kind may, however, inflict a wound on the faith of individuals. Should this be the case with theologians, they have in their science the means of healing such wounds, from which, if they would not remain behind the development of their age, they cannot possibly be exempt. For the laity the subject is certainly not adequately prepared; and for this reason the present work is so framed, that at least the unlearned among them will quickly and often perceive that the book is not destined for them. If from curiosity or excessive zeal against heresy they persist in their persual, they will then have, as Schleiermacher says on a similar occasion, to bear the punishment in their conscience, since their feelings directly urge on them the conviction that they understand not that of which they are ambitious to speak.

A new opinion, which aims to fill the place of an older one, ought fully to adjust its position with respect to the latter. Hence the way to the mythical view is here taken in each particular point through the supranaturalistic and rationalistic opinions and their respective refutations; but, as becomes a valid refutation, with an acknowledgment of what is true in the opinions combated, and an adoption of this truth into the new theory. This method also brings with it the extrinsic advantage, that the work may now serve as a repertory of the principal opinions and treatises concerning all parts of the evangelical history. The author has not, however, aimed to give a complete bibliographical view of this department of theological literature, but, where it was possible, has adhered to the chief works in each separate class of opinions. For the rationalistic system the works of Paulus remain classical, and are therefore preeminently referred to; for the orthodox opinions, the commentary of Olshausen is especially important, as the most recent and approved attempt to render the supranaturel interpretation philosophical and modern; while as a preliminary to a critical investigation of the life of Jesus, the commentaries of Fritzsche are excellently adapted, since they exhibit, together with uncommon philological learning, that freedom from prejudice and scientific indifference to results and consequences, which form the first condition of progress in this region of inquiry.

The second volume, which will open with a detailed examination of the miracles of Jesus, and which will conclude the whole work, is already prepared and will be in the press immediately on the completion of the first.

THE AUTHOR.

Tübingen, 24th May, 1835.

PREFACE

TO THE FOURTH GERMAN EDITION.

———

As this new edition of my critical examination of the life of
Jesus appears simultaneously with the first volume of my *Dogmatik*,
it will not be expected to contain any essential alterations. Indeed,
even in the absence of other labours, I should scarcely have been
inclined to undertake such on the present occasion. The critical
researches prompted by the appearance of my work have, after the
stormy reaction of the first few years, at length entered on that
quiet course, which promises the most valuable assistance towards
the confirmation and more precise determination of the negative results at which I have arrived. But these fruits still require some
years for their maturing; and it must therefore be deferred to a future opportunity to enrich this work by the use of them. I could
not persuade myself to do so, at least in the present instance, by
prosecuting a polemic against opposite opinions. Already in the
last edition there was more of a polemical character than accorded
with the unity and calmness proper to such a work; hence I was in
this respect admonished rather to abridge than to amplify. But
that edition also contained too much of compliance. The intermingling voices of opponents, critics, and fellow-labourers, to which I
held it a duty attentively to listen, had confused the idea of the
work in my mind; in the diligent comparison of divergent opinions
I had lost sight of the subject itself. Hence on coming with a more
collected mind to this last revision, I found alterations at which I
could not but wonder, and by which I had evidently done myself
injustice. In all these passages the earlier readings are now restored, and thus my labour in this new edition has chiefly consisted in
whetting, as it were, my good sword, to free it from the notches
made in it rather by my own grinding, than by the blows of my
enemies.

THE AUTHOR.

Stuttgard, 17th October, 1840.

CONTENTS.

THE LIFE OF JESUS.

INTRODUCTION.

DEVELOPMENT OF THE MYTHICAL POINT OF VIEW IN RELATION TO THE GOSPEL HISTORIES.

§ 1. INEVITABLE RISE OF DIFFERENT MODES OF EXPLAINING SACRED HISTORIES.

WHEREVER a religion, resting upon written records, prolongs and extends the sphere of its dominion, accompanying its votaries through the varied and progressive stages of mental cultivation, a discrepancy between the representations of those ancient records, referred to as sacred, and the notions of more advanced periods of mental development, will inevitably sooner or later arise. In the first instance this disagreement is felt in reference only to the unessential—the external form: the expressions and delineations are seen to be inappropriate; but by degrees it manifests itself also in regard to that which is essential; the fundamental ideas and opinions in these early writings fail to be commensurate with a more advanced civilization. As long as this discrepancy is either not in itself so considerable, or else is not so universally discerned and acknowledged, as to lead to a complete renunciation of these Scriptures as of sacred authority, so long will a system of reconciliation by means of interpretation be adopted and pursued by those who have a more or less distinct consciousness of the existing incongruity.

A main element in all religious records is sacred history: a history of events in which the divine enters, without intermediation, into the human: the ideal thus assuming an immediate embodiment. But as the progress of mental cultivation mainly consists in the gradual recognition of a chain of causes and effects connecting natural phenomena with each other; so the mind in its development becomes ever increasingly conscious of those mediate links which are indispensable to the realization of the ideal;* and hence the discrepancy between the modern culture and the ancient records, with regard to their historical portion, becomes so apparent, that the immediate intervention of the divine in human affairs loses its probability. Besides, as the humanity of these records is the humanity of an early period, consequently of an age comparatively undeveloped and necessarily rude, a sense of repulsion is likewise excited. The incongruity may be thus expressed. *The divine cannot so have happened;* (not immediately, not in forms so rude;) or, *that which has so happened cannot have been divine:*—and if a reconciliation be sought by means of interpretation, it will be attempted to prove, either that the divine did not manifest itself in the manner related,—which is to deny the historical validity of the ancient Scriptures; or, that the actual occurrences were not divine,—which is to explain away the absolute contents of these books. In both cases the interpretation may be partial or impartial: partial, if undertaken with a determination to close the eyes to the secretly recognized fact of the disagreement between the modern culture and the ancient records, and to see only in such interpretation the original signification of these records; impartial, if it unequivocally acknowledges and openly avows that the matters narrated in these books must be viewed in a light altogether different from that in which they were regarded by the authors themselves. This latter method, however, by no means involves the entire rejection of the religious documents; on the contrary, the essential may be firmly retained, whilst the unessential is unreservedly abandoned.

§ 2. DIFFERENT EXPLANATIONS OF SACRED LEGENDS AMONG THE GREEKS.

THOUGH the Hellenic religion cannot be said to have rested upon written records, it became enshrined in the Greek poems, for example, in those of Homer and Hesiod; and these, no less than its orally transmitted legends, did not fail to receive continually varying interpretations, successively adapted to the progressive intellectual culture of the Greeks. At an early period the rigid philosophy of the Greeks, and under its influence even some of the Greek poets, recognized the impossibility of ascribing to Deity manifestations so grossly human, so immediate, and so barbarous, as those exhibited and represented as divine in the wild conflicts of Hesiod's Theogony, and in the domestic occupations and trivial pursuits of the Homeric deities. Hence arose the quarrel of Plato, and prior to him of Pindar, with Homer;† hence the cause which induced Anaxagoras, to whom the invention of the allegorical mode of interpretation is ascribed, to apply the Homeric delineations to virtue and to justice;‡

---

* [This passage varies slightly from the original, a subsequent amplification by Dr. Strauss being incorporated with it.—TR.] † Plato, de Republ. ii. p. 377. Steph.; Pindar, Nem. vii. 31. ‡ Diog. Laërt. L. ii. c. iii. No. 7.

hence it was that the Stoics understood the Theogony of Hesiod as relating to the action of the elements, which, according to their notions, constituted, in their highest union, the divine nature.* Thus did these several thinkers, each according to his own peculiar mode of thought, succeed in discovering an absolute meaning in these representations : the one finding in them a physical, the other an ethical signification, whilst, at the same time, they gave up their external form, ceasing to regard them as strictly historical.

On the other hand, the more popular and sophistical culture of another class of thinkers led them to opposite conclusions. Though, in their estimation, every semblance of the divine had evaporated from this histories ; though they were convinced that the proceedings ascribed to the gods were not godlike, still they did not abandon the historical sense of these narratives. With Evemerus† they transformed the subjects of these histories from gods to men, to heroes and sages of antiquity, kings and tyrants, who, through deeds of might and valour, had acquired divine honours. Some indeed went still further, and, with Polybius,‡ considered the whole system of heathen theology as a fable, invented by the founders of states to awe the people into subjection.

§ 3. ALLEGORICAL INTERPRETATIONS AMONG THE HEBREWS—PHILO.

WHILST, on the one hand, the isolation and stability of the Hebrews served to retard the development of similar manifestations amongst this people, on the other hand, when once actually developed, they were the more marked ; because, in proportion to the high degree of authority ascribed to the sacred records, was the skill and caution required in their interpretation. Thus, even in Palestine, subsequent to the exile, and particularly after the time of the Maccabees, many ingenious attempts were made to interpret the Old Testament so as to remove offensive literalities, supply deficiencies, and introduce the notions of a later age. Examples of this system of interpretation occur in the writings of the Rabbins, and even in the New Testament :§ but it was at that place where the Jewish mind came into contact with Greek civilization, and under its influence was carried beyond the limits of its own national culture,—namely, at Alexandria,—that the allegorical mode of interpretation was first consistently applied to the whole body of historical narrative in the Old Testament. Many had prepared the way, but it was Philo who first fully developed the doctrine of both a common and a deeper sense of the Holy Scriptures. He was by no means inclined to cast away the former, but generally placed the two together, side by side, and even declared himself opposed to those who, everywhere and without necessity, sacrificed the literal to the higher

* Cic. de Nat. Deor. i. 10. 15.   Comp. Athenag. Leg. 22.   Tatian, c. Graec. Orat. 21. Clement. homil. 6, 1 f.   † Diodor. Sic.   Bibl. Fragm. L. vi.   Cic. de Nat. Deor. i. 42. ‡ Hist. vi. 56. § Döpke, die Hermeneutik der neutestamentlichen Schriftsteller, S. 123. ff.

signification. * In many cases, however, he absolutely discarded the verbal meaning and historical conception, and considered the narrative merely as the figurative representation of an idea. He did so, for example, whenever the sacred story appeared to him to present delineations unworthy of Deity, tending either to materialism or anthropomorphism, or otherwise to contain contradictions.*

The fact that the Jews, whilst they adopted this mode of explaining the Old Testament, (which, in order to save the purity of the intrinsic signification, often sacrificed the historical form,) were never led into the opposite system of Evemerus, (which preserved the historical form by divesting the history of the divine, and reducing it to a record of mere human events,) is to be ascribed to the tenacity with which that people ever adhered to the supernatural point of view. The latter mode of interpretation was first brought to bear upon the Old Testament by the Christians.

§ 4. ALLEGORICAL INTERPRETATIONS AMONG THE CHRISTIANS—ORIGEN.

To the early Christians who, antecedent to the fixing of the christian canon, made especial use of the Old Testament as their principal sacred record, an allegorical interpretation was the more indispensable, inasmuch as they had made greater advances beyond the views of the Old Testament writers than even the most enlightened of the Jews. It was no wonder therefore that this mode of explanation, already in vogue among the Jews, was almost universally adopted by the primitive christian churches. It was however again in Alexandria that it found the fullest application amongst the Christians, and that in connexion with the name of Origen. Origen attributes a treefold meaning to the Scriptures, corresponding with his distribution of the human being into three parts: the literal sense answering to the body; the moral, to the soul; and the mystical, to the spirit.† The rule with him was to retain all three meanings, though differing in worth; in some particular cases, however, he was of opinion that the literal interpretation either gave no sense at all, or else a perverted sense, in order the more directly to impel the reader to the discovery of its mystical signification. Origen's repeated observation that it is not the purpose of the biblical narratives to transmit old tales, but to instruct in the rules of life;‡ his assertion that the merely literal acceptation of many of the narratives would prove destructive of the christian religion;§ and his application of the passage "The letter killeth, but the spirit giveth life,"‖ to the relative worth of the allegorical and the literal modes of biblical interpretation, may be understood as indicating only the

---

* Gfrörer. Dähne. † Homil. 5. in Levit. § 5. ‡ Homil 2. in Exod. iii.: *Nolite putare, ut sæpe jam diximus, veterum vobis fabulas recitari, sed doceri vos per hæc, ut agnoscatis ordinem vitæ.* § Homil. 5. in Levit. i.: *Hæc omnia, nisi alio sensu accipiamus quam titeræ textus ostendit, obstaculum magis et subversionem Christianæ religioni, quam hortationem ædificationemque prestabunt.* ‖ Contra Cels. vi. 70.

inferiority of the literal to the deeper signification. But the literal
sense is decidedly given up when it is said, "Every passage of
Scripture has a spiritual element, but not every one has a corporeal
element;"* "A spiritual truth often exists embodied in a corporeal
falsehood;"† "The Scriptures contain many things which never
came to pass, interwoven with the history, and he must be dull
indeed who does not of his own accord observe that much which
the Scriptures represent as having happened never actually occurred."‡ Among the passages which Origen regarded as admitting
no other than an allegorical interpretation, besides those which too
sensibly humanized the Deity,§ he included those which attributed
unworthy action to individuals who had held intimate communion
with God.‖

It was not however from the Old Testament views alone that
Origen had, in consequence of his christian training, departed so
widely that he felt himself compelled, if he would retain his reverence for the sacred records, to allegorize their contents, as a means
of reconciling the contradiction which had arisen between them and
his own mind. There was much likewise in the New Testament
writings which so little accorded with his philosophical notions, that
he found himself constrained to adopt a similar proceeding in reference to them. He reasoned thus:—the New Testament and the Old
are the work of the same spirit, and this spirit would proceed in
the same manner in the production of the one and of the other, in-
terweaving fiction with reality, in order thereby to direct the mind,
to the spiritual signification.¶ In a remarkable passage of his work
against Celsus, Origen classes together, and in no ambiguous language, the partially fabulous stories of profane history, and of heathen
mythology, with the gospel narratives.** He expresses himself as
follows: "In almost every history it is a difficult task, and not
unfrequently an impossible one, to demonstrate the reality of the
events recorded, however true they may in fact be. Let us suppose
some individual to deny the reality of a Trojan war on account of the
incredibilities mixed up with the history; as, for example, the birth
of Achilles from a goddess of the sea. How could we substantiate
the fact, encumbered as it is with the numerous and undeniable

* De principp. I. iv. § 20: πᾶσα μὲν (γραφή) ἔχει τὸ πνευματικὸν, οὐ πᾶσα δὲ τὸ σωματικόν. † Comm. in Joann. Tom. x. § 4 :—σωζομένου πολλάκις τοῦ ἀληθοῦς πνευ-ματικοῦ ἐν τῷ σωματικῷ, ὡς ἂν εἴποι τις, ψεύδει. ‡ De principp. iv. 15: συντέθηνεν ἡ γραφῇ τῇ ἱστορίᾳ τὸ μὴ γενόμενον, πῆ μὲν μὴ δυνατὸν γενέσθαι, πῆ δὲ δυνατὸν μὲν γενέσθαι, οὐ μὴν γεγενημένον. De principp. iv. 16: καὶ τί δεῖ πλείω λέγειν; τῶν μὴ πάνυ ἀμβλέων μυρία ὅσα τοιαῦτα δυναμένων συναγαγεῖν, γεγραμμένα μὲν ὡς γεγονότα, οὐ γεγονητμένα δὲ κατὰ τὴν λέξιν. § De principp. iv. 16. ‖ Homil. 6, in Gen. iii.: Quae nobis aedificatio erit, legentibus, Abraham, tantum patriarcham, non solum mentitum esse Abimelech regi, sed et pudicitiam conjugis prodidisse ? Quid nos aedificat tanti patriarchae uxor, si putetur contami-nationibus exposita per conniventiam maritalem ? Haec Judaei putent et si qui cum eis sunt literae amici, non spiritus. ¶ De principp. iv. 16: οὐ μόνον δὲ περὶ τῶν πρὸ τῆς παρουσίας ταῦτα τὸ πνεῦμα ᾠκονόμησεν, ἀλλ', ἅτε τὸ αὐτὸ τυγχάνον καὶ ἀπὸ τοῦ ἑνὸς θεοῦ, τὸ ὅμοιον καὶ ἐπὶ τῶν εὐαγγελίων πεποίηκε καὶ ἐπὶ τῶν ἀποστόλων, οὐδὲ τοί των πάντη ἄκρατον τὴν ἱστορίαν τῶν προσιφασμένων κατὰ τὸ σωματικὸν ἐχόντων, μὴ γεγενημένων. ** Contra Cel-sum, i. 40.

poetical fictions which have, in some unascertainable manner, become interwoven with the generally admitted account of the war between the Greeks and the Trojans? There is no alternative: he who would study history with understanding, and not suffer himself to be deluded, must weigh each separate detail, and consider what is worthy of credit and may be believed without further evidence; what, on the contrary, must be regarded as merely figurative; (τίνα δὲ τροπολογήσει) always bearing in mind the aim of the narrator,—and what must be wholly mistrusted as being written with intent to please certain individuals." In conclusion Origen says, "I was desirous of making these preliminary observations in relation to the entire history of Jesus given in the Gospels, not with the view of exacting from the enlightened a blind and baseless belief, but with design to show how indispensable to the study of this history are not only judgment and diligent examination, but, so to speak, the very penetrating into the mind of the author, in order to discover the particular aim with which each narrative may have been written."

We here see Origen almost transcending the limits of his own customary point of view, and verging towards the more modern mythical view. But if his own prepossessions in favour of the supernatural, and his fear of giving offence to the orthodox church, combined to hinder him from making a wider application of the allegorical mode of interpretation to the Old Testament, the same causes operated still more powerfully in relation to the New Testament; so that when we further inquire of which of the gospel histories in particular did Origen reject the historical meaning, in order to hold fast a truth worthy of God? the instances will prove to be meager in the extreme. For when he says, in illustration of the above-mentioned passage, that amongst other things, it is not to be unterstood literally that Satan showed to Jesus all the kingdoms of the earth from a mountain, because this is impossible to the bodily eye; he here gives not a strictly allegorical interpretation, but merely a different turn to the literal sense, which, according to him, relates not to an external fact, but to the internal fact of a vision. Again, even where the text offers a tempting opportunity of sacrificing the literal to the spiritual meaning, as, for example, the cursing of the fig-tree,* Origen does not speak out freely. He is most explicit when speaking of the expulsion of the buyers and sellers from the temple; he characterizes the conduct of Jesus according to the literal interpretation, as assuming and seditious.† He moreover expressly remarks that the Scriptures contain many more historical than merely scriptural truths.‡

---

* Comm. in Matth. Tom. xvi. 26.
† Comm. in Joann. Tom. x. 17.
‡ De principp. iv. 19. After Origen, that kind of allegory only which left the historical sense unimpaired was retained in the church; and where, subsequently, a giving up of the verbal meaning is spoken of, this refers merely to a trope or a simile.

§ 5. TRANSITION TO MORE MODERN TIMES—DEISTS AND NATURAL-
ISTS OF THE 17TH AND 18TH CENTURIES—THE WOLFENBUETTEL
FRAGMENTIST.

THUS was developed one of those forms of interpretation to which
the Hebrew and Christian Scriptures, in common with all other religious records, in relation to their historical contents, became necessarily subjected; that, namely, which recognizes in them the divine, but denies it to have actually manifested itself in so immediate
a manner. The other principal mode of interpretation, which, to a
certain extent, acknowledges the course of events to have been historically true, but assigns it to a human and not a divine origin, was
developed amongst the enemies of Christianity by a Celsus, a Porphyry, and a Julian. They indeed rejected much of the history as
altogether fabulous : but they admitted many of the incidents related
of Moses, Jesus, and others, to be historical facts : these facts were
however considered by them as originating from common motives ;
and they attributed their apparently supernatural character either to
gross fraud or impious sorcery.

It is worthy of observation that the circumstances attending the
introduction of these several modes of interpretation into the heathen
and Jewish religions, on the one hand, and into the christian religion, on the other, were different. The religion and sacred literature of the Greeks and Hebrews had been gradually developed with
the development of the nation, and it was not until the intellectual
culture of the people had outgrown the religion of their fathers, and
the latter was in consequence verging towards decay, that the discrepancy which is the source of these varying interpretations became
apparent. Christianity, on the contrary, came into a world of already
advanced civilization ; which was, with the exception of that of Palestine, the Judaico-Hellenistic and the Greek. Consequently a disagreement manifested itself at the very beginning ; it was not now
however, as in former times, between modern culture and an ancient
religion, but between a new religion and ancient culture. The production of allegorical interpretations among the Pagans and the Hebrews, was a sign that their religion had lost its vitality : the allegories of Origen and the attacks of Celsus, in reference to Christianity,
were evidences rather that the world had not as yet duly accommodated itself to the new religion. As however with the christianizing
of the Roman empire, and the overthrow of the chief heresies, the
christian principle gained an ever-increasing supremacy : as the
schools of heathen wisdom closed : and the uncivilized Germanic
tribes lent themselves to the teaching of the church :—the world,
during the tedious centuries of the middle ages, was satisfied with
Christianity, both in form and in substance. Almost all traces of
those modes of interpretation which presuppose a discrepancy between the culture of a nation, or of the world, and religion, in consequence disappeared. The reformation effected the first breach in

the solid structure of the faith of the church. It was the first vital expression of a culture, which had now in the heart of Christendom itself, as formerly in relation to Paganism and Judaism, acquired strength and independence sufficient to create a reaction against the soil of its birth, the prevailing religion. This reaction, so long as it was directed against the dominant hierarchy, constituted the sublime, but quickly terminated, drama of the reformation. In its later direction against the Bible, it appeared again upon the stage in the barren revolutionary efforts of deism; and many and various have been the forms it has assumed in its progress down to the present time.

The deists and naturalists of the seventeenth and eighteenth centuries renewed the polemic attacks of the pagan adversaries of Christianity in the bosom of the christian church; and gave to the public an irregular and confused mass of criticisms, impugning the authenticity and credibility of the Scriptures, and exposing to contempt the events recorded in the sacred volume. Toland,* Bolingbroke,† and others, pronounced the Bible to be a collection of unauthentic and fabulous books; whilst some spared no pains to despoil the biblical histories, and the heroes whose actions they celebrate, of every ray of divine light. Thus, according to Morgan,‡ the law of Moses is a miserable system of superstition, blindness, and slavery; the Jewish priests are deceivers; and the Jewish prophets the originators of the distractions and civil wars of the two kingdoms of Judah and Israel. According to Chubb,§ the Jewish religion cannot be a revelation from God, because it debases the moral character of the Deity by attributing to him arbitrary conduct, partiality for a particular people, and above all, the cruel command to exterminate the Canaanitish nations. Assaults were likewise made by these and other deists upon the New Testament: the apostles were suspected of being actuated by selfish and mercenary motives :‖ the character of Jesus himself was not spared,¶ and the fact of his resurrection was denied.** The miracles of Jesus, wrought by an immediate exercise of divine power in human acts and concerns, were made the particular objects of attack by Woolston.†† This writer is also worthy of notice on account of the peculiar position taken by him between the ancient allegorists and the modern naturalists. His whole reasoning turns upon the alternative; either to retain the historical reality of the miracles narrated in the Bible, and thus to sacrifice the divine character of the narratives, and reduce the miracles to mere artifices, miserable juggleries, or common-place deceptions; or, in order to hold fast the divine character of these narratives, to reject them entirely as details of actual occurrences, and regard them as historical

* In his Amyntor, 1698. See Leland's View of the Deistical Writers. † See Leland. ‡ In his work entitled The Moral Philosopher. § Posthumous Works, 1748. ‖ Chubb, Posthumous Works, i. 102. ¶ Ibid. ii. 269. ** The Resurrection of Jesus Considered, by a Moral Philosopher, 1744. †† Six Discourses on the Miracles of our Saviour. Published singly, from 1727—1729.

representations of certain spiritual truths. Woolston cites the authority of the most distinguished allegorists among the fathers in support of this view. He is wrong however in representing them as supplanting the literal by the figurative meaning. These ancient fathers, on the contrary, were disposed to retain both the literal and the allegorical meaning. (A few examples in Origen, it is true, are an exception to this rule.) It may be doubted, from the language of Woolston, which alternative was adopted by himself. If we reason from the fact, that before he appeared as the opponent of the commonly entertained views of Christianity, he occupied himself with allegorical interpretations of the Scriptures,* we may be led to consider the latter alternative as expressing his real conviction. On the other hand, he enlarges with so evident a predilection on the absurdities of the miracles, when literally understood, and the manner in which he treats the whole subject is so tinged with levity, that we may suspect the Deist to put forward the allegorical interpretations merely as a screen, from behind which he might inveigh the more unreservedly against the literal signification.

Similar deistical objections against the Bible, and the divine character of its history, were propagated in Germany, chiefly by an anonymous author (Reimarus) whose manuscripts were discovered by Lessing in the Wolfenbüttel library. Some portions of these manuscripts, called the "Wolfenbüttel Fragments," were published by Lessing in 1774. They consist of Essays, one of which treats of the many arguments which may be urged against revealed religion in general; the others relate partly to the Old and partly to the New Testament. 'It is the opinion of the Fragmentist, in relation to the Old Testament, first, that the men, of whom the Scriptures narrate that they had immediate communications with God, were so unworthy, that such intercourse, admitting its reality, compromised the character of Deity; secondly, that the result of this intercourse,—the instructions and laws alleged to have been thus divinely communicated,—were so barbarous and destructive, that to ascribe them to God is impossible: and thirdly, that the accompanying miracles were at once absurd and incredible. From the whole, it appears to him clear, that the divine communications were only pretended; and that the miracles were delusions, practised with the design of giving stability and efficiency to certain laws and institutions highly advantageous to the rulers and priests. The author finds much to condemn in the conduct of the patriarchs, and their simulations of divine communications: such as the command to Abraham to sacrifice his son. But it is chiefly Moses upon whom he seeks, in a long section, to cast all the obloquy of an impostor, who did not scruple to employ the most disgraceful means in order to make himself the despotic ruler of a free people: who, to effect his purpose, feigned divine apparitions, and pretended to have received the command of God to perpetrate acts which, but for this divine sanction, would

* Schröckh, Kirchengesch. seit der Reform. 6 Th. S. 191.

have been stigmatized as fraudulent, as highway robbery, as inhuman barbarity. For instance, the spoiling of the Egyptians, and the extirpation of the inhabitants of Canaan: atrocities which, when introduced by the words "*Jehovah hath said it*," became instantly transformed into deeds worthy of God. The Fragmentist is as little disposed to admit the divinity of the New Testament histories. He considers the aim of Jesus to have been political; and his connexion with John the Baptist a preconcerted arrangement, by which the one party should recommend the other to the people. He views the death of Jesus as an event by no means foreseen by himself, but which frustrated all his plans; a catastrophe which his disciples knew not how else to repair than by the fraudulent pretence that Jesus was risen from the dead, and by an artful alteration of his doctrines.*

§ 6.   NATURAL MODE OF EXPLANATION ADOPTED BY THE RATIONAL-ISTS—EICHHORN—PAULUS.

WHILST the reality of the biblical revelation, together with the divine origin and supernatural character of the Jewish and Christian histories, were tenaciously maintained in opposition to the English deists by numerous English apologists, and in opposition to the Wolfenbüttel Fragmentist by the great majority of German theologians, there arose a distinct class of theologians in Germany, who struck into a new path. The ancient pagan mythology, as understood by Evemerus, admitted of two modes of explanation, each of which was in fact adopted. The deities of the popular worship might, on the one hand, be regarded as good and benevolent men; as wise lawgivers, and just rulers, of early times, whom the gratitude of their contemporaries and posterity had encircled with divine glory: or they might, on the other hand, be viewed as artful impostors and cruel tyrants, who had veiled themselves in a nimbus of divinity, for the purpose of subjugating the people to their dominion. So, likewise, in the purely human explanation of the bible histories, besides the method of the deists to regard the subjects of these narratives as wicked and deceitful men, there was yet another course open: to divest these individuals of their immediate divinity, but to accord to them an undegraded humanity; not indeed to look upon their deeds as miraculous;—as little on the other hand to decry them as impositions;—but to explain their proceedings as altogether natural, yet morally irreprehensible. If the Naturalist was led by his special enmity to the Christianity of the church to the former explanation, the Rationalist, anxious, on the contrary, to remain within the pale of the church, was attracted towards the latter.

Eichhorn, in his critical examination of the Wolfenbüttel Fragments,† directly opposes this rationalistic view to that maintained by the Naturalist. He agrees with the Fragmentist in refusing to

* Fragmente des Wolfenbüttelschen Ungenannten von G. E. Lessing herausgegeben.
† Recension der übrigen, noch ungedruckten Werke des Wolfenbüttler Fragmentisten, in Eichhorns allgemeiner Bibliothek, erster Band 1. u. 2. Stück.

recognize an immediate divine agency, at all events in the narratives of early date. The mythological researches of a Heyne had so far enlarged his circle of vision as to lead Eichhorn to perceive that divine interpositions must be alike admitted, or alike denied, in the primitive histories of all people. It was the practice of all nations, of the Grecians as well as the Orientals, to refer every unexpected or inexplicable occurrence immediately to the Deity. The sages of antiquity lived in continual communion with superior intelligences. Whilst these representations (such is Eichhorn's statement of the matter) are always, in reference to the Hebrew records, understood verbally and literally, it has hitherto been customary to explain similar representations in the pagan histories, by presupposing either deception and gross falsehood, or the misinterpretation and corruption of tradition. But Eichhorn thinks justice evidently requires that Hebrew and pagan history should be treated in the same way; so that intercourse with celestial beings during a state of infancy, must either be accorded to all nations, pagan and Hebrew, or equally denied to all. The mind hesitates to make so universal an admission : first, on account of the not unfrequent errors contained in religions claiming to have been divinely communicated; secondly, from a sense of the difficulty of explaining the transition of the human race from a state of divine tutelage to one of self-dependence; and lastly, because in proportion as intelligence increases, and the authenticity of the records may be more and more confidently relied upon, in the same proportion do these immediate divine influences invariably disappear. If, accordingly, the notion of supernatural interposition is to be rejected with regard to the Hebrews, as well as to all other people, the view generally taken of pagan antiquity presents itself, at first sight, as that most obviously applicable to the early Hebrews; namely, that their pretended revelations were based upon deceit and falsehood, or that their miraculous histories should be referred to the misrepresentations and corruptions of tradition. This is the view of the subject actually applied by the Fragmentist to the Old Testament; a representation, says Eichhorn, from which the mind on a nearer contemplation recoils. Is it conceivable that the greatest men of antiquity, whose influence operated so powerfully and so beneficially upon their age, should one and all have been impostors, and yet have escaped the detection of their contemporaries?

According to Eichhorn, so perverted a view could arise only in a mind that refused to interpret the ancient records in the spirit of their age. Truly, had they been composed with all the philosophical accuracy of the writers of the present day, we should have been compelled to find in them either actual divine interpositions, or a fraudulent pretence. But they are the production of an infant and unscientific age : and treat, without reserve of divine interventions, in accordance with the conceptions and phraseology of that early period. So that, in point of fact, we have neither miracles to wonder at, on the one hand, nor deceptions to unmask on the other; but simply the language of a former age to translate into that of our own day. Eichhorn observes that before the human race had gained a knowledge of the true causes of things, all occurrences were referred to supernatural agencies, or to the interposition of superhuman beings. Lofty conceptions, noble resolves, useful inventions and regulations, but more especially vivid dreams, were the operations of that Deity under whose immediate influence they believed themselves placed. Manifestations of distinguished intelligence and skill, by which some individual excited the wonder of the people, were regarded as miraculous; as signs of supernatural endowments, and of a particular intercourse with higher beings. And this was the belief, not of the people only, but also of these eminent individuals, who entertained no doubt of the fact, and who exulted in the full conviction of being in mysterious connexion with the Deity. Eichhorn is of opinion that no objection can be urged against the attempt to resolve all the Mosaic narratives into natural occurrences, and thus far he concedes to the Fragmentist his primary position; but he rejects his inference that Moses was an impostor, pronouncing the conclusion to be over-hasty and unjust. Thus Eichhorn agreed with the Naturalists in divesting the biblical narratives of all their immediately divine contents, but he differed from them in this, that he explained the supernatural lustre which adorns these histories, not as a fictitious colouring imparted with design to deceive, but as a natural and as it were spontaneous illumination reflected from antiquity itself.

In conformity with these principles Eichhorn sought to explain naturally the histories of Noah, Abraham, Moses, &c. Viewed in the light of that age, the appointment of Moses to be the leader of the Israelites was nothing more than the long cherished project of the patriot to emancipate his people, which when presented before his mind with more than usual vividness in his dreams, was believed by him to be a divine inspiration. The flame and smoke which ascended from Mount Sinai, at the giving of the law, was merely a fire which Moses kindled in order to make a deeper impression upon the imagination of the people, together with an accidental thunderstorm which arose at that particular moment. The shining of his countenance was the natural effect of being overheated; but it was supposed to be a divine manifestation, not only by the people, but by Moses himself, he being ignorant of the true cause.

Eichhorn was more reserved in his application of this mode of interpretation to the New Testament. Indeed, it was only to a few of the narratives in the Acts of the Apostles, such as the miracle of the day of Pentecost, the conversion of the Apostle Paul, and the many apparitions of angels, that he allowed himself to apply it. Here too, he refers the supernatural to the figurative language of the Bible; in which, for example, a happy accident is called—a protecting angel; a joyous thought—the salutation of an angel, and a

peaceful state of mind—a comforting angel. It is however remarkable that Eichhorn was conscious of the inapplicability of the natural
explanation to some parts of the gospel history, and with respect to
many of the narratives took a more elevated view.

Many writings in a similar spirit, which partially included the
New Testament within the circle of their explanations, appeared;
but it was Dr. Paulus who by his commentary on the Gospels* in
1800, first acquired the full reputation of a *christian Evemerus*.
In the introduction to this work he states it to be the primary requisite of the biblical critic to be able to distinguish between what
is *fact*, and what is *opinion*. That which has been actually experienced, internally or externally, by the participants in an event, he
calls *fact*. The interpretation of an event, the supposed causes
to which it is referred either by the participants or by the narrators, he calls *opinion*. But, according to Dr. Paulus, these
two elements become so easily blended and confounded in the
minds both of the original sharers in an event, and of the subsequent relators and historians, that fact and opinion lose their distinction; so that the one and the other are believed and recorded
with equal confidence in their historical truth. This intermixture
is particularly apparent in the historical books of the New Testament; since at the time when Jesus lived, it was still the prevailing
disposition to derive every striking occurrence from an invisible and
superhuman cause. It is consequently the chief task of the historian
who desires to deal with matters of fact, that is to say, in reference
to the New Testament, to separate these two constituent elements
so closely amalgamated, and yet in themselves so distinct: and to
extricate the pure kernel of fact from the shell of opinion. In order
to this, in the absence of any more genuine account which would
serve as a correcting parallel, he must transplant himself in imagination upon the theatre of action, and strive to the utmost to contemplate the events by the light of the age in which they occurred.
And from this point of view he must seek to supply the deficiencies
of the narration, by filling in those explanatory collateral circumstances, which the relator himself is so often led by his predilection
for the supernatural to leave unnoticed. It is well known in what
manner Dr. Paulus applies these principles to the New Testament
in his Commentary, and still more fully in his later production,
"The Life of Jesus." He firmly maintains the historical truth of
the gospel narratives, and he aims to weave them into one consecutive chronologically-arranged detail of facts; but he explains
away every trace of immediate divine agency, and denies all supernatural intervention. Jesus is not to him the *Son of God* in the
sense of the Church, but a wise and virtuous human being: and
the effects he produced are not miracles, but acts sometimes of benevolence and friendship, sometimes of medical skill, sometimes
also the results of accident and good fortune.

* Paulus's Commentar über das neue Testament.

This view proposed by Eichhorn, and more completely developed by Paulus, necessarily presupposes the Old and New Testament writings to contain a minute and faithful narration, composed shortly after the occurrence of the events recorded, and derived, wherever this was possible, from the testimony of eye-witnesses. For it is only from an accurate and original report that the ungarbled fact can be disentangled from interwoven opinion. If the report be later and less original, what security is there that what is taken for the matter-of-fact kernel does not belong to opinion or tradition? To avoid this objection, Eichhorn sought to assign a date to the Old Testament histories approximating as nearly as possible to the events they record: and here he, and other theologians of the same school, found no difficulty in admitting suppositions the most unnatural: for example, that the Pentateuch was written during the passage through the wilderness. However this critic admits that some portions of the Old Testament, the Book of Judges, for instance, could not have been written contemporaneously with the events; that the historian must have contemplated his heroes through the dim mist of intervening ages, which might easily have magnified them into giant forms. No historian who had either witnessed the circumstances, or had been closely connected with them in point of time, could embellish after such fashion, except with the express aim to amuse at the expense of truth. But with regard to remote occurrences it is quite different. The imagination is no longer restricted by the fixed limits of historical reality, but is aided in its flight by the notion that in earlier times all things were better and nobler; and the historian is tempted to speak in loftier phrase and to use hyperbolical expressions. Least of all is it possible to avoid embellishment, when the compiler of a subsequent age derives his materials from the orally transmitted traditions of antiquity. The adventures and wondrous exploits of ancestors, handed down by father to son, and by son to grandson, in glowing and enthusiastic representations, and sung by the poet in lofty strains, are registered in the written records of the historian in similar terms of high flowing diction. Though Eichhorn took this view of a portion of the Old Testament Books, he believed he was not giving up their historical basis, but was still able, after clearing away the more or less evident legendary additions, to trace out the natural course of the history.

But in one instance at least, this master of the natural mode of interpretation in reference to the Old Testament, took a more elevated view:—namely, of the history of the creation and the fall. In his influential work on primitive history,[*] although he had from the first declared the account of the creation to be poetry, he nevertheless maintained that of the fall to be neither mythology nor allegory, but true history. The historical basis that remained after the removal of the supernatural, he stated to be this: that the human constitution had at the very beginning become impaired by the eating of a poisonous fruit. He thought it indeed very possible in itself, and confirmed by numerous examples in profane history, that purely historical narratives might be overlaid by a mythical account; but owing to a supranaturalistic notion, he refused to allow the same possibility to the Bible, because he thought it unworthy of the Deity to admit a mythological fragment into a book, which bore such incontestable traces of its divine origin. Later, however, Eichhorn himself declared that he had changed his opinion with regard to the second and third chapters of Genesis.* He no longer saw in them an historical account of the effects of poison, but rather the mythical embodying of a philosophical thought; namely, that the desire for a better condition than that in which man actually is, is the source of all the evil in the world. Thus, in this point at least, Eichhorn preferred to give up the history in order to hold fast the idea, rather than to cling to the history with the sacrifice of every more elevated conception. For the rest, he agreed with Paulus and others in considering the miraculous in the sacred history as a drapery which needs only to be drawn aside, in order to disclose the pure historic form.

§ 7.　MORAL INTERPRETATION OF KANT.

AMIDST these natural explanations which the end of the eighteenth century brought forth in rich abundance, it was a remarkable interlude to see the old allegorical system of the christian fathers all at once called up from its grave, and revived in the form of the moral interpretation of Kant. He, as a philosopher, did not concern himself with the history, as did the rationalist theologians, but like the fathers of the church, he sought the idea involved in the history: not however considering it as they did an absolute idea, at once theoretical as well as practical, but regarding it only on its practical side, as what he called *the moral imperative* and consequently belonging to the finite. He moreover attributed these ideas wrought into the biblical text, not to the Divine Spirit, but to its philosophical interpreters, or in a deeper sense, to the moral condition of the authors of the book themselves. This opinion Kant† bases upon the fact, that in all religions old and new which are partly comprised in sacred books, intelligent and well-meaning teachers of the people have continued to explain them, until they have brought their actual contents into agreement with the universal principles of morality. Thus did the moral philosophers amongst the Greeks and Romans with their fabulous legends; till at last they explained the grossest polytheism as mere symbolical representations of the attributes of the one divine Being, and gave a

* Allgem. Biblioth. 1 Bd. S. 989, und Einleitung in das A. T. 3 Thl. S. 82.　† Religion innerhalb der Grenzen der blossen Vernunft, drittes Stück, No. VI.: Der Kirchenglaube hat zu seinem höchsten Ausleger den reinen Religionsglauben

mystical sense to the many vicious actions of their gods, and to
the wildest dreams of their poets, in order to bring the popular faith,
which it was not expedient to destroy, into agreement with the doctrines of morality. The later Judaism and Christianity itself he
thinks have been formed upon similar explanations, occasionally
much forced, but always directed to objects undoubtedly good and
necessary for all men. Thus the Mahometans gave a spiritual
meaning to the sensual descriptions of their paradise, and thus the
Hindoos, or at least the more enlightened part of them, interpreted
their Vedas. In like manner, according to Kant, the Christian
Scriptures of the Old and New Testament, must be interpreted
throughout in a sense which agrees with the universal practical
laws of a religion of pure reason: and such an explanation, even
though it should, apparently or actually, do violence to the text,
which is the case with many of the biblical narratives, is to be pre
ferred to a literal one, which either contains no morality at all or is
in opposition to the moral principle. For example, the expressions
breathing vengeance against enemies in many of the Psalms are
made to refer to the desires and passions which we must strive by
all means to bring into subjection; and the miraculous account in
the New Testament of the descent of Jesus from heaven, of his
relationship to God, &c., is taken as an imaginative description of
the ideal of humanity well-pleasing to God. That such an interpretation is possible, without even always too offensive an opposition
to the literal sense of these records of the popular faith, arises according to the profound observations of Kant from this: that long
before the existence of these records, the disposition to a moral religion was latent in the human mind; that its first manifestations
were directed to the worship of the Deity, and on this very account
gave occasion to those pretended revelations; still, though unintentionally, imparting even to these fictions somewhat of the spiritual
character of their origin. In reply to the charge of dishonesty
brought against his system of interpretation, he thinks it a sufficient
defence to observe, that it does not pretend that the sense now given
to the sacred books, always existed in the intention of the authors;
this question it sets aside, and only claims for itself the right to
interpret them after its own fashion.

Whilst Kant in this manner sought to educe moral thoughts
from the biblical writings, even in their historical part, and was
even inclined to consider these thoughts as the fundamental object
of the history: on the one hand, he derived these thoughts only
from himself and the cultivation of his age, and therefore could
seldom assume that they had actually been laid down by the authors of those writings: and on the other hand, and for the same
reason, he omitted to show what was the relation between these
thoughts and those symbolic representations, and how it happened
that the one came to be expressed by the other.

§ 8. RISE OF THE MYTHICAL MODE OF INTERPRETING THE SACRED HISTORY, IN REFERENCE FIRST TO THE OLD TESTAMENT.

It was impossible to rest satisfied with modes of proceeding so unhistorical on the one hand, and so unphilosophical on the other. Added to which, the study of mythology, now become far more general and more prolific in its results, exerted an increasing influence on the views taken of biblical history. Eichhorn had indeed insisted that all primitive histories, whether Hebrew or Pagan, should be treated alike, but this equality gradually disappeared; for though the mythical view became more and more developed in relation to profane history, the natural mode of explanation was still rigidly adhered to for the Hebrew records. All could not imitate Paulus, who sought to establish consistency of treatment by extending the same natural explanation which he gave to the Bible, to such also of the Greek legends as presented any points of resemblance; on the contrary, opinion in general took the opposite course, and began to regard many of the biblical narratives as mythi. Semler had already spoken of a kind of Jewish mythology, and had even called the histories of Samson and Esther mythi; Eichhorn too had done much to prepare the way, now further pursued by Gabler, Schelling, and others, who established the notion of the mythus as one of universal application to ancient history, sacred as well as profane, according to the principle of Heyne: *A mythis omnis priscorum hominum cum historia tum philosophia procedit.*[*] And Bauer in 1820 ventured so far as to publish a Hebrew mythology of the Old and New Testament.[†] The earliest records of all nations are, in the opinion of Bauer, mythical: why should the writings of the Hebrews form a solitary exception?—whereas in point of fact a cursory glance at their sacred books proves that they also contain mythical elements. A narrative he explains, after Gabler and Schelling, to be recognizable as mythus, first, when it proceeds from an age in which no written records existed, but in which facts were transmitted through the medium of oral tradition alone; secondly, when it presents an historical account of events which are either absolutely or relatively beyond the reach of experience, such as occurrences connected with the spiritual world, and incidents to which, from the nature of the circumstances, no one could have been witness; or thirdly, when it deals in the marvellous and is couched in symbolical language. Not a few narratives of this description occur in the Bible; and an unwillingness to regard them as mythi can arise only from a false conception of the nature of a mythus, or of the character of the biblical writings. In the one case mythi are confounded with fables, premeditated fictions, and wilful falsehoods, instead of being recognised as the necessary vehicle of expression for the first efforts of the human mind: in the

---

[*] Ad. Apollod. Athen. Biblioth. notæ, p. 3 f.   [†] Hebräische Mythologie des alten und neuen Testaments. G. L. Bauer, 1802.

other case it certainly does appear improbable, (the notion of inspiration presupposed,) that God should have admitted the substitution of mythical for actual representations of facts and ideas, but a nearer examination of the scriptures shows that this very notion of inspiration, far from being any hindrance to the mythical interpretation, is itself of mythical origin.

Wegscheider ascribed this greater unwillingness to recognise mythi in the early records of the Hebrew and Christian religion than in the heathen religions, partly to the prevailing ignorance respecting the progress of historical and philosophical science: partly to a certain timidity which dares not call things manifestly identical by the same name. At the same time he declared it impossible to rescue the Bible from the reproaches and scoffs of its enemies except by the acknowledgment of mythi in the sacred writings, and the separation of their inherent meaning from their unhistorical form.*

These biblical critics gave the following general definition of the mythus. It is the representation of an event or of an idea in a form which is historical, but, at the same time characterized by the rich pictorial and imaginative mode of thought and expression of the primitive ages. They also distinguished several kinds of mythi.†

1st. *Historical mythi:* narratives of real events coloured by the light of antiquity, which confounded the divine and the human, the natural and the supernatural.

2nd. *Philosophical mythi:* such as clothe in the garb of historical narrative a simple thought, a precept, or an idea of the time.

3rd. *Poetical mythi:* historical and philosophical mythi partly blended together, and partly embellished by the creations of the imagination, in which the original fact or idea is almost obscured by the veil which the fancy of the poet has woven around it.

To classify the biblical mythi according to these several distinctions is a difficult task, since the mythus which is purely symbolical wears the semblance of history equally with the mythus which represents an actual occurrence. These critics however laid down rules by which the different mythi might be distinguished. The first essential is, they say, to determine whether the narrative have a distinct object, and what that object is. Where no object, for the sake of which the legend might have been invented, is discoverable, every one would pronounce the mythus to be *historical.* But if all the principal circumstances of the narrative concur to symbolize a particular truth, this undoubtedly was the object of the narrative, and the mythus is *philosophical.* The blending of the historical and philosophical mythus is particularly to be recognised when we can detect in the narrative an attempt to derive

* Institutiones Theol. Chr. Dogm. § 42,   † Ammon, Progr. quo inquiritur in narra-tionum de vitæ Jesu Christi primordiis fontes, etc., in Pott's and Ruperti's Sylloge Comm. theol. No. 5, und Gabler's n. theol. Journal, 5 Bd. S. 83 und 397.

events from their causes. In many instances the existence of an historical foundation is proved also by independent testimony; sometimes certain particulars in the mythus are intimately connected with known genuine history, or bear in themselves undeniable and inherent characteristics of probability : so that the critic, while he rejects the external form, may yet retain the groundwork as historical. The *poetical* mythus is the most difficult to distinguish, and Bauer gives only a negative criterion. When the narrative is so wonderful on the one hand as to exclude the possibility of its being a detail of facts, and when on the other it discovers no attempt to symbolize a particular thought, it may be suspected that the entire narrative owes its birth to the imagination of the poet. Schelling particularly remarks on the unartificial and spontaneous origin of mythi in general. The unhistorical which is interwoven with the matters of fact in the historical mythus is not, he observes, the artistical product of design and invention. It has on the contrary glided in of itself, as it were, in the lapse of time and in the course of transmission. And, speaking of philosophical mythi, he says: the sages of antiquity clothed their ideas in an historical garb, not only in order to accommodate those ideas to the apprehension of a people who must be awakened by sensible impressions, but also on their own account : deficient themselves in clear abstract ideas, and in ability to give expression to their dim conceptions, they sought to illumine what was obscure in their representations by means of sensible imagery.*

We have already remarked, that the natural mode of interpreting the Old Testament could be maintained only so long as the records were held to be contemporaneous, or nearly so, with the events recorded. Consequently it was precisely those theologians, Vater, De Wette, and others who controverted this opinion, who contributed to establish the mythical view of the sacred histories. Vater† expressed the opinion that the peculiar character of the narrations in the Pentateuch could not be rightly understood, unless it were conceded that they are not the production of an eye witness, but are a series of transmitted traditions. Their traditional origin being admitted, we cease to feel surprised at the traces which they discover of a subsequent age ; at numerical exaggerations, together with other inaccuracies and contradictions ; at the twilight which hangs over many of the occurrences : and at representations such as, that the clothes of the Israelites waxed not old during their passage through the wilderness. Vater even contends, that unless we ascribe a great share of the marvellous contained in the Pentateuch to tradition, we do violence to the original sense of the compilers of these narratives.

* Ueber Mythen, historische Sagen und Philosopheme der ältesten Welt. In Paulus Memorabilien, 5. Stück, 1793.
† Vid. die Abhandlung über Moses und die Verfasser des Pentateuch im 3. Band des Comm. über den Pent., S. 660.

The natural mode of explanation was still more decidedly opposed by De Wette than by Vater. He advocated the mythical interpretation of a large proportion of the Old Testament histories. In order to test the historical credibility of a narrative, he says,[*] we must ascertain the intention of the narrator. If that intention be not to satisfy the natural thirst for historical truth by a simple narration of facts, but rather to delight or touch the feelings, or to illustrate some philosophical or religious truth, then his narrative has no pretension to historical validity. Even when the narrator is conscious of strictly historical intentions, nevertheless his point of view may not be the historical: he may be a poetical narrator, not indeed subjectively, as a poet drawing inspiration from himself, but objectively, as enveloped by and depending on poetry external to himself. This is evidently the case when the narrator details as bona fide matter of fact things which are impossible and incredible, which are contrary not only to experience, but to the established laws of nature. Narrations of this description spring out of tradition. Tradition, says De Wette, is uncritical and partial; its tendency is not historical, but rather patriotic and poetical. And since the patriotic sentiment is gratified by all that flatters national pride, the more splendid, the more honourable, the more wonderful the narrative, the more acceptable it is; and where tradition has left any blanks, imagination at once steps in and fills them up. And since, he continues, a great part of the historical books of the Old Testament bear this stamp, it has hitherto been believed possible (on the part of the natural interpreters) to separate the embellishments and transformations from the historical substance, and still to consider them available as records of facts. This might indeed be done, had we, besides the marvellous biblical narratives, some other purely historical account of the events. But this is not the case with regard to the Old Testament history; we are solely dependent on those accounts which we cannot recognize as purely historical. They contain no criterion by which to distinguish between the true and the false; both are promiscuously blended, and set forth as of equal dignity. According to De Wette, the whole natural mode of explanation is set aside by the principle that the only means of acquaintance with a history is the narrative which we possess concerning it, and that beyond this narrative the historian cannot go. In the present case, this reports to us only a supernatural course of events, which we must either receive or reject: if we reject it, we determine to know nothing at all about it, and are not justified in allowing ourselves to invent a natural course of events, of which the narrative is totally silent. It is moreover inconsistent and arbitrary to refer the dress in which the events of the Old Testament are clothed to poetry, and to preserve the events themselves as historical; much rather do the particular details and the dress in which they appear, constitute a whole belonging to the province of poetry and mythus. For

* Kritik der Mosaischen Geschichte, Einl, S. 10, ff.

example, if God's covenant with Abraham be denied in the form of fact, whilst at the same time it is maintained that the narrative had an historical basis.—that is to say, that though no objective divine communications took place, the occurrence had a subjective reality in Abraham's mind in a dream or in a waking vision; in other words, that a natural thought was awakened in Abraham which he, in the spirit of the age, referred to God:—of the naturalist who thus reasons, De Wette asks, how he knows that such thoughts arose in Abraham's mind? The narration refers them to God; and if we reject the narration, we know nothing about these thoughts of Abraham, and consequently cannot know that they had arisen naturally in him. According to general experience, such hopes as are described in this covenant, that he should become the father of a mighty nation which should possess the land of Canaan, could not have sprung up naturally in Abraham's mind: but it is quite natural that the Israelites when they had become a numerous people in possession of that land, should have invented the covenant in order to render their ancestor illustrious. Thus the natural explanation, by its own unnaturalness, ever brings us back to the mythical.

Even Eichhorn, who so extensively employed the natural explanation in reference to the Old Testament, perceived its inadmissibility in relation to the gospel histories. Whatever in these narratives has a tendency to the supernatural, he remarks,[*] we ought not to attempt to transform into a natural occurrence, because this is impossible without violence. If once an event has acquired a miraculous colouring, owing to the blending together of some popular notion with the occurrence, the natural fact can be disentangled only when we possess a second account which has not undergone the like transformation; as, concerning the death of Herod Agrippa, we have not only the narrative in the Acts, but also that of Josephus.[†] But since we have no such controlling account concerning the history of Jesus, the critic who pretends to discover the natural course of things from descriptions of supernatural occurrences, will only weave a tissue of indemonstrable hypotheses:—a consideration which, as Eichhorn observes, at once annihilates many of the so-called psychological interpretations of the Gospel histories.

It is this same difference between the natural and mythical modes of interpretation which Krug intends to point out, referring particularly to the histories of miracles, when he distinguishes the physical or material, from the genetic or formal, mode of explaining them. Following the former mode, according to him, the inquiry is: how can the wonderful event here related have possibly taken place with all its details by natural means and according to natural laws? Whereas, following the latter, the question is: whence arose the narrative of the marvellous event? The former explains the natural possibility of the thing related (the substance of the narrative); the latter traces the origin of the existing record (the form of the narrative). Krug considers attempts of the former kind to be fruitless, because they produce interpretations yet more wonderful than the fact itself; far preferable is the other mode, since it leads to results which throw light upon miraculous histories collectively. He gives the preference to the exegetist, because in his explanation of the text he is not obliged to do violence to it, but may accept it altogether literally as the author intended, even though the thing related be impossible; whereas the interpreter, who follows the material or physical explanation, is driven to ingenious subtleties which make him lose sight of the original meaning of the authors, and substitute something quite different which they neither could nor would have said.

In like manner Gabler recommended the mythical view, as the best means of escaping from the so called natural, but forced explanation, which had become the fashion. The natural interpreter, he remarks, commonly aims to make the whole narrative natural; and as this can but seldom succeed, he allows himself the most violent measures, owing to which modern exegesis has been brought into disrepute even amongst laymen. The mythical view, on the contrary, needs no such subtleties; since the greater part of a narrative frequently belongs to the mythical representation merely, while the nucleus of fact, when divested of the subsequently added miraculous envelopments, is often very small.

Neither could Horst reconcile himself to the atomistic mode of proceeding, which selected from the marvellous narratives of the Bible, as unhistorical, isolated incidents merely, and inserted natural ones in their place, instead of recognizing in the whole of each narrative a religious moral mythus in which a certain idea is embodied.

An anonymous writer in Bertholdt's Journal has expressed himself very decidedly against the natural mode of explaining the sacred history, and in favour of the mythical. The essential defect of the natural interpretation, as exhibited in its fullest development by Paulus's Commentary, is, according to that writer, its unhistorical mode of procedure. He objects: that it allows conjecture to supply the deficiencies of the record; adopts individual speculations as a substitute for real history; seeks by vain endeavours to represent that as natural which the narrative describes as supernatural; and lastly, evaporates all sacredness and divinity from the Scriptures, reducing them to collections of amusing tales no longer meriting the name of history. According to our author, this insufficiency of the natural mode of interpretation, whilst the supernatural also is felt to be unsatisfactory, leads the mind to the mythical view, which leaves the substance of the narrative unassailed; and instead of venturing to explain the details, accepts the whole, not indeed as true history, but as a sacred legend. This view is supported by the analogy of all antiquity, political and religious, since the closest resemblance exists between many of the narratives of the Old and New Testament, and the mythi of profane antiquity. But the most convincing argument is this: if the mythical view be once admitted, the innumerable, and never otherwise to be harmonized, discrepancies and chronological contradictions in the gospel histories disappear, as it were, at one stroke.*

§ 9. THE MYTHICAL MODE OF INTERPRETATION IN REFERENCE TO THE NEW TESTAMENT.

THUS the mythical mode of interpretation was adopted not only in relation to the Old Testament, but also to the New; not, however, without its being felt necessary to justify such a step. Gabler has objected to the Commentary of Paulus, that it concedes too little to the mythical point of view, which must be adopted for certain New Testament narratives. For many of these narratives present not only those mistaken views of things which might have been taken by eye witnesses, and by the rectification of which a natural course of events may be made out; but frequently, also, false facts and impossible consequences which no eye witness could have related, and which could only have been the product of tradition, and must therefore be mythically understood.†

The chief difficulty which opposed the transference of the mythical point of view from the Old Testament to the New, was this:—it was customary to look for mythi in the fabulous primitive ages only, in which no written records of events as yet existed: whereas, in the time of Jesus, the mythical age had long since passed away, and writing had become common among the Jews. Schelling had however conceded (at least in a note) that the term mythi, in a more extended sense, was appropriate to those narratives which, though originating in an age when it was usual to preserve documentary records, were nevertheless transmitted by the mouth of the people. Bauer‡ in like manner asserted, that though a connected series of mythi,—a history which should be altogether mythical,—was not to be sought in the New Testament, yet there might occur in it single mythi, either transferred from the Old Testament to the New, or having originally sprung up in the latter. Thus he found, in the details of the infancy of Jesus, much which requires to be regarded from a mythical point of view. As after the decease of celebrated personages, numerous anecdotes are circulated concerning them, which fail not to receive many and wondrous amplifications in the legends of a wonder-loving people; so, after Jesus had become distinguished by his life, and yet more glorified by his death, his early years, which had been passed in obscurity, became adorned with miraculous embellishments. And, according to Bauer, whenever in

* Die verschiedenen Rücksichten, in welchen und für welche der Biograph Jesu arbeiten kann.   In Bertholdt's krit. Journal, 5 Bd. S. 235 ff.   † Recens. von Paulus Commentar, im neuesten theol. Journal 7, 4, S. 395 ff. (1801).   ‡ Hebräische Mythologie. 1. Thl. Einl. § 5.

this history of the infancy we find celestial beings, called by name and bearing the human shape, predicting future occurrences, &c., we have a right to suppose a mythus: and to conjecture as its origin, that the great actions of Jesus being referred to superhuman causes, this explanation came to be blended with the history. On the same subject, Gabler* remarked that the notion of ancient is relative; compared with the Mosaic religion Christianity is certainly young: but in itself it is old enough to allow us to refer the original history of its founder to ancient times. That at that time written documents on other subjects existed, proves nothing, whilst it can be shown that for a long period there was no written account of the life of Jesus, and particularly of his infancy. Oral narratives were alone transmitted, and they would easily become tinged with the marvellous, mixed with Jewish ideas, and thus grow into historical mythi. On many other points there was no tradition, and here the mind was left to its own surmises. The more scanty the historical data, the greater was the scope for conjecture; and historical guesses and inferences of this description, formed in harmony with the Jewish-Christian tastes, may be called the philosophical, or rather, the dogmatical mythi of the early christian Gospel. The notion of the mythus, concludes Gabler, being thus shown to be applicable to many of the narratives of the New Testament, why should we not dare to call them by their right name; why—that is to say in learned discussion—avoid an expression which can give offence only to the prejudiced or the misinformed?

As in the Old Testament Eichhorn had been brought over by the force of internal evidence from his earlier natural explanation, to the mythical view of the history of the fall; so in the New Testament, the same thing happened to Usteri in relation to the history of the temptation. In an earlier work he had, following Schleiermacher, considered it as a parable spoken by Jesus but misunderstood by his disciples.† Soon however he perceived the difficulties of this interpretation; and since both the natural and the supernatural views of the narrative appeared to him yet more objectionable, he had no alternative but to adopt the mythical. Once admit, he remarks, a state of excitement, particularly of religious excitement, among a not unpoetical people, and a short time is sufficient to give an appearance of the marvellous not only to obscure and concealed, but even to public and well-known facts. It is therefore by no means conceivable that the early Jewish Christians, gifted with the spirit, that is, animated with religious enthusiasm, as they were, and familiar with the Old Testament, should not have been in a condition to invent symbolical scenes such as the temptation and other New Testament mythi. It is not however to be imagined that any

---

* Ist es erlaubt, in der Bibel, und sogar im N. T., Mythen anzunehmen? Im Journal für auserlesene theol. Literatur, 2, 1, S. 49 ff.   † Ueber den Täufer Johannes, die Taufe und Versuchung Christi, in Ullmann's u. Umbreit's theol. Studien u. Kritiken, 2, 3, S. 456 ff.

one individual seated himself at his table to invent them out of his own head, and write them down, as he would a poem: on the contrary, these narratives like all other legends were fashioned by degrees, by steps which can no longer be traced: gradually acquired consistency, and at length received a fixed form in our written Gospels.

We have seen that in reference to the early histories of the Old Testament, the mythical view could be embraced by those only who doubted the composition of these Scriptures by eye witnesses or contemporaneous writers. This was equally the case in reference to the New. It was not till Eichhorn* became convinced that only a slender thread of that primitive Gospel believed by the Apostles ran through the three first Gospels, and that even in Matthew this thread was entangled in a mass of unapostolic additions, that he discarded as unhistorical legends, the many narratives which he found perplexing, from all share in the history of Jesus; for example, besides the Gospel of the Infancy, the details of the temptation: several of the miracles of Jesus; the rising of the saints from their graves at his crucifixion: the guard at the sepulchre: &c.† Particularly since the opinion, that the three first Gospels originated from oral traditions, became firmly established,‡ they have been found to contain a continually increasing number of mythi and mythical embellishments.§ On this account the authenticity of the Gospel of John, and consequently its historical credibility, is confidently maintained by most of the theologians of the present day: he only who, with Bretschneider,‖ questions its apostolic composition, may cede in this Gospel also a considerable place to the mythical element.

§ 10. THE NOTION OF THE MYTHUS IN ITS APPLICATION TO SACRED HISTORIES NOT CLEARLY APPREHENDED BY THEOLOGIANS.

Thus, indeed, did the mythical view gain application to the biblical history: still the notion of the mythus was for a long time neither clearly apprehended nor applied to a due extent.

Not clearly apprehended. The characteristic which had been recognised as constituting the distinction between historical and philosophical mythi, however just that distinction might in itself be, was of a kind which easily betrayed the critic back again into the scarcely abandoned natural explanation. His task, with regard to historical mythi, was still to separate the natural fact—the nucleus of historical reality—from its unhistorical and miraculous embellishments. An essential difference indeed existed: the natural explanation attributed the embellishments to the opinion of the actors concerned, or of the narrator; the mythical interpretation derived

* Beitrag zur Erklärung der Versuchungsgeschichte, in ders. Zeitschrift, 1832, 4. Hft. † Einleitung in das N. T. 1, S. 422 ff. 453. ‡ Besonders durch Gieseler, über die Entstehung und die frühsten Schicksale der schriftlichen Evangelien. § Vid. den Anhang der Schulz'schen Schrift über das Abendmahl, und die Schriften von Sieffert und Schneckenburger über den Ursprung des ersten kanonischen Evangeliums. ‖ In den Probabilien.

them from tradition; but the mode of proceeding was left too little
determined.   If the Rationalist could point out historical mythi in
the Bible, without materially changing his mode of explanation; so
the Supernaturalist on his part felt himself less offended by the admission of historical mythi, which still preserved to the sacred narratives a basis of fact, than by the supposition of philosophical mythi,
which seemed completely to annihilate every trace of historical
foundation.   It is not surprising, therefore, that the interpreters
who advocated the mythical theory spoke almost exclusively of historical mythi; that Bauer, amongst a considerable number of mythi
which he cites from the New Testament, finds but one philosophical
mythus; and that a mixed mode of interpretation, partly mythical
and partly natural, (a medley far more contradictory than the pure
natural explanation, from the difficulties of which these critics sought
to escape,) should have been adopted.   Thus Bauer* thought that
he was explaining Jehovah's promise to Abraham as an historical
mythus, when he admitted as the fundamental fact of the narrative,
that Abraham's hopes of a numerous posterity were re-awakened by
the contemplation of the star-sown heavens.   Another theologian†
imagined he had seized the mythical point of view, when, having
divested the anouncement of the birth of the Baptist of the supernatural, he still retained the dumbness of Zachariah as the historical
groundwork.   In like manner Krug,‡ immediately after assuring us
that his intention is not to explain the substance of the history, (according to the natural mode,) but to explain the origin of the narrative, (according to the mythical view,) constitutes an accidental
journey of oriental merchants the basis of the narrative of the visit
of the wise men from the east.   But the contradiction is most glaring when we meet with palpable misconceptions of the true nature
of a mythus in a work on the mythology of the New Testament,
such as Bauer's; in which for instance he admits, in the case of the
parents of John the Baptist, a marriage which had actually been
childless during many years;—in which he explains the angelic appearance at the birth of Jesus as a meteoric phenomenon; supposes
the occurrence of thunder and lightning and the accidental descent
of a dove at his baptism; constitutes a storm the groundwork of
the transfiguration; and converts the angels at the tomb of the risen
Jesus into white grave-clothes.   Kaiser also, though he complains
of the unnaturalness of many of the natural explanations, accords
to a very considerable proportion of natural explanations a place by
the side of the mythical; remarking—and the remark is in itself
just—that to attempt to explain all the miracles of the New
Testament in one and the same manner betrays a limited and partial comprehension of the subject.   Let it be primarily admitted
that the ancient author intended to narrate a miracle, and the nat-

* Geschichte der hebräischen Nation, Theil i. S. 123.   † In Henke's Magazin, 5ten
Bdes. 1tes Stück, S. 163.   ‡ Versuch über die genetische oder formelle Erklärungsart der
Wunder. In Henke's Museum, i. 3. 1803.

ural explanation is in many instances admissible. This may be either a physical-historical explanation, as in the narrative of the leper whose approaching recovery Jesus doubtless perceived; or it may be a psychological explanation; since, in the case of many sick persons, the fame of Jesus and faith in him were mainly instrumental in effecting the cure; sometimes indeed good fortune must be taken into the account, as where one apparently dead revived in the presence of Jesus, and he became regarded as the author of the sudden re-animation. With respect to other miracles Kaiser is of opinion that the mythical interpretation is to be preferred; he, however, grants a much larger space to historical, than to philosophical mythi. He considers most of the miracles in the Old and New Testament real occurrences mythically embellished: such as the narrative of the piece of money in the fish's mouth: and of the changing of water into wine: which latter history he supposes to have originated from a friendly jest on the part of Jesus. Few only of the miracles are recognised by this critic as pure poetry embodying Jewish ideas; as the miraculous birth of Jesus, and the murder of the innocents.*

Gabler in particular calls attention to the error of treating philosophical mythi as if they were historical, and of thus converting into facts things that never happened.† He is however as little disposed to admit the exclusive existence of philosophical, as of historical mythi in the New Testament, but adopting a middle course, he decides in each case that the mythus is of this kind or of that according to its intrinsic character. He maintains that it is as necessary to guard against the arbitrary proceeding of handling as philosophical a mythus through which a fact unquestionably glimmers, as it is to avoid the opposite tendency to explain naturally or historically that which belongs properly to the mythical clothing. In other words: when the derivation of a mythus from a thought is easy and natural, and when the attempt to educe from it a matter of fact and to give the wonderful history a natural explanation, does violence to the sense or appears ridiculous, we have, according to Gabler, certain evidence that the mythus is philosophical and not historical. He remarks in conclusion that the philosophical-mythical interpretation is in many cases far less offensive than the historical-mythical explanation.‡

Yet, notwithstanding this predilection in favour of the philosophical mythus in relation to biblical history, one is surprised to find that Gabler himself was ignorant of the true nature both of the historical and of the philosophical mythus. Speaking of the mythological interpreters of the New Testament who had preceded him, he says that some of them, such as Dr. Paulus, discover in the history of Jesus historical mythi only; whilst others, the anonymous E. F. in Henke's Magazine for instance, find only philosophical mythi. From this we see that he confounded not only the natural explanation with the historical-mythical view, (for in Paulus's "Commentar" the former only is adopted,) but also historical with philosophical mythi: for the author E. F. is so exclusively attached to the historical-mythical view that his explanations might almost be considered as naturalistic.

De Wette has some very cogent observations directed equally against the arbitrary adoption either of the historical-mythical or of the natural explanation in relation to the Mosaic history. In reference to the New Testament an anonymous writer in Bertholdt's Critical Journal* is the most decided in his condemnation of every attempt to discover an historical groundwork even in the Gospel mythi. To him likewise the midway path struck out by Gabler, between the exclusive adoption of historical mythi on the one hand and of philosophical mythi on the other, appears inapplicable; for though a real occurence may in fact constitute the basis of most of the New Testament narratives, it may still be impossible at the present time to separate the element of fact from the mythical adjuncts which have been blended with it, and to determine how much may belong to the one and how much to the other. Usteri likewise expressed the opinion that it is no longer possible to discriminate between the historical and the symbolical in the gospel mythi; no critical knife however sharp is now able to separate the one element from the other. A certain measure of *probability* respecting the preponderance of the historical in one legend, and of the symbolical in another, is the ultimate point to which criticism can now attain.

Opposed however to the onesidedness of those critics who found it so easy to disengage the historical contents from the mythical narratives of the Scriptures, is the onesidedness of other critics, who, on account of the difficulty of the proposed separation, despaired of the possibility of success, and were consequently led to handle the whole mass of gospel mythi as philosophical, at least in so far as to relinquish the endeavour to extract from them a residuum of historical fact. Now it is precisely this latter onesidedness which has been attributed to my cristicism of the life of Jesus; consequently, several of the reviewers of this work have taken occasion repeatedly to call attention to the varying proportions in which the historical and the ideal in the pagan religion and primitive history, (the legitimate province of the mythus,) alternate; an interchange with the historical which in the christian primitive history, presupposing the notion of the mythus to be admitted here, must unquestionably take place in a far greater degree. Thus Ullmann distinguishes not only firstly the *philosophical*, and secondly the *historical mythus*, but makes a further distinction between the latter (that is the *historical mythus*, in which there is always a preponderance of the fictitious,) and thirdly the *mythical history*, in which the historical element, though wrought into the ideal, forms the predominating constituent; whilst fourthly in *histories of which the legend is a component element* we tread properly speaking upon historical ground, since in these histories we meet only with a few faint echoes of mythical fiction. Ullmann is moreover of opinion, and Bretschneider and others agree with him, that independently of the repulsion and confusion which must inevitably be caused by the application of the term *mythus* to that which is Christian—a term originally conceived in relation to a religion of a totally different character—it were more suitable, in connexion with the primitive Christian records, to speak only of Gospel *legend*, (𝕾𝖆𝖌𝖊) and the legendary element.*

George on the contrary has recently attempted not only more accurately to define the notions of the mythus and of the legend, but likewise to demonstrate that the gospel narratives are mythical rather than legendary. Speaking generally, we should say, that he restricts the term *mythus* to what had previously been distinguished as philosophical mythi; and that he applies the name *legend* to what had hitherto been denominated historical mythi. He handles the two notions as the antipodes of each other; and grasps them with a precision by which the notion of the mythus has unquestionably gained. According to George, *mythus* is the creation of a fact out of an idea: *legend* the seeing of an idea in a fact, or arising out of it. A people, a religious community, finds itself in a certain condition or round of institutions of which the spirit, the idea, lives and acts within it. But the mind following a natural impulse, desires to gain a complete representation of that existing condition, and to know its origin. This origin however is buried in oblivion, or is too indistinctly discernible to satisfy present feelings and ideas. Consequently an image of that origin, coloured by the light of existing ideas, is cast upon the dark wall of the past, which image is however but a magnified reflex of existing influences.

If such be the rise of the *mythus*, the *legend*, on the contrary, proceeds from given facts: represented, indeed, sometimes in an incomplete and abridged, sometimes in an amplified form, in order to magnify the heroes of the history—but disjoined from their true connexion: the points of view from which they should be contemplated, and the ideas they originally contained, having in the course of transmission wholly disappeared. The consequence is, that new ideas, conceived in the spirit of the different ages through which the legend has passed down, become substituted in the stead of the original ideas. For example, the period of Jewish history subsequent to the time of Moses, which was in point of fact pervaded by a gradual elevation of ideas to monotheism and to a theocracy, is, in a later legend, represented in the exactly opposite light, as a state of falling away from the religious constitution of Moses. An idea so unhistorical will infallibly here and there distort facts transmitted by tradition, fill up blanks in the history, and su'join new and

* Ullmann, Recens. meiner L. J., in den Theol. Studien u. Kritiken 1836, 3.

significant features—and then the mythus reappears in the legend. It is the same with the mythus: propagated by tradition, it, in the process of transmission, loses its distinctive character and completeness, or becomes exaggerated in its details—as for example in the matter of numbers—and then the mythus comes under the influence of the legend. In such wise do these two formations, so essentially distinct in their origin, cross each other and mingle together. Now, if the history of the life of Jesus be of mythical formation, inasmuch as it embodies the vivid impression of the original idea which the first christian community had of their founder, this history, though unhistorical in its form, is nevertheless a faithful representation of the idea of the Christ. If instead of this, the history be legendary—if the actual external facts are given in a distorted and often magnified form—are represented in a false light and embody a false idea,—then, on the contrary, the real tenor of the life of Jesus is lost to us. So that, according to George, the recognition of the mythical element in the Gospels is far less prejudicial to the true interests of the Christian faith than the recognition of the legendary element.[*]

With respect to our own opinion, without troubling ourselves here with the dogmatic signification, we need only remark in this introduction, that we are prepared to meet with both legend and mythus in the gospel history; and when we undertake to extract the historical contents which may possibly exist in narratives recognized as mythical, we shall be equally careful neither on the one part by a rude and mechanical separation, to place ourselves on the same ground with the natural interpreter; nor on the other by a hypercritical refusal to recognize such contents where they actually exist, to lose sight of the history.

§ 11.   THE APPLICATION OF THE NOTION OF THE MYTHUS TOO CIRCUMSCRIBED.

THE notion of the mythus, when first admitted by theologians, was not only imperfectly apprehended, but also too much limited in its application to biblical history.

As Eichhorn recognized a genuine mythus only on the very threshold of the Old Testament history, and thought himself obliged to explain all that followed in a natural manner; as, some time later, other portions of the Old Testament were allowed to be mythical, whilst nothing of the kind might be suspected in the New; so, when the mythus was once admitted into the New Testament, it was here again long detained at the threshold, namely, the history of the infancy of Jesus, every farther advance being contested.   Ammon,[†]

* George, Mythus und Sage; Versuch einer wissenschaftlichen Entwicklung dieser Begriffe und ihres Verhältnisses zum christlichen Glauben, S, 11. ff. 108. ff.   † Work cited, § 8, note 4. Hase, Leben Jesu, § 32. Tholuck, S. 208. ff. Kern, die Hauptsachen der evangelischen Geschichte, 1st Article, Tübinger Zeitschrift für Theol. 1836, ii. S. 39.

the anonymous E. F. in Henke's Magazine, Usteri, and others maintained a marked distinction between the historical worth of the narratives of the public life and those of the infancy of Jesus. The records of the latter could not, they contend, have been contemporaneous; for particular attention was not at that time directed towards him ; and it is equally manifest that they could not have been written during the last three years of his life, since they embody the idea of Jesus glorified, and not of Jesus in conflict and suffering. Consequently their composition must be referred to a period subsequent to his resurrection. But at this period accurate data concerning his childhood were no longer to be obtained. The apostles knew him first in manhood. Joseph was probably dead; and Mary, supposing her to be living when the first and third gospels were composed, had naturally imparted an imaginative lustre to every incident treasured in her memory, whilst her embellishments were doubtless still further magnified in accordance with the Messianic ideas of those to whom her communications were made. Much also that is narrated had no historical foundation, but originated entirely from the notions of the age, and from the Old Testament predictions—that a virgin should conceive—for example. But, say these critics, all this does not in any degree impair the credibility of what follows. The object and task of the Evangelists was merely to give an accurate account of the three last years of the life of Jesus : and here they merit implicit confidence, since they were either themselves spectators of the details they record, or else had learned them from the mouth of trustworthy eye witnesses. This boundary line between the credibility of the history of the public life, and the fabulousness of the history of the infancy of Jesus, became yet more definitely marked, from the circumstance that many theologians were disposed to reject the two first chapters of Matthew and Luke as spurious and subsequent additions.*

Soon, however, some of the theologians who had conceded the commencement of the history to the province of mythi, perceived that the conclusion, the history of the ascension, must likewise be regarded as mythical.† Thus the two extremities were cut off by the pruning knife of criticism, whilst the essential body of the history, the period from the baptism to the resurrection, remained, as yet, unassailed ; or in the words of the reviewer of Greiling's Life of Jesus :‡ the entrance to the gospel history was through the decorated portal of mythus, and the exit was similar to it, whilst the intermediate space was still traversed by the crooked and toilsome paths of natural interpretations.

In Gabler's§ writings we meet with a somewhat more extended application of the mythical view. He distinguishes (and recently Rosenkranz‖ has agreed with him) between the miracles wrought

* Comp. Kuinöl, Prolegom. in Matthaeum, § 3; in Lucam, § 6. † e. g. Ammon, in der Diss.: Ascensus J. C. in coelum historia biblica, in seinen Opusc. nov. ‡ In Bertholdt's Krit. Journ. v. Bd. S. 248. § Gabler's neuestes theol. Journal, 1 B l. vii. S. 395. ‖ Encyclopädie der theol. Wissenschaften, S. 161.

by Jesus and those operated *on him* or *in relation to him*, interpreting the latter mythically, but the former naturally. Subsequently however, we find Gabler expressing himself as if with the
above mentioned theologians he restricted the mythical interpretation to the miraculous narratives of the childhood of Jesus, but this
restriction is in fact a limitation merely of the admitted distinction:
since though all the miracles connected with the early history of
Jesus were operated in relation to him and not wrought by him,
many miracles of the same character occur in the history of his
public life. Bauer appears to have been guided by the same rule
in his Hebrew mythology. He classes as mythical the narratives
of the conception and birth of Jesus of the Baptism, the transfiguration, the angelic apparitions in Gethsemane and at the sepulchre:
miracles selected from all periods of the life of Jesus, but all operated in relation to him and not by him. This enumeration, however, does not include all the miracles of this kind.

The often referred to author of the treatise "Upon the different
views with which and for which a Biographer of Jesus may work,"
has endeavoured to show that so limited an application of the notion
of the mythus to the history of the life of Jesus is insufficient and
inconsequent. This confused point of view from which the gospel
narrative is regarded as partly historical and partly mythical owes
its origin, according to him, to those theologians who neither give
up the history, nor are able to satisfy themselves with its clear results, but who think to unite both parties by this middle course—
a vain endeavour which the rigid supranaturalist pronounces heretical, and the rationalist derides. The attempt of these reconcilers,
remarks our author, to explain as intelligible everything which is
not impossible, lays them open to all the charges so justly brought
against the natural interpretation; whilst the admission of the existence of mythi in the New Testament subjects them to the direct
reproach of being inconsequent: the severest censure which can be
passed upon a scholar. Besides, the proceeding of these Eclectics
is most arbitrary, since they decide respecting what belongs to the
history and what to the mythus almost entirely upon subjective
grounds. Such distinctions are equally foreign to the evangelists,
to logical reasoning, and to historical criticism. In consistency with
these opinions, this writer applies the notion of the mythus to the
entire history of the life of Jesus; recognizes mythi or mythical
embellishments in every portion, and ranges under the category of
mythus not merely the miraculous occurrences during the infancy
of Jesus; but those also of his public life; not merely miracles
operated on Jesus but those wrought by him.

The most extended application of the notion of the philosophical or dogmatical mythus to the Gospel histories which has yet been
made, was published in 1799 in an anonymous work concerning
Revelation and Mythology. The writer contends that the whole life
of Jesus, all that he should and would do, had an ideal existence in

the Jewish mind long prior to his birth. Jesus as an individual was
not actually such as according to Jewish anticipations he should have
been. Not even that, in which all the records which recount his
actions agree, is absolutely matter of fact. A popular idea of the
life of Jesus grew out of various popular contributions, and from
this source our written Gospels were first derived. A reviewer objects that this author appears to suppose a still smaller portion of
the historical element in the gospels than actually exists. It would,
he remarks, have been wiser to have been guided by a sober criticism of details, than by a sweeping scepticism.*

§ 12.   OPPOSITION TO THE MYTHICAL VIEW OF THE GOSPEL
HISTORY.

IN adopting the mythical point of view as hitherto applied to
Biblical history, our theologians had again approximated to the
ancient allegorical interpretation. For as both the natural explanations of the Rationalists, and the jesting expositions of the Deists,
belong to that form of opinion which, whilst it sacrifices all divine
meaning in the sacred record, still upholds its historical character;
the mythical mode of interpretation agrees with the allegorical, in
relinquishing the historical reality of the sacred narratives, in order
to preserve to them an absolute inherent truth. The mythical and
the allegorical view (as also the moral) equally allow that the historian apparently relates that which is historical, but they suppose
him, under the influence of a higher inspiration known or unknown
to himself, to have made use of this historical semblance merely as
the shell of an *idea*—of a religious conception. The only essential
distinction therefore between these two modes of explanation is,
that according to the allegorical this higher intelligence is the immediate divine agency; according to the mythical, it is the spirit of
a people or a community. (According to the moral view it is generally the mind of the interpreter which suggest the interpretation.)
Thus the allegorical view attributes the narrative to a supernatural
source, whilst the mythical view ascribes it to that *natural* process
by which legends are originated and developed. To which it should
be added, that the allegorical interpreter (as well as the moral) may
with the most unrestrained arbitrariness separate from the history
every thought he deems to be worthy of God, as constituting its inherent meaning; whilst the mythical interpreter, on the contrary,
in searching out the ideas which are embodied in the narrative, is
controlled by regard to conformity with the spirit and modes of
thought of the people and of the age.
This new view of the sacred Scriptures was opposed alike by the
orthodox and by the rationalistic party. From the first, whilst the
mythical interpretation was still restricted to the primitive history

* In Gabler's neuestem theolog. Journal, Bd. vi. 4. Stück, S. 350.

of the Old Testament, Hess* on the orthodox side, protested against it. The three following conclusions may be given as comprising, however incredible this may appear, the substance of this book, a work of some compass; upon which however it is unnecessary to remark further than that Hess was by no means the last orthodox theologian who pretended to combat the mythical view with such weapons. He contends, 1st, that mythi are to be understood figuratively; now the sacred historians intended their writings to be understood literally: consequently they do not relate mythi. 2ndly, Mythology is something heathenish; the Bible is a christian book; consequently it contains no mythology. The third conclusion is more complex, and, as will appear below, has more meaning. If, says Hess, the marvellous were confined to those earliest biblical records of which the historical validity is less certain, and did not appear in any subsequent writings, the miraculous might be considered as a proof of the mythical character of the narrative; but the marvellous is no less redundant in the latest and undeniably historical records, than in the more ancient; consequently it cannot be regarded as a criterion of the mythical. In short the most hollow natural explanation, dit it but retain the slightest vestige of the historical—however completely it annihilated every higher meaning,—was preferable, in the eyes of the orthodox, to the mythical interpretation. Certainly nothing could be worse than Eichhorn's natural explanation of the fall. In considering the tree of knowledge as a poisonous plant, he at once destroyed the intrinsic value and inherent meaning of the history; of this he afterwards became fully sensible, and in his subsequent mythical interpretation, he recognized in the narrative the incorporation of a worthy and elevated conception. Hess however declared himself more content with Eichhorn's original explanation, and defended it against his later mythical interpretation. So true is it that supranaturalism clings with childlike fondness to the empty husk of historical semblance, though void of divine significance, and estimates it higher than the most valuable kernel divested of its variegated covering.

Somewhat later De Wette's bold and thorough application of the mythical view to the Mosaic writings; his decided renunciation of the so-called *historical-mythical*, or more properly speaking of the natural mode of interpretation; and his strict opposition to the notion of the possibility of arriving at any certainty respecting the residue of fact preserved in these writings, gave rise to much controversy. Some agreed with Steudel in totally rejecting the mythical view in relation to the Bible, and in upholding the strictly historical and indeed supranatural sense of the Scriptures: whilst Meyer and others were willing to follow the guidance of De Wette, at least as far as the principles of Vater, which permitted the attempt to extract some, if only probable, historical data from the mythical

* Gränzbestimmung dessen, was in der Bibel Mythus, u. s. f., und was wirkliche Geschichte ist. In seiner Bibliothek der heiligen Geschichte, ii. Bd. S. 155. ff.

investment. If, says Meyer,* the marvellousness and irrationality of many of the narratives contained in the Pentateuch, (narratives which no one would have thought of inventing,) together with the want of symmetry and connexion in the narration, and other considerations, permit us not to mistake the historical groundwork of the record; surely, allowing the existence of an historical basis, a modest and cautious attempt to seek out or at any rate to approximate towards a discovery of that historical foundation is admissible. In the hope of preserving those who adopted the historical mythical view from relapsing into the inconsistencies of the natural interpretres, Meyer laid down the following rules, which however serve rather to exhibit afresh the difficulty of escaping this danger. 1. To abstract every thing which is at once recognizable as mythical representation as opposed to historical fact; that is the extraordinary, the miraculous, accounts of immediate divine operation, also the religious notions of the narrators in relation to final causes. 2. To proceed from that which is simple to that which is more complicated. Let a case be supposed where we have two accounts of the same event, the one natural, the other supernatural, as, for instance, the gathering of the elders by Moses, attributed, Numbers, xi. 16., to the suggestion of Jehovah, and Exodus, xviii. 14., to the counsel of Jethro. According to this rule all divine inspiration must be subtracted from the known decisions of Noah, Abraham, Moses, and others. (Precisely the proceeding which met with the censure of De Wette quoted above.) 3. As far as possible to contemplate the fact which forms the basis of a narrative, in its simple and common character, apart from all collateral incidents. (This however, is going too far where no basis of fact exists.) For example. The story of the deluge may be reduced thus: a great inundation in Asia Minor, according to the legend, destroyed many wicked. (Here the supposed final cause is not abstracted.) Noah the father of Shem, a devout man, (*the teleological* notion again!) saved himself by swimming. The exact circumstances of this preservation, the character of the vessel, if such there were, which saved him, are left undetermined in order to avoid arbitrary explanations. Thus, in reference to the birth of Isaac, Meyer is satisfied with saying, that the wish and hope of the wealthy and pious Emir Abraham to possess an heir by his wife Sara was fulfilled unusually late, and in the eyes of others very unexpectedly. (Here again De Wette's censure is quite applicable.)

In like manner Eichhorn, in his Introduction to the New Testament, declared in yet stronger terms his opposition to the view advocated by De Wette. If the orthodox were displeased at having their historical faith disturbed by the progressive inroads of the mythical mode of interpretation, the rationalists were no less dis-

---

* Meyer Apologie der geschichtlichen Auffassung der historischen Bücher des A. T., besonders des Pentateuchs, im Gegensatz gegen die blos mythische Deutung des letztern. Fritzsche. Kelle.

concerted to find the web of facts they had so ingeniously woven together torn asunder, and all the art and labour expended on the natural explanation at once declared useless. Unwillingly does Dr. Paulus admit to himself the presentiment that the reader of his Commentary may possibly exclaim: "Wherefore all this labour to give an historical explanation to such legends? how singular thus to handle mythi as history, and to attempt to render marvellous fictions intelligible according to the rules of causality!" Contrasted with the toilsomeness of his natural explanation, the mythical interpretation appears to this theologian merely as the refuge of mental indolence, which, seeking the easiest method of treating the gospel history, disposes of all that is marvellous, and all that is difficult to comprehend, under the vague term—mythus, and which, in order to escape the labour of disengaging the natural from the supernatural, fact from opinion, carries back the whole narration into tho *camera-obscura* of ancient sacred legends.*

Still more decided was Greiling's† expression of disapprobation, elicited by Krug's commendation of the *genetic*—that is to say, mythical theory; but each stroke levelled by him at the mythical interpretation may be turned with far greater force against his own natural explanation. He is of opinion that among all the attempts to explain obscure passages in the New Testament, scarcely any can be more injurious to the genuine historical interpretation, to the ascertaining of actual facts and their legitimate objects (that is, more prejudicial to the pretensions of the natural expounder) than the endeavour to supply, by aid of an inventive imagination, the deficiencies of the historical narrative. (The inventive imagination is that of the natural interpreter, which suggests to him collateral incidents of which there is no trace in the text. The imagination of the mythical interpreter is not inventive; his part is merely the recognizing and detecting of the fictitious.) According to Greiling the *genetic*, or mythical mode of explaining miracles, is a needless and arbitrary invention of the imagination. (Let a groping spirit of inquiry be added, and the natural explanation is accurately depicted.) Many facts, he continues, which might be retained as such are thus consigned to the province of fable, or replaced by fictions the production of the interpreter. (But it is the *historical* mythical mode of interpretation alone which substitutes such inventions, and this only in so far as it is mixed up with the natural explanation.) Greiling thinks that the explanation of a miracle ought not to change the fact, and by means of interpretation, as by sleight of hand, substitute one thing for another; (which is done by the natural explanation only,) for this is not to explain that which shocks the reason, but merely to deny the fact, and leave the difficulty unsolved. (It is false to say we have a fact to explain: what immediately lies before us is a statement, respecting which we have to discover whether it embody a fact or not.) According to this learned critic the miracles wrought by Jesus should be naturally, or rather psychologically, explained; by which means all occasion to change, clip, and amplify by invention the recorded facts, till at length they become metamorphosed into fiction, is obviated—(with how much justice this censure may be applied to the natural mode of explanation has been sufficiently demonstrated.)

Heydenreich has lately written a work expressly on the inadmissibility of the mythical interpretation of the historical portions of the New Testament. He reviews the external evidences concerning the origin of the Gospels, and finds the recognition of a mythical element in these writings quite incompatible with their substantiated derivation from the Apostles, and the disciples of the Apostles. He also examines the character of the gospel representations, and decides, in reference to their form, that narratives at once so natural and simple, so complete and exact, could be expected only from eye witnesses, or those connected with them; and, with respect to their contents, that those representations which are in their nature miraculous are so worthy of God, that nothing short of an abhorrence of miracles could occasion a doubt as to their historical truth. The divine operations are indeed generally mediate, but according to Heydenreich this by no means precludes the possibility of occasional intermediate exertions of the divine energy, when requisite to the accomplishment of some particular object; and, referring to each of the divine attributes in succession, he shows that such intervention in nowise contradicts any of them; and that each individual miracle is a peculiarly appropriate exercise of divine power.

These, and similar objections against the mythical interpretation of the gospel histories, which occur in recent commentaries and in the numerous writings in opposition to my work on the life of Jesus, will find their place and refutation in the following pages.

§ 13. THE POSSIBILITY OF THE EXISTENCE OF MYTHI IN THE NEW TESTAMENT CONSIDERED IN REFERENCE TO THE EXTERNAL EVIDENCES.

THE assertion that the Bible contains mythi is, it is true, directly opposed to the convictions of the believing christian. For if his religious view be circumscribed within the limits of his own community, he knows no reason why the things recorded in the sacred books should not literally have taken place: no doubt occurs to him, no reflection disturbs him. But, let his horizon be so far widened as to allow him to contemplate his own religion in relation to other religions, and to draw a comparison between them, the conclusion to which he then comes is that the histories related by the heathens of their deities, and by the Mussulman of his prophet, are so many fictions, whilst the accounts of God's actions, of Christ and other Godlike men contained in the Bible are, on the contrary, true. Such is the general notion expressed in the theological position:

that which distinguishes Christianity from the heathen religions is this, they are mythical, it is historical.

But this position, thus stated without further definition and proof, is merely the product of the limitation of the individual to that form of belief in which he has been educated, which renders the mind incapable of embracing any but the affirmative view in relation to its own creed, any but the negative in reference to every other—a prejudice devoid of real worth, and which cannot exist in conjunction with an extensive knowledge of history. For let us transplant ourselves among other religious communities; the believing Mohammedan is of opinion that truth is contained in the Koran alone, and that the greater portion of our Bible is fabulous; the Jew of the present day, whilst admitting the truth and divine origin of the Old Testament, rejects the New; and, the same exclusive belief in the truth of their own creed and the falsity of every other was entertained by the professors of most of the heathen religions before the period of the Syncretism. But which community is right? Not all, for this is impossible, since the assertion of each excludes the others. But which particular one? Each claims for itself the true faith. The pretensions are equal; what shall decide? The origin of the several religions? Each lays claim to a divine origin. Not only does the Christian religion profess to be derived from the Son of God, and the Jewish from God himself, through Moses; the Mohammedan religion asserts itself to be founded by a prophet immediately inspired by God; in like manner the Greeks attributed the institution of their worship to the gods.

"But in no other religion" it is urged "are the vouchers of a divine origin so unequivocal as in the Jewish and the Christian. The Greek and Roman mythologies are the product of a collection of unauthenticated legends, whilst the Bible history was written by eye witnesses; or by those whose connexion with eye witnesses afforded them opportunities of ascertaining the truth; and whose integrity is too apparent to admit of a doubt as to the sincerity of of their intentions." It would most unquestionably be an argument of decisive weight in favour of the credibility of the biblical history, could it indeed be shown that it was written by eye witnesses, or even by persons nearly contemporaneous with the events narrated. For though errors and false representations may glide into the narrations even of an eye witness, there is far less probability of unintentional mistake (intentional deception may easily be detected) than where the narrator is separated by a long interval from the facts he records, and is obliged to derive his materials through the medium of transmitted communications.

But this alleged ocular testimony, or proximity in point of time of the sacred historians to the events recorded, is mere assumption, an assumption originating from the titles which the biblical books bear in our Canon. Those books which describe the departure of the Israelites from Egypt, and their wanderings through the wilder-

ness, bear the name of Moses, who being their leader would un
doubtedly give a faithful history of these occurrences, unless he designed to deceive; and who, if his intimate connexion with Deity
described in these books be historically true, was likewise eminently
qualified, by virtue of such connexion, to produce a credible history
of the earlier periods. In like manner, of the several accounts of
the life and fate of Jesus, the superscriptions assign one to Matthew
and one to John: two men who having been eye witnesses of the
public ministry of Jesus from its commencement to its close were
particularly capable of giving a report of it; and who, from their
confidential intercourse with Jesus and his mother, together with
that supernatural aid which, according to John, Jesus promised to
his disciples to teach them and bring all things to their remembrance,
were enabled to give information of the circumstances of his earlier
years; of which some details are recorded by Matthew.

But that little reliance can be placed on the headings of ancient
manuscripts, and of sacred records more especially, is evident, and
in reference to biblical books has long since been proved. In the
so-called books of Moses mention is made of his death and burial:
but who now supposes that this was written beforehand by Moses
in the form of prophecy? Many of the Psalms bear the name of
David which presuppose an acquaintance with the miseries of the
exile; and predictions are put into the mouth of Daniel, a Jew living at the time of the Babylonish captivity, which could not have
been written before the reign of Antiochus Epiphanes. It is an
incontrovertible position of modern criticism that the titles of the
Biblical books represent nothing more than the design of their author, or the opinion of Jewish or Christian antiquity respecting their
origin: points the first of which proves nothing; and as to the second every thing depends upon the following considerations: 1. the
date of the opinion and the authority on which it rests; 2. the degree of harmony existing between this opinion and the internal
character of the writings in question. The first consideration includes an examination of the external, the second of the internal
grounds of evidence respecting the authenticity of the biblical books.
To investigate the internal grounds of credibility in relation to each
detail given in the Gospels, (for it is with them alone we are here
concerned) and to test the probability or improbability of their being
the production of eye witnesses, or of competently informed writers,
is the sole object of the present work. The *external grounds* of evidence may be examined in this introduction, only so far however
as is necessary in order to judge whether they yield a definite result,
which may perhaps be in opposition to the internal grounds of evidence: or whether the external evidence, insufficient of itself, leaves
to the internal evidence the decision of the question.

We learn from the works of Irenæus, of Clemens Alexandrinus,
and of Tertullian, that at the end of the second century after Christ
our four Gospels were recognized by the orthodox church as the

writings of the Apostles and the disciples of the Apostles; and were separated from many other similar productions as authentic records of the life of Jesus. The first Gospel according to our Canon is attributed to Matthew, who is enumerated among the twelve Apostles; the fourth to John the beloved disciple of our Lord; the second to Mark the interpreter of Peter; and the third to Luke the companion of Paul.* We have, besides, the authority of earlier authors, both in their own works and in quotations cited by others.

It is usual, in reference to the first Gospel to adduce the testimony of Papias, Bishop of Hierapolis, said to have been an auditor ἀκουστὴς of John, (probably the presbyter) and to have suffered martyrdom under Mark Aurelius. (161—180.) Papias asserts that Matthew the Apostle wrote τὰ λόγια (τὰ κυριακὰ.†) Schleiermacher, straining the meaning of λόγια, has latterly understood it to signify merely a collection of the sayings of Jesus. But when Papias speaks of Mark, he seems to use σύνταξιν τῶν κυριακῶν λογίων ποιεῖσθαι, and τὰ ὑπὸ τοῦ Χριστου ἢ λεχθέντα ἢ πραχθέντα γράφειν as equivalent expressions. Whence it appears that the word λόγια designates a writing comprehending the acts and fate of Jesus; and the fathers of the church were justified in understanding the testimony of Papias as relating to an entire Gospel.‡ They did indeed apply this testimony decidedly to our first Gospel; but the words of the Apostolic father contain no such indication, and the manuscript, of which he speaks, cannot be absolutely identical with our Gospel; for, according to the statement given by Papias, Matthew wrote in the Hebrew language; and it is a mere assumption of the christian fathers that our Greek Matthew is a translation of the original Hebrew Gospel.§ Precepts of Jesus, and narratives concerning him, corresponding more or less exactly with passages in our Matthew, do indeed occur in the works of other of the apostolic fathers: but then these works are not wholly genuine, and the quotations themselves are either in a form which indicates that they might have been derived from oral traditions; or where these authors refer to written sources, they do not mention them as being directly apostolic. Many citations in the writings of Justin Martyr (who died 166) agree with passages in our Matthew; but there are also, mixed up with these, other elements which are not to be found in our Gospels; and he refers to the writings from which he derives them generally as ἀπομνημονεύματα τῶν ἀποστόλων, or εὐαγγέλια, without naming any author in particular. Celsus,‖ the opponent of Christianity, (subsequent to 150) mentions that the disciples of Jesus had written his history, and he alludes to our present Gospels when he speaks of the divergence of the accounts respecting the number of angels seen at the resurrection; but we find no more precise refer-

* See the quotations given by De Wette in his "Einleitung in d. N. T." § 76.
† Euseb. H. E., iii. 39.   ‡ Ullmann, Credner, Lücke, De Wette.
§ Hieron de vir. illustr. 3.
‖ Contra Celsum, ii. 16. v. 56.

ence to any one Evangelist in his writings, so far as we know them through Origen.

We have the testimony of the same Papias who has the notice concerning Matthew, a testimony from the mouth of John (πρεσβύτερος), that Mark, who according to him was the interpreter of Peter (ἑρμηνευτὴσ Πέτρου), wrote down the discourses and actions of Jesus from his recollections of the instructions of that Apostle.* Ecclesiastical writers have likewise assumed that this passage from Papias refers to our second Gospel, though it does not say any thing of the kind, and is besides inapplicacle to it. For our second Gospel cannot have originated from recollections of Peter's instructions, i. e. from a source peculiar to itself, since it is evidently a compilation, whether made from memory or otherwise, from the first and third Gospels.† As little will the remark of Papias that Mark wrote without order (οὐ τάξει) apply to our Gospel. For he cannot by this expression intend a false chronological arrangement, since he ascribes to Mark the strictest love of truth, which, united with the consciousness that he had not the means of fixing dates, must have withheld him from making the attempt. But a total renunciation of chronological connexion, which Papias can alone have meant to attribute to him, is not to be found in the second Gospel. This being the case, what do those echoes which our second Gospel, in like manner as our first, seems to find in the most ancient ecclesiastical writers, prove?

That Luke, the companion of Paul, wrote a Gospel, is not attested by any authority of corresponding weight or antiquity with that of Papias in relation to Matthew and to Mark. The third Gospel however possesses a testimony of a particular kind in the "Acts of the Apostles:" not indeed authenticating it as the composition of Luke, but attributing it to an occasional companion of the Apostle Paul. According to the proem to the Acts and that to the Gospel of Luke, these two books proceeded from the same author or compiler: an origin which these writings do not, in other respects, contradict. In several chapters in the second half of the Book of the Acts the author, speaking of himself together with Paul, makes use of the first person plural,‡ and thus identifies himself with the companion of that apostle. The fact is, however, that many of the details concerning Paul, contained in other parts of the book of the Acts, are so indefinite and marvellous, and are moreover so completely at variance with Paul's genuine epistles, that it is extremely difficult to reconcile them with the notion that they were written by a companion of that apostle. It is also not a little remarkable that the author, neither in the introduction to the Acts, nor in that to the Gospel, alludes to his connexion with one of the most distin-

* Euseb. H. E. iii. 39. † This is clearly demonstrated by Griesbach in his "Commentatio, quâ Marci Evangelium totum e Matthaei et Lucae commentariis decerptum esse demonstratur." ‡ Chap. xvi. 10—17; xx. 5—15; xxi. 1—17; xxvii. 1—28; xxviii. 10—16.

guished of the Apostles, so that it is impossible not to suspect that the passages in which the writer speaks of himself as an actor in the scenes described, belong to a distinct memorial by another hand, which the author of the Acts has merely incorporated into his history. But leaving this conjecture out of the question, it is indeed possible that the companion of Paul may have composed his two works at a time, and under circumstances, when he was no longer protected by Apostolic influence against the tide of tradition; and that he saw no reason why, because he had not heard them previously from this Apostle, he should therefore reject the instructive, and (according to his notions, which certainly would not lead him to shun the marvellous,) credible narratives derived from that source. Now, it is asserted that because the Book of the Acts terminates with the two years imprisonment of Paul at Rome, therefore this second work of the disciple of that apostle, must have been written during that time, (63—65. A. D.) before the decision of Paul's trial, and that consequently, the Gospel of Luke, the earlier work of the same author, could not have been of later date. But, the breaking off of the Acts at that particular point might have been the result of many other causes; at all events such testimony, standing alone, is wholly insufficient to decide the historial worth of the Gospel.

It were to be wished that Polycarp. (he died 167) who both heard and saw the Apostle John,* had left us a testimony respecting him similar to that of Papias concerning Matthew. Still his silence on this subject, in the one short epistle which has come down to us, is no evidence against the authenticity of that Gospel, any more than the more or less ambiguous allusions in several of the Apostolic fathers to the *Epistles* of John are proofs in its favour. But it is matter of surprise that Irenæus the disciple of Polycarp, who was called upon to defend this Gospel from the attacks of those who denied its composition by John, should neither on this occasion, nor once in his diffuse work, have brought forward the weighty authority of his Apostolic master, as to this fact. Whether or not the fourth Gospel originally bore the name of John remains uncertain. We meet with it first among the Valentinians and the Montanists, about the middle of the second century. Its Apostolic origin was however (immediately after) denied by the so-called Alogi, who ascribed it to Cerinthus; partly because the Montanists derived from it their idea of the Paraclete; partly also because it did not harmonize with the other Gospels.† The earliest quotation expressly stated to be from the Gospel of John is found in Theophilus of Antioch, about the year 172.‡ How little reason the numerous theologians of the present day have to boast of the evidences in favour of the fourth Gospel, whilst they deny the not less well attested Apocalypse, has been well remarked by Tholuck. Lastly, that there were two Johns, the Apostle and the Presbyter, living contemporaneously at Ephesus, is a circumstance which has not received sufficient attention in con-

* Euseb. II. E. v. 20. 24.   † De Wette, Gieseler.   ‡ Ad. Autol. ii., 22.

nexion with the most ancient testimonies in favour of the derivation from John, of the Apocalypse on the one hand, and of the Gospels and Epistles on the other.

Thus these most ancient testimonies tell us, firstly, that an apostle, or some other person who had been acquainted with an apostle, wrote a Gospel history; but not whether it was identical with that which afterwards came to be circulated in the church under his name; secondly, that writings similar to our Gospels were in existence: but not that they were ascribed with certainty to any one individual apostle or companion of an apostle. Such is the uncertainty of these accounts, which after all do not reach further back than the third or fourth decade of the second century. According to all the rules of probability, the Apostles were all dead before the close of the first century: not excepting John, who is said to have lived till A. D. 100: concerning whose age and death, however, many fables were early invented. What an ample scope for attributing to the Apostles manuscripts they never wrote! The Apostles, dispersed abroad, had died in the latter half of the first century; the Gospel became more widely preached throughout the Roman empire, and by degrees acquired a fixed form in accordance with a particular type. It was doubtless from this orally circulated Gospel that the many passages agreeing accurately with passages in our Gospels, which occur without any indication of their source in the earliest ecclesiastical writers, were actually derived. Before long this oral traditionary Gospel became deposited in different manuscripts: this person or that, possibly an apostle, furnishing the principal features of the history. But these manuscripts were not at first compiled according to a particular form and order, and consequently had to undergo many revisions and re-arrangements, of which we have an example in the Gospel of the Hebrews and the citations of Justin. It appears that these manuscripts did not originally bear the names of their compilers, but either that of the community by whom they were first read, as the Gospel of Hebrews: or that of the Apostle or disciple after whose oral discourses or notes some other person had composed a connected history. The latter seems to have been the original meaning attached to the word κατὰ; as in the title to our first Gospel.* Nothing however was more natural than the supposition which arose among the early christians, that the histories concerning Jesus which were circulated and used by the churches had been written by his immediate disciples. Hence the ascription of the gospel writings generally to the apostles by Justin and by Celsus: and also of particular gospels to those particular apostles and disciples, whose oral discourses or written notes might possibly have formed the groundwork of a gospel manuscript, or who had perhaps been particularly connected with some certain district, or had been held in especial esteem by some particular community. The Gospel of the Hebrews successively received all three kinds of

* See Schleiermacher.

appellations; being first called εὐαγγέλιον καθ᾽ Ἑβραίους, after the community by which it was read; somewhat later, *Evangelium juxta duodecim apostolos;* and finally, *secundum Matthæum.*

Admitting however that we do not possess the immediate record of an eye witness in any one of the four Gospels, it is still very incomprehensible, replies the objector, how in Palestine itself, and at a time when so many eye witnesses yet lived, unhistorical legends and even collections of them should have been formed. But, in the first place, the fact that many such compilations of narratives concerning the life of Jesus were already in general circulation during the lifetime of the Apostles, and more especially that any one of our gospels was known to an Apostle and acknowledged by him, can never be proved. With respect to insolated anecdotes, it is only necessary to form an accurate conception of Palestine and of the real position of the eye witnesses referred to, in order to understand that the origination of legends, even at so early a period, is by no means incomprehensible. Who informs us that they must necessarily have taken root in that particular district of Palestine where Jesus tarried longest, and where his actual history was well known? And with respect to eye witnesses, if by these we are to understand the Apostles, it is to ascribe to them absolute ubiquity, to represent them as present here and there, weeding out all the unhistorical legends concerning Jesus in whatever places they had chanced to spring up and flourish. Eye witnesses in the more extended sense, who had only seen Jesus occasionally and not been his constant companions, must, on the contrary, have been strongly tempted to fill up their imperfect knowledge of his history with mythical representations.

But it is inconceivable, they say, that such a mass of mythi should have originated in an age so historical as that of the first Roman emperors. We must not however be misled by too comprehensive a notion of an historical age. The sun is not visible at the same instant to every place on the same meridian at the same time of year; it gleams upon the mountain summits and the high plains before it penetrates the lower valleys and the deep ravines. No less true is it that the historic age dawns not upon all people at the same period. The people of highly civilized Greece, and of Rome the capital of the world, stood on an eminence which had not been reached in Galilee and Judæa. Much rather may we apply to this age an expression become trite among historians, but which seems in the present instance willingly forgotten: namely, that incredulity and superstition, scepticism and fanaticism go hand in hand.

But the Jews, it is said, had long been accustomed to keep written records; nay, the most flourishing period of their literature was already past, they were no longer a progressing and consequently a productive people, they were a nation verging to decay. But the fact is, the pure historic idea was never developed among the Hebrews during the whole of their political existence; their latest historical works, such as the Books of the Maccabees, and even the writings of Josephus, are not free from marvellous and extravagant tales. Indeed no just notion of the true nature of history is possible, without a perception of the inviolability of the chain of finite causes, and of the impossibility of miracles. This perception which is wanting to so many minds of our own day was still more deficient in Palestine, and indeed throughout the Roman empire. And to a mind still open to the reception of the marvellous, if it be once carried away by the tide of religious enthusiasm, all things will appear credible, and should this enthusiasm lay hold of a yet wider circle, it will awaken a new creative vigour, even in a decayed people. To account for such an enthusiasm it is by no means necessary to presuppose the gospel miracles as the exciting cause. This may be found in the known religious dearth of that period, a dearth so great that the cravings of the mind after some religious belief excited a relish for the most extravagant forms of worship: secondly in the deep religious satisfaction which was afforded by the belief in the resurrection of the deceased Messiah, and by the essential principles of the doctrine of Jesus.

§ 14. THE POSSIBILITY OF MYTHI IN THE NEW TESTAMENT CONSIDERED ON INTERNAL GROUNDS.

SEEING from what has already been said that the external testimony respecting the composition of our Gospels, far from forcing upon us the conclusion that they proceeded from eye witnesses or well-informed contemporaries, leaves the decision to be determined wholly by internal grounds of evidence, that is, by the nature of the Gospel narratives themselves: we might immediately proceed from this introduction to the peculiar object of the present work, which is an examination of those narratives in detail. It may however appear useful, before entering upon this special inquiry, to consider the general question, how far it is consistent with the character of the Christian religion that mythi should be found in it, and how far the general construction of the Gospel narratives authorizes us to treat them as mythi. Although, indeed, if the following critical examination of the details be successful in proving the actual existence of mythi in the New Testament, this preliminary demonstration of their possibility becomes superfluous.

If with this view we compare the acknowledged mythical religions of antiquity with the Hebrew and Christian, it is true that we are struck by many differences between the sacred histories existing in these religious forms and those in the former. Above all, it is commonly alleged that the sacred histories of the Bible are distinguished from the legends of the Indians, Greeks, Romans, &c., by their moral character and excellence. "In the latter, the stories of the battles of the gods, the loves of Krishna, Jupiter, &c., contain much which was offensive to the moral feeling even of enlightened heathens, and which is revolting to ours: whilst in the former, the whole course of the narration, offers only what is worthy of God, instructive, and ennobling." To this it may be answered with regard to the heathens, that the appearance of immorality in many of their narratives is merely the consequence of a subsequent misconception of their original meaning: and with regard to the Old Testament, that the perfect moral purity of its history has been contested. Often indeed, it has been contested without good grounds, because a due distinction is not made between that which is ascribed to individual men, (who, as they are represented, are by no means spotless examples of purity,) and that which is ascribed to God:* nevertheless it is true that we have commands called divine, which, like that to the Israelites on their departure out of Egypt to purloin vessels of gold, are scarcely less revolting to an enlightened moral feeling, than the thefts of the Grecian Hermes. But even admitting this difference in the morality of the religions to its full extent, (and it must be admitted at least with regard to the New Testament,) still it furnishes no proof of the historical character of the Bible; for though every story relating to God which is immoral is necessarily fictitious, even the most moral is not necessarily true.

"But that which is incredible and inconceivable forms the staple of the heathen fables; whilst in the biblical history, if we only presuppose the immediate intervention of the Deity, there is nothing of the kind." Exactly, if this be presupposed. Otherwise, we might very likely find the miracles in the life of Moses, Elias, or Jesus, the Theophany and Angelophany of the Old and New Testament, just as incredible as the fables of Jupiter, Hercules, or Bacchus: presuppose the divinity or divine descent of these individuals, and their actions and fate become as credible as those of the biblical personages with the like presupposition. Yet not quite so, it may be returned. Vishnu appearing in his three first avatars as a fish, a tortoise, and a boar; Saturn devouring his children: Jupiter turning himself into a bull, a swan, &c.—these are incredibilities of quite another kind from Jehovah appearing to Abraham in a human form under the terebinth tree, or to Moses in the burning bush. This extravagant love of the marvellous is the character of the heathen mythology. A similar accusation might indeed be brought against many parts of the Bible, such as the tales of Balaam, Joshua, and Samson; but still it is here less glaring, and does not form as in the Indian religion and in certain parts of the Grecian, the prevailing character. What however does this prove? Only that the biblical history *might* be true, sooner than the Indian or Grecian fables; not in the least that on this account it *must* be true, and can contain nothing fictitious.

"But the subjects of the heathen mythology are for the most

* This same want of distinction has led the Alexandrians to allegorize, the Deists to scoff, and the Supernaturalists to strain the meaning of words; as was done lately by Hoffmann in describing David's behaviour to the conquered Amonites. (Christoterpe auf 1838, S. 184.)

part such, as to convince us beforehand that they are mere inventions: those of the Bible such as at once to establish their own reality. A Brahma, an Ormusd, a Jupiter, without doubt never existed; but there still is a God, a Christ, and there have been an Adam, a Noah, an Abraham, a Moses." Whether an Adam or a Noah, however, were such as they are represented, has already been doubted, and may still be doubted. Just so, on the other side, there may have been something historical about Hercules, Theseus, Achilles, and other heroes of Grecian story. Here, again, we come to the decision that the biblical history *might* be true sooner than the heathen mythology, but is not necessarily so. This decision however, together with the two distinctions already made, brings us to an important observation. How do the Grecian divinities approve themselves immediately to us as non-existing beings, if not because things are ascribed to them which we cannot reconcile with our idea of the divine? whilst the God of the Bible is a reality to us just in so far as he corresponds with the idea we have formed of him in our own minds. Besides the contradiction to our notion of the divine involved in the plurality of heathen gods, and the intimate description of their motives and actions, we are at once revolted to find that the gods themselves have a history: that they are born, grow up, marry, have children, work out their purposes, suffer difficulties and weariness, conquer and are conquered. It is irreconcileable with our idea of the Absolute to suppose it subjected to time and change, to opposition and suffering: and therefore where we meet with a narrative in which these are attributed to a divine being, by this test we recognize it as unhistorical or mythical.

It is in this sense that the Bible, and even the Old Testament, is said to contain no mythi. The story of the creation with its succession of each day's labour ending in a rest after the completion of the task; the expression often recurring in the farther course of the narrative, God repented of having done so and so:—these and similar representations cannot indeed be entirely vindicated from the charge of making finite the nature of the Deity, and this is the ground which has been taken by mythical interpreters of the history of the creation. And in every other instance where God is said to reveal himself exclusively at any definite place or time, by celestial apparition, or by miracle wrought immediately by himself, it is to be presumed that the Deity has become finite and descended to human modes of operation. It may however be said in general, that in the Old Testament the divine nature does not appear to be essentially affected by the temporal character of its operation, but that the temporal shows itself rather as a mere form, an unavoidable appearance, arising out of the necessary limitation of human, and especially of uncultivated powers of representation. It is obvious to every one, that there is something quite different in the Old Testament declarations, that God made an alliance with Noah, and Abraham, led his people out of Egypt, gave them laws, brought them into the promised land, raised up for them judges, kings, and prophets, and punished them at last for their disobedience by exile;—from the tales concerning Jupiter, that he was born of Rhea in Crete, and hidden from his father Saturn in a cave; that afterwards he made war upon his father, freed the Uranides, and with their help and that of the lightning with which they furnished him, overcame the rebellious Titans, and at last divided the world amongst his brothers and children. The essential difference between the two representations is, that in the latter, the Deity himself is the subject of progression, becomes another being at the end of the process from what he was at the beginning, something being effected in himself and for his own sake: whilst in the former, change takes place only on the side of the world; God remains fixed in his own identity as the I AM, and the temporal is only a superficial reflection cast back upon his acting energy by that course of mundane events which he both originated and guides. In the heathen mythology the gods have a history: in the Old Testament, God himself has none, but only his people: and if the proper meaning of mythology be the history of gods, then the Hebrew religion has no mythology.

From the Hebrew religion, this recognition of the divine unity and immutability was transmitted to the Christian. The birth, growth, miracles, sufferings, death, and resurrection of Christ, are circumstances belonging to the destiny of the Messiah, above which God remains unaffected in his own changeless identity. The New Testament therefore knows nothing of mythology in the above sense. The state of the question is however somewhat changed from that which it assumed in the Old Testament: for Jesus is called the Son of God, not merely in the same sense as kings under the theocracy were so called, but as actually begotten by the divine spirit, or from the incarnation in his person of the divine λόγος. Inasmuch as he is one with the Father, and in him the whole fullness of the godhead dwells bodily, he is more than Moses. The actions and sufferings of such a being are not external to the Deity: though we are not allowed to suppose a *theopaschitic* union with the divine nature, yet still, even in the New Testament, and more in the later doctrine of the Church, it is a divine being that here lives and suffers, and what befals him has an absolute worth and significance. Thus according to the above accepted notion of the mythus, the New Testament has more of a mythical character than the Old. But to call the history of Jesus mythical in this sense, is as unimportant with regard to the historical question as it is unexceptionable; for the idea of God is in no way opposed to such an intervention in human affairs as does not affect his own immutability; so that as far as regards this point, the gospel history, notwithstanding its mythical designation, might be at the same time throughout historically true.

Admitting that the biblical history does not equally with the

heathen mythology offend our idea of Deity, and that consequently
it is not in like manner characterized by this mark of the unhistorical, however far it be from bearing any guarantee of being historical,—we are met by the further question whether it be not less
accordant with our idea of the world, and whether such discordancy
may not furnish a test of its unhistorical nature.

In the ancient world, that is, in the east, the religious tendency
was so preponderating, and the knowledge of nature so limited, that
the law of connexion between earthly finite beings was very loosely
regarded. At every link there was a disposition to spring into the
Infinite, and to see God as the immediate cause of every change in
nature or the human mind. In this mental condition the biblical
history was written. Not that God is here represented as doing all
and every thing himself:—a notion which, from the manifold direct
evidence of the fundamental connexion between finite things, would
be impossible to any reasonable mind:—but there prevails in the
biblical writers a ready disposition to derive all things down to the
minutest details, as soon as they appear particularly important, immediately from God. He it is who gives the rain and sunshine ;
he sends the east wind and the storm ; he dispenses war, famine,
pestilence ; he hardens hearts and softens them ; suggests thoughts
and resolutions. And this is particularly the case with regard to
his chosen instruments and beloved people. In the history of the
Israelites we find traces of his immediate agency at every step:
through Moses, Elias, Jesus, he performs things which never would
have happened in the ordinary course of nature.

Our modern world, on the contrary, after many centuries of
tedious research, has attained a conviction, that all things are linked
together by a chain of causes and effects, which suffers no interruption. It is true that single facts and groups of facts, with their
conditions and processes of change, are not so circumscribed as to
be unsusceptible of external influence ; for the action of one existence or kingdom in nature intrenches on that of another: human
freedom controls natural development, and material laws react on
human freedom. Nevertheless the totality of finite things forms a
vast circle, which, except that it owes its existence and laws to a
superior power, suffers no intrusion from without. This conviction
is so much a habit of thought with the modern world, that in actual
life, the belief in a supernatural manifestation, an immediate divine
agency, is at once attributed to ignorance or imposture. It has
been carried to the extreme in that modern explanation, which, in
a spirit exactly opposed to that of the Bible, has either totally removed the divine causation, or has so far restricted it that it is immediate in the act of creation alone, but mediate from that point
onwards ;—i. e. God operates on the world only in so far as he
gave to it this fixed direction at the creation. From this point of
view, at which nature and history appear as a compact tissue of
finite causes and effects, it was impossible to regard the narratives

of the Bible, in which this tissue is broken by innumerable instances
of divine interference, as historical.

It must be confessed on nearer investigation, that this modern
explanation, although it does not exactly deny the existence of God,
yet puts aside the idea of him, as the ancient view did the idea of
the world. For this is, as it has been often and well remarked, no
longer a God and Creator, but a mere finite Artist, who acts immediately upon his work only during its first production, and then
leaves it to itself; who becomes excluded with his full energy from
one particular sphere of existence. It has therefore been attempted
to unite the two views so as to maintain for the world its law of
sequence, and for God his unlimited action, and by this means to
preserve the truth of the biblical history. According to this view,
the world is supposed to move in obedience to the law of consecutive
causes and effects bound up with its constitution, and God to act
upon it only mediately: but in single instances, where he finds it
necessary for particular objects, he is not held to be restricted from
entering into the course of human changes immediately. This is
the view of modern Supranaturalism;[*] evidently a vain attempt to
reconcile two opposite views, since it contains the faults of both,
and adds a new one in the contradiction between the two ill-assorted
principles. For here the consecutiveness of nature and history is
broken through as in the ancient biblical view; and the action of
God limited as in the contrary system. The proposition that God
works sometimes mediately, sometimes immediately, upon the world,
introduces a changeableness, and therefore a temporal element, into
the nature of his action, which brings it under the same condemnation as both the other systems; that, namely, of distinguishing the ·
maintaining power, in the one case from individual instances of the
divine agency, and in the other from the act of creation.[†]

Since then our idea of God requires an immediate, and our idea
of the world a mediate divine operation; and since the idea of combination of the two species of action is inadmissible :—nothing remains for us but to regard them both as so permanently and immov-
ably united, that the operation of God on the world continues for
ever and every where twofold, both immediate and mediate : which
comes just to this, that it is neither of the two, or this distinction
loses its value. To explain more closely: if we proceed from the
idea of God, from which arose the demand for his immediate operation, then the world is to be regarded in relation to him as a Whole:

---

* Heydenreich, über die Unzulässigkeit, u. s, f. 1. Stück. Compare Storr, doctr.
christ. § 35 ff.   † If the Supranatural view contains a theological contradiction, so the
new evangelical theology, which esteems itself raised so far above the old supranatural
view, contains a logical contradiction.   To say that God acts only mediately upon the
world as the general rule, but sometimes, by way of exception, immediately,—has some
meaning, though perhaps not a wise one.   But to say that God acts always immediately
on the world, but in some cases more particularly immediately,—is a flat contradiction
in itself.   On the principle of the immanence or immediate agency of God in the world,
to which the new evangelical theology lays claim, the idea of the miraculous is impossible,
Comp. my Streitschriften, i. 3, S. 46 f.

on the contrary, if we proceed from the idea of the finite, the world is a congeries of separate parts, and hence has arisen the demand for a merely mediate agency of God:—so that we must say—God acts upon the world as a Whole immediately, but on each part only by means of his action on every other part, that is to say, by the laws of nature.*

This view brings us to the same conclusion with regard to the historical value of the Bible as the one above considered. The miracles which God wrought for and by Moses and Jesus, do not proceed from his immediate operation on the Whole, but presuppose an immediate action in particular cases, which is a contradiction to the type of the divine agency we have just given. The supranaturalists indeed claim an exception from this type on behalf of the biblical history; a presupposition which is inadmissible from our point of view,† according to which the same laws, although varied by various circumstances, are supreme in every sphere of being and action, and therefore every narrative which offends against these laws, is to be recognized as so far unhistorical.

The result, then, however surprising, of a general examination of the biblical history, is that the Hebrew and Christian religions, like all others, have their mythi. And this result is confirmed, if we consider the inherent nature of religion, what essentially belongs to it and therefore must be common to all religions, and what on the other hand is peculiar and may differ in each. If religion be defined as the perception of truth, not in the form of an idea, which is the philosophic perception, but invested with imagery; it is easy to see that the mythical element can be wanting only when religion either falls short of, or goes beyond, its peculiar province, and that in the proper religious sphere it must necessarily exist.

It is only amongst the lowest and most barbarous people, such as the Esquimaux, that we find religion not yet fashioned into an objective form, but still confined to a subjective feeling. They know nothing of gods, of superior spirits and powers, and their whole piety consists in an undefined sentiment excited by the hurricane, the eclipse, or the magician. As it progresses however, the religious principle loses more and more of this indefiniteness, and ceasing to be subjective, becomes objective. In the sun, moon, mountains, animals, and other objects of the sensible world, higher powers are discovered and revered; and in proportion as the signifi-

* In this view essentially coincide Wegscheider, instit. theol. dogm. § 12 ; De Wette, bibl. Dogm., Vorbereitung ; Schleiermacher, Glaubensl. § 46 f.; Markeineke, Dogm. § 260 ff. Comp. George, S. 78 f.   † To a freedom from this presupposition we lay claim in the following work ; in the same sense as a state might be called free from presupposition where the privileges of station, &c., were of no account. Such a state indeed has one presupposition, that of the natural equality of its citizens ; and similarly do we take for granted the equal amenability to law of all events : but this is merely an affirmative form of expression for our former negation. But to claim for the biblical history especial laws of its own, is an affirmative proposition, which, according to the established rule, is that which requires proof, and not our denial of it, which is merely negative. And if the proof cannot be given, or be found insufficient, it is the former and not the latter, which is to be considered a presupposition. See my Streitschriften i. 3. S. 36 ff.

cance given to these objects is remote from their actual nature, a new world of mere imagination is created, a sphere of divine existences whose relations to one another, actions, and influences, can be represented only after human analogy, and therefore as temporal and historical. Even when the mind has raised itself to the conception of the Divine unity, still the energy and activity of God are considered only under the form of a series of acts: and on the other hand, natural events and human actions can be raised to a religious significance only by the admission of divine interpositions and miracles. It is only from the philosophic point of view that the world of imagination is seen again to coincide with the actual, because the thought of God is comprehended to be his essence, and in the regular course itself of nature and of history, the revelation of the divine idea is acknowledged.

It is certainly difficult to conceive, how narratives which thus speak of imagination as reality can have been formed without intentional deceit, and believed without unexampled credulity; and this difficulty has been held an invincible objection to the mythical interpretation of many of the narratives of the Old and New Testament. If this were the case, it would apply equally to the Heathen legends ; and on the other hand, if profane Mythology have steered clear of the difficulty, neither will that of the Bible founder upon it. I shall here quote at length the words of an experienced inquirer into Grecian mythology and primitive history, Otfried Müller, since it is evident that this preliminary knowledge of the subject which must be derived from general mythology, and which is necessary for the understanding of the following examination of the evangelic mythus, is not yet familiar to all theologians. "How," says Müller,* "shall we reconcile this combination of the true and the false, the real and ideal, in mythi, with the fact of their being believed and received as truth? The ideal, it may be said, is nothing else than poetry and fiction clothed in the form of a narration. But a fiction of this kind cannot be invented at the same time by many different persons without a miracle, requiring, as it does, a peculiar coincidence of intention, imagination, and expression. It is therefore the work of one person:—but how did he convince all the others that his fiction had an actual truth? Shall we suppose him to have been one who contrived to delude by all kinds of trickery and deception, and perhaps allied himself with similar deceivers, whose part it was to afford attestation to the people of his inventions as having been witnessed by themselves? Or shall we think of him as a man of higher endowments than others, who believed him upon his word; and received the mythical tales under whose veil he sought to impart wholesome truths, as a sacred revelation?

* Prolegomena zu einer wissenschaftlichen Mythologie, S. 110 ff. With this Ullmann and J. Muller in their reviews of this work, Hoffmann, S. 113, f., and others are agreed as far as relates to the heathen mythi. Especially compare George, Mythus und Sage, S. 15, ff. 103.

But it is impossible to prove that such a caste of deceivers existed in ancient Greece (or Palestine): on the contrary, this skilful system of deception, be it gross or refined, selfish or philanthropic, if we are not misled by the impression we have received from the earliest productions of the Grecian (or Christian) mind, is little suited to the noble simplicity of those times. Hence an inventer of the mythus in the proper sense of the word is inconceivable. This reasoning brings us to the conclusion, that the idea of a deliberate and intentional fabrication, in which the author clothes that which he knows to be false in the appearance of truth, must be entirely set aside as insufficient to account for the origin of the mythus. Or in other words, that there is a certain necessity in this connexion between the ideal and the real, which constitutes the mythus; that the mythical images were formed by the influence of sentiments common to all mankind; and that the different elements grew together without the author's being himself conscious of their incongruity. It is this notion of a certain necessity and unconsciousness in the formation of the ancient mythi, on which we insist. If this be once understood, it will also be perceived that the contention whether the mythus proceed from one person or many, from the poet or the people, though it may be started on other grounds, does not go to the root of the matter. For if the one who invents the mythus is only obeying the impulse which acts also upon the minds of his hearers, he is but the mouth through which all speak, the skilful interpreter who has the address first to give form and expression to the thoughts of all. It is however very possible that this notion of necessity and unconsciousness, might appear itself obscure and mystical to our antiquarians (and theologians), from no other reason than that this mythicising tendency has no analogy in the present mode of thinking. But is not history to acknowledge even what is strange, when led to it by unprejudiced research?"

As an example to show that even very complicated mythi, in the formation of which many apparently remote circumstances must have combined, may yet have arisen in this unconscious manner, Müller then refers to the Grecian mythus of Apollo and Marsyas. "It was customary to celebrate the festivals of Apollo with playing on the lyre, and it was necessary to piety, that the god himself should be regarded as its author. In Phrygia, on the contrary, the national music was the flute, which was similarly derived from a demon of their own, named Marsyas. The ancient Grecians perceived that the tones of these two instruments were essentially opposed: the harsh shrill piping of the flute must be hateful to Apollo, and therefore Marsyas his enemy. This was not enough: in order that the lyre-playing Grecian might flatter himself that the invention of his god was the more excellent instrument, Apollo must triumph over Marsyas. But why was it necessary in particular that the unlucky Phrygian should be flayed? Here is the simple origin of the mythus. Near the castle of Celene in Phrygia, in a cavern whence flowed a stream or torrent named Marsyas, was suspended a skin flask, called by the Phrygians, the bottle of Marsyas; for Marsyas was, like the Grecian Silenus, a demi-god symbolizing the exuberance of the juices of nature. Now where a Grecian, or a Phrygian with Grecian prepossessions, looked on the bottle, he plainly saw the catastrophe of Marsyas: here was still suspended his skin, which had been torn off and made into a bottle:—Apollo had flayed him. In all this there is no arbitrary invention: the same ideas might have occurred to many, and if one first gave expression to them, he knew well that his auditors, imbued with the same prepossessions, would not for an instant doubt his accuracy."

"The chief reason of the complicated character of mythi in general, is their having been formed for the most part, not at once, but successively and by degrees, under the influence of very different circumstances and events both external and internal. The popular traditions, being orally transmitted and not restricted by any written document, were open to receive every new addition, and thus grew in the course of long centuries to the form in which we now find them. (How far this applies to a great part of the New Testament mythi, will be shown hereafter.) This is an important and luminous fact, which however is very frequently overlooked in the explanation of mythi; for they are regarded as allegories invented by one person, at one stroke, with the definite purpose of investing a thought in the form of a narration."

The view thus expressed by Müller, that the mythus is founded not upon any individual conception, but upon the more elevated and general conception of a whole people (or religious community), is said by a competent judge of Müller's work to be the necessary condition for a right understanding of the ancient mythus, the admission or rejection of which henceforth ranges the opinions on mythology into two opposite divisions.*

It is not however easy to draw a line of distinction between intentional and unintentional fiction. In the case where a fact lay at the foundation, which, being the subject of popular conversation and admiration, in the course of time formed itself into a mythus, we readily dismiss all notion of wilful fraud, at least in its origin. For a mythus of this kind is not the work of one man, but of a whole body of men, and of succeeding generations; the narrative passing from mouth to mouth, and like a snowball growing by the involuntary addition of one exaggerating feature from this and another from that narrator. In time however these legends are sure to fall into the way of some gifted minds, which will be stimulated by them to the exercise of their own poetical, religious, or didactic powers. Most of the mythical narratives which have come down to us from antiquity, such as the Trojan, and the Mosaic series of legends, are presented to us in this elaborated form. Here then it

---

* The words of Bauer in his review of Müller's Prolegomena, in Jahn's Jahrbüchern f. Philol. u. Pädag. 1838, 1 Heft, S. 7.

would appear there must have been intentional deception : this however is only the result of an erroneous assumption. It is almost impossible, in a critical and enlightened age like our own, to carry ourselves back to a period of civilization in which the imagination worked so powerfully, that its illusions were believed as realities by the very minds that created them. Yet the very same miracles which are wrought in less civilized circles by the imagination, are produced in the more cultivated by the understanding. Let us take one of the best didactic historians of ancient or modern times, Livy, as an example. "Numa," he says, "gave to the Romans a number of religious ceremonies, *ne luxuriarentur otio animi*, and because he regarded religion as the best means of bridling *multitudinem imperitum et illis seculis rudem. Idem,*" he continues, "*nefastos dies fastosque fecit, quia aliquando nihil cum populo agi utile futurum erat.*"* How did Livy know that these were the motives of Numa? In point of fact they certainly were not. But Livy believed them to be so. The inference of his own understanding appeared to him so necessary, that he treated it with full conviction as an actual fact. The popular legend, or some ancient poet, had explained this fertility of religious invention in Numa otherwise ; namely, that it arose from his communication with the nymph Egeria, who revealed to him the forms of worship that would be most acceptable to the gods. It is obvious, that the case is pretty nearly the same with regard to both representations. If the latter had an individual author, it was his opinion that the historical statement could be accounted for only upon the supposition of a communication with a superior being ; as it was that of Livy, that its explanation must lie in political views. The one mistook the production of his imagination, the other the inference of his understanding, for reality.

Perhaps it may be admitted that there is a possibility of unconscious fiction, even when an individual author is assigned to it, provided that the mythical consists only in the filling up and adorning some historical event with imaginary circumstances : but that where the whole story is invented, and not any historical nucleus is to be found, this unconscious fiction is impossible. Whatever view may be taken of the heathen mythology, it is easy to show with regard to the New Testament, that there was the greatest antecedent probability of this very kind of fiction having arisen respecting Jesus without any fraudulent intention. The expectation of a Messiah had grown up amongst the Israelitish people long before the time of Jesus, and just then had ripened to full maturity. And from its beginning this expectation was not indefinite, but determined, and characterized by many important particulars. Moses was said to have promised his people a prophet like unto himself (Deut. xviii. 15), and this passage was in the time of Jesus applied to the Messiah (Acts iii. 22 ; vii. 37). Hence the rabbinical prin-

* I. 19.

ciple: as the first redeemer (*Goel*), so shall be the second; which principle was carried out into many particulars to be expected in the Messiah after his prototype Moses.* Again, the Messiah was to come of the race of David, and as a second David take possession of his throne (Matt. xxii. 42; Luke i. 32; Acts ii. 30): and therefore in the time of Jesus it was expected that he, like David, should be born in the little village of Bethlehem (John vii. 42; Matt. ii. 5 f.). In the above passage Moses describes the supposed Messiah as a prophet; so in his own idea, Jesus was the greatest and last of the prophetic race. But in the old national legends the prophets were made illustrious by the most wonderful actions and destiny. How could less be expected of the Messiah? Was it not necessary beforehand, that his life should be adorned with that which was most glorious and important in the lives of the prophets? Must not the popular expectation give him a share in the bright portion of their history, as subsequently the sufferings of himself and his disciples were attributed by Jesus when he appeared as the Messiah, to a participation in the dark side of the fate of the prophets (Matt. xxiii. 29 ff.; Luke xiii. 33 ff.; compare Matt. v. 12.)? Believing that Moses and all the prophets had prophesied of the Messiah (John v. 46; Luke iv. 21; xxiv. 27), it was as natural for the Jews, with their allegorizing tendency, to consider their actions and destiny as types of the Messiah, as to take their sayings for predictions. In general the whole Messianic era was expected to be full of signs and wonders. The eyes of the blind should be opened, the ears of the deaf should be unclosed, the lame should leap, and the tongue of the dumb praise God (Isaiah xxxv. 5 f.; xlii. 7; comp. xxxii. 3, 4). These merely figurative expressions, soon came to be understood literally (Matt. xi. 5; Luke vii. 21 f.), and thus the idea of the Messiah was continually filled up with new details, even before the appearence of Jesus.† Thus many of the legends respecting him had not to be newly invented; they already existed in the popular hope of the Messiah, having been mostly derived with various modifications‡ from the Old Testament, and had

---

* Midrasch Koheleth f. 73, 3. (in Schöttgen, *horæ hebraicæ et talmudicæ*, 2, S. 251. f.) *R. Berechias nomine R. Isaaci dixit: Quemadmodum Goel primus (Moses), sic etiam postremus (Messias) comparatus est. De Goele primo quidnam scriptura dixit?* Exod. iv. 20: *et sumsit Moses uxorem et filios, eosque asino imposuit. Sic Goel postremus, Zacharias ix. 9: pauper et insidens asino. Quidnam de Goele primo nosti? Is descendere fecit Man, q. d.* Exod. xvi. 14: *ecce ego pluere faciam vobis panem de cœlo. Sic etiam Goel postremus manua descendere faciet, q. d.* Ps. lxxii. 16: *erit multitudo frumenti in terra. Quomodo Goel primus comparatus fuit? Is ascendere fecit puteum: sic quoque Goel postremus ascendere faciet aquas, q. d.* Joel iv. 18: *et fons e domo Domini egredietur, et torrentem Sittim irrigabit.*

† Tanchuma f. 54, 4. (in Schöttgen, p. 74): *R. Acha nomine R. Samuelis bar Nachmani dixit: Quæcumque Deus S. B. facturus est* לבא ריתל *(tempore messiano) ea jam ante fecit per manus justorum* חיה בימי *(seculo ante Messiam elapso). Deus S. B. suscitabit mortuos, id quod jam ante fecit per Eliam, Elisam et Ezechielem. Mare exsiccabit, prout per Mosen factum est. Oculos cæcorum aperiet, id quod per Elisam fecit. Deus S. B. futuro tempore visitabit steriles, quemadmodum in Abrahamo et Sara fecit.*

‡ The Old Testament legends have undergone many changes and amplifications, even without any reference to the Messiah, so that the partial discrepancy between the narra-

merely to be transferred to Jesus,* and accommodated to his character and doctrines. In no case could it be easier for the person who first added any new feature to the description of Jesus, to believe himself its genuineness, since his argument would be: Such and such things must have happened to the Messiah; Jesus was the Messiah; therefore such and such things happened to him.†

Truly it may be said that the middle term of this argument, namely, that Jesus was the Messiah, would have failed in proof to his contemporaries all the more on account of the common expectation of miraculous events, if that expectation had not been fulfilled by him. But the following critique on the Life of Jesus does not divest it of all those features to which the character of miraculous has been appropriated: and besides we must take into account the overwhelming impression which was made upon those around him by the personal character and discourse of Jesus, as long as he was living amongst them, which did not permit them deliberately to scrutinize and compare him with their previous standard. The belief in him as the Messiah extended to wider circles only by slow degrees; and even during his lifetime the people may have reported many wonderful stories of him (comp. Matt. xiv. 2). After his death, however, the belief in his resurrection, however that belief may have arisen, afforded a more than sufficient proof of his Messiahship; so that all the other miracles in his history need not be considered as the foundation of the faith in this, but may rather be adduced as the consequence of it.

It is however by no means necessary to attribute this same freedom from all conscious intention of fiction, to the authors of all those narratives in the Old and New Testament which must be considered as unhistorical. In every series of legends, especially if any patriotic or religious party interest is associated with them, as soon as they become the subject of free poetry or any other literary composition, some kind of fiction will be intentionally mixed up with them. The authors of the Homeric songs could not have believed that every particular which they related of their gods and heroes had really happened; and just as little could the writer of the Chronicles have been ignorant that in his deviation from the books of Samuel and of the Kings, he was introducing many events of later occurrence

tives concerning Jesus with those relating to Moses and the prophets, is not a decisive proof that the former were not derived from the latter. Compare Acts vii. 22, 53, and the corresponding part of Josephus Antiq. ii. & iii. with the account of Moses given in Exodus. Also the Biblical account of Abraham with Antiq. i. 8. 2; of Jacob with i. 19, 6; of Joseph with ii. 5, 4.

* George, S. 125: If we consider the firm conviction of the disciples, that all which had been prophesied in the Old Testament of the Messiah must necessarily have been fulfilled in the person of their master; and moreover that there were many blank spaces in the history of Christ; we shall see that it was impossible to have happened otherwise than that these ideas should have embodied themselves, and thus the mythi have arisen which we find. Even if a more correct representation of the life of Jesus had been possible by means of tradition, this conviction of the disciples must have been strong enough to triumph over it.

† Compare O. Müller, Prolegomena, S. 7, on a similar conclusion of Grecian poets.

into an earlier period; or the author of the book of Daniel* that he was modelling his history upon that of Joseph, and accommodating prophecies to events already past; and exactly as little may this be said of all the unhistorical narratives of the Gospels, as for example, of the first chapter of the third, and many parts of the fourth Gospel. But a fiction, although not undesigned, may still be without evil design. It is true, the case is not the same with the supposed authors of many fictions in the Bible, as with poets properly so called, since the latter write without any expectation that their poems will be received as history: but still it is to be considered that in ancient times, and especially amongst the Hebrews, and yet more when this people was stirred up by religious excitement, the line of distinction between history and fiction, prose and poetry, was not drawn so clearly as with us. It is a fact also deserving attention that amongst the Jews and early Christians, the most reputable authors published their works with the substitution of venerated names, without an idea that they were guilty of any falsehood or deception by so doing.

The only question that can arise here is whether to such fictions, the work of an individual, we can give the name of mythi? If we regard only their own intrinsic nature, the name is not appropriate; but it is so when these fictions, having met with faith, come to be received amongst the legends of a people or religious party, for this is always a proof that they were the fruit, not of any individual conception, but of an accordance with the sentiments of a multitude.†

A frequently raised objection remains, for the refutation of which the remarks above made, upon the date of the origin of many of the gospel mythi, are mainly important: the objection, namely, that the space of about thirty years, from the death of Jesus to the destruction of Jerusalem, during which the greater part of the narratives must have been formed; or even the interval extending to the beginning of the second century, the most distant period which can be allowed for the origin of even the latest of these gospel narratives, and for the written composition of our gospels;—is much too short to admit of the rise of so rich a collection of mythi. But, as we

* The comparison of the first chapter of this book with the history of Joseph in Genesis gives an instructive view of the tendency of the later Hebrew legend and poetry to form new relations upon the pattern of the old. As Joseph was carried captive to Egypt, so was Daniel to Babylon; (i. 2.) like Joseph he must change his name; (7.) God makes the הַסָּרִיסִים שַׂר favourable to him, as the הַטַּבָּחִים שַׂר סָרִיס to Joseph; (9.) he abstains from polluting himself with partaking of the king's meats and drinks, which are pressed upon him; (8.) a self-denial held as meritorious in the time of Antiochus Epiphanes, as that of Joseph with regard to Potiphar's wife; like Joseph he gains eminence by the interpretation of a dream of the king, which his חַרְטֻמִּים were unable to explain to him, (ii.); whilst the additional circumstance that Daniel is enabled to give not only the interpretation, but the dream itself, which had escaped the memory of the king, appears to be a romantic exaggeration of that which was attributed to Joseph. In the account of Josephus, the history of Daniel has reacted in a singular manner upon that of Joseph; for as Nebuchadnezzar forgets his dream, and the interpretation according to Josephus revealed to him at the same time, so does he make Pharaoh forget the interpretation shown to him with the dream. Antiq. ii. 5. 4.   † Thus J. Müller, theol. Studien und Kritiken, 1836, iii. S. 839, ff.

have shown, the greater part of these mythi did not arise during that period, for their first foundation was laid in the legends of the Old Testament, before and after the Babylonish exile; and the transference of these legends with suitable modifications to the expected Messiah, was made in the course of the centuries which elapsed between that exile and the time of Jesus. So that for the period between the formation of the first christian community and the writing of the Gospels, there remains to be effected only the transference of Messianic legends, almost all ready formed, to Jesus, with some alterations to adapt them to christian opinions, and to the individual character and circumstances of Jesus; only a very small proportion of mythi having to be formed entirely new.

§. 15. DEFINITION OF THE EVANGELICAL MYTHUS AND ITS DISTINCTIVE CHARACTERISTICS.

The precise sense in which we use the expression *mythus*, applied to certain parts of the gospel history, is evident from all that has already been said; at the same time the different kinds and gradations of the mythi which we shall meet with in this history may here by way of anticipation be pointed out.

We distinguish by the name *evangelical mythus* a narrative relating directly or indirectly to Jesus, which may be considered not as the expression of a fact, but as the product of an idea of his earliest followers; such a narrative being mythical in proportion as it exhibits this character. The mythus in this sense of the term meets us, in the Gospel as elsewhere, sometimes in its pure form, constituting the substance of the narrative, and sometimes as an accidental adjunct to the actual history.

The pure mythus in the Gospel will be found to have two sources, which in most cases contributed simultaneously, though in different proportions, to form the mythus. The one source is, as already stated, the Messianic ideas and expectations existing according to their several forms in the Jewish mind before Jesus, and independently of him; the other is that particular impression which was left by the personal character, actions, and fate of Jesus, and which served to modify the Messianic idea in the minds of his people. The account of the Transfiguration, for example, is derived almost exclusively from the former source; the only amplification taken from the latter source being—that they who appeared with Jesus on the Mount spake of his decease. On the other hand, the narrative of the rending of the veil of the temple at the death of Jesus seems to have had its origin in the hostile position which Jesus, and his church after him, sustained in relation to the Jewish temple worship. Here already we have something historial, though consisting merely of certain general features of character, position &c.; we are thus at once brought upon the ground of the historical mythus.

The historical mythus has for its groundwork a definite individual fact which has been seized upon by religious enthusiasm, and twined around with mythical conceptions culled from the idea of the Christ. This fact is perhaps a saying of Jesus such as that concerning "fishers of men" or the barren fig-tree, which now appear in the Gospels transmuted into marvellous histories; or, it is perhaps a real transaction or event taken from his life; for instance, the mythical traits in the account of the baptism were built upon such a reality. Certain of the miraculous histories may likewise have had some foundation in natural occurrences, which the narrative has either exhibited in a supernatural light, or enriched with miraculous incidents.

All the species of imagery here enumerated may justly be designated as mythi, even according to the modern and precise definition of George, inasmuch as the unhistorical which they embody—whether formed gradually by tradition, or created by an individual author—is in each case the product of an *idea*. But for those parts of the history which are characterized by indefiniteness and want of connexion, by misconstruction and transformation, by strange combinations and confusion,—the natural results of a long course of oral transmission; or which, on the contrary, are distinguished by highly coloured and pictorial representations, which also seem to point to a traditionary origin;—for these parts the term *legendary* is certainly the more appropriate.

Lastly. It is requisite to distinguish equally from the mythus and the legend, that which, as it serves not to clothe an idea on the one hand, and admits not of being referred to tradition on the other, must be regarded as *the addition of the author*, as purely individual, and designed merely to give clearness, connexion, and climax, to the representation.

It is to the various forms of the unhistorical in the gospels that this enumeration exclusively refers; it does not involve the renunciation of the *historical* which they may likewise contain.

§ 16.   CRITERIA BY WHICH TO DISTINGUISH THE UNHISTORICAL IN
THE GOSPEL NARRATIVE.

HAVING shown the possible existence of the mythical and the legendary in the gospels, both on extrinsic and intrinsic grounds, and defined their distinctive characteristics, it remains in conclusion to inquire how their actual presence may be recognized in individual cases?

The mythus presents two phases; in the first place it is not history; in the second it is fiction, the product of the particular mental tendency of a certain community. These two phases afford the one a negative, the other a positive criterion, by which the mythus is to be recognized.

I. *Negative.* That an account is not historical—that the matter related could not have taken place in the manner described is evident.

First. When the narration is irreconcileable with the known and universal laws which govern the course of events. Now according to these laws, agreeing with all just philosophical conceptions and all credible experience, the absolute cause never disturbs the chain of secondary causes by single arbitrary acts of interposition, but rather manifests itself in the production of the aggregate of finite causalities, and of their reciprocal action. When therefore we meet with an account of certain phenomena or events of which it is either expressly stated or implied that they were produced immediately by God himself (divine apparitions—voices from heaven and the like), or by human beings possessed of supernatural powers (miracles, prophecies), such an account is *in so far* to be considered as not historical. And inasmuch as, in general, the intermingling of the spiritual world with the human is found only in unauthentic records, and is irreconcileable with all just conceptions ; so narratives of angels and of devils, of their appearing in human shape and interfering with human concerns, cannot possibly be received as historical.

Another law which controls the course of events is the law of succession, in accordance with which all occurrences, not excepting the most violent convulsions and the most rapid changes, follow in a certain order of sequence of increase and decrease. If therefore we are told of a celebrated individual that he attracted already at his birth and during his childhood that attention which he excited in his manhood ; that his followers at a single glance recognized him as being all that he actually was ; if the transition from the deepest despondency to the most ardent enthusiasm after his death is represented as the work of a single hour ; we must feel more than doubtful whether it is a real history which lies before us. Lastly, all those psychological laws, which render it improbable that a human being should feel, think, and act in a manner directly opposed to his own habitual mode and that of men in general, must be taken into consideration. As for example, when the Jewish Sanhedrim are represented as believing the declaration of the watch at the grave that Jesus was risen, and instead of accusing them of having suffered the body to be stolen away whilst they were asleep, bribing them to give currency to such a report. By the same rule it is contrary to all the laws belonging to the human faculty of memory, that long discourses, such as those of Jesus given in the fourth Gospel, could have been faithfully recollected and reproduced.

It is however true that effects are often far more rapidly produced, particularly in men of genius and by their agency, than might be expected ; and that human beings frequently act inconsequently, and in opposition to their general modes and habits : the two last mentioned tests of the mythical character must therefore be cautiously applied, and in conjunction only with other tests.

Secondly. An account which shall be regarded as historically valid, must neither be inconsistent with itself, nor in contradiction with other accounts.

The most decided case falling under this rule, amounting to a positive contradiction, is when one account affirms what another denies. Thus, one gospel represents the first appearance of Jesus in Galilee as subsequent to the imprisonment of John the Baptist, whilst another Gospel remarks, long after Jesus had preached both in Galilee and in Judea, that "John was not yet cast into prison." When on the contrary, the second account, without absolutely contradicting the first, differs from it, the disagreement may be merely between the incidental particulars of the narrative; such as *time*, (the clearing of the Temple,) *place*, (the original residence of the parents of Jesus:) *number*, (the Gadarenes, the angels at the sepulchre:) *names*, (Matthew and Levi); or it may concern the essential substance of the history. In the latter case, sometimes the character and circumstances in one account differ altogether from those in another. Thus, according to one narrator, the Baptist recognizes Jesus as the Messiah destined to suffer; according to the other, John takes offence at his suffering condition. Sometimes an occurrence is represented in two or more ways, of which one only can be consistent with the reality; as when in one account Jesus calls his first disciples from their nets whilst fishing on the sea of Galilee, and in the other meets them in Judea on his way to Galilee. We may class under the same head instances where events or discourses are represented as having occurred on two distinct occasions, whilst they are so similar that it is impossible to resist . the conclusion that both the narratives refer to the same event or discourse.

It may here be asked: is it to be regarded as a contradiction if one account is wholly silent respecting a circumstance mentioned by another? In itself, apart from all other considerations, the argumentum ex silentio is of no weight; but it is certainly to be accounted of moment when, at the same time, it may be shown that had the author known the circumstance he could not have failed to mention it, and also that he must have known it had it actually occurred.

II. *Positive.* The positive characters of legend and fiction are to be recognized sometimes in the form, sometimes in the substance of a narrative.

If the form be poetical, if the actors converse in hymns, and in a more diffuse and elevated strain than might be expected from their training and situations, such discourses, at all events, are not to be regarded as historical. The absence of these marks of the unhistorical do not however prove the historical validity of the narration, since the mythus often wears the most simple and apparently historical form: in which case the proof lies in the substance.

If the contents of a narrative strikingly accords with certain ideas existing and prevailing within the circle from which the narrative proceeded, which ideas themselves seem to be the product of preconceived opinions rather than of practical experience, it is more or less probable, according to circumstances, that such a narrative is of mythical origin. The knowledge of the fact, that the Jews were fond of representing their great men as the children of parents who had long been childless, cannot but make us doubtful of the historical truth of the statement that this was the case with John the Baptist; knowing also that the Jews saw predictions every where in the writings of their prophets and poets, and discovered types of the Messiah in all the lives of holy men recorded in their Scriptures; when we find details in the life of Jesus evidently sketched after the pattern of these prophecies and prototypes, we cannot but suspect that they are rather mythical than historical.

The more simple characteristics of the legend, and of additions by the author, after the observations of the former section, need no further elucidation.

Yet each of these tests, on the one hand, and each narrative on the other, considered apart, will rarely prove more than the possible or probable unhistorical character of the record. The concurrence of several such indications, is necessary to bring about a more definite result. The accounts of the visit of the Magi, and of the murder of the innocents at Bethlehem, harmonize remarkably with the Jewish Messianic notion, built upon the prophecy of Balaam, respecting the star which should come out of Jacob; and with the history of the sanguinary command of Pharaoh. Still this would not alone suffice to stamp the narratives as mythical. But we have also the corroborative facts that the described appearance of the star is contrary to the physical, the alleged conduct of Herod to the psychological laws; that Josephus, who gives in other respects so circumstantial an account of Herod, agrees with all other historical authorities in being silent concerning the Bethlehem massacre; and that the visit of the Magi together with the flight into Egypt related in the one Gospel, and the presentation in the temple related in another Gospel, mutually exclude one another. Wherever, as in this instance, the several criteria of the mythical character concur, the result is certain, and certain in proportion to the accumulation of such grounds of evidence.

It may be that a narrative, standing alone, would discover but slight indications, or perhaps, might present no one distinct feature of the mythus; but it is connected with others, or proceeds from the author of other narratives which exhibit unquestionable marks of a mythical or legendary character: and consequently suspicion is reflected back from the latter, on the former. Every narrative, however miraculous, contains some details which might in themselves be historical, but which, in consequence of their connexion with the other supernatural incidents, necessarily become equally doubtful.

In these last remarks we are, to a certain extent, anticipating the question which is, in conclusion, to be considered: viz., whether the mythical character is restricted to those features of the narrative, upon which such character is actually stamped; and whether a contradiction between two accounts invalidate one account only, or both? That is to say, what is the precise boundary line between the historical and the unhistorical?— the most difficult question in the whole province of criticism.

In the first place, when two narratives mutually exclude one another, one only is thereby proved to be unhistorical. If one be true the other must be false, but though the one be false the other may be true. Thus, in reference to the original residence of the parents of Jesus, we are justified in adopting the account of Luke which places it at Nazareth, to the exclusion of that of Matthew, which plainly supposes it to have been at Bethlehem; and, generally speaking, when we have to choose between two irreconcileable accounts, in selecting as historical that which is the least opposed to the laws of nature, and has the least correspondence with certain national or party opinions. But upon a more particular consideration it will appear that, since one account is false, it is possible that the other may be so likewise: the existence of a mythus respecting some certain point, shows that the imagination has been active in reference to that particular subject; (we need only refer to the genealogies); and the historical accuracy of either of two such accounts cannot be relied upon, unless substantiated by its agreement with some other well authenticated testimony.

Concerning the different parts of one and the same narrative: it might be thought for example, that though the appearance of an angel, and his announcement to Mary that she should be the Mother of the Messiah, must certainly be regarded as unhistorical, still, that Mary should have indulged this hope before the birth of the child, is not in itself incredible. But what should have excited this hope in Mary's mind? It is at once apparent that that which is credible in itself is nevertheless unhistorical when it is so intimately connected with what is incredible that, if you discard the latter, you at the same time remove the basis on which the former rests. Again, any action of Jesus represented as a miracle, when divested of the marvellous, might be thought to exhibit a perfectly natural occurrence; with respect to some of the miraculous histories, the expulsion of devils for instance, this might with some limitation, be possible. But for this reason alone: in these instances, a cure, so instantaneous, and effected by a few words merely, as it is described in the Gospels, is not psychologically incredible; so that, the essential in these narratives remains untouched. It is different in the case of the healing of a man born blind. A natural cure could not have been effected otherwise than by a gradual process; the narrative states the cure to have been immediate; if therefore the history be understood to record a natural occurrence, the most essential particular is incorrectly represented, and consequently all security for the truth of the otherwise natural remainder is gone, and the real fact cannot be discovered without the aid of arbitrary conjecture.

The following examples will serve to illustrate the mode of deciding in such cases. According to the narrative, as Mary entered the house and saluted her cousin Elizabeth, who was then pregnant, the babe leaped in her womb, she was filled with the Holy Ghost, and she immediately addressed Mary as the Mother of the Messiah. This account bears indubitable marks of an unhistorical character. Yet, it is not, in itself, impossible that Mary should have paid a visit to her cousin, during which every thing went on quite naturally. The fact is however that there are psychological difficulties connected with this journey of the betrothed; and that the visit, and even the relationship of the two women, seem to have originated entirely in the wish to exhibit a connexion between the mother of John the Baptist, and the mother of the Messiah. Or when in the history of the transfiguration it is stated, that the men who appeared with Jesus on the Mount were Moses and Elias; and that the brilliancy which illuminated Jesus was supernatural; it might seem here also that, after deducting the marvellous, the presence of two men and a bright morning beam might be retained as the historical facts. But the legend was predisposed, by virtue of the current idea concerning the relation of the Messiah to these two prophets, not merely to make any two men (whose persons, object, and conduct, if they were not what the narrative represents them, remain in the highest degree mysterious) into Moses and Elias, but to create the whole occurrence; and in like manner not merely to conceive of some certain illumination as a supernatural effulgence (which, if a natural one, is much exaggerated and misrepresented), but to create it at once after the pattern of the brightness which illumined the face of Moses on Mount Sinai.

Hence is derived the following rule. Where not merely the particular nature and manner of an occurrence is critically suspicious, its external circumstances represented as miraculous and the like; but where likewise the essential substance and groundwork is either inconceivable in itself, or is in striking harmony with some Messianic idea of the Jews of that age, then not the particular alleged course and mode of the transaction only, but the entire occurrence must be regarded as unhistorical. Where on the contrary, the form only, and not the general contents of the narration, exhibits the characteristics of the unhistorical, it is at least possible to suppose a kernel of historical fact; although we can never confidently decide whether this kernel of fact actually exists, or in what it consists; unless, indeed, it be discoverable from other sources. In legendary narratives, or narratives embellished by the writer, it is less difficult,—by divesting them of all that betrays itself as fictitious imagery, exaggeration, &c.—by endeavouring to abstract from them every extraneous adjunct and to fill up every hiatus—to succeed, proximately at least, in separating the historical groundwork.

The boundary line, however, between the historical and the unhistorical, in records, in which as in our Gospels this latter element is incorporated, will ever remain fluctuating and unsusceptible of precise attainment. Least of all can it be expected that the first comprehensive attempt to treat these records from a critical point of view should be successful in drawing a sharply defined line of demarcation. In the obscurity which criticism has produced, by the extinction of all lights hitherto held historical, the eye must accustom itself by degrees to discriminate objects with precision; and at all events the author of this work, wishes especially to guard himself, in those places where he declares he knows not what happened, from the imputation of asserting that he knows that nothing happened.

FIRST PART.

HISTORY OF THE BIRTH AND CHILDHOOD OF JESUS.

CHAPTER I.

ANNUNCIATION AND BIRTH OF JOHN THE BAPTIST.

---

§ 17. ACCOUNT GIVEN BY LUKE.* IMMEDIATE, SUPERNATURAL CHARACTER OF THE REPRESENTATION.

EACH of the four Evangelists represents the public ministry of Jesus as preceded by that of John the Baptist; but it is peculiar to Luke to make the Baptist the precursor of the Messiah in reference also to the event of his birth. This account finds a legitimate place in a work devoted exclusively to the consideration of the life of Jesus: firstly, on account of the intimate connexion which it exhibits as subsisting from the very commencement between the life of John and the life of Jesus; and secondly, because it constitutes a valuable contribution, aiding essentially towards the formation of a correct estimate of the general character of the gospel narratives. The opinion that the two first chapters of Luke, of which this particular history forms a portion, are a subsequent and unauthentic addition, is the uncritical assumption of a class of theologians who felt that the history of the childhood of Jesus seemed to require a mythical interpretation, but yet demurred to apply the comparatively modern mythical view to the remainder of the Gospel.†

A pious sacerdotal pair had lived and grown old in the cherished, but unrealized hope, of becoming parents, when, on a certain day,

---

* It may here be observed, once for all, that whenever in the following inquiry the names "Matthew," "Luke," &c., are used, it is the author of the several Gospels who is thus briefly indicated, quite irrespective of the question whether either of the Gospels was written by an apostle or disciple of that name, or by a later unknown author.   † See Kuinöl Comm. in Luc., Proleg. p. 217.

as the priest is offering incense in the sanctuary, the angel Gabriel appears to him, and promises him a son, who shall live consecrated to God, and who shall be the harbinger of the Messiah, to prepare his way when he shall visit and redeem his people. Zacharias, however, is incredulous, and doubts the prediction on account of his own advanced age and that of his wife; whereupon the angel, both as a sign and as a punishment, strikes him dumb until the time of its accomplishment; an infliction which endures until the day of the circumcision of the actually born son, when the father, being called upon to assign to the child the name predetermined by the angel, suddenly recovers his speech, and with the regained powers of utterance, breaks forth in a hymn of praise. (Luke i. 5—25. 57—80.)

It is evidently the object of this gospel account to represent a series of external and miraculous occurrences. The announcement of the birth of the forerunner of the Messiah is divinely communicated by the apparition of a celestial spirit; the conception takes place under the particular and preternatural blessing of God; and the infliction and removal of dumbness are effected by extraordinary means. But it is quite another question, whether we can accede to the view of the author, or can feel convinced that the birth of the Baptist was in fact preceded by such a series of miraculous events.

The first offence against our modern notions in this narrative is the appearance of the angel: the event contemplated in itself, as well as the peculiar circumstances of the apparition. With respect to the latter, the angel announces himself to be *Gabriel that stands in the presence of God*. Now it is inconceivable that the constitution of the celestial hierarchy should actually correspond with the notions entertained by the Jews subsequent to the exile; and that the names given to the angels should be in the language of this people.* Here the supranaturalist finds himself in a dilemma, even upon his own ground. Had the belief in celestial beings, occupying a particular station in the court of heaven, and distinguished by particular names, originated from the revealed religion of the Hebrews,—had such a belief been established by Moses, or some later prophet,—then, according to the views of the supranaturalist, they might, nay they must, be admitted to be correct. But it is in the Maccabæan Daniel† and in the apocryphal Tobit,‡ that this doctrine of angels, in its more precise form, first appears; and it is evidently a product of the influence of the Zend religion of the Persians on the Jewish mind. We have the testimony of the Jews themselves, that they brought the names of the angels with them from Babylon.§

* Paulus, exeget. Handbuch, 1 A. S. 78 f. 96. Bauer, hebr. Mythol. 2 Bd. S. 218 f.
† Here Michael is called *one of the chief princes*.   ‡ Here Raphael is represented as one *of the seven angels which go in and out before the glory of the holy One;* (Tobit, xii. 15.), almost the same as Gabriel in Luke i. 19., excepting the mention of the number.   This number is in imitation of the Persian Amschaspands.   Vid. De Wette, bibl. Dogmatik, § 171. b.
§ Hieros. rosch haschanah f. lvi. 4.   (Lightfoot, horæ hebr. et talmud. in IV. Evangg., p. 723.): *R. Simeon ben Lachisch dicit: nomina angelorum ascenderunt in manu Israelis ex Babylone.   Nam antea dictum est: advolavit ad me unus τῶν Seraphim, Seraphim steterunt ante eum*, Jes. vi.; *at post: vir Gabriel*, Dan. ix. 21, *Michael princeps vester*, Dan. x. 21.

Hence arises a series of questions extremely perplexing to the supranaturalist. Was the doctrine false so long as it continued to be the exclusive possession of the heathens, but true as soon as it became adopted by the Jews? or was it at all times equally true, and was an important truth discovered by an idolatrous nation sooner than by the people of God? If nations shut out from a particular and divine revelation, arrived at truth by the light of reason alone, sooner than the Jews who were guided by that revelation, then either the revelation was superfluous, or its influence was merely negative: that is, it operated as a check to the premature acquisition of knowledge. If, in order to escape this consequence, it be contended that truths were revealed by the divine influence to other people besides the Israelites, the supranaturalistic point of view is annihilated; and, since all things contained in religions which contradict each other cannot have been revealed, we are compelled to exercise a critical discrimination. Thus, we find it to be by no means in harmony with an elevated conception of God to represent him as an earthly monarch, surrounded by his court: and when an appeal is made, in behalf of the reality of angels standing round the throne, to the reasonable belief in a graduated scale of created intelligences,* the Jewish representation is not thereby justified, but merely a modern conception substituted for it. We should, thus, be driven to the expedient of supposing an accommodation on the part of God: that he sent a celestial spirit with the command to simulate a rank and title which did not belong to him, in order that, by this conformity to Jewish notions, he might insure the belief of the father of the Baptist. Since however it appears that Zacharias did not believe the angel, but was first convinced by the result, the accommodation proved fruitless, and consequently could not have been a divine arrangement. With regard to the name of the angel, and the improbability that a celestial being should bear a Hebrew name, it has been remarked that the word Gabriel, taken appellatively in the sense of *Man of God*, very appropriately designates the nature of the heavenly visitant; and since it may be rendered with this signification into every different language, the name cannot be said to be restricted to the Hebrew.† This explanation however leaves the difficulty quite unsolved, since it converts into a simple appellative a name evidently employed as a proper name. In this case likewise an accommodation must be supposed, namely, that the angel, in order to indicate his real nature, appropriated a name which he did not actually bear: an accommodation already judged in the foregoing remarks.

But it is not only the name and the alleged station of the angel which shock our modern ideas, we also feel his discourse and his conduct to be unworthy. Paulus indeed suggests that none but a levitical priest, and not an angel of Jehovah, could have conceived it

* Olshausen, biblischer Commentar zum N. T., 1 Thl. S. 29. (2te Auflage). Comp. Hoffmann, S. 121 f.   † Olshausen, ut sup. Hoffmann, S. 135.

necessary that the boy should live in nazarite abstemiousness,* but
to this it may be answered that the angel also might have known
that under this form John would obtain greater influence with the
people. But there is a more important difficulty. When Zacharias,
overcome by surprise, doubts the promise and asks for a sign, this
natural incredulity is regarded by the angel as a crime, and immediately punished with dumbness. Though some may not coincide
with Paulus that a real angel would have lauded the spirit of inquiry
evinced by the priest, yet all will agree in the remark, that conduct
so imperious is less in character with a truly celestial being than
with the notions the Jews of that time entertained of such. Moreover we do not find in the whole province of supranaturalism a parallel severity.

The instance, cited by Paulus, of Jehovah's far milder treatment
of Abraham, who asks precisely the same question unreproved, Gen.
xv. 8, is refuted by Olshausen, because he considers the words of
Abraham, chap. v. 6, an evidence of his faith; but this observation
does not apply to chap. xviii. 12, where the greater incredulity of
Sarah, in a similar case, remains unpunished; nor to chap. xvii. 17,
where Abraham himself is not even blamed, though the divine
promise appears to him so incredible as to excite laughter. The
example of Mary is yet closer, who (Luke i. 34.) in regard to a still
greater improbability, but one which was similarly declared by a
special divine messenger to be no impossibility, puts exactly the
same question as Zacharias; so that we must agree with Paulus that
such inconsistency certainly cannot belong to the conduct of God or
of a celestial being, but merely to the Jewish representation of
them. Feeling the objectionableness of the representation in its existing form, orthodox theologians have invented various motives to
justify this infliction of dumbness. Hess has attempted to screen
it from the reproach of an arbitrary procedure by regarding it as the
only means of keeping secret, even against the will of the priest, an
event, the premature proclamation of which might have been followed by disastrous consequences, similar to those which attended
the announcement by the wise men of the birth of the child Jesus.†
But, in the first place, the angel says nothing of such an object, he
inflicts the dumbness but as a sign and punishment; secondly, the
loss of speech did not hinder Zacharias from communicating, at any
rate to his wife, the main features of the apparition, since we see
that she was acquainted with the destined name of the child before
appeal was made to the father. Thirdly, what end did it serve thus
to render difficult the communication of the miraculous annunciation
of the unborn babe, since no sooner was it born than it was at once
exposed to all the dreaded dangers?—for the father's sudden recovery of speech, and the extraordinary scene at the circumcision
excited attention and became noised abroad in all the country. Ols-

---

* Ut sup. S. 77.   † Geschichte der drei lesten Lebensjahre Jesu, sammt dessen Ju-
gendgeschichte. Tübingen 1779. 1. Bd, S. 12.

hausen's view of the thing is more admissible. He regards the whole proceeding, and especially the dumbness, as a moral training destined to teach Zacharias to know and conquer his want of faith.* But of this too we have no mention in the text: besides, the unexpected accomplishment of the prediction would have made Zacharias sufficiently ashamed of his unbelief, if instead of inflicting dumbness the angel had merely remonstrated with him.

But however worthy of God we might grant the conduct of his messenger to have been, still many of the present day will find an angelic apparition, as such, incredible. Bauer insists that wherever angels appear, both in the New Testament and in the Old, the narrative is mythical.† Even admitting the existence of angels, we cannot suppose them capable of manifesting themselves to human beings, since they belong to the invisible world, and spiritual existences are not cognizable by the organs of sense; so that it is always advisable to refer their pretended apparitions to the imagination.‡ It is not probable, it is added, that God should make use of them according to the popular notion, for these apparitions have no apparent adequate object, they serve generally only to gratify curiosity, or to encourage man's disposition passively to leave his affairs in higher hands.§ It is also remarkable that in the old world these celestial beings show themselves active upon the smallest occasions, whilst in modern times they remain idle even during the most important occurrences.‖ But to deny their appearance and agency among men is to call in question their very being, because it is precisely this occupation which is a main object of their existence. (Heb. i., 14.) According to Schleiermacher¶ we cannot indeed actually disprove the existence of angels, yet the conception is one which could not have originated in our time, but belongs wholly to the ancient ideas of the world. The belief in angels has a twofold root or source: the one the natural desire of the mind to presuppose a larger amount of intelligence in the universe than is realized in the human race. We who live in these days find this desire satisfied in the conviction that other worlds exist besides our own, and are peopled by intelligent beings; and thus the first source of the belief in angels is destroyed. The other source, namely, the representation of God as an earthly monarch surrounded by his court, contradicts all enlightened conceptions of Deity; and further, the phenomena in the natural world and the transitions in human life, which were formerly thought to be wrought by God himself through ministering angels, we are now able to explain by natural causes; so that the belief in angels is without a link by which it can attach itself to rightly apprehended modern ideas: and it exists only as a lifeless tradition. The result is the same if, with one of the latest writers on the doctrine of angels,* we consider as the origin of this repre-

* Bibl. Comm. 1, S. 115.   † Heb. Mythol. ii. S. 218.   ‡ Bauer, ut sup. i. S. 129. Paulus, exeget. Handbuch, i. a 74.   § Paulus, Commentar. i. S. 12.   ‖ Bauer, ut sup. ¶ Glaubenslehre, 1 Thl. § 42 und 43 (2te Ausgabe).   * Binder, Studien der evang. Geistlichkeit Wurtembergs, ix. 2, 5, 11 ff.

sentation, man's desire to separate the two sides of his moral nature, and to contemplate, as beings existing external to himself, angels and devils. For, the origin of both representations remains merely subjective, the angel being simply the ideal of created perfection: which, as it was formed from the subordinate point of view of a fanciful imagination, disappears from the higher and more comprehensive observation of the intellect.*

Olshausen, on the other hand, seeks to deduce a positive argument in favour of the reality of the apparation in question, from those very reasonings of the present day which, in fact, negative the existence of angels; and he does so by viewing the subject on its speculative side. He is of opinion that the gospel narrative does not contradict just views of the world, since God is immanent in the universe and moves it by his breath.† But if it be true that God is immanent in the world, precisely on that account is the intervention of angels superfluous. It is only a Deity who dwells apart, throned in heaven, who requires to send down his angels to fulfil his purposes on earth. It would excite surprise to find Olshausen arguing thus, did we not perceive from the manner in which this interpreter constantly treats of angelology and demonology, that he does not consider angels to be independent personal entities; but regards them rather as divine powers, transitory emanations and fulgurations of the Divine Being. Thus Olshausen's conception of angels, in their relation to God, seems to correspond with the Sabellian doctrine of the Trinity; but as his is not the representation of the Bible, as also the arguments in favour of the former prove nothing in relation to the latter, it is useless to enter into further explanation. The reasoning of this same theologian, that we must not require the ordinariness of every day life for the most pregnant epochs in the life of the human race; that the incarnation of the eternal word was accompanied by extraordinary manifestations from the world of spirits, uncalled for in times less rich in momentous results,‡ rests upon a misapprehension. For the ordinary course of every day life is interrupted in such moments, by the very fact that exalted beings like the Baptist are born into the world, and it would be puerile to designate as ordinary those times and circumstances which gave birth and maturity to a John, because they were unembellished by angelic apparitions. That which the spiritual world does for ours at such periods is to send extraordinary human intelligences, not to cause angels, to ascend and descend.

Finally, if, in vindication of this narrative, it be stated that such an exhibition by the angel, of the plan of education for the unborn child, was necessary in order to make him the man he should become,§ the assumption includes too much: namely, that all great men, in order by their education to become such, must have been introduced into the world in like manner, or cause must be shown why that which was unnecessary in the case of great men of other ages and countries was indispensable for the Baptist. Again, the assumption attaches too much importance to external training, too little to the internal development of the mind. But in conclusion, many of the circumstances in the life of the Baptist, instead of serving to confirm a belief in the truth of the miraculous history, are on the contrary, as has been justly maintained, altogether irreconcileable with the supposition, that his birth was attended by these wonderful occurrences. If it were indeed true, that John was from the first distinctly and miraculously announced as the forerunner of the Messiah, it is inconceivable that he should have had no acquaintance with Jesus prior to his baptism ; and that, even subsequent to that event, he should have felt perplexed concerning his Messiahship. (John i., 30 ; Matth. xi., 2.*)

Consequently the *negative* conclusion of the rationalistic criticism and controversy must, we think, be admitted, namely, that the birth of the Baptist could not have been preceded and attended by these supernatural occurrences. The question now arises, what *positive* view of the matter is to replace the rejected literal orthodox explanation ?

§ 18.   NATURAL EXPLANATION OF THE NARRATIVE.

In treating the narrative before us according to the rationalistic method, which requires the separation of the pure fact from the opinion of interested persons, the simplest alteration is this : to retain the two leading facts, the apparition and the dumbness, as actual external occurrences ; but to account for them in a natural manner. This were possible with respect to the apparition, by supposing that a man, mistaken by Zacharias for a divine messenger, really appeared to him, and addressed to him the words he believed he heard. But this explanation viewed in connexion with the attendant circumstances, being too improbable, it became necessary to go a step further, and to transform the event from an external to an internal one ; to remove the occurrence out of the physical into the psychological world. To this view the opinion of Bahrdt, that a flash of lightning was perhaps mistaken by Zacharias for an angel,† forms a transition ; since he attributes the greater part of the scene to Zacharias's imagination. But that any man, in an ordinary state of mind, could have created so long and consecutive a dialogue out of a flash of lightning is incredible. A peculiar mental state must be supposed ; whether it be a swoon, the effect of fright occasioned by the lightning,‡ but of this there is no trace in the text : (no falling down as in Acts ix., 4.) ; or, abandoning the notion of the lightning, a dream, which, however, could scarcely

---

* Horst in Henke's Museum i, 4, S. 733 f.   Gabler in seinem neuest. theol. Journal, vii. 1. S. 403.   † Briefe über die Bibel im Volkstone (Ausg. Frankfurt und Leipzig, 1800), Iter Bändchen, 6ter Brief, S. 51 f.   ‡ Bahrdt, ut sup. S. 52.

occur whilst burning incense in the temple. Hence, it has been found necessary, with Paulus, to call to mind that there are waking visions or ecstasies, in which the imagination confounds internal images with external occurrences.* Such ecstasies, it is true, are not common; but says Paulus, in Zacharias's case many circumstances combined to produce so unusual a state of mind. The exciting causes were, firstly, the long-cherished desire to have a posterity; secondly, the exalted vocation of administering in the Holy Place, offering up with the incense the prayers of the people to the throne of Jehovah, which seemed to Zacharias to foretoken the acceptance of his own prayer; and thirdly, perhaps an exhortation from his wife as he left his house, similar to that of Rachel to Jacob. Gen. xxx., I. (!) In this highly excited state of mind, as he prays in the dimly-lighted sanctuary, he thinks of his most ardent wish, and expecting that now or never his prayer shall be heard, he is prepared to discern a sign of its acceptance in the slightest occurrence. As the glimmer of the lamps falls upon the ascending cloud of incense, and shapes it into varying forms, the priest imagines he perceives the figure of an angel. The apparition at first alarms him; but he soon regards it as an assurance from God that his prayer is heard. No sooner does a transient doubt cross his mind, than the sensitively pious priest looks upon himself as sinful, believes himself reproved by the angel, and—here two explanations are possible—either an apoplectic seizure actually deprives him of speech, which he receives as the just punishment of his incredulity, till the excessive joy he experiences at the circumcision of his son restores the power of utterance: so that the dumbness is retained as an external, physical, though not miraculous, occurrence;† or the proceeding is psychologically understood, namely, that Zacharias, in accordance with a Jewish superstition, for a time denied himself the use of the offending member.‡ Re-animated in other respects by the extraordinary event, the priest returns home to his wife, and she becomes a second Sarah.

With regard to this account of the angelic apparition given by Paulus,—and the other explanations are either of essentially similar character, or are so manifestly untenable, as not to need refutation—it may be observed that the object so laboriously striven after is not attained. Paulus fails to free the narrative of the marvellous; for by his own admission, the majority of men have no experience of the kind of vision here supposed.§ If such a state of ecstasy occur in particular cases, it must result either from a predisposition in the individual, of which we find no sign in Zacharias, and which his advanced age must have rendered highly improbable; or it must have been induced by some peculiar circumstances, which totally fail in the present instance.‖ A hope which has been long indulged

* Exeget. Handb. 1, a. S. 74 ff.   † Bahrdt, ut sup. 7ter Brief, S. 60.—E. F. über die beiden ersten Kapitel des Matthäus und Lukas, in Henke's Magazin, v. 1. S. 163. Bauer, hebr. Mythol, 2, S. 220.   ‡ Exeget. Handb, 1, a. S. 77—80.   § Ut sup. S. 73. ‖ Comp. Schleiermacher über die Schriften des Lukas, S. 25.

is inadequate to the production of ecstatic vehemence, and the act of burning incense is insufficient to cause so extraordinary an excitement, in a priest who has grown old in the service of the temple. Thus Paulus has in fact substituted a miracle of chance for a miracle of God. Should it be said that to God nothing is impossible, or to chance nothing is impossible, both explanations are equally precarious and unscientific.

Indeed, the dumbness of Zacharias as explained from this point of view is very unsatisfactory. For had it been, as according to one explanation, the result of apoplexy; admitting Paulus's reference to Lev. xxi., 16, to be set aside by the contrary remark of Lightfoot,* still, we must join with Schleiermacher in wondering how Zacharias, notwithstanding this apoplectic seizure, returned home in other respects healthy and vigorous:† and that in spite of partial paralysis his general strength was unimpaired, and his long-cherished hope fulfilled. It must also be regarded as a strange coincidence, that the father's tongue should have been loosed exactly at the time of the circumcision; for if the recovery of speech is to be considered as the effect of joy,‡ surely the father must have been far more elated at the birth of the earnestly-desired son, than at the circumcision; for by that time he would have become accustomed to the possession of his child.

The other explanation: that Zacharias's silence was not from any physical impediment, but from a notion, to be psychologically explained, that he ought not to speak, is in direct contradiction to the words of Luke. What do all the passages, collected by Paulus to show that οὐ δύναμαι may signify not only a positive *non posse*, but likewise a mere *non sustinere*,§ prove against the clear meaning of the passage and its context? If perhaps the narrative phrase, (v. 22.) οὐκ ἠδύνατο λαλῆσαι αὐτοῖς might be forced to bear this sense, yet certainly in the supposed vision of Zacharias, had the angel only forbidden him to speak, instead of depriving him of the power of speech, he would not have said: καὶ ἔσῃ σιωπῶν, μὴ δυνάμενος λαλῆσαι, but ἴσθι σιωπῶν μηδ' ἐπιχειρήσῃς λαλῆσαι. The words διέμενε κωφὸς (v. 21.) also most naturally mean actual dumbness. This view assumes, and indeed necessarily so, that the gospel history is a correct report of the account given by Zacharias himself: if then it be denied that the dumbness was actual, as Zacharias affirms that actual dumbness was announced to him by the angel, it must be admitted that, though perfectly able to speak, he believed himself to be dumb: which leads to the conclusion that he was mad: an imputation not to be laid upon the father of the Baptist without compulsory evidence in the text.

Again, the natural explanation makes too light of the incredibly accurate fulfilment of a prediction originating, as it supposes, in an unnatural, over-excited state of mind. In no other province of inquiry would the realization of a prediction which owed its birth to a vision be found credible, even by the Rationalist. If Dr. Paulus were to read that a somnambulist, in a state of ecstasy, had foretold the birth of a child, under circumstances in the highest degree improbable; and not only of a child, but of a boy; and had moreover, with accurate minuteness, predicted his future mode of life, character, and position in history; and that each particular had been exactly verified by the result: would he find such a coincidence credible? Most assuredly to no human being, under any conditions whatsoever, would he concede the power thus to penetrate the most mysterious workings of nature; on the contrary he would complain of the outrage on human free-will, which is annihilated by the admission that a man's entire intellectual and moral development may be predetermined like the movements of a clock. And he would on this very ground complain of the inaccuracy of observation, and untrustworthiness of the report, which represented, as matters of fact, things in their very nature impossible. Why does he not follow the same rule with respect to the New Testament narrative? Why admit in the one case what he rejects in the other? Is biblical history to be judged by one set of laws, and profane history by another?—An assumption which the Rationalist is compelled to make, if he admits as credible in the Gospels that which he rejects as unworthy of credit in every other history—which is in fact to fall back on the supranaturalistic point of view, since the assumption, that the natural laws which govern in every other province are not applicable to sacred history, is the very essential of supranaturalism.

No other rescue from this self annihilation remains to the anti-supernatural mode of explanation, than to question the verbal accuracy of the history. This is the simplest expedient, felt to be such by Paulus himself, who remarks, that his efforts may be deemed superfluous to give a natural explanation of a narrative, which is nothing more than one of those stories invented either after the death or even during the lifetime of every distinguished man to embellish his early history. Paulus, however, after an impartial examination, is of opinion that the analogy, in the present instance, is not applicable. The principal ground for this opinion is the too short interval between the birth of the Baptist, and the composition of the Gospel of Luke.* We, on the contrary, in harmony with the observations in the introduction, would reverse the question and inquire of this interpreter, how he would render it credible, that the history of the birth of a man so famed as the Baptist should have been transmitted, in an age of great excitement, through a period of more than sixty years, in all its primitive accuracy of detail? Paulus's answer is ready: an answer approved by others (Heidenreich, Olshausen):—the passage inserted by Luke (i. 5; ii. 39.)

* Ut sup. S. 72 f.

was possibly a family record, which circulated among the relatives of the Baptist and of Jesus; and of which Zacharias was probably the author.*

K. Ch. L. Schmidt controverts this hypothesis with the remark, that it is impossible that a narrative so disfigured, (we should rather say, so embellished,) could have been a family record; and that, if it does not belong altogether to the class of legends, its historical basis, if such there be, is no longer to be distinguished.† It is further maintained, that the narrative presents certain features which no poet would have conceived, and which prove it to be a direct impression of facts; for instance, the Messianic expectations expressed by the different personages introduced by Luke (chap. i. and ii.) correspond exactly with the situation and relation of each individual.‡ But these distinctions are by no means so striking as Paulus represents; they are only the characteristics of a history which goes into details, making a transition from generalities to particulars, which is natural alike to the poet and to the popular legend; besides, the peculiar Judaical phraseology in which the Messianic expectations are expressed, and which it is contended confirm the opinion that this narrative was written, or received its fixed form, before the death of Jesus, continued to be used after that event. (Acts i. 6.§) Moreover we must agree with Schleiermacher when he says:‖ least of all is it possible to regard these utterances as strictly historical; or to maintain that Zacharias, in the moment that he recovered his speech, employed it in a song of praise, uninterrupted by the exultation and wonder of the company, sentiments which the narrator interrupts himself to indulge. It must, at all events, be admitted, that the author has made additions of his own, and has enriched the history by the lyric effusions of his muse. Kuinöl supposes that Zacharias composed and wrote down the canticle subsequent to the occasion; but this strange surmise contradicts the text. There are some other features which, it is contended, belong not to the creations of the poet: such as, the signs made to the father, the debate in the family, the position of the angel on the right hand of the altar.¶ But this criticism is merely a proof that these interpreters have, or determine to have, no just conception of poetry or popular legend; for the genuine characteristic of poetry and mythus is natural and pictorial representation of details.**

§ 19. MYTHICAL VIEW OF THE NARRATIVE IN ITS DIFFERENT STAGES.

THE above exposition of the necessity, and lastly, of the possibility of doubting the historical fidelity of the gospel narrative,

* Ut sup. S. 69. † In Schmidt's Bibliothek für Kritik und Exegese, iii. 1, S. 119.
‡ Paulus, ut sup. § Comp. De Wette, exeg. Handb. i. 2, S. 9. ‖ Ueber die Schriften des Lukas, S. 23. * Paulus und Olshausen, z. d. St., Heydenreich, a. a. O. 1, S. 87.
** Comp. Horst, in Henke's Museum, i. 4, S. 705; Vater, Commentar zum Pentateuch, 3, S. 597 ff.; Hase L. J., § 35; auch George, S. 33 f. 91.

has led many theologians to explain the account of the birth of the
Baptist as a poetical composition; suggested by the importance attributed by the Christians to the forerunner of Jesus, and by the
recollection of some of the Old Testament histories, in which the
births of Ishmael, Isaac, Samuel, and especially of Samson, are
related to have been similarly announced. Still the matter was not
allowed to be altogether invented. It may have been historically
true that Zacharias and Elizabeth lived long without offspring; that,
on one occasion whilst in the temple, the old man's tongue was
suddenly paralyzed; but that soon afterwards his aged wife bore
him a son, and he, in his joy at the event, recovered the power of
speech. At that time, but still more when John became a remarkable man, the history excited attention, and out of it the existing
legend grew.*

It is surprising to find an explanation almost identical with the
natural one we have criticised above, again brought forward under
a new title; so that the admission of the possibility of an admixture
of subsequent legends in the narrative has little influence on the
view of the matter itself. As the mode of explanation we are now
advocating denies all confidence in the historical authenticity of the
record, all the details must be in themselves equally problematic;
and whether historical validity can be retained for this or that particular incident, can be determined only by its being either less
improbable than the rest, or else less in harmony with the spirit,
interest, and design of the poetic legend, so as to make it probable
that it had a distinct origin. The barenness of Elizabeth and the
sudden dumbness of Zacharias are here retained as incidents of this
character: so that only the appearing and prediction of the angel
are given up. But by taking away the angelic apparition, the sudden infliction and as sudden removal of the dumbness loses its only
adequate supernatural cause, so that all difficulties which beset the
natural interpretation remain in full force: a dilemma into which
these theologians are, most unnecessarily, brought by their own
inconsequence: for the moment we enter upon mythical ground, all
obligation to hold fast the assumed historical fidelity of the account
ceases to exist. Besides, that which they propose to retain as historical fact, namely, the long barenness of the parents of the Baptist, is so strictly in harmony with the spirit and character of Hebrew
legendary poetry, that of this incident the mythical origin is least
to be mistaken. How confused has this misapprehension made,
for example, the reasoning of Bauer! It was a prevailing opinion,
says he, consonant with Jewish ideas, that all children born of aged
parents who had previously been childless became distinguished personages. John was the child of aged parents, and became a notable
preacher of repentance; consequently it was thought justifiable to
infer that his birth was predicted by an angel. What an illogical

---

* E. F. über die zwei ersten Kapitel u. s. w. in Henke's Magazin, v. 1, S. 162 ff. und
Bauer hebr. Mythol. ii. 220 f.

conclusion! for which he has no other ground than the assumption that John was the son of aged parents. Let this be made a settled point, and the conclusion follows without difficulty. It was readily believed, he proceeds, of remarkable men that they were born of aged parents and that their birth, no longer in the ordinary course of nature to be expected, was announced by a heavenly messenger;* John was a great man and a prophet; consequently, the legend represented him to have been born of an aged couple, and his birth to have been proclaimed by an angel.

Seeing that this explanation of the narrative before us, as a half (so called historical) mythus, is encumbered with all the difficulties of a half measure, Gabler has treated it as a pure philosophical, or dogmatical mythus.† Horst likewise considers it, and indeed the entire two first chapters of Luke of which it forms a part, as an ingenious fiction, in which the birth of the Messiah, together with that of his precursor, and the predictions concerning the character and ministry of the latter, framed after the event, are set forth; it being precisely the loquacious circumstantiality of the narration which betrays the poet.‡ Schleiermacher likewise explains the first chapter as a little poem, similar in character to many of the Jewish poems which we meet with in their apocrypha. He does not however consider it altogether a fabrication. It might have had a foundation in fact, and in a wide spread tradition; but the poet has allowed himself so full a license in arranging, and combining, in moulding and embodying the vague and fluctuating representations of tradition, that the attempt to detect the purely historical in such narratives, must prove a fruitless and useless effort.§ Horst goes so far as to suppose the author of the piece to have been a Judaising Christian; whilst Schleiermacher imagines it to have been composed by a Christian of the famed Jewish school, at a period when it comprised some who still continued strict disciples of John; and whom it was the object of the narrative to bring over to Christianity, by exhibiting the relationship of John to the Christ as his peculiar and highest destiny; and also by holding out the expectation of a state of temporal greatness for the Jewish people at the re-appearance of Christ.

An attentive consideration of the Old Testament histories, to which, as most interpreters admit, the narrative of the annunciation and birth of the Baptist bears a striking affinity, will render it

---

* The adoption of this opinion is best explained by a passage—with respect to this matter classical—in the Evang. de nat. Mariæ, in Fabr. cod. apocryph. N. Ti. 1, p. 22 f., and in Thilo 1. p. 322, "Deus" it is here said, cum alicujus uterum claudit, ad hoc facit, ut mirabilius denuo aperiat, et non libidinis esse, quod nascitur, sed divini numeris cognoscatur. Prima enim gentes nostræ Sara mater nonne usque ad octogesimum annum infecunda fuit? et tamen in ultima senectutis ætate genuit Isaac, cui repromissa erat benedictio omnium gentium. Rachel quoque, tantum Domino grata tantumque a sancto Jacob amata, diu sterilis fuit, et tamen Joseph genuit, non solum dominum Ægypti, sed plurimarum gentium. fame perituarum liberatorem. Quis in ducibus vel fortior Sampsone, vel sanctior Samuele? et tamen hi ambo steriles matres habuere.—ergo—credo—dilatos diu conceptus et steriles partus mirabiliores esse solere.   † Neustes theol. Journal, vii. 1, S. 402 f.   ‡ In Henke's Museum, i. 1, S. 702 ff.   § Hase in his Leben Jesu makes the same admission; compare § 52 with § 32.

abundantly evident that this is the only just view of the passage in
question.   But it must not here be imagined, as is now so readily
affirmed in the confutation of the mythical view of this passage, that
the author of our narrative first made a collection from the Old
Testament of its individual traits; much rather had the scattered
traits respecting the late birth of different distinguished men, as recorded in the Old Testament, blended themselves into a compound
image in the mind of their reader, whence he selected the features
most appropriate to his present subject.   Of the children born of
aged parents Isaac is the most ancient prototype.   As it is said of
Zacharias and Elizabeth "they both were advanced in their days"
(v. 7.) προβεβηκότες ἐν ταῖς ἡμέραις αὐτῶν, so Abraham and Sarah
"were advanced in their days" בָּאִים בַּיָּמִים ((Gen. xviii; LXX:
προβεβηκότες ἡμερῶν), when they were promised a son.   It is likewise from this history that the incredulity of the father, on account
of the advanced age of both parents, and the demand of a sign, are
borrowed in our narrative.   As Abraham, when Jehovah promises
him he shall have a son and a numerous posterity who shall inherit
the land of Canaan, doubtingly inquires "Whereby shall I know
that I shall inherit it?" κατὰ τί γνώσομαι, ὅτι πληρονομήσω αὐτήν;
(sc. τὴν γῆν.   Gen. xv. 8. LXX): so Zacharias—"Whereby shall
I know this?" κατὰ τί γνώσομαι τᾶτο; (v. 18.)   The incredulity of
Sarah is not made use of for Elizabeth; but she is said to be of the
daughters of Aaron, and the name Elizabeth may perhaps have been
suggested by that of Aaron's wife. (Exod. vi. 23. LXX.)   The incident of the angel announcing the birth of the Baptist is taken from
the history of another late-born child, Samson.   In our narrative
indeed, the angel appears first to the father in the temple, whereas
in the history of Samson he shows himself first to the mother, and
afterwards to the father in the field.   This, however, is an alteration
arising naturally out of the different situations of the respective parents. (Judges xiii.)   According to popular Jewish notions it was
no unusual occurrence for the priest to be visited by angels and divine apparitions whilst offering incense in the temple.*   The command which before his birth predestined the Baptist—whose later
ascetic mode of life was known—to be a Nazarite, is taken from the
same source.   As, to Samson's mother during her pregnancy, wine,
strong drink, and unclean food, were forbidden, so a similar diet is
prescribed for her son,† adding, as in the case of John, that the
child shall be consecrated to God from the womb.‡   The blessings

* Wetstein zu Luke i. 11, S. 647 f. adduces passages from Josephus and from the
Rabbins recording apparitions seen by the high priests.   How readily it was presumed
that the same thing happened to ordinary priests is apparent from the narrative before us.
† Judges xiii. 14 (LXX.):   Luc. i. 15:
καὶ οἶνον καὶ σίκερα (al. μέθυσμα, hel r. שֵׁכָר)   καὶ οἶνον καὶ σίκερα οὐ μὴ πίῃ.
μὴ πιέτω.
‡ Judg. xiii. 5:   Luc. i. 15:
ὅτι ἡγιασμένον ἔσται τῷ θεῷ (al. Ναζὶρ θεοῦ   καὶ πνεύματος ἁγίου πλησθήσεται ἔτι ἐκ κοιλί-
ἔσται) τὸ παιδάριον οὐκ τῆς γαστρός (al. ἀπὸ   ας μητρὸς αὐτρίου.
τῆς κοιλίας).

which it is predicted that these two men shall realize for the people of Israel are similar, (comp. Luke i. 16, 17, with Judges xiii. 5.) and each narrative concludes with the same expression respecting the hopeful growth of the child.[*] It may be too bold to derive the Levitical descent of the Baptist from a third Old Testament history of a late-born son—from the history of Samuel: (compare 1 Sam. i. 1; Chron. vii. 27.) but the lyric effusions in the first chapter of Luke are imitations of this history. As Samuel's mother, when consigning him to the care of the high priests, breaks forth into a hymn, (1 Sam. ii. 1.) so the father of John does the same at the circumcision; though the particular expressions in the Canticle uttered by Mary—of which we shall have to speak hereafter—have a closer resemblance to Hannah's song of praise than that of Zacharias. The significant appellation *John* (יְהוֹחָנָן=Θεοχαρις) predetermined by the angel, had its precedent in the announcements of the names of Ishmael and Isaac:[†] but the ground of its selection was the apparently providential coincidence between the signification of the name and the historical destination of the man. The remark, that the name of John was not in the family, (v. 61.) only brought its celestial origin more fully into view. The tablet (πινακίδιον) upon which the father wrote the name (v. 63.) was necessary on account of his incapacity to speak; but it also had its type in the Old Testament. Isaiah was commanded to write the significant names of the child Maher-shalal-hash-baz upon a tablet. (Isaiah viii. 1, ff.) The only supernatural incident of the narrative, of which the Old Testament may seem to offer no precise analogy, is the dumbness; and this is the point fixed upon by those who contest the mythical view.[‡] But if it be borne in mind that the asking and receiving a sign from heaven in confirmation of a promise or prophecy was usual among the Hebrews (comp. Isaiah vii. 11, ff.); that the temporary loss of one of the senses was the peculiar punishment inflicted after a heavenly vision (Acts ix. 8, 17, ff.); that Daniel became dumb whilst the angel was talking with him, and did not recover his speech till the angel had touched his lips and opened his mouth: (Dan. x. 15, f.) the origin of this incident also will be found in the legend and not in historical fact. Of two ordinary and subordinate features of the narrative, the one, the righteousness of the parents of the Baptist, (v. 6.) is merely a conclusion founded upon the belief that to a pious couple alone would the blessing of such a son be vouchsafed, and consequently is void of all historical worth;

---

* Judg. xiii. 24 f.:
καὶ ἠλόγησεν αὐτὸν Κύριος, καὶ ηὐξήθη (al. ηὐλόγηθη) τὸ παιδάριον· καὶ ἤρξατο πνεῦμα Κυρίου συμπορεύεσθαι αὐτῷ ἐν παρεμβολῇ Δαν, ἀναμέσον Σαρὰ καὶ ἀναμέσον Ἐσθαόλ.

Comp. Gen. xxi. 20.

† Gen. xvi. 11, (LXX.:
καὶ καλέσεις τὸ ὄνομα αὐτοῦ Ἰσμαήλ.
xvii. 19: — — Ἰσαάκ.

Luc. i. 80:
τὸ δὲ παιδίον ηὔξανε καὶ ἐκραταιοῦτο πνεύματι, καὶ ἦν ἐν ταῖς ἐρήμοις, ἕως ἡμέρας ἀναδείξεως αὐτοῦ πρὸς τὸν Ἰσραήλ.

Luc. i. 13.
καὶ καλέσεις τὸ ὄνομα αὐτοῦ Ἰωάννην.

‡ Olshausen, Bibl. Commentar, 1. S. 116. Hoffmann, S. 116.

the other, the statement that John was born in the reign of Herod (the Great) (v. 5.) is without doubt a correct calculation.

So that we stand here upon purely mythical-poetical ground; the only historical reality which we can hold fast as positive matter of fact being this :—the impression made by John the Baptist, by virtue of his ministry and his relation to Jesus, was so powerful as to lead to the subsequent glorification of his birth in connection with the birth of the Messiah in the Christian legend.*

CHAPTER II.

DAVIDICAL DESCENT OF JESUS, ACCORDING TO THE GENEALOGICAL TABLES OF MATTHEW AND LUKE.

§ 20. THE TWO GENEALOGIES OF JESUS CONSIDERED SEPARATELY AND IRRESPECTIVELY OF ONE ANOTHER.

In the history of the birth of the Baptist we had the single account of Luke; but regarding the genealogical descent of Jesus we have also that of Matthew; so that in this case the mutual control of two narrators in some respects multiplies, whilst in others it lightens, our critical labour. It is indeed true that the authenticity of the two first chapters of Matthew, which contain the history of the birth and childhood of Jesus, as well as that of the parallel section of Luke, has been questioned: but as in both cases the question has originated merely in a prejudiced view of the subject, the doubt has been silenced by a decisive refutation.†

Each of these two gospels contains a genealogical table designed to exhibit the Davidical descent of Jesus, the Messiah. That of Matthew (i. 1—17.) precedes, that of Luke (iii. 23—38.) follows, the history of the announcement and birth of Jesus. These two tables, considered each in itself, or both compared together, afford so important a key to the character of the evangelic records in this section, as to render a close examination of them imperative. We shall first consider each separately, and then each, but particularly that of Matthew, in comparison with the passages in the Old Testament to which it is parallel.

In the Genealogy given by the author of the first Gospel, there is a comparison of the account with itself which is important as it gives a result, a sum at its conclusion, whose correctness may be proved by comparing it with the previous statements. In the sum-

---

* With this view of the passage compare De Wette, Exeg. Handbuch zum N. T., i. 2, S. 12. † Kuinöl, Comm. in Matth. Proleg. p. xxvii. f.

ming up it is said, that from Abraham to Christ there are three divisions of fourteen generations each, the first from Abraham to David, the second from David to the Babylonish exile, the third from the exile to Christ. Now if we compute the number of names for ourselves, we find the first fourteen from Abraham to David, both included, complete (2—5.); also that from Solomon to Jechonias, after whom the Babylonish exile is mentioned (6—11.); but from Jechonias to Jesus, even reckoning the latter as one, we can discover only thirteen. (12—16.) How shall we explain this discrepancy? The supposition that one of the names has escaped from the third division by an error of a transcriber,* is in the highest degree improbable, since the deficiency is mentioned so early as by Porphyry.† The insertion, in some manuscripts and versions, of the name *Jehoiakim*‡ between Josias and Jechonias, does not supply the deficiency of the third division; it only adds a superfluous generation to the second division which was already complete. As also there is no doubt that this deficiency originated with the author of the genealogy, the question arises: in what manner did he reckon so as to count fourteen generations for his third series? Truly it is possible to count in various ways, if an arbitrary inclusion and exclusion of the first and last members of the several series be permitted. It might indeed have been presupposed, that a generation already included in one division was necessarily excluded from another: but the compiler of the genealogy may perhaps have thought otherwise; and since David is twice mentioned in the table, it is possible that the author counted him twice: namely, at the end of the first series, and again at the beginning of the second. This would not indeed, any more than the insertion of Jehoiakim, fill up the deficiency in the third division, but give too many to the second; so that we must, with some commentators,§ conclude the second series not with Jechonias, as is usually done, but with his predecessor Josias: and now, by means of the double enumeration of David, Jechonias, who was superfluous in the second division, being available for the third, the last series, including Jesus, has its fourteen members complete. But it seems very arbitrary to reckon the concluding member of the first series twice, and not also that of the second:—to avoid which inconsistency some interpreters have proposed to count Josias twice, as well as David, and thus complete the fourteen members of the third series without Jesus. But whilst this computation escapes one blunder it falls into another; namely, that whereas the expression ἀπὸ ᾿Αβραὰμ ἕως Δαβίδ κ. τ. λ. (v. 17.) is supposed to include the latter, in ἀπὸ μετοικεσίας Βαβυλῶνος ἕως τοῦ Χριστοῦ, the latter is excluded. This difficulty may be avoided by counting Jechonias twice instead of Josias, which gives us fourteen names for the third division, including Jesus: but then, in order not to have too many in the second, we must drop

* Paulus, p. 292. † Hieron, in Daniel. init. ‡ See Wetstein. § e. g. Frische, Comm. in Matth. p. 13.

the double enumeration of David, and thus be liable to the same charge of inconsistency as in the former case, since the double enumeration is made between the second and third divisions, and not between the first and second. Perhaps De Wette has found the right clue when he remarks, that in v. 17, in both transitions some member of the series is mentioned twice, but in the first case only that member is a *person* (David), and therefore to be twice reckoned. In the second case it is the *Babylonish captivity* occurring between Josias and Jechonias, which latter, since he had reigned only three months in Jerusalem, (the greater part of his life having passed after the carrying away to Babylon,) was mentioned indeed at the conclusion of the second series for the sake of connexion, but was to be reckoned only at the beginning of the third.*

If we now compare the genealogy of Matthew, (still without reference to that of Luke,) with the corresponding passages of the Old Testament, we shall also find discrepancy, and in this case of a nature exactly the reverse of the preceding : for as the table considered in itself required the duplication of one member in order to complete its scheme, so when compared with the Old Testament, we find that many of the names there recorded have been omitted, in order that the number fourteen might not be exceeded. That is to say, the Old Testament affords data for comparison with this genealogical table as the famed pedigree of the royal race of David, from Abraham to Zorobabel and his sons; after whom the Davidical line begins to retire into obscurity, and from the silence of the Old Testament the genealogy of Matthew ceases to be under any control. The series of generations from Abraham to Judah, Pharez, and Hezron, is sufficiently well known from Genesis ; from Pharez to David we find it in the conclusion of the book of Ruth, and in the 2nd chapter of the 1st Chronicles ; that from David to Zerubbabel in the 3rd chapter of the same book ; besides passages that are parallel with separate portions of the series.

To complete the comparison : we find the line from Abraham to David, that is, the whole first division of fourteen in our genealogy, in exact accordance with the names of men given in the Old Testament : leaving out however the names of some women, one of which makes a difficulty. It is said v. 5 that Rahab was the mother of Boaz. Not only is this without confirmation in the Old Testament, but even if she be made the great grandmother of Jesse, the father of David, there are too few generations between her time and that of David (from about 1450 to 1050 B. C.) that is, counting either Rahab or David as one, four for 400 years. Yet this error falls back upon the Old Testament genealogy itself, in so far as Jesse's great grandfather Salmon, whom Matthew calls the husband of Rahab, is said Ruth iv. 20, as well as by Matthew, to be the son of a Nahshon, who according to Numbers i. 7, lived in the time of the march through the wilderness:* from which circumstance the idea was naturally suggested, to marry his son with that Rahab who saved the Israelitish spies, and thus to introduce a woman for whom the Israelites had an especial regard (compare James ii. 25, Heb. xi. 31) into the lineage of David and the Messiah.

Many discrepancies are found in the second division from David to Zorababel and his son, as well as in the beginning of the third. Firstly, it is said v. 8 *Joram begat Ozias ;* whereas we know from 1 Chron. iii. 11, 12, that Uzziah was not the son, but the grandson of the son of Joram, and that three kings occur between them, namely, Ahaziah, Joash, and Amaziah, after whom comes Uzziah, (2 Chron. xxvi. 1, or as he is called 1 Chron. iii. 12, and 2 Kings xiv. 21, Azariah.) Secondly: our genealogy says v. 11, *Josias begat Jechonias and his brethren.* But we find from 1 Chron. iii. 16, that the son and successor of Josiah was called Jehoiakim, after whom came his son and successor Jechoniah or Jehoiachin. Moreover *brethren* are ascribed to Jechoniah, whereas the Old Testament mentions none. Jehoiakim, however, had brothers : so that the mention of the *brethren of Jechonias* in Matthew appears to have originated in an exchange of these two persons.—A third discrepancy relates to Zorobabel. He is here called, v. 12, a son of Salathiel ; whilst in 1 Chron. iii. 19, he is descended from Jechoniah, not through Shealtiel, but through his brother Pedaiah. In Ezra v. 2, and Haggai i. 1, however, Zerubbabel is designated, as here, the son of Shealtiel.—In the last place, Abiud, who is here called the son of Zorobabel, is not to be found amongst the children of Zerubbabel mentioned 1 Chron. iii. 19 f. : perhaps because Abiud was only a surname derived from a son of one of those there mentioned.†

The second and third of these discrepancies may have crept in without evil intention, and without any great degree of carelessness, for the omission of Jehoiakim may have arisen from the similar sound of the names יְהוֹיָקִים יְהוֹיָכִין and which accounts also for the transposition of the brothers of Jechoniah ; whilst respecting Zorobabel the reference to the Old Testament is partly adverse, partly favourable. But the first discrepancy we have adduced, namely, the omission of three known kings, is not so easily to be set aside. It has indeed been held that the similarity of names may here also have led the author to pass unintentionally from Joram to Ozias, instead of to the similar sounding Ahaziah, (in the LXX Ochozias.) But this omission falls in so happily with the author's design of the threefold fourteen, (admitting the double enumeration of David,) that we cannot avoid believing, with Jerome, that the oversight was made on purpose with a view to it.‡ From

* The expedient of Kuinöl, Comm. in Matth. p. 3, to distinguish the Rahab here mentioned from the celebrated one, becomes hence superfluous, besides that it is perfectly arbitrary. † Hoffmann, S. 151, according to Hug, Einl. ii, S. 271. ‡ Compare Fritsche, Comm. in Matth. p. 19; Paulus, exeget. Handbuch, i, S. 289; De Wette, exeg. Handb. in loco.

Abraham to David, where the first division presented itself, having found fourteen members, he seems to have wished that those of the following divisions should correspond in number. In the whole remaining series the Babylonish exile offered itself as the natural point of separation. But as the second division from David to the exile gave him four supernumerary members, therefore he omitted four of the names. For what reason these particular four were chosen would be difficult to determine, at least for the three last mentioned.

The cause of the compiler's laying so much stress on the threefold equal numbers, may have been simply, that by this adoption of the Oriental custom of division into equal sections, the genealogy might be more easily committed to memory :* but with this motive a mystical idea was probably combined. The question arises whether this is to be sought in the number which is thrice repeated, or whether it consists in the threefold repetition? Fourteen is the double of the sacred number seven ; but it is improbable that it was selected for this reason,† because otherwise the seven would scarcely have been so completely lost sight of in the fourteen. Still more improbable is the conjecture of Olshausen, that the number fourteen was specially chosen as being the numeric value of the name of David ;‡ for puerilities of this kind, appropriate to the rabbinical gematria, are to be found in no other part of the Gospels. It is more likely that the object of the genealogists consisted merely in the repetition of an equal number by retaining the fourteen which had first accidentally presented itself: since it was a notion of the Jews that signal divine visitations, whether of prosperity or adversity, recurred at regular periodical intervals. Thus, as fourteen generations had intervened between Abraham, the founder of the holy people, and David the king after God's own heart, so fourteen generations must intervene between the re-establishment of the kingdom and the coming of the son of David, the Messiah.§ The most ancient genealogies in Genesis exhibit the very same uniformity. As according to the βίβλος γενέσεως ἀνθρώπων, cap. v., from Adam the first, to Noah the second, father of men, were ten generations : so from Noah, or rather from his son, the tenth is Abraham the father of the faithful.‖

This *a priori* treatement of his subject, this Procrustes-bed upon which the author of our genealogy now stretches, now curtails it, almost like a philosopher constructing a system,—can excite no predisposition in his favour. It is in vain to appeal to the custom

* Fritsche in Matth. p. 11.　† Paulus, S. 292.　‡ Bibl. Comm. p. 56, note.　§ See Schneckenburger, Beiträge zur Einleitung in das N. T., S. 41 f., and the passage cited from Josephus, B. j. vi. 8. Also may be compared the passage cited by Schöttgen, horæ hebr. et talm. zu Matth. i. from Synopsis Sohar, p. 132, n. 18.　*Ab Abrahamo usque ad Salomonem XV sunt generationes ; atque tunc luna fuit in plenilunio. A Salomone usque ad Zedekiam iterum sunt XV generationes, et tunc luna defecit, et Zedekiæ effossi sunt oculi.* ‖ De Wette has already called attention to the analogy between these Old Testament genealogies and those of the Gospels, with regard to the intentional equality of numbers. Kritik der mos. Geschichte, S. 69. Comp. S. 43.

of Oriental genealogists to indulge themselves in similar license: for when an author presents us with a pedigree expressly declaring that *all the generations* during a space of time were fourteen, whereas, through accident or intention, many members are wanting,— he betrays an arbitrariness and want of critical accuracy, which must shake our confidence in the certainty of his whole genealogy.

The genealogy of Luke, considered separately, does not present so many defects as that of Matthew. It has no concluding statement of the number of generations comprised in the genealogy, to act as a check upon itself, neither can it be tested, to much extent, by a comparison with the Old Testament. For, from David to Nathan, the line traced by Luke has no correspondence with any Old Testament genealogy, excepting in two of its members, Salathiel and Zorobabel; and even with respect to these two, there is a contradiction between the statement of Luke and that of 1 Chron. iii. 17. 19. f.: for the former calls Salathiel a son of Neri, whilst according to the latter, he was the son of Jechoniah. Luke also mentions one Resa as the son of Zorobabel, a name which does not appear amongst the children of Zerubbabel in 1 Chron. iii. 17. 19. Also, in the series before Abraham, Luke inserts a Cainan, who is not to be found in the Hebrew text, Gen. x. 24; xi. 12 ff., but who was however already inserted by the LXX. In fact the original text has this name in its first series as the third from Adam, and thence the translation appears to have transplanted him to the corresponding place in the second series as the third from Noah.

§ 21.   COMPARISON OF THE TWO GENEALOGIES—ATTEMPT TO
RECONCILE THEIR CONTRADICTIONS.

If we compare the genealogies of Matthew and Luke together, we become aware of still more striking discrepancies. Some of these differences indeed are unimportant, as the opposite direction of the two tables, the line of Matthew descending from Abraham to Jesus, that of Luke ascending from Jesus to his ancestors. Also the greater extent of the line of Luke: Matthew deriving it no farther than from Abraham, while Luke (perhaps lengthening some existing document in order to make it more consonant with the universalism of the doctrines of Paul:*) carries it back to Adam and to God himself. More important is the considerable difference in the number of generations for equal periods, Luke having 41 between David and Jesus, whilst Matthew has only 26. The main difficulty, however, lies in this: that in some parts of the genealogy, in Luke totally different individuals are made the ancestors of Jesus from those in Matthew. It is true, both writers agree in deriving the lineage of Jesus through Joseph from David and Abraham, and that the names of the individual members of the series

* See Chrysostom and Luther, in Credner, Einleitung in das N. T., 1, S. 143 f.
Winer, bibl. Realwörterbuch, 1 S. 659.

7

correspond from Abraham to David, as well as two of the names in the subsequent portion: those of Salathiel and Zorobabel. But the difficulty becomes desperate when we find that, with these two exceptions about midway, the whole of the names from David to the foster-father of Jesus are totally different in Matthew and in Luke. In Matthew, the father of Joseph is called Jacob; in Luke, Heli. In Matthew, the son of David through whom Joseph descended from that king is Solomon; in Luke, Nathan: and so on, the line descends, in Matthew, through the race of known kings: in Luke, through an unknown collateral branch, coinciding only with respect to Salathiel and Zorobabel, whilst they still differ in the names of the father of Salathiel and the son of Zorobabel. Since this difference appears to offer a complete contradiction, the most industrious efforts have been made at all times to reconcile the two. Passing in silence explanations evidently unsatisfactory, such as a mystical signification,* or an arbitrary change of names,† we shall consider two pairs of hypotheses which have been most conspicuous, and are mutually supported, or at least bear affinity to one another.

The first pair is formed upon the presupposition of Augustine, that Joseph was an adopted son, and that one evangelist gave the name of his real, the other that of his adopted father:‡ and the opinion of the old chronologist Julius Africanus, that a Levirate marriage had taken place between the parents of Joseph, and that the one genealogy belonged to the natural, the other to the legal, father of Joseph, by the one of whom he was descended from David through Solomon, by the other through Nathan.§ The farther question: to which father do the respective genealogies belong? is open to two species of criticism, the one founded upon literal expressions, the other upon the spirit and character of each gospel: and which lead to opposite conclusions. Augustine as well as Africanus, has observed, that Matthew makes use of an expression in describing the relationship between Joseph and his so-called father, which more definitely points out the natural filial relationship than that of Luke: for the former says Ἰακὼβ ἐγέννησε τὸν Ἰωσήφ: whilst the expression of the latter, Ἰωσὴφ τοῦ Ἡλί, appears equally applicable to a son by adoption, or by virtue of a Levirate marriage. But since the very object of a Levirate marriage was to maintain the name and race of a deceased childless brother, it was the Jewish custom to inscribe the firstborn son of such a marriage, not on the family register of his natural father, as Matthew has done here, but on that of his legal father, as Luke has done on the above supposition. Now that a person so entirely imbued with Jewish opinions as the author of the first gospel, should have made a mistake of this kind, cannot be held probable. Accordingly, Schleiermacher and others conceive themselves bound by the spirit of the two gospels to admit that Matthew, in spite of his ἐγέννησε, must have given the lineage of the legal father, according to Jewish custom : whilst Luke, who perhaps was not born a Jew, and was less familiar with Jewish habits, might have fallen upon the genealogy of the younger brothers of Joseph, who were not, like the firstborn, inscribed amongst the family of the deceased legal father, but with that of their natural father, and might have taken this for the genealogical table of the first-born Joseph, whilst it really belonged to him only by natural descent, to which Jewish genealogists paid no regard.* But, besides the fact which we shall show hereafter, that the genealogy of Luke can with difficulty be proved to be the work of the author of that gospel ;—in which case the little acquaintance of Luke with Jewish customs ceases to afford any clue to the meaning of this genealogy ;—it is also to be objected, that the genealogist of the first gospel could not have written his ἐγέννησε thus without any addition, if he was thinking of a mere legal paternity. Wherefore these two views of the genealogical relationship are equally difficult.

However, this hypothesis, which we have hitherto considered only in general, requires a more detailed examination in order to judge of its admissibility. In considering the proposition of a Levirate marriage, the argument is essentially the same if, with Augustine and Africanus, we ascribe the naming of the natural father to Matthew, or with Schleiermacher, to Luke. As an example we shall adopt the former statement ; the rather because Eusebius, according to Africanus, has left us a minute account of it. According to this representation, then, the mother of Joseph was first married to that person whom Luke calls the father of Joseph, namely Heli. But since Heli died without children, by virtue of the Levirate law, his brother, called by Matthew Jacob the father of Joseph, married the widow, and by her begot Joseph, who was legally regarded as the son of the deceased Heli, and so described by Luke, whilst naturally he was the son of his brother Jacob, and thus described by Matthew.

But, merely thus far, the hypothesis is by no means adequate. For if the two fathers of Joseph were real brothers, sons of the same father, they had one and the same lineage, and the two genealogies would have differed only in the father of Joseph, all the preceding portion being in agreement. In order to explain how the discordancy extends so far back as to David, we must have recourse to the second proposition of Africanus, that the fathers of Joseph were only half-brothers, having the same mother, but not the same father. We must also suppose that this mother of the two fathers of Joseph, had twice married ; once with the Matthan of Matthew, who was descended from David through Solomon and the line of kings, and to whom she bore Jacob : and also, either before or after, with the

* S. 53.　Comp. Winer bibl. Realwörterbuch, I Bd. S. 660.

Matthan of Luke, the offspring of which marriage was Heli: which Heli, having married and died childless, his half-brother Jacob married his widow, and begot for the deceased his legal child Joseph.

This hypothesis of so complicated a marriage in two successive generations, to which we are forced by the discrepancy of the two genealogies, must be acknowledged to be in no way impossible, but still highly improbable: and the difficulty is doubled by the untoward agreement already noticed, which occurs midway in the discordant series, in the two members Salathiel and Zorobabel. For to explain how Neri in Luke, and Jechonias in Matthew, are both called the father of Salathiel, who was the father of Zorobabel;—not only must the supposition of the Levirate marriage be repeated, but also that the two brothers who successively married the same wife, were brothers only on the mother's side. The difficulty is not diminished by the remark, that any nearest blood-relation, not only a brother, might succeed in a Levirate marriage,—that is to say, though not obligatory, it was at least open to his choice. (Ruth iii. 12 f. iv. 4 f.*) For since even in the case of two cousins, the concurrence of the two branches must take place much earlier than here for Jacob and Heli, and for Jechonias and Neri, we are still obliged to have recourse to the hypothesis of half-brothers; the only amelioration in this hypothesis over the other being, that these two very peculiar marriages do not take place in immediately consecutive generations. Now that this extraordinary double incident should not only have been twice repeated, but that the genealogists should twice have made the same selection in their statements respecting the natural and the legal father, and without any explanation,—is so improbable, that even the hypothesis of an adoption which is burdened with only one-half of these difficulties, has still more than it can bear. For in the case of adoption, since no fraternal or other relationship is required, between the natural and adopting fathers, the recurrence to a twice-repeated half-brotherhood is dispensed with; leaving only the necessity for twice supposing a relationship by adoption, and twice the peculiar circumstance, that the one genealogist from want of acquaintance with Jewish customs was ignorant of the fact, and the other, although he took account of it, was silent respecting it.

It has been thought by later critics that the knot may be loosed in a much easier way, by supposing that in one gospel we have the genealogy of Joseph, in the other that of Mary, in which case there would be no contradiction in the disagreement:† to which they are pleased to add the assumption that Mary was an heiress.‡ The opinion that Mary was of the race of David as well as Joseph has been long held. Following indeed the idea, that the Messiah, as a second Melchizedec, ought to unite in his person the priestly with

---

* Comp. Michaelis, Mos. Recht, ii, S. 200. Winer, bibl. Realwörterb. ii. S. 22 f.
† Thus e. g. Spanheim, dubia evang. p. 1, S. 13 ff. Lightfoot, Michaelis, Paulus, Kuinöl, Olshausen, lately Hoffmann and others. ‡ Epiphanius, Grotius. Olshausen, S. 43.

the kingly dignity,* and guided by the relationship of Mary with Elizabeth, who was a daughter of Aaron (Luke i. 36); already in early times it was not only held by many that the races of Judah and Levi were blended in the family of Joseph:† but also the opinion was not rare that Jesus, deriving his royal lineage from Joseph, descended also from the priestly race through Mary.‡ The opinion of Mary's descent from David, soon however became the more prevailing. Many apocryphal writers clearly state this opinion,§ as well as Justin Martyr, whose expression, that the virgin was of the race of David, Jacob, Isaac, and Abraham, may be considered an indication that he applied to Mary one of our genealogies, which are both traced back to Abraham through David.‖

On inquiring which of these two genealogies is to be held that of Mary? we are stopped by an apparently insurmountable obstacle, since each is distinctly announced as the genealogy of Joseph: the one in the words Ἰακὼβ ἐγέννησε τὸν Ἰωσήφ the other by the phrase υἱὸς Ἰωσήφ τοῦ Ἠλί. Here also, however, the ἐγέννησε of Matthew is more definite than the τοῦ of Luke, which according to those interpreters may mean just as well a son-in-law or grandson; so that the genetive of Luke in iii. 23 was either intended to express that Jesus was in common estimation a son of Joseph, who was the son-in-law of Heli, the father of Mary⁶:—or else, that Jesus was, as was believed, a son of Joseph, and through Mary a grandson of Heli.** As it may here be objected, that the Jews in their genealogies were accustomed to take no account of the female line,†† a farther hypothesis is had recourse to, namely, that Mary was an heiress, i. e. the daughter of a father without sons; and that in this case, according to Numbers xxxvi. 6, and Nehemiah vii. 63, Jewish custom required that the person who married her should not only be of the same race with herself, but that he should henceforth sink his own family in hers, and take her ancestors as his own. But the first point only is proved by the reference to Numbers; and the passage in Nehemiah, compared with several similar ones, (Ezra ii. 61: Numbers xxxii. 41; comp. with 1 Chron. ii. 21 f.) shows only that sometimes, by way of exception, a man took the name of his maternal ancestors. This difficulty with regard to Jewish customs, however, is cast into shade by one much more important. Although undeniably the genitive case used by Luke, expressing simply derivation in a general

* Testament. XII Patriarch., Test. Simeon c. 71. In Fabric. Codex pseudepigr. V. T. p. 542; ἐξ αὐτῶν (the races of Levi and Juda) ἀνατελεῖ ἡμῖν τὸ σωτήριον τοῦ θεοῦ. Ἀναστήσει γὰρ Κύριος ἐκ τοῦ Λευὶ ὡς ἀρχιερέα, καὶ ἐκ τοῦ Ἰούδα ὡς βασιλέα κ. τ. λ. † Comp. Thilo, cod. apocr. N. T. 1, S. 374 ff. ‡ Thus e. g. the Manichæan Faustus in Augustin. contra Faust. L. xxiii. 1. § Protevang. Jacobi c. 1 f. u. 10. de nativitate Mariæ c. 1. Joachim and Anna, of the race of David, are here mentioned as the parents of Mary. Faustus on the contrary, in the above cited passage, gives Joachim the title of S record s. ‖ Dial. c. Tryph. 43. 100. (Paris 1712.) ● Paulus, The Jews also in their representation of a Mary, the daughter of Heli, tormented in the lower world, (see Lightfoot,) appear to have taken the genealogy of Luke, which sets out from Heli, for that of Mary. ** e. g. Lightfoot horæ p. 750; Osiander, S. 86. †† Juchasin f. 55, 2. in Lightfoot S. 183. and Bava bathra, f. 110, 2. in Westein S. 230 f. Comp. Joseph. Vita, 1.

sense, may signify any degree of relationship, and consequently that of son-in-law or grandson : yet this interpretation destroys the consistency of the whole passage. In the thirty-four preceding members, which are well known to us from the Old Testament, this genitive demonstrably indicates throughout the precise relationship of a son: likewise when it occurs between Salathiel and Zorobabel : how could it be intended in the one instance of Joseph to indicate that of son-in-law? or, according to the other interpretation, supposing the nominative υἱὸς to govern the whole series, how can we suppose it to change its signification from son to grandson, great-grandson, and so on to the end? If it be said the phrase Ἀδὰμ τοῦ θεοῦ is a proof that the genitive does not necessarily indicate a son in the proper sense of the word, we may reply that it bears a signification with regard to the immediate Author of existence equally inapplicable to either father-in-law or grandfather.

A further difficulty is encountered by this explanation of the two genealogies in common with the former one, in the concurrence of the two names of Salathiel and Zorobabel. The supposition of a Levirate marriage is as applicable to this explanation as the other, but the interpreters we are now examining prefer for the most part to suppose, that these similar names in the different genealogies belong to different persons. When Luke however, in the twenty-first and twenty-second generations from David, gives the very same names that Matthew (including the four omitted generations,) gives in the nineteenth and twentieth, one of these names being of great notoriety, it is certainly impossible to doubt that they refer to the same persons.

Moreover, in no other part of the New Testament is there any trace to be found of the Davidical descent of Mary: on the contrary, some passages are directly opposed to it. In Luke i. 27, the expression ἐξ οἴκου Δαβὶδ refers only to the immediately preceding ἀνδρὶ ᾧ ὄνομα Ἰωσήφ, not to the more remote παρθένου μεμνηστευμένην. And more pointed still is the turn of the sentence Luke ii. 4, ἀνέβη δὲ καὶ Ἰωσήφ—διὰ τό εἶναι αὐτὸν ἐξ οἴκου καὶ πατριᾶς Δαβὶδ, ἀπογράψασθαι σὺν Μαρίᾳ κ. τ. λ., where αὐτούς might so easily have been written instead of αὐτὸν, if the author had any thought of including Mary in the descent from David. These expressions fill to overflowing the measure of proof already adduced, that it is impossible to apply the genealogy of the third Evangelist to Mary.

§ 22. THE GENEALOGIES UNHISTORICAL.

A CONSIDERATION of the insurmountable difficulties, which unavoidably embarrass every attempt to bring these two genealogies into harmony with one another, will lead us to despair of reconciling them, and will incline us to acknowledge, with the more free-thinking class of critics, that they are mutually contradictory.* Consequently they cannot both be true : if, therefore, one is to be preferred before the other, several circumstances would seem to decide in favour of the genealogy of Luke, rather than that of Matthew. It does not exhibit an arbitrary adherence to a fixed form and to equal periods : and whilst the ascribing of twenty generations to the space of time from David to Jechonias or Neri, in Luke, is at least not more offensive to probability, than the omission of four generations in Matthew to historical truth : Luke's allotment of twenty-two generations for the period from Jechonias (born 617 B. C.) to Jesus. i. e. about 600 years, forming an average of twenty-seven years and a half to each generation, is more consonant with natural events, particularly amongst eastern nations, than the thirteen generations of Matthew, which make an average of forty-two years for each. Besides the genealogy of Luke is less liable than that of Matthew to the suspicion of having been written with a design to glorify Jesus, since it contents itself with ascribing to Jesus a descent from David, without tracing that descent through the royal line. On the other hand, however, it is more improbable that the genealogy of the comparatively insignificant family of Nathan should have been preserved, than that of the royal branch. Added to which, the frequent recurrence of the same names is, as justly remarked by Hoffmann, an indication that the genealogy of Luke is fictitious.

In fact then neither table has any advantage over the other. If the one is unhistorical, so also is the other, since it is very improbable that the genealogy of an obscure family like that of Joseph, extending through so long a series of generations, should have been preserved during all the confusion of the exile, and the disturbed period that followed. Yet, it may be said, although we recognize in both, so far as they are not copied from the Old Testament, an unrestrained play of the imagination, or arbitrary applications of other genealogies to Jesus,—we may still retain as an historical basis that Jesus was descended from David, and that only the intermediate members of the line of descent were variously filled up by different writers. But the one event on which this historical basis is mainly supported, namely, the journey of the parents of Jesus to Bethlehem in order to be taxed, so far from sufficing to prove them to be of the house and lineage of David, is itself, as we shall presently show, by no means established as matter of history. Of more weight is the other ground, namely, that Jesus is universally represented in the New Testament, without any contradiction from his adversaries, as the descendant of David. Yet even the phrase υἱὸς Δαβὶδ is a predicate that may naturally have been applied to Jesus, not on historical, but on dogmatical grounds. According to the

* Thus Eichorn, Einl. in das N. T. 1 Bd. S. 425. Kaiser, bibl. Theol. 1, S. 232. Wegscheider, Institut. § 123, not. d. de Wette, bibl. Dogm. § 279, and exeget. Handbuch 1, 2, S. 32. Winer, bibl. Realworterb. 1, S. 660 f. Hase, Leben Jesu, § 35. Fritzsche, Comm. in Matt. p. 35. Ammon, Fortbildung des Christenthums zur Weltreligion, 1, S. 196 ff.

prophecies, the Messiah could only spring from David. When therefore a Galilean, whose lineage was utterly unknown, and of whom consequently no one could prove that he was not descended from David, had acquired the reputation of being the Messiah; what more natural than that tradition should under different forms have early ascribed to him a Davidical descent, and that genealogical tables, corresponding with this tradition should have been formed? which, however, as they were constructed upon no certain data, would necessarily exhibit such differences and contradictions as we find actually existing between the genealogies in Matthew and in Luke.*

If, in conclusion, it be asked, what historical result is to be deduced from these genealogies? we reply: a conviction, (arrived at also from other sources,) that Jesus, either in his own person or through his disciples, acting upon minds strongly imbued with Jewish notions and expectations, left among his followers so firm a conviction of his Messiahship, that they did not hesitate to attribute to him the prophetical characteristic of Davidical descent, and more than one pen was put in action, in order, by means of a genealogy which should authenticate that descent, to justify his recognition as the Messiah.†

CHAPTER III.

ANNOUNCEMENT OF THE CONCEPTION OF JESUS—ITS SUPERNATURAL CHARACTER—VISIT OF MARY TO ELIZABETH.

§ 23.   SKETCH OF THE DIFFERENT CANONICAL AND APOCRYPHAL ACCOUNTS.

THERE is a striking gradation in the different representations of the conception and birth of Jesus given in the canonical and in the apocryphal gospels. They exhibit the various steps, from a simple statement of a natural occurrence, to a minute and miraculously embellished history, in which the event is traced back to its very earliest date. Mark and John presuppose the fact of the birth of Jesus, and

---

* See De Wette, bibl. Dogm. and exeg. Handbuch 1, 1, S. 14 ; Hase. L. J. Eusebius gives a not improbable explanation of this disagreement (ad. Steph. quæst. iii, pointed out by Credner, 1. p. 68 f.) that besides the notion amongst the Jews, that the Messiah must spring from the royal line of David, another had arisen, that this line having become polluted and declared unworthy of continuing on the throne of David, (Jerem. xxii. 30,) by the wickedness of its later reigning members, a line more pure though less famed was to be preferred to it.   † The farther considerations on the origin and import of these genealogies, which arise from their connexion with the account of the miraculous birth of Jesus, must be reserved till after the examination of the latter point.

content themselves with the incidental mention of Mary as the
mother (Mark vi. 3), and of Joseph as the father of Jesus (John i.
46). Matthew and Luke go further back, since they state the particular circumstances attending the conception as well as the birth
of the Messiah. But of these two evangelists Luke mounts a step
higher than Matthew. According to the latter Mary, the betrothed
of Joseph, being *found with child*, Joseph is offended and determines to put her away; but the angel of the Lord visits him in a
dream, and assures him of the divine origin and exalted destiny of
Mary's offspring; the result of which is that Joseph takes unto him
his wife: but knows her not till she has brought forth her first-born
son. (Matt. i. 18—25.) Here the pregnancy is discovered in the
first place, and then afterwards justified by the angel; but in Luke
the pregnancy is prefaced and announced by a celestial apparition.
The same Gabriel, who had predicted the birth of John to Zacharias, appears to Mary, the betrothed of Joseph, and tells her that
she shall conceive by the power of the Holy Ghost: whereupon the
destined mother of the Messiah pays a visit full of holy import to
the already pregnant mother of his forerunner: upon which occasion
both Mary and Elizabeth pour forth their emotions to one another
in the form of a hymn, (Luke i. 26—56). Matthew and Luke are
content to presuppose the connexion between Mary and Joseph: but
the apocryphal gospels, the *Protevangelium Jacobi*, and the *Evangelium de Nativitate Mariae,** (books with the contents of which
the Fathers partially agree), seek to represent the origin of this connexion; indeed they go back to the birth of Mary, and describe it
to have been preceded, equally with that of the Messiah and the
Baptist, by a divine annunciation. As the description of the birth
of John in Luke is principally borrowed from the Old Testament
accounts of Samuel and of Samson, so this history of the birth of
Mary is an imitation of the history in Luke, and of the Old Testament histories.

Joachim, so says the apocryphal narrative, and Anna (the name
of Samuel's mother†) are unhappy on account of their long childless
marriage (as were the parents of the Baptist); when an angel appears
to them both (so in the history of Samson) at different places, and
promises them a child, who shall be the mother of God, and commands that this child shall live the life of a Nazarite (like the Baptist). In early childhood Mary is brought by her parents to the
temple (like Samuel); where she continues till her twelfth year, visited and fed by angels and honoured by divine visions. Arrived at
womanhood she is to quit the temple, her future provision and destiny being revealed by the oracle to the high priest. In conformity
with the prophecy of Isaiah, xi. 1 f.: *egredietur virga de radice*

* Fabricius, Codex apocryphus N. T. 1, p. 19 ff. 66 ff.; Thilo, 1, p. 161 ff. 319 ff.
† Gregory of Nyssa or his interpolator is reminded of this mother of Samuel by the
apocryphal Anna when he says of her: Μιμεῖται τοίνυν καὶ αὕτη τὰ περὶ τῆς μητρὸς τοῦ
Σαμουὴλ διηγήματα κ. τ. λ. Fabricius 1, p. 6.

Jesse, et flos de radice ejus ascendet, et requiescet super eum spiritus Domini; this oracle commanded, according to one gospel*, that all the unmarried men of the house of David,—according to the other,† that all the widowers among the people,—should bring their rods and that he on whose rod a sign should appear (like the rod of Aaron, Numb. xvii.), namely the sign predicted in the prophecy, should take Mary unto himself. This sign was manifested upon Joseph's rod : for, in exact accordance with the oracle, it put forth a blossom and a dove lighted upon it.‡ The apocryphal gospels and the fathers agree in representing Joseph as an old man :§ but the narrative is somewhat differently told in the two apocryphal gospels. According to the *Evang. de nativ. Mariae*, notwithstanding Mary's alleged vow of chastity, and the refusal of Joseph on account of his great age, betrothment took place at the command of the priest, and subsequently a marriage—(which marriage, however, the author evidently means to represent also as chaste). According to the *Protevang. Jacobi*, on the contrary, neither betrothment nor marriage are mentioned, but Joseph is regarded merely as the chosen protector of the young virgin,‖ and Joseph on the journey to Bethlehem doubts whether he shall describe his charge as his wife or as his daughter; fearing to bring ridicule upon himself, on account of his age, if he called her his wife. Again, where in Matthew Mary is called ἡ γυνὴ of Joseph, the apocryphal gospel carefully designates her merely as ἡ παῖς, and even avoids using the term παραλαβεῖν or substitutes διαφυλάξαι, with which many of the Fathers concur.¶ In the *Protevangelicum* it is further related that Mary, having been received into Joseph's house, was charged, together with other young women, with the fabrication of the veil for the temple, and that it fell to her lot to spin the true purple. But whilst Joseph was absent on business Mary was visited by an angel, and Joseph on his return found her with child and called her to account, not as a husband, but as the guardian of her honour. Mary, however, had forgotten the words of the angel and protested her ignorance of the cause of her pregnancy. Joseph was perplexed and determined to remove her secretly from under his protection; but an angel appeared to him in a dream and reassured him by his explanation. The matter was then brought before the priest, and both Joseph and Mary being charged with incontinence were condemned to drink the "bitter water,"** ὕδωρ τῆς ἐλέγξεως, but as they remained uninjured by it, they were declared innocent. Then follows the account of the taxing and of the birth of Jesus.††

---

* Evang. de nativ. Mar. c. 7: *cunctos de domo et familia David nuptui habiles, non conjugatos.* † Protev. Jac. c. 8: τοῖς χηρεύοντας τοῦ λαοῦ. ‡ It is thus in the Evang. de nativ. Mariae vii. and viii.; but rather different in the Protev. Jac. c. ix. § Protev. c. 9: πρεσβύτης. Evang. de nativ. Mar. 8.: grandaevus. Epiphan. adv. haeres. 78, 8: λαμβάνει τὴν Μαρίαν χῆρος, κατάγων ἡλικίαν περί που ὀγδοήκοντα ἐτῶν καὶ πρόσω ὁ ἀνήρ. ‖ Παράλαβε αὐτὴν εἰς τήρησιν σεαυτῷ. c. ix. Compare with Evang. de nativ. Mar. viii. and x. ¶ See the variations in *Thilo* p. 227. and the quotations from the Fathers at p. 365 not. ** Numb. v. 18. †† Protev. J. x—xvi. The account in the Evang. de nativ. Mar. is less characteristic.

CONCEPTION OF JESUS—ITS SUPERNATURAL CHARACTER. 107

Since these apocryphal narratives were for a long period held as historical by the church, and were explained, equally with those of the canonical accounts, from the supranaturalistic point of view as miraculous, they were entitled in modern times to share with the New Testament histories the benefit of the natural explanation. If, on the one hand, the belief in the marvellous was so superabundantly strong in the ancient church, that it reached beyond the limits of the New Testament even to the embracing of the apocryphal narratives, blinding the eye to the perception of their manifestly unhistorical character: so, on the other hand, the positive rationalism of some of the heralds of the modern modes of explanation was so overstrong that they believed it adequate to explain even the apocryphal miracles. Of this we have an example in the author of the natural history of the great Prophet of Nazareth:* who does not hesitate to include the stories of the lineage and early years of Mary within the circle of his representations, and to give them a natural explanation. If we in our day, with a perception of the fabulous character of such narratives, look down alike upon the Fathers of the church and upon these naturalistic interpreters, we are certainly so far in the right, as it is only by gross ignorance that this character of the apocryphal accounts is here to be mistaken; more closely considered, however, the difference between the apocryphal and the canonical narratives concerning the early history of the Baptist and of Jesus, is seen to be merely a difference of form: they have sprung, as we shall here-after find, from the same root, though the one is a fresh and healthy sprout, and the other an artificially nurtured and weak aftergrowth. Still, the Fathers of the church and these naturalistic interpreters had this superiority over most of the theologians of our own time; that they did not allow themselves to be deceived respecting the inherent similarity by the difference of form, but interpreted the kindred narratives by the same method; treating both as miraculous or both as natural; and not, as is now usual, the one as fiction and the other as history.

§ 24. DISAGREEMENTS OF THE CANONICAL GOSPELS IN RELATION TO THE FORM OF THE ANNUNCIATION.

AFTER the foregoing general sketch, we now proceed to examine the external circumstances which, according to our gospels, attended the first communication of the future birth of Jesus to Mary and Joseph. Leaving out of sight, for the present, the special import of the annunciation, namely, that Jesus should be supernaturally begotten of the Holy Ghost, we shall, in the first place, consider merely the form of the announcement; by whom, when, and in what manner it was made.

As the birth of the Baptist was previously announced by an angel, so the conception of Jesus was, according to the gospel his-

* "Die natürliche Geschichte des grossen Propheten von Nazareth," 1ter Band S. 119 ff.

tories, proclaimed after the same fashion. But whilst in the one case, we have but one history of the apparition, that of Luke; in the other we have two accounts, accounts however which do not correspond, and which we must now compare. Apart from the essential signification the two accounts exhibit the following differences. 1. The individual who appears is called in Matthew by the indefinite appellation, *angel of the Lord*, ἄγγελος Κυρίου: in Luke by name, *the angel Gabriel*, ὁ ἄγγελος Γαβριὴλ. 2. The person to whom the angel appears is, according to Matthew, Joseph, according to Luke, Mary. 3. In Matthew the apparation is seen in a dream, in Luke whilst awake. 4. There is a disagreement in relation to the time at which the apparition took place: according to Matthew, Joseph receives the heavenly communication after Mary was already pregnant: according to Luke it is made to Mary prior to her pregnancy. 5. Lastly, both the purpose of the apparition and the effect produced are different: it was designed, according to Matthew, to comfort Joseph, who was troubled on account of the pregnancy of his betrothed: according to Luke to prevent, by a previous announcement, all possibility of offence.

Where the discrepancies are so great and so essential, it may, at first sight, appear altogether superfluous to inquire whether the two Evangelists record one and the same occurrence, though with considerable disagreement; or whether they record distinct occurrences, so that the two accounts can be blended together, and the one be made to amplify the other? The first supposition cannot be admitted without impeaching the historical validity of the narrative; for which reason most of our theologians, indeed all who see in the narrative a true history, whether miraculous or natural, have decided in favour of the second supposition. Maintaining, and justly, that the silence of one Evangelist concerning an event which is narrated by the other, is not a negation of the event,* they blend the two accounts together in the following manner: 1, First, the angel makes known to Mary her approaching pregnancy (Luke): 2, she then journeys to Elizabeth (the same gospel); 3, after her return her situation being discovered, Joseph takes offence (Matthew); whereupon, 4, he likewise is visited by an angelic apparition (the same gospel.†)

But this arrangement of the incidents is, as Schleiermacher has already remarked, full of difficulty :‡ and it seems that what is related by one Evangelist is not only not presupposed, but excluded, by the other. For, in the first place, the conduct of the angel who appears to Joseph is not easily explained, if the same or another angel had previously appeared to Mary. The angel (in Matthew) speaks altogether as if his communication were the first in this affair: he neither refers to the message previously received by Mary, nor reproaches Joseph because he had not believed it; but more

* Augustin, *de consens. evangelist*, ii. 5.   † Paulus, Olshausen, Fritzsche, Comm. in Matth. p. 56.   ‡ Comp. de Wette's exeg. Handbuch i. 1, S. 18.   Schleiermacher über die Schriften des Lukas, S. 42 ff.

than all, the informing Joseph of the name of the expected child, and the giving him a full detail of the reasons why he should be so called, (Matt. i. 21.) would have been wholly superfluous had the angel (according to Luke i. 31.) already indicated this name to Mary.

Still more incomprehensible is the conduct of the betrothed parties according to this arrangement of events. Had Mary been visited by an angel, who had made known to her an approaching supernatural pregnancy, would not the first impulse of a delicate woman have been, to hasten to impart to her betrothed the import of the divine message, and by this means to anticipate the humiliating discovery of her situation, and an injurious suspicion on the part of her affianced husband. But exactly this discovery Mary allows Joseph to make from others, and thus excites suspicions; for it is evident that the expression εὑρέθη ἐν γαστρὶ ἔχουσα (Matth. i. 18.) signifies a discovery made independent of any communication on Mary's part, and it is equally clear that in this manner only does Joseph obtain the knowledge of her situation, since his conduct is represented as the result of that discovery (εὑρίσκεσθαι). The apocryphal *Protevangelium Jacobi* felt how enigmatical Mary's conduct must appear, and sought to solve the difficulty in a manner which, contemplated from the supranaturalistic point of view, is, perhaps the most consistent. Had Mary retained a recollection of the import of the heavenly message—upon this point the whole ingenious representation of the apocryphal gospel rests—she ought to have imparted it to Joseph; but since it is obvious from Joseph's demeanour that she did not acquaint him with it, the only remaining alternative is, to admit that the mysterious communication made to Mary had, owing to her excited state of mind, escaped her memory, and that she was herself ignorant of the true cause of her pregnancy.* In fact, nothing is left to supranaturalism in the present case but to seek refuge in the miraculous and the incomprehensible. The attempts which the modern theologians of this class have made to explain Mary's silence, and even to find in it an admirable trait in her character, are so many rash and abortive efforts to make a virtue of necessity. According to Hess† it must have cost Mary much self-denial to have concealed the communication of the angel from Joseph; and this reserve, in a matter known only to herself and to God, must be regarded as a proof of her firm trust in God. Without doubt Mary communed thus with herself: It is not without a purpose that this apparition has been made to me alone, had it been intended that Joseph should have participated in the communication, the angel would have appeared to him also (if each individual favoured with a divine revelation were of this opinion, how many special revelations would it not require?); besides it is an affair of

* Protev. Jac. c. 12: Μαριὰμ δὲ ἐπιλάθετο τῶν μυστηρίων ὧν εἶπε πρὸς αὐτὴν Γαβριήλ. When questioned by Joseph she assures him with tears: οὐ γινώσκω, πόθεν ἐστί τοῦτο τὸ ἐν τῇ γαστρί μου. c. 13.   †. Geschichte der drei letzten Lebensjahre Jesu u. s. w. 1. Thl. S. 36. Comp. Hoffmann, S. 176 f.

God alone, consequently it becomes me to leave it with him to convince Joseph (the argument of indolence). Olshausen concurs, and adds his favourite general remark, that in relation to events so extraordinary the measure of the ordinary occurrences of the world is not applicable: a category under which, in this instance, the highly essential considerations of delicacy and propriety are included.

More in accordance with the views of the natural interpreters, the *Evangelium de nativitate Mariæ,** and subsequently some later writers, for example, the author of the natural history of the great prophet of Nazareth, have sought to explain Mary's silence, by supposing Joseph to have been at a distance from the abode of his affianced bride at the time of the heavenly communication. According to them Mary was of Nazareth, Joseph of Bethlehem : to which latter place Joseph departed after the betrothing, and did not return to Mary until the expiration of three months: when he discovered the pregnancy which had taken place in the interim. But since the assumption that Mary and Joseph resided in different localities has no foundation, as will presently be seen, in the canonical gospels, the whole explanation falls to the ground. Without such an assumption, Mary's silence towards Joseph might, perhaps, have been accounted for from the point of view of the naturalistic interpreters, by imagining her to have been held back through modesty from confessing a situation so liable to excite suspicion. But one who, like Mary, was so fully convinced of the divine agency in the matter, and had shown so ready a comprehension of her mysterious destination (Luke i. 38.) could not possibly have been tongue-tied by petty considerations of false shame.

Consequently, in order to rescue Mary's character, without bringing reproach upon Joseph's, and at the same time to render his unbelief intelligible, interpreters have been compelled to assume that a communication, though a tardy one, was actually made by Mary, to Joseph. Like the last-named apocryphal gospel, they introduce a journey, not of Joseph, but of Mary—the visit to Elizabeth mentioned in Luke—to account for the postponement of the communication. It is probable, says Paulus, that Mary did not open her heart to Joseph before this journey, because she wished first to consult with her older friend as to the mode of making the disclosure to him, and whether she, as the mother of the Messiah, ought to marry.

It was not till after her return, and then most likely through the medium of others, that she made Joseph acquainted with her situation, and with the promises she had received. But Joseph's mind was not properly attuned and prepared for such a disclosure ; he became haunted by all kinds of thoughts: and vacillated between suspicion and hope till a length a dream decided him.† But in the first place a motive is here given to Mary's journey which is foreign to the account in Luke. Mary sets off to Elizabeth, not

* Ch. viii.—x.   † Paulus, exeg. Handb. 1 A., S. 121. 145

to take counsel of her, but to assure herself regarding the sign appointed by the angel. No uneasiness which the friend is to dissipate, but a proud joy, unalloyed by the smallest anxiety, is expressed in her salutation to the future mother of the Baptist. But besides, a confession so tardily made can in nowise justify Mary. What behaviour on the part of an affianced bride—after having received a divine communication, so nearly concerning her future husband, and in a matter so delicate—to travel miles away, to absent herself for three months, and then to permit her betrothed to learn through third persons that which could no longer be concealed!

Those, therefore, who do not impute to Mary a line of conduct which certainly our Evangelists do not impute to her, must allow that she imparted the message of the angel to her future husband as soon as it had been revealed to her; but that he did not believe her.* But now let us see how Joseph's character is to be dealt with! Even Hess is of opinion that, since Joseph was acquainted with Mary, he had no cause to doubt her word, when she told him of the apparition she had had. This scepticism presupposes a mistrust of his betrothed which is incompatible with his character as a *just man* (Matt. i. 19.) and an incredulity respecting the marvellous which is difficult to reconcile with a readiness on other occasions to believe in angelic apparitions; nor, in any case, would this want of faith have escaped the censure of the angel who subsequently appeared to himself.

Since then, to suppose that the two accounts are parallel, and complete one another, leads unavoidably to results inconsistent with the sense of the Gospels, in so far as they evidently meant to represent the characters of Joseph and Mary as free from blemish; the supposition cannot be admitted, but the accounts mutually exclude each other. An angel did not appear, first to Mary, and also afterwards to Joseph; he can only have appeared either to the one or to the other. Consequently, it is only the one or the other relation which can be regarded as historical. And here different considerations would conduct to opposite decisions. The history in Matthew might appear the more probable from the rationalistic point of view, because it is more easy to interpret naturally an apparition in a dream; whilst that in Luke might be preferred by the supranaturalistic, because the manner in which the suspicion cast upon the holy virgin is refuted is more worthy of God. But in fact, a nearer examination proves, that neither has any essential claim to be advanced before the other. Both contain an angelic apparition, and both are therefore encumbered with all the difficulties which, as was stated above in relation to the annunciation of the birth of the Baptist, oppose the belief in angels and apparitions. Again, in both narrations the import of the angelic message is, as we shall presently see, an impossibility. Thus every criterion which might determine the adoption of the one, and the rejection of the other, dis-

* To this opinion Neander inclines L. J. ch. S. 18.

appears; and we find ourselves, in reference to both accounts, driven back by necessity to the mythical view.

From this point of view, all the various explanations, which the Rationalists have attempted to give of the two apparitions, vanish of themselves. Paulus explains the apparition in Matthew as a natural dream, occasioned by Mary's previous communication of the announcement which had been made to her: and with which Joseph must have been acquainted, because this alone can account for his having heard the same words in his dream, which the angel had beforehand addressed to Mary: but much rather, is it precisely this similarity in the language of the presumed second angel to that of the first, with the absence of all reference by the latter to the former, which proves that the words of the first angel were not presupposed by the second. Besides, the natural explanation is annihilated the moment the narratives are shown to be mythical. The same remark applies to the explanation, expressed guardedly indeed by Paulus, but openly by the author of the "Natural history of the great prophet of Nazareth," namely, that the angel who visited Mary (in Luke) was a human being; of which we must speak hereafter.

According to all that has been said, the following is the only judgment we can form of the origin of the two narratives of the angelic apparitions. The conception of Jesus through the power of the Holy Ghost ought not to be grounded upon a mere uncertain suspicion; it must have been clearly and positively asserted; and to this end a messenger from heaven was required, since theocratic decorum seemed to demand it far more in relation to the birth of the Messiah, than of a Samson or a John. Also the words which the angels use, correspond in part with the Old Testament annunciations of extraordinary children.* The appearing of the angel in the one narrative beforehand to Mary, but in the other at a later period to Joseph, is to be regarded as a variation in the legend or in the composition, which finds an explanatory counterpart in the history of the annunciation of Isaac. Jehovah (Gen. xvii. 15.) promises Abraham a son by Sarah, upon which the Patriarch cannot refrain from laughing; but he receives a repetition of the assurance; Jehovah (Gen. xviii. 1, ff.) makes this promise under the Terebinth tree at Mamre, and Sarah laughs as if it were something altogether novel and unheard of by her; lastly, according to Gen.

---

* Gen. xvii. 19; LXX. (Annunciation of Isaac):
ἰδοὺ Σάῤῥα ἡ γυνή σου τέξεταί σοι υἱὸν, καὶ καλέσεις τὸ ὄνομα αὐτοῦ Ἰσαακ.
Judg. xiii. 5. (Annunciation of Samson):
καὶ αὐτὸς ἄρξεται σῶσαι τὸν Ἰσραὴλ ἐκ χειρὸς Φυλιστίμ.
Gen. xvi. 11 ff. (Annunciation of Ishmael):
κα εἶπ εν αὐτῇ ὁ ἄγγελος Κυρίου ἰδοὺ σὺ ἐν γαστρὶ ἔχεις, καὶ τέξῃ υἱὸν καὶ καλέσεις τὸ ὄνομα αὐτοῦ Ἰσμαὴλ Οὗτος ἔσται — —

Matth. i. 21
(μὴ φοβηθῇς παραλαβεῖν Μαριὰμ τὴν γυναῖκα σου —) τέξεται δὲ υἱὸν, καὶ καλέσεις τὸ ὄνομα αὐτοῦ Ἰησοῦν αὐτὸς γὰρ σώσει τὸν λαὸν αὐτοῦ ἀπὸ τῶν ἁμαρτιῶν αὐτῶν.

Luke i. 10 ff.
καὶ εἶπεν ὁ ἄγγελος αὐτῇ ἰδοὺ συλλήψῃ ἐν γαστρὶ, καὶ τέξῃ υἱὸν, καὶ καλέσεις τὸ ὄνομα αὐτοῦ Ἰησοῦν Οὗτος ἔσται.

xxi. 5 ff. it is first after Isaac's birth that Sarah mentions the laughing of the people, which is said to have been the occasion of his name: whereby it appears that this last history does not presuppose the existence of the two other accounts of the annunciation of the birth of Isaac.* As in relation to the birth of Isaac, different legends or poems were formed without reference to one another, some simpler, some more embellished: so we have two discordant narratives concerning the birth of Jesus. Of these the narrative in Matthew† is the simpler and ruder style of composition, since it does not avoid, though it be but by a transient suspicion on the part of Joseph, the throwing a shade over the character of Mary which is only subsequently removed; that in Luke, on the contrary, is a more refined and artistical representation, exhibiting Mary from the first in the pure light of a bride of heaven.‡

§ 25. IMPORT OF THE ANGEL'S MESSAGE—FULFILLMENT OF THE PROPHECY OF ISAIAH.

ACCORDING to Luke, the angel who appears to Mary, in the first place informs her only that she shall become pregnant, without specifying after what manner: that she shall bring forth a son and call his name Jesus; he shall be great, and shall be called the Son of the Highest (υἱὸς ὑψίστου); and God shall give unto him the throne of his father David, and he shall reign over the house of Jacob for ever. The subject, the Messiah, is here treated precisely in the language common to the Jews, and even the term *Son of the Highest*, if nothing further followed, must be taken in the same sense; as according to 2 Sam. vii. 14. Ps. ii. 7. an ordinary king of Israel might be so named; still more, therefore, the greatest of these kings, the Messiah, even considered merely as a man. This Jewish language reflects in addition a new light upon the question of the historic validity of the angelic apparition; for we must agree with Schleiermacher that the real angel Gabriel would hardly have proclaimed the advent of the Messiah in a phraseology so strictly Jewish :§ for which reason we are inclined to coincide with this theologian, and to ascribe this particular portion of the history, as also that which precedes and relates to the Baptist, to one and the same Jewish-christian author. It is not till Mary opposes the fact of her

* Comp. de Wette, Kritik der mosaischen Geschichte, S. 86 ff.
† The vision, which according to Matthew, Joseph had in his sleep, had besides a kind of type in the vision by which, according to the Jewish tradition related by Josephus, the father of Moses was comforted under similar circumstances, when suffering anxiety concerning the pregnancy of his wife, although for a different reason. Joseph. Antiq. II, ix., 3. "A man whose name was Amram, one of the nobler sort of Hebrews, was afraid for his whole nation, lest it should fail, by the want of young men to be brought up hereafter, and was very uneasy at it, his wife being then with child, and he knew not what to do. Hereupon he betook himself to prayer to God . . . Accordingly God had mercy on him, and was moved by his supplication. He stood by him in his sleep, and exhorted him not to despair of his future favours. . . For this child of thine shall deliver the Hebrew nation from the distress they are under from the Egyptians. His memory shall be famous while the world lasts." ‡ Compare Ammon, Fortbildung des Christenthums, i. S. 208 f. § Ueber die Schriften des Lukas S. 23.

virginity to the promises of a son, that the angel defines the nature of the conception: that it shall be by the Holy Ghost, by the power of the Highest; after which the appellation *υἱος ὑψίστου* receives a more precise metaphysical sense. As a confirmatory sign that a matter of this kind is nowise impossible to God, Mary is referred to that which had occurred to her relative Elizabeth: whereupon, she resigns herself in faith to the divine determination respecting her.

In Matthew, where the main point is to dissipate Joseph's anxiety, the angel begins at once with the communication, that the child conceived by Mary is, (as the Evangelist had already stated of his own accord, chap. i. 18.), of the *Holy Ghost* (*πνεῦμα ἅγιον*); and hereupon the Messianic destination of Jesus is first pointed out by the expression, *He shall save his people from their sins.* This language may seem to sound less Jewish than that by which the Messianic station of the child who should be born, is set forth in Luke; it is however to be observed, that under the term *sins* (*ἁμαρτίαις*) is comprehended *the punishment* of those sins, namely, the subjection of the people to a foreign yoke; so that here also the Jewish element is not wanting; as neither in Luke, on the other hand, is the higher destination of the Messiah left wholly out of sight, since under the term *to reign βασιλεύειν*, the rule over an obedient and regenerated people is included. Next is subjoined by the angel, or more probably by the narrator, an oracle from the Old Testament, introduced by the often recurring phrase, *all this was done, that it might be fulfilled which was spoken of the Lord by the prophet.* [v. 22.]. It is the prophecy from Isaiah, (chap. vii. 14.) which the conception of Jesus after this manner should accomplish: namely, *a virgin shall be with child, and shall bring forth a son, and they shall call his name Emmanuel*—God-with-us.

The original sense of this passage in Isaiah is, according to modern research,[*] this. The prophet is desirous of giving Ahaz, who, through fear of the kings of Syria and Israel, was disposed to make a treaty with Assyria, a lively assurance of the speedy destruction of his much dreaded enemies; and he therefore says to him: suppose that an unmarried woman now on the point of becoming a wife[†] shall conceive; or categorically: a certain young woman is, or is about to be with child; (perhaps the prophet's own wife); now, before this child is born, the political aspect of affairs shall be so much improved, that a name of good omen shall be given to the child; and before he shall be old enough to use his reason, the power of these enemies shall be completely annihilated. That is to say, prosaically expressed: before nine months shall have passed away, the condition of the kingdom shall be amended, and within about three years the danger shall have disappeared. Thus much, at all events, is demonstrated by modern criticism, that, under the circumstances stated by Isaiah in the introduction to the oracle, it is only a sign having reference to the actual moment and the near future, which could have any meaning. How ill chosen, according to Hengstenberg's* interpretation, is the prophet's language : As certainly as the day shall arrive when, in fulfilment of the covenant, the Messiah shall be born, so impossible is it that the people among whom he shall arise, or the family whence he shall spring, shall pass away. How ill-judged, on the part of the prophet, to endeavour to make the improbability of a speedy deliverance appear less improbable, by an appeal to a yet greater improbability in the far distant future!—And then the given limit of a few years! The overthrow of the two kingdoms, such is Hengstenberg's explanation, shall take place—not in the immediately succeeding years, before the child specified shall have acquired the use of his reason but—within such a space of time, as in the far future will elapse between the birth of the Messiah and the first development of his mental powers : therefore in about three years. What a monstrous confounding of times! A child is to be born in the distant future, and that which shall happen before this child shall know how to use his reason, is to take place in the nearest present time.

Thus Paulus and his party are decidedly right in opposing to Hengstenberg and his party, that the prophecy of Isaiah has relation, in its original local signification, to the then existing circumstances, and not to the future Messiah, still less to Jesus. Hengstenberg, on the other hand, is equally in the right, when in opposition to Paulus he maintains, that the passage from Isaiah is adopted by Matthew as a prophecy of the birth of Jesus of a virgin. Whilst the orthodox commentators explain the often recurring *that it might be fulfilled* (ἵνα πληρωθῇ), and similar expressions as signifying: this happened by divine arrangement, in order that the Old Testament prophecy, which in its very origin had reference to the New Testament occurrence, might be fulfilled:—the rationalistic interpreters, on the contrary understand merely: this took place after such a manner, that it was so constituted, that the Old Testament words, which, originally indeed, had relation to something different, should admit of being so applied : and in such application alone do they receive their full verification. In the first explanation, the relation between the Old Testament passage and the New Testament occurrence is objective, arranged by God himself: in the last it is only subjective, a relation perceived by the later author : according to the former it is a relationship at once precise and essential : according to the latter both inexact and adventitious. But opposed to this latter interpretation of New Testament passages, which point out an Old Testament prophecy as

fulfilled, is the language, and equally so the spirit of the New Testament writers. The language: for neither can πληροῦθαι signify
in such connexion any thing than *ratum fieri, eventu comprobari*,
nor ἵνα ὅπως any thing than *eo consilio ut*, whilst the extensive adoption of ἵνα ἐκβατικὸν has arisen only from dogmatic perplexity.*
But such an interpretation is altogether at variance with the Judaical
spirit of the authors of the gospels. Paulus maintains that the
Orientalist does not seriously believe that the ancient prophecy was
designedly spoken, or was accomplished by God, precisely in order
that it should prefigure a modern event, and vice versa; but this is to
carry over our sober European modes of thought into the imaginative life of the Orientals. When however Paulus adds: much
rather did the coincidence of a later event with an earlier prophecy
assume only the *form* of a designed coincidence in the mind of the
Oriental: he thus, at once, annuls his previous assertion; for this
is to admit, that, what in our view is mere coincidence, appeared to
the oriental mind the result of design; and we must acknowledge
this to be the meaning of an oriental representation, if we would
interpret it according to its original signification. It is well known
that the later Jews found prophecies, of the time being and of the
future, everywhere in the Old Testament; and that they constructed
a complete image of the future Messiah, out of various, and in part
falsely interpreted, Old Testament passages.† And the Jew believed he saw in the application he gave to the Scripture, however
perverted it might be, an actual fulfilment of the prophecy. In the
words of Olshausen: it is a mere dogmatic prejudice to attribute to
this formula, when used by the New Testament writers, an altogether different sense from that which it habitually bears among
their countrymen; and this solely with the view to acquit them of
the sin of falsely interpreting the Scripture.

Many theologians of the present day are sufficiently impartial to
admit, with regard to the Old Testament, in opposition to the ancient orthodox interpretation, that many of the prophecies originally
referred to near events; but they are not sufficiently rash, with regard to the New Testament, to side with the rationalistic commentators, and to deny the decidedly Messianic application which the
New Testament writers make of these prophecies; they are still too
prejudiced to allow, that here and there the New Testament has
falsely interpreted the Old. Consequently, they have recourse to
the expedient of distinguishing a double sense in the prophecy; the
one relating to a near and minor occurrence, the other to a future
and more important event; and thus they neither offend against the
plain grammatical and historical sense of the Old Testament passage
on the one hand, nor distort or deny the signification of the New
Testament passage on the other.‡ Thus, in the prophecy of Isaiah

---

* See Winer, Grammatik des neutest. Sprachidioms, 3te Aufl. S. 382 ff. Fritzsche,
Comm. in Matth. p. 49, 317 und Excurs. I, p. 836 ff. † See the Introduction, § 14.
‡ See Bleck in den theol. Studien u. Kritiken, 1835, 2, S. 441 ff.

under consideration, the spirit of prophecy, they contend, had a double intention : to announce a near occurrence, the delivery of the affianced bride of the prophet, and also a distinct event in the far distant future, namely the birth of the Messiah of a virgin.   But a double sense so monstrous owes its origin to dogmatic perplexity alone.   It has been adopted, as Olshausen himself remarks, in order to avoid the offensive admission that the New Testament writers, and Jesus himself, did not interpret the Old Testament rightly, or, more properly speaking, according to modern principles of exegesis, but explained it after the manner of their own age, which was not the most correct.   But so little does this offence exist for the unprejudiced, that the reverse would be the greater difficulty, that is, if, contrary to all the laws of historical and national development, the New Testament writers had elevated themselves completely above the modes of interpretation common to their age and nation. Consequently, with regard to the prophecies brought forward in the New Testament, we may admit, according to circumstances, without further argument, that they are frequently interpreted and applied by the evangelists, in a sense which is totally different from that they originally bore.

We have here in fact a complete table of all the four possible views on this point : two extreme and two conciliatory ; one false and one, it is to be hoped, correct.

1. *Orthodox view* (Hengstenberg and others) : Such Old Testament passages had in their very origin an exclusive prophetic reference to Christ, for the New Testament writers so understand them : and they must be in the right even should human reason be confounded.

2. *Rationalistic view* (Paulus and others) : The New Testament writers do not assign a strictly Messianic sense to the Old Testament prophecies, for this reference to Christ is foreign to the original signification of these prophecies viewed by the light of reason ; and the New Testament writings must accord with reason, whatever ancient beliefs may say to the contrary.

3. *Mystical conciliatory view* (Olshausen and others) : The Old Testament passages originally embody both the deeper signification ascribed to them by the New Testament writers, and that more proximate meaning which common sense obliges us to recognize : thus sound reason and the ancient faith are reconcileable.

4. *Decision of criticism :* Very many of the Old Testament prophecies had, originally, only an immediate reference to events belonging to the time : but they came to be regarded by the men of the New Testament as actual predictions of Jesus as the Messiah, because the intelligence of these men was limited by the manner of thinking of their nation, a fact recognized neither by Rationalism nor the ancient faith.[*]

* The whole rationalistic interpretation of Scripture rests upon a sufficiently palpable paralogism, by which it stands er falls :

Accordingly we shall not hesitate for a moment to allow, in relation to the prophecy in question, that the reference to Jesus is obtruded upon it by the Evangelists. Whether the actual birth of Jesus of a virgin gave rise to this application of the prophecy, or whether this prophecy, interpreted beforehand as referring to the Messiah, originated the belief that Jesus was born of a virgin, remains to be determined.

§. 26.   JESUS BEGOTTEN OF THE HOLY GHOST—CRITICISM OF THE ORTHODOX OPINION.

THE statement of Matthew and of Luke concerning the mode of Jesus's conception has, in every age, received the following interpretation by the church; that Jesus was conceived in Mary not by a human father, but by the Holy Ghost. And truly the gospel expressions seem, at first sight, to justify this interpretation; since the words πρὶν ἢ συνελθεῖν αὐτοὺς (Matth. i. 18.) and ἐπεὶ ἄνδρα οὐ γινώσκω (Luke i. 34.) preclude the participation of Joseph or any other man in the conception of the child in question. Nevertheless the terms πνεῦμα ἅγιον and δύναμις ὑψίστου do not represent the Holy Ghost in the sense of the Church, as the third person in the Godhead, but rather the אֱלֹהִים רוּחַ *Spiritus Dei* as used in the Old Testament: God in his agency upon the world, and especially upon man. In short the words ἐν γαστρὶ ἔχουσα ἐκ πνεύματος ἁγίου in Matthew, and πνεῦμα ἅγιον ἐπελεύσεται ἐπὶ σὲ κ. τ. λ. in Luke, express with sufficient clearness that the absence of human agency was supplied—not physically after the manner of heathen representations—but by the divine creative energy.

Though this seems to be the representation intended by the evangelists in the passages referred to concerning the origin of the life of Jesus, still it cannot be completed without considerable difficulties. We may separate what we may term the *physico-theological* from the *historical-exegetical* difficulties.

The physiological difficulties amount to this, that such a conception would be a most remarkable deviation from all natural laws. However obscure the physiology of the fact, it is proved by an exceptionless experience that only by the concurrence of the two sexes is a new human being generated; on which account, Plutarch's remark, "παιδίον οὐδεμία ποτὲ γυνὴ λέγεται ποιῆσαι δίχα κοινωνίας

The New Testament authors are not to be interpreted as if they said something irrational (certainly not something contrary to *their own* modes of thinking).

Now according to a particular interpretation their assertions are irrational (that is, contrary to *our* modes of thinking).

Consequently the interpretation cannot give the original sense, and a different interpretation must be given.

Who does not here perceive the *quaternio terminorum* and the fatal inconsequence, when Rationalism takes its stand upon the same ground with supernaturalism; that, namely, whilst with regard to all other men the first point to be examined is whether they speak or write what is just and true, to the New Testament writers the prerogative is granted of this being, in their case, already presupposed?

ἀνδρὸς,"* and Cerinthus's "*impossibile*" become applicable.† It is only among the lowest species of the animal kingdom that generation takes place without the union of sexes :‡ so that regarding the matter purely physiologically, what Origen says, in the supranaturalistic sense, would indeed be true of a man of the like origin : namely, that the words in Ps. xxii, 7, *I am a worm and no man* is a prophecy of Jesus in the above respect.§ But to the merely physical consideration a theological one is subjoined by the angel (Luke i. 37.), when he appeals to the divine omnipotence to which nothing is impossible. But since the divine omnipotence, by virtue of its unity with divine wisdom, is never exerted in the absence of an adequate motive, the existence of such, in the present instance, must be demonstrated. But nothing less than an object worthy of the Deity, and at the same time necessarily unattainable except by a deviation from the ordinary course of nature, could constitute a sufficient cause for the suspension by God of a natural law which he had established. Only here, it is said, the end, the redemption of mankind required impeccability on the part of Jesus ; and in order to render him exempt from sin, a divinely wrought conception, which excluded the participation of a sinful father, and severed Jesus from all connexion with original sin, was necessary.‖ To which it has been answered by others,¶ (and Schleiermacher has recently most decisively argued this side of the question,**) that the exclusion of the paternal participation is insufficient, unless, indeed, the inheritance of original sin, on the maternal side, be obviated by the adoption of the Valentinian assertion, that Jesus only passed through the body of Mary. But that the gospel histories represent an actual maternal participation is undeniable ; consequently a divine intervention which should sanctify the participation of the sinful human mother in the conception of Jesus must be supposed in order to maintain his assumed necessary impeccability. But if God determined on such a purification of the maternal participation, it had been easier to do the same with respect to that of the father, than by his total exclusion, to violate the natural law in so unprecedented a manner ; and consequently, a fatherless conception cannot be insisted upon as the necessary means of compassing the impeccability of Jesus.

Even he who thinks to escape the difficulties already specified, by enveloping himself in a supranaturalism, inaccessible to arguments based on reason or the laws of nature, must nevertheless admit the force of the *exegetical-historical* difficulties meeting him upon his own ground, which likewise beset the view of the supernatural conception of Jesus. Nowhere in the New Testament is such an origin

* Conjugial. praecept. Opp. ed. Hutten, Vol. 7, S. 428. † Irenäus adv. haer, 1, 26 : Cerinthus Jesum subjecit non ex virgine natum, impossibile enim hoc ei visum est. ‡ In Henke's neuem Magazin iii. 3, S. 369. § Homil. in Lucam xiv. Comp. my Streitschriften i. 2, S. 72 f.
‖ Olshausen Bibl. Comm. S. 49. Neander, L. J. Ch., S. 16 f.
¶ e. g. by Eichhorn, Einleitung in das N. T. 1. Bd. S. 407.
** Glaubenslehre, 2 Thl. § 97, S. 73. f. der zweiten Auflage.

ascribed to Jesus, or even distinctly alluded to, except in these two accounts of his infancy in Matthew and in Luke.* The history of the conception is omitted not only by Mark, but also by John, the supposed author of the fourth gospel and an alleged inmate with the mother of Jesus subsequent to his death, who therefore would have been the most accurately informed concerning these occurences. It is said that John sought rather to record the heavenly than the earthly origin of Jesus ; but the question arises, whether the doctrine which he sets forth in his prologue, of a divine hypostasis actually becoming flesh and remaining immanent in Jesus, is reconcileable with the view given in the passages before us, of a simple divine operation determining the conception of Jesus; whether therefore John could have presupposed the history of the conception contained in Matthew and Luke ? This objection, however, loses its conclusive force, if in the progress of our investigation the apostolic origin of the fourth gospel is not established. The most important consideration therefore is, that no retrospective allusion to this mode of conception occurs throughout the four gospels ; not only neither in John nor in Mark, but also neither in Matthew nor in Luke. Not only does Mary herself designate Joseph simply as the father of Jesus (Luke ii. 48.), and the Evangelist speak of both as his parents, γονεῖς (Luke ii. 41.),—an appellation which could only have been used in a wider sense by one who had just related the miraculous conception,—but all his contemporaries in general, according to our Evangelists, regarded him as a son of Joseph, a fact which was not unfrequently alluded to contemptuously and by way of reproach in his presence (Matt. xiii. 55; Luke iv. 22 ; John vi. 42.), thus affording him an opportunity of making a decisive appeal to his miraculous conception, of which, however, he says not a single word. Should it be answered, that he did not desire to convince respecting the divinity of his person by this external evidence, and that he could have no hope of making an impression by such means on those who were in heart his opponents,—it must also be remembered, that, according to the testimony of the fourth gospel, his own disciples, though they admitted him to be the son of God, still regarded him as the actual son of Joseph. Philip introduces Jesus to Nathaniel *as the son of Joseph*, Ἰησοῦν τὸν υἱὸν Ἰωσήφ (John i. 46.), manifestly in the same sense of real paternity which the Jews attached to the designation ; and nowhere is this represented as an erroneous or imperfect notion which these Apostles had subsequently to relinquish ; much rather does the whole sense of the narrative, which is not to be mistaken, exhibit the Apostles as having a right belief on this point. The enigmatical presupposition, with which, at the marriage in Cana, Mary

---

* This side is particulary considered in der Skiagraphie des Dogma's von Jesu übernatürlicher Geburt, in Schmidt's Bibliothek i. 3, S. 400 ff.; in den Bemerkungen über den Glaubenspunkt : Christus ist empfangen vom heil. Geist, in Henke's neuem Magazin, iii. 3, 365, ff.; in Kaiser's bibl. Theol. 1, S. 231 f.; De Wette's bibl. Dogmatik, § 281 ; Schleiermacher's Glaubenslehre, 2 Thl. § 97.

addressed herself to Jesus,* is far too vague to prove a recollection of his miraculous conception on the part of the mother: at all events this feature is counterbalanced by the opposing one that the family of Jesus, and, as appears from Matt. xii. 46 ff. compared with Mark iii. 21 ff., his mother also were, at a later time, in error respecting his aims; which is scarcely explicable, even of his brothers, supposing them to have had such recollections.

Just as little as in the Gospels, is any thing in confirmation of the view of the supernatural conception of Jesus, to be found in the remaining New Testament writings. For when the Apostle Paul speaks of Jesus as *made of a woman, γενόμενον ἐκ γυναικὸς* (Gal. iv. 4.), this expression is not to be understood as an exclusion of parternal participation; since the addition *made under the law*, γενόμενον ὑπὸ νόμον, clearly shows that he would here indicate (in the form which is frequent in the Old and New Testament, for example Job xiv. 1; Matt. xi. 11.) human nature with all its conditions. When Paul (Rom. i. 3. 4. compared with ix. 5.) makes Christ *according to the flesh*, κατὰσάρκα, descend from David, but declares him to be the son of God *according to the Spirit of Holiness*, κατὰ πνεῦμα ἁγιωσύνης; no one will here identify the antithesis *flesh* and *spirit* with the maternal human participation, and the divine energy superseding the paternal participation in the conception of Jesus. Finally when in the Epistle to the Hebrews (vii. 3.) Melchisedec is compared with *the son of God*, υἱὸς τοῦ θεοῦ, because *without father*, ἀπάτωρ, the application of the literally interpreted ἀπάτωρ to Jesus, as he appeared upon earth, is forbidden by the addition *without mother* ἀμήτωρ, which agrees as little with him as the immediately following *without descent*, ἀγενεαλόγητος.

§ 27.   RETROSPECT OF THE GENEALOGIES.

THE most conclusive exegetical ground of decision against the supernatural conception of Jesus, which bears more closely on the point than all the hitherto adduced passages, is found in the two genealogies previously considered.   Even the Manichaean Faustus asserted that it is impossible without contradiction to trace the descent of Jesus from David through Joseph, as is done by our two genealogists, and yet assume that Joseph was not the father of Jesus: and Augustine had nothing convincing to answer when he remarked that it was necessary, on account of the superior dignity of the masculine gender, to carry the genealogy of Jesus through Joseph, who was Mary's husband if not by a natural by a spiritual alliance.† In modern times also the construction of the genealogical tables in Matthew and in Luke has led many theologians to observe, that these authors considered Jesus as the actual son of Joseph.‡   The

---

* Brought to bear upon this point by Neander L. J. Ch., S. 12.   Augustinus contra Faustum Manichaeum L. 23. 3. 1. 8.   † See Schmidt, Schleiermacher, and Wegscheider, Instit. ‡ 123 (not d.)

very design of these tables is to prove Jesus to be of the lineage of
David through Joseph; but what do they prove, if indeed Joseph
was not the father of Jesus? The assertion that Jesus was the son
of David, υἱὸς Δαυίδ, which in Matthew (i. 1.) prefaces the genealogy
and announces its object, is altogether annulled by the subsequent
denial of his conception by means of the Davidical Joseph. It is
impossible, therefore, to think it probable that the genealogy and
the history of the birth of Jesus emanate from the same author;*
and we must concur with the theologians previously cited, that the
genealogies are taken from a different source. Scarcely could it satisfy to oppose the remark, that as Joseph doubtlessly adopted Jesus,
the genealogical table of the former became fully valid for the latter.
For adoption might indeed suffice to secure to the adopted son the
reversion of certain external family rights and inheritances; but
such a relationship could in no wise lend a claim to the Messianic
dignity, which was attached to the true blood and lineage of David.
He, therefore, who had regarded Joseph as nothing more than the
adopted father of Jesus, would hardly have given himself the trouble
to seek out the Davidical descent of Joseph; but if indeed, besides
the established belief that Jesus was the son of God, it still remained
important to represent him as the son of David, the pedigree of Mary
would have been preferred for this purpose; for, however contrary to
custom, the maternal genealogy must have been admitted in a case
where a human father did not exist. Least of all is it to be believed, that several authors would have engaged in the compilation
of a genealogical table for Jesus which traced his descent through
Joseph, so that two different genealogies of this kind are still preserved to us, if a closer relationship between Jesus and Joseph had
not been admitted at the time of their composition.

Consequently, the decision of the learned theologians who agree
that these genealogies were composed in the belief that Jesus was
the actual son of Joseph and Mary, can hardly be disputed; but
the authors or compilers of our gospels, notwithstanding their own
conviction of the divine origin of Jesus, received them among their
materials; only that Matthew (i. 16.) changed the original *Joseph
begat Jesus of Mary*—'Ιωσήφ δὲ ἐγέννησε τὸν 'Ιησοῦν ἐκ τῆς Μαρίας
(comp. verses 3. 5. 6.) according to his own view; and so likewise
Luke (iii. 23.) instead of commencing his genealogy simply with,
Jesus—the son of Joseph—'Ιησοῦς υἱὸς 'Ιωσήφ, inserts *being as was
supposed*, ὢν, ὡς ἐνομίζετο κ. τ. λ.

Let it not be objected that the view for which we contend,
namely, that the genealogies could not have been composed under
the notion that Joseph was not the father of Jesus, leaves no conceivable motive for incorporating them into our present gospels. The
original construction of a genealogy of Jesus, even though in the case
before us is consisted simply in the adapting of foreign already ex-

---

* Eichhorn thinks this probable, Einl. in das N. T. i. S. 425. De Wette possible,
exeg. Handb. i. 1, S. 7.

isting genealogical tables to Jesus, required a powerful and direct inducement: this was the hope thereby to gain—the corporeal descent of Jesus from Joseph being presupposed— a main support to the belief in his Messiahship; whilst, on the other hand, a less powerful inducement was sufficient to incite to the admission of the previously constructed genealogies: the expectation that, notwithstanding the non-existence of any real relationship between Joseph and Jesus, they might nevertheless serve to link Jesus to David. Thus we find, that in the histories of the birth both in Matthew and in Luke, though they each decidedly exclude Joseph from the conception, great stress is laid upon the Davidical descent of Joseph (Matt. i. 20, Luke i. 27, ii. 4); that which in fact had no real significance, except in connexion with the earlier opinion, is retained even after the point of view is changed.

Since, in this way, we discover both the genealogies to be memorials belonging to the time and circle of the primitive church, in which Jesus was still regarded as a naturally begotten man, the sect of the Ebionites cannot fail to occur to us; as we are told concerning them, that they held this view of the person of Christ at this early period * We should therefore have expected, more especially, to have found these genealogies in the old Ebionitish gospels, of which we have still knowledge, and are not a little surprised to learn that precisely in these gospels the genealogies were wanting. It is true Epiphanius states that the gospel of the Ebionites commenced with the public appearance of the Baptist;† accordingly, by the genealogies, γενεαλογίαις, which they are said to have cut away, might have been meant, those histories of the birth and infancy comprised in the two first chapters of Matthew; which they could not have adopted in their present form, since they contained the fatherless conception of Jesus, which was denied by the Ebionites: and it might also have been conjectured that this section which was in opposition to their system had alone perhaps been wanting in their gospel: and that the genealogy which was in harmony with their view might nevertheless have been somewhere inserted. But this supposition vanishes as soon as we find that Epiphanius in reference to the Nazarenes, defines the genealogies, (of which he is ignorant whether they possessed them or not, as *reaching from Abraham to Christ*, τὰς ἀπὸ τοῦ Ἀβραὰμ ἕως Χριστοῦ;‡ consequently by the genealogies which were wanting to some heretics, he evidently understood the genealogical tables, though, in relation to the Ebionites, he might likewise have included under this expression the history of the birth.

How is the strange phenomenon, that these genealogies are not found among that very sect of Christians who retained the particular opinion upon which they were constructed, to be explained? A modern investigator has advanced the supposition, that the Jewish-

* Justin. Mart. Dial. cum Tryphone, 48; Origenes contra Celsum L. 5, 51. Euseb. H. E. 3, 27. † Epihan. haeres. 30, 14. ‡ Haeres. 29, 9.

christians omitted the genealogical tables from prudential motives, in order not to facilitate or augment the persecution which, under Domitian, and perhaps even earlier, threatened the family of David.* But explanations, having no inherent connexion with the subject, derived from circumstances in themselves of doubtful historical validity, are admissible only as a last refuge, when no possible solution of the questionable phenomenon is to be found in the thing itself, as here in the principles of the Ebionitish system.

But in this case the matter is by no means so difficult. It is known that the Fathers speak of two classes of Ebionites, of which the one, besides strenuously maintaining the obligation of the Mosaic law, held Jesus to be the naturally begotten Son of Joseph and Mary; the other, from that time called also Nazarenes, admitted with the orthodox church the conception by the Holy Ghost.† But besides this distinction there existed yet another. The most ancient ecclesiastic writers, Justin Martyr and Irenæus for example, are acquainted with those Ebionites only, who regarded Jesus as a naturally born man first endowed with divine powers at his baptism.‡ In Epiphanius and the Clementine Homilies, on the other hand, we meet with Ebionites who had imbibed an element of speculative Gnosticism. This tendency, which according to Epiphanius is to be dated from one Elxai, has been ascribed to Essenic influence,§ and traces of the same have been discovered in the heresies referred to in the Epistle to the Colossians; whereas the first class of Ebionites evidently proceeded from Common Judaism. Which form of opinion was the earlier and which the later developed is not so easily determined; with reference to the last detailed difference, it might seem, since the speculative Ebionites are mentioned first by the Clementines and Epiphanius, whilst Ebionites holding a simpler view are spoken of by Justin and by Irenæus, that the latter were the earlier; nevertheless as Tertullian already notices in his time the Gnosticising tendency of the opinions of the Ebionites respecting Christ,‖ and as the germ of such views existed among the Essenes in the time of Jesus, the more probable assumption is, that both opinions arose side by side about the same period.¶ As little can it be proved with regard to the other difference, that the views concerning Christ held by the Nazarenes became first, at a later period, lowered to those of the Ebionites;** since the notices, partly confused and partly of late date, of the ecclesiastical writers, may be naturally explained as arising out of what may be called an optical delusion of the church, which,—whilst she in fact made con-

* Credner, in den Beiträgen zur Einleitung in das N. T. 1, S. 443. Anm.   † Orig. ut sup.   ‡ See Neander, K. G. 1, 2, S. 615 f.   § Credner, über Essener und Ebioniten und einen theilweisen Zusammenhang beider, in Winer's Zeitschrift f. wissenschaftliche Theologie, 1. Bd. 2tes und 3tes Heft; see Bauer, Progr. de Ebionitarum origine et doctrina ab Essenis repetenda, und christl. Gnosis, S. 403.   ‖ De carne Christi, c. 14 : Poterit hæc opinio convenire, qui nudum hominem, et tantum ex semine David, i. e. non et Dei filium, constituit Jesum, ut in illo angelum fuisse edicat.   ¶ Neander and Schneckenburg-r are of the latter, Gieseler and Credner of the former opinion.   ** I here refer to the account of Hegesippus in Eusebius, H. E. iv. 22.

tinual advances in the glorification of Christ, but a part of the Jewish Christians remained stationary,—made it appear to her as if she herself remained stationary, whilst the others fell back into heresy.

By thus distinguishing the simple and the speculative Ebionites, so much is gained, that the failure of the genealogies among the latter class, mentioned by Epiphanius, does not prove them to have been also wanting among the former. And the less if we should be able to make it appear probable, that the grounds of their aversion to the genealogical table, and the grounds of distinction between them and the other class of Ebionites, were identical. One of these grounds was evidently the unfavourable opinion, which the Ebionites of Epiphanius and of the Clementine Homilies had of David, from whom the genealogy traces the descent of Jesus. It is well known that they distinguished in the Old Testament a twofold prophecy, male and female, pure and impure, of which the former only promised things heavenly and true, the latter things earthly and delusive; that proceeding from Adam and Abel, this from Eve and Cain; and both constituted and under current through the whole history of the revelation.* It was only the pious men from Adam to Joshua whom they acknowledged as true prophets : the later prophets and men of God, among whom David and Solomon are named, were not only not recognized, but abhorred.† We even find positive indications that David was an object of their particular aversion. There were many things which created in them a detestation of David (and Solomon). David was a bloody warrior; but to shed blood was, according to the doctrines of these Ebionites, one of the greatest of sins; David was known to have committed adultery, (Solomon to have been a voluptuary): and adultery was even more detested by this sect than murder. David was a performer on stringed instruments; this art, the invention of the Canaanites (Gen. iv. 21), was held by these Ebionites to be a sign of false prophecy; finally, the prophecies announced by David and those connected with him, (and Solomon,) had reference to the kingdoms of this world, of which the Gnosticising Ebionites desired to know nothing.‡ Now the Ebionites who had sprung from common Judaism could not have shared this ground of aversion to the genealogies; since to the orthodox Jew David was an object of the highest veneration.

Concerning a second point the notices are not so lucid and accordant as they should be; namely, whether it was a further development of the general Ebionitish doctrine concerning the person

---

* Homil. 3, 23—27.   † Epiphan. haeres. 30, 18, comp. 15.   ‡ That these were the traits in David's character, which displeased the Christian sect in question, is sufficiently evident from a passage in the Clementine Homilies, though the name is not given : Homil. 3, 25 : ἐπὶ μὴν καὶ οἱ ἀπὸ τῆς τούτου (τοῦ Κάϊν) διαδοχῆς προεληλυθότες πρῶτοι μοιχοὶ ἐγένοντο, καὶ ψαλτήρια, καὶ κιθάραι, καὶ χαλκεῖς ὅπλων πολεμικῶν ἐγένοντο. Διὸ καὶ ἡ τῶν ἐγγόνων προφητεία, μοιχῶν καὶ ψαλτηρίων γίνουσα, γαυδανούντως διὰ τῶν ἡδυπαθειῶν ὡς τοῖς πολέμους ἐγείρει.

of the Christ, which led these Ebionites to reject the genealogies. According to Epiphanius, they fully recognized the Gnostic distinction between Jesus the son of Joseph and Mary, and the Christ who descended upon him ;* and consequently might have been withheld from referring the genealogy to Jesus only perhaps by their abhorrence of David. On the other hand, from the whole tenor of the Clementines, and from one passage in particular,† it has recently been inferred, and not without apparent reason, that the author of these writings had himself abandoned the view of a natural conception, and even birth of Jesus ;‡ whereby it is yet more manifest that the ground of the rejection of the genealogies by this sect was peculiar to it, and not common to the other Ebionites.

Moreover positive indications, that the Ebionites who proceeded from Judaism possessed the genealogies, do not entirely fail. Whilst the Ebionites of Epiphanius and of the Clementines called Jesus only Son of God, but rejected the appellation Son of David, as belonging to the common opinion of the Jews ;§ other Ebionites were censured by the Fathers for recognizing Jesus only as the Son of David, to whom he is traced in the genealogies, and not likewise as the Son of God.‖ Further, Epiphanius relates of the earliest Judaising Gnostics Cerinthus and Carpocrates, that they used a gospel the same in other respects indeed as the Ebionites, but that they adduced the genealogies, which they therefore read in the same, in attestation of the human conception of Jesus by Joseph.¶ Also the ἀπομνημονεύματα cited by Justin, and which originated upon Judæo-christian ground, appear to have contained a genealogy similar to that in our Matthew; since Justin as well as Matthew speaks, in relation to Jesus, of a γένος τοῦ Δαβὶδ καὶ Ἀβραάμ, of a σπέρμα ἐξ Ἰακὼβ, διὰ Ἰούδα, καὶ Φαρὲς καὶ Ἰεσσαὶ καὶ Δαβὶδ κατερχόμενον ;** only that at the time, and in the circle of Justin, the opinion of a supernatural conception of Jesus had already suggested the reference of the genealogy to Mary, instead of to Joseph.

Hence it appears that we have in the genealogies a memorial, agreeing with indications from other sources, of the fact that in the very earliest christian age, in Palestine, a body of Christians, numerous enough to establish upon distinct fundamental opinions two different Messianic tables of descent, considered Jesus to have been a naturally conceived human being. And no proof is furnished to us in the apostolic writings, that the Apostles would have declared

---

* Epiphan. Haer. 30, 14, 16, 34. † Homil. 3, 17. ‡ Schneckenburger, über das Evangelium der Aegypter, S. 7; Bauer, christliche Gnosis, S. 760 ff. See on the other side Credner und Hoffmann. § Orig. Comm. in Matth. T. 16, 12. Tertullian, De carne Christi, 14, S. Anm. 13 (a passage in which indeed the speculative and ordinary Ebionites are mingled together). ‖ Clement. homil. 18, 13. They referred the words of Matth. xi, 27 : οὐδεὶς ἔγνω τὸν πατέρα, εἰ μὴ ὁ υἱός κ. τ. λ. to τοὺς πατέρα νομίζοντας Χριστοῦ τὸν Δαβίδ, καὶ αὐτὸν δὲ τὸν χριστὸν υἱὸν ὄντα, καὶ υἱὸν θεοῦ μὴ ἐγνωκότας, and complained that αἰτὶ τοῦ θεοῦ τὸν Δαβὶδ πάντες ἔλεγον. ¶ Haeres. 30, 14 : ὁ μὲν γὰρ Κήρινθος καὶ Καρποκρας τῷ αὐτῷ χρώμενοι παρ' αὐτοῖς (τοῖς Ἐβιωναίοις) εὐαγγελίῳ, ἀπὸ τῆς ἀρχῆς τοῦ κατὰ Ματθαῖον εὐαγγελίου διὰ τῆς γενεαλογίας βούλονται παριστᾶν ἐκ σπέρματος Ἰωσὴφ καὶ Μαρίας εἶναι τὸν χριστόν. ** Dial. c. Tryph. 100, 120.

this doctrine to be unchristian: it appeared so first from the point of view adopted by the authors of the histories of the birth in the first and third Gospels: notwithstanding which however, it is treated with surprising lenity by the Fathers of the church.

§ 28. NATURAL EXPLANATION OF THE HISTORY OF THE CONCEPTION.

IF, as appears from the foregoing statements, so many weighty difficulties, philosophical as well as exegetical, beset the supranaturalistic explanation, it is well worth while to examine whether it be not possible to give an interpretation of the gospel history which shall obviate these objections. Recourse has been had to the natural explanation, and the two narratives singly and conjointly have been successively subjected to the rationalistic mode of interpretation.

In the first place, the account in Matthew seemed susceptible of such an interpretation. Numerous rabbinical passages were cited to demonstrate, that it was consonant with Jewish notions to consider a son of pious parents to be conceived by the divine co-operation, and that he should be called the son of the Holy Spirit, without its being ever imagined that paternal participation was thereby excluded. It was consequently contended, that the section in Matthew represented merely the intention of the angel to inform Joseph, not indeed that Mary had become pregnant in the absence of all human intercourse, but that notwithstanding her pregnancy she was to be regarded as pure, not as one fallen from virtue. It was maintained that the exclusion of paternal participation—which is an embellishment of the original representation—occurs first in Luke in the words ἄνδρα οὐ γινώσκω (i. 34.)* When however this view was justly opposed by the remark, that the expression πρὶν ἢ συνελθεῖν αὐτούσ in Matthew (i. 18) decidedly excludes the participation of the only individual in question, namely Joseph; it was then thought possible to prove that even in Luke the paternal exclusion was not so positive: but truly this could be done only by an unexegetical subversion of the clear sense of the words, or else by uncritically throwing suspicion on a part of a well-connected narrative. The first expedient is to interpret Mary's inquiry of the angel i. 34, thus: Can I who am already betrothed and married give birth to the Messiah, for as the mother of the Messiah I must have no husband? whereupon the angel replies, that God, through his power, could make something distinguished even of the child conceived of her and Joseph.† The other proceeding is no less arbitrary. Mary's inquiry of the angel is explained as an unnatural interruption of his communication, which being abstracted, the pas-

---

* Br . . . , die Nachricht, dass Jesus durch den heil. Geist und von einer Jungfrau geboren sei, aus Zeitbegriffen erlautert. In Schmidt's Bibl. I, I. S. 101 ff. Horst, in Henke's Museum I, I, 197 ff., über die beiden ersten Kapitel in Evang. Lukas.   † Bemerkungen über den Glaubenspunkt: Christus ist empfangen vom heil. Geist. In Henke's neuem Magazin 3, 3. 399.

sage is found to contain no decided intimation of the supernatural conception.*

If consequently, the difficulty of the natural explanation of the two accounts be equally great, still, with respect to both it must be alike attempted or rejected; and for the consistent Rationalist, a Paulus for example, the latter is the only course. This commentator considers the participation of Joseph indeed excluded by Matt. i. 18, but by no means that of every other man; neither can he find a supernatural divine intervention in the expression of Luke i. 35. The *Holy Ghost* πνεῦμα ἅγιον is not with him objective, an external influence operating upon Mary, but her own pious imagination. The *power of the Highest*—δύναμις ὑψίστον is not the immediate divine omnipotence, but every natural power employed in a manner pleasing to God may be so called. Consequently, according to Paulus, the meaning of the angelic announcement is simply this: prior to her union with Joseph, Mary, under the influence of a pure enthusiasm in sacred things on the one hand, and by a human co-operation pleasing to God on the other, became the mother of a child who on account of this holy origin was to be called a son of God.

Let us examine rather more accurately the view which this representative of rationalistic interpretation takes of the particulars of the conception of Jesus. He begins with Elizabeth, the patriotic and wise daughter of Aaron, as he styles her. She, having conceived the hope that she might give birth to one of God's prophets, naturally desired moreover that he might be the first of prophets, the forerunner of the Messiah; and that the latter also might speedily be born. Now there was among her own kinsfolk a person suited in every respect for the mother of the Messiah, Mary, a young virgin, a descendant of David; nothing more was needful than to inspire her likewise with such a special hope. Whilst these intimations prepare us to anticipate a cleverly concerted plan on the part of Elizabeth in reference to her young relative, in which we hope to become initiated; Paulus here suddenly lets fall the curtain, and remarks, that the exact manner in which Mary was convinced that she should become the mother of the Messiah must be left historically undetermined: thus much only is certain, that Mary remained pure, for she could not with a clear conscience have stationed herself, as she afterwards did, under the Cross of her Son, had she felt that a reproach rested on her concerning the origin of the hopes she had entertained of him. The following is the only hint subsequently given of the particular view held by Paulus. It is probable, he thinks, that the angelic messenger visited Mary in the evening or even at night; indeed according to the correct reading of Luke i. 28, which has not the word angel, καὶ εἰσελθὼν πρὸς αὐτὴν εἶπε, without ὁ ἄγγελος, the evangelist here speaks only of some one who had come in. (As if in this case, the participle εἰσελθὼν must not necessarily be accompanied by τίς; or, in the absence of the pronoun be

---

* Schleiermacher über den Lukas, S. 26 f.

referred to the subject, the angel Gabriel—ὁ ἄγγελος Γαβριήλ, v. 26.!) Paulus adds: that this visitant was the angel Gabriel was the subsequent suggestion of Mary's own mind, after she had heard of the vision of Zacharias.

Gabler in a review of Paulus's Commentary[*] has fully exposed, with commensurate plainness of speech, the transaction which lies concealed under this explanation. It is impossible, says he, to imagine any other interpretation of Paulus's view than that some one passed himself off for the angel Gabriel, and as the pretended Messenger of God remained with Mary in order that she might become the mother of the Messiah. What! asks Gabler, Is Mary, at the very time she is betrothed, to become pregnant by another and is this to be called an innocent holy action, pleasing to God and irreprochable? Mary is here pourtrayed as a pious visionary, and the pretended messenger of heaven as a deceiver, or he too is a gross fanatic. The reviewer most justly considers such an assertion as revolting, if contemplated from the christian point of view: if from the scientific, as at variance both with the principles of interpretation and of criticism.

The author of the "Natural History of the Great Prophet of Nazareth" is, in this instance, to be considered as the most worthy interpreter of Paulus: for though the former could not, in this part of his work, have made use of Paulus's Commentary, yet, in exactly the same spirit, he unreservedly avows what the latter carefully veils. He brings into comparison a story in Josephus,[†] according to which, in the very time of Jesus, a Roman knight won the chaste wife of a Roman noble to his wishes, by causing her to be invited by a priest of Isis into the temple of the Goddess, under the pretext that the god Anubis desired to embrace her. In innocence and faith, the woman resigned herself, and would perhaps afterwards have believed she had given birth to the child of a god, had not the intriguer, with bitter scorn, soon after discovered to her the true state of the case. It is the opinion of the author that Mary, the betrothed bride of the aged Joseph, was in like manner deceived by some amorous and fanatic young man (in the sequel to the history he represents him to be Joseph of Arimathea), and that she on her part, in perfect innocence, continued to deceive others.[‡] It is evident that this interpretation does not differ from the ancient Jewish blasphemy, which we find in Celsus and in the Talmud; that Jesus falsely represented himself as born of a pure virgin, whereas, in fact, he was the offspring of the adultery of Mary with a certain Panthera.[§] This whole view, of which the culminating point is in the cal-

---

[*] Im neuesten theol. Journal 7. Bd. 4. St. S. 107 f.   [†] Antiq. xviii. 3, 4.   [‡] Iter Theil, S. 140 ff.   [§] The legend has undergone various modifications, but the name of Panthera or Pandira has been uniformly retained. Vil. Origenes c. C ls. 1, 28. 32. Schöttgen, Horæ 2, 693 ff, aus Tract. Sanhedrin u. A.; Eisenmenger, entdecktes Judenthum, 1, S. 105 ff, aus der Schmahschrift: Toledoth Jeschu; Thilo, cod. apocr. S. 528. Comp. my Abhandlung über die Namen Panther, Pantheras, Pandera, in judischen und patristischen Erzählungen von der Abstammung Jesu. Athenäum, Febr. 1839, S. 15 ff.

umny of the Jews, cannot be better judged than in the words of
Origen. If, says this author, they wished to substitute something
else in the place of the history of the supernatural conception of
Jesus, they should at any rate have made it happen in a more probable manner; they ought not, as it were against their will, to admit
that Mary knew not Joseph, but they might have denied this feature, and yet have allowed Jesus to have been born of an ordinary
human marriage; whereas, the forced and extravagant character of
their hypothesis betrays its falsehood.* Is not this as much as to
say, that if once some particular features of a marvellous narrative
are doubted, it is inconsequent to allow others to remain unques-
tioned? each part of such an account ought to be subjected to critical examination. The correct view of the narrative before us is to
be found, that is indirectly, in Origen. For when at one time he
places together, as of the same kind, the miraculous conception of
Jesus and the story of Plato's conception by Apollo (though here,
indeed, the meaning is that only ill-disposed persons could doubt such
things †), and when at another time he says of the story concerning
Plato, that it belongs to those mythi by which it was sought to exhibit the distinguished wisdom and power of great men (but here
he does not include the narrative of Jesus's conception), he in fact
states the two premises, namely, the similarity of the two narratives
and the mythical character of the one;‡ from which the inference of
the merely mythical worth of the narrative of the conception of
Jesus follows; a conclusion which can never indeed have occurred
to his own mind.

§ 29.   HISTORY OF THE CONCEPTION OF JESUS VIEWED AS A MYTHUS.

IF, says Gabler in his review of the Commentary of Paulus, we
must relinquish the supernatural origin of Jesus, in order to escape
the ridicule of our contemporaries, and if, on the other hand, the
natural explanation leads to conclusions not only extravagant, but
revolting: the adoption of the mythus, by which all these difficulties are obviated, is to be preferred. In the world of mythology
many great men had extraordinary births, and were sons of the gods.
Jesus himself spoke of his heavenly origin, and called God his father; besides, his title as Messiah was—Son of God. From Matthew i. 22., it is further evident that the passage of Isaiah, vii. 14.
was referred to Jesus by the early Christian Church. In conformity
with this passage the belief prevailed that Jesus, as the Messiah,
should be born of a virgin by means of divine agency; it was therefore taken for granted that what was to be actually did occur; and
thus originated a philosophical (dogmatical) mythus concerning the
birth of Jesus. But according to historical truth, Jesus was the
offspring of an ordinary marriage, between Joseph and Mary; an

explanation which, it has been justly remarked, maintains at once the dignity of Jesus and the respect due to his mother.*

The proneness of the ancient world to represent the great men and benefactors of their race as the sons of the gods, has therefore been referred to, in order to explain the origin of such a mythus. Our theologians have accumulated examples from the Greco-Roman mythology and history. They have cited Hercules, and the Dioscuri; Romulus, and Alexander; but above all Pythagoras,† and Plato. Of the latter philosopher Jerome speaks in a manner quite applicable to Jesus: sapientiæ principem non aliter arbitrantur, nisi de partu virginis editum.‡

From these examples it might have been inferred that the narratives of the supernatural conception had possibly orginated in a similar tendency, and had no foundation in history. Here however the orthodox and the rationalists are unanimous in denying, though indeed upon different grounds, the validity of the analogy. Origen, from a perception of the identical character of the two classes of narratives, is not far from regarding the heathen legends of the sons of the gods as true supernatural histories. Paulus on his side is more decided, and is so logical as to explain both classes of narratives in the same manner, as natural, but still as true histories. At least he says of the narrative concerning Plato: it cannot be affirmed that the groundwork of the history was a subsequent creation: it is far more probable that Perictione believed herself to be pregnant by one of her gods. The fact that her son became a Plato might indeed have served to confirm that belief, but not to have originated it. Tholuck invites attention to the important distinction that the mythi concerning Romulus and others were formed many centuries after the lifetime of these men: the mythi concerning Jesus, on the contrary, must have existed shortly after his death.§ He cleverly fails to remember the narrative of Plato's birth, since he is well aware that precisely in that particular, it is a dangerous point. Osiander however approaches the subject with much pathos, and affirms that Plato's apotheosis as son of Apollo did not exist till several centuries after him : ‖ whereas in fact Plato's sister's son speaks of it as a prevailing legend in Athens.¶ Olshausen, with whom Neander coincides, refuses to draw any detrimental inference from this analogy of the mythical sons of the gods; remarking that though these narratives are unhistorical, they evince a general anticipation and desire

* Gabler, in seinem neuesten theol. Journal, 7, 3. S. 408 f; Eichhorn, Einleit. in das N. T. 1, S. 428 f; Bauer, hebr. Mythol. 1, 192 c. ff; Kaiser, bibl. Theologie, 1, S. 231 f; Wegscheider, Instit. § 123; De Wette, bibl. Dogmat. § 281, und exeg. Handbuch 1, 1, S. 18 f; Ammon, Fortbildung des Christenth. S. 201 ff; Hase, L. J. § 33; Fritzsche, Comment. in Matth. S. 56. The latter justly remarks in the title to the first chapter: non milus ille (Jesus) ab ferunt doctorum Judæicorum de Messiæ sententiæ, patrem habet spiritum divinum, matrem virginem. † Jamblich, vita Pythagoræ, cap. 2, ed. Kiessling. ‡ Adv. Jovin. 1, 26. Diog. Laërt, 3, 1, 2. § Glaubwürdigkeit S. 61. ‖ Apologie des L. J. S. 92. • Diog. Laërt. u. a. O.: Σπεύσιππος (Sororis Platonis filius, Hieron.) δ᾽ ἐν τῷ ἐπιγραφομένῳ Πλάτωνος περιδείπνῳ καὶ Κλέαρχος ἐν τῷ Πλάτωνος ἐγκωμίῳ καὶ Ἀναξιλίδης ἐν τῷ δευτέρῳ περὶ φιλοσόφων, φασίν, Ἀθήνῃσιν ἦν λόγος, κ. τ. λ.

of such a fact, and therefore guarantee its reality, at least in one historical manifestation. Certainly, a general anticipation and representation must have truth for its basis; but the truth does not consist in any one individual fact, presenting an accurate correspondence with that notion, but in *an idea* which realizes itself in a series of facts, which often bear no resemblance to the general notion. The widely spread notion of a golden age does not prove the existence of a golden age: so the notion of divine conceptions does not prove that some one individual was thus produced. The truth which is the basis of this notion is something quite different.

A more essential objection* to the analogy is, that the representations of the heathen world prove nothing with respect to the isolated Jews; and that the idea of sons of the gods, belonging to polytheism, could not have exerted an influence on the rigidly monotheistic notion of the Messiah. At all events such an inference must not be too hastily drawn from the expression "sons of God," found likewise among the Jews, which as applied in the Old Testament to magistrates, (Ps. lxxxii. 6., or to theocratic kings, 2 Sam. vii. 14, Ps. ii. 7.), indicates only a theocratic, and not a physical or metaphysical relation. Still less is importance to be attached to the language of flattery used by a Roman, in Josephus, who calls beautiful children of the Jewish princes children of God.† It was, however, a notion among the Jews, as was remarked in a former section, that the Holy Spirit co-operated in the conception of pious individuals; moreover, that God's choicest instruments were conceived by divine assistance of parents, who could not have had a child according to the natural course of things. And if, according to the believed representation, the extinct capability on both sides was renewed by divine intervention (Rom. iv. 19.), it was only one step further to the belief that in the case of the conception of the most distinguished of all God's agents, the Messiah, the total absence of participation on the one side was compensated by a more complete superadded capability on the other. The latter is scarcely a degree more marvellous than the former. And thus must it have appeared to the author of Luke i., since he dissipates Mary's doubts by the same reply with which Jehovah repelled Sara's incredulity. ‡ Neither the Jewish reverence for marriage, nor the prevalent representation of the Messiah as a human being, could prevent the advance to this climax; to which, on the other hand, the ascetic estimation of celibacy, and the idea, derived from Daniel, of the Christ as a superhuman being, contributed. But decided impulse to the development of the representations embodied in our histories of the birth, consisted partly in the title, *Son of God*, at one time usually given to the Messiah. For it is the nature of such originally figurative expressions, after a while to come to be interpreted according

---

* Neander, L. J. Ch. S. 10.   † Ant. 15. 2. 6.
‡ Gen. xviii. 14. Sept.   Luke i. 37.
μὴ ἀδυνατήσει παρὰ τῷ θεῷ ῥῆμα;   ὅτι οὐκ ἀδυνατήσει παρὰ τῷ θεῷ πᾶν ῥῆμα.

to their more precise and literal signification; and it was a daily occurrence, especially among the later Jews, to attach a sensible signification to that which originally had merely a spiritual or figurative meaning. This natural disposition to understand the Messianic title *Son of God* more and more literally, was fostered by the expression in the Psalms (ii. 7.), interpreted of the Messiah : *Thou art my son ; this day have I begotten thee :* words which can scarcely fail to suggest a physical relation; it was also nurtured by the prophecy of Isaiah respecting the virgin who should be with child, which it appears was applied to the Messiah; as were so many other prophecies of which the immediate signification had become obscure. This application may be seen in the Greek word chosen by the Septuagint, παρθένος, a pure unspotted virgin, whereas by Aquila and other Greek translators the word νεανις is used.* Thus did the notions of a *son of God* and a *son of a virgin* complete one another, till at last the divine agency was substituted for human paternal participation. Wetstein indeed affirms that no Jew ever applied the prophecy of Isaiah to the Messiah; and it was with extreme labour that Schoettgen collected traces of the notion that the Messiah should be the son of a virgin from the Rabbinical writings. This however, considering the paucity of records of the Messianic ideas of that age,† proves nothing in opposition to the presumption that a notion then prevailed, of which we have the groundwork in the Old Testament, and an inference hardly to be mistaken in the New.

One objection yet remains, which I can no longer designate as peculiar to Olshausen, since other theologians have shown themselves solicitous of sharing the fame. The objection is, that the mythical interpretation of the gospel narrative is especially dangerous, it being only too well fitted to engender, obscurely indeed, profane and blasphemous notions concerning the origin of Jesus; since it cannot fail to favour an opinion destructive of the belief in a Redeemer, namely, that Jesus came into being through unholy means; since, in fact, at the time of her pregnancy Mary was not married.‡ In Olshausen's first edition of his work, he adds that he willingly allows that these interpreters know not what they do : it is therefore but just to give him the advantage of the same concession, since he certainly appears not to know what mythical interpretation means. How otherwise would he say, that the mythical interpretation is fitted only to favour a blasphemous opinion; therefore that all who understand the narrative mythically, are disposed to commit the absurdity with which Origen reproaches the Jewish calumniators: the retaining one solitary incident, namely, that Mary was not married, whilst the remainder of the narrative is held to be unhistorical; a particular incident which evidently serves only as a support

* De Wette, Exg. Handb., 1, 1, S. 17.   † They are to be found however in the more modern Rabbins, s. Matthæi, Religionsgl. der Apostel 2, a, S. 555 ff.   ‡ Bibl. Comm. 1, S. 47.   Also Daub, 2 a. S. 311 f.; Theile, § 14. Neander, S. 9.

to the other, that Jesus was conceived without human paternal participation, and with it, therefore, stands or falls. No one among the
interpreters who, in this narrative, recognise a mythus in the full
signification of that term, has been thus blind and inconsistent; all
have supposed a legitimate marriage between Joseph and Mary; and
Olshausen merely paints the mythical mode of interpretation in cari-
cature, in order the more easily to set it aside; for he confesses that
in relation to this portion of the gospel in particular, it has much
that is dazzling.

§ 30.   RELATION OF JOSEPH TO MARY—BROTHERS OF JESUS.

OUR Gospels, in the true spirit of the ancient legend, find it un-
becoming to allow the mother of Jesus, so long as she bore the heavenly germ, to be approached or profaned by an earthly husband.
Consequently Luke (ii. 5.) represents the connexion between Joseph
and Mary, prior to the birth of Jesus, as a betrothment merely.
And, as it is stated respecting the father of Plato, after his wife had
become pregnant by Apollo: ὅθεν καθαρὰν γάμου φυλάξαι ἕως τῆς
ἀποκυήσεως,* so likewise it is remarked of Joseph in Matthew (i. 25.):
καὶ οὐκ ἐγίνωσκεν αὐτὴν (τὴν γυναῖκα αὐτοῦ) ἕως οὗ ἔτεκε τὸν υἱὸν αὐτῆς τὸν πρωτότοκον. In each of these kindred passages the Greek
word ἕως (till) must evidently receive the same interpretation. Now
in the first quotation the meaning is incontestably this:—that till
the time of Plato's birth his father abstained from intercourse with
his wife, but subsequently assumed his conjugal rights, since we
hear of Plato's brothers. In reference, therefore, to the parents of
Jesus, the ἕως cannot have a different signification; in each case it
indicates precisely the same limitation. So again the expression
πρωτότοκος (firstborn) used in reference to Jesus in both the Gospels
(Matt. i. 25, Luke ii. 7.) supposes that Mary had other children, for
as Lucian says: εἰ μὲν πρῶτος, οὐ μόνος εἰ δὲ μόνος, οὐ πρῶτος.† Even
in the same Gospels (Matt. xiii. 55, Luke viii. 19.) mention is made
of ἀδελφοῖς Ἰησοῦ, (the brothers of Jesus.) In the words of Fritzsche: Lubentissime post Jesu natales Mariam concessit Matthæus
(Luke does the same) uxorem Josepho, in hoc uno occupatus, ne
quis ante Jesu primordia mutua venere usos suspicaretur. But
this did not continue to satisfy the orthodox: as the veneration for
Mary rose even higher, she who had once become fruitful by divine
agency was not subsequently to be profaned by the common relations
of life.‡ The opinion that Mary after the birth of Jesus became the
wife of Joseph, was early ranked among the heresies,§ and the orthodox Fathers sought every means to escape from it and to combat

---

* Diog. Laërt. a, a. O.   See Origenes c. Cels. 1, 37.   † Demonax, 29.   ‡ S. Origenes
in Matthæum according to Photius taught, τὸν Ἰωσὴφ μετὰ τὴν ἄφραστον κυοφορίαν συνάπ-
τεσθαι τῇ παρθένῳ. This was also, according to Epiphanias, the doctrine of those called
by him Dimœrites and Antidicomarianites, and in the time of Jerome, of Helvidius and
his followers. Compare on this point the Sammlung von Suicer, im Thesaurus ii., s. v.
Mαρία, Fol. 365 f.

it. They contended that according to the exegetical interpretation of ἕως οὖ, it sometimes affirmed or denied a thing, not merely up to a certain limit, but beyond that limitation and for ever; and that the words of Matthew οὐν ἐγίνωσκεν αὐτὴν ἕως οὖ ἔτεκε κ. τ. λ. excluded a matrimonial connexion between Joseph and Mary for all time.[*] In like manner it was asserted of the term πρωτότοκος, that it did not necessarily include the subsequent birth of other children, but that it merely excluded any previous birth.[†] But in order to banish the thought of a matrimonial connexion between Mary and Joseph, not only grammatically but physiologically, they represented Joseph as a very old man, under whom Mary was placed for control and protection only; and the brothers of Jesus mentioned in the New Testament they regarded as the children of Joseph by a former marriage.[‡] But this was not all: soon it was insisted not only that Mary never became the wife of Joseph, but that in giving birth to Jesus she did not lose her virginity.[§] But even the conservation of Mary's virginity did not long continue to satisfy: perpetual virginity was likewise required on the part of Joseph. It was not enough that he had no connexion with Mary; it was also necessary that his entire life should be one of celibacy. Accordingly, though Epiphanius allows that Joseph had sons by a former marriage, Jerome rejects the supposition as an impious and audacious invention; and from that time the brothers of Jesus were degraded to the rank of cousins.[‖]

Some modern theologians agree with the Fathers of the Church in maintaining that no matrimonial connexion subsisted at any time between Joseph and Mary, and believe themselves able to explain the gospel expressions which appear to assert the contrary. In reference to the term *first born*, Olshausen contends that it signifies an only son: no less than the eldest of several. Paulus allows that here he is right, and Clemen[¶] and Fritzsche seek in vain to demonstrate the impossibility of this signification. For when it is said in Exod. xiii. 2, כָּל־בְּכוֹר פֶּטֶר כָּל־רֶחֶם בִּבְנֵי יִשְׂרָאֵל (πρωτότοκον πρωτογενὲς LXXX.) it was not merely a firstborn followed by others subsequently born, who was sanctified to Jehovah, but the fruit of the body of that mother of whom no other child had previously been born. Therefore the term πρωτότοκος must of necessity bear also this signification. Truly however we must confess with Winer[**] and others, on the other side, that if a narrator who was acquainted with the whole sequel of the history used that expression, we should be tempted to understand it in its primitive sense; since had the author intended to exclude other children, he would rather have em-

* Comp. Hieron. adv. Helv. 6, 7, Theophylact and Suidas in Suicer, 1. s. v. ἕως, Fol. 1291 f.   † Hieron. z. d. St.   ‡ See Orig. in Matth. Tom. 10, 17; Epiphan. hæres. 78, 7; Historia Josephi, c. 2; Protev. Jac. 9, 18.   § Chrysostomus, hom. 112. in Suicer, s. v. Μαρία, most repulsively described in the Protev. Jac. xix. and xx.   ‖ Hieron. ad Matth. 12, und advers. Helvid. 15.   ¶ Die Bruder Jesu.   In Winer's Zeitschrift für wissenschaftliche Theologie, 1. 3. S. 364 f.   ** Biblisches Realwörterbuch, 1. Bd. S. 661, Anm.   De Wette, z. d. St.   Neander L. J. Ch., S. 34.

ployed the word μονογενής, or would have connected it with πρωτό-τοκος. If this be not quite decisive, the reasoning of Fritzsche in reference to the ἕως οὗ, κ. τ. λ., is more convincing. He rejects the citations adduced in support of the interpretation of the Fathers of the Church, proving that this expression according to its primitive signification affirms only to a given limit, and beyond that limit supposes the logical opposite of the affirmation to take place; a signification which it loses only when the context shows clearly that the opposite is impossible in the nature of things.* For example, when it is said οὐκ ἐγίνωσκεν αὐτὴν, ἕως οὗ ἀπέθανεν, it is self-evident that the negation, during the time elapsed till death—cannot be transformed after death into an affirmation; but when it is said, as in Matthew, οὐκ ἐ. ἀ. ἕως οὗ ἔτεκεν, the giving birth to the divine fruit opposes no impossibility to the establishment of the conjugal relations; on the contrary it renders it possible i. e. suitable† for them now to take place.

Olshausen, impelled by the same doctrinal motives which influenced the Fathers, is led in this instance to contradict both the evidence of grammar and of logic. He thinks that Joseph, without wishing to impair the sanctity of marriage, must have concluded after the experiences he had had (?) that his marriage with Mary had another object than the production of children: besides it was but natural (?) in the last descendant of the house of David, and of that particular branch from which the Messiah should come forth, to terminate her race in this last and eternal offshoot.

A curious ladder may be formed of these different beliefs and superstitions in relation to the connexion between Mary and Joseph.

1. Contemporaries of Jesus and composers of the genealogies: Joseph and Mary man and wife—Jesus the offspring of their marriage.

2. The age and authors of our histories of the birth of Jesus: Mary and Joseph betrothed only; Joseph having no participation in the conception of the child, and previous to its birth no conjugal connexion with Mary.

3. Olshausen and others: subsequent to the birth of Jesus, Joseph, though then the husband of Mary, relinquishes his matrimonial rights.

4. Epiphanius, Protevangelium Jacobi and others: Joseph a decrepit old man, no longer to be thought of as a husband: the children attributed to him are of a former marriage. More especially it is not as a bride and wife that he receives Mary; he takes her merely under his guardianship.

5. Protevang., Chrysostom and others: Mary's virginity was not only not destroyed by any subsequent births of children by Jo-

* Comment. in Matth. S. 53 ff., vgl. auch S. 835.   † Olshausen is exceedingly unhappy in the example chosen by him in support of his interpretation of ἕως οὗ. For when it is said, *we waited till midnight but no one came,* certainly this by no means implies that after midnight some one did come, but it does imply that after midnight we waited no longer; so that here the expression *till* retains its signification of exclusion.

seph, it was not in the slightest degree impaired by the birth of
Jesus.

6. Jerome : not Mary only but Joseph also observed an absolute virginity, and the pretended brothers of Jesus were not his sons
but merely cousins to Jesus.

The opinion that the ἀδελφοὶ (brothers) and ἀδελφαὶ Ἰησοῦ (sisters of Jesus) mentioned in the New Testament, were merely half
brothers or indeed cousins, appears in its origin, as shown above,
together with the notion that no matrimonial connexion ever subsisted between Joseph and Mary, as the mere invention of superstition, a circumstance highly prejudicial to such an opinion. It is
however no less true that purely exegetical grounds exist, in virtue
of which theologians who were free from prejudice have decided,
that the opinion that Jesus actually had brothers is untenable.*
Had we merely the following passages—Matth. xiii. 55, Mark vi. 3,
where the people of Nazareth astonished at the wisdom of their coun-
tryman, in order to mark his well known origin, immediately after
having spoken of τέκτων (the carpenter) his father, and his mother
Mary, mention by name his ἀδελφοὺς (brothers) James, Joses, Simon, and Judas, together with his sisters whose names are not
given ;† again Matth. xii. 46, Luke viii. 19, when his mother and
his brethren come to Jesus ; John ii. 12, where Jesus journeys with
his mother and his brethren to Capernaum ; Acts i. 14, where they
are mentioned in immediate connexion with his mother—if we had
these passages only, we could not for a moment hesitate to recognize here real brothers of Jesus at least on the mother's side, children of Joseph and Mary; not only on account of the proper signification of the word ἀδελφὸς, but also in consequence of its continual
conjunction with Mary and Joseph. Even the passages—John vii.
5, in which it is remarked that his brethren did not believe on
Jesus, and Mark iii. 21, compared with 31, where according to the
most probable explanation, the brothers of Jesus with his mother
went out to lay hold of him as one beside himself—furnish no adequate grounds for relinquishing the proper signification of ἀδελφὸς.
Many theologians have interpreted ἀδελφοὺς Ἰησοῦ in the last cited
passage *half brothers, sons of Joseph by a former marriage*, alleging that the real brothers of Jesus must have believed on him,
but this is a mere assumption. The difficulty seems greater when
we read in John xix. 26 f. that Jesus on the cross, enjoined John
to be a son to his mother ; an injunction it is not easy to regard as
suitable under the supposition that Mary had other children, except
indeed these were half brothers and unfriendly to Jesus. Nevertheless we can imagine the existence both of external circumstances
and of individual feelings which might have influenced Jesus to con-

* On this subject compare in particular Clemen, die Brüder Jesu, in Winer's Zeitschrift für wissensch. Theol. 1, 3, S. 329 ff.; Paulus, exeg. Handbuch 1 Bd. S. 557 ff.;
Fritzsche, a. a. O. S. 480 ff.; Winer bibl. Realwörterbuch, in den A. A.: Jesus, Jacobus,
Apostel.   † See the different names assigned them in the legend in Thilo, Codex apocryphus N. T., 1 S. 363 note.

side his mother to John rather than to his brothers. That these brothers appeared in company with his Apostles after the ascension (Acts i. 14,) is no proof that they must have believed on Jesus at the time of his death.

The real perplexity in the matter, however, originates in this: that besides the James and Joses spoken of as the brothers of Jesus, two men of the same name are mentioned as the sons of another Mary (Mark xv. 40, 47, xvi. 1, Matt. xxvii. 56,) without doubt that Mary who is designated, John xix. 25, as the sister of the mother of Jesus, and the wife of Cleophas: so that we have a James and a Joses not only among the children of Mary the mother of Jesus, but again among her sister's children. We meet with several others among those immediately connected with Jesus, whose names are identical. In the lists of the Apostles (Matth. x. 2 ff., Luke vi. 14 ff.) we have two more of the name of James: that is four, the brother and cousin of Jesus included; two more of the name of Judas: that is three, the brother of Jesus included; two of the name of Simon, also making three with the brother of Jesus of the same name. The question naturally arises, whether the same individual is not here taken as distinct persons? The suspicion is almost unavoidable in reference to James. As James the son of Alpheus is, in the list of the Apostles, introduced after the son of Zebedee, as the second, perhaps the younger; and as James the cousin of Jesus is called ὁ μικρος ("the less") Mark. xv. 40; and since by comparing John xix. 25, we find that the latter is called the son of Cleophas, it is possible that the name Κλωπᾶς (Cleophas) given to the husband of Mary's sister, and the name Ἀλφαῖος (Alpheus) given to the father of the apostle, may be only different forms of the Hebrew חלפי. Thus would the second James enumerated among the Apostles and the cousin of Jesus of that name be identical, and there would remain besides him only the son of Zebedee and the brother of Jesus. Now in the Acts (xv. 13) a James appears who takes a prominent part in the so-called apostolic council, and as, according to Acts xii. 2, the son of Zebedee had previously been put to death, and as in the foregoing portion of the book of the Acts no mention is made of any other James besides the son of Alpheus (i. 13) so this James, of whom (Acts xv. 13,) no more precise description is given, can be no other than the son of Alpheus. But Paul speaks of a James (Gal. i. 19) *the Lord's brother*, whom he saw at Jerusalem, and it is doubtless he of whom he speaks in connexion with Cephas and John as the στύλοι (pillars) of the church—for this is precisely in character with the (Apostle) James as he appeared at the apostolic council—so that this James may be considered as identical with the Lord's brother, and the rather as the expression ἕτερον δὲ τῶν ἀποστόλων οὐκ εἶδον, εἰ μὴ Ἰάκωβον τὸν ἀδελφὸν τοῦ Κυρίου (*but other of the apostles saw I none, save James the Lord's brother.* Gal. i. 19,) makes it appear as if the Lord's brother were reckoned among the apostles; with which also the ancient tradition which represents James the Just, a brother of Jesus, as the first head of the church at Jerusalem, agrees.* But admitting the James of the Acts to be identical with the distinguished Apostle of that name, then is he the son of Alpheus, and not the son of Joseph; consequently if he be at the same time ἀδελφός τοῦ Κυρίου, then ἀδελφὸς cannot signify a brother. Now if Alpheus and Cleophas are admitted to be the same individual, the husband of the sister of Mary the mother of Jesus, it is obvious that ἀδελφὸς, used to denote the relationship of his son to Jesus, must be taken in the signification, cousin. If, after this manner, James the Apostle the son of Alpheus be identified with the cousin, and the cousin be identified with the brother of Jesus of the same name, it is obvious that Ἰούδας Ἰακώβου in the catalogue of the Apostles in Luke (Luke vi. 16, Acts i. 13,) must be translated *brother of James* (son of Alpheus); and this Apostle Jude must be held as identical with the Jude ἀδελφὸς Ἰησοῦ, that is, with the cousin of the Lord and son of Mary Cleophas: (though the name of Jude is never mentioned in connexion with this Mary.) If the Epistle of Jude in our canon be authentic, it is confirmatory of the above deduction, that the author (verse 1) designates himself as the ἀδελφὸς Ἰακώβου (*brother of James*). Some moreover have identified the Apostle Simon ὁ ζηλωτὴς or Κανανίτης (*Zelotes or the Cananite*) with the Simon enumerated among the brothers of Jesus (Mark vi. 3,) and who according to a tradition of the church succeeded James as head of the church at Jerusalem;† so that Joses alone appears without further designation or appellative.

If, accordingly, those spoken of as ἀδελφοὶ Ἰησοῦ were merely cousins, and three of these were Apostles, it must excite surprise that not only in the Acts, (i. 14,) after an enumeration of the Apostles, the brothers of Jesus are separately particularized, but that also (1 Cor. ix. 5,) they appear to be a class distinct from the Apostles. Perhaps, also, the passage Gal. 1. 19 ought to be understood as indicating that James, the Lord's brother, was not an Apostle.‡ If therefore, the ἀδελφοὶ Ἰησοῦ seem thus to be extruded from the number of the Apostles, it is yet more difficult to regard them merely as the cousins of Jesus, since they appear in so many places immediately associated with the mother of Jesus, and in two or three passages only are two men bearing the same names mentioned in connexion with the other Mary, who accordingly would be their real mother. The Greek word ἀδελφὸς, may indeed signify, in language which pretends not to precision, as well as the Hebrew אח a more distant relative; but as it is repeatedly used to express the relationship of these persons to Jesus, and is in no instance replaced by ἀνεψιὸς—a word which is not foreign to the New Testament language when the relationship of cousin is to be denoted (Col. iv. 10,) it cannot well be taken in any other than its proper signification. Further, it need only be pointed out that the highest degree of uncertainty exists respecting not only the identity of the names Alpheus and Cleophas, upon which the identity of James the cousin of Jesus and of the Apostle James the Less rests, but also regarding the translation of Ἰουδᾶς Ἰακώβου by the *brother of James;* and likewise respecting the assumed identity of the author of the last Catholic Epistle with the Apostle Jude.

Thus the web of this identification gives way at all points, and we are forced back to the position whence we set out; so that we have again real brothers of Jesus, also two cousins distinct from these brothers, though bearing the same names with two of them, besides some Apostles of the same names with both brothers and cousins. To find two pairs of sons of the same names in a family is, indeed, not so uncommon as to become a source of objection. It is, however, remarkable that the same James who in the Epistle to the Galatians is designated ἀδελφὸσ Κυρίυν (*the Lord's brother*), must unquestionably, according to the Acts of the Apostles, be regarded as the son of Alpheus; which he could not be if this expression signified a brother. So that there is perplexity on every side, which can be solved only (and then, indeed, but negatively and without historical result) by admitting the existence of obscurity and error on this point in the New Testament writers, and even in the very earliest Christian traditions: error which, in matters of involved relationships and family names, is far more easily fallen into than avoided.*

We have consequently no ground for denying that the mother of Jesus bore her husband several other children besides Jesus, younger, and perhaps also older: the latter, because the representation in the New Testament that Jesus was the first-born may belong no less to the mythus than the representation of the Fathers that he was an only son.

§ 31. VISIT OF MARY TO ELIZABETH.

THE angel who announced to Mary her own approaching pregnancy, at the same time informed her (Luke i. 36.) of that of her relative Elizabeth, with whom it was already the sixth month. Hereupon Mary immediately set out on a journey to her cousin, a visit which was attended by extraordinary occurrences; for when Elizabeth heard the salutation of Mary, the babe leaped in her womb for joy: she also became inspired, and in her exultation poured forth an address to Mary as the future mother of the Messiah, to which Mary responded by a hymn of praise (Luke i. 39—56).

The rationalistic interpreter believes it to be an easy matter to give a natural explanation of this narrative of the Gospel of Luke. He is of opinion† that the unknown individual who excited such peculiar anticipations in Mary, had at the same time acquainted her with the similar situation of her cousin Elizabeth. This it was

* Theile, Biographie Jesu, § 18.   † Paulus exeg. Handb. 1, a, S. 120 ff.

which impelled Mary the more strongly to confer on the subject with her older relative. Arrived at her cousin's dwelling, she first of all made known what had happened to herself; but upon this the narrator is silent, not wishing to repeat what he had just before described. And here the Rationalist not only supposes the address of Elizabeth to have been preceded by some communication from Mary, but imagines Mary to have related her history piecemeal, so as to allow Elizabeth to throw in sentences during the intervals. The excitement of Elizabeth—such is the continuation of the rationalistic explanation—communicated itself, according to natural laws, to the child, who, as is usual with an embryo of six months, made a movement, which was first regarded by the mother as significant, and as the consequence of the salutation, after Mary's farther communications. Just as natural does it appear to the Rationalist that Mary should have given utterance to her Messianic expectations, confirmed as they were by Elizabeth, in a kind of psalmodic recitative, composed of reminiscences borrowed from various parts of the Old Testament.

But there is much in this explanation which positively contradicts the text. In the first place, that Elizabeth should have learned the heavenly message imparted to Mary from Mary herself. There is no trace in the narrative either of any communication preceding Elizabeth's address, or of interruptions occasioned by farther explanations on the part of Mary. On the contrary, as it is a supernatural revelation which acquaints Mary with the pregnancy of Elizabeth, so also it is to a revelation that Elizabeth's immediate recognition of Mary, as the chosen mother of the Messiah, is attributed.* As little will the other feature of this narrative—that the entrance of the mother of the Messiah occasioned a responsive movement in his mother's womb on the part of his forerunner—bear a natural explanation. In modern times indeed even orthodox interpreters have inclined to this explanation, but with the modification, that Elizabeth in the first place received a revelation, in which however the child, owing to the mother's excitement, a matter to be physiologically explained, likewise took part.† But the record does not represent the thing as if the excitement of the mother were the determining cause of the movement of the child; on the contrary (v. 41.) the emotion of the mother follows the movement of the child, and Elizabeth's own account states, that it was the salutation of Mary (v. 44.), not indeed from its particular signification, but merely as the voice of the mother of the Messiah, which produced the movement of the unborn babe: undeniably assuming something supernatural. But even herein the supranaturalistic view of this miracle is not free from objection, even on its own ground; and hence the anxiety of the above mentioned modern orthodox interpreters to evade it. It may be possible to conceive the human mind immediately acted upon by the divine mind, to which it is related, but how solve the difficulty of an immediate communication of the divine mind to an unintelligent embryo? And if we inquire the object of so strange a miracle, none which is worthy presents itself. Should it be referred to the necessity that the Baptist should receive the earliest possible intimation of the work to which he was destined; still we know not how such an impression could have been made upon an embryo. Should the purpose be supposed to centre in the other individuals, in Mary or Elizabeth; they had been the recipients of far higher revelations, and were consequently already possessed of an adequate measure of insight and faith.

No fewer difficulties oppose the rationalistic than the supranaturalistic explanation of the hymn pronounced by Mary. For though it is not, like the Canticle of Zacharias (v. 67.) and the address of Elizabeth (v. 41.) introduced by the formula ἐπλήσθη πνεύματος ἁγίου *she was filled with the Holy Ghost*, still the similarity of these utterances is so great, that the omission cannot be adduced as a proof that the narrator did not intend to represent this, equally with the other two, as the operation of the πνεῦμα (spirit). But apart from the intention of the narrator, can it be thought natural that two friends visiting one another should, even in the midst of the most extraordinary occurrences, break forth into long hymns, and that their conversation should entirely lose the character of dialogue, the natural form on such occasions? By a supernatural influence alone could the minds of the two friends be attuned to a state of elevation, so foreign to their every day life. But if indeed Mary's hymn is to be understood as the work of the Holy Spirit, it is surprising that a speech emanating immediately from the divine source of inspiration should not be more striking for its originality, but should be so interlarded with reminiscences from the Old Testament, borrowed from the song of praise spoken by the mother of Samuel (1 Sam. ii.) under analogous circumstances.* Accordingly we must admit that the compilation of this hymn, consisting of recollections from the Old Testament, was put together in a natural way: but allowing its composition to have been perfectly natural, it cannot be ascribed to the artless Mary, but to him who poetically wrought out the tradition in circulation respecting the scene in question.

Since then we find all the principal incidents of this visit inconceivable according to the supernatural interpretation; also that they will not bear a natural explanation; we are led to seek a mythical exposition of this as well as the preceding portions of the gospel history. This path has already been entered upon by others. The view of this narrative given by the anonymous E. F. in Henke's Magazine† is, that it does not portray events as they actually did

* Compare Luke i. 47 with 1 Sam. ii. 1.   Particularly Luke i. 48 with 1 Sam, i. 11.
  i. 49   ii. 2.   Compare Luke i. 50 with Deut. vii, 9.
  i. 51   ii. 3, 4.   i. 52   Ecclesiasticus x. 14.
  i. 52   ii. 8.   i. 54   Psa. xcviii. 3.
  i. 53   ii. 5.   † 5 Band, 1. Stück. S. 161 f.

occur, but as they might have occurred ; that much which the sequel taught of the destiny of their sons was carried back into the speeches of these women, which were also enriched by other features gleaned from tradition ; that a true fact however lies at the bottom, namely an actual visit of Mary to Elizabeth, a joyous conversation, and the expression of gratitude to God ; all which might have happened solely in virtue of the high importance attached by Orientals to the joys of maternity, even though the two mothers had been at that time ignorant of the destination of their children.   This author is of opinion that Mary, when pondering over at a later period the remarkable life of her son, may often have related the happy meeting with her cousin and their mutual expressions of thankfulness to God, and that thus the history gained currency.   Horst also, who has a just conception of the fictitious nature of this section in Luke, and ably refutes the natural mode of explanation, yet himself slides unawares half-way back into it.   He thinks it not improbable that Mary during her pregnancy, which was in many respects a painful one, should have visited her older and more experienced cousin, and that Elizabeth should during this visit have felt the first movement of her child ; an occurrence which as it was afterwards regarded as ominous, was preserved by the oral tradition.[*]

These are farther examples of the uncritical proceeding which pretends to disengage the mythical and poetical from the narrative, by plucking away a few twigs and blossoms of that growth, whilst it leaves the very root of the mythus undisturbed as purely historical.   In our narrative the principal mythical feature (the remainder forms only its adjuncts) is precisely that which the above mentioned authors, in their pretended mythical explanations, retain as historical : namely the visit of Mary to the pregnant Elizabeth.   For, as we have already seen, the main tendency of the first chapter of Luke is to magnify Jesus by connecting the Baptist with him from the earliest possible point in a relation of inferiority.   Now this object could not be better attained than by bringing about a meeting, not in the first instance of the sons, but of the mothers in reference to their sons, during their pregnancy, at which meeting some occurrence which should prefigure the future relative positions of these two men should take place.   Now the more apparent the existence of a dogmatical motive as the origin of this visit, the less probability is there that it had an historical foundation.   With this principal feature the other details are connected in the following order:— The visit of the two women must be represented as possible and probable by the feature of family relationship between Mary and Elizabeth (v. 36.), which would also give a greater suitability to the subsequent connexion of the sons.   Further a visit, so full of import, made precisely at that time, must have taken place by special divine appointment ; therefore it is an angel who refers Mary to her cousin.   At the visit the subservient position of the Baptist to Jesus is to be particularly exhibited;—this could have been effected by the mother as indeed it is in her address to Mary, but it were better if possible that the future Baptist himself should give a sign. The mutual relation of Esau and Jacob had been prefigured by their struggles and position in their mother's womb. (Gen. xxv. 22. ff.) But, without too violent an offence against the laws of probability an ominous movement would not be attributed to the child prior to that period of her pregnancy at which the motion of the fœtus is felt; hence the necessity that Elizabeth should be in the sixth month of her pregnancy when Mary, in consequence of the communication of the angel, set out to visit her cousin (v. 36.). Thus as Schleiermacher remarks* the whole arrangement of times had reference to the particular circumstance the author desired to contrive—the joyous responsive movement of the child in his mother's womb at the moment of Mary's entrance. To this end only must Mary's visit be delayed till after the fifth month; and the angel not appear to her before that period.

Thus not only does the visit of Mary to Elizabeth with all the attendant circumstances disappear from the page of history, but the historical validity of the further details—that John was only half a year older than Jesus; that the two mothers were related; that an intimacy subsisted between the families;—cannot be affirmed on the testimony of Luke, unsupported by other authorities: indeed, the contrary rather will be found substantiated in the course of our critical investigations.

CHAPTER IV.

BIRTH AND EARLIEST EVENTS OF THE LIFE OF JESUS.

---

§ 32.   THE CENSUS.

WITH respect to the birth of Jesus, Matthew and Luke agree in representing it as taking place at Bethlehem: but whilst the latter enters into a minute detail of all the attendant circumstances, the former merely mentions the event as it were incidentally, referring to it once in an appended sentence as the sequel to what had gone before, (i. 25.) and again as a presupposed occurrence. (ii. 1.) The one Evangelist seems to assume that Bethlehem was the habitual residence of the parents; but according to the other they are led thither by very particular circumstances. This point of difference between the Evangelists however can only be discussed after

Ueber den Lukas. S. 23 f.

we shall have collected more data; we will therefore leave it for the present, and turn our attention to an error into which Luke, when compared with himself and with dates otherwise ascertained seems to have fallen. This is the statement, that the census, decreed by Augustus at the time when Cyrenius (Quirinus) was governor of Syria, was the occasion of the journey of the parents of Jesus, who usually resided at Nazareth, to Bethlehem where Jesus was born (Luke ii. 1. ff.)

The first difficulty is that the ἀπογραφὴ (namely, the inscription of the name and amount of property in order to facilitate the taxation) commanded by Augustus, is extended to *all the world* πᾶσαν τὴν οἰκουμένην. This expression, in its common acceptation at that time, would denote the *orbis Romanus.* But ancient authors mention no such general census decreed by Augustus; they speak only of the assessment of single provinces decreed at different times. Consequently, it was said Luke meant to indicate by οἰκουμένη merely the land of Judea, and not the Roman world according to its ordinary signification. Examples were forthwith collected in proof of the possibility of such an interpretation,[*] but they in fact prove nothing. For supposing it could not be shown that in all these citations from the Septuagint, Josephus, and the New Testament, the expression really does signify, in the extravagant sense of these writers, the whole known world: still in the instance in question where the subject is a decree of the Roman emperor, πᾶσα ἡ οἰκουμένη must necessarily be understood of the regions which he governed, and therefore of the *orbis Romanus.* This is the reason that latterly the opposite side has been taken up, and it has been maintained, upon the authority of Savigny, that in the time of Augustus a census of the whole empire was actually undertaken.[†] This is positively affirmed by late christian writers:[‡] but the statement is rendered suspicious by the absence of all more ancient testimony;[§] and it is even contradicted by the fact, that for a considerable lapse of time an equal assessment throughout the empire was not effected. Finally, the very expressions of these writers show that their testimony rests upon that of Luke.[‖] But, it is said, Augustus at all events attempted an equal assessment of the empire by means of an universal census: and he began the carrying out his project by an assessment of individual provinces, but he left the further execution and completion to his successors.[¶] Admit that the gospel term δόγμα (*decree*) may be interpreted as a mere design, or, as Hoffmann thinks, an undetermined project expressed in an imperial decree:

* Olshausen, Paulus, Kuinöl.   † Tholuck, S. 194 ff.   Neander, S. 10.   ‡ Cassiodor. Variarum 3, 52.   Isidor.   Orig. 5, 36.   § To refer here to the *Monumentum Ancyranum,* which is said to record a census of the whole empire in the year of Rome 746, (Osiander, p. 95.) is proof of the greatest carelessness.   For he who examines this inscription will find mention only of three assessments *census civium Romanorum,* which Suetonius designates *census populi* and of which Dio Cassius speaks, at least of one of them, as ἀπογραφὴ τῶν ἐν τῇ Ἰταλίᾳ κατοικοῦντων.   See Ideler, Chronol. 2, S. 339.   ‖ In the authoritative citation in Suidas are the words taken from Luke, αὕτη ἡ ἀπογραφὴ πρώτη ἐγένετο.   ¶ Hoffmann, S. 231.

still the fulfilment of this project in Judea at the time of the birth of Jesus was impossible.

Matthew places the birth of Jesus shortly before the death of Herod the Great, whom he represents (ii. 19.) as dying during the abode of Jesus in Egypt. Luke says the same indirectly, for when speaking of the announcement of the birth of the Baptist, he refers it to the days of Herod the Great, and he places the birth of Jesus precisely six months later; so that according to Luke, also, Jesus was born, if not, like John, previous to the death of Herod I., shortly after that event. Now, after the death of Herod the country of Judea fell to his son Archelaus, (Matt. ii. 22.) who, after a reign of something less than ten years, was deposed and banished by Augustus,* at which time Judea was first consituted a Roman province, and began to be ruled by Roman functionaries.† Thus the Roman census in question must have been made either under Herod the Great, or at the commencement of the reign of Archelaus. This is in the highest degree improbable, for in those countries which were not reduced *in formam provinciæ*, but were governed by *regibus sociis*, the taxes were levied by these princes, who paid a tribute to the Romans;‡ and this was the state of things in Judea prior to the deposition of Archelaus. It has been the object of much research to make it appear probable that Augustus decreed a census, as an extraordinary measure, in Palestine under Herod. Attention has been directed to the circumstance that the *breviarium imperii*, which Augustus left behind him, contained the financial state of the whole empire, and it has been suggested that, in order to ascertain the financial condition of Palestine, he caused a statement to be prepared by Herod.§ Reference has been made first to the record of Josephus, that on account of some disturbance of the relations between Herod and Augustus, the latter threatened for the future to make him feel his subjection;‖ secondly, also to the oath of allegiance to Augustus which, according to Josephus, the Jews were forced to take even during the lifetime of Herod.¶ From which it is inferred that Augustus, since he had it in contemplation after the death of Herod to restrict the power of his sons, was very likely to have commanded a census in the last years of that prince. ** But

* Joseph. Antiq. 17, 13, 2. B. j. 2, 7, 3. † Antiq. 17, 13, 5, 18, 1, 1. B. j. 2, 8, 1. ‡ Paulus, exeg. Handb. 1, a, S. 171. Winer, bibl. Realwörterbuch. § Tacit. Annal. 1, 11. Sueton. Octav. 101. But if in this document *opes publicæ continebantur: quantum civium sociorumque in armis; quot classes, regna, provinciæ, tributa aut vectigalia, et necessitates ac largitiones:* the number of troops and the sum which the Jewish prince had to furnish, might have been given without a Roman tax being levied in their land. For Judea in particular Augustus had before him the subsequent census made by Quirinus. ‖ Ὅτι, πάλαι χρώμενος αὐτῷ φίλῳ, νῦν ὑπηκόῳ χρήσεται. Joseph. Antiq. 16, 9, 3. But the difference was adjusted long before the death of Herod. Antiq. 16, 10, 9. ¶ Joseph. Antiq. 17, 2, 4. παντὸς τοῦ Ἰουδαικοῦ βεβαιώσαντος δι' ὅρκων, ἦ μὴν εὐνοήσαι Καίσαρι καὶ τοῖς βασιλέως πράγμασι. That this oath, far from being a humiliating measure for Herod, coincided with his interest, is proved by the zeal with which he punished the Pharisees who refused to take it. ** Tholuck, S. 192 f. But the insurrection which the ἀπογραφὴ after the depositions of Archelaus actually occasioned—a fact which outweighs all Tholuck's surmises—proves it to have been the first Roman measure of the kind in Judea.

it seems more probable that it took place shortly after the death of Herod, from the circumstance that Archelaus went to Rome concerning the matter of succession, and that during his absence, the Roman procurator Sabinus occupied Jerusalem, and oppressed the Jews by every possible means.*

The Evangelist relieves us from a farther inquiry into this more or less historical or arbitrary combination by adding, that this taxing was first made when Cyrenius (Quirinus) *was governor of Syria*, ἡγεμονεύοντος τῆς Συρίασ Κυρηνίου: for it is an authenticated point that the assessment of Quirinus did not take place either under Herod or early in the reign of Archelaus, the period at which, according to Luke, Jesus was born. Quirinus was not at that time governor of Syria, a situation held during the last years of Herod by Sentius Saturninus, and after him by Quintilius Varus: and it was not till long after the death of Herod that Quirinus was appointed governor of Syria. That Quirinus undertook a census of Judea we know certainly from Josephus,† who, however, remarks that he was sent to execute this measure, τῆς Ἀρχελάου χώρας εἰς ἐπαρχίαν περιγραφείσης, or ὑποτελοῖς προσνεμηθείσμι τῇ Σύρων:‡ thus about ten years after the time at which, according to Matthew and Luke, Jesus must have been born.

Yet commentators have supposed it possible to reconcile this apparently undeniable contradiction between Luke and history. The most dauntless explain the whole of the second verse as a gloss, which was early incorporated into the text.§ Some change the reading of the verse; either of the *nomen proprium*, by substituting the name of Saturninus or Quintilius,‖ according to the example of Tertullian, who ascribed the census to the former :¶ or of the other words, by various additions and modifications. Paulus's alteration is the most simple. He reads, instead of αὕτη, αὐτή, and concludes, from the reasons stated above, that Augustus actually gave orders for a census during the reign of Herod I., and that the order was so far carried out as to occasion the journey of Joseph and Mary to Bethlehem; but that Augustus being afterwards conciliated, the measure was abandoned, and αὐτὴ ἡ ἀπογραφή was only carried into effect a considerable time later, by Quirinus. Trifling as this alteration, which leaves the letters unchanged, may appear, in order to render it admissible it must be supported by the context. The reverse, however, is the fact. For if one sentence narrates a command issued by a prince, and the very next sentence its execution, it is not probable that a space of ten years intervened. But chiefly, according to this view the Evangelist speaks, verse 1, of the decree of the emperor: verse 2, of the census made ten years later: but verse 3, without any remark, again of a journey performed at the time the command was issued; which, in a rational narrative, is impossible. Opposed to such arbitrary conjectures, and always to be ranked above them, are the attempts to solve a difficulty by legitimate methods of interpretation. Truly, however, to take πρώτη in this connexion for προτέρα, and ἡγεμονεύοντος K. not for a genitive absolute, but for a genitive governed by a comparative, and thus to understand an enrolment *before* that of Quirinus,* is to do violence to grammatical construction; and to insert πρὸ τῆς after πρώτη† is no less uncritical. As little is it to be admitted that some preliminary measure, in which Quirinus was not employed, perhaps the already mentioned oath of allegiance, took place during the lifetime of Herod, in reference to the census subsequently made by Quirinus ; and that this preliminary step and the census were afterwards comprised under the same name. In order in some degree to account for this appellation, Quirinus is said to have been sent into Judea, in Herod's time, as an extraordinary tax-commissioner;‡ but this interpretation of the word ἡγεμονεύοντος is rendered impossible by the addition of the word Συρίας, in combination with which the expression can denote only the *Præses Syriæ.*

Thus at the time at which Jesus, according to Matth. ii., 1, and Luke i., 5, 26. was born, the census of which Luke ii., 1 f. speaks could not have taken place; so that if the former statements are correct, the latter must be false. But may not the reverse be the fact, and Jesus have been born after the banishment of Archelaus, and at the time of the census of Quirinus? Apart from the difficulties in which this hypothesis would involve us in relation to the chronology of the future life of Jesus, a Roman census, subsequent to the banishment of Archelaus, would not have taken the parents of Jesus from Nazareth in Galilee to Bethlehem in Judea. For Judea only, and what otherwise belonged to the portion of Archelaus, became a Roman province and subjected to the census. In Galilee Herod Antipas continued to reign as an allied prince, and none of his subjects dwelling at Nazareth could have been called to Bethlehem by the census. The Evangelist therefore, in order to get a census, must have conceived the condition of things such as they were after the deposition of Archelaus; but in order to get a census extending to Galilee, he must have imagined the kingdom to have continued undivided, as in the time of Herod the Great. Thus he deals in manifest contradictions; or rather he has an exceedingly sorry acquaintance with the political relations of that period; for he extends the census not only to the whole of Palestine, but also, (which we must not forget,) to the whole Roman world.

Still these chronological incongruities do not exhaust the difficulties which beset this statement of Luke. His representation of the manner in which the census was made is subject to objection.

---

* Storr, opusc. acad. 3, S. 126 f.   Süskind, vermischte Aufsätze, S. 63.   Tholuck S. 182 f.   † Michaelis, Anm. z. d. St. und Einl. in d. N. T. 1, 71.   ‡ Münter, Stern der Weisen, S. 88.

In the first place it is said, the taxing took Joseph to Bethlehem, *because he was of the house and lineage of David,* διὰ τὸ εἶναι αὐτὸν ἐξ οἴκου καὶ πατριᾶς Δαβίδ, and likewise every one into his own city, εἰς τὴν ἰδίαν πόλιν, i. e. according to the context, to the place whence his family had originally sprung. Now, that every individual should be registered in his own city was required in all Jewish inscriptions, because among the Jews the organization of families and tribes constituted the very basis of the state. The Romans, on the contrary, were in the habit of taking the census at the residences, and at the principal cities in the district.* They conformed to the usages of the conquered countries only in so far as they did not interfere with their own objects. In the present instance it would have been directly contrary to their design, had they removed individuals—Joseph for example—to a great distance, where the amount of their property was not known, and their statement concerning it could not be checked.† The view of Schleiermacher is the more admissible, that the real occasion which took the parents to Bethlehem was a sacerdotal inscription, which the Evangelist confounded with the better known census of Quirinus. But this concession does not obviate the contradiction in this dubious statement of Luke. He allows Mary to be inscribed with Joseph, but according to Jewish customs inscriptions had relation to men only. Thus, at all events, it is an inaccuracy to represent Mary as undertaking the journey, in order to be inscribed with her betrothed in his own city. Or, if with Paulus we remove this inaccuracy by a forced construction of the sentence, we can no longer perceive what inducement could have instigated Mary, in her particular situation, to make so long a journey, since, unless we adopt the airy hypothesis of Olshausen and others, that Mary was the heiress of property in Bethlehem, she had nothing to do there.

The Evangelist, however, knew perfectly well what she had to do there ; namely, to fulfil the prophecy of Micah (v. 1), by giving birth, in the city of David, to the Messiah. Now as he set out with the supposition that the habitual abode of the parents of Jesus was Nazareth, so he sought after a lever which should set them in motion towards Bethlehem, at the time of the birth of Jesus. Far and wide nothing presented itself but the celebrated census ; he seized it the more unhesitatingly because the obscurity of his own view of the historical relations of that time, veiled from him the many difficulties connected with such a combination. If this be the true history of the statement in Luke, we must agree with K. Ch. L. Schmidt when he says, that to attempt to reconcile the statement of Luke concerning the ἀπογραφή with chronology, would be to do the narrator too much honour ; he wished to place Mary in Bethlehem, and therefore times and circumstances were to accommodate themselves to his pleasure.‡

* Paulus, Wettstein. † Credner. ‡ In Schmidt's Bibliothek für Kritik und Exegese, 3, 1. S. 121. See Kaiser, bibl. Theol. 1, S. 230; Ammon, Fortbildung, 1, S. 196; Credner, Einleitung in d. N. T., 1, S. 155; De Wette, exeget. Handbuch.

Thus we have here neither a fixed point for the date of the birth of Jesus, nor an explanation of the occasion which led to his being born precisely at Bethlehem. If then—it may justly be said—no other reason why Jesus should have been born at Bethlehem can be adduced than that given by Luke, we have absolutely no guarantee that Bethlehem was his birth-place.

§ 33. PARTICULAR CIRCUMSTANCES OF THE BIRTH OF JESUS—THE CIRCUMCISION.

THE basis of the narrative, the arrival of Joseph and Mary as strangers in Bethlehem on account of the census, being once chosen by Luke, the farther details are consistently built upon it. In consequence of the influx of strangers brought to Bethlehem by the census, there is no room for the travellers in the inn, and they are compelled to put up with the accommodation of a stable where Mary is forthwith delivered of her first-born. But the child, who upon earth comes into being in so humble an abode, is highly regarded in heaven. A celestial messenger announces the birth of the Messiah, to shepherds who are guarding their flocks in the fields by night, and directs them to the child in the manger. A choir of the heavenly host singing hymns of praise next appears to them, after which they seek and find the child. (Luke ii. 6—20.)

The apocryphal gospels and the traditions of the Fathers still further embellished the birth of Jesus. According to the *Protevangelium Jacobi*,[*] Joseph conducts Mary on an ass to Bethlehem to be taxed. As they approach the city she begins to make now mournful, now joyous gestures, and upon inquiry explains that—(as once in Rebecca's womb the two hostile nations struggled, (Gen. xxv. 23)—she sees two people before her, the one weeping, the other laughing: *i. e.* according to one explanation, the two portions of Israel, to one of whom the advent of Jesus *was set* (Luke ii. 34) εἰς πτῶσιν, *for the fall*, to the other εἰς ἀνάστασιν, *for the rising again*. According to another interpretation, the two people were the Jews who should reject Jesus, and the heathens who should accept him.[†] Soon, however, whilst still without the city—as appears from the context and the reading of several MSS—Mary is seized with the pains of child-bearing, and Joseph brings her into a cave situated by the road side, where veiled by a cloud of light, all nature pausing in celebration of the event, she brings her child into the world, and after her delivery is found, by women called to her assistance, still a virgin.[‡] The legend of the birth of Jesus in a cave was known to Justin[§] and to Origen,[||] who, in order to reconcile it with the account in Luke that he was laid in a manger, suppose a manger situated within the cave. Many modern commentators

* Chap. 17. Compare Historia de nativ. Mariae et de infantia Servatoris, c. 13.
† Fabricius, im Codex Apocryph. N. T. 1, S. 105. not. y. ‡ Ambrosius and Jerome. See Gieseler K. G. 1, S. 516. § Dial. c. Tryph. 78. || C. Cels. 1, 51.

agree with them ;* whilst others prefer to consider the cave itself as
φάτνη, in the sense of foddering-stall.† For the birth of Jesus in a
cave, Justin appeals to the prophecy in Isaiah xxviii. 16: οὗτος (the
righteous) οἰκήσει ἐν ὑψηλῷ σπηλαίῳ πέτρας ἰσχυρᾶς. In like manner,
for the statement that on the third day the child Jesus, when brought
from the cave into the stable, was worshipped by the oxen and the
asses, the *Historia de Nativitate Mariae‡* &c. refers to Isaiah i. 3:
cognovit bos possessorem suum, et asinus praesepe domini sui. In
several apocryphas, between the Magi and the women who assist at
the birth, the shepherds are forgotten ; but they are mentioned in
the *Evangelium infantiae arabicum,§* where it says, that when they
arrived at the cave, and had kindled a fire of rejoicing, the heavenly
host appeared to them.

If we take the circumstances attending the birth of Jesus, narrated by Luke, in a supranaturalistic sense, many difficulties occur.
First, it may reasonably be asked, to what end the angelic apparition? The most obvious answer is, to make known the birth of
Jesus; but so little did it make it known that, in the neighbouring
city of Jerusalem, it is the Magi who give the first information of
the new-born king of the Jews; and in the future history of Jesus,
no trace of any such occurrence at his birth is to be found. Consequently, the object of that extraordinary phenomenon was not to
give a wide-spreading intimation of the fact: for if so, God failed
in his object. Must we then agree with Schleiermacher, that the
aim was limited to an immediate operation upon the shepherds?
Then we must also suppose with him, that the shepherds, equally
with Simeon, were filled with Messianic expectations, and that God
designed by this apparition to reward and confirm their pious belief.
The narrative however says nothing of this heavenly frame of mind,
neither does it mention any abiding effects produced upon these men.
According to the whole tenor of the representation, the apparition
seems to have had reference, not to the shepherds, but exclusively
to the glorification and the proclaiming of the birth of Jesus, as the
Messiah. But as before observed, the latter aim was not accomplished, and the former, by itself, like every mere empty display, is
an object unworthy of God. So that this circumstance in itself
presents no inconsiderable obstacle to the supranaturalistic conception
of the history. If, to the above considerations, we add those already
stated which oppose the belief in apparitions and the existence of
angels in general, it is easy to understand that with respect to this
narrative also refuge has been sought in a natural explanation.

The results of the first attempts at a natural explanation were
certainly sufficiently rude. Thus Eck regarded the angel as a messenger from Bethlehem, who carried a light which caught the eye of
the shepherds, and the song of the heavenly host as the merry tones of
a party accompanying the messenger.‖ Paulus has woven together

a more refined and matter of fact explanation. Mary, who had met with a hospitable reception in a herdsman's family, and who was naturally elated with the hope of giving birth to the Messiah, told her expectations to the members of this family; to whom as inhabitants of a city of David the communication could not have been indifferent. These shepherds therefore on perceiving, whilst in the fields by night, a luminous appearance in the air,—a phenomenon which travellers say is not uncommon in those regions—they interpret it as a divine intimation that the stranger in their foddering-stall is delivered of the Messiah; and as the meteoric light extends and moves to and fro, they take it for a choir of angels chaunting hymns of praise. Returning home they find their anticipations confirmed by the event, and that which at first they merely conjectured to be the sense and interpretation of the phenomenon, they now, after the manner of the East, represent as words actually spoken.*

This explanation rests altogether on the assumption, that the shepherds were previously acquainted with Mary's expectation that she should give birth to the Messiah. How otherwise should they have been led to consider the sign as referring particularly to the birth of the Messiah in their manger? Yet this very assumption is the most direct contradiction of the gospel account. For, in the first place, the Evangelist evidently does not suppose the manger to belong to the shepherds: since after he has narrated the delivery of Mary in the manger, he then goes on to speak of the shepherds as a new and distinct subject, not at all connected with the manger. His words are: *and there were in the same country shepherds*, καὶ ποιμένες ἦσαν ἐν τῇ χώρᾳ τῇ αὐτῇ. If this explanation were correct he would, at all events, have said, *the shepherds &c.* οἱ δὲ ποιμένες κ. τ. λ.; besides he would not have been wholly silent respecting the comings and goings of these shepherds during the day, and their departure to guard the flock at the approach of night. But, grant these presupposed circumstances, is it consistent in Paulus to represent Mary, at first so reserved concerning her pregnancy as to conceal it even from Joseph, and then so communicative that, just arrived among strangers, she parades the whole history of her expectations? Again the sequel of the narrative contradicts the assumption that the shepherds were informed of the matter by Mary herself, before her delivery. For, according to the gospel history, the shepherds receive the first intelligence of the birth of the Saviour σωτήρ from the angel who appears to them, and who tells them, as a sign of the truth of his communication, that they shall find the babe lying in a manger. Had they already heard from Mary of the approaching birth of the Messiah, the meteoric appearance would have been a confirmation to them of Mary's words, and not the finding of the child a proof of the truth of the apparition. Finally, may we so far confide in the investigations already made as to

---

* Exeg. Handb. S. 180 ff. As Paulus supposes an external natural phenomenon so Matthæi imagines a mental vision of angels. Synopse der vier Evangelien, S. 3.

inquire, whence, if neither a miraculous announcement nor a supernatural conception actually occurred, could Mary have derived the confident anticipation that she should give birth to the Messiah?

In opposition to this natural explanation, so full of difficulties on every side, Bauer announced his adoption of the mythical view;* in fact, however, he did not advance one step beyond the interpretation of the Rationalists, but actually repeated Paulus's exposition point for point. To this mixed mythical explanation Gabler justly objected that it, equally with the natural interpretation, multiplies improbabilities: by the adoption of the pure, dogmatic mythus, every thing appears simpler: thereby, at the same time, greater harmony is introduced into the early christian history, all the preceding narratives of which ought equally to be interpreted as pure mythi.† Gabler, accordingly, explained the narrative as the product of the ideas of the age, which demanded the assistance of angels at the birth of the Messiah. Now had it been known that Mary was delivered in a dwelling belonging to shepherds, it would also have been concluded that angels must have brought the tidings to these good shepherds that the Messiah was born in their manger; and the angels, who cease not praising God, must have sung a hymn of praise on the occasion. Gabler thinks it impossible, that a Jewish christian who should have known some of the data of the birth of Jesus, could have thought of it otherwise than as here depicted.‡

This explanation of Gabler shows, in a remarkable manner, how difficult it is entirely to extricate oneself from the natural explanation, and to rise completely to the mythical; for whilst this theologian believes he treads on pure mythical ground, he still stands with one foot upon that of the natural interpretation. He selects from the account of Luke one incident as historical which, by its connexion with other unhistorical statements and its conformity to the spirit of the primitive christian legend, is proved to be merely mythical: namely, that Jesus was really born in a shepherd's dwelling. He also borrows an assumption from the natural explanation, which the mythical needs not to obtrude on the text: that the shepherds to whom it is alleged the angels appeared, were the possessors of the manger in which Mary was delivered. The first detail, upon which the second is built, belongs to the same machinery by which Luke, with the help of the census, transported the parents of Jesus from Nazareth to Bethlehem. Now we know what is the fact respecting the census; it crumbles away inevitably before criticism, and with it the datum built entirely upon it, that Jesus was born in a manger. For had not the parents of Jesus been strangers, and had they not come to Bethlehem in company with so large a concourse of strangers as the census might have occasioned, the

* Hebraische Mythologie, 2. Thl. S. 223 ff. † Recension von Bauer's hebr. Mythologie in Gabler's Journal für auserlesene theol. Literatur, 2, 1, S. 58 f. ‡ Neuestes theol. Journal, 7, S. 112 f.

cause which obliged Mary to accept a stable for her place of delivery
would no longer have existed. But, on the other hand, the incident,
that Jesus was born in a stable and saluted in the first instance by
shepherds, is so completely in accordance with the spirit of the ancient legend, that it is evident the narrative may have been derived
purely from this source.   Theophylact, in his time, pointed out its
true character, when he says : the angels did not appear to the
scribes and pharisees of Jerusalem who were full of all malice, but
to the shepherds, in the fields, on account of their simplicity and
innocence, and because they by their mode of life were the successors of the patriarchs.* It was in the field by the flocks that Moses
was visited by a heavenly apparition (Exod. iii. 1 ff.); and God took
David, the forefather of the Messiah, from his sheepfolds (at Bethlehem), to be the shepherd of his people. Psalm lxxviii. 70. (comp.
1 Sam. xvi. 11.).   The mythi of the ancient world more generally
ascribed divine apparitions to countrymen† and shepherds; ‡ the
sons of the gods, and of great men were frequently brought up
among shepherds.§   In the same spirit of the ancient legend is the
apocryphal invention that Jesus was born in a cave, and we are at
once reminded of the cave of Jupiter and of the other gods ; even
though the misunderstood passage of Isaiah xxxiii. 16. may have
been the immediate occasion of this incident.‖ Moreover the night,
in which the scene is laid,—(unless one refers here to the rabbinical
representations, according to which, the deliverance by means of the
Messiah, like the deliverance from Egypt, should take place by
night,¶)—forms the obscure background against which the manifested *glory of the Lord* shone so much the more brilliantly, which,
as it is said to have glorified the birth of Moses,** could not have
been absent from that of the Messiah, his exalted antitype.

The mythical interpretation of this section of the gospel history
has found an opponent in Schleiermacher.†† He thinks it improbable that this commencement of the second chapter of Luke is a
continuation of the first, written by the same author; because the frequent opportunities of introducing lyrical effusions—as for example,
when the shepherds returned glorifying and praising God, v. 20—
are not taken advantage of as in the first chapter; and here indeed we can in some measure agree with him. But when he adds
that a decidedly poetical character cannot be ascribed to this narrative, since a poetical composition would of necessity have contained
more of the lyrical, this only proves that Schleiermacher has not
justly apprehended the notion of that kind of poetry of which he
here treats, namely, the poetry of the mythus. In a word, mythical poetry is objective: the poetical exists in the substance of

---

* In Luc. 2. in Suicer 2, p. 789 f.   † Servius ad Virg. Ecl. 10, 26.   ‡ Liban pro-
gymn. p. 138, in Wetstein, S. 662.   § Thus Cyrus, see Herod. 1, 110 ff.   Romulus, see
Livy, 1, 4.   ‖ Thilo, Codex, Apocr. N. T. 1, S. 383, not.   ¶ Vid. Schöttgen, 2, S. 531.
** Sota, 1, 48 : *Sapientes nostri perhibent, circa horam nativitatis Mosis totam domum
repletam fuisse luce* (Wetstein).   †† Ueber den Lukas, S. 29 f.   With whom Neander
and others now agree.—L. J. Ch., S. 21 f.

the narrative, and may therefore appear in the plainest form, free from all the adornments of lyrical effusions; which latter are rather only the subsequent additions of a more intelligent and artificially elaborated subjective poetry.* Undoubtedly this section seems to have been preserved to us more nearly in its original legendary form, whilst the narratives of the first chapter in Luke bear rather the stamp of having been re-wrought by some poetical individual; but historical truth is not on that account to be sought here any more than there. Consequently the obligation which Schleiermacher further imposes upon himself, to trace out the source of this narrative in the gospel of Luke, can only be regarded as an exercise of ingenuity. He refuses to recognize that source in Mary, though a reference to her might have been found in the observation, v. 19, *she kept all these sayings in her heart;* wherein indeed he is the more right, since that observation (a fact to which Schleiermacher does not advert) is merely a phrase borrowed from the history of Jacob and his son Joseph.† For as the narrative in Genesis relates of Jacob, the father of Joseph, that child of miracle, that, when the latter told his significant dreams, and his brethren envied him, *his father observed the saying:* so the narrative in Luke, both here and at verse 51, relates of Mary, that she, whilst others gave utterance aloud to their admiration at the extraordinary occurrences which happened to her child, *kept all these things and pondered them in her heart.* But the above named theologian points out the shepherds instead of Mary as the source of our narrative, alleging that all the details are given, not from Mary's point of view, but from that of the shepherds. More truly however is the point of view that of the legend which supersedes both. If Schleiermacher finds it impossible to believe that this narrative is an air bubble conglomerated out of *nothing;* he must include under the word *nothing* the Jewish and early christian ideas—concerning Bethlehem, as the necessary birthplace of the Messiah; concerning the condition of the shepherd, as being peculiarly favoured by communications from heaven; concerning angels, as the intermediate agents in such communications—notions, we on our side cannot possibly hold in so little estimation, but we find it easy to conceive that something similar to our narrative might have formed itself out of them. Finally, when he finds an adventitious or designed invention impossible, because the Christians of that district might easily have inquired of Mary or of the disciples concerning the truth of the matter: he speaks too nearly the language of the ancient apologists, and pre-

* Comp. De Wette, Kritik der mosaischen Geschichte, s. 116; George, Mythus u. Sage, s. 33 f.

† Gen. xxxvii. 11 (LXX): Luc. 2, 18 f. Ἐζήλωσαν δὲ αὐτὸν οἱ ἀδελφοὶ αὐτοῦ, ὁ δὲ πατὴρ αὐτοῦ διετήρησε τὸ ῥῆμα.—Schleiermacher, horæ, 1, 262. καὶ πάντες οἱ ἀκούσαντες ἐθαύμασαν. — — ἡ δὲ Μαριὰμ πάντα συνετήρει τὰ ῥήματα ταῦτα, συμβάλλουσα ἐν τῇ καρδίᾳ αὐτῆς. 2, 51: καὶ ἡ μήτηρ αὐτοῦ διετήρει πάντα τὰ ῥήματα ταῦτα ἐν τῇ καρδίᾳ αὐτῆς.

supposes the ubiquity of these persons,* already alluded to in the
Introduction, who however could not possibly have been in all
places rectifying the tendency to form christian legends, wherever
it manifested itself.

The notice of the circumcision of Jesus (Luke ii. 21.), evidently
proceeds from a narrator who had no real advice of the fact, but
who assumed as a certainty that, according to Jewish custom, the
ceremony took place on the eighth day, and who was desirous of
commemorating this important event in the life of an Israelitish
boy :† in like manner as Paul (Phil. iii. 5.) records his circumcision
on the eighth day. The contrast however between the fullness of
detail with which this point is elaborated and coloured in the life of
the Baptist, and the barrenness and brevity with which it is stated
in reference to Jesus, is striking, and may justify an agreement
with the remark of Schleiermacher, that here, at least the author of
the first chapter is no longer the originator. Such being the state
of the case, this statement furnishes nothing for our object, which
we might not already have known; only we have till now had no
opportunity of observing, distinctly, that the pretented appointment
of the name of Jesus before his birth likewise belongs merely to the
mythical dress of the narrative. When it is said *his name was
called Jesus, which was so named of the angel before he was conceived in the womb*, the importance attached to the circumstance is
a clear sign, that a dogmatic interest lies at the bottom of this feature in the narrative; which interest can be no other than that
which gave rise to the statement—in the Old Testament concerning
an Isaac and Ishmael, and in the New Testament concerning a John—
that the names of these children were, respectively, revealed to
their parents prior to their birth, and on account of which interest
the rabbins in particular, expected that the same thing should occur
in relation to the name of the Messiah.‡ Without doubt there were
likewise other far more natural reasons which induced the parents
of Jesus to give him this name (חלבי an abbreviation of יְשִׁיב ὁ Κύριος
σωτηρία;) a name which was very common among his countrymen;
but because this name agreed in a remarkable manner with the path
of life subsequently chosen by him as Messiah and σωτήρ, it was
not thought possible that this coincidence could have been accidental.
Besides it seemed more appropriate that the name of the Messiah
should have been determined by divine command than by human
arbitration, and consequently the appointment of the name was ascribed to the same angel who had announced the conception of
Jesus.

---

* See Introduction.   † Perhaps as a precautionary measure to obviate objections on
the part of the Jews. (Ammon, Fortbildung 1, S. 217.)   ‡ Pirke R. Elieser, 33 : *Sex
hominum nomina dicta sunt, antequam nascerentur : Isaaci nempe, Ismaelis, Mosis, Salo-
monis, Josiæ et nomen regis Messiæ.* Bereschith rabba, sect. 1, fol. 3, 3.—(Schöttgen, horæ, 2, s. 436.) : *Sex res prævenerunt creationem mundi : quædam ex illis creatæ sunt,
nempe lex et thronus gloriæ ; aliæ ascenderunt in cogitationem (Dei) ut crearentur, nimirum Patriarchæ, Israël, templum, et nomen Messiæ.*

§ 34.   THE MAGI AND THEIR STAR—THE FLIGHT INTO EGYPT AND
THE MURDER OF THE CHILDREN IN BETHLEHEM—CRITICISM OF THE
SUPRANATURALISTIC VIEW.

In the Gospel of Matthew also we have a narrative of the Messiah's entrance into the world : it differs considerably in detail from that of Luke, which we have just examined, but in the former part of the two accounts there is a general similarity (Matt. ii. 1 ff.). The object of both narratives is to describe the solemn introduction of the Messianic infant, the heralding of his birth undertaken by heaven itself, and his first reception among men.* In both, attention is called to the new-born Messiah by a celestial phenomenon; according to Luke, it is an angel clothed in brightness, according to Matthew, it is a star.   As the apparitions are different, so accordingly are the recipients; the angel addresses simple shepherds: the star is discovered by eastern magi, who are able to interpret for themselves the voiceless sign.   Both parties are directed to Bethlehem; the shepherds by the words of the angel, the magi by the instructions they obtain in Jerusalem; and both do homage to the infant; the poor shepherds by singing hymns of praise, the magi by costly presents from their native country.   But from this point the two narratives begin to diverge widely.   In Luke all proceeds happily; the shepherds return with gladness in their hearts, the child experiences no molestation, he is presented in the temple on the appointed day, thrives and grows up in tranquillity.   In Matthew, on the contrary, affairs take a tragical turn.   The inquiry of the wise men in Jerusalem concerning the new-born King of the Jews, is the occasion of a murderous decree on the part of Herod against the children of Bethlehem, a danger from which the infant Jesus is rescued only by a sudden flight into Egypt, whence he and his parents do not return to the Holy Land till after the death of Herod.

Thus we have here a double proclamation of the Messianic child: we might, however, suppose that the one by the angel, in Luke, would announce the birth of the Messiah to the immediate neighbourhood ; the other, by means of the star, to distant lands.   But as according to Matthew, the birth of Jesus became known at Jerusalem, which was in the immediate vicinity, by means of the star; if this representation be historical, that of Luke, according to which the shepherds were the first to spread abroad with praises to God (v. 17, 20.), that which had been communicated to them as glad tidings for all people (v. 10.), cannot possibly be correct.   So, on the other hand, if it be true that the birth of Jesus was made known in the neighbourhood of Bethlehem as Luke states, by an angelic communication to the shepherds, Matthew must be in error when he represents the first intelligence of the event as subsequently brought to Jerusalem (which is only from two to three hours distant from Bethlehem) by the magi.   But as we have recognized many indications of the unhistorical character of the announcement by the

* Comp. Schneckenburger, über den Ursprung des ersten kanonischen Evangeliums, s. 69 ff.

shepherds given in Luke, the ground is left clear for that of Matthew, which must be judged of according to its inherent credibility.

Our narrative commences as if it were an admitted fact, that astrologers possessed the power of recognizing a star announcing the birth of the Messiah. That eastern magi should have knowledge of a King of the Jews to whom they owed religious homage might indeed excite our surprise; but contenting ourselves here with remarking, that seventy years later an expectation did prevail in the east that a ruler of the world would arise from among the Jewish people,* we pass on to a yet more weighty difficulty. According to this narrative it appears, that astrology is right when it asserts that the birth of great men and important revolutions in human affairs are indicated by astral phenomena; an opinion long since consigned to the region of superstition. It is therefore to be explained, how this deceptive science could in this solitary instance prove true, though in no other case are its inferences to be relied on. The most obvious explanation, from the orthodox point of view, is an appeal to the supernatural intervention of God: who, in this particular instance, in order to bring the distant magi unto Jesus, accommodated himself to their astrological notions, and caused the anticipated star to appear. But the adoption of this expedient involves very serious consequences. For the coincidence of the remarkable sequel with the astrological prognostic could not fail to strengthen the belief, not only of the magi and their fellow-countrymen, but also of the Jews and Christians who were acquainted with the circumstances, in the spurious science of astrology, thereby creating incalculable error and mischief. If therefore it be unadvisable to admit an extraordinary divine intervention,† and if the position that in the ordinary course of nature, important occurrences on this earth are attended by changes in the heavenly bodies, be abandoned, the only remaining explanation lies in the supposition of an accidental coincidence. But to appeal to chance is in fact either to say nothing, or to renounce the supranaturalistic point of view.

But the orthodox view of this account not only sanctions the false science of astrology, but also confirms the false interpretation of a passage in the prophets. For as the magi, following their star, proceed in the right direction, so the chief priests and scribes of Jerusalem whom Herod, on learning the arrival and object of the magi, summons before him and questions concerning the birth-place of the King of the Jews, interpret the passage in Micah v. 1. as signifying that the Messiah should be born in Bethlehem; and to this signification the event corresponds. Now such an application of the above

---

* Joseph. B. J. vi. vi. 4 : Tacit. Histor. v. 13; Sueton. Vespas. 4. All the extant allusions to the existence of such a hope at the era of Christ's birth, relate only in an indeterminate manner to a ruler of the world. Virg. Eclog. 4; Sueton. Octav. 94. † In saying that it is inadmissible to suppose a divine intervention directly tending to countenance superstition, I refer to what is called *immediate* intervention. In the doctrine of *mediate* intervention, which includes the co-operation of man, there is doubtless a mixture of truth and error, Neander confuses the two. L. J. Ch. S. 29.

passage can only be made by forcing the words from their true meaning and from all relation with the context, according to the well-known practice of the rabbins. For independently of the question whether or not under the word בֵּית in the passage cited, the Messiah be intended, the entire context shows the meaning to be, not that the expected governor who was to come forth out of Bethlehem would actually be born in that city, but only that he would be a descendant of David, whose family sprang from Bethlehem.[*] Thus allowing the magi to have been rightly directed by means of the rabbinical exegesis of the oracle, a false interpretation must have hit on the truth, either by means of divine intervention and accommodation, or by accident. The judgment pronounced in the case of the star is applicable here also.

After receiving the above answer from the Sanhedrim, Herod summons the magi before him, and his first question concerns the time at which the star appeared (v. 7.). Why did he wish to know this?[†] The 16th verse tells us; that he might thereby calculate the age of the Messianic child, and thus ascertain up to what age it would be necessary for him to put to death the children of Bethlehem, so as not to miss the one announced by the star. But this plan of murdering all the children of Bethlehem up to a certain age, that he might destroy the one likely to prove fatal to the interests of his family, was not conceived by Herod until after the magi had disappointed his expectation that they would return to Jerusalem: a deception which, if we may judge from his violent anger on account of it (v. 16) Herod had by no means anticipated. Prior to this, according to v. 8, it had been his intention to obtain from the magi, on their return, so close a description of the child, his dwelling and circumstances, that it would be easy for him to remove his infantine rival without sacrificing any other life. It was not until he had discovered the stratagem of the magi, that he was obliged to have recourse to the more violent measure for the execution of which it was necessary for him to know the time of the star's appearance.[‡] How fortunate for him, then, that he had ascertained this time before he had decided on the plan that made the information important; but how inconceivable that he should make a point which was only indirectly connected with his original project, the subject of his first and most eager interrogation (v. 7.)!

Herod, in the second place, commissions the magi to acquaint themselves accurately with all that concerns the royal infant, and to impart their knowledge to him on their return, that he also may go and tender his homage to the child, that is, according to his real meaning, take sure measures for putting him to death (v. 8.). Such a proceeding on the part of an astute monarch like Herod has long been held improbable.* Even if he hoped to deceive the magi, while in conference with them, by adopting this friendly mask, he must necessarily foresee that others would presently awaken them to the probability that he harboured evil designs against the child, and thus prevent them from returning according to his injunction. He might conjecture that the parents of the child on hearing of the ominous interest taken in him by the king, would seek his safety by flight, and finally, that those inhabitants of Bethlehem and its environs who cherished Messianic expectations, would be not a little confirmed in them by the arrival of the magi. On all these grounds, Herod's only prudent measure would have been either to detain the magi in Jerusalem,† and in the meantime by means of secret emissaries to dispatch the child to whom such peculiar hopes were attached, and who must have been easy of discovery in the little village of Bethlehem : or to have given the magi companions who, so soon as the child was found, might at once have put an end to his existence. Even Olshausen thinks that these strictures are not groundless, and his best defence against them is the observation that the histories of all ages present unaccountable instances of forgetfulness—a proof that the course of human events is guided by a supreme hand. When the supernaturalist invokes the supreme hand in the case before us, he must suppose that God himself blinded Herod to the surest means of attaining his object, in order to save the Messianic child from a premature death. But the other side of this divine contrivance is, that instead of the one child, many others must die. There would be nothing to object against such a substitution in this particular case, if it could be proved that there was no other possible mode of rescuing Jesus from a fate inconsistent with the scheme of human redemption. But if it be once admitted, that God interposed supernaturally to blind the mind of Herod and to suggest to the magi that they should not return to Jerusalem, we are constrained to ask, why did not God in the first instance inspire the magi to shun Jerusalem and proceed directly to Bethlehem, whither Herod's attention would not then have been so immediately attracted, and thus the disastrous sequel perhaps have been altogether avoided ?‡ The supranaturalist has no answer to this question but the old-fashioned argument that it was good for the infants to die, because they were thus freed by transient suffering from much misery, and more especially from the danger of sinning against Jesus with the unbelieving Jews ; whereas now they had the honour of losing their lives for the sake of Jesus, and thus of ranking as martyrs, and so forth.§

* K. Ch. L. Schmidt, exeg. Beiträge, 1, S. 150 f. Comp. Fritzsche and De Wette in loc.   † Hoffmann thinks that Herod shunned this measure as a breach of hospitality; yet this very Herod he represents as a monster of cruelty, and that justly, for the conduct attributed to the monarch in chap. ii. of Matth. is not unworthy of his heart, against which Neander superfluously argues (p. 30 f.), but of his head.   ‡ Schmidt, ut sup. p. 155 f. § Stark, Synops. bibl. exeg. in N. T. p. 62.

The magi leave Jerusalem by night, the favourite time for travelling in the east. The star, which they seem to have lost sight of since their departure from home, again appears and goes before them on the road to Bethlehem, until at length it remains stationary over the house that contains the wondrous child and its parents. The way from Jerusalem to Bethlehem lies southward: now the true path of erratic stars is either from west to east, as that of the planets and of some comets, or from east to west, as that of other comets; the orbits of many comets do indeed tend from north to south, but the true motion of all these bodies is so greatly surpassed by their apparent motion from east to west produced by the rotation of the earth on its axis, that it is imperceptible except at considerable intervals. Even the diurnal movement of the heavenly bodies, however, is less obvious on a short journey than the merely optical one, arising from the observer's own change of place, in consequence of which a star that he sees before him seems, as long as he moves forward, to pass on in the same direction through infinite space; it cannot therefore stand still over a particular house and thus induce a traveller to halt there also: on the contrary, the traveller himself must halt before the star will appear stationary. The star of the magi could not then be an ordinary, natural star, but must have been one created by God for that particular exigency, and impressed by him with a peculiar law of motion and rest.* Again, this could not have been a true star, moving among the systems of our firmament, for such an one, however impelled and arrested, could never, according to optical laws, appear to pause over a particular house. It must therefore have been something lower, hovering over the earth's surface: hence some of the Fathers and apocryphal writers† supposed it to have been an angel, which, doubtless, might fly before the magi in the form of a star, and take its station at a moderate height above the house of Mary in Bethlehem: more modern theologians have conjectured that the phenomenon was a meteor.‡ Both these explanations are opposed to the text of Matthew: the former, because it is out of keeping with the style of our Gospels to designate any thing purely supernatural, such as an angelic appearance, by an expression that implies a merely natural object, as ἀστήρ (a star): the latter, because a mere meteor would not last for so long a time as must have elapsed between the departure of the magi from their remote home and their arrival in Bethlehem. Perhaps, however, it will be contended that God created one meteor for the first monition, and another for the second.

Many, even of the orthodox expositors, have found these difficulties in relation to the star so pressing, that they have striven to escape at any cost from the admission that it preceded the magi in their way towards Bethlehem, and took its station directly over a

---

* This was the opinion of some of the Fathers, e. g. Euseb. Demonstr. evang. 9, ap. Suicer, 1, S. 559; Joann. Damasc, de fide orthod. ii. 7.   † Chrysostomus and others ap. Suicer, ut sup. and the Evang. infant. arab. c. vii.   ‡ See Kuinol, Comm. in Matth. p. 23.

11

particular house. According to Süskind, whose explanation has been much approved, the verb προῆγεν (*went before*) (v. 9) which is in the imperfect tense, does not signify that the star visibly led the magi on their way, but is equivalent to the pluperfect, which would imply that the star had been invisibly transferred to the destination of the magi before their arrival, so that the Evangelist intends to say: the star which the magi had seen in the east and subsequently lost sight of, suddenly made its appearance to them in Bethlehem above the house they were seeking; it had therefore preceded them.* But this is a transplantation of rationalistic artifice into the soil of orthodox exegesis. Not only the word προῆγεν, but the less flexible expressions ἕως ἐλθὼν κ. τ. λ. (*till it came*, &c.) denotes that the transit of the star was not an already completed phenomenon, but one brought to pass under the observation of the magi. Expositors who persist in denying this must, to be consistent, go still farther, and reduce the entire narrative to the standard of merely natural events. So when Olshausen admits that the position of a star could not possibly indicate a single house, that hence the magi must have inquired for the infant's dwelling, and only with child-like simplicity referred the issue as well as the commencement of their journey to a heavenly guide :† he deserts his own point of view for that of the rationalists, and interlines the text with explanatory particulars, an expedient which he elsewhere justly condemns in Paulus and others.

The magi then enter the house, offer their adoration to the infant, and present to him gifts, the productions of their native country. One might wonder that there is no notice of the astonishment which it must have excited in these men to find, instead of the expected prince, a child in quite ordinary, perhaps indigent circumstances. ‡ It is not fair, however, to heighten the contrast by supposing, according to the common notion, that the magi discovered the child in a stable lying in the manger; for this representation is peculiar to Luke, and is altogether unknown to Matthew, who merely speaks of a *house*, οἰκία, in which the child was found. Then follows (v. 10.) the warning given to the magi in a dream, concerning which, as before remarked, it were only to be wished that it had been vouchsafed earlier, so as to avert the steps of the magi from Jerusalem, and thus perchance prevent the whole subsequent massacre.

While Herod awaits the return of the magi, Joseph is admonished by an angelic apparition in a dream to flee with the Messianic child and its mother into Egypt for security (v. 13—15.). Adopting the evangelist's point of view, this is not attended with any difficulty: it is otherwise, however, with the prophecy which the above event is said to fulfil, Hosea xi. 1. In this passage the prophet, speaking in the name of Jehovah, says : *When Israel was a child, then I loved him, and called my son out of Egypt.* We may venture to attribute, even to the most orthodox expositor,

---

* Vermischte Aufsätze, S. 8.   † Bibl. Comm. in loc. Hoffmann, S. 261.   ‡ Schmidt, exeg. Beiträge, I, 152 ff.

enough clear-sightedness to perceive that the subject of the first half of the sentence is also the object of the second, namely the people of Israel, who here, as elsewhere, (e. g. Exod. iv. 22. Sirach xxxvi, 14.) are collectively called the Son of God, and whose past deliverance under Moses out of their Egyptian bondage is the fact referred to : that consequently, the prophet was not contemplating either the Messiah or his sojourn in Egypt. Nevertheless as our evangelist says, v. 15. that the flight of Jesus into Egypt took place expressly that the above words of Hosea might be fulfilled, he must have understood them as a prophecy relating to Christ—must, therefore, have misunderstood them. It has been pretended that the passage has a twofold application, and, though referring primarily to the Israelitish people, is not the less a prophecy relative to Christ, because the destiny of Israel "after the flesh" was a type of the destiny of Jesus. But this convenient method of interpretation is not applicable here, for the analogy would, in the present case, be altogether external and inane, since the only parallel consists in the bare fact in both instances of a sojourn in Egypt, the circumstances under which the Israelitish people and the child Jesus sojourned there being altogether diverse.*

When the return of the magi has been delayed long enough for Herod to become aware that they have no intention to keep faith with him, he decrees the death of all the male children in Bethlehem and its environs up to the age of two years, that being, according to the statements of the magi as to the time of the star's appearance, the utmost interval that could have elapsed since the birth of the Messianic child. (16—18.) This was, beyond all question, an act of the blindest fury, for Herod might easily have informed himself whether a child who had received rare and costly presents was yet to be found in Bethlehem: but even granting it not inconsistent with the disposition of the aged tyrant to the extent that Schleiermacher supposed, it were in any case to be expected that so unprecedented and revolting a massacre would be noticed by other historians than Matthew.† But neither Josephus, who is very minute in his account of Herod, nor the rabbins, who were assiduous in blackening his memory, give the slightest hint of this decree. The latter do, indeed, connect the flight of Jesus into Egypt with a murderous scene, the author of which, however, is not Herod but King Jannæus, and the victims not children, but rabbins.‡ Their story is evidently founded on a confusion of the occurrence gathered from the Christian history, with an earlier event; for Alexander Jannæus died 40 years before the birth of Christ. Macrobius, who lived in the fourth century, is the only author who notices the slaughter of the infants, and he introduces it obliquely in a passage which loses all credit by confounding the execution of Antipater, who was so far from a child that he complained of his grey hairs,[*] with the murder of the infants, renowned among the Christians.[†] Commentators have attempted to diminish our surprise at the remarkable silence in question, by reminding us that the number of children of the given age in the petty village of Bethlehem, must have been small, and by remarking that among the numerous deeds of cruelty by which the life of Herod was stained, this one would be lost sight of as a drop in the ocean.[‡] But in these observations the specific atrocity of murdering innocent children, however few, is overlooked; and it is this that must have prevented the deed, if really perpetrated, from being forgotten.[§] Here also the evangelist cites (v. 17, 18) a prophetic passage (Jerem. xxxi. 15), as having been fulfilled by the murder of the infants; whereas it originally referred to something quite different, namely the transportation of the Jews to Babylon, and had no kind of reference to an event lying in remote futurity.

While Jesus and his parents are in Egypt, Herod the Great dies, and Joseph is instructed by an angel, who appears to him in a dream, to return to his native country; but as Archelaus, Herod's successor in Judæa, was to be feared, he has more precise directions in a second oracular dream, in obedience to which he fixes his abode at Nazareth in Galilee, under the milder government of Herod Antipas. (19—23.) Thus in the compass of this single chapter, we have five extraordinary interpositions of God; an anomalous star, and four visions. For the star and the first vision, we have already remarked, one miracle might have been substituted, not only without detriment, but with advantage; either the star or the vision might from the beginning have deterred the magi from going to Jerusalem, and by this means perhaps have averted the massacre ordained by Herod. But that the two last visions are not united in one is a mere superfluity; for the direction to Joseph to proceed to Nazareth instead of Bethlehem, which is made the object of a special vision, might just as well have been included in the first. Such a disregard, even to prodigality, of the *lex parsimoniæ* in relation to the miraculous, one is tempted to refer to human imagination rather than to divine providence.

The false interpretations of Old Testament passa⬤ in this chapter are crowned by the last verse, where it is said that by the settlement of the parents of Jesus at Nazareth was fulfilled the saying of the prophets: *He shall be called a Nazarene.* Now this passage is not to be found in the Old Testament, and unless expositors, losing courage, take refuge in darkness by supposing that it is extracted from a canonical[‖] or apocryphal[¶] book now lost, they must

* Joseph. B. j. I. xxx. 3. Comp. Antiq. xvii. iv. 1.   † Macrob. Saturnal. ii. 4 : *Quum audisset (Augustus) inter pueros, quos in Syria Herodes rex Judæorum intra bimatum jussit interfici, filium quoque ejus occisum, ait: melius est, Herodis porcum (ὑν) esse quam filium (υἱόν),*   ‡ Vid. Wetstein, Kuinöl, Olshausen in loc. Winer d. A. Herodes. § Fritzsche, Comm. in Matt. p. 93 f.   ‖ Chrysostom and others.   ¶ Vid. Gratz, Comm. zum Ev. Matth. 1, S. 115.

admit the conditional validity of one or other of the following charges against the evangelist. If, as it has been alleged, he intended to compress the Old Testament prophecies that the Messiah would be despised, into the oracular sentence, He shall be called a Nazarene, i. e. the citizen of a despised city,[*] we must accuse him of the most arbitrary mode of expression ; or, if he be supposed to give a modification of נָזִיר (*nasir*) we must tax him with the most violent transformation of the word and the grossest perversion of its meaning, for even if, contrary to the fact, this epithet were applied to the Messiah in the Old Testament, it could only mean either that he would be a Nazarite,[†] which Jesus never was, or that he would be crowned,[‡] as Joseph Gen. xlix. 26, in no case that he would be brought up in the petty town of Nazareth. The most probable interpretation of this passage, and that which has the sanction of the Jewish Christians questioned on the subject by Jerome, is, that the evangelist here alludes to Isa. xi. 1, where the Messiah is called נֵצֶר יִשַׁי (*surculus Jesse*) as elsewhere נֵצֶר.[§] But in every case there is the same violence done to the word by attaching to a mere appellative of the Messiah, an entirely fictitious relation to the name of the city of Nazareth.

§ 35. ATTEMPTS AT A NATURAL EXPLANATION OF THE HISTORY OF THE MAGI—TRANSITION TO THE MYTHICAL EXPLANATION.

To avoid the many difficulties which beset us at every step in interpreting this chapter after the manner of the supranaturalists, it is quite worth our while to seek for another exposition which may suffice to explain the whole according to physical and psychological laws, without any admixture of supranaturalism. Such an exposition has been the most successfully attempted by Paulus.

How could heathen magi, in a remote country of the east, know any thing of a Jewish king about to be born ? This is the first difficulty, and it is removed on the above system of interpretation by supposing that the magi were expatriated Jews. But this, apparently, is not the idea of the evangelist. For the question which he puts into the mouth of the magi, " *Where is he that is born King of the Jews?*" distinguishes them from that people, and as regards the tendency of the entire narrative, the church seems to have apprehended it more correctly than Paulus thinks, in representing the visit of the magi as the first manifestation of Christ to the Gentiles. Nevertheless, as we have above remarked, this difficulty may be cleared away without having recourse to the supposition of Paulus.

Further, according to the natural explanation, the real object of the journey of these men was not to see the new-born king, nor was its cause the star which they had observed in the east ; but they

* Kuinöl, ad Matth. p. 44 f. † Wetstein, in loc. ‡ Schneckenburger, Beitrage zur Einleitung in das N. T. S. 12. § Gieseler, Studien und Kritiken, 1831, 3. Heft, S.588 f. Fritzsche S. 104. Comp. Hieron. ad Jesai. XI. 1.

happened to be travelling to Jerusalem perhaps with mercantile views, and hearing far and wide in the land of a new-born king, a celestial phenomenon which they had recently observed occured to their remembrance, and they earnestly desired to see the child in question. By this means, it is true, the difficulty arising from the sanction given to astrology by the usual conception of the story is diminished, but only at the expense of unprejudiced interpretation. For even if it were admissible unceremoniously to transform magi μαγοὺς into merchants, their purpose in this journey cannot have been a commercial one, for their first inquiry on arriving at Jerusalem is after the new-born king, and they forthwith mention a star, seen by them in the east, as the cause not only of their question, but also of their present journey, the object of which they aver to be the presentation of their homage to the new-born child. (v. 2.)

The ἀστὴρ (star) becomes, on this method of interpretation, a natural meteor, or a comet,* or finally, a constellation, that is, a conjunction of planets.† The last idea was put forth by Kepler, and has been approved by several astronomers and theologians. Is it more easy, on any one of these suppositions, to conceive that the star could precede the magi on their way, and remain stationary over a particular house, according to the representation of the text? We have already examined the two first hypotheses; if we adopt the third, we must either suppose the verb προάγειν (v. 9) to signify the disjunction of the planets, previously in apparent union,‡ though the text does not imply a partition but a forward movement of the entire phenomenon; or we must call Süskind's pluperfect to our aid, and imagine that the constellation, which the magi could no longer see in the valley between Jerusalem and Bethlehem, again burst on their view over the place where the child dwelt.§ For the expression, ἐπάνω οὗ ἦν τὸ παιδίον (v. 9.), denotes merely the place of abode, not the particular dwelling of the child and his parents. This we grant; but when the evangelist proceeds thus: καὶ εἰσελθόντες εἰς τὴν οἰκίαν, (v. 9,) he gives the more general expression the precise meaning of dwelling-house, so that this explanation is clearly a vain effort to abate the marvellousness of the evangelical narrative.

The most remarkable supposition adopted by those who regard ἀστὴρ as a conjunction of planets, is that they had hereby obtain a fixed point in accredited history, to which the narrative of Matthew may be attached. According to Kepler's calculation, corrected by Ideler, there occurred, three years before the death of Herod, in the year of Rome 747, a conjunction of Jupiter and Saturn in the sign Pisces. The conjunction of these planets is repeated in the above sign, to which astrologers attribute a special relation to Palestine, about every 800 years, and according to the computation of the Jew Abarbanel (1463) it took place three years before the birth of

---

* For both these explanations, see Kuinöl, in loc. † Kepler, in various treatises; Münster, der Stern der Weisen; Ideler, Handbuch der mathem. und technischen Chronologie, 2. Bd. S. 399 ff. ‡ Olshausen, S. 67. § Paulus, ut sup. S. 202, 221.

Moses; hence it is probable enough that the hope of the second great deliverer of the nation would be associated with the recurrence of this conjunction in the time of Herod, and that when the phenomenon was actually observed, it would occasion inquiry on the part of Babylonian Jews. But that the star mentioned by Matthew was this particular planetary conjunction, is, from our uncertainty as to the year of Christ's birth, and also as to the period of the above astrological calculation, an extremely precarious conjecture; and as, besides, there are certain particulars in the evangelical text, for instance, the words προῆγεν and ἔστη, which do not accord with such an explanation,—so soon as another, more congruous with Matthew's narrative, presents itself, we are justified in giving it the preference.

The difficulties connected with the erroneous interpretations of passages from the Old Testament are, from the natural point of view, eluded by denying that the writers of the New Testament are responsible for the falsity of these interpretations. It is said that the prophecy of Micah is applied to the Messiah and his birth in Bethlehem by the Sanhedrim alone, and that Matthew has not committed himself to their interpretation by one word of approval. But when the evangelist proceeds to narrate how the issue corresponded with the interpretation, he sanctions it by the authoritative seal of fact. In relation to the passage from Hosea, Paulus and Steudel[*] concur in resorting to a singular expedient. Matthew, say they, wished to guard against the offence which it might possibly give to the Jews of Palestine to learn that the Messiah had once left the Holy Land; he therefore called attention to the fact that Israel, in one sense the first-born of God, had been called out of Egypt, for which reason, he would imply, no one ought to be astonished that the Messiah, the son of God in a higher sense, had also visited a profane land. But throughout the passage there is no trace[†] of such a negative, precautionary intention on the part of the evangelist in adducing this prophecy; on the contrary, all his quotations seem to have the positive object to confirm the Messiahship of Jesus by showing that in him the Old Testament prophecies had their fulfilment. It has been attempted with reference to the two other prophecies cited in this chapter, to reduce the signification of the verb πληρωθῆναι (to be fulfilled) to that of mere similitude or applicability; but the futility of the effort needs no exposure.

The various directions conveyed to the persons of our narrative by means of visions are, from the same point of view, all explained psychologically, as effects of waking inquiries and reflections. This appears, indeed, to be indicated by the text itself, v. 22, according to which Joseph, hearing that Archelaus was master of Judea, feared to go thither, and not until then did he receive an intimation from

* Bengel's Archiv, vii. ii. p. 424.   † At a later period, it is true, this journey of Jesus was the occasion of calumnies from the Jews, but those were of an entirely different nature, as will be seen in the following chapter.

a higher source in a dream. Nevertheless, on a closer examination we find that the communication given in the dream was something new, not a mere repetition of intelligence received in waking moments. Only a negative conclusion, that on account of Archelaus it was not advisable to settle at Bethlehem, was attained by Joseph when awake; the positive injunction to proceed to Nazareth was superadded in his dream. To explain the other visions in the above way is a direct interpolation of the text, for this represents both the hostility and death of Herod as being first made known to Joseph by dreams; in like manner, the magi have no distrust of Herod until a dream warns them against his treachery.

Thus, on the one hand, the sense of the narrative in Matt. ii. is opposed to the conception of its occurrence as natural: on the other hand, this narrative, taken in its original sense, carries the supernatural into the extravagant, the improbable into the impossible. We are therefore led to doubt the historical character of the narrative, and to conjecture that we have before us something mythical. The first propounders of this opinion were so unsuccessful in its illustration, that they never liberated themselves from the sphere of the natural interpretation, which they sought to transcend. Arabian merchants (thinks Krug, for example) coming by chance to Bethlehem, met with the parents of Jesus, and learning that they were strangers in distress, (according to Matthew the parents of Jesus were not strangers in Bethlehem,) made them presents, uttered many good wishes for their child, and pursued their journey. When subsequently, Jesus was reputed to be the Messiah, the incident was remembered and embellished with a star, visions, and believing homage. To these were added the flight into Egypt and the infanticide; the latter, because the above incident was supposed to have had some effect on Herod, who, on other grounds than those alleged in the text, had caused some families in Bethlehem to be put to death; the former, probably because Jesus had with some unknown object, actually visited Egypt at a later period.[*]

In this as in the purely naturalistic interpretation, there remain as so many garb, the arrival of some oriental travellers, the flight into Egypt, and the massacre in Bethlehem; divested, however, of the marvellous garb with which they are enveloped in the evangelical narrative. In this unadorned form, these occurrences are held to be intelligible and such as might very probably happen, but in point of fact they are more incomprehensible even than when viewed through the medium of orthodoxy, for with their supernatural embellishments vanishes the entire basis on which they rest. Matthew's narrative adequately accounts for the relations between the men of the east and the parents of Jesus; this attempt at mythical exposition reduces them to a wonderful chance. The massacre at

* Ueber formelle oder Genetische Erklärungen der Wunder. In Henke's Museum, 1, 3, 399 ff. Similar essays see in the Abhandlungen über die beiden ersten Kapitel des Matthäus und Lukas, in Henke's Magazin, 5, 1, 171 ff., and in Matthäi, Religionsgl. der Apostel, 2, S. 422 ff.

Bethlehem has, in the evangelical narrative, a definite cause; here, we are at a loss to understand how Herod came to ordain such an enormity; so, the journey into Egypt which had so urgent a motive according to Matthew, is on this scheme of interpretation, totally inexplicable. It may indeed be said: these events had their adequate causes in accordance with the regular course of things, but Matthew has withheld this natural sequence and given a miraculous one in its stead. But if the writer or legend be capable of environing occurrences with fictitious motives and accessory circumstances, either the one or the other is also capable of fabricating the occurrences themselves, and this fabrication is the more probable, the more clearly we can show that the legend had an interest in depicting such occurrences, though they had never actually taken place.

This argument is equally valid against the attempt, lately made from the supranaturalistic point of view, to separate the true from the false in the evangelical narrative. In a narrative like this, says Neander, we must carefully distinguish the kernel from the shell, the main fact from immaterial circumstances, and not demand the same degree of certitude for all its particulars. That the magi by their astrological researches were led to anticipate the birth of a Saviour in Judea, and hence journeyed to Jerusalem that they might offer him their homage, is, according to him, the only essential and certain part of the narrative. But how, when arrived in Jerusalem, did they learn that the child was to be born in Bethlehem? From Herod, or by some other means? On this point Neander is not equally willing to guarantee the veracity of Matthew's statements, and he regards it as unessential. The magi, he continues, in so inconsiderable a place as Bethlehem, might be guided to the child's dwelling by many providential arrangements in the ordinary course of events; for example, by meeting with the shepherds or other devout persons who had participated in the great event. When however they had once entered the house, they might represent the circumstances in the astrological guise with which their minds were the most familiar. Neander awards an historical character to the flight into Egypt and the infanticide.* By this explanation of the narrative, only its heaviest difficulty, namely, that the star preceded the magi on their way and paused above a single house, is in reality thrown overboard; the other difficulties remain. But Neander has renounced unlimited confidence in the veracity of the evangelist, and admitted that a part of his narrative is unhistorical. If it be asked how far this unhistorical portion extends, and what is its kind—whether the nucleus around which legend has deposited its crystallizations be historical or ideal,—it is easy to show that the few and vague data which a less lenient criticism than that of Neander can admit as historical, are far less adapted to give birth to our narrative, than the very precise circle of ideas and types which we are about to exhibit.

* L. J. Ch. s. 29 ff.

§. 36. THE PURELY MYTHICAL EXPLANATION OF THE NARRATIVE
CONCERNING THE MAGI, AND OF THE EVENTS WITH WHICH IT IS
CONNECTED.

SEVERAL Fathers of the Church indicated the true key to the
narrative concerning the magi when, in order to explain from what
source those heathen astrologers could gather any knowledge of a
Messianic star, they put forth the conjecture that this knowledge
might have been drawn from the prophecies of the heathen Balaam,
recorded in the Book of Numbers.*   K. Ch. L. Schmidt justly
considers it a deficiency in the exposition of Paulus, that it takes
no notice of the Jewish expectation that a star would become visible
at the appearance of the Messiah; and yet, he adds, this is the only
thread to guide us to the true origin of this narrative.†   The prophecy of Balaam (Num. xxiv. 17.) *A star shall come out of Jacob*,
was the cause—not indeed, as the Fathers supposed, that magi
actually recognized a newly-kindled star as that of the Messiah, and
hence journeyed to Jerusalem,—but that legend represented a star
to have appeared at the birth of Jesus, and to have been recognized
by astrologers as the star of the Messiah.   The prophecy attributed
to Balaam originally referred to some fortunate and victorious ruler
of Israel; but it seems to have early received a Messianic interpretation.   Even if the translation in the Targum of Onkelos, *surget
rex ex Jacobo, et Messias (unctus) ungetur ex Israele*, prove nothing, because here the word *unctus* is synonymous with *rex*, and might
signify an ordinary king,—it is yet worthy of notice that, according to the testimony of Aben Ezra‡ and the passages cited by
Wetstein and Schoettgen, many rabbins applied the prophecy to
the Messiah.   The name Bar-Cocheba (*son of a star*), assumed by
a noted pseudo-Messiah under Hadran, was chosen with reference
to the Messianic interpretation of Balaam's prophecy.

It is true that the passage in question, taken in its original
sense, does not speak of a real star, but merely compares to a star
the future prince of Israel, and this is the interpretation given to it
in the Targum above quoted.   But the growing belief in astrology,
according to which every important event was signalized by sidereal
changes, soon caused the prophecy of Balaam to be understood no
longer figuratively, but literally, as referring to a star which was to
appear contemporaneously with the Messiah.   We have various proofs
that a belief in astrology was prevalent in the time of Jesus.   The
future greatness of Mithridates was thought to be prognosticated by
the appearance of a comet in the year of his birth, and in that of
his accession to the throne ;§ and a comet observed shortly after the
death of Julius Cæsar, was supposed to have a close relation to that
event.‖   These ideas were not without influence on the Jews ; at

* Orig. c. Cels. i. 60.   Auctor, op. imperf. in Matth. ap. Fabricius Pseudepigr. V,
T. p. 807 ff.   † Schmidt's Bibliothek, 3, 1, S. 130.   ‡ In loc. Num. (Schöttgen, horæ,
ii. p. 152): *Multi interpretati sunt hæc de Messia.*   § Justin. Hist. 37.   ‖ Sueton. Jul.
Cæs. 88.

least we find traces of them in Jewish writings of a later period, in which it is said that a remarkable star appeared at the birth of Abraham.* When such ideas were afloat, it was easy to imagine that the birth of the Messiah must be announced by a star, especially as, according to the common interpretation of Balaam's prophecy, a star was there made the symbol of the Messiah. It is certain that the Jewish mind effected this combination; for it is a rabbinical idea that at the time of the Messiah's birth, a star will appear in the east and remain for a long time visible.† The narrative of Matthew is allied to this simpler Jewish idea; the apocryphal descriptions of the star that announced the birth of Jesus, to the extravagant fictions about the star said to have appeared in the time of Abraham.‡ We may therefore state the opinion of K. Ch. L. Schmidt,§ recently approved by Fritzsche and De Wette, as the nearest approach to truth on the subject of Matthew's star in the east. In the time of Jesus it was the general belief that stars were always the forerunners of great events: hence the Jews of that period thought that the birth of the Messiah would necessarily be announced by a star, and this supposition had a specific sanction in Num. xxiv. 17. The early converted Jewish Christians could confirm their faith in Jesus, and justify it in the eyes of others, only by labouring to prove that in him were realized all the attributes lent to the Messiah by the Jewish notions of their age—a proposition that might be urged the more inoffensively and with the less chance of refutation, the more remote lay the age of Jesus, and the more completely the history of his childhood was shrouded in darkness. Hence it soon ceased to be matter of doubt that the anticipated appearance of a star was really coincident with the birth of Jesus.‖ This being once presupposed, it followed as a matter of course that the observers of this appearance were eastern magi; first, because none could better interpret the sign than astrologers, and the east was supposed to be the native region of their science; and secondly, because it must have seemed fitting that the Messianic star which had been seen by the spiritual eye of the ancient magus Ba-

---

* Jalkut Rubeni, f. xxxii, 3 (ap. Wetstein): *qua hora natus est Abrahamus, pater noster, super quem sit pax, stetit quoddam sidus in oriente et deglutirit quatuor astra, quae erant in quatuor cœli plagis.* According to an Arabic writing entitled Maallem, this star, prognosticating the birth of Abraham, was seen by Nimrod in a dream. Fabric. Cod. pseudepigr. V. T. i. S. 345. † Testamentum XII Patriarcharum, test. Levi, 18 (Fabric. Cod. pseud. V. T. p. 581 f.): καὶ ἀνατελεῖ ἄστρον αὐτοῦ (of the Messianic Ιερευς καιτὸς) ἐν οὐρανῷ—φωτίζον φῶς γνωσεως κ. τ. λ. Pesikta Sotarta f. xlviii. 1 (ap. Schottgen ii. p. 531): *Et prodibit stella ab oriente, quae est stella Messiae, et in oriente versabitur dies XV.* Comp. Sohar Genes. f. 74, Schottgen ii. 524, and some other passages which are pointed out by Ideler in the Handbuch der Chronologie, 2 Bd. S. 409, Anm. 1. and Bertholdt, Christologia Judæorum, § 11. ‡ Compare with the passages cited Note 7. Protevang. Jac. cap. xxi.: *εἴδομεν ἀστερα παμμεγίθη, λαμψαντα ἐν τοῖς ἀστροις τούτοις καὶ ἀμβλύνοντα αὐτους τον φαινειν.* Still more exaggerated in Ignat. ep. ad. Ephes. 19. See the collection of passages connected with this subject in Thilo, cod. apocr. i. p. 390 f.

§ Exeg. Beitrage i. S. 159 ff. ‖ Fritzsche in the paraphrase of chap. ii. *Etiam stella, quam judaica disciplina sub Messiae natale risum iri dicit, quo Jesus nascebatur tempore exorta est.*

laam, should, on its actual appearance be first recognized by the bodily eyes of later magi.

This particular, however, as well as the journey of the magi into Judea, and their costly presents to the child, bear a relation to other passages in the Old Testament. In the description of the happier future, given in Isaiah, chap. lx., the prophet foretels that, at that time, the most remote people and kings will come to Jerusalem to worship Jehovah, with offerings of gold and incense and all acceptable gifts.* If in this passage the messianic times alone are spoken of, while the Messiah himself is wanting, in Psalm lxxii. we read of a king who is to be feared as long as the sun and moon endure, in whose times the righteous shall flourish, and whom all nations shall call blessed; this king might easily be regarded as the Messiah, and the Psalm says of him nearly in the words of Isai. lx., that foreign kings shall bring him gold and other presents. To this it may be added, that the pilgrimage of foreign people to Jerusalem is connected with a risen light,† which might suggest the star of Balaam. What was more natural, when on the one hand was presented Balaam's messianic star out of Jacob, (for the observation of which magian astrologers were the best adapted,) on the other, a light which was to arise on Jerusalem, and to which distant nations would come, bringing gifts,—than to combine the two images and to say: In consequence of the star which had risen over Jerusalem, astrologers came from a distant land with presents for the Messiah whom the star announced? But when the imagination once had possession of the star, and of travellers attracted by it from a distance, there was an inducement to make the star the immediate guide of their course, and the torch to light them on their way. This was a favourite idea of antiquity: according to Virgil, a star, *stella facem ducens*, marked out the way of Æneas from the shores of Troy to the west;‡ Thrasybulus and Timoleon were led by celestial fires; and a star was said to have guided Abraham on his way to Moriah.§ Besides, in the prophetic passage itself, the heavenly light seems to be associated with the pilgrimage of the offerers as the guide of their course; at all events the originally figurative language of the prophet would probably, at a latter period, be understood literally, in accordance with the rabbinical spirit of interpretation. The magi are not conducted by the star directly to Bethlehem where Jesus was; they first proceed to Jerusalem. One reason for this might be, that the prophetic passage connects the risen light and the offerers with Jerusalem; but the chief reason lies in the fact, that in Jerusalem Herod was to be found; for

---

* As in Matt. ii. 11. it is said of the magi προσήνεγκαν αὐτῷ—χρυσὸν καὶ λίβανον : so in Isai. lx, 6 (LXX): ἥξουσι, φέροντες χρυσίον, καὶ λίβανον οἴσουσι. The third present is in Matth. σμύρνα, in Isai. λιθὸς τίμιος.

† V. 1. und 3: קוּמִי אוֹרִי וּכְבוֹד (LXX: Ἱερουσαλήμ.) כִּי בָא אוֹרֵךְ יְהוָה עָלַיִךְ זָרָה:—וְהָלְכוּ גוֹיִם לְאוֹרֵךְ וּמְלָכִים לְנֹגַהּ זַרְחֵךְ:

‡ Æneid. ii. 693 ff.   § Wetstein, in loc.

what was better adapted to instigate Herod to his murderous decree, than the alarming tidings of the magi, that they had seen the star of the great Jewish king ?

To represent a murderous decree as having been directed by Herod against Jesus, was the interest of the primitive Christian legend. In all times legend has glorified the infancy of great men by persecutions and attempts on their life ; the greater the danger that hovered over them, the higher seems their value : the more unexpectedly their deliverance is wrought, the more evident is the esteem in which they are held by heaven. Hence in the history of the childhood of Cyrus in Herodotus, of Romulus in Livy,* and even later of Augustus in Suetonius,† we find this trait ; neither has the Hebrew legend neglected to assign such a distinction to Moses.‡ One point of analogy between the narrative in Exod. i. ii., and that in Matthew, is that in both cases the murderous decree does not refer specially to the one dangerous child, but generally to a certain class of children : in the former, to all new-born males, in the latter to all of and under the age of two years. It is true that, according to the narrative in Exodus, the murderous decree is determined on without any reference to Moses, of whose birth Pharaoh is not supposed to have had any presentiment, and who is therefore only by accident implicated in its consequences. But this representation did not sufficiently mark out Moses as the object of hostile design to satisfy the spirit of Hebrew tradition, and by the time of Josephus it had been so modified as to resemble more nearly the legends concerning Cyrus and Augustus, and above all the narrative of Matthew. According to the later legend, Pharaoh was incited to issue his murderous decree by a communication from his interpreters of the sacred writings, who announced to him the birth of an infant destined to succour the Israelites and humble the Egyptians.§ The interpreters of the sacred writings here play the same part as the interpreters of dreams in Herodotus, and the astrologers in Matthew. Legend was not content with thus signalizing the infancy of the lawgiver alone—it soon extended the same distinction to the great progenitor of the Israelitish nation, Abraham, whom it represented as being in peril of his life from the murderous attempt of a jealous tyrant, immediately after his birth. Moses was opposed to Pharaoh as an enemy and oppressor : Abraham held the same position with respect to Nimrod. This monarch was forewarned by his sages, whose attention had been excited by a remarkable star, that Tharah would have a son from

* Herod. i. 108 ff. Liv. 1. 4. † Octav. 94 :—*ante paucos quam nasceretur menses prodigium Romæ factum publice, quo denuntiabatur, regem populi Romani naturam parturire. Senatum exterritum, censuisse, ne quis illo anno genitus educaretur. Eos, qui gravidas uxores haberent, quo ad se quisque spem traheret, curasse, ne Senatus consultum ad ærarium deferretur.* ‡ Bauer (über das Mythische in der früheren Lebensper. des Moses, in the n. Theol. Journal 13, 3) had already compared the marvellous deliverance of Moses with that of Cyrus and Romulus ; the comparison of the infanticides was added by De Wette, Kritik der Mos. Geschichte, s. 176. § Joseph. Antiq. ii. ix. 2.

whom a powerful nation would descend. Apprehensive of rivalry, Nimrod immediately issues a murderous command, which, however, Abraham happily escapes.* What wonder, then, that, as the great progenitor and the lawgiver of the nation had their Nimrod and Pharaoh, a corresponding persecutor was found for the restorer of the nation, the Messiah, in the person of Herod :—that this tyrant was said to have been apprised of the Messiah's birth by wise men, and to have laid snares against his life, from which, however, he happily escapes? The apocryphal legend, indeed, has introduced an imitation of this trait after its own style, into the history of the Fore-runner ; he, too, is endangered by Herod's decree, a mountain is miraculously cleft asunder to receive him and his mother, but his father, refusing to point out the boy's hidingplace, is put to death.†

Jesus escapes from the hostile attempts of Herod by other means than those by which Moses, according to the mosaic history, and Abraham, according to the Jewish legend, elude the decree issued against them ; namely, by a flight out of his native land, into Egypt. In the life of Moses also there occurs a flight into a foreign land ; not, however, during his childhood, but after he had slain the Egyptian, when, fearing the vengeance of Pharaoh, he takes refuge in Midian (Exod. ii. 15.). That reference was made to this flight of the first Goël in that of the second, our text expressly shows, for the words, which it attributes to the angel, who encourages Joseph to return out of Egypt into Palestine, are those by which Moses is induced to return out of Midian into Egypt.‡ The choice of Egypt as a place of refuge for Jesus, may be explained in the simplest manner: the young Messiah could not, like Moses, flee *out of* Egypt; hence, that his history might not be destitute of so significant a feature as a connexion with Egypt, that ancient retreat of the patriarchs, the relation was reversed, and he was made to flee *into* Egypt, which, besides, from its vicinity, was the most appropriate asylum for a fugitive from Judea. The prophetic passage which the evangelist cites from Hosea xi. 1. *Out of Egypt have I called my son—* is less available for the elucidation of this particular in our narrative. For the immediate proofs that the Jews referred this passage to the Messiah are very uncertain ;§ though, if we compare such passage as Ps. ii. 7. in which the words בְּנִי אָתָּה (*thou art my son*) are interpreted of the Messiah, it cannot appear incredible that the expression בְּנִי (*my son*) in Hosea was supposed to have a messianic signification.

* Jalkut Rubeni (cont. of the passage cited in No. 6): *dixerunt sapientes Nimrodi ; natus est Tharæ filius hac ipsa hora, ex quo egressus est populus, qui hæredit ibit præsens et futurum seculum ; si tibi placuerit, detur patri ipsius domus argento auroque plena, et occidat ipsum.* Comp. the passage of the Arabic book quoted by Fabric, Cod. pseudepigr. ut sup.   † Protev. Jacobi, c, xxii. f.

‡ Ex. iv. 19, LXX :   Matt. ii. 20 :
βάδιζε, ἄπελθε εἰς Αἴγυπτον, τεθνήκασι γὰρ   ἐγερθεὶς—πορεύου εἰς γῆν Ἰσραήλ· Τεθνή-
πάντες οἱ ζητοῦντές σου τὴν ψυχήν.   κασι γὰρ οἱ ζητοῦντες τὴν ψυχὴν τοῦ παιδίου.
We may remark that the inapropriate use of the plural in the evangelical passage, can only be explained on the supposition of a reference to the passage in Exod. See Winer,

Against this mythical derivation of the narrative, two objections have been recently urged. First, if the history of the star originated in Balaam's prophecy, why, it is asked, does not Matthew, fond as he is of showing the fulfilment of Old Testament predictions in the life of Jesus, make the slightest allusion to that prophecy?* Because it was not he who wove this history out of the materials furnished in the Old Testament; he received it, already fashioned, from others, who did not communicate to him its real origin. For the very reason that many narratives were transmitted to him without their appropriate keys, he sometimes tries false ones; as in our narrative, in relation to the Bethlehem massacre, he quotes, under a total misconception of the passage, Jeremiah's image of Rachel weeping for her children.† The other objection is this: how could the communities of Jewish Christians, whence this pretended mythus must have sprung, ascribe so high an importance to the heathen as is implied in the star of the magi?‡ As if the prophets had not, in such passages as we have quoted, already ascribed to them this importance, which, in fact, consists but in their rendering homage and submission to the Messiah, a relation that must be allowed to correspond with the ideas of the Jewish Christians, not to speak of the particular conditions on which the heathen were to be admitted into the kingdom of the Messiah.

We must therefore abide by the mythical interpretation of our narrative, and content ourselves with gathering from it no particular fact in the life of Jesus, but only a new proof how strong was the impression of his messiahship left by Jesus on the minds of his contemporaries, since even the history of his childhood received a messianic form.§

Let us now revert to the narrative of Luke, chap. ii., so far as it runs parallel with that of Matthew. We have seen that the narrative of Matthew does not allow us to presuppose that of Luke as a series of prior incidents: still less can the converse be true, namely, that the magi arrived before the shepherds: it remains then to be asked, whether the two narratives do not aim to represent the same fact, though they have given it a different garb? From the older orthodox opinion that the star in Matthew was an angel, it was an easy step to identify that apparition with the angel in Luke, and to suppose that the angels, who appeared to the shepherds of Bethlehem on the night of the birth of Jesus, were taken by the distant magi for a star vertical to Judea,‖ so that both the accounts might be essentially correct. Of late, only one of the Evangelists

N. T. Gramm. s. 119. Comp. also Exod. iv. 20 with Matt. ii. 11, 21.   § Vide e. g. Schöttgen, horæ, ii. p 209.
    * Theile, zur Biographie Jesu, § 15, Anm. 9. Hoffmann, S. 269.   † Comp. my Streitschriften, i. 1, S. 12 f.; George, s. 39.   ‡ Neander, L. J. Ch. s. 27.   Schleiermacher, (uber den Lukas, s. 47) explains the narrative concerning the magi as a symbolical one ; but he scorns to take into consideration the passages from the O. T. and other writings, which have a bearing on the subject, and by way of retribution, his exposition at one time rests in generalities, at another, takes a wrong path.   § Lightfoot, horæ, p. 202.

has been supposed to give the true circumstances, and Luke has had the preference, Matthew's narrative being regarded as an embellished edition.

According to this opinion, the angel clothed in heavenly brightness, in Luke, became a star in the tradition recorded by Matthew, the ideas of angels and stars being confounded in the higher Jewish theology; the shepherds were exalted into royal magi, kings being in antiquity called the shepherds of their people.* This derivation is too elaborate to be probable, even were it true, as it is here assumed, that Luke's narrative bears the stamp of historical credibility. As, however, we conceive that we have proved the contrary, and as, consequently, we have before us two equally unhistorical narratives, there is no reason for preferring a forced and unnatural derivation of Matthew's narrative from that of Luke, to the very simple derivation which may be traced through Old Testament passages and Jewish notions. These two descriptions of the introduction of Jesus into the world, are, therefore, two variations on the same theme, composed, however, quite independently of each other.

§ 37. CHRONOLOGICAL RELATION BETWEEN THE VISIT OF THE MAGI, TOGETHER WITH THE FLIGHT INTO EGYPT, AND THE PRESENTATION IN THE TEMPLE RECORDED BY LUKE.

It has been already remarked, that the narratives of Matthew and Luke above considered at first run tolerably parallel, but afterwards widely diverge ; for instead of the tragical catastrophe of the massacre and flight, Luke has preserved to us the peaceful scene of the presentation of the child Jesus in the temple. Let us for the present shut our eyes to the result of the preceding inquiry—the purely mythical character of Matthew's narrative—and ask : In what chronological relation could the presentation in the temple stand to the visit of the magi and the flight into Egypt?

Of these occurrences the only one that has a precise date is the presentation in the temple, of which it is said that it took place at the expiration of the period appointed by the law for the purification of a mother, that is, according to Levit. xii. 2—4, forty days after the birth of the child (Luke ii. 22). The time of the other incidents is not fixed with the same exactness ; it is merely said that the magi came to Jerusalem, τοῦ Ἰησοῦ γεννηθέντος ἐν Βηθλεὲμ (Matt. ii. 1)—how long after the birth the Evangelist does not decide. As, however, the participle connects the visit of the magi with the birth of the child, if not immediately, at least so closely that nothing of importance can be supposed to have intervened, some expositors have been led to the opinion that the visit ought to be regarded as prior to the presentation in the temple.† Admitting this arrangement we

* Schneckenburger, über den Ursprung des ersten kanonischen Evangeliums S. 69 ff.
† Thus, e. g. Augustin de consensu evangelistarum ii. 5. Storr, opusc. acad. iii. S. 96 ff. Süskind, in Bengel's Archiv. i. 1, S. 216 ff.

have to reconcile it with one of two alternatives: either the flight into Egypt also preceded the presentation in the temple; or, while the visit of the magi preceded, the flight followed that event. If we adopt the latter alternative, and thrust the presentation in the temple between the visit of the magi and the flight, we come into collision at once with the text of Matthew and the mutual relation of the facts. The evangelist connects the command to flee into Egypt with the return of the magi, by a participial construction (v. 13) similar to that by which he connects the arrival of the oriental sages with the birth of Jesus: hence those, who in the one instance hold such a construction to be a reason for placing the events which it associates in close succession, must in the other instance be withheld by it from inserting a third occurrence between the visit and the flight. As regards the mutual relation of the facts, it can hardly be considered probable, that at the very point of time in which Joseph received a divine intimation, that he was no longer safe in Bethlehem from the designs of Herod he should be permitted to take a journey to Jerusalem, and thus to rush directly into the lion's mouth. At all events, the strictest precautions must have been enjoined on all who were privy to the presence of the messianic child in Jerusalem, lest a rumour of the fact should get abroad. But there is no trace of this solicitous incognito in Luke's narrative; on the contrary, not only does Simeon call attention to Jesus in the temple, unchecked either by the Holy Spirit or by the parents, but Anna also thinks she is serving the good cause, by publishing as widely as possible the tidings of the Messiah's birth (Luke ii. 28 ff. 38). It is true that she is said to have confined her communications to those who were like-minded with herself (ἐλάλει περὶ αὐτοῦ πᾶσι τοῖς προσδεχομένοις λύτρωσιν ἐν Ἱερουσαλήμ), but this could not hinder them from reaching the ears of the Herodian party, for the greater the excitement produced by such news on the minds of those *who looked for redemption*, the more would the vigilance of the government be aroused, so that Jesus would inevitably fall into the hands of the tyrant who was lying in wait.

Thus in any case, they who place the presentation in the temple after the visit of the magi, must also determine to postpone it until after the return from Egypt. But even this arrangement clashes with the evangelical statement; for it requires us to insert, between the birth of Jesus and his presentation in the temple, the following events: the arrival of the magi, the flight into Egypt, the Bethlehem massacre, the death of Herod, and the return of the parents of Jesus out of Egypt —obviously too much to be included in the space of forty days. It must therefore be supposed that the presentation of the child, and the first appearance of the mother in the temple, were procrastinated beyond the time appointed by the law. This expedient, however, runs counter to the narrative of Luke, who expressly says, that the visit to the temple took place at the legal time. But in either case the difficulty is the same; the parents of

Jesus could, according to Matthew's account, as little think of a journey to Jerusalem after their return from Egypt, as immediately previous to their departure thither.   For if Joseph, on his return from Egypt was warned not to enter Judea, because Archelaus was Herod's successor in that province, he would least of all venture to Jerusalem, the very seat of the government.

On neither of the above plans, therefore, will the presentation in the temple bear to be placed after the visit of the magi, and the only remaining alternative, which is embraced by the majority of commentators,* is to make the incident noticed by Luke, precede both those narrated by Matthew.   This is so far the most natural, that in Matthew there is at least an indirect intimation of a considerable interval between the birth of Jesus and the arrival of the magi. For we are told that Herod's decree included all the children in Bethlehem up to the age of two years; we must therefore necessarily infer, that even if Herod, to make sure of his object, exceeded the term fixed by the magi, the star had been visible to these astrologers for more than a year.   Now the narrator seems to suppose the appearance of the star to have been cotemporary with the birth of Jesus. Viewing the narratives in this order, the parents of Jesus first journeyed from Bethlehem, where the child was born, to Jerusalem, there to present the legal offerings; they next returned to Bethlehem, where (according to Matt. ii. 1 and 5.) they were found by the magi; then followed the flight into Egypt, and after the return from thence, the settlement at Nazareth.   The first and most urgent question that here suggests itself is this: What had the parents of Jesus to do a second time in Bethlehem, which was not their home, and where their original business connected with the census must surely have been despatched in the space of forty days? The discussion of this question must be deferred, but we can find an ample substitute for this argument, drawn from the nature of the fact, in one which rests on the words of the evangelical narrative. Luke (v. 39) says, in the most definite manner, that after the completion of the legal observance, the parents of Jesus returned to Nazareth, as to their proper home, not to Bethlehem, which, according to him was merely a temporary residence.†   If, then, the magi arrived after the presentation in the temple, they must have met with the parents of Jesus in Nazareth, and not in Bethlehem, as Matthew states.   Moreover, had the arrival of the magi really been preceded by the presentation in the temple, together with the attention which must have been excited by the language of Simeon and Anna; it is impossible that at the period of that arrival the birth of the messianic child could have been so much a secret in Jerusalem, that the announcement of it by the magi should be, as Matthew relates, a source of general astonishment.‡

---

* E. g. Hess, Geschichte Jesu, 1, S. 51 ff. Paulus, Olshausen, in loc.   † Süskind, ut sup. S. 222.   ‡ The same difference as to the chronological relation of the two incidents exists between the two different texts of the apocryphal book: Historia de navitate Mariæ et de inf. Serv., see Thilo, p. 385, not.

If, then, the presentation of Jesus in the temple can have taken place neither earlier nor later than the visit of the magi and the flight into Egypt; and if the flight into Egypt can have taken place neither earlier nor later than the presentation in the temple; it is impossible that both these occurrences really happened, and, at the very utmost, only one can be historical.[*]

To escape from this dangerous dilemma, supranaturalism has lately been induced to take a freer position, that by the surrender of what is no longer tenable, the residue may be saved. Neander finds himself constrained to admit, that neither did Luke know any thing of what Matthew communicates concerning the childhood of Jesus, nor did the Greek editor of Matthew (to be distinguished from the apostle) know any thing of the events detailed by Luke. But, he contends, it does not therefore follow that both the different series of incidents cannot have happened.[†] By giving this turn to the matter, the difficulties arising from the words of the evangelist are certainly avoided: not so, the difficulties arising from the nature of the facts. The first evangelist ranges in close succession the visit of the magi and the flight into Egypt, as though no change of place had intervened; the author of the third gospel represents the parents of Jesus as returning with the child, after the presentation in the temple, directly to Nazareth. We cannot, on this ground, argue from one evangelist against the other: for it is inadmissible to maintain that certain events never happened, because they were unknown to a remote narrator. But viewing the two narratives in another light, we perceive how improbable it is that, after the scene in the temple, the birth of the messianic child should be so entirely unknown in Jerusalem as the conduct of Herod on the arrival of the magi implies; how incredible (reversing the order of the events) that Joseph should be permitted to go to Jerusalem, with the child which Herod had just sought to kill; how inconceivable, finally, that the parents of Jesus should have returned to Bethlehem, after the presentation in the temple (of which more hereafter). All these difficulties, lying in the nature of the facts, difficulties not less weighty than those connected with the words of the evangelists, still subsist in Neander's explanation, and prove its inadequacy.

Thus the dilemma above stated remains, and were we compelled to choose under it, we should, in the present stage of our inquiry, on no account decide in favour of Matthew's narrative, and against that of Luke: on the contrary, as we have recognized the mythical character of the former, we should have no resource but to adhere, with our modern critics,[‡] to the narrative of Luke, and surrender that of Matthew. But is not Luke's narrative of the same nature as that of Matthew, and instead of having to choose between the

* This incompatibility of the two narratives was perceived at an early period by some opponents of Christianity. Epiphanius names one Philosabbatius, together with Celsus and Porphyry (haeres. li. S). † Neander, L. J. Ch. S. 33, Anm. ‡ Schleiermacher, uber den Lukas, S. 47. Schneckenburger, ut sup.

two, must we not deny to both an historical character? The answer to this question will be found in the succeeding examination.

§ 38.   THE PRESENTATION OF JESUS IN THE TEMPLE.

THE narrative of the presentation of Jesus in the temple (Luke ii. 22) seems, at the first glance, to bear a thoroughly historical stamp. A double law, on the one hand prescribing to the mother an offering of purification, on the other, requiring the redemption of the first-born son, leads the parents of Jesus to Jerusalem and to the temple. Here they meet with a devout man, absorbed in the expectation of the Messiah, named Simeon. Many expositors hold this Simeon to be the same with the Rabbi Simeon, the son of Hillel, his successor as president of the Sanhedrim, and the father of Gamaliel; some even identify him with the Sameas of Josephus,* and attach importance to his pretended descent from David, because this descent makes him a relative of Jesus, and helps to explain the following scene naturally: but this hypothesis is improbable, for Luke would hardly have introduced so celebrated a personage by the meagre designation, ἄνθρωπός τις, (a certain man.†) Without this hypothesis, however, the scene between the parents of Jesus and Simeon, as also the part played by Anna the prophetess, seems to admit of a very natural explanation. There is no necessity for supposing, with the author of the Natural History,‡ that Simeon was previously aware of the hope cherished by Mary that she was about to give birth to the Messiah; we need only, with Paulus and others, conceive the facts in the following manner. Animated, like many of that period, with the hope of the speedy advent of the Messiah, Simeon receives, probably in a dream, the assurance that before his death he will be permitted to see the expected deliverer of his nation. One day, in obedience to an irresistible impulse, he visited the temple, and on this very day Mary brought thither her child, whose beauty at once attracted his notice; on learning the child's descent from David, the attention and interest of Simeon were excited to a degree that induced Mary to disclose to him the hopes which were reposed on this scion of ancient royalty, with the extraordinary occurrences by which they had been called into existence. These hopes Simeon embraced with confidence, and in enthusiastic language gave utterance to his messianic expectations and forebodings, under the conviction that they would be fulfilled in this child. Still less do we need the supposition of the author of the Natural History with respect to Anna, namely, that she was one of the women who assisted at the birth of the infant Jesus, and was thus acquainted beforehand with the marvels and the hopes that had clustered round his cradle;—she had heard the words of Simeon,

* Antiq. xiv. ix. 4, xv. i. 1 and x. 4.   † The Evang. Nicodemi indeed calls him, c. xvi. ὁ μέγας διδάσκαλος, and the Protev. Jacobi, c. xxiv. makes him a priest or even high priest, vid. Varr. ap. Thilo Cod. Apocr. N. T. 1, S. 271, comp. 203.   ‡ 1 Th. S. 205 ff.

and being animated by the same sentiments, she gave them her approval.

Simple as this explanation appears, it is not less arbitrary than we have already found other specimens of natural interpretation. The evangelist nowhere says, that the parents of Jesus had communicated anything concerning their extraordinary hopes to Simeon, before he poured forth his inspired words; on the contrary, the point of his entire narrative consists in the idea that the aged saint had, by virtue of the spirit with which he was filled, instantaneously discerned in Jesus the messianic child, and the reason why the co-operation of the Holy Spirit is insisted on, is to make it evident how Simeon was enabled, without any previous information, to recognise in Jesus the promised child, and at the same time to foretel the course of his destiny. Our canonical Gospel refers Simeon's recognition of Jesus to a supernatural principle resident in Simeon himself; the *Evangelium infantiæ arabicum* refers it to something objective in the appearance of Jesus[*]—far more in the spirit of the original narrative than the natural interpretation, for it retains the miraculous element. But, apart from the general reasons against the credibility of miracles, the admission of a miracle in this instance is attended with a special difficulty, because no worthy object for an extraordinary manifestation of divine power is discoverable. For, that the above occurrence during the infancy of Jesus served to disseminate and establish in more distant circles the persuasion of his Messiahship, there is no indication; we must therefore, with the evangelist, limit the object of these supernatural communications to Simeon and Anna, to whose devout hopes was vouchsafed the special reward of having their eyes enlightened to discern the messianic child. But that miracles should be ordained for such occasional and isolated objects, is not reconcileable with just ideas of divine providence.

Thus here again we find reason to doubt the historical character of the narrative, especially as we have found by a previous investigation that it is annexed to narratives purely mythical. Simeon's real expressions, say some commentators, were probably these: Would that I might yet behold the newborn Messiah, even as I now bear this child in my arms!—a simple wish which was transformed *ex eventu* by tradition, into the positive enunciations now read in Luke[†]. But this explanation is incomplete, for the *reason why* such stories became current concerning Jesus, must be shown in the relative position of this portion of the evangelical narrative, and in the interest of the primitive Christian legend. As to the former, this scene at the presentation of Jesus in the temple is obviously parallel with that at the circumcision of the Baptist, narrated by the same evangelist: for on both occasions, at the inspiration

* Cap. 6. *Viditque il un Simeon senex instar columnæ lucis refulgentem, cum Domina Maria virgo, mater ejus, illuis suis cum gestaret, ut circumdibuit cum angeli instar circuli, celebrantes illum etc.* Ap. Thilo, p. 71.   † Thus E. F. in the treatise, on the two first chapters of Matth. and Luke.   In Henke's Mag. 5. B I. S. 169 f.   A similar half-measure is in Matthai, Synopse der 4 Evang. S. 3, 5 f.

of the Holy Spirit, God is praised for the birth of a national deliverer, and the future destiny of the child is prophetically announced, in the one case by the father, in the other by a devout stranger. That this scene is in the former instance connected with the circumcision, in the latter with the presentation in the temple, seems to be accidental; when however the legend had once, in relation to Jesus, so profusely adorned the presentation in the temple, the circumcision must be left, as we have above found it, without embellishment.

As to the second spring in the formation of our narrative, namely, the interest of the Christian legend, it is easy to conceive how this would act. He who, as a man, so clearly proved himself to be the Messiah, must also, it was thought, even as a child have been recognisable in his true character to an eye rendered acute by the Holy Spirit; he who at a later period, by his powerful words and deeds, manifested himself to be the Son of God, must surely, even before he could speak or move with freedom, have borne the stamp of divinity. Moreover if men, moved by the Spirit of God, so early pressed Jesus with love and reverence in their arms, then was the spirit that animated him not an impious one, as his enemies alleged; and if a holy seer had predicted, along with the high destiny of Jesus, the conflict which he had to undergo, and the anguish which his fate would cause his mother,[*] then it was assuredly no chance, but a divine plan, that led him into the dephts of abasement on the way to his ultimate exaltation.

This view of the narrative is thus countenanced positively by the nature of the fact,—and negatively by the difficulties attending any other explanation. One cannot but wonder, therefore, how Schleiermacher can be influenced against it by an observation which did not prevent him from taking a similar view of the history of the Baptist's birth, namely, that the narrative is too natural to have been fabricated;[†] and how Neander can argue against it, from exaggerated ideas of the more imposing traits which the mythus would have substituted for our narrative. Far from allowing a purification for the mother of Jesus, and a redemption for himself, to take place in the ordinary manner, Neander thinks the mythus would have depicted an angelic appearance, intended to deter Mary or the priest from an observance inconsistent with the dignity of Jesus.[‡] As though even the Christianity of Paul did not maintain that Christ was *born under the law*, γενόμενος ὑπὸ νόμου (Gal. iv. 4.); how much more then the Judaic Christianity whence these narratives are derived! As though Jesus himself had not, agreeably to this view of his position, submitted to baptism, and according to the Evangelist

---

[*] With the words of Simeon addressed to Mary: καὶ σοῦ δε αὐτῆς τὴν ψυχὴν διελεύσεται ῥομφαία (V. 35,) comp. the words in the messianic psalm of sorrow, xxii. 21: ῥῦσαι ἀπὸ ῥομφαίας τὴν ψυχήν μου.   [†] Schleiermacher, über den Lukas, s. 37. Compare on the other hand the observations in § 18, with those of the authors there quoted, Note 19.   [‡] Neander here (s. 21 f.) mistakes the apocryphal for the mythical, as he had before done the poetical.

whose narrative is in question, without any previous expostulation
on the part of the Baptist! Of more weight is Schleiermacher's
other observation, that supposing this narrative to be merely a poetical creation, its author would scarcely have placed by the side of
Simeon Anna, of whom he makes no poetical use, still less would
he have characterized her with minuteness, after designating his
principal personage with comparative negligence. But to represent
the dignity of the child Jesus as being proclaimed by the mouth of
two witnesses, and especially to associate a prophetess with the
prophet—this is just the symmetrical grouping that the legend loves.
The detailed description of Anna may have been taken from a real
person who, at the time when our narrative originated, was yet held
in remembrance for her distinguished piety. As to the Evangelist's
omission to assign her any particular speech, it is to be observed
that her office is to spread abroad the glad news, while that of Simeon is to welcome Jesus into the temple: hence as the part of the
prophetess was to be performed behind the scenes, her precise words
could not be given. As in a former instance Schleiermacher supposes the Evangelist to have received his history from the lips of
the shepherds, so here he conceives him to have been indebted to
Anna, of whose person he has so vivid a recollection: Neander approves this opinion—not the only straw thrown out by Schleiermacher, to which this theologian has clung in the emergencies of
modern criticism.

At this point also, where Luke's narrative leaves Jesus for a
series of years, there is a concluding sentence on the prosperous
growth of the child (v. 40): a similar sentence occurs at the corresponding period in the life of the Baptist, and both recall the analogous form of expression found in the history of Sampson (Judg.
xiii. 24 f.).

§ 39. RETROSPECT—DIFFERENCE BETWEEN MATTHEW AND LUKE AS TO THE ORIGINAL RESIDENCE OF THE PARENTS OF JESUS.

IN the foregoing examinations we have called in question the
historical credibility of the Gospel narratives concerning the genealogy, birth, and childhood of Jesus, on two grounds: first, because
the narratives taken separately contain much that will not bear an
historical interpretation; and secondly, because the parallel narratives of Matthew and Luke exclude each other, so that it is impossible for both to be true, and one must necessarily be false: this
imputation however may attach to either, and consequently to both.
One of the contradictions between the two narratives extends from
the commencement of the history of the childhood to the point we
have now reached: it has therefore often come in our way, but we
have been unable hitherto to give it our consideration, because only
now that we have completely reviewed the scenes in which it figures,
have we materials enough on which to found a just estimate of its

consequences. We refer to the divergency that exists between
Matthew and Luke, in relation to the original dwelling-place of the
parents of Jesus.

Luke, from the very beginning of his history, gives Nazareth
as the abode of Joseph and Mary; here the angel seeks Mary (i. 26);
here we must suppose Mary's house οἶκος, to be situated (i. 56);
from hence the parents of Jesus journey to Bethlehem on account
of the census (ii. 4); and hither, when circumstances permit, they
return as to their own city πόλις αὐτῶν (v. 39). Thus in Luke, Nazareth is evidently the proper residence of the parents of Jesus, and
they only visit Bethlehem for a short time, owing to a casual circumstance.

In Matthew, it is not stated in the first instance where Joseph
and Mary resided. According to ii. 1. Jesus was born in Bethlehem,
and since no extraordinary circumstances are said to have led his
parents thither, it appears as if Matthew supposed them to have
been originally resident in Bethlehem. Here he makes the parents
with the child receive the visit of the magi; then follows the flight
into Egypt, on returning from which Joseph is only deterred from
again seeking Judea by a special divine admonition, which directs
him to Nazareth in Galilee (ii. 22). This last particular renders
certain what had before seemed probable, namely, that Matthew did
not with Luke suppose Nazareth, but Bethlehem, to have been
the original dwelling-place of the parents of Jesus, and that he conceived their final settlement at Nazareth to have been the result of
unforeseen circumstances.

This contradiction is generally glided over without suspicion.
The reason of this lies in the peculiar character of Matthew's Gospel, a character on which a modern writer has built the assertion
that this Evangelist does not contradict Luke concerning the original residence of the parents of Jesus, for he says nothing at all on
the subject, troubling himself as little about topographical as chronological accuracy. He mentions the later abode of Joseph and
Mary, and the birth-place of Jesus, solely because it was possible
to connect with them Old Testament prophecies; as the abode of
the parents of Jesus prior to his birth furnished no opportunity for a
similar quotation, Matthew has left it entirely unnoticed, an omission
which however, in his style of narration, is no proof that he was
ignorant of their abode, or that he supposed it to have been Bethlehem.* But even admitting that the silence of Matthew on the earlier residence of the parents of Jesus in Nazareth, and on the peculiar circumstances that caused Bethlehem to be his birth-place, proves
nothing: yet the above supposition requires that the exchange of
Bethlehem for Nazareth should be so represented as to give some
intimation, or at least to leave a possibility, that we should understand the former to be a merely temporary abode, and the journey
to the latter a return homeward. Such an intimation would have

* Olshausen, bibl. Comm. 1. S. 112 f.

been given, had Matthew attributed to the angelic vision, that determined Joseph's settlement in Nazareth after his return from Egypt, such communications as the following: Return now into the land of Israel and into your native city Nazareth, for there is no further need of your presence in Bethlehem, since the prophecy that your messianic child should be born in that place is already fulfilled. But as Matthew is alleged to be generally indifferent about localities, we will be moderate, and demand no positive intimation from him, but simply make the negative requisition, that he should not absolutely exclude the idea, that Nazareth was the original dwelling-place of the parents of Jesus. This requisition would be met if, instead of a special cause being assigned for the choice of Nazareth as a residence, it had been merely said that the parents of Jesus returned by divine direction into the land of Israel and betook themselves to Nazareth. It would certainly seem abrupt enough, if without any preamble Nazareth were all at once named instead of Bethlehem: of this our narrator was conscious, and for this reason he has detailed the causes that led to the change (ii. 22). But instead of doing this, as we have shown that he must have done it, had he, with Luke, known Nazareth to be the original dwelling-place of the parents of Jesus, his account has precisely the opposite bearing, which undeniably proves that his supposition was the reverse of Luke's. For when Matthew represents Joseph on his return from Egypt as being prevented from going to Judea solely by his fear of Archelaus, he ascribes to him an inclination to proceed to that province—an inclination which is unaccountable if the affair of the census alone had taken him to Bethlehem, and which is only to be explained by the supposition that he had formerly dwelt there. On the other hand as Matthew makes the danger from Archelaus (together with the fulfilment of a prophecy) the sole cause of the settlement of Joseph and Mary at Nazareth, he cannot have supposed that this was their original home, for in that case there would have been an independently decisive cause which would have rendered any other superfluous.

Thus the difficulty of reconciling Matthew with Luke, in the present instance, turns upon the impossibility of conceiving how the parents of Jesus could, on their return from Egypt, have it in contemplation to proceed a second time to Bethlehem unless this place had formerly been their home. The efforts of commentators have accordingly been chiefly applied to the task of finding other reasons for the existence of such an inclination in Joseph and Mary. Such efforts are of a very early date. Justin Martyr, holding by Luke, who, while he decidedly states Nazareth to be the dwelling-place of the parents of Jesus, yet does not represent Joseph as a complete stranger in Bethlehem, (for he makes it the place from which he lineally sprang,) seems to suppose that Nazareth was the dwelling-place, and Bethlehem the birth-place of Joseph,[*] and Cred-

---

[*] Dial. c. Trypho, 78: Joseph came from Nazareth, *where he lived*, to Bethlehem,

ner thinks that this passage of Justin points out the source, and presents the reconciliation of the divergent statements of our two evangelists.* But it is far from presenting a reconciliation. For as Nazareth is still supposed to be the place which Joseph had chosen as his home, no reason appears why, on his return from Egypt, he should all at once desire to exchange his former residence for his birth-place, especially as, according to Justin himself, the cause of his former journey to Bethlehem had not been a plan of settling there, but simply the census—a cause which, after the flight, no longer existed. Thus the statement of Justin leans to the side of Luke and does not suffice to bring him into harmony with Matthew. That it was the source of our two evangelical accounts is still less credible; for how could the narrative of Matthew, which mentions neither Nazareth as a dwelling-place, nor the census as the cause of a journey to Bethlehem, originate in the statement of Justin, to which these facts are essential? Arguing generally, where on the one hand, there are two diverging statements, on the other, an insufficient attempt to combine them, it is certain that the latter is not the parent and the two former its offspring, but vice versa. Moreover, in this department of attempting reconciliations, we have already, in connexion with the genealogies, learned to estimate Justin or his authorities.

A more thorough attempt at reconciliation is made in the *Evangelium de nativitate Mariæ*, and has met with much approval from modern theologians. According to this apocryphal book, the house of Mary's parents was at Nazareth, and although she was brought up in the temple at Jerusalem and there espoused to Joseph, she returned after this occurence to her parents in Galilee. Joseph, on the contrary, was not only born at Bethlehem, as Justin seems to intimate, but also lived there, and thither brought home his betrothed.† But this mode of conciliation, unlike the other, is favourable to Matthew and disadvantageous to Luke. For the census with its attendant circumstances is left out, and necessarily so, because if Joseph were at home in Bethlehem, and only went to Nazareth to fetch his bride, the census could not be represented as the reason why he returned to Bethlehem, for he would have done so in the ordinary course of things, after a few days' absence. Above all, had Bethlehem been his home, he would not on his arrival have sought an inn where there was no room for him, but would have taken Mary under his own roof. Hence modern expositors who wish to avail themselves of the outlet presented by the apocryphal book, and yet to save the census of Luke from rejection, maintain that Joseph did indeed dwell, and carry on his trade, in Beth-

whence he was, to be enrolled, ἀνελήλυθει ('Ιωσήφ) ἀπὸ Ναζαρὲτ, ἐνθαώκει, εἰς Βηθλέμ, ὅθεν ἦν, ἀπογράψασθαι. The words ὅθεν ἦν might however be understood as signifying merely the place of his tribe, especially if Justin's addition be considered: *For his race was of the tribe of Judah, which inhabit that land, ἀπὸ γὰρ τῆς κατοικούσης τὴν γῆν ἐκείνην φυλῆς 'Ιούδα τὸ γένος ἦν.* * Beiträge zur Einleit. in das N. T. 1. S. 217. Comp. Hoffmann, S. 238 f. 277 ff. † C. I. 8. 10.

lehem, but that he possessed no house of his own in that place, and the census recalling him thither sooner than he had anticipated, he had not yet provided one.* But Luke makes it appear, not only that the parents of Jesus were not yet settled in Bethlehem, but that they were not even desirous of settling there; that, on the contrary, it was their intention to depart after the shortest possible stay. This opinion supposes great poverty on the part of Joseph and Mary; Olshausen, on the other hand, prefers enriching them, for the sake of conciliating the difference in question. He supposes that they had property both in Bethlehem and Nazareth, and could therefore have settled in either place, but unknown circumstances inclined them, on their return from Egypt, to fix upon Bethlehem, until the divine warning came as a preventive. Thus Olshausen declines particularizing the reason why it appeared desirable to the parents of Jesus to settle in Bethlehem; but Heydenreich and others have supplied his omission, by assuming that it must have seemed to them most fitting for him, who was pre-eminently the Son of David, to be brought up in David's own city.

Here, however, theologians would do well to take for their model the honesty of Neander,† and to confess with him that of this intention on the part of Joseph and Mary to settle at Bethlehem, and of the motives which induced them to give up the plan, Luke knows nothing, and that they rest on the authority of Matthew alone. But what reason does Matthew present for this alleged change of place? The visit of the magi, the massacre of the infants, visions in dreams—events whose evidently unhistorical character quite disqualifies them from serving as proofs of a change of residence on the part of the parents of Jesus. On the other hand Neander, while confessing that the author of the first Gospel was probably ignorant of the particular circumstances which, according to Luke, led to the journey to Bethlehem, and hence took Bethlehem to be the original residence of the parents of Jesus, maintains that there may be an essential agreement between the two accounts though that agreement did not exist in the consciousness of the writers.‡ But, once more, what cause does Luke assign for the journey to Bethlehem? The census, which our previous investigations have shown to be as frail a support for this statement, as the infanticide and its consequences for that of Matthew. Hence here again it is not possible by admitting the inacquaintance of the one narrator with what the other presents to vindicate the statements of both; since each has against him, not only the ignorance of the other, but the improbability of his own narrative.

But we must distinguish more exactly the respective aspects and elements of the two accounts. As, according to the above observations, the change of residence on the part of the parents of Jesus, is in Matthew so linked with the unhistorical data of the infanticide

* Paulus, exeg. Handb. I, a, S. 178. † Ueber die Unzulässigkeit der mythischen Auffassung u. s. f. 1, S. 101. ‡ L. J Ch S. 33.

and the flight into Egypt, that without these every cause for the
migration disappears, we turn to Luke's account, which makes the
parents of Jesus resident in the same place, both after and before
the birth of Jesus. But in Luke, the circumstance of Jesus being
born in another place than where his parents dwelt, is made to depend on an event as unhistorical as the marvels of Matthew, namely
the census. If this be surrendered, no motive remains that could induce the parents of Jesus to take a formidable journey at so critical
a period for Mary, and in this view of the case Matthew's representation seems the more probable one, that Jesus was born in the
home of his parents and not in a strange place. Hitherto, however,
we have only obtained the negative result, that the evangelical statements, according to which the parents of Jesus lived at first in another place than that in which they subsequently settled, and Jesus
was born elsewhere than in the home of his parents, are destitute
of any guarantee; we have yet to seek for a positive conclusion by
inquiring what was really the place of his birth.

On this point we are drawn in two opposite directions. In both
Gospels we find Bethlehem stated to be the birth-place of Jesus,
and there is, as we have seen, no impediment to our supposing that
it was the habitual residence of his parents; on the other hand,
the two Gospels again concur in representing Nazareth as the ultimate dwelling-place of Joseph and his family, and it is only an unsupported statement that forbids us to regard it as their original
residence, and consequently as the birth-place of Jesus. It would
be impossible to decide between these contradictory probabilities
were both equally strong, but as soon as the slightest inequality
between them is discovered, we are warranted to form a conclusion.
Let us first test the opinion, that the Galilean city Nazareth was the
final residence of Jesus. This is not supported barely by the passages immediately under consideration, in the 2nd chapters of Matthew and Luke;—it rests on an uninterrupted series of data drawn
from the Gospels and from the earliest church history. The Galilean, the Nazarene—were the epithets constantly applied to Jesus.
As Jesus of Nazareth he was introduced by Philip to Nathaniel,
whose responsive question was, Can any good thing come out of Nazareth? Nazareth is described, not only as the place where he was
brought up, οὖ ἦν τεθραμμένος (Luke iv. 16 f.), but also as his country, πατρὶς (Matt. xiii. 34, Mark vi. 1.). He was known among the
populace as Jesus of Nazareth (Luke xviii. 37.), and invoked under
this name by the demons (Mark i. 24.). The inscription on the
cross styles him a Nazarene (John xix. 19.), and after his resurrection his apostles everywhere proclaimed him as Jesus of Nazareth
(Acts ii. 22.) and worked miracles in his name (Acts iii. 6.) His
disciples too were long called Nazarenes, and it was not until a late
period that this name was exclusively applied to a heretical sect.[*]
This appellation proves, if not that Jesus was born in Nazareth, at

* Tertull. ad. Marcion. iv. 8. Epiphan. hær. xxix. 1.

least that he resided in that place for a considerable time ; and as, according to a probable tradition (Luke iv. 16 f. parall.), Jesus, during his public life, paid but transient visits to Nazareth, this prolonged residence must be referred to the earlier part of his life, which he passed in the bosom of his family. Thus his family, at least his parents, must have lived in Nazareth during his childhood ; and if it be admitted that they once dwelt there, it follows that they dwelt there always, for we have no historical grounds for supposing a change of residence : so that this one of the two contradictory propositions has as much certainty as we can expect, in a fact belonging to so remote and obscure a period.

Neither does the other proposition, however, that Jesus was born in Bethlehem, rest solely on the statement of our Gospels ; it is sanctioned by an expectation, originating in a prophetic passage, that the Messiah would be born at Bethlehem. (Comp. with Matt. ii. 5. f., John vii. 42). But this is a dangerous support, which they who wish to retain as historical the gospel statement, that Jesus was born in Bethlehem, will do well to renounce. For wherever we find a narrative which recounts the accomplishment of a long-expected event, a strong suspicion must arise, that the narrative owes its origin solely to the pre-existent belief that that event would be accomplished. But our suspicion is converted into certainty when we find this belief to be groundless; and this is the case here, for the alleged issue must have confirmed a false interpretation of a prophetic passage. Thus this prophetic evidence of the birth of Jesus in Bethlehem, deprives the historical evidence, which lies in the 2nd chapters of Matthew and Luke, of its value, since the latter seems to be built on the former, and consequently shares its fall. Any other voucher for this fact is however sought in vain. Nowhere else in the New Testament is the birth of Jesus at Bethlehem mentioned; nowhere does he appear in any relation with his alleged birth-place, or pay it the honour of a visit, which he yet does not deny to the unworthy Nazareth ; nowhere does he appeal to the fact as a concomitant proof of his messiahship, although he had the most direct inducements to do so, for many were repelled from him by his Galilean origin, and defended their prejudice by referring to the necessity that the Messiah should come out of Bethlehem, the city of David (John vii. 42).[*] John does not, it is true, say that these objections were uttered in the presence of Jesus;[†] but as, immediatly before, he had annexed to a discourse of Jesus a comment of his own, to the effect that the Holy Ghost was not yet given, so here he might very suitably have added, in explanation of the doubts expressed by the people, that they did not yet know that Jesus was born in Bethlehem. Such an observation will be thought too superficial and trivial for an apostle like John : thus much however must be admitted : he had occasion *repeatedly* to mention the popular notion that Jesus

was a native of Nazareth, and the consequent prejudice against him ;
had he then known otherwise, he must have added a corrective remark, if he wished to avoid leaving the false impression, that he also
believed Jesus to be a Nazarene. As it is, we find Nathanael, John
i. 46, alleging this objection, without having his opinion rectified either mediately or immediately, for he nowhere learns that the *good
thing* did not really come out of Nazareth, and the conclusion he is
left to draw is, that even out of Nazareth something good can come.
In general, if Jesus were really born in Bethlehem, though but fortuitously, (according to Luke's representation,) it is incomprehensible, considering the importance of this fact to the article of his messiahship, that even his own adherents should always call him the Nazarene, instead of opposing to this epithet, pronounced by his opponents with polemical emphasis, the honourable title of the Bethle-
hemite.

Thus the evangelical statement that Jesus was born at Bethlehem is destitute of all valid historical evidence ; nay, it is contra-
vened by positive historical facts. We have seen reason to conclude that the parents of Jesus lived at Nazareth, not only after
the birth of Jesus, but also, as we have no counter evidence, prior
to that event, and that, no credible testimony to the contrary existing, Jesus was probably not born at any other place than the home
of his parents. With this twofold conclusion, the supposition that
Jesus was born at Bethlehem is irreconcileable : it can therefore
cost us no further effort to decide that Jesus was born, not in Bethlehem, but, as we have no trustworthy indications that point elsewhere, in all probability at Nazareth.

The relative position of the two evangelists on this point may be
thus stated. Each of their accounts is partly correct, and partly
incorrect ; Luke is right in maintaining the identity of the earlier
with the later residence of the parents of Jesus, and herein Matthew
is wrong; again, Matthew is right in maintaining the identity of the
birth-place of Jesus with the dwelling-place of his parents, and here
the error is on the side of Luke. Further, Luke is entirely correct
in making the parents of Jesus reside in Nazareth before, as well as
after, the birth of Jesus, while Matthew has only half the truth,
namely, that they were established there after his birth ; but in the
statement that Jesus was born at Bethlehem both are decidedly
wrong. The source of all the error of their narratives, is the Jewish
opinion with which they fell in, that the Messiah must be born at
Bethlehem; the source of all their truth, is the fact which lay before
them, that he always passed for a Nazarene ; finally, the cause of
the various admixture of the true and the false in both, and the
preponderance of the latter in Matthew, is the different position held
by the two writers in relation to the above data. Two particulars
were to be reconciled—the historical fact that Jesus was universally
reputed to be a Nazarene, and the prophetic requisition that, as
Messiah, he should be born at Bethlehem. Matthew, or the legend

which he followed, influenced by the ruling tendency to apply the prophecies, observable in his Gospel, effected the desired reconciliation in such a manner, that the greatest prominence was given to Bethlehem, the locality pointed out by the prophet; this was represented as the original home of the parents of Jesus, and Nazareth merely as a place of refuge, recommended by a subsequent turn of events. Luke, on the contrary, more bent on historic detail, either adopted or created that form of the legend, which attaches the greatest importance to Nazareth, making it the original dwelling-place of the parents of Jesus, and regarding the sojourn in Bethlehem as a temporary one, the consequence of a casual occurrence.

Such being the state of the case, no one, we imagine, will be inclined either with Schleiermacher,* to leave the question concerning the relation of the two narratives to the real facts undecided, or with Sieffert,† to pronounce exclusively in favour of Luke.‡

CHAPTER V.

THE FIRST VISIT TO THE TEMPLE, AND THE EDUCATION OF JESUS.

---

§ 40. JESUS, WHEN TWELVE YEARS OLD, IN THE TEMPLE.

THE Gospel of Matthew passes in silence over the entire period from the return of the parents of Jesus out of Egypt, to the baptism of Jesus by John; and even Luke has nothing to tell us of the long interval between the early childhood of Jesus and his maturity, beyond a single incident—his demeanour on a visit to the temple in his twelfth year (ii. 41—52). This anecdote, out of the early youth of Jesus is, as Hess has truly remarked,§ distinguished from the narratives hitherto considered, belonging to his childhood, by the circumstance that Jesus no longer, as in the latter, holds a merely passive position, but presents an active proof of his high destination: a proof which has always been especially valued, as indicating the moment in which the consciousness of that destination was kindled in Jesus.‖

In his twelfth year, the period at which, according to Jewish

---

* Ueber den Lukas, S. 49. There is a similar hesitation in Theile, Biographie Jesu, §. 15. † Ueber den Ursprung u. s. w., S. 68 f. u. S. 158. ‡ Comp. Ammon, Fortbildung, 1, S. 191 ff.; De Wette, exeget. Handb., 1, 2, S. 21 f.; George, S. 84 ff. That different narrators may give different explanations of the same fact, and that these different explanations may afterwards be united in one book, is proved by many examples in the O. T. Thus in Genesis, three derivations are given of the name of Isaac; two of that of Jacob,(xxv. 26. xxvii. 16). and so of Edom and Beersheba (xxvi. 33). Comp. De Wette, Kritik der mos. Gesch., S. 110, 118 ff., and my Streitschriften, 1, 1, S. 83 ff. § Hess, Geschichte Jesu, 1, S. 110. ‖ Olshausen, bibl. Comm. 1, S. 115 f.

usage, the boy became capable of an independent participation in
the sacred rites, the parents of Jesus, as this narrative informs us,
took him for the first time to the Passover. At the expiration of
the feast, the parents bent their way homewards ; that their son
was missing gave them no immediate anxiety, because they supposed him to be among their travelling companions, and it was not
until after they had accomplished a day's journey, and in vain sought
their son among their kinsfolk and acquaintance, that they turned
back to Jerusalem to look for him there. This conduct on the part
of the parents of Jesus may with reason excite surprise. It seems
inconsistent with the carefulness which it has been thought incumbent on us to attribute to them, that they should have allowed the
divine child entrusted to their keeping, to remain so long out of
their sight; and hence they have on many sides been accused of
neglect and a dereliction of duty, in the instance before us.* It has
been urged, as a general consideration in vindication of Joseph and
Mary, that the greater freedom permitted to the boy is easily conceivable as part of a liberal method of education ;† but even according to our modern ideas, it would seem more than liberal for parents
to let a boy of twelve years remain out of their sight during so long
an interval as our narrative supposes ; how far less reconcileable
must it then be with the more rigid views of education held by the
ancients, not excepting the Jews ? It is remarked however, that
viewing the case as an extraordinary one, the parents of Jesus knew
their child, and they could therefore very well confide in his understanding and character, so far as to be in no fear that any danger
would accrue to him from his unusual freedom ;‡ but we can perceive from their subsequent anxiety, that they were not so entirely
at ease on that head. Thus their conduct must be admitted to be
such as we should not have anticipated ; but it is not consequently
incredible, nor does it suffice to render the entire narrative improbable, for the parents of Jesus are no saints to us, that we should
not impute to them any fault.

Returned to Jerusalem, they find their son on the third day in
the temple, doubtless in one of the outer halls, in the midst of an
assembly of doctors, engaged in a conversation with them, and exciting universal astonishment (v. 45 f.) From some indications it
would seem that Jesus held a higher position in the presence of the
doctors, than could belong to a boy of twelve years. The word
καθεζόμενον (*sitting*) has excited scruples, for according to Jewish
records, it was not until after the death of the Rabbi Gamaliel, an
event long subsequent to the one described in our narrative. that the
pupils of the rabbins sat, they having previously been required to
stand§ when in the school ; but this Jewish tradition is of doubtful
authority.|| It has also been thought a difficulty, that Jesus does

* Olshausen, ut sup. 1. 150.   † Hase, Leben Jesu, § 37.   ‡ Heydenreich, über die
Unzulässigkeit u. s. f. 1, S. 103.   § Megillah, f. 21, apud Lightfoot in loc. || Vid. Kuinöl,
in Luc. p. 353.

not merely hear the doctors, but also asks them questions, thus appearing to assume the position of their teacher. Such is indeed the representation of the apocryphal Gospels, for in them Jesus, before he is twelve years old, perplexes all the doctors by his questions,[*] and reveals to his instructor in the alphabet the mystical significance of the characters;[†] while at the above visit to the temple he proposes controversial questions,[‡] such as that touching the Messiah's being at once David's Son and Lord, (Matth. xxii. 41) and proceeds to throw light on all departments of knowledge.[§] If the expressions ἐρωτᾶν and ἀποκρίνεσθαι implied that Jesus played the part of a teacher in this scene, so unnatural a feature in the evangelical narrative would render the whole suspicious.[‖] But there is nothing to render this interpretation of the words necessary, for according to Jewish custom, rabbinical teaching was of such a kind that not only did the masters interrogate the pupils, but the pupils interrogated the masters, when they wished for explanations on any point.[¶] We may with the more probability suppose that the writer intended to attribute to Jesus such questions as suited a boy, because he, apparently not without design, refers the astonishment of the doctors, not to his questions, but to that in which he could best show himself in the light of an intelligent pupil—namely, to his answers. A more formidable difficulty is the statement, that the boy Jesus sat *in the midst of the doctors*, ἐν μέσῳ τῶν διδασκάλων. For we learn from Paul (Acts xxii. 3.) the position that became a pupil, when he says that he was brought up *at the feet* (παρὰ τοὺς πόδας) of Gamaliel: it being the custom for the rabbins to be placed on chairs, while their pupils sat on the ground,[**] and did not take their places among their masters. It has indeed been thought that ἐν μέσῳ might be so explained as to signify, either that Jesus sat between the doctors, who are supposed to have been elevated on chairs, while Jesus and the other pupils are pictured as sitting on the ground between them,[††] or merely that he was in the company of doctors, that is, in the synagogue:[‡‡] but according to the strict sense of the words, the expression καθέζεσθαι ἐν μέσῳ τινῶν appears to signify, if not as Schöttgen believes,[§§] *in majorem Jesu gloriam*, a place of pre-eminent honour, at least a position of equal dignity with that occupied by the rest. It need only be asked, would it harmonize with the spirit of our narrative to substitute καθεζόμενον παρὰ τοὺς πόδας τῶν διδασκάλων for καθ. ἐν μέσω τ. δ.? the answer will certainly be in the negative, and it will then be inevitable to admit, that our narrative places Jesus in another relation to the doctors than that of a learner, though the latter is the only natural one for a boy of twelve, however highly gifted. For Olshausen's

* Evang. Thomæ, c. vi. ff. Ap. Thilo, p. 288 ff. and Evang. infant. arab. c. xlviii. p. 123. Thilo, † Ibid. ‡ Evang. infant. arab. c. l. § Ibid. c. l. and li; comp. ev. Thomæ, c. xix. ‖ Olshausen confesses this, S. 151. ¶ For proofs (e. g. Hieros. Taanith, lxvii. 4) see Westein and Lightfoot, in loc. ** Lightfoot, Horæ, p. 712. †† Paulus, S. 279. ‡‡ Kuinöl, S. 353 f. §§ Horæ, ii. p. 886.

position,*—that in Jesus nothing was formed from without, by the instrumentality of another's wisdom, because this would be inconsistent with the character of the Messiah, as absolutely self-determined,—contradicts a dogma of the church which he himself advances, namely, that Jesus in his manifestation as man, followed the regular course of human development. For not only is it in the nature of this development to be gradual, but also, and still more essentially, to be dependent, whether it be mental or physical, on the interchange of reception and influence. To deny this in relation to the physical life of Jesus—to say, for example, that the food which he took did not serve for the nourishment and growth of his body by real assimilation, but merely furnished occasion for him to reproduce himself from within, would strike every one as Docetism; and is the analogous proposition in relation to his spiritual development, namely, that he appropriated nothing from without, and used what he heard from others merely as a voice to evoke one truth after another from the recesses of his own mind—is this anything else than a more refined Docetism? Truly, if we attempt to form a conception of the conversation of Jesus with the doctors in the temple according to this theory, we make anything but a natural scene of it. It is not to be supposed that he taught, nor properly speaking that he was taught, but that the discourse of the doctors merely gave an impetus to his power of teaching himself, and was the occasion for an ever-brightening light to rise upon him, especially on the subject of his own destination. But in that case he would certainly have given utterance to his newly acquired knowledge; so that the position of a teacher on the part of the boy would return upon us, a position which Olshausen himself pronounces to be preposterous. At least such an indirect mode of teaching is involved as Ness subscribes to, when he supposes that Jesus, even thus early, made the first attempt to combat the prejudices which swayed in the synagogue, exposing to the doctors, by means of good-humoured questions and requests for explanation, such as are willingly permitted to a boy, the weakness of many of their dogmas.* But even such a position on the part of a boy of twelve, is inconsistent with the true process of human development, through which it behoved the God-Man himself to pass. Discourse of this kind from a boy must, we grant, have excited the astonishment of all the hearers; nevertheless the expression ἐξίσταντο πάντες οἱ ἀκούοντες αὐτοῦ (v. 47.), looks too much like a panegyrical formula.§

The narrative proceeds to tell us how the mother of Jesus reproached her son when she had found him thus, asking him why he had not spared his parents the anguish of their sorrowful search?

* Bibl. Comm. p. 151.   † Geschichte Jesu, S. 112.   ‡ In the similar account also which Josephus gives us of himself when fourteen, it is easy to discern the exaggeration of a self-complacent man. Life, 2: *Moreover, when I was a child, and about fourteen years of age, I was commended by all for the love I had to learning, on which account the high priests and principal men of the city came there frequently to me together, in order to know my opinion about the accurate understanding of points of the law.*

To this Jesus returns an answer which forms the point of the entire narrative; he asks whether they might not have known that he was to be sought nowhere else than in the house of his Father, in the temple? (v. 48 f.) One might be inclined to understand this designation of God as τοῦ πατρὸς generally, as implying that God was the Father of all men, and only in this sense the Father of Jesus. But this interpretation is forbidden, not only by the addition of the pronoun μοῦ, the above sense requiring ἡμῶν (as in Matt. vi. 9.), but still more absolutely by the circumstance that the parents of Jesus did not understand these words (v. 50), a decided indication that they must have a special meaning, which can here be no other than the mystery of the Messiahship of Jesus, who as Messiah, was υἱὸς Θεοῦ in a peculiar sense. But that Jesus in his twelfth year had already the consciousness of his Messiahship is a position which, although it may be consistently adopted from the orthodox point of view, and although it is not opposed to the regular human form of the development of Jesus, which even orthodoxy maintains, we are not here bound to examine. So also the natural explanation, which retains the above narrative as a history, though void of the miraculous, and which accordingly supposes the parents of Jesus, owing to a particular combination of circumstances, to have come even before his birth to a conviction of his Messiahship, and to have instilled this conviction into their son from his earliest childhood,—this too may make it plain how Jesus could be so clear as to his messianic relation to God; but it can only do so by the hypothesis of an unprecedented coincidence of extraordinary accidents. We, on the contrary, who have renounced the previous incidents as historical, either in the supernatural or the natural sense, are unable to comprehend how the consciousness of his messianic destination could be so early developed in Jesus. For though the consciousness of a more subjective vocation, as that of a poet or an artist, which is dependent solely on the internal gifts of the individual, (gifts which cannot long remain latent,) may possibly be awakened very early; an objective vocation, in which the conditions of external reality are a chief co-operator, as the vocation of the statesman, the general, the reformer of religion, can hardly be so early evident to the most highly endowed individual, because for this a knowledge of contemporary circumstances would be requisite, which only long observation and mature experience can confer. Of the latter kind is the vocation of the Messiah, and if this is implied in the words by which Jesus in his twelfth year justified his lingering in the temple, he cannot have uttered the words at that period.

In another point of view also, it is worthy of notice that the parents of Jesus are said (v. 50) not to have understood the words which he addressed to them. What did these words signify? That God was his Father, in whose house it behoved him to be. But that her son would in a specific sense be called a υἱὸς Θεοῦ had been already made known to Mary by the annunciating angel (Luke i. 32.

35), and that he would have a peculiar relation to the temple she might infer, both from the above-title, and from the striking reception which he had met with at his first presentation in the temple, when yet an infant. The parents of Jesus, or at least Mary, of whom it is repeatedly noticed that she carefully kept in her heart the extraordinary communications concerning her son, ought not to have been in the dark a single moment as to the meaning of his language on this occasion. But even at the presentation in the temple, we are told that the parents of Jesus marvelled at the discourse of Simeon (v. 33.), which is merely saying in other words that they did not understand him. And their wonder is not referred to the declaration of Simeon that their boy would be a cause not only of the rising again, but of the fall of many in Israel, and that a sword would pierce through the heart of his mother (an aspect of his vocation and destiny on which nothing had previously been communicated to the parents of Jesus, and at which therefore they might naturally wonder); for these disclosures are not made by Simeon until after the wonder of the parents, which is caused only by Simeon's expressions of joy at the sight of the Saviour, who would be the glory of Israel, and a light even to the Gentiles. And here again there is no intimation that the wonder was excited by the idea that Jesus would bear this relation to the heathens, which indeed it could not well be, since this more extended destination of the Messiah had been predicted in the Old Testament. There remains therefore as a reason for the wonder in question, merely the fact of the child's Messiahship, declared by Simeon; a fact which had been long ago announced to them by angels, and which was acknowledged by Mary in her song of praise. We have just a parallel difficulty in the present case, it being as inconceivable that the parents of Jesus should not understand his allusion to his messianic character, as that they should wonder at the declaration of it by Simeon. We must therefore draw this conclusion: if the parents of Jesus did not understand these expressions of their son when twelve years old, those earlier communications cannot have happened; or, if the earlier communications really occurred, the subsequent expressions of Jesus cannot have remained incomprehensible to them. Having done away with those earlier incidents as historical, we might content ourselves with this later want of comprehension, were it not fair to mistrust the whole of a narrative whose later portions agree so ill with the preceding. For it is the character not of an historical record, but of a marvellous legend, to represent its personages as so permanently in a state of wonder, that they not only at the first appearance of the extraordinary, but even at the second, third, tenth repetition, when one would expect them to be familiarized with it, continually are astonished and do not understand—obviously with the view of exalting the more highly the divine impartation by this lasting incomprehensibleness. So, to draw an example from the later history of Jesus, the divine decree of his suffering and death is set forth in all its loftiness in the evangelical narratives by the circumstance, that even the repeated, explicit disclosures of Jesus on this subject, remain throughout incomprehensible to the disciples; as here the mystery of the Messiahship of Jesus is exalted by the circumstance, that his parents, often as it has been announced to them, at every fresh word on the subject are astonished anew and do not understand.

The twofold form of conclusion, that the mother of Jesus kept all these sayings in her heart (v. 51), and that the boy grew in wisdom and stature, and so forth, we have already recognised as a favourite form of conclusion and transition in the heroic legend of the Hebrews; in particular, that which relates to the growth of the boy is almost verbally parallel with a passage relating to Samuel, as in two former instances similar expressions appeared to have been borrowed from the history of Samson.*

§. 41. THIS NARRATIVE ALSO MYTHICAL.

THUS here again we must acknowledge the influence of the legend; but as the main part of the incident is thoroughly natural, we might in this instance prefer the middle course, and after disengaging the mythical, seek to preserve a residue of history. We might suppose that the parents of Jesus really took their son to Jerusalem in his early youth, and that after having lost sight of him, (probably before their departure,) they found him in the temple where, eager for instruction, he sat at the feet of the rabbins. When called to account, he declared that his favourite abode was in the house of God;† a sentiment which rejoiced his parents, and won the approbation of the bystanders. The rest of the story we might suppose to have been added by the aggrandizing legend, after Jesus was acknowledged as the Messiah. Here all the difficulties in our narrative,—the idea of the boy sitting in the midst of the doctors, his claiming God as his father in a special sense, and the departure of the parents without their son, would be rejected; but the journey of Jesus when twelve years old, the eagerness for knowledge then manifested by him, and his attachment to the temple, are retained. To these particulars there is nothing to object negatively, for they contain nothing improbable in itself; but their historical truth must become doubtful if we can shew, positively, a strong interest of the legend, out of which the entire narrative, and especially these intrinsically not improbable particulars, might have arisen.

That in the case of great men who in their riper age have been distinguished by mental superiority, the very first presaging move-

* 1 Sam. ii. 26 (LXX):
καὶ τὸ παιδάριον Σαμουὴλ ἐπορεύετο μεγαλυνόμενον, καὶ ἀγαθὸν καὶ μετὰ Κυρίου καὶ μετὰ ἀνθρώπων.

Luc. ii. 52:
καὶ Ἰησοῦς προέκοπτε σοφίᾳ καὶ ἡλικίᾳ, καὶ χάριτι παρὰ θεῷ καὶ ἀνθρώποις.

Compare also what Josephus says Antiq. ii. ix. 6, of the χάρις παιδικὴ of Moses.   † Gabler neuest. theol. Journal 3, 1, S. 39.

ments of their mind are eagerly gleaned, and if they are not to be ascertained historically, are invented under the guidance of probability, is well known. In the Hebrew history and legend especially, we find manifold proofs of this tendency. Thus of Samuel it is said in the Old Testament itself, that even as a boy he received a divine revelation and the gift of prophecy (1 Sam. iii.), and with respect to Moses, on whose boyish years the Old Testament narrative is silent, a subsequent tradition, followed by Josephus and Philo, had striking proofs to relate of his early development. As in the narrative before us Jesus shews himself wise beyond his years; so this tradition attributes a like precocity to Moses;* as Jesus turning away from the idle tumult of the city in all the excitement of festival time, finds his favourite entertainment in the temple among the doctors; so the boy Moses was not attracted by childish sports, but by serious occupation, and very early it was necessary to give him tutors, whom, however, like Jesus in his twelfth year, he quickly surpassed.†

According to Jewish custom and opinion, the twelfth year formed an epoch in development to which especial proofs of awakening genius were the rather attached, because in the twelfth year, as with us in the fourteenth, the boy was regarded as having outgrown the period of childhood.‡ Accordingly it was believed of Moses, that in his twelfth year he left the house of his father, to become an independent organ of the divine revelations.§ The Old Testament leaves it uncertain how early the gift of prophecy was imparted to Samuel, but he was said by a later tradition to have prophesied from his twelfth year:‖ and in like manner the wise judgments of Solomon and Daniel (1 Kings iii. 23 ff. Susann. 45 ff.) were supposed to have been given when they were only twelve.¶ If in the case of these Old Testament heroes, the spirit that impelled them manifested itself according to common opinion so early as in their twelfth year, it was argued that it could not have remained longer concealed in Jesus; and if Samuel and David shewed themselves at

---

* Joseph. Ant. ii. ix. 6. † Philo, de vita Mosis, Opp. ed. Mangey, V. 2. p. 83 f. οὐχ οἷα κομιδῇ νήπιος ἤρετο τωθασμοῖς καὶ γέλωσι καὶ παιδιαῖς—ἀλλ' αἰδὼ καὶ σεμνότητα παραφαίνων. ἀπούσμασι καὶ θεάμασιν, ἃ τὴν ψυχὴν ἔμελλεν ὠφελήσειν προσεῖχε. διδάσκαλοι δ' οἱ ϑὺς, ἀλλαχόϑεν ἄλλος, παρῆσαν.—ὧν ἐν οὐ μακρῷ χρόνῳ τὰς δυνάμεις ὑπερέβαλεν, εὐμοιρίᾳ φύσεως φϑάνων τὰς ὑφηγήσεις. ‡ Chagiga, ap. Wetstein, in loc. A XII anno filius censetur maturus. So Joma f. lxxxii. 1. Berachoth f. xxiv. 1; whereas Bereschith Rabba lxii. mentions the 13th year as the critical one. § Schemoth R. ap. Wetstein: Dixit R. Chama: Moses duodenarius avulsus est a domo patris sui etc. ‖ Joseph. Antiq. v. x. 4; Σαμούηλος δὲ πεπληρωκὼς ἔτος ἤδη δωδέκατον, προεφήτευε. ¶ Ignat. ep. (interpol.) ad Magnes. c. iii.: Σολομῶν δὲ — δωδηκαετὴς βασιλεύσας, τὴν φοβερὰν ἐκείνην καὶ δυσερμήνευτον ἐπὶ ταῖς γυναιξὶ κρίσιν ἕνεκα τῶν παιδίων ἐποιήσατο. — Δανιὴλ ὁ σοφὸς δωδεκαετὴς γέγονε κάτοχος τῷ θείῳ πνεύματι, καὶ τοὺς μάτην τὴν πολιὰν φέροντας πρεσβύτας συκοφάντας καὶ ἐπιϑυμητὰς ἀλλοτρίου κάλλους ἀπήλεγξε. But Solomon . . . . . being king at the age of twelve years, gave that terrible and profound judgment between the women with respect to the children . . . . Daniel, the wise man, when twelve years old, was possessed by the divine spirit, and convicted those calumniating old men who, carrying gray hairs in vain, coveted the beauty that belonged to another. This, it is true, is found in a Christian writing, but on comparing it with the above data, we are led to believe that is was drawn from a more ancient Jewish legend.

that age in their later capacity of divinely inspired seers, Solomon in that of a wise ruler, so Jesus at the corresponding period in his life must have shewn himself in the character to which he subsequently established his claim, that namely, of the Son of God and Teacher of Mankind. It is, in fact, the obvious aim of Luke to pass over no epoch in the early life of Jesus, without surrounding him with divine radiance, with significant prognostics of the future; in this style he treats his birth, mentions the circumcision at least emphatically, but above all avails himself of the presentation in the temple. There yet remained according to Jewish manners one epoch, the twelfth year, with the first journey to the passover; how could he do otherwise than, following the legend, adorn this point in the development of Jesus as we find that he has done in his narrative? and how could we do otherwise than regard his narrative as a legendary embellishment of this period in the life of Jesus,[*] from which we learn nothing of his real development,[†] but merely something of the exalted notions which were entertained in the primitive church of the early ripened mind of Jesus?

But how this anecdote can be numbered among mythi is found by some altogether inconceivable. It bears, thinks Heydenreich,[‡] a thoroughly historical character (this is the very point to be proved) and the stamp of the highest simplicity (like every popular legend in its original form); it contains no tincture of the miraculous, wherein the primary characteristic of a mythus (but not of every mythus) is held to consist; it is so remote from all embellishment that there is not the slightest detail of the conversation of Jesus with the doctors (the legend was satisfied with the dramatic trait, *sitting in the midst of the doctors:* as a dictum, v. 49. was alone important, and towards this the narrator hastens without delay); nay, even the conversation between Jesus and his mother is only given in a fragmentary aphoristic manner (there is no trace of an omission); finally, the inventor of a legend would have made Jesus speak differently to his mother, instead of putting into his mouth words which might be construed into irreverence and indifference. In this last observation Heydenreich agrees with Schleiermacher, who finds in the behaviour of Jesus to his mother, liable as it is to be misinterpreted, a sure guarantee that the whole history was not invented to supply something remarkable concerning Jesus, in connexion with the period at which the holy things of the temple and the law were first opened to him.[§]

In combating the assertion, that an inventor would scarcely have attributed to Jesus so much apparent harshness towards his mother, we need not appeal to the apocryphal *Evangelium Thomæ,* which

---

* This Kaiser has seen, bibl. Theol. 1, 231.   † Neither do we learn what Hase (Leben Jesu § 37) supposes to be conveyed in this narrative, namely, that as it exhibits the same union with God that constituted the idea of the later life of Jesus, it is an intimation that his later excellence was not the result of conversion from youthful errors, b. t of the uninterrupted development of his freedom.   ‡ Ueber die Unzulässigkeit u. s. f. 1, S. 92.   § Ueber den Lukas, S. 33 f.

makes the boy Jesus say to his fosterfather Joseph: *insipientissime fecisti;** for even in the legend or history of the canonical gospels, corresponding traits are to be found. In the narrative of the wedding at Cana, we find this rough address to his mother: τὶ ἐμοὶ καὶ σοὶ γύναι (John ii. 4); and in the account of the visit paid to Jesus by his mother and brethren, the striking circumstance that he apparently wishes to take no notice of his relatives (Matt. xii. 46). If these are real incidents, then the legend had an historical precedent to warrant the introduction of a similar feature, even into the early youth of Jesus; if, on the other hand, they are only legends, they are the most vivid proofs that an inducement was not wanting for the invention of such features. Where this inducement lay, it is easy to see. The figure of Jesus would stand in the higher relief from the obscure background of his contracted family relations, if it were often seen that his parents were unable to comprehend his elevated mind, and if even he himself sometimes made them feel his superiority—so far as this could happen without detriment to his filial obedience, which, it should be observed, our narrative expressly preserves.

§ 42. ON THE EXTERNAL LIFE OF JESUS UP TO THE TIME OF HIS PUBLIC APPEARANCE.

WHAT were the external conditions under which Jesus lived, from the scene just considered up to the time of his public appearance? On this subject our canonical Gospels give scarcely an indication.

First, as to his place of residence, all that we learn explicitly is this: that both at the beginning and at the end of this obscure period he dwelt at Nazareth. According to Luke ii. 51.. Jesus when twelve years old returned thither with his parents, and according to Matthew iii. 13. Mark i. 9, he, when thirty years old (comp. Luke iii. 23), came from thence to be baptized by John. Thus our evangelists appear to suppose, that Jesus had in the interim resided in Galilee, and, more particularly, in Nazareth. This supposition, however, does not exclude journeys, such as those to the feasts in Jerusalem.

The employment of Jesus during the years of his boyhood and youth seems, from an intimation in our Gospels, to have been determined by the trade of his father, who is there called a τέκτων (Matt. xiii. 55.). This Greek word, used to designate the trade of Joseph, is generally understood in the sense of *faber lignarius* (carpenter):† a few only, on mystical grounds, discover in it a *faber ferrarius (blacksmith)*, *aurarius (goldsmith)*, or *caementarius (ma-*

---

* Cap. v. In the Greek text also the more probable reading is καὶ μάλιστα οὐ σοφῶς. vid. Thilo, p. 287. † Hence the title of an Arabian apocryphal work (according to the Latin translation in Thilo, 1, p. 3): *historia Josephi, fabri lignarii.*

son).* The works in wood which he executed are held of different magnitude by different authors: according to Justin and the *Evangelium Thomæ*,† they were *ploughs and yokes*, ἄροτρα καὶ ζυγὰ, and in that case he would be what we call a wheelwright; according to the *Evangelium infantiæ arabicum*,‡ they were doors, milkvessels, sieves and coffers, and once Joseph makes a throne for the king; so that here he is represented partly as a cabinet-maker and partly as a cooper. The *Protevangelium Jacobi*, on the other hand, makes him work at *buildings*, οἰκοδομαῖς,§ without doubt as a carpenter. In these labours of the father Jesus appears to have shared, according to an expression of Mark, who makes the Nazarenes ask concerning Jesus, not merely as in the parallel passage of Matthew: *Is not this the carpenter's son?* οὐκ αὐτός ἐστιν ὁ τοῦ τέκτόνος υἱός; but *Is not this the carpenter?* οὐκ αὐτός ἐστιν ὁ τέκτων; (vi. 3.) It is true that in replying to the taunt of Celsus that the teacher of the Christians was a carpenter by trade, τέκτων ἦν τὴν τέχνην, Origen says, he must have forgotten *that in none of the Gospels received by the churches is Jesus himself called a carpenter*, ὅτι οὐδαμοῦ τῶν ἐν ταῖς ἐκκλησίαις φερομένων εὐαγγελίων τέκτων αὐτὸς ὁ Ἰησοῦς ἀναγέγραπται. ‖ The above passage in Mark has in fact the various reading, ὁ τοῦ τέκτονος υἱός; which Origen must have taken, unless he be supposed altogether to have overlooked the passage, and which is preferred by some modern critics.¶ But here Beza has justly remarked that *fortasse mutavit aliquis, existimans, hanc artem Christi majestati parum convenire;* whereas there could hardly be an interest which would render the contrary alteration desirable.** Moreover Fathers of the Church and apocryphal writings represent Jesus, in accordance with the more generally accepted reading, as following the trade of his father. Justin attaches especial importance to the fact that Jesus made ploughs and yokes or scales, as symbols of active life and of justice.†† In the *Evangelium infantiæ Arabicum*, Jesus goes about with Joseph to the places where the latter has work, to help him in such a manner that if Joseph made anything too long or too short, Jesus, by a touch or by merely stretching out his hand, gave to the object its right size; an assistance which was very useful to his foster-father, because, as the apocryphal text naively remarks: *nec admodum peritus erat artis fabrilis*.‡‡

Apart from the apocryphal descriptions, there are many reasons for believing that the above intimation as to the youthful employment of Jesus is correct. In the first place, it accords with the

* Vid. Thilo, Cod. Apocr. N. T. p. 368 f. not.   † Justin. Dial c. Tryph. 88.   According to him Jesus makes these implements, doubtless under the direction of Joseph. In the *Evang. Thomæ* c. xiii. Joseph is the workman.   ‡ Cap. xxxviii. ap. Thilo, p. 112 ff.   § C. ix. and xiii.   ‖ C. Cels. vi. 36.   ¶ Fritzsche, in Marc. p. 200.   ** Vid. Wetstein and Paulus, in loc.; Winer, Realworterbuch, 1, S. 665.   Note: Neander, L. J. Chr. S. 46 f. Note.   †† Ut sup.: ταῦτα γὰρ τὰ τεκτονικὰ ἔργα εἰργάζετο ἐν ἀνθρώποις ὤν, ἄροτρα καὶ ζυγὰ διὰ τούτων καὶ τὰ τῆς δικαιοσύνης συμβόλα διδάσκων, καὶ ἐνεργῆ βίον.   ‡‡ Cap. xxxviii.

Jewish custom which prescribed even to one destined to a learned career, or in general to any spiritual occupation, the acquisition of some handicraft; thus Paul, the pupil of the rabbins, was also a tent-maker, σκηνοποιὸς τὴν τέχνην (Acts xviii. 3.). Next, as our previous examinations have shown that we know nothing historical of extraordinary expectations and plans on the part of the parents of Jesus in relation to their son, so nothing is more natural than the supposition that Jesus early practised the trade of his father. Further, the Christians must have had an interest in denying, rather than inventing, this opinion as to their Messiah's youthful occupation, since it often drew down upon them the ridicule of their opponents. Thus Celsus, as we have already mentioned, could not abstain from a reflection on this subject, for which reason Origen will know nothing of any designation of Jesus as a τέκτων in the New Testament; and every one knows the scoffing question of Libanius about the carpenter's son, a question which seems to have been provided with so striking an answer, only *ex eventu.** It may certainly be said in opposition to this, that the notion of Jesus having been a carpenter, seems to be founded on a mere inference from the trade of the father as to the occupation of the son, whereas the latter was just as likely to apply himself to some other branch of industry; nay, that perhaps the whole tradition of the carpentry of Joseph and Jesus owes its origin to the symbolical significance exhibited by Justin. As however the allusion in our Gospels to the trade of Joseph is very brief and bare, and is nowhere used allegorically in the New Testament, nor entered into more minutely: it is not to be contested that he was really a carpenter; but it must remain uncertain whether Jesus shared in this occupation.

What were the circumstances of Jesus and his parents as to fortune? The answer to this question has been the object of many dissertations. It is evident that the ascription of pressing poverty to Jesus, on the part of orthodox theologians, rested on dogmatical and æsthetic grounds. On the one hand, they wished to maintain even in this point the *status exinanitionis*, and on the other, they wished to depict as strikingly as possible the contrast between the μορφὴ Θεοῦ (*form of God*) and the μορφὴ δούλου (*form of a servant*). That this contrast as set forth by Paul, Phil. ii. 6. ff., as well as the expression ἐπτώχευσε, which this apostle applies to Christ, (2 Cor. viii. 9.) merely characterizes the obscure and laborious life to which he submitted after his heavenly pre-existence, and instead of playing the part of king which the Jewish imagination attributed to the Messiah, is also to be regarded as established.[†] The expression of Jesus himself, *The Son of man hath not where to lay his head*, τοῦ τὴν κεφαγὴν κλίνη (Matt. viii. 20), may possibly import merely his voluntary renunciation of the peaceful enjoyment of fortune, for the sake of devoting himself to the wandering life of the Messiah. There is only one other particular bearing on the point in question,

* Theod. II. E. iii. 23.   † Hase, L. J., § 70; Winer, bibl. Realwörterb., 1, S. 665.

namely, that Mary presented, as an offering of purification, doves (Luke ii. 24),—according to Lev. xii. 8, the offering of the poor: which certainly proves that the author of this information conceived the parents of Jesus to have been in by no means brilliant circumstances :* but what shall assure us that he also was not induced to make this representation by unhistorical motives? Meanwhile we are just as far from having tenable ground for maintaining the contrary proposition, namely, that Jesus possessed property: at least it is inadmissible to adduce the coat without seam † (John xix. 23), untill we shall have inquired more closely what kind of relation it has to the subject.

§. 43. THE INTELLECTUAL DEVELOPMENT OF JESUS.

OUR information concerning the external life of Jesus during his youth is very scanty : but we are almost destitute of any concerning his intellectual development. For the indeterminate phrase, twice occurring in Luke's history of the childhood, concerning the increase of his spiritual strength and his growth in wisdom, tells us no more than we must necessarily have presupposed without it ; while on the expectations which his parents cherished with respect to him before his birth, and on the sentiment which his mother especially then expressed, no conclusion is to be founded, since those expectations and declarations are themselves unhistorical. The narrative just considered, of the appearance of Jesus in the temple at twelve years of age, rather gives us a result—the early and peculiar development of his religious consciousness,—than an explanation of the causes and conditions by which this development was favoured. But we at least learn from Luke ii. 41., (what however is to be of course supposed of pious Israelites,) that the parents of Jesus used to go to Jerusalem every year at the Passover. We may conjecture, then, that Jesus from his twelfth year generally accompanied them, and availed himself of this excellent opportunity, amid the concourse of Jews and Jewish proselytes of all countries and all opinions, to form his mind, to become acquainted with the condition of his people and the false principles of the Pharisaic leaders, and to extend his survey beyond the narrow limits of Palestine.‡

Whether or in what degree Jesus received the learned education of a rabbin, is also left untold in our canonical Gospels. From such passages as Matt. vii. 29., where it is said that Jesus taught *not as the scribes*, οὐχ ὡς οἱ γραμματεῖς, we can only infer that he did not adopt the method of the doctors of the law, and it does not follow that he had never enjoyed the education of a *scribe* (γραμματεύς). On the other hand, not only was Jesus called ῥαββί and ῥαββουνί by his disciples (Matth. xxvi. 25. 49. Marc. ix. 5. xi. 21. xiv. 45. John iv. 31. ix. 2. xi. 8. xx. 16. comp. i. 38. 40. 50.) and by supplicat-

* Winer, ut sup. † This is done by both the above named theologians. ‡ Paulus, exeget. Handb. 1 a, S. 273 ff.

ing sufferers (Mark x. 5.), but even the pharisaic αρχων Nicodemus (John iii. 2.) did not refuse him this title. We cannot however conclude from hence that Jesus had received the scholastic instruction of a rabbin;* for the salutation Rabbi, as also the privilege of reading in the synagogue (Luke iv. 16 ff.), a particular which has likewise been appealed to, belonged not only to graduated rabbins, but to every teacher who had given actual proof of his qualifications.† The enemies of Jesus explicitly assert, and he does not contradict them, that he had never learned letters: πῶς οὗτος γράμματα οἶδε μὴ μεμαθηκὼς; (John vii. 15.) and the Nazarenes are astonished to find so much wisdom in him, whence we infer that he had not to their knowledge been a student. These facts cannot be neutralized by the discourse of Jesus in which he represents himself as the model of a scribe well-instructed unto the kingdom of heaven.‡ (Matt. xiii. 52.) for the word γραμματεὺς here means a doctor of the law in general, and not directly a doctor qualified in the schools. Lastly, the intimate acquaintance with the doctrinal traditions, and the abuses of the rabbins, which Jesus exhibits,§ especially in the sermon on the mount and the anti-pharisaic discourse Matt. xxiii., he might acquire from the numerous discourses of the Pharisees to the people, without going through a course of study under them. Thus the data on our present subject to be found in the Gospels, collectively yield the result that Jesus did not pass formally through a rabbinical school; on the other hand, the consideration that it must have been the interest of the Christian legend to represent Jesus as independent of human teachers, may induce a doubt with respect to these statements in the New Testament, and a conjecture that Jesus may not have been so entirely a stranger to the learned culture of his nation. But from the absence of authentic information we can arrive at no decision on this point.

Various hypotheses, more or less independent of the intimations given in the New Testament, have been advanced both in ancient and modern times concerning the intellectual development of Jesus: they may be divided into two principal classes, according to their agreement with the natural or the supernatural view. The supernatural view of the person of Jesus requires that he should be the only one of his kind, independent of all external, human influences, self-taught or rather taught of God; hence, not only must its advocates determinedly reject every supposition implying that he borrowed or learned anything, and consequently place in the most glaring light the difficulties which lay in the way of the natural development of Jesus;|| but, the more surely to exclude every kind of reception, they must also be disposed to assign as early an appearance as possible to that spontaneity which we find in Jesus in his

---

* Such, however, are the arguments of Paulus, ut. sup. 275 ff.   † Comp. Hase, Leben Jesu, § 38;   Neander, L. J. Chr. S. 45 f.   ‡ Paulus, ut sup.   § To this Schöttgen appeals, *Christus rabbinorum summus*, in his horæ, ii. p. 890 f. || As e. g. Reinhard does, in his Plan Jesu.

mature age. This spontaneous activity is twofold; it is theoretical and practical. As regards the theoretical side, comprising judgment and knowledge, the effort to give as early a date as possible to its manifestation in Jesus, displays itself in the apocryphal passages which have been already partly cited, and which describe Jesus as surpassing his teachers long before his twelfth year, for according to one of them he spoke in his cradle and declared himself to be the Son of God.[*] The practical side, too, of that superior order of spontaneity attributed to Jesus in his later years, namely, the power of working miracles, is attached by the apocryphal gospels to his earliest childhood and youth. The *Evangelium Thomæ* opens with the fifth year of Jesus the story of his miracles,[‡] and the Arabian *Evangelium Infantiæ* fills the journey into Egypt with miracles which the mother of Jesus performed by means of the swaddling bands of her infant, and the water in which he was washed.[†] Some of the miracles which according to these apocryphal gospels were wrought by Jesus when in his infancy and boyhood, are analogous to those in the New Testament—cures and resuscitations of the dead; others are totally diverse from the ruling type in the canonical Gospels—extremely revolting retributive miracles, by which every one who opposes the boy Jesus in any matter whatever is smitten with lameness, or even with death, or else mere extravagancies, such as the giving of life to sparrows formed out of mud.[‡]

The natural view of the person of Jesus had an opposite interest, which was also very early manifested both among Jewish and heathen opponents of Christianity, and which consisted in explaining his appearance conformably to the laws of causality, by comparing it with prior and contemporaneous facts to which it had a relation, and thus exhibiting the conditions on which Jesus depended, and the sources from which he drew. It is true that in the first centuries of the Christian era, the whole region of spirituality being a supernatural one for heathens as well as Jews, the reproach that Jesus owed his wisdom and seemingly miraculous powers, not to himself or to God, but to a communication from without, could not usually take the form of an assertion that he had acquired natural skill and wisdom in the ordinary way of instruction from others.[§] Instead of the natural and the human, the unnatural and the demoniacal were opposed to the divine and the supernatural (comp. Matt. xii. 24.), and Jesus was accused of working his miracles by the aid of magic acquired in his youth. This charge was the most easily attached to the journey of his parents with him into Egypt, that native land of magic and secret wisdom, and thus we find it both in Celsus and in the Talmud. The former makes a Jew allege

* Evang. infant. arab. c. i. p. 60 f. ap. Thilo, and the passages quoted § 40. out of the same Gospel and the Evang. Thomæ. † Cap. ii. p. 278 Thilo. ‡ Cap. x. ff. § E. g. Evang. Thomæ, c. iii.—v. Evang. infant. arab. c. xlvi. f. Evang. Thomæ, c. ii. Evang. inf. arab. c. xxxvi. ‖ Yet some isolated instances occur, vid. Semler, Baumgarten's Glaubenslehre, 1, S. 42, Anm. 8.

against Jesus, amongst other things, that he had entered into service for wages in Egypt, that he had there possessed himself of some magic arts, and on the strength of these had on his return vaunted himself for a God.* The Talmud gives him a member of the Jewish Sanhedrim as a teacher, makes him journey to Egypt with this companion, and bring magic charms from thence into Palestine.†

The purely natural explanation of the intellectual development of Jesus could only become prevalent amid the enlightened culture of modern times. In working out this explanation, the chief points of difference are the following: either the character of Jesus is regarded in too circumscribed a view, as the result of only one among the means of culture which his times afforded, or more comprehensively, as the result of all these combined; again, in tracing this external influence, either the internal gifts and self-determination of Jesus are adequately considered, or they are not.

In any case, the basis of the intellectual development of Jesus was furnished by the sacred writings of his people, of which the discourses preserved to us in the Gospels attest his zealous and profound study. His Messianic ideas seem to have been formed chiefly on Isaiah and Daniel: spiritual religiousness and elevation above the prejudices of Jewish nationality were impressively shadowed forth in the prophetic writings generally, together with the Psalms.

Next among the influences affecting mental cultivation in the native country of Jesus, must be reckoned the three sects under which the spiritual life of his fellow-countrymen may be classified. Among these, the Pharisees, whom Jesus at a later period so strenuously combated, can apparently have had only a negative influence over him; yet along with their fondness for tradition and legal pedantry, their sanctimoniousness and hypocrisy, by which Jesus was repelled from them, we must remember their belief in angels and in immortality, and their constant admission of a progressive development of the Jewish religion after Moses, which were so many points of union between them and Jesus. Still as these tenets were only peculiar to the Pharisees in contradistinction to the Sadducees, and, for the rest, were common to all orthodox Jews, we abide by the opinion that the influence of the Pharisaic sect on the development of Jesus was essentially negative.

In the discourses of Jesus Sadduceeism is less controverted, nay, he agrees with it in rejecting the Pharisaic traditions and hypocrisy;

* Orig. c. Cels. I. 28: καὶ (λέγει) ὅτι οὗτος (ὁ Ἰησοῦς) διὰ πενίαν εἰς Αἴγυπτον μισθαρνήσας, κἀκεῖ δυνάμεων τινῶν πειραθείς, ἐφ' αἷς Αἰγύπτιοι σεμνύνονται, ἐπανῆλθεν, ἐν ταῖς δυνάμεσι μέγα φρονῶν, καὶ δι' αὐτὰς θεὸν αὑτὸν ἀνηγόρευσε. † Sanhedr. f. cvii. 2:— R. Josua f. Perachja et ... Alexandriam Aegypti profecti sunt — — ... ex il'o tempore magiam excrcuit, et Isra.litas ad pessima quaeis perduit. (An important anachronism, as this Josua Ben Perachja lived about a century earlier. See Jost, Geschichte der Isr., 3, S. 80 ff. and 112 of the Appendices.) Schabbath f. civ. 2: Traditio est, R. Eliesercm dixisse ad viros doctos: annon f. Satdæ (i. e. Jesus) magicam ex Aegypto adduxit per incisionem in carne sua factam? vid. Schöttgen, horæ, ii. p. 697 ff. Eisenmenger, entdecktes Judenthum, 1, S. 149 f.

hence a few of the learned have wished to find him a school in this sect.* But the merely nagative agreement against the errors of the Pharisees,—an agreement which, moreover, proceeded from quite another principle in Jesus than in the Sadducees,—is more than counterbalanced by the contrast which their religious indifference, their unbelief in immortality and in spiritual existences, formed with the disposition of Jesus, and his manner of viewing the world. That the controversy with the Sadducees is not prominent in the Gospels, may be very simply explained by the fact that their sect had very slight influence on the circle with which Jesus was immediately connected, the adherents of Sadduceeism belonging to the higher ranks alone.†

Concerning one only of the then existing Jewish sects can the question seriously arise, whether we ought not to ascribe to it a positive influence on the development and appearance of Jesus—the sect, namely, of the Essenes.‡ In the last century the derivation of Christianity from Essenism was very much in vogue; not only English deists, and among the Germans, Bahrdt and Venturini, but even theologians, such as Städlin, embraced the idea.§ In the days of freemasonry and secret orders, there was a disposition to transfer their character to primitive Christianity. The concealment of an Essene lodge appeared especially adapted to explain the sudden disappearance of Jesus after the brilliant scenes of his infancy and boyhood, and again after his restoration to life. Besides the forerunner John, the two men on the Mount of Transfiguration, and the angels clothed in white at the grave, and on the Mount of Ascension, were regarded as members of the Essene brotherhood, and many cures of Jesus and the Apostles were referred to the medical traditions of the Essenes. Apart, however, from these fancies of a bygone age, there are really some essential characteristics which seem to speak in favour of an intimate relation between Essenism and Christianity. The most conspicuous as such are the prohibition of oaths and the community of goods: with the former was connected fidelity, peaceableness, obedience to every constituted authority: with the latter, contempt of riches, and the custom of travelling without provisions. These and other features, such as the sacred meal partaken in common, the rejection of sanguinary sacrifices and of slavery, constitute so strong a resemblance between Essenism and Christianity, that even so early a writer as Eusebius mistook the Therapeutæ, a sect allied to the Essenes, for Christians.‖ But there are very essential dissimilarities which must not be overlooked. Leaving out of consideration the *contempt of marriage*, ἐπερϊφία γάμου, since Josephus ascribes it to a part only of the Essenes: the asceticism, the punctilious observance of the Sab-

* E. g. Des Côtes, Schutzschrift für Jesus von Nazaret, S. 128 ff. † Neander, L. J. Chr. S. 39 ff. ‡ Vid. Joseph. B. j. ii. vii. 2—13. Antiq. xviii. i. 5. Comp. Philo, *quod omnis probus liber und de vita contemplativa*. § This opinion is judiciously developed by Städlin, Geschichte der Sittenlehre Jesu I, S. 570 ff.; and in a romantic manner in the Geschichte des Grossen Prophet n von Nazaret, I. Band. ‖ H. E. ii. 16 f.

bath, the purifications, and other superstitious usages of this sect, their retention of the names of the angels, the mystery which they affected, and their contracted, exclusive devotion to their order, are so foreign, nay so directly opposed to the spirit of Jesus, that, especially as the Essenes are nowhere mentioned in the New Testament, the aid which this sect also contributed to the development of Jesus, must be limited to the uncertain influence which might be exercised over him by occasional intercourse with Essenes.*

Did other elements than such as were merely Jewish, or at least confined to Palestine, operate upon Jesus? Of the heathens settled in *Galilee of the Gentiles*, Γαλιλαία τῶν ἐθνῶν, there was hardly much to be learned beyond patience under frequent intercourse with them. On the other hand, at the feasts in Jerusalem not only foreign Jews, some of whom, as for example the Alexandrian and Cyrenian Jews, had synagogues there (Acts vi. 9.), but also devout heathens were to be met with (John xii. 20.); and that intercourse with these had some influence in extending the intellectual horizon of Jesus, and spiritualizing his opinions, has, as we have already intimated, all historical probability.†

But why do we, in the absence of certain information, laboriously seek after uncertain traces of an influence which cotemporary means of development may have exercised on Jesus? and yet more, why, on the other side, are these labours so anxiously repudiated? Whatever amount of intellectual material may be collected, the spark by which genius kindles it, and fuses its various elements into a consistent whole, is neither easier to explain nor reduced in value. Thus it is with Jesus. Allow him to have exhausted the means of development which his age afforded: a comprehensive faculty of reception is with great men ever the reverse side of their powerful originality; allow him to have owed far more to Essenism and Alexandrianism, and whatever other schools and tendencies existed, than we, in our uncertainty, are in a condition to prove:— still for the reformation of a world these elements were all too little; the leaven necessary for this he must obtain from the depth of his own mind.‡

But we have not yet spoken of an appearance to which our Gospels assign a most important influence in developing the activity of Jesus—that of John the Baptist. As his ministry is first noticed in the Gospels in connexion with the baptism and public appearance of Jesus, our inquiry concerning him, and his relation to Jesus, must open the second part.

---

* Comp. Bengel, Bemerkungen über den Versuch, das Christenthum aus dem Essäismus abzuleiten, in Flatt's Magazin, 7, S. 126 ff.; Neander, L. J. Chr. S. 41 ff.   † This is stated with exaggeration by Bahrdt, Briefe über die Bibel, zweites Bändchen, 18ter, 20ster Brief ff. 4tes Bändchen, 49ster Brief.   ‡ Comp. Paulus ut sup. 1, a, 273 ff. Planck, Geschichte des Christenthums in der Periode seiner ersten Einführung I, S. 84. De Wette, bibl. Dogm. § 212. Hase L. J. § 38. Winer, bibl. Realw. S. 677 f. Neander, L. J. Chr. S. 38 ff.

SECOND PART.

HISTORY OF THE PUBLIC LIFE OF JESUS.

CHAPTER I.

RELATIONS BETWEEN JESUS AND JOHN THE BAPTIST.

§ 44. CHRONOLOGICAL RELATIONS BETWEEN JOHN AND JESUS.

For the ministry of John the Baptist, mentioned in all the Gospels, the second and fourth evangelists fix no epoch; the first gives us an inexact one; the third, one apparently precise. According to Matt. iii. 1. John appeared as a preacher of repentance, *in those days, ἐν ταῖς ἡμέραις ἐκείναις,* that is, if we interpret strictly this reference to the previous narrative, about the time when the parents of Jesus settled at Nazareth, and when Jesus was yet a child. We are told, however, in the context, that Jesus came to John for baptism; hence between the first appearance of the Baptist, which was cotemporary with the childhood of Jesus, and the period at which the latter was baptized, we must intercalculate a number of years, during which Jesus might have become sufficiently matured to partake of John's baptism. But Matthew's description of the person and work of the Baptist is so concise, the office attributed to him is so little independent, so entirely subservient to that of Jesus, that it was certainly not the intention of the evangelist to assign a long series of years to his single ministry. His meaning incontestably is, that John's short career early attained its goal in the baptism of Jesus.

It being thus inadmissible to suppose between the appearance of John and the baptism of Jesus, that is, between verses 12 and 13 of the 3rd chapter of Matthew, the long interval which is in every case indispensable, nothing remains but to insert it between the close of the second and the beginning of the third chapter, namely, between the settlement of the parents of Jesus at Nazareth and the appearance of the Baptist. To this end we may presume, with Paulus, that Matthew has here introduced a fragment from a history of the Baptist, narrating many particulars of his life immediately preceding his public agency, and very properly proceeding

I 4

with the words, *in those days*, ἐν ταῖς ἡμέραις ἐκείναις, which connecting phrase Matthew, although he omitted that to which it referred, has nevertheless retained ;* or we may, with Süskind, apply the words, not to the settlement, but to the subsequent residence of Jesus at Nazareth ;† or better still, ἐν ταῖς ἡμέραις ἐκείναις, like the corresponding Hebrew expression, בַּיָּמִים הָהֵם e. g., Exod. ii. 11. is probably to be interpreted as relating indeed to the establishment at Nazareth, but so that an event happening thirty years afterwards may yet be said, speaking indefinitely, to occur *in those days*.‡ In neither case do we learn from Matthew concerning the time of John's appearance more than the very vague information, that it took place in the interval between the infancy and manhood of Jesus.

Luke determines the date of John's appearance by various synchronisms, placing it in the time of Pilate's government in Judea ; in the sovereignty of Herod (Antipas), of Philip and of Lysanias over the other divisions of Palestine ; in the high priesthood of Annas and Caiaphas ; and, moreover, precisely in the 15th year of the reign of Tiberius, which, reckoning from the death of Augustus, corresponds with the year 28—29 of our era§ (iii. 1. 2). With this last and closest demarcation of time all the foregoing less precise ones agree. Even that which makes Annas high priest together with Caiaphas appears correct, if we consider the peculiar influence which, according to John xviii. 13. Acts iv. 6., that ex-high priest retained, even when deposed, especially after the assumption of office by his son-in-law, Caiaphas.

A single exception occurs in the statement about Lysanias, whom Luke makes cotemporary with Antipas and Philip as tetrarch of Abilene. Josephus, it is true, speaks of an Ἀβίλα ἡ Λυσανίου, and mentions a Lysanias as governor of Chalcis in Lebanon, near to which lay the territory of Abila ; so that the same Lysanias was probably master of the latter. But this Lysanias was, at the instigation of Cleopatra, put to death 34 years before the birth of Christ, and a second Lysanias is not mentioned either by Josephus, or by any other writer on the period in question.‖ Thus, not only is the time of his government earlier by 60 years than the 15th year of Tiberius, but it is also at issue with the other dates associated with it by Luke. Hence it has been conjectured that Luke here speaks of a younger Lysanias, the descendant of the earlier one, who possessed Abilene under Tiberius, but who, being less famous, is not noticed by Josephus.¶ We cannot indeed prove what Süskind

* Exeget. Handbuch. 1, a, S. 46. Schneckenburger agrees with him, über den Ursprung des ersten kanon. Evang. S. 30. † Vermischte Aufsätze, S. 76 ff. Compare Schneckenburger, ut sup. ‡ De Wette and Fritzsche, in loc. § See Paulus, ut sup. 336. ‖ I here collect all the passages in Josephus relative to Lysanias, with the parallel passages in Dio Cassius. Antiq. xiii. xvi. 3, xiv. iii. 2, vii. 8—Antiq. xv. iv. 1, B. j.i. xiii. 1 (Dio Cassius xlix. 32). Antiq. xv. x. 1—3. B. j. i. xx. 4 (Dio Cass. liv. 9). Antiq. xvii. xi. 4. B. j. ii. vi. 3. Antiq. xviii. vi. 10. B. j. ii. ix. 6 (Dio Cass. lix. 8) Antiq. xix. v. 1. B j. ii. xi. 5. Antiq. xx. v. 2, vii. 1. B. j. ii. xii. 8. ¶ Süskind, vermischte Aufsätze, S. 15 ff. 93 ff.

demands for the refutation of this hypothesis, namely, that had such a younger Lysanias existed, Josephus must have mentioned him : yet that he had more than one inducement to do so, Paulus has satisfactorily shown.   Especially, when in relation to the times of the first and second Agrippa he designates Abila, ἡ Λυσανίου, he must have been reminded that he had only treated of the elder Lysanias, and not at all of the younger, from whom, as the later ruler, the country must at that time have derived its second appellation.* If, according to this, the younger Lysanias is but an historic fiction, the proposed alternative is but a philological one.† For when it is said in the first place: Φιλίππου—τετραρχοῦντος τῆς Ἰτουραίας, κ. τ. λ., and when it follows : καὶ Λυσανίου τῆς Ἀβιληνῆς τετραρχοῦντος : we cannot possibly understand from this, that Philip reigned also over the Abilene of Lysanias.   For in that case the word τετραρχοῦντος ought not to have been repeated,‡ and τῆς ought to have been placed before Lysanias, if the author wished to avoid misconstruction. The conclusion is therefore inevitable that the writer himself erred, and, from the circumstance that Abilene, even in recent times, was called, after the last ruler of the former dynasty, ἡ Λυσανίου, drew the inference that a monarch of that name was still existing ; while, in fact, Abilene either belonged to Philip, or was immediately subject to the Romans.§

The above chronological notation relates directly to John the Baptist alone ; a similar one is wanting when Luke begins farther on (v. 21 ff.) to speak of Jesus. Of him it is merely said that he was *about thirty years of age*, ὡσεὶ ἐτῶν τριάκοντα, on his public appearance, (ἀρχόμενος), but no date is given ; while, in the case of John, there is a contrary omission. Thus even if John commenced his ministry in the 15th year of Tiberius, we cannot thence gather anything as to the time when Jesus commenced his, as it is nowhere said how long John had been baptizing when Jesus came to him on the Jordan ; while on the other hand, although we know that Jesus, at his baptism, was about 30 years old, this does not help us to ascertain the age of John when he entered on his ministry as Baptist. Remembering, however, Luke i. 26, according to which John was just half a year older than Jesus, and calling to our aid

* Tholuck thinks he has found a perfectly corresponding example in Tacitus. When this historian, Annal. ii. 42 (A. D. 17), mentions the death of an Archelaus, king of Cappadocia, and yet, Annal. vi. 41 (A. D. 36), cites an Archelaus, also a Cappadocian, as ruler of the Clitæ, the same historical conjecture, says Tholuck, is necessary, viz. that there were two Cappadocians named Archelaus. But when the same historian, after noticing the death of a man, introduces another of the same name, under different circumstances, it is no conjecture, but a clear historic datum, that there were two such persons. It is quite otherwise when, as in the case of Lysanias, two writers have each one of the same name, but assign him distinct epochs. Here it is indeed a conjecture to admit two successive persons ; a conjecture so much the less historial, the more improbable it is shown to be that one of the two writers would have been silent respecting the second of the like-named men, had such an one existed.   † Michaelis, Paulus, in loc. Schneckenburger, in Ullmann's und Umbreit's Studien, 1833, 4. Heft. S. 1056 ff. Tholuck, S. 201 ff.   ‡ For, on the authority of a single manuscript to erase, with Schneckenburger and others, the second πετραρχοῦντος, is too evident violence.   § Compare with this view, Allgem. Lit. Ztg., 1803, No 311, S. 552: De Wette, exeg. Handbuch, in loc.

the fact that Jewish usage would scarcely permit the exercise of public functions before the thirtieth year, we might infer that the Baptist could only have appeared half a year before the arrival of Jesus on the banks of the Jordan, since he would only so much earlier have attained the requisite age. But no express law forbade a public appearance previous to the thirtieth year; and it has been justly questioned whether we can apply to the freer office of a Prophet a restriction which concerned the Priests and Levites, for whom the thirtieth year was fixed for their entrance on regular service* (Num. iv. 3. 47. Compare besides 2 Chron. xxxi. 17. where the 20th year is named). This then would not hinder us from placing the appearance of John considerably prior to that of Jesus, even presupposing the averred relation between their ages. Hardly, however, could this be the intention of the Evangelist. For to ascertain so carefully the date of the Forerunner's appearance, and leave that of the Messiah himself undetermined, would be too great an oversight,† and we cannot but suppose that his design, in the particulars he gives concerning John, was to fix the time for the appearance of Jesus. To agree with this purpose, he must have understood that Jesus came to the banks of the Jordan and began to teach, shortly after the appearance of John.‡ For that the above chronological determination was originally merely the introduction to a document concerning John, quoted by Luke, is improbable, since its exactness corresponds with the style of him *who had perfect understanding of all things from the very first*, παρηκολουθηκότι ἄνωθεν πᾶσιν ἀκριβῶς, and who sought to determine, in like manner, the epoch of the Messiah's birth.

It is not easy, however, to imagine, in accordance with this statement, that John was by so little the predecessor of Jesus, nor is it without reason that the improbability of his having had so short an agency is maintained. For he had a considerable number of disciples, whom he not only baptized but taught (Luke xi. 1.), and he left behind a party of his peculiar followers (Acts xviii. 25. xix. 3.), all which could hardly be the work of a few months. There needed time, it has been observed, for the Baptist to become so well known, that people would undertake a journey to him in the wilderness; there needed time for his doctrine to be comprehended, time for it to gain a footing and establish itself, especially as it clashed with the current Jewish ideas; in a word, the deep and lasting veneration in which John was held by his nation, according to Josephus§ as well as the evangelists, could not have been so hastily won.∥

But the foregoing considerations, although they demand, in general, a longer agency for the Baptist, do not prove that the evangelists err in placing the commencement of his ministry shortly before

* See Paulus, S. 294.   † See Schleiermacher, über den Lukas, S. 62.   ‡ Bengel was also of this opinion.   Ordo temporum, S. 204 f. ed. 2.   § Antiq. xviii. v. 2.   ∥ So Cludius, über die Zeit und Lebensdauer Johannis und Jesu. In Henke's Museum, ii. iii. 502 ff.

that of Jesus, since they might suppose the required prolongation as a sequel, instead of an introduction, to the appearance of Jesus. Such a prolongation of the Baptist's ministry, however, is not to be found, at least in the first two Gospels; for not only do these contain no details concerning John, after the baptism of Jesus, except his sending two disciples (Matt. xi.), which is represented as a consequence of his imprisonment; but we gather from Matt. iv. 12. Mark i. 14. that during or shortly after the forty days' abode of Jesus in the wilderness, the Baptist was arrested, and thereupon Jesus went into Galilee, and entered on his public career. Luke, it is true, (iv. 14.) does not mention the imprisonment of John as the cause of the appearance of Jesus in Galilee, and he seems to regard the commission of the two disciples as occurring while John was at large (vii. 18 ff.); and the fourth Evangelist testifies yet more decisively against the notion that John was arrested so soon after the baptism of Jesus; for in chap. iii. 24. it is expressly stated, that John was actively engaged in his ministry after the first passover, attended by Jesus during his public life. But on the one hand, as it appears from Luke ix. 9. Matt. xiv. 1 ff. Mark xiv. 16. that John was put to death long before Jesus, the continuance of his agency after the rise of the latter could not be very protracted (Luke ix. 9. Matt. xiv. 1 ff. Mark xiv. 16.); and on the other, that which may be added to the agency of John after the appearance of Jesus, will not make amends for that which is subtracted from it before that epoch. For, apart from the fact implied by the fourth Evangelist (i. 35.) that the Baptist had formed a definite circle of familiar disciples before the appearance of Jesus, it would be difficult to account for the firm footing acquired by his school, if he had laboured only a few months, to be, at their close, eclipsed by Jesus.

There is yet one resource, namely, to separate the baptism of Jesus from the commencement of his ministry, and to say: It was indeed after the first half year of John's agency that Jesus was so attracted by his fame, as to become a candidate for his baptism; but for some time subsequently, he either remained among the followers of the Baptist, or went again into retirement, and did not present himself independently until a considerable interval had elapsed. By this means we should obtain the requisite extension of John's ministry prior to the more brilliant career of Jesus, without impugning the apparent statement of our evangelists that the baptism of Jesus followed close upon the public appearance of John. But the idea of a long interim, between the baptism of Jesus and the commencement of his ministry, is utterly foreign to the New Testament writers. For that they regard the baptism of Jesus as his consecration to the Messianic office, is proved by the accompanying descent of the spirit and the voice from heaven; the only pause which they allow to intervene, is the six weeks' fast in the wilderness, immediately after which, according to Luke, or after the apparently cotemporary arrest of the Baptist, according to Matthew and Mark, Jesus appears in Galilee. Luke, in particular, by designating (iii. 23.) the baptism of Jesus as his ἄρχεσθαι, his assumption of office, and by dating the intercourse of Jesus with his disciples from the βάπτισμα Ἰωάννου (Acts i. 22.), evinces his persuasion that the baptism and public manifestation of Jesus were identical.

Thus the gospel narrative is an obstacle to the adoption of the two most plausible expedients for the prolongation of John's ministry, viz., that Jesus presented himself for baptism later, or that his public appearance was retarded longer after his baptism, than has been generally inferred. We are not, however, compelled to renounce either of these suppositions, if we can show that the New Testament writers might have been led to their point of view even without historical grounds. A sufficient motive lies close at hand, and is implied in the foregoing observations. Let the Baptist once be considered, as was the case in the Christian church (Acts xix. 4.), not a person of independent significance, but simply a Forerunner of the Christ; and the imagination would not linger with the mere Precursor, but would hasten forward to the object at which he pointed. Yet more obvious is the interest which primitive Christian tradition must have had in excluding, whatever might have been the fact, any interval between the baptism of Jesus and the beginning of his public course. For to allow that Jesus, by his submission to John's baptism, declared himself his disciple, and remained in that relation for any length of time, was offensive to the religious sentiment of the new church, which desired a Founder instructed by God, and not by man: another turn, therefore, would soon be given to the facts, and the baptism of Jesus would be held to signify, not his initiation into the school of John, but a consecration to his independent office. Thus the diverging testimony of the evangelists does not preclude our adopting the conclusion to which the nature of the case leads us; viz., that the Baptist had been long labouring, anterior to the appearance of Jesus.

If, in addition to this, we accept the statement of Luke (i. 26. and iii. 23.), that Jesus, being only half a year younger than John, was about in his thirtieth year at his appearance, we must suppose that John was in his twentieth year when he began his ministry. There is, as we have seen, no express law against so early an exercise of the prophetic office; neither do I, so decidedly as Cludius*, hold it improbable that so young a preacher of repentance should make an impression, or even that he should be taken for a prophet of the olden time—an Elias; I will only appeal to the ordinary course of things as a sanction for presuming, that one who entered so much earlier upon the scene of action was proportionately older, especially when the principles and spirit of his teaching tell so plainly of a mature age as do the discourses of John. There are exceptions to this rule; but the statement of Luke (i. 26.), that John was only six months older than Jesus, is insufficient to establish one in this

* Cludius, ut sup.

instance, as it accords with the interest of the poetical legend, and must therefore be renounced for the slightest improbability.

The result then of our critique on the chronological data Luke iii. 1. 2. comp. 23. and i. 26. is this: if Jesus, as Luke seems to understand, appeared in the fifteenth year of Tiberius, the appearance of John occurred, not in the same year, but earlier; and if Jesus was in his thirtieth year when he began his ministry, the Baptist, so much his predecessor, could hardly be but six months his senior.

§ 45. APPEARANCE AND DESIGN OF THE BAPTIST—HIS PERSONAL RELATIONS WITH JESUS.

JOHN, a Nazarite, according to our authorities (Matt. iii. 4. ix. 14. xi. 18. Luke i. 15.), and in the opinion of several theologians,[*] an Essene, is said by Luke (iii. 2.) to have been summoned to his public work by the *word of God* ῥῆμα Θεοῦ, which came to him in the wilderness. Not possessing the Baptist's own declaration, we cannot accept as complete the dilemma stated by Paulus,[†] when he says, that we know not whether John himself interpreted some external or internal fact as a divine call, or whether he received a summons from another individual; and we must add as a third possibility, that his followers sought to dignify the vocation of their Teacher by an expression which recalls to mind the ancient Prophets.

While from the account of Luke it appears that the divine call came to John *in the wilderness*, ἐν τῇ ἐρήμῳ, but that for the purpose of teaching and baptizing he resorted to *the country about Jordan*, περίχωρος τοῦ Ἰορδάνου (ver. 3.): Matthew (iii. 1f.) makes the wilderness of Judea the scene of his labours, as if the Jordan in which he baptized flowed through that wilderness. It is true that, according to Josephus, the Jordan before emptying itself into the Dead Sea traverses a *great wilderness*, πολλὴν ἐρημίαν,[‡] but this was not the wilderness of Judea, which lay farther south.[§] Hence it has been supposed that Matthew, misled by his application of the prophecy, *the voice of one crying in the wilderness*, φωνὴ βοῶντος ἐν τῇ ἐρήμῳ, to John, who issued from *the wilderness of Judea*, ἔρημος τῆς Ἰουδαίας, placed there his labours as a preacher of repentance and a baptizer, although their true scene was the blooming valley of the Jordan.[‖]   In the course of Luke's narrative, however, this evangelist ceases to intimate that John forsook the wilderness after receiving his call, for on the occasion of John's message to Jesus, he makes the latter ask, *Whom went ye out into the wilderness to see?* Οἱ ἐξεληλύθατε εἰς τὴν ἔρημον θεάσασθαι (vii. 24.).   Now as the

* Stäudlin, Geschichte der Sittenlehre Jesu, 1, S. 580.   Paulus, exeg. Handb. 1 a, S. 136.   Comp. also Creuzer, Symbolik, 4, S. 413 ff.   † Ut sup. p. 317.   ‡ Bell. jud. iii. x. 7.   § See Winer, bibl. Realwörterbuch, A. Wüste.   Schneckenburger, über den Ursprung des ersten kanonischen Evangeliums, S. 39.   ‖ Schneckenburger, ut sup. S. 38 f.

valley of the Jordan in the vicinity of the Dead Sea was in fact a
barren plain, the narrow margin of the river excepted, no greater
mistake may belong to Matthew than that of specifying the wilderness as the ἔρημος τῆς 'Ιουδαίας; and even that may be explained
away by the supposition, either that John, as he alternately preached
and baptized, passed from the wilderness of Judea to the borders of
the Jordan,* or that the waste tract through which that river flowed,
being a continuation of the wilderness of Judea, retained the same
name.†

The baptism of John could scarcely have been derived from the
baptism of proselytes,‡ for this rite was unquestionably posterior to
the rise of Christianity. It was more analogous to the religious
lustrations in practice amongst the Jews, especially the Essenes,
and was apparently founded chiefly on certain expressions used by
several of the prophets in a figurative sense, but afterwards understood literally. According to these expressions, God requires from
the Israelitish people, as a condition of their restoration to his favour,
a washing and purification from their iniquity, and he promises that
he will himself cleanse them with water (Isa. i. 16. Ez. xxxvi. 25.
comp. Jer. ii. 22). Add to this the Jewish notion that the Messiah
would not appear with his kingdom until the Israelites repented,§
and we have the combination necessary for the belief that an ablu-
tion, symbolical of conversion and forgiveness of sins, must precede
the advent of the Messiah.

Our accounts are not unanimous as to the signification of John's
baptism. They all, it is true, agree in stating *repentance*, μετάνοια,
to be one of its essential requirements; for even what Josephus says
of the Baptist, that he admonished the Jews, *practising virtue,*
just towards each other, and devout towards God, to come to his
baptism, ἀρετὴν ἐπασκοῦντας, καὶ τῇ πρὸς ἀλλήλους δικαιοσύνῃ καὶ πρὸς
τὸν Θεον εὐσεβείᾳ χρωμένους βαπτισμῷ συνιέναι,‖ has the same sense
under a Greek form. Mark and Luke, however, while designating
the baptism of John βάπτισμα μετανοίας, add, εἰς ἄφεσιν ἁμαρτιῶν (i. 4.
iii. 3). Matthew has not the same addition; but he, with Mark,
describes the baptized as *confessing their sins,* ἐξομολογούμενοι τὰς
ἁμαρτίας αὐτῶν (iii. 6.) Josephus, on the other hand, appears in
direct contradiction to them, when he gives it as the opinion of the
Baptist, that *baptism is pleasing to God, not when we ask pardon*
for some transgressions, but when we purify the body, after hav-
ing first purified the mind by righteousness, οὕτω γὰρ καὶ τὴν
βάπτισιν ἀποδεκτὴν αὐτῷ (τῷ Θεῷ) φανεῖσθαι, μὴ ἐπί τίνων ἁμαρτάδων
παραιτήσει χρωμένων, ἀλλ' ἐφ' ἁγνείᾳ τοῦ σώματος, ἅτε δὴ καὶ τῆς ψυχῆς
δικαιοσύνῃ προεκκεκαθαρμένης. We might here be led to the supposition that the words *for the remission of sins,* εἰς ἄφεσιν ἁμαρτιῶν,
as in Acts ii. 38. and other passages, was commonly used in relation

* Winer, ut sup. S. 691.   † Paulus, ut sup. S. 301.   ‡ Schneckenburger, über das
Alter der Judischen Proselytentaufe.   §. Sanhedr. f. xcvii. 2 : R. Eliser dixit : si Israë-
litæ pænitentiam agunt, tunc per Goelem liberantur; sin vero, non liberantur.   Schöttgen,
horæ, 2, p. 780 ff.   ‖ Antiq. xviii. v. 2.

to Christian baptism, and was thence transferred unhistorically to that of John; but as in the passages quoted from Ezekiel the washing typified not only reformation but forgiveness, the probabilities are in favour of the evangelical statement.   Moreover, it is possible to reconcile Josephus and the Evangelists, by understanding the words of the former to mean that the baptism of John was intended to effect a purification, not from particular or merely Levitical transgressions, but of the entire man, not immediately and mysteriously through the agency of water, but by means of the moral acts of reformation.*

The several accounts concerning John are farther at variance, as to the relation in which they place his baptism to the *kingdom of heaven*, βασιλεία τῶν οὐρανῶν.   According to Matthew, the concise purport of the appeal with which he accompanied his baptism was, *Repent, for the kingdom of heaven is at hand*, μετανοεῖτε ἤγγικε γὰρ ἡ βασιλεία τῶν οὐρανῶν (iii. 2.); according to Luke, the Baptist in the first instance mentions only repentance and remission of sins, but no kingdom of heaven; and it is the conjecture of the people, that he might be the Messiah, by which he is first led to direct them to one who was coming after him (iii. 15 ff.).   In Josephus, there is no trace of a relation between the ministry of John and the Messianic idea.   Yet we must not therefore conclude that the Baptist himself recognized no such relation, and that its only source was the Christian legend.   For the baptism of John, waiving the opinion that it was derived from the baptism of proselytes, is not quite explicable without a reference to the above-mentioned expiatory lustrations of the people—lustrations which were to usher in the times of the Messiah; moreover, the appearance of Jesus is made more comprehensible by the supposition, that John had introduced the idea of the proximity of the Messiah's kingdom.   That Josephus should keep back the Messianic aspect of the fact, is in accordance with his general practice, which is explained by the position of his people with respect to the Romans.   Besides, in the expression, *to assemble for baptism*, βαπτισμῷ συνιέναι, in his mention of popular *assemblages*, συστρέφεσθαι, and in the fear of Antipas lest John should excite a *revolt*, ἀπόστασις, there lies an intimation of precisely such a religious and political movement as the hope of the Messiah was calculated to produce.   That the Baptist should so distinctly foretell the immediate appearance of the Messiah's kingdom must create surprise, and (Luke's reference to a divine call and revelation being held unsatisfactory) might lead to the supposition that the Christian narrator, believing that the true Messiah was actually manifested in the person of Jesus, the cotemporary of John, gave to the language of the latter a definiteness which did not belong to it originally; and while the Baptist merely said, consonantly with the Jewish notion already mentioned: *Repent, that the kingdom of heaven may come*, μετανοεῖτε, ἵνα ἔλθῃ ἡ βασ. τ. οὐρ., a later edition of his words gave

* Thus Paulus, ut sup. S. 314 and 361, Anm.

γὰρ (*for*) instead of ἵνα (*that*). But such a supposition is needless. In those times of commotion, John might easily believe that he discerned signs, which certified to him the proximity of the Messiah's kingdom; the exact degree of its proximity he left undecided.

According to the Evangelists, the coming of the *kingdom of heaven*, βασιλεία τῶν οὐρανῶν, was associated by John with a Messianic individual to whom he ascribed, in distinction from his own baptism with water, a *baptism with the Holy Ghost and with fire*, βαπτίζειν πνεύματι ἁγίῳ καὶ πυρὶ (Matt. iii. 11. parall.), the outpouring of the Holy Spirit being regarded as a leading feature of the Messianic times (Joel ii. 28; Acts ii. 16 ff.) Of this personage he farther predicted, in imagery akin to that used by the prophets on the same subject, that he would winnow the people as wheat (Mal. iii. 2, 3. Zech. xiii. 9.). The Synoptical Gospels state the case as if John expressly understood this Messianic individual to be Jesus of Nazareth. According to Luke, indeed, the mothers of these two men were cousins, and aware of the destination of their sons. The Baptist while yet unborn acknowledged the divinity of Jesus, and all the circumstances imply that both were early acquainted with their relative position, predetermined by a heavenly communication. Matthew, it is true, says nothing of such a family connexion between John and Jesus; but when the latter presents himself for baptism, he puts into the mouth of John words which seem to presuppose an earlier acquaintance. His expression of astonishment that Jesus should come to him for baptism, when he had need to be baptized of Jesus, could only arise from a previous knowledge or instantaneous revelation of his character. Of the latter there is no intimation; for the first visible sign of the Messiahship of Jesus did not occur till afterwards. While in the first and third Gospels (in the second, the facts are so epitomized that the writers view on the subject is not evident), John and Jesus seem to have been no strangers to each other prior to the baptism; in the fourth, the Baptist pointedly asserts that he knew not Jesus before the heavenly appearance, which, according to the Synoptical Gospels, was coincident with his baptism (i. 31, 33.). Simply considered, this looks like a contradiction. By Luke, the previous acquaintance of the two is stated objectively, as an external matter of fact; by Matthew, it is betrayed in the involuntary confession of the astonished Baptist; in the fourth Gospel, on the contrary, their previous unacquaintance is attested subjectively, by his premeditated assertion. It was not, therefore, a very farfetched idea of the Wolfenbüttel fragmentist, to put down the contradiction to the account of John and Jesus, and to presume that they had in fact long known and consulted each other, but that in public (in order better to play into one another's hands) they demeaned themselves as if they had hitherto been mutual strangers, and each·delivered an unbiassed testimony to the other's excellence.[*]

* Fragment von dem Zwecke Jesu und seiner Jünger, herausgeg. v. Lessing, S. 133 ff.

That such premeditated dissimulation might not be imputed to John, and indirectly to Jesus, it has been sought to disprove the existence of the contradiction in question exegetically. What John learned from the heavenly sign was the Messiahship of Jesus ; to this therefore, and not to his person, refer the words, *I knew him not,* κἀγὼ οὐκ ᾔδειν αὐτόν.* But it may be questioned whether such an acquaintance as John must have had with Jesus, presupposing the narrative of Matthew and Luke, was separable from a knowledge of his Messiahship. The connexion and intercourse of the two families, as described by Luke, would render it impossible for John not to be early informed how solemnly Jesus had been announced as the Messiah, before and at his birth : he could not therefore say at a later period that, prior to the sign from heaven, he had not *known*, but only that he had not *believed*, the story of former wonders, one of which relates to himself.† It being thus unavoidable to acknowledge that by the above declaration in the fourth Gospel, the Baptist is excluded, not only from a knowledge of the Messiahship of Jesus, but also from a personal acquaintance with him ; it has been attempted to reconcile the first chapter of Luke with this ignorance, by appealing to the distance of residence between the two families, as a preventive to the continuance of their intercourse.‡ But if the journey from Nazareth to the hill country of Judea was not too formidable for the betrothed Mary, how could it be so for the two sons when ripening to maturity? What culpable indifference is hereby supposed in both families to the heavenly communications they had received! nay, what could be the object of those communications, if they had no influence on the early life and intercourse of the two sons?§

Let it be granted that the fourth gospel excludes an acquaintance with the Messiahship only of Jesus, and that the third presupposes an acquaintance with his person only, on the part of John ; still the contradiction is not removed. For in Matthew, John, when required to baptize Jesus, addresses him as if he knew him, not generally and personally alone, but specially, in his character of Messiah. It is true that the words : *I have need to be baptized of thee, and comest thou to me?* (iii. 14.) have been interpreted, in the true spirit of harmonizing, as referring to the general superior excellence of Jesus, and not to his Messiahship.‖ But the right to undertake the baptism which was to prepare the way for the Messiah's king-

dom, was not to be obtained by moral superiority in general, but
was conferred by a special call, such as John himself had received,
and such as could belong only to a prophet, or to the Messiah and
his Forerunner (John i. 19 ff.) If then John attributed to Jesus
authority to baptize, he must have regarded him not merely as an
excellent man, but as indubitably a prophet, nay, since he held him
worthy to baptize himself, as his own superior: that is, since John
conceived himself to be the Messiah's Forerunner, no other than
the Messiah himself. Add to this, that Matthew had just cited a
discourse of the Baptist, in which he ascribes to the coming Messiah a baptism more powerful than his own; how then can we understand his subsequent language towards Jesus otherwise than
thus: "Of what use is my water baptism to thee, O Messiah? Far
more do I need thy baptism of the Spirit!"*

The contradiction cannot be cleared away; we must therefore,
if we would not lay the burthen of intentional deception on the
agents, let the narrators bear the blame; and there will be the less
hindrance to our doing so, the more obvious it is how one or both
of them might be led into an erroneous statement. There is in the
present case no obstacle to the reconciliation of Matthew with the
fourth evangelist, farther than the words by which the Baptist seeks
to deter Jesus from receiving baptism; words which, if uttered before the occurrence of any thing supernatural, presuppose a knowledge of Jesus in his character of Messiah. Now the Gospel of the
Hebrews, according to Epiphanius, places the entreaty of John that
Jesus would baptize him, as a sequel to the sign from heaven;† and
this account has been recently regarded as the original one, abridged
by the writer of our first Gospel, who, for the sake of effect, made
the refusal and confession of the Baptist coincident with the first
approach of Jesus.‡ But that we have not in the Gospel of the
Hebrews the original form of the narrative, is sufficiently proved by
its very tedious repetition of the heavenly voice and the diffuse style
of the whole. It is rather a very traditional record, and the insertion of John's refusal after the sign and voice from heaven, was not
made with the view of avoiding a contradiction of the fourth Gospel,
which cannot be supposed to have been recognized in the circle of
the Ebionite Christians, but from the very motive erroneously attributed to Matthew in his alleged transposition, namely, to give
greater effect to the scene. A simple refusal on the part of the

* Comp. the Fragmentist, ut sup.   † Hæres. xxx. 13: Καὶ ὡς ἀνῆλθεν ἀπὸ τοῦ ὕδατος, ἠνοίχησαν οἱ οὐρανοὶ, καὶ εἶδε τὸ πνεῦμα τοῦ Θεοῦ τὸ ἅγιον ἐν εἴδει περιστερᾶς κ. τ. λ. καὶ φωνὴ ἐγένετο κ. τ. λ. καὶ εὐθὺς περιέλαμψε τὸν τόπον φῶς μέγα· ὃν ἰδὼν, φησὶν, ὁ Ἰωάννης λέγει αὐτῷ οὐ τίς εἶ, Κύριε; καὶ πάλιν φωνὴ κ. τ. λ. καὶ τότε, φησὶν, ὁ Ἰωάννης παραπεσὼν αὐτῷ ἔλεγε δέομαι σοῦ Κύριε, σύ με βάπτισον. And when he came from the water, the heavens were opened, and he saw the holy spirit of God in the form of a dove, &c., and a voice was heard, &c., and immediately a great light illuminated the place; seeing which, John said to him, Who art thou, Lord? and again a voice, &c. And then, John falling at his feet, said to him, I beseech thee, Lord, baptize me.   ‡ Schneckenburger, uber den Ursprung des ersten kanonischen Evangeliums, S. 121 f.; Lücke, Comm. z. Ev. Joh., 1, S. 361. Usteri, über den Täufer Johannes u. s. w., Studien, 2, 3. S. 416.

Baptist appeared too weak; he must at least fall at the feet of Jesus; and a more suitable occasion could not be given than that of the sign from heaven, which accordingly must be placed beforehand. This Hebrew Gospel, therefore, will not help us to understand how Matthew was led into contradiction with John; still less will it avail for the explanation of Luke's narrative.

All is naturally explained by the consideration, that the important relation between John and Jesus must have been regarded as existing at all times, by reason of that ascription of pre-existence to the essential which is a characteristic of the popular mind. Just as the soul, when considered as an essence, is conceived more or less clearly as pre-existent; so in the popular mind, every relation pregnant with consequences is endowed with pre-existence. Hence the Baptist, who eventually held so significant a relation to Jesus, must have known him from the first, as is indistinctly intimated by Matthew, and more minutely detailed by Luke; according to whom, their mothers knew each other, and the sons themselves were brought together while yet unborn. All this is wanting in the fourth Gospel, the writer of which attributes an opposite assertion to John, simply because in his mind an opposite interest preponderated; for the less Jesus was known to John by whom he was afterwards so extolled, the more weight was thrown on the miraculous scene which arrested the regards of the Baptist—the more clearly was his whole position with respect to Jesus demonstrated to be the effect, not of the natural order of events, but of the immediate agency of God.

§. 46.   WAS JESUS ACKNOWLEDGED BY JOHN AS THE MESSIAH? AND IN WHAT SENSE?

To the foregoing question whether Jesus was known to John before the baptism, is attached another, namely, What did John think of Jesus and his Messiahship? The evangelical narratives are unanimous in stating, that before Jesus had presented himself for baptism, John had announced the immediate coming of One to whom he stood in a subordinate relation; and the scene at the baptism of Jesus marked him, beyond mistake, as the personage of whom John was the forerunner. According to Mark and Luke, we must presume that the Baptist gave credence to this sign: according to the fourth Gospel, he expressly attested his belief (i. 34.), and moreover uttered words which evince the deepest insight into the higher nature and office of Jesus (i. 29 ff. 36; iii. 27 ff.): according to the first Gospel, he was already convinced of these before the baptism of Jesus. On the other hand, Matthew (xi. 2 ff.) and Luke (vii. 18.) tell us that at a later period, the Baptist, on hearing of the ministry of Jesus, despatched some of his disciples to him with the inquiry, whether he (Jesus) was the promised Messiah, or whether another must be expected.

The first impression from this is, that the question denoted an uncertainty on the part of the Baptist whether Jesus were really the Messiah; and so it was early understood.* But such a doubt is in direct contradiction with all the other circumstances reported by the evangelists. It is justly regarded as psychologically impossible that he whose belief was originated or confirmed by the baptismal sign, which he held to be a divine revelation, and who afterwards pronounced so decidedly on the Messianic call and the superior nature of Jesus, should all at once have become unsteady in his conviction; he must then indeed have been like a reed shaken by the wind, a comparison which Jesus abnegates on this very occasion (Matt. xi. 7.). A cause for such vacillation is in vain sought in the conduct or fortunes of Jesus at the time; for the rumor of *the works of Christ*, ἔργα τοῦ Χριστοῦ, which in Luke's idea were miracles, could not awaken doubt in the Baptist, and it was on this rumour that he sent his message. Lastly, how could Jesus subsequently (John v. 33. ff.) so confidently appeal to the testimony of the Baptist concerning him, when it was known that John himself was at last perplexed about his Messiahship?†

Hence it has been attempted to give a different turn to the facts, and to show that John's inquiry was not made on his own account, but for the sake of his disciples, to overcome in them the doubt with which he was himself untainted.‡ Hereby it is true, the above-named difficulties are removed; in particular it is explained why the Baptist should contrive to send this message precisely on hearing of the miracles of Jesus: he plainly hoping that his disciples, who had not believed his testimony to the Messiahship of Jesus, would be convinced of its truth by beholding the marvellous works of the latter. But how could John hope that his envoys would chance to find Jesus in the act of working miracles? According to Matthew, indeed, they did not so find him, and Jesus appeals (v. 4.) only to his former works, many of which they had seen, and of which they might hear wherever he had presented himself. Luke alone, in giving his evidently second-hand narrative,§ misconstrues the words of Jesus to require that the disciples of John should have found him in the exercise of his supernatural power. Further, if it had been the object of the Baptist to persuade his disciples by a sight of the works of Jesus, he would not have charged them with a question which could be answered by the mere words, the authentic declaration of Jesus. For he could not hope by the assertion of the person whose Messiahship was the very point in debate, to convince the disciples whom his own declaration, in other cases, au-

* Tertull. adv. Marcion, iv. 18. Comp. Bengel, historico-exegetical remarks in Matt. xi. 2—19, in his Archiv. I, iii. p. 754 ff. † See Paulus, Kuinöl. in loc. Bengel, ut sup. p 763. ‡ Calvin, Comm. in harm. ex. Matth., Marc. et Luc. in loc. § We agree with Schleiermacher, (uber den Lukas, S. 106 f.) in thus designating the narrative of the third evangelist, first, on account of the idle repetition of the Baptist's words, ver. 20; secondly on account of the mistake in ver. 18 and 21, of which we shall presently treat, and to which ver. 29, 30. seem to betray a similar one.

thoritative, had failed to satisfy. On the whole, it would have been a singular course in the Baptist to lend his own words to the doubts of others, and thereby, as Schleiermacher well observes, to compromise his early and repeated testimony in favour of Jesus. It is clear that Jesus understood the question proposed to him by the messengers as proceeding from John himself; ($\dot{a}\pi a\gamma\gamma\epsilon\iota\lambda a\tau\epsilon$ 'Iω-άννη, Matt. xi. 4 :) and he indirectly complained of the want of faith in the latter by pronouncing those blessed who were not offended in him (ver. 6).*

If then it must be granted that John made his inquiry on his own behalf, and not on that of his disciples, and if nevertheless we cannot impute to him a sudden lapse into doubt after his previous confidence : nothing remains but to take the positive instead of the negative side of the question, and to consider its scepticism as the mere garb of substantial encouragement.† On this interpretation, the time which Jesus allowed to escape without publicly manifesting himself as the Messiah, seemed too tedious to John in his imprisonment : he sent therefore to inquire how long Jesus would allow himself to be waited for, how long he would delay winning to himself the better part of the people by a declaration of his Messiahship, and striking a decisive blow against the enemies of his cause, a blow that might even liberate the Baptist from his prison. But if the Baptist, on the strength of his belief that Jesus was the Messiah, hoped and sued for a deliverance, perhaps miraculous, by him from prison, he would not clothe in the language of doubt an entreaty which sprang out of his faith. Now the inquiry in our evangelical text is one of unmixed doubt, and encouragement must be foisted in, before it can be found there. How great a violence must be done to the words is seen by the way in which Schleiermacher handles them in accordance with this interpretation. The dubitative question, $\sigma\dot{v}$ $\epsilon\dot{\iota}$ $\dot{o}$ $\dot{\epsilon}\rho\chi\dot{o}\mu\epsilon\nu o\varsigma$; he changes into the positive assumption, *thou art he who was to come ;* the other still more embarrassing interrogatory, $\dot{\eta}$ $\dot{\epsilon}\tau\epsilon\rho o\nu$ $\pi\rho o\sigma\delta o\kappa\tilde{\omega}\mu\epsilon\nu$; he completely transfigures thus: *wherefore (seeing that thou performest so great works) do we yet await thee?—shall not John with all his authority command, through us, all those who have partaken of his baptism to obey thee as the Messiah, and be attentive to thy signs?* Even if we allow, with Neander, the possibility of truth to this interpretation, a mere summons to action will not accord with the earlier representation of Jesus given by the Baptist. The two enunciations are at issue as to form : for if John doubted not the Messiahship of Jesus, neither could he doubt his better knowledge of the fitting time and manner of his appearance : still farther are they at issue as to matter ; for the Baptist could not take offence at what is termed the delay of Jesus in manifesting himself as the Messiah, or wish to animate him to bolder conduct, if he retained his early view of the destination of Jesus. If he still, as formerly, conceived Jesus to be *the Lamb of God that taketh away the sins of the world*, ὁ ἀμνὸς τοῦ Θεοῦ, ὁ αἴρων τὴν ἁμαρτίαν τοῦ κόσμου, no thought could occur to him of a blow to be struck by Jesus against his enemies, or in general, of a violent procedure to be crowned by external conquest; rather, the quiet path which Jesus trod must appear to him the right one—the path befitting the destination of the Lamb of God. Thus if the question of John conveyed a mere summons to action, it contradicted his previous views.

These expedients failing, the original explanation returns upon us; namely, that the inquiry was an expression of uncertainty respecting the messianic dignity of Jesus, which had arisen in the Baptist's own mind; an explanation which even Neander allows to be the most natural. This writer seeks to account for the transient apostacy of the Baptist from the strong faith in which he gave his earlier testimony, by the supposition that a dark hour of doubt had overtaken the man of God in his dismal prison; and he cites instances of men who, persecuted for their Christian faith or other convictions, after having long borne witness to the truth in the face of death, at length yielded to human weakness and recanted. But on a closer examination, he has given a false analogy. Persecuted Christians of the first centuries, and, later, a Berengarius or a Galileo, were false to the convictions for which they were imprisoned, and by abjuring which they hoped to save themselves: the Baptist, to be compared with them, should have retracted his censure of Herod, and not have shaken his testimony in favour of Christ, which had no relation to his imprisonment. However that may be, it is evident here that these doubts cannot have been preceded by a state of certainty.

We come again to the difficulty arising from the statement of Matthew that John sent his two disciples on hearing of the *works of Christ*, ἀκούσας τὰ ἔργα τοῦ Χριστοῦ, or as Luke has it, because his disciples *showed him of all these things*, ἀπήγγειλαν περὶ πάντων τούτων. The latter evangelist has narrated, immediately before, the raising of the widow's son, and the healing of the centurion's servant. Could John, then, believe Jesus to be the Messiah before he had performed any messianic works, and be seized with doubt when he began to legitimatize his claim by miracles such as were expected from the Messiah?[*] This is so opposed to all psychological probability, that I wonder Dr. Paulus, or some other expositor versed in psychology and not timid in verbal criticism, has not started the conjecture that a negative has slipped out of Matt. xi. 2, and that its proper reading is, ὁ δὲ Ἰωάννης οὐκ ἀκούσας ἐν τῷ δεσμωτηρίῳ τὰ ἔργα τοῦ Χριστοῦ, κ. τ. λ. It might then be conceived, that John had indeed been convinced, at a former period, of the Messiahship of Jesus; now, however, in his imprisonment, the works of Jesus came no longer to his ears, and imagining him inactive, he was as-

---

[*] This difficulty occurred to Bengel also, ut sup. p. 769.

sailed with doubt. But had John been previously satisfied of the Messiahship of Jesus, the mere want of acquaintance with his miracles could not have unhinged his faith. The actual cause of John's doubt, however, was the report of these miracles ;—a state of the case which is irreconcilable with any previous confidence.

But how could he become uncertain about the Messiahship of Jesus, if he had never recognized it ? Not indeed in the sense of beginning to suspect that Jesus was *not* the Messiah ; but quite possibly in the sense of beginning to conjecture that a man of such deeds *was* the Messiah.

We have here, not a decaying, but a growing certainty, and this discrimination throws light on the whole purport of the passages in question. John knew nothing of Jesus before, but that he had, like many others, partaken of his baptism, and perhaps frequented the circle of his disciples ; and not until after the imprisonment of the Baptist did Jesus appear as a teacher, and worker of miracles. Of this John heard, and then arose in his mind a conjecture, fraught with hope, that as he had announced the proximity of the Messiah's kingdom, this Jesus might be he who would verify his idea.* So interpreted, this message of the Baptist excludes his previous testimony ; if he had so spoken formerly, he could not have so inquired latterly, and *vice versâ*. It is our task, therefore, to compare the two contradictory statements, that we may ascertain which has more traces than the other, of truth or untruth.

The most definite expressions of John's conviction that Jesus was the Messiah are found in the fourth Gospel, and these suggest two distinct questions: first, whether it be conceivable that John had such a notion of the Messiah as is therein contained ; and, secondly, whether it be probable that he believed it realized in the person of Jesus.

With respect to the former, the fourth Gospel makes the Baptist's idea of the Messiah include the characteristics of expiatory suffering, and of a premundane, heavenly existence. It has been attempted, indeed, so to interpret the expressions with which he directs his disciples to Jesus, as to efface the notion of expiatory suffering. Jesus, we are told, is compared to a lamb on account of his meekness and patience ; αἴρειν τὴν ἁμαρτίαν τοῦ κόσμου, is to be understood either of a patient endurance of the world's malice, or of an endeavour to remove the sins of the world by reforming it ; and the sense of the Baptist's words is this: "How moving is it that this meek and gentle Jesus should have undertaken so difficult and painful an office!"† But the best critics have shown that even

---

* The gospel writers, after what they had narrated of the relations between Jesus and the Baptist, of course understood the question to express doubt, whence probably v. 6 (Matt.) and v. 23 (Luke) came in this connection. Supposing these passages authentic, they suggest another conjecture ; viz. that Jesus spoke in the foregoing verses of spiritual miracles, and that the Baptist was perplexed by the absence of corporeal ones. The ἀκούσας τὰ ἔργα τ. Χ. must then be set down to the writer's misapprehension of the expressions of Jesus.   † Gabler and Paulus.

15

if αἴρειν by itself might bear this interpretation, still ἀμνὸς, not merely with the article but with the addition τοῦ Θεοῦ, must signify, not a lamb in general, but a special, holy Lamb; and if, as is most probable, this designation has reference to Isai. liii. 7., αἴρειν τὴν ἁμαρτίαν can only be expounded by what is there predicated of the lamblike servant of God, that he τὰς ἁμαρτίας ἡμῶν φέρει, καὶ περὶ ἡμῶν ὀδυνᾶται (V. 4, LXX.), words which must signify vicarious suffering.* Now that the Baptist should have referred the above prophetic passage to the Messiah, and hence have thought of him as suffering, has been recently held more than doubtful.†

For so foreign to the current opinion, at least, was this notion of the Messiah, that the disciples of Jesus, during the whole period of their intercourse with him, could not reconcile themselves to it; and when his death had actually resulted, their trust in him as the Messiah was utterly confounded (Luke xxiv. 20 ff.). How, then, could the Baptist, who, according to the solemn declaration of Jesus, Matt. xi. 11., confirmed by the allusions in the Gospels to his strict ascetic life, ranked below the least in the kingdom of heaven, to which the apostles already belonged—how could this alien discern, long before the sufferings of Jesus, that they pertained to the character of the Messiah, when the denizens were only taught the same lesson by the issue? Or, if the Baptist really had such insight, and communicated it to his disciples, why did it not, by means of those who left his circle for that of Jesus, win an entrance into the latter—nay, why did it not, by means of the great credit which John enjoyed, mitigate the offence caused by the death of Jesus, in the public at large?‡ Add to this, that in none of our accounts of the Baptist, with the exception of the fourth Gospel, do we find that he entertained such views of the Messiah's character; for, not to mention Josephus, the Synoptical Gospels confine his representation of the Messianic office to the spiritual baptism and winnowing of the people. Still it remains possible that a penetrating mind, like that of the Baptist, might, even before the death of Jesus, gather from Old Testament phrases and types the notion of a suffering Messiah, and that his obscure hints on the subject might not be comprehended by his disciples and cotemporaries.

Thus the above considerations are not decisive, and we therefore turn to the expressions concerning the premundane existence and heavenly origin of the Messiah, with the question: Could the Baptist have really held such tenets? That from the words, John i. 15, 27, 30: *He that cometh after me is preferred before me; for he was before me,* ὁ ὀπίσω μοῦ ἐρχόμενος ἔμπροσθέν μοῦ γέγονεν, ὅτι πρῶτός μου ἦν, nothing but dogmatical obstinacy can banish the notion of pre-existence, is seen by a mere glance at such expositions as this of Paulus: "He who in the course of time comes after me;

---

* De Wette, de morte Christi expiatoria, in his Opusc. theol. S. 77 ff. Lücke, Comm. zum Ev. Joh. 1, S. 347 ff. Winer, bibl. Realwörterbuch 1, S. 693, Anm. † Gabler and Paulus. De Wette. ‡ De Wette, ut sup. p. 76.

has so appeared in my eyes, ἔμπροσθέν μοῦ, that he (ὅτι—ὥστε, premiss—conclusion!) deserves rather from his rank and character to be called the first."* With preponderating arguments more un-prejudiced commentators have maintained, that the reason here given why Jesus, who appeared after the Baptist in point of time, had the precedence of him in dignity, is the pre-existence of the former.† We have here obviously the favourite dogma of the fourth evangelist, the eternal pre-existence of the λόγος, present indeed to the mind of that writer, who had just been inditing his proem, but that it was also present to the mind of the Baptist is another ques-tion. The most recent expositor allows that the sense in which the evangelist intends πρῶτος μοῦ, must have been very remote from the Baptist's point of view, at least so far as the λόγος is concerned. The Baptist, he thinks, held the popular Jewish notion of the pre-existence of the Messiah, as the subject of the Old Testament theophanies.‡ There are traces of this Jewish notion in the writings of Paul (e. g. 1 Cor. x. 4. Col. i. 15 f.) and the rabbins;§ and allowing that it was of Alexandrian origin, as Bretschneider argues,‖ we may yet ask whether even before the time of Christ, the Alexan-drian-judaic theology may not have modified the opinions of the mother country?¶ Even these expressions then, taken alone, are not conclusive, although it begins to appear suspicious that the Baptist, otherwise conspicuous for exhibiting the practical side of the idea of the Messiah's kingdom, should have ascribed to him by the fourth evangelist solely, two notions which at that time undoubtedly belonged only to the deepest messianic speculations; and that the form in which those notions are expressed is too peculiarly that of the writer, not to be put to his account.

We arrive at a more decisive result by taking into examination the passage John iii. 27—36, where John replies to the complaints of his disciples at the rival baptism of Jesus, in a way that reduces all commentators to perplexity. After showing how it lay at the foundation of their respective destinies, which he desired not to overstep, that he must decrease, while Jesus must increase, he proceeds (ver. 31) to use forms of expression precisely similar to those in which the evangelist makes Jesus speak of himself, and in which he delivers his own thoughts concerning Jesus. Our most recent commentator** allows that this discourse of John seems the echo of the foregoing conversation between Jesus and Nicodemus.††

* Paulus, Leben Jesu, 2, a, die Uebers. S. 29, 31.   † Tholuck and Lücke, in loc.
‡ Lücke, ut sup.   § See Bertholdt, Christologia Judæorum Jesu apostolorumque ætate, §
23—26.   ‖ Probabilia, p. 44.   ¶ See Gfrörer, Philo und die Alexandr. Theosophie,
part ii. p. 180.   ** Lücke, ut sup. p. 500.
†† Compare especially :
Joh. iii. 11 (Jesu to Nicodemus): ἀμὴν,
ἀμὴν, λέγω σοι, ὅτι ὃ οἴδαμεν, λαλοῦμεν καὶ
ὃ ἑωράκαμεν, μαρτυροῦμεν καὶ τὴν μαρτυρίαν
ἡμῶν οὐ λαμβάνετε.

V. 18 : ὁ πιστεύων εἰς αὐτὸν οὐ κρίνεται·
ὁ δὲ μὴ πιστεύων, ἤδη κέκριται ὅτι μὴ πε-

Joh. iii. 32 (the Baptist): καὶ ὃ ἑώρακε καὶ
ἤκουσε, τοῦτο μαρτυρεῖ καὶ τὴν μαρτυρίαν
αἰτοῦ οὐδεὶς λαμβάνει

V. 36 : ὁ πιστεύων εἰς τὸν υἱὸν ἔχει ζωὴν
αἰώνιον· ὁ δὲ ἀπειθῶν τῷ υἱῷ, οὐκ ὄψεται

The expressions in the speech lent to the Baptist are peculiarly those of the apostle John; for instance, σφραγίζω (*to seal*), μαρτυρία (*testimony*), the antithesis of ἄνωθεν and ἐκ τῆς γῆς (*from above* and of *the earth*), the phrase ἔχειν ζωήν αἰώνιον (*to have eternal life*); and the question presents itself: Is it more probable that the evangelist, as well as Jesus, in whose mouth these expressions are so often put, borrowed them from the Baptist, or that the evangelist lent them (I will only at present say) to the latter? This must be decided by the fact that the ideas, to which the Baptist here gives utterance, lie entirely within the domain of Christianity, and belong specially to the Christianity of the apostle John. Take for example that antithesis of ἄνω (*from above*), and ἐκ τῆς γῆς (*of the earth*), the designation of Jesus as ἄνωθεν ἐρχόμενος (*he that cometh from above*), as ὃν ἀπέστειλεν ὁ Θεὸς (*he whom God had sent*), who consequently τὰ ῥήματα τοῦ Θεοῦ λαλεῖ (*speaketh the words of God*), the relation of Jesus to God as the υἱὸς (*son*), whom ὁ πατὴρ ἀγαπᾷ (*the Father loveth*):—what can be characteristic of Christianity, and of the Apostle John's mode of presenting it, if these ideas are not so? and could they belong to the Baptist? *Christianismus ante Christum!* And then, as Olshausen well observes,[*] is it consistent for John, who, even on the fourth evangelist's own showing, remained separate from Jesus, to speak of the blessedness of a believing union with him? (v. 33 and 36.)

Thus much then is certain, and has been acknowledged by the majority of modern commentators: the words v. 31—36, cannot have been spoken by the Baptist. Hence theologians have concluded, that the evangelist cannot have intended to ascribe them to him, but from v. 31 speaks in his own person.[†] This sounds plausible, if they can only point out any mark of division between the discourse of the Baptist and the addenda of the evangelist. But none such is to be found. It is true that the speaker from v. 31. uses the third person, and not the first as in v. 30., when referring to the Baptist: but in the former passage the Baptist is no longer alluded to directly and individually, but as one of a class, in which case he must, though himself the speaker, choose the third person. Thus there is no definitive boundary, and the speech glides imperceptibly from those passages which might have been uttered by the Baptist, into those which are altogether incongruous with his position; moreover from v. 30. Jesus is spoken of in the present tense, as the evangelist might represent the Baptist to speak during the lifetime of Jesus, but could not in his own person have written after the death of Jesus. In other passages, when presenting his own re-

---

πίστευκεν εἰς τὸ ὄνομα τοῦ μονογενοῖς υἱοῦ   ζωὴν, ἀλλ' ἡ ὀργὴ τοῦ Θεοῦ μένει ἐπ' αὐτόν.
τοῦ Θεοῦ.

Comp. also the words of the Baptist v. 31, with Joh. iii. 6. 12 f. viii. 23; v. 32 with viii. 26; v. 33 with vi. 27; v. 34 with xii. 49, 50; v. 35 with v. 22, 27. x. 28 f. xvii. 2.

* Bibl. Comm. 2, p. 105.

† Paulus, Olshausen, in loc.

flections concerning Jesus, he uses the preterite.* Thus, grammatically, the Baptist continues to speak from v. 31, and yet, historically, it is impossible that he should have uttered the sequel; a contradiction not to be solved, if it be added that, dogmatically, the evangelist cannot have ascribed to the Baptist words which he never really pronounced. Now if we do not choose to defy the clear rules of grammar, and the sure data of history, for the sake of the visionary dogma of inspiration, we shall rather conclude from the given premises, with the author of the Probabilia, that the evangelist falsely ascribes the language in question to the Baptist, putting into his mouth a Christology of his own, of which the latter could know nothing. This is no more than Lücke† confesses, though not quite so frankly, when he says that the reflections of the evangelist are here more than equally mixed with the discourse of the Baptist, in such a way as to be undistinguishable. In point of fact, however, the reflections of the evangelist are easily to be recognized; but of the fundamental ideas of the Baptist there is no trace, unless they are sought for with a good will which amounts to prejudice, and to which therefore we make no pretension. If then we have a proof in the passages just considered, that the fourth evangelist did not hesitate to lend to the Baptist messianic and other ideas which were never his; we may hence conclude retrospectively concerning the passages on which we formerly suspended our decision, that the ideas expressed in them of a suffering and pre-existent Messiah belonged, not to the Baptist, but to the evangelist.

In giving the above reply to our first question, we have, in strictness, answered the remaining one; for if the Baptist had no such messianic ideas, he could not refer them to the person of Jesus. But to strengthen the evidence for the result already obtained, we will make the second question the object of a special examination. According to the fourth evangelist the Baptist ascribed to Jesus all the messianic attributes above discussed. If he did this so enthusiastically, publicly, and repeatedly, as we read in John, he could not have been excluded by Jesus from the kingdom of heaven (Matt. xi. 11.), nor have been placed below the least of its citizens. For such a confession as that of the Baptist, when he calls Jesus the υἱὸς τοῦ Θεοῦ, who was before him,—such refined insight into the messianic economy, as is shown by his designating Jesus ὁ ἀμνὸς τοῦ Θεοῦ, ὁ αἴρων τὴν ἁμαρτίαν τοῦ κόσμου, Peter himself had not to produce, though Jesus not only receives him into the kingdom of heaven for his confession, Matt. xvi. 16., but constitutes him the rock on which that kingdom was to be founded. But we have something yet more incomprehensible. John, in the fourth Gospel, gives it as the object of his baptism, ἵνα φανερωθῇ (Jesus as Messiah) τῷ Ἰσραήλ (i. 31.), and acknowledges it to be the divine ordinance, that by the side of the increasing Jesus, he must decrease

---

* E. g. here, v. 32, it is said : τὴν μαρτυρίαν αὐτοῦ οὐδεὶς λαμβάνει, but in the Prolog. v. 11 : καὶ οἱ ἴδιοι αὐτὸν οὐ παρέλαβον.   Com. Lücke, S. 501.   † Ut sup.

(iii. 30.); nevertheless after Jesus had begun to baptize by the instrumentality of his disciples, John continues to practise his baptism (iii. 32.). Why so, if he knew the object of his baptism to be fulfilled by the introduction of Jesus, and if he directed his followers to him as the Messiah? (i. 36 f.).* The continuance of his baptism would be to no purpose; for Lüke's supposition, that John's baptism was still of effect in those places where Jesus had not appeared, he himself overthrows by the observation, that at least at the period treated of in John iii. 22 ff., Jesus and John must have been baptizing near to each other, since the disciples of John were jealous of the concourse to the baptism of Jesus. But the continuance of John's baptism appears even to counteract his aim, if that aim were merely to point out Jesus as the Messiah. He thereby detained a circle of individuals on the borders of the Messiah's kingdom, and retarded or hindered their going over to Jesus (and that through his own fault, not theirs alone,† for he nullified his verbal direction to Jesus by his contradictory example). Accordingly we find the party of John's disciples still existing in the time of the Apostle Paul (Acts xviii. 24 f. xix. 1 ff.); and, if the Sabæans are to be credited concerning their own history, the sect remains to this day.‡ Certainly, presupposing the averred conviction of the Baptist relative to Jesus, it would seem most natural for him to have attached himself to the latter; this, however, did not happen, and hence we conclude that he cannot have had that conviction.§

But chiefly the character and entire demeanour of the Baptist render it impossible to believe that he placed himself on that footing with Jesus, described by the fourth evangelist. How could the man of the wilderness, the stern ascetic, who fed on locusts and wild honey, and prescribed severe fasts to his disciples, the gloomy, threatening preacher of repentance, animated with the spirit of Elias—how could he form a friendship with Jesus, in every thing his opposite? He must assuredly, with his disciples, have stumbled at the liberal manners of Jesus, and have been hindered by them from recognizing him as the Messiah. Nothing is more unbending than ascetic prejudice; he who, like the Baptist, esteems it piety to fast and mortify the body, will never assign a high grade in things divine to him who disregards such asceticism. A mind with narrow views can never comprehend one whose vision takes a wider range, al-

---

* De Wette, de morte Christi expiatoria, in s. Opusc. theol. p. 81 ; biblische Dogmatik, § 209 ; Winer, bibl. Realwörterbuch I, S. 692.   † Neander, p. 75.   This author erroneously supposes that there is an indication of the Baptist having directed his disciples to Jesus in Acts xviii. 25, where it is said of Apollos: ἐδίδασκεν ἀκριβῶς τὰ περὶ τοῦ Κυρίου, ἐπιστάμενος τὸ βάπτισμα Ἰωάννου.   For on comparing the following chapter, we find that Paul had to teach the disciples of John, that by the ἐρχόμενος announced by their master, they were to understand Jesus ; whence it is clear that the things of the Lord expounded by Apollos, consisted only in the messianic doctrine, purified by John into an expectation of one who was to come, and that the more accurate instruction which he received from the Christians, Aquila and Priscilla, was the doctrine of its fulfilment in the person of Jesus.   ‡ Gesenius, Probeheft der Gruber'schen Encyclopädie, d. A. Zabier.   § Bretschneider, Probab. S. 46 f. ; comp. Lücke, S. 493 f. ; De Wette, Opusc. a. a. O.

though the latter may know how to do justice to its inferior; hence Jesus could value and sanction John in his proper place, but the Baptist could never give the precedence to Jesus, as he is reported to have done in the fourth Gospel. The declaration of the Baptist (John iii. 30.), that he must decrease, but Jesus must increase, is frequently praised as an example of the noblest and sublimest resignation.* The beauty of this representation we grant; but not its truth. The instance would be a solitary one, if a man whose life had its influence on the world's history, had so readily yielded the ascendant, in his own æra, to one who came to eclipse him and render him superfluous. Such a step is not less difficult for individuals than for nations, and that not from any vice, as egotism or ambition, so that an exception might be presumed (though not without prejudice) in the case of a man like the Baptist; it is a consequence of that blameless limitation which, as we have already remarked, is proper to a low point of view in relation to a higher, and which is all the more obstinately maintained if the inferior individual is, like John, of a coarse, rugged nature. Only from the divine point of view, or from that of an historian, bent on establishing religious doctrines, could such things be spoken, and the fourth evangelist has in fact put into the mouth of the Baptist the very same thoughts concerning the relation between him and Jesus, that the compiler of the 2nd book of Samuel has communicated, as his own observation, on the corresponding relation between Saul and David.† Competent judges have recently acknowledged that there exists a discrepancy between the Synoptical Gospels and the fourth, the blame of which must be imputed to the latter;‡ and this opinion is confirmed and strengthened by the fact, that the fourth evangelist transforms the Baptist into a totally different character from that in which he appears in the Synoptical Gospels and in Josephus; out of a practical preacher he makes a speculative christologist; out of a hard and unbending, a yielding and self-renunciating nature.

The style in which the scenes between John and Jesus (John i. 29 ff. 35 ff.) are depicted, shows them to have originated partly in the free composition of the imagination, partly in a remodelling of the synoptical narratives with a view to the glorification of Jesus. With respect to the former : Jesus is walking, v. 35, near to John ; in v. 29 he is said to come directly to him ; yet on neither occasion is there any account of an interview between the two. Could Jesus really have avoided contact with the Baptist, that there might be no appearance of preconcerted action? This is Lampe's conjecture: but it is the product of modern reflections, foreign to the time and circumstances of Jesus. Or shall we suppose that the narrator,

---

* Greiling, Leben Jesu von Nazaret, S. 132 f.
† 2 Sam iii. 1.

נָתוֹן הָלוֹךְ וְקָשֵׁ֑ה
בֵּית שָׁאוּל הֹלְכִים וְדַלִּֽים׃

John iii. 30.
ἐκεῖνον δεῖ αὐξάνειν.
ἐμὲ δὲ ἐλαττοῦσθαι.

‡ Schulz, die Lehre vom Abendmahl, S. 115.   Winer Realwörterbuch 1. S. 693.

whether fortuitously or purposely, omitted known details? But
the meetings of Jesus and John must have furnished him with peculiarly interesting matter, so that, as Lücke allows,* his silence is
enigmatical. From our point of view the enigma is solved. The
Baptist had, in the evangelist's idea, pointed to Jesus as the Messiah. This, understood as a visible pointing, required that Jesus
should pass by or approach John; hence this feature was inserted
in the narrative: but the particulars of an actual meeting being unnecessary, were, though very awkwardly, omitted. The incident
of some disciples attaching themselves to Jesus in consequence of
the Baptist's direction, seems to be a free version of the sending of
two disciples by John from his prison. Thus, as in Matthew xi.
2, and Luke vii. 18, John despatches two disciples to Jesus with
the dubitative question, "Art thou *he that should come?*" so in
the fourth Gospel he likewise sends two disciples to Jesus, but with
the positive assertion that he (Jesus) is *the Lamb of God,* ἀμνὸς
Θεοῦ; as Jesus in the former case gives to the disciples, after the
delivery of their message, the direction: "Go and tell John *the
things ye have seen and heard,*" ἃ εἴδετε καὶ ἠκούσατε: so in the
latter, he gives to the inquiry concerning his abode, the answer:
come and see, ἔρχεσθε καὶ ἴδετε. But while in the synoptical gospels the two disciples return to John, in the fourth, they permanently
attach themselves to Jesus.

From the foregoing considerations, it is inconceivable that John
should ever have held and pronounced Jesus to be the Messiah: but
it is easy to show how a belief that he did so might obtain, without
historical foundation. According to Acts xix. 4, the apostle Paul
declares what seems sufficiently guaranteed by history, that John
baptized εἰς τὸν ἐρχόμενον, and this coming Messiah, adds Paul, to
whom John pointed was Jesus (τουτέστιν εἰς Χριστὸν Ἰησοῦν). This
was an interpretation of the Baptist's words by the issue; for Jesus
had approved himself to a great number of his cotemporaries, as the
Messiah announced by John. There was but a step to the notion
that the Baptist himself had, under the ἐρχόμενος, understood the
individual Jesus,—had himself the τουτεστιν, κ. τ. λ. in his mind;
a view which, however unhistorical, would be inviting to the early
Christians, in proportion to their wish to sustain the dignity of Jesus by the authority of the Baptist, then very influential in the
Jewish world.† There was yet another reason, gathered from the

---

* Commentar, S. 380.   † The passage above quoted from the Acts gives us also
some explanation, why the fourth evangelist of all others should be solicitous to place the
Baptist in a more favourable relation to Jesus, than history allows us to conceive. According to v. 1 ff. there were persons in Ephesus who knew only of John's baptism, and were
therefore rebaptized by the apostle Paul in the name of Jesus. Now an old tradition represents the fourth gospel to have been written in Ephesus (Irenæus adv. hær. iii. 1.). If
we accept this, (and it is certainly correct in assigning a Greek locality for the composition of this Gospel,) and presuppose, in accordance with the intimation in the Acts, that
Ephesus was the seat of a number of the Baptist's followers, all of whom Paul could hardly
have converted; the endeavour to draw them over to Jesus would explain the remarkable
stress laid by the fourth evangelist on the μαρτυρία Ἰωάννου. Storr has very judiciously

Old Testament. The ancestor of the Messiah, David, had likewise in the old Hebrew legend a kind of forerunner in the person of Samuel, who by order from Jehovah anointed him to be king over Israel (1 Sam. xvi.), and afterwards stood in the relation of a witness to his claims. If then it behoved the Messiah to have a forerunner, who, besides, was more closely characterized in the prophecy of Malachi as a second Elias, and if, historically, Jesus was preceded by John, whose baptism as a consecration corresponded to an anointing; the idea was not remote of conforming the relation between John and Jesus to that between Samuel and David.

We might have decided with tolerable certainty which of the two incompatible statements concerning the relation between the Baptist and Jesus is to be renounced as unhistorical, by the universal canon of interpretation, that where, in narratives having a tendency to aggrandize a person or a fact, (a tendency which the Gospels evince at every step,) two contradictory statements are found, that which best corresponds to this aim is the least historical; because if, in accordance with it, the original fact had been so dazzling, it is inconceivable that the other less brilliant representation should afterwards arise; as here, if John so early acknowledged Jesus, it is inexplicable how a story could be fabricated, which reports him to have been in doubt on the same subject at a very late period. We have, however, by a separate examination of the narrative in the fourth gospel, ascertained that it is self-contradictory and contains its own solution; hence our result, found independently of the above canon, serves for its confirmation.

Meanwhile that result is only the negative, that all which turns upon the early acknowledgment of Jesus by John has no claim to be received as historical; of the positive we know nothing, unless the message out of prison may be regarded as a clue to the truth, and we must therefore subject this side of the matter to a separate examination. We will not extend our arguments against the probability of an early and decided conviction on the part of the Baptist, to a mere conjecture awakened in him at a later period that Jesus was the Messiah; and therefore we leave uncontested the proper contents of the narrative. But as regards the form, it is not to be conceived without difficulty. That the Baptist in prison, ἐν τῷ δεσμωτηρίῳ, should have information of the proceedings of Jesus: that he should from that locality send his disciples to Jesus: and that these, as we are led to infer, should bring him an answer in his imprisonment.

According to Josephus,[*] Herod imprisoned John from fear of disturbances; allowing this to be merely a joint cause with that given by the evangelist, it is yet difficult to believe that to a man, one motive of whose imprisonment was to seclude him from his followers, his disciples should have retained free access; although we cannot

remarked and discussed this, über den Zweck der Evangelischen Geschichte und der Briefe Johannis S. 5 ff. 21 f. Compare Hug. Einleitung in das N. T. S. 190 3te Ausg.
    [*] Antiq. xviii. v. 2.

prove it an impossibility that circumstances might favour the admission of certain individuals. Now that the message was sent from prison we learn from Matthew alone; Luke says nothing of it, although he tells of the message. We might hence, with Schleiermacher,* consider Luke's account the true one, and the δεσμωτηρίῳ of Matthew an unhistorical addition. But that critic has himself very convincingly shown, from the tedious amplifications, partly betraying even misunderstanding, which the narrative of Luke contains (vii. 20, 21, 29, 30), that Matthew gives the incident in its original, Luke in a revised form.† It would indeed be singular if Matthew had supplied the δεσμωτηρίῳ when it was originally wanting; it is far more natural to suppose that Luke, who in the whole paragraph appears as a reviser, expunged the original mention of the prison.

In judging of Luke's motives for so doing, we are led to notice the difference in the dates given by the evangelists for the imprisonment of John. Matthew, with whom Mark agrees, places it before the public appearance of Jesus in Galilee; for he gives it as the motive for the return of Jesus into that province (Matt. iv. 12; Mark i. 14.). Luke assigns no precise date to the arrest of the Baptist (iii. 19 f.), yet it is to be inferred from his silence about the prison, in connexion with the sending of the two disciples, that he regarded it as a later occurrence; but John expressly says, that after the first passover attended by Jesus in his public character, *John was not yet cast into prison* (iii. 24.). If it be asked, who is right? we answer that there is something on the face of the account of the first evangelist, which has inclined many commentators to renounce it in favour of the two last. That Jesus, on the report of John's imprisonment in Galilee by Herod Antipas, should have returned into the dominions of that prince for the sake of safety, is, as Schneckenburger well maintains,‡ highly improbable, since there, of all places, he was the least secure from a similar fate. But even if it be held impossible to dissociate the ἀνεχώρησεν (*he withdrew*) from the connate idea of seeking security, we may still ask whether, disregarding the mistake in the motive, the fact itself may not be maintained. Matthew and Mark connect with this journey into Galilee after John's imprisonment, the commencement of the public ministry of Jesus; and that this was consequent on the removal of the Baptist, I am quite inclined to believe. For it is in itself the most natural that the exit of the Baptist should incite Jesus to carry on in his stead the preaching of μετανοεῖτε ἤγγικε γὰρ ἡ βασιλεία τῶν οὐρανῶν; and the canon cited above is entirely in favour of Matthew. For if it be asked which fiction best accords with the aggrandizing spirit of the Christian legend,—that of John's removal before the appearance of Jesus, or that of their having long laboured in conjunction?—the answer must be, the latter. If he to whom the hero of a narrative is superior disappears from the scene before the entrance of the latter, the crowning opportunity for the hero to demonstrate his ascendancy

* Ueber den Lukas, S. 109. † Ibid. p. 106. ‡ Ueber den Ursprung u. s. w. S. 79.

is lost—the full splendour of the rising sun can only be appreciated, when the waning moon is seen above the horizon, growing paler and paler in the presence of the greater luminary.   Such is the case in the Gospels of Luke and John, while Matthew and Mark rest satisfied with the less effective representation.   Hence, as the least calculated to magnify Jesus, the account of Matthew has the advantage in historical probability.

Thus at the time when the two disciples must have been sent to Jesus, the Baptist was already imprisoned, and we have remarked above, that he could hardly, so situated, transmit and receive messages.   But popular legend might be prompted to fabricate such a message that the Baptist might not depart without at least an incipient recognition of Jesus as the Messiah; so that neither the one nor the other of the two incompatible statements is to be regarded as historical.

§. 47. OPINION OF THE EVANGELISTS AND JESUS CONCERNING THE BAPTIST, WITH HIS OWN JUDGMENT ON HIMSELF—RESULT OF THE INQUIRY INTO THE RELATIONSHIP BETWEEN THESE TWO INDIVIDUALS.

The Evangelists apply to John, as the preparer of the Messiah's kingdom, several passages of the Old Testament.

The abode of the preacher of repentance in the wilderness, his activity in preparing the way for the Messiah, necessarily recalled the passage of Isaiah (xl. 3 ff. LXX.): φωνὴ βοῶντος ἐν ἐρήμῳ· ἑτοιμάσατε τὴν ὁδὸν Κυρίῳ, κ. τ. λ.   This passage, which in its original connection related not to the Messiah and his forerunner, but to Jehovah, for whom a way was to be prepared through the wilderness toward Judea, that he might return with his people from exile, is quoted by the first three evangelists as a prophecy fulfilled by the appearance of the Baptist (Matt. iii. 3; Mark i. 3; Luke iii. 4 ff.). This might be thought a later and Christian application, but there is nothing to controvert the statement of the fourth evangelist, that the Baptist had himself characterized his destination by those prophetic words.

As the synoptical gospels have unanimously borrowed this passage from the Baptist himself, so Mark has borrowed the application of another prophetic passage to the Baptist from Jesus.   Jesus had said (Matt. xi. 10. Luke vii. 27.): οὗτος γάρ ᾽ἐστι περὶ οὗ γέγραπται· ἰδοὺ ἀποστέλλω τὸν ἄγγελόν μου πρὸ προσώπου σου ὃς κατασκευάσει τὴν ὁδόν σου ἔμπροσθέν σου·   *This is he of whom it is written, Behold, I send my messenger before thy face, to prepare thy way before thee;* and Mark, in the introduction to his Gospel, applies these words of Malachi (iii. 1.), together with the above passage from Isaiah, without distinguishing their respective sources, to the forerunner, John.   The text is a messianic one; Jehovah, however, does not therein speak of sending a messenger before the Messiah, but before himself; and it is only in the New Testament citations in all

these instances that the second person (σου) is substituted for the
first (לְכֶם).

Another notable passage of the same prophet (iii. 23. LXX. iv. 4.:
καὶ ἰδοὺ ἐγὼ ἀποστελῶ ὑμῖν Ἠλίαν τὸν Θεσβίτην, πρὶν ἐλθεῖν τὴν ἡμέραν
Κυρίου, κ. τ. λ : *Behold, I will send you Elijah the Tishbite be-*
fore the coming of the day of the Lord, &c.) suggested to the
evangelists the assimilation of John the Baptist to Elias. That
John, labouring for the reformation of the people, in the spirit and
power of Elias, should prepare the way for the Divine visitation in
the times of the Messiah, was, according to Luke i. 17, predicted
before his birth. In John i. 21, when the emissaries of the Sanhedrim ask, "Art thou Elias?" the Baptist declines this dignity:
according to the usual explanation, he only extended his denial to
the rude popular notion, that he was the ancient Seer corporeally
resuscitated, whereas he would have admitted the view of the Synoptical Gospels, that he had the spirit of Elias. Nevertheless, it
appears improbable that if the fourth evangelist had been familiar
with the idea of the Baptist as a second Elias, he would have put
into his mouth so direct a negative.

This scene, peculiar to the fourth Gospel, in which John rejects
the title of Elias, with several others, demands a yet closer examination, and must be compared with a narrative in Luke (iii. 15.), to
which it has a striking similarity. In Luke, the crowd assembled
round the Baptist begin to think : *Is not this the Christ?* μήποτε
αὐτὸς εἴη ὁ Χριστός; in John the deputies of the Sanhedrim* ask
him, *Who art thou?* σὺ τίς εἶ; which we infer from the Baptist's
answer to mean: "Art thou, as is believed, the Messiah?"† According to Luke, the Baptist answers, *I indeed baptize you with
water; but one mightier than I cometh, the latchet of whose shoes
I am not worthy to unloose.* According to John he gives a similar
reply: *I baptize with water; but there standeth one among you
whom ye know not; He it is who coming after me is preferred
before me, whose shoes's latchet I am not worthy to unloose:* the
latter evangelist adding his peculiar propositions concerning the pre-
existence of Jesus, and deferring to another occasion (v. 33.) the
mention of the Messiah's spiritual baptism, which Luke gives in
immediate connexion with the above passage. In Luke, and still
more decidedly in John, this whole scene is introduced with a design to establish the Messiahship of Jesus, by showing that the
Baptist had renounced that dignity, and attributed it to one who
should come after him. If at the foundation of two narratives so
similar, there can scarcely be more than one fact,‡ the question is,
which gives that fact the most faithfully? In Luke's account there
is no intrinsic improbability; on the contrary it is easy to imagine
that the people, congregated round the man who announced the Messiah's kingdom, and baptized with a view to it, should, in moments

---

* The expression οἱ Ἰουδαῖοι is thus interpreted by the most learned exegetists.
Comp. Paulus, Lücke, Tholuck in loc.   † Lücke, Commentar, S. 327.   ‡ Lücke, S. 339.

of enthusiasm, believe him to be the Messiah. But that the San-hedrim should send from Jerusalem to John on the banks of the Jordan, for the sake of asking him whether he were the Messiah, seems less natural. Their object could only be what, on a later oc-casion, it was with respect to Jesus, (Matt. xxi. 23 ff.), namely, to challenge the authority of John to baptize, as appears from v. 25. Moreover, from the hostile position which John had taken towards the sects of the Pharisees and Sadducees (Matt. iii. 7.), to whom the members of the Sanhedrim belonged, they must have prejudged that he was not the Messiah, nor a prophet, and consequently, that he had no right to undertake a βάπτισμα. But in that case, they could not possibly have so put their questions as they are reported to have done in the fourth Gospel. In the passage from Matthew above cited, they ask Jesus, quite consistently with their impression that he had no prophetic authority: ἐν ποίᾳ ἐξουσίᾳ ταῦτα ποιεῖς; *By what authority doest thou these things?* but in John, they question the Baptist precisely as if they presupposed him to be the Messiah, and when he, apparently to their consternation, has denied this, they tender him successively the dignities of Elias, and of another prophetic forerunner, as if they earnestly wished him to accept one of these titles. Searching opponents will not thus thrust the high-est honours on the man to whom they are inimical;—this is the representation of a narrator who wishes to exhibit the modesty of the man, and his subordination to Jesus, by his rejection of those brilliant titles. To enable him to reject them, they must have been offered ; but this could in reality only be done by well-wishers, as in Luke, where the conjecture that the Baptist was the Messiah is attributed to the people.

Why then did not the fourth evangelist attribute those questions likewise to the people, from whom, with a slight alteration, they would have seemed quite natural ? Jesus, when addressing the un-believing Jews in Jerusalem, John v. 33., appeals to their message to the Baptist, and to the faithful testimony then given by the lat-ter. Had John given his declaration concerning his relation to Jesus before the common people merely, such an appeal would have been impossible ; for if Jesus were to refer his enemies to the tes-timony of John, that testimony must have been delivered before his enemies : if the assertions of the Baptist were to have any diplo-matic value, they must have resulted from the official inquiry of a magisterial deputation. Such a remodelling of the facts appears to have been aided, by the above-mentioned narrative from the synop-tical traditions, wherein the high priests and scribes ask Jesus, by what authority he does such things (as the casting out of the buyers and sellers). Here also Jesus refers to John, asking for their opinion as to the authority of his baptism, only, it is true, with the nega-tive view of repressing their further inquiries (Matt. xxi. 23. ff. parall.); but how easily might this reference be made to take an affirmative sense, and instead of the argument, "If ye know not

what powers were entrusted to John, ye need not know whence
mine are given,"—the following be substituted: "Since ye know
what John has declared concerning me, ye must also know what
power and dignity belong to me;" whereupon what was originally
a question addressed to Jesus, transformed itself into a message to
the Baptist.*

The judgment of Jesus on the character of John is delivered on
two occasions in the Synoptical Gospels; first, after the departure
of John's messengers (Matt. xi. 7 ff.); secondly, after the appearance
of Elias at the transfiguration (Matt. xvii. 12 ff.), in reply to the
question of a disciple. In the fourth Gospel, after an appeal to the
Baptist's testimony, Jesus pronounces an eulogium on him in the
presence of the Jews (v. 35.), after referring, as above remarked, to
their sending to John. In this passage he calls the Baptist a burning and a shining light, in whose beams the fickle people were for
a season willing to rejoice. In one synoptical passage, he declares
John to be the promised Elias; in the other, there are three points
to be distinguished. First, with respect to the character and agency
of John,—the severity and firmness of his mind, and the pre-eminence which as the messianic forerunner, who with forcible hand
had opened the kingdom of heaven, he maintained even over the
prophets, are extolled (v. 7—14.); secondly, in relation to Jesus
and the citizens of the *kingdom of heaven*, the Baptist, though exalted above all the members of the Old Testament economy, is declared to be in the rear of every one on whom, through Jesus, the
new light had arisen (v. 11.). We see how Jesus understood this
from what follows (v. 18.), when we compare it with Matt. ix. 16 f.
In the former passage Jesus describes John as μήτε ἐσθίων μήτε
πίνων, *neither eating nor drinking;* and in the latter it is this very
asceticism which is said to liken him to the ἱματίοις and ἀσκοῖς πα-
λαιοῖς, the *old garments* and *old bottles*, with which the new, introduced by Jesus, will not agree. What else then could it be, in
which the Baptist was beneath the children of the kingdom of Jesus, but (in connexion with his non-recognition or only qualified
acknowledgment of Jesus as Messiah,) the spirit of external observance, which still clung to fasting and similar works, and his gloomy
asceticism? And, in truth, freedom from these is the test of transition from a religion of bondage, to one of liberty and spirituality.†
Thirdly, with respect to the relation in which the agency of John
and Jesus stood to their cotemporaries, the same inaptitude to receive the ministrations of both is complained of v. 16 ff., although in
v. 12 it is observed, that the violent zeal of some βιασταὶ had, under

* Whether the dialogue between John and his complaining disciples (John iii. 25
ff.) be likewise a transmutation of the corresponding scene, Matt. ix. 14 f., as Bretschneider seeks to show, must remain uncertain. Probab. p. 66 ff.

† That Jesus, as many suppose, assigns a low rank to the Baptist, because the latter
thought of introducing the new order of things by external violence, is not to be detected
in the Gospels.

the guidance of John, wrested for them an entrance into the kingdom of the Messiah.*

In conclusion, we must take a review of the steps by which tradition has gradually annexed itself to the simple historical traits of the relation between John and Jesus. Thus much seems to be historical: that Jesus, attracted by the fame of the Baptist, put himself under the tuition of that preacher, and that having remained some time among his followers, and been initiated into his ideas of the approaching messianic kingdom, he, after the imprisonment of John, carried on, under certain modifications, the same work, never ceasing, even when he had far surpassed his predecessor, to render him due homage.

The first addition to this in the Christian legend, was, that John had taken approving notice of Jesus. During his public ministry, it was known that he had only indefinitely referred to one coming after him; but it behoved him, at least in a conjectural way, to point out Jesus personally, as that successor. To this it was thought he might have been moved by the fame of the works of Jesus, which, loud as it was, might even penetrate the walls of his prison. Then was formed Matthew's narrative of the message from prison; the first modest attempt to make the Baptist a witness for Jesus, and hence clothed in an interrogation, because a categorical testimony was too unprecedented.

But this late and qualified testimony was not enough. It was a late one, for prior to it there was the baptism which Jesus received from John, and by which he, in a certain degree, placed himself in subordination to the Baptist; hence those scenes in Luke, by which the Baptist was placed even before his birth in a subservient relation to Jesus.

Not only was it a late testimony, which that message contained; it was but half a one: for the question implied uncertainty, and ὁ ἐρχόμενος, conveyed indecision. Hence in the fourth Gospel there is no longer a question about the Messiahship of Jesus, but the most solemn asseverations on that head, and we have the most pointed declarations of the eternal, divine nature of Jesus, and his character as the suffering Messiah.

In a narrative aiming at unity, as does the fourth Gospel, these very pointed declarations could not stand by the side of the dubious message, which is therefore only found in this Gospel under a totally reorganized form. Neither does this message accord with that which in the synoptical gospels is made to occur at the baptism of Jesus, and even earlier in his intercourse with John; but the first three evangelists, in their loose compositions, admitted, along with the more recent form of the tradition, the less complete one, because they attached less importance to the question of John, than to the consequent discourse of Jesus.

* For a different explanation see Schneckenburger, Beiträge, S. 48 ff.

§. 48. THE EXECUTION OF JOHN THE BAPTIST.

WE here take under our examination, by way of appendix, all
that has been transmitted to us concerning the tragic end of the
Baptist. According to the unanimous testimony of the synoptical
evangelists and Josephus,* he was executed, after a protracted imprisonment, by order of Herod Antipas, tetrarch of Galilee; and in
the New Testament accounts he is said to have been beheaded.
(Matt. xiv. 3 ff. ; Mark vi. 17 ff. ; Luke ix. 9.)

But Josephus and the evangelists are at variance as to the cause
of his imprisonment and execution. According to the latter, the
censure which John had pronounced on the marriage of Herod with
his (half) brother's† wife, was the cause of his imprisonment, and
the revengeful cunning of Herodias, at a court festival, of his death:
Josephus gives the fear of disturbances, which was awakened in
Herod by the formidable train of the Baptist's followers, as the cause
at once of the imprisonment and the execution.‡ If these two accounts be considered as distinct and irreconcileable, it may be doubted which of the two deserves the preference. It is not here as in
the case of Herod Agrippa's death, Acts xii. 23., viz., that the New
Testament narrative, by intermixing a supernatural cause where Josephus has only a natural one, enables us to prejudge it as unhistorical; on the contrary, we might here give the palm to the evangelical narrative, for the particularity of its details. But on the other
hand, it must be considered that that very particularity, and especially the conversion of a political into a personal motive, corresponds
fully to the development of the legendary spirit among the people,
whose imagination is more at home in domestic than in political
circles.§ Meanwhile it is quite possible to reconcile the two narratives. This has been attempted by conjecturing, that the fear of insurrection was the proper cabinet motive for the imprisonment of the
Baptist, while the irreverent censure passed on the ruler was thrust
forward as the ostensible motive.‖ But I greatly doubt whether
Herod would designedly expose the scandalous point touched on by
John; it is more likely, if a distinction is to be here made between
a private and ostensible cause, that the censure of the marriage was
the secret reason, and the fear of insurrection disseminated as an
excuse for extreme severity.¶ Such a distinction, however, is not
needed; for Antipas might well fear, that John, by his strong censure of the marriage and the whole course of the tetrarch's life, might
stir up the people into rebellion against him.

But there is a diversity even between the evangelical narratives
themselves, not only in this, that Mark gives the scene at the feast

---

* Antiq. xviii. v. 2.   † This former husband of Herodias is named by the evangelists
Philip, by Josephus, Herod. He was the son of the high priest's daughter, Mariamne, and
lived as a private person. V. Antiq. xv. ix. 3: xviii. v. 1. 4. B. j. i. xxix. 2. xxx. 7.
‡ Antiq. xviii. v. 4.   § Hase, Leben Jesu, S. 88.   ‖ Fritzsche, Comm. in Matth. in loc.
Winer, bibl. Realwörterb. 1, S. 694.   ¶ Paulus, exeg. Handb. 1, a, S. 361 ; Schleier-
macher, über den Lukas, S. 109

with the most graphic details, while Luke is satisfied with a concise
statement (iii. 18—20; ix. 9), and Matthew takes a middle course;
but Mark's representation of the relation between Herod and the
Baptist differs essentially from that of Matthew.   While according
to the latter, Herod wished to kill John, but was withheld by his
dread of the people, who looked on the Baptist as a prophet (v. 5):
according to Mark, it was Herodias who conspired against his life,
but could not attain her object, because her husband was in awe of
John as a holy man, sometimes heard him gladly, and not seldom
followed his counsel (v. 19).* Here, again, the individualizing characteristic of Mark's narrative has induced commentators to prefer it
to that of Matthew.† But in the finishing touches and alterations
of Mark we may detect the hand of tradition; especially as Josephus
merely says of the people, that *they gave ear to the sound of his
words*, ἤρθησαν τῇ ἀκροάσει τῶν λόγων, while he says of Herod, that
*having conceived fears of John, he judged it expedient to put him
to death*, δείσας κρεῖττον ἡγεῖται (τὸν Ἰωάννην) ἀναιρεῖν.   How near
lay the temptation to exalt the Baptist, by representing the prince
against whom he had spoken, and by whom he was imprisoned, as
feeling bound to venerate him, and only, to his remorse, seduced
into giving his death-warrant, by his vindictive wife!   It may be
added, that the account of Matthew is not inconsistent with the
character of Antipas, as gathered from other sources.‡

The close of the evangelical narratives leaves the impression that
the dissevered head of John was presented at table, and that the
prison was consequently close at hand.   But we learn from the passage in Josephus above cited, that the Baptist was confined in Machaerus, a fortress on the southern border of Persia, whereas the
residence of Herod was in Tiberias,§ a day's journey distant from
Machaerus.   Hence the head of John the Baptist could only be presented to Herod after two day's journey, and not while he yet sat
at table.   The contradiction here apparent is not to be removed by
the consideration, that it is not expressly said in the Gospels that
John's head was brought in during the meal, for this is necessarily
inferred from the entire narrative.   Not only are the commission of
the executioner and his return with the head, detailed in immediate
connexion with the incidents of the meal; but, only thus has the
whole dramatic scene its appropriate conclusion:—only thus is the
contrast complete, which is formed by the death-warrant and the
feast: in fine, the πίναξ, on which the dissevered head is presented,
marks it as the costliest viand which the unnatural revenge of a
woman could desire at table.   But we have, as a probable solution,
the information of Josephus,‖ that Herod Antipas was then at war
with the Arabian king, Aretas, between whose kingdom and his own

* Vergl. Fritzsche, Comm. in Marc. p. 225.   † E. g. Schneckenburger, über den Ursprung des ersten kanonischen Evangeliums, S. 86 f.   That the ἐκπηδῇ of Matthew, v.
9, is not contradictory to his own narrative, see Fritzsche, in loc.   ‡ Winer, bibl. Realwörterb. d. A. Herodes Antipas.   § Fritzsche, Commentar. in Matt. p. 191.   ‖ Antiq.
xviii. v. 1.

lay the fortress of Machærus; and there Herod might possibly have resided with his court at that period.

Thus we see that the life of John in the evangelical narratives is, from easily conceived reasons, overspread with mythical lustre on the side which is turned toward Jesus, while on the other its historical lineaments are more visible.

CHAPTER II.

BAPTISM AND TEMPATION OF JESUS.

§. 49.   WHY DID JESUS RECEIVE BAPTISM FROM JOHN?

In conformity with the evangelical view of the fact, the customary answer given by the orthodox to this question is, that Jesus, by his submission to John's baptism, signified his consecration to the messianic office; an explanation which is supported by a passage in Justin, according to which it was the Jewish notion, that the Messiah would be unknown as such to himself and others, until Elias as his forerunner should anoint him, and thereby make him distinguishable by all.* The Baptist himself, however, as he is represented by the first evangelist, could not have partaken of this design; for had he regarded his baptism as a consecration which the Messiah must necessarily undergo, he would not have hesitated to perform it on the person of Jesus (iii. 14.).

Our former inquiries have shown that John's baptism related partly εἰς τὸν ἐρχόμενον, its recipients promising a believing preparation for the expected Messiah; how then could Jesus, if he was conscious of being himself the ἐρχόμενος, submit himself to this baptism? The usual answer from the orthodox point of view is, that Jesus, although conscious of his Messiahship, yet, so long as it was not publicly attested by God, spoke and acted, not as the Messiah, but merely as an Israelite, who held himself bound to obey every divine ordinance relative to his nation.† But, here, there is a distinction to be made. Negatively, it became Jesus to refrain from performing any messianic deeds, or using any of the Messiah's prerogatives, before his title was solemnly attested; even positively, it became him to submit himself to the ordinances which were incumbent on every Israelite; but to join in a new rite, which symbolized the expectation of another and a future Messiah, could never, without dissimulation, be the act of one who was conscious of being the actual Messiah himself. More recent theologians have

* Dial. c. Tryph. 8, S. 110, der Mauriner Ausg.   † Hess, Geschichte Jesu, 1. B. S. 118.

therefore wisely admitted, that when Jesus came to John for baptism, he had not a decided conviction of his Messiahship.[*] They indeed regard this uncertainty as only the struggle of modesty. Paulus, for instance, observes that Jesus, notwithstanding he had heard from his parents of his messianic destination, and had felt this first intimation confirmed by many external incidents, as well as by his own spiritual development, was yet not over eager to appropriate the honour, which had been as it were thrust upon him. But, if the previous narratives concerning Jesus be regarded as a history, and therefore, of necessity, as a supernatural one ; then must he, who was heralded by angels, miraculously conceived, welcomed into the world by the homage of magi and prophets, and who in his twelfth year knew the temple to be his Father's house, have long held a conviction of his Messiahship, above all the scruples of a false modesty. If on the contrary it be thought possible, by criticism, to reduce the history of the childhood of Jesus to a merely natural one, there is no longer anything to account for his early belief that he was the Messiah ; and the position which he adopted by the reception of John's baptism becomes, instead of an affected diffidence, a real ignorance of his messianic destiny. Too modest, continue these commentators, to declare himself Messiah on his own authority, Jesus fulfilled all that the strictest self-judgment could require, and wished to make the decisive experiment, whether the Deity would allow that he, as well as every other, should dedicate himself to the coming Messiah, or whether a sign would be granted, that he himself was the ἐρχόμενος. But to do something seen to be inappropriate, merely to try whether God will correct the mistake, is just such a challenging of the divine power as Jesus, shortly after his baptism, decidedly condemns. Thus it must be allowed that, the baptism of John being a baptism εἰς τὸν ἐρχόμενον, if Jesus could submit himself to it without dissimulation or presumption, he could not at the time have held himself to be that ἐρχόμενος, and if he really uttered the words οὕτω πρέπον ἐστι, κ. τ. λ. *Suffer it to be so now*, &c. (which, however, could only be called forth by the refusal of the Baptist—a refusal that stands or falls with his previous conviction of the Messiahship of Jesus,) he could only mean by them, that it became him, with every pious Israelite, to devote himself by anticipation to the expected Messiah, in baptism, although the evangelist, instructed by the issue, put on them a different construction.

But the relation hitherto discussed is only one aspect of John's baptism ; the other, which is yet more strongly attested by history, shows it as a βάπτισμα μετανοίας, *a baptism of repentance.* The Israelites, we are told Matt. iii. 6, were baptized of John, *confessing their sins :* shall we then suppose that Jesus made such a confession ? They received the command to repent : did Jesus acknowledge such a command ? This difficulty was felt even in the early church. In the gospel of the Hebrews, adopted by the Nazarenes,

[*] Paulus, ut sup. S. 362 ff. 337. Hase, L. J. S. 48, erste Ausg.

Jesus asks his mother and brother, when invited by them to receive John's baptism, wherein he had sinned, that this baptism was needful for him ?* and an heretical apocryphal work appears to have attributed to Jesus a confession of his own sins at his baptism.†

The sum of what modern theologians have contributed towards the removal of this difficulty, consists in the application to Jesus of the distinction between what a man is as an individual, and what he is as a member of the community. He needed, say they, no repentance on his own behalf, but, aware of its necessity for all other men, the children of Abraham not excepted, he wished to demonstrate his approval of an institute which confirmed this truth, and hence he submitted to it. But let the reader only take a nearer view of the facts. According to Matt. iii. 6, John appears to have required a confession of sins previous to baptism; such a confession Jesus, presupposing his impeccability, could not deliver without falsehood; if he refused, John would hardly baptize him, for he did not yet believe him to be the Messiah, and from every other Israelite he must have considered a confession of sins indispensable. The non-compliance of Jesus might very probably originate the dispute to which Matthew gives a wholly different character; but certainly, if the refusal of John had such a cause, the matter could scarcely have been adjusted by mere *suffer it to be so now*, for no confession being given, the Baptist would not have perceived that *all righteousness was fulfilled*. Even supposing that a confession was not required of every baptized person, John would not conclude the ceremony of baptism without addressing the neophyte on the subject of repentance. Could Jesus tacitly sanction such an address to himself, when conscious that he needed no regeneration? and would he not, in so doing, perplex the minds which were afterwards to believe in him as the sinless one? We will even abandon the position that John so addressed the neophytes, and only urge that the gestures of those who plunged into the purifying water must have been those of contrition; yet if Jesus conformed himself to these even in silence, without referring them to his own condition, he cannot be absolved from the charge of dissimulation.

There is then no alternative but to suppose, that as Jesus had not, up to the time of his baptism, thought of himself as the Messiah, so with regard to the μετάνοια (*repentance*), he may have justly ranked himself amongst the most excellent in Israel, without excluding himself from what is predicated in Job iv. 18; xv. 15. There is little historical ground for controverting this: for the words, *which*,

---

* Hieron. adv. Pelagian. iii. 2: In Evangelio juxta Hebræos—narrat historia: *Ecce mater Domini et fratres ejus dicebant ei: Joannes baptista baptizat in remissionem peccatorum; eamus et baptizemur ab eo. Dixit autem eis: quid peccavi ut vadam et baptizer ab eo? nisi forte hoc ipsum quod dixi, ignorantia est.* † The author of the *Tractatus de non iterando baptismo* in Cyprian's works, Rigalt. p. 139, says (the passage is also found in Fabric. Cod. apocr. N. T., S. 799 f.): *Est—liber, qui inscribitur Pauli prædicatio. In quo libro, contra omnes scripturas et de peccato proprio confitentem invenies Christum, qui solus omnino nihil deliquit, et ad accipiendum Joannis baptisma pœne invitum a matre sua Maria esse compulsum.*

of you convinceth me of sin? (John viii. 46.) could only refer to open delinquencies, and to a later period in the life of Jesus. The scene in his twelfth year, even if historical, could not by itself prove a sinless development of his powers.

§. 50. THE SCENE AT THE BAPTISM OF JESUS CONSIDERED AS SUPERNATURAL AND AS NATURAL.

AT the moment that John had completed his baptim of Jesus, the synoptical gospels tell us that the heavens were opened, the Holy Spirit descended on Jesus in the form of a dove, and a voice from heaven designated him the Son of God, in whom the Father was well pleased. The fourth evangelist (i. 32 ff.) makes the Baptist narrate that he saw the Holy Spirit descend like a dove, and remain on Jesus: but as in the immediate context John says of his baptism, that it was destined for the manifestation of the Messiah, and as the description of the descending dove corresponds almost verbally with the synoptical accounts, it is not to be doubted that the same event is intended. The old and lost Gospels of Justin and the Ebionites give, as concomitants, a heavenly light, and a flame bursting out of the Jordan;* in the dove and heavenly voice also, they have alterations, hereafter to be noticed. For whose benefit the appearance was granted, remains doubtful on a comparison of the various narratives. In John, where the Baptist recites it to his followers, these seem not to have been eye-witnesses; and from his stating that he who sent him to baptize, promised the descend and repose of the Spirit as a mark of the Messiah, we gather that the appearance was designed specially for the Baptist. According to Mark it is Jesus, who, in ascending from the water, sees the heavens open and the Spirit descend. Even in Matthew it is the most natural to refer εἶδε, *he saw,* and ἀνεῴχθησαν αὐτῷ, *were opened to him,* to ὁ Ἰησοῦς, *Jesus,* the subject immediately before; but as it is said, in continuation, that he saw the Holy Spirit ἐρχόμενον ἐπ'αὐτὸν, not ἐφ'αὐτόν, (Mark's ἐπ'αὐτὸν, which does not agree with his construction, is explained by his dependance on Matthew,) the beholder seems not to be the same as he on whom the Spirit descended, and we are obliged to refer εἶδε and ἀνεῴχθησαν αὐτῷ to the more remote antecedent, namely the Baptist, who, as the heavenly voice speaks of Jesus in the third person, is most naturally to be regarded as also a witness. Luke appears to give a much larger number of spectators to the scene, for according to him, Jesus was baptized ἐν τῷ βαπτισθῆναι ἅπαντα τὸν λαὸν, *when all the people were baptized,* and consequently he must have supposed that the scene described occurred in their presence.†

---

* Justin. Mart. dial. c. Tryph. 88 : κατελθόντος τοῦ Ἰησοῦ ἐπὶ τὸ ὕδωρ, καὶ πῦρ ἀνήφθη ἐν τῷ Ἰορδάνῃ, κ. τ. λ. Epiphan. hæres. 30, 13 (after the heavenly voice): καὶ εὐθὺς περιέλαμψε τὸν τόπον φῶς μέγα. † See Usteri, über den Täufer Johannes, die Taufe und Versuchung Christi, in the theolog. Studien und Kritiken, 2. B, 3. Heft, S. 442 ff. and Bleek, in the same periodical, 1833, 2, S. 428 ff.

The narrations directly convey no other meaning, than that the whole scene was externally visible and audible, and thus they have been always understood by the majority of commentators. But in endeavouring to conceive the incident as a real one, a cultivated and reflecting mind must stumble at no insignificant difficulties. First, that for the appearance of a divine being on earth, the visible heavens must divide themselves, to allow of his descent from his accustomed seat, is an idea that can have no objective reality, but must be the entirely subjective creation of a time when the dwelling-place of Deity was imagined to be above the vault of heaven. Further, how is it reconcileable with the true idea of the Holy Spirit as the divine, all-pervading Power, that he should move from one place to another, like a finite being, and embody himself in the form of a dove? Finally, that God should utter articulate tones in a national idiom, has been justly held extravagant.*

Even in the early church, the more enlightened fathers adopted the opinion, that the heavenly voices spoken of in the biblical history were not external sounds, the effect of vibrations in the air, but inward impressions produced by God in the minds of those to whom he willed to impart himself: thus of the appearance at the baptism of Jesus, Origen and Theodore of Mopsuestia maintain that it was *a vision, and not a reality*, ὀπτασία, οὐ φύσις.† To the simple indeed, says Origen, in their simplicity, it is a light thing to set the universe in motion, and to sever a solid mass like the heavens; but those who search more deeply into such matters, will, he thinks, refer to those higher revelations, by means of which chosen persons, even waking, and still more frequently in their dreams, are led to suppose that they perceive something with their bodily senses, while their minds only are affected : so that consequently, the whole appearance in question should be understood, not as an external incident, but as an inward vision sent by God ; an interpretation which has also met with much approbation among modern theologians.

In the first two Gospels and in the fourth, this interpretation is favoured by the expressions, *were opened to him*, ἀνεῴχθησαν αὐτῷ, *he saw*, εἶδε, and *I beheld*, τεθέαμαι, which seem to imply that the appearance was subjective, in the sense intended by Theodore, when he observes that the descent of the Holy Spirit *was not seen by all present, but that, by a certain spiritual contemplation, it was visible to John alone*, οὐ πᾶσιν ὤφθη τοῖς παροῦσιν, ἀλλὰ κατά τινα πνευματικὴν θεωρίαν ὤφθη μόνῳ τῷ 'Ιωάννῃ : to John however we must add Jesus, who, according to Mark, participated in the vision. But in opposition to this stands the statement of Luke: the expressions which he uses, ἐγένετο—ἀνεῳχθῆναι—καὶ καταβῆναι—καὶ φωνὴν—γενέσθαι, *it came to pass—was opened—and descended—and a*

<hr>

* Bauer, hebr. Mythologie, 2 S. 225 f. Comp. Gratz, Comm. zum Evang. Matth. i. S. 172 ff.

† These are Theodore's words, in Münter's Fragmenta patr. græc. Fasc. 1, S. 142. Orig. c. Cels. i. 48. Basil. M. in Suicer's Thesaurus, 2, p. 1479.

voice came, bear a character so totally objective and exterior,* especially if we add the words, *in a bodily form*, σωματικῷ εἴδει, that (abiding by the notion of the perfect truthfulness of all the evangelical records,) the less explicit narratives must be interpreted by the unequivocal one of Luke, and the incident they recount must be understood as something more than an inward revelation to John and Jesus. Hence it is prudent in Olshausen to allow, in concession to Luke, that there was present on the occasion a crowd of persons, who saw and heard something, yet to maintain that this was nothing distinct or comprehensible. By this means, on the one hand, the occurence is again transferred from the domain of subjective visions to that of objective phenomena; while on the other, the descending dove is supposed visible, not to the bodily eye, but only to the open spiritual one, and the words audible to the soul, not to the bodily ear. Our understanding fails us in this pneumatology of Olshausen, wherein there are sensible realities transcending the senses; and we hasten out of this misty atmosphere into the clearer one of those, who simply tell us, that the appearance was an external incident, but one purely natural.

This party appeals to the custom of antiquity, to regard natural occurrences as divine intimations, and in momentous crises, where a bold resolution was to be taken, to adopt them as guides. To Jesus, spiritually matured into the Messiah, and only awaiting an external divine sanction, and to the Baptist who had already ceded the superiority to the friend of his youth, in their solemn frame of mind at the baptism of the former by the latter, every natural phenomenon that happened at the time, must have been pregnant with meaning, and have appeared as a sign of the divine will. But what the natural appearance actually was, is a point on which the commentators are divided in opinon. Some, with the synoptical writers, include a sound as well as an appearance; others give, with John, an appearance only. They interpret the opening of the heavens, as a sudden parting of the clouds, or a flash of lightning: the dove they consider as a real bird of that species, which by chance hovered over the head of Jesus; or they assume that the lightning or some meteor was compared to a dove, from the manner of its descent. They who include a sound as a part of the machinery in the scene, suppose a clap of thunder, which was imagined by those present to be a Bath Kol, and interpreted into the words given by the first evangelist. Others, on the contrary, understand what is said of audible words, merely as an explanation of the visible sign, which was regarded as an attestation that Jesus was the Son of God. This last opinion sacrifices the synoptical writers, who undeniably speak of an audible voice, to John, and thus contains a critical doubt as to the historical character of the narratives, which, consistently followed out, leads to quite other ground than that of the naturalistic inter-

* As even Lücke confesses, Comm. zum Evang. Joh. i. S. 370, and Bleek, ut sup. S. 437.

pretation. If the sound was mere thunder, and the words only an interpretation put upon it by the bystanders ; then, as in the synoptical accounts the words are evidently supposed to have been audibly articulated, we must allow that there is a traditional ingredient in these records. So far as the appearance is concerned, it is not to be denied that the sudden parting of clouds, or a flash of lightning, might be described as an opening of heaven ; but in nowise could the form of a dove be ascribed to lightning or a meteor. The form is expressly the point of comparison in Luke only, but it is doubtless so intended by the other narrators ; although Fritzsche contends that the words *like a dove*, ὡσεὶ περιστερὰν, in Matthew refer only to the rapid motion. The flight of the dove has nothing so peculiar and distinctive, that, supposing this to be the point of comparison, there would not be in any of the parallel passages **a** variation, a substitution of some other bird, or an entirely new figure. As, instead of this, the mention of the dove is invariable through all the four Gospels, the simile must turn upon something exclusively proper to the dove, and this can apparently be nothing but its form. Hence those commit the least violence on the text, who adopt the supposition of a real dove. Paulus, however, in so doing, incurred the hard task of shewing by a multitude of facts from natural history and other sources, that the dove might be tame enough to fly towards a man ;[*] how it could linger so long over one, that it might be said, ἔμεινεν ἐπ᾽ αὐτὸν, *it abode upon him*, he has not succeeded in explaining, and he thus comes into collision with the narrative of John, by which he had sustained his supposition of the absence of a voice.[†]

§ 51.   AN ATTEMPT AT A CRITICISM AND MYTHICAL INTERPRETATION OF THE NARRATIVES.

IF then a more intelligible representation of the scene at the baptism of Jesus is not to be given, without doing violence to the evangelical text, or without supposing it to be partially erroneous, we are necessarily driven to a critical treatment of the accounts ; and indeed, according to DeWette and Schleiermacher,[‡] this is the prevalent course in relation to the above point in the evangelical history. From the narrative of John, as the pure source, it is sought to derive the synoptical accounts, as turbid streams. In the former, it is said, there is no opening heaven, no heavenly voice ; only the descent of the Spirit is, as had been promised, a divine witness to John that Jesus is the Messiah ; but in what manner the Baptist perceived that the Spirit rested on Jesus, he does not tell us, and possibly the only sign may have been the discourse of Jesus.

* Comp. Eusebius, II. E. vi. 29.   † See Paulus, Bauer, Kuinöl, Hase and Theile.
‡ DeWette, bibl. Dogmatik, § 208. Anm. 6. exeg. Handbuch 1, 1, S. 31 f. 1, 3 S. 20 f.
Schleiermacher, über den Lukas, S. 58 f.   Usteri, Bleek, Hase, Kern, Neander.

One cannot but wonder at Schleiermacher's assertion, that the manner in which the Baptist perceived the descending spirit is not given in the fourth Gospel, when here also the expression ὡσεὶ περιστερὰν, *like a dove*, tells it plainly enough ; and this particular marks the descent as a visible one, and not a mere inference from the discourse of Jesus. Usteri, indeed, thinks that the Baptist mentioned the dove, merely as a figure, to denote the gentle, mild spirit which he had observed in Jesus. But had this been all, he would rather have compared Jesus himself to a dove, as on another occasion he did to a lamb, than have suggested the idea of a sensible appearance by the picturesque description, *I saw the Spirit descending from heaven like a dove*. It is therefore not true in relation to the dove, that first in the more remote tradition given by the synoptical writers, what was originally figurative, was received in a literal sense ; for in this sense it is understood by John, and if he have the correct account, the Baptist himself must have spoken of a visible dove-like appearance, as Bleek, Neander, and others, acknowledge.

While the alleged distinction in relation to the dove, between the first three evangelists and the fourth, is not to be found ; with respect to the voice, the difference is so wide, that it is inconceivable how the one account could be drawn from the other. For it is said that the testimony which John gave concerning Jesus, after the appearance: *This is the Son of God* (John i. 34.), taken in connexion with the preceding words: *He that sent me to baptize, the same said unto me*, &c., became, in the process of tradition, an immediate heavenly declaration, such as we see in Matthew: *This is my beloved Son, in whom I am well pleased.* Supposing such a transformation admissible, some instigation to it must be shown. Now in Isaiah xlii. 1, Jehovah says of his servant : (בּוֹ־אֶרְצְתָה נַפְשִׁי) הֵן עַבְדִּי אֶתְמָךְ־בּוֹ בְּחִירִי רָצְתָה נַפְשִׁי; words which, excepting those between the parentheses, are almost literally translated by the declaration of the heavenly voice in Matthew. We learn from Matt. xii. 17 ff. that this passage was applied to Jesus as the Messiah ; and in it God himself is the speaker, as in the synoptical account of the baptism.

Here then was what would much more readily prompt the fiction of a heavenly voice, than the expressions of John. Since, therefore, we do not need a misapprehension of the Baptist's language, to explain the story of the divine voice, and since we cannot use it for the derivation of the allusion to the dove ; we must seek for the source of our narrative, not in one of the evangelical documents, but beyond the New Testament,—in the domain of cotemporary ideas, founded on the Old Testament, the total neglect of which has greatly diminished the value of Schleiermacher's critique on the New Testament.

To regard declarations concerning the Messiah, put by poets into the mouth of Jehovah, as real, audible voices from heaven, was wholly in the spirit of the later Judaism, which not seldom

supposed such vocal communications to fall to the lot of distinguished rabbins,* and of the messianic prejudices, which the early
Christians both shared themselves, and were compelled, in confront-
ing the Jews, to satisfy. In the passage quoted from Isaiah, there
was a divine declaration, in which the present Messiah was pointed
to as it were with the finger, and which was therefore specially
adapted for a heavenly annunciation concerning him. How could
the spirit of Christian legend be slow to imagine a scene, in which
these words were audibly spoken from heaven of the Messiah? But
we detect a farther motive for such a representation of the case by
observing, that in Mark and Luke, the heavenly voice addresses
Jesus in the second person, and by comparing the words which,
according to the Fathers, were given in the old and lost gospels as
those of the voice. Justin, following his *Memoirs of the Apostles*,
ἀπομνημονεύματα τῶν ἀποστόλον, thus reports them : υἱός μου εἰ σύ,
ἐγὼ σήμερον γεγέννηκα σε ;† *Thou art my Son, this day have I begotten thee.* In the gospel of the Hebrews, according to Epiphanius,‡
this declaration was combined with that which our gospels contain.
Clement of Alexandria§ and Augustin‖ seem to have read the words
even in some copies of the latter ; and it is at least certain that some
of our present manuscripts of Luke have this addition.¶ Here were
words uttered by the heavenly voice, drawn, not from Isaiah, but
from Psalm ii. 7, a passage considered messianic by Jewish interpreters ;** in Heb. i. 5, applied to Christ ; and, from their being
couched in the form of a direct address, containing a yet stronger
inducement to conceive it as a voice sent to the Messiah from heaven.
If then the words of the psalm were originally attributed to the
heavenly voice, or if they were only taken in connexion with the
passage in Isaiah, (as is probable from the use of the second person,
σὺ εἰ, in Mark and Luke, since this form is presented in the psalm,
and not in Isaiah,) we have a sufficient indication that this text,
long interpreted of the Messiah, and easily regarded as an address
from heaven to the Messiah on earth, was the source of our narrative of the divine voice, heard at the baptism of Jesus. To unite
it with the baptism, followed as a matter of course, when this was
held to be a consecration of Jesus to his office.

We proceed to the descent of the spirit in the form of a dove.
In this examination, we must separate the descent of the Spirit from
the form of the dove, and consider the two particulars apart. That
the Divine Spirit was to rest in a peculiar measure on the Messiah,
was an expectation necessarily resulting from the notion, that the
messianic times were to be those of the outpouring of the Spirit upon
all flesh (Joel iii. 1 ff.) ; and in Isaiah xi. 1 f. it was expressly said

---

* According to Bava Mezia, f. lix. 1, (in Wetstein, p. 427), R. Elieser appealed to
a heavenly sign, in proof that he had tradition in his favour: *tum personuit echo cœlestis:
quid robis cum R. Eliesere? nam ubicis secundum illum obtinet traditio.* † Dial. c. Tryph.
88. ‡ Hæres, xxx. 13. § Pædagog. i. 6. ‖ De consens. Evangg. ii. 14. ¶ S. Wetstein in loc. des Lukas, and De Wette Einl. in das N. T. S. 100. ** See Rosenmüller's
Schol. in Psalm ii.

of the stem of Jesse, that the spirit of the Lord would rest on it in all its fulness, as the Spirit of wisdom and understanding, of might, and of the fear of the Lord. The communication of the Spirit, considered as an individual act, coincident with the baptism, had a type in the history of David, on whom, when anointed by Samuel the spirit of God came from that day forward (1 Sam. xvi. 13). Further, in the Old Testament phrases concerning the imparting of the Divine Spirit to men, especially in that expression of Isaiah, נחה על, which best corresponds to the μένειν ἐπὶ of John, there already lay the germ of a symbolical representation: for that Hebrew verb is applied also to the halting of armies, or, like the parallel Arabic word, even of animals. The imagination, once stimulated by such an expression, would be the more strongly impelled to complete the picture, by the necessity for distinguishing the descent of the Spirit on the Messiah,—in the Jewish view, from the mode in which it was imparted to the prophets (e. g. Isaiah lxi. 1)—in the Christian view, from its ordinary communication to the baptized (e. g. Acts xix. 1 ff.).* The position being once laid down, that the Spirit was to descend on the Messiah, the question immediately occurred: *How would it descend?* This was necessarily decided according to the popular Jewish idea, which always represented the Divine Spirit under some form or other. In the Old Testament, and even in the New (Acts ii. 3), fire is the principal symbol of the Holy Spirit; but it by no means follows that other sensible objects were not similarly used. In an important passage of the Old Testament (Gen. i. 2), the Spirit of God is described as hovering (מרחפת), a word which suggests, as its sensible representation, the movement of a bird, rather than of fire. Thus the expression רחף, Deut. xxxii. 11, is used of the hovering of a bird over its young. But the imagination could not be satisfied with the general figure of a bird; it must have a specific image, and every thing led to the choice of the dove.

In the east, and especially in Syria, the dove is a sacred bird,† and it is so for a reason which almost necessitated its association with the Spirit moving on the face of the primitive waters (Gen. i. 2). The brooding dove was a symbol of the quickening warmth of nature:‡ it thus perfectly represented the function which, in the Mosaic cosmogony, is ascribed to the Spirit of God,—the calling forth of the world of life from the chaos of the first creation. Moreover, when the earth was a second time covered with water, it is a dove, sent by Noah, which hovers over its waves, and which, by plucking an olive leaf, and at length finally disappearing, announces the renewed possibility of living on the earth. Who then can wonder that in Jewish writings, the Spirit hovering over the primeval

* Schleiermacher, über den Lukas, S. 57.
† Tibull. Carm. L. 1, eleg. 8, v. 17 f. See the remark of Broeckhuis on this passage; Creuzer, Symbolik, ii. S. 70 f.; Paulus, exeg. Handb. 1, a, S. 369.
‡ Creuzer, Symbolik, ii. S. 80.

waters is expressly compared to a dove,* and that, apart from the narrative under examination, the dove is taken as a symbol of the Holy Spirit?† How near to this lay the association of the hovering dove with the Messiah, on whom the dove-like spirit was to descend, is evident, without our having recourse to the Jewish writings, which designate the Spirit hovering over the waters, Gen. 1. 2, as the Spirit of the Messiah,‡ and also connect with him its emblem, the Noachian dove.§

When, in this manner, the heavenly voice, and the Divine Spirit down-hovering like a dove, gathered from the cotemporary Jewish ideas, had become integral parts of the Christian legend concerning the circumstances of the baptism of Jesus; it followed, of course, that the heavens should open themselves, for the Spirit, once embodied, must have a road, before it could descend through the vault of heaven. ‖

The result of the preceding inquiries, viz., that the alleged miraculous circumstances of the baptism of Jesus have merely a mythical value, might have been much more readily obtained, in the way of inference from the preceding chapter; for if, according to that, John had not acknowledged Jesus to be the Messiah, there could have been no appearances at the baptism of Jesus, demonstrative to John of his Messiahship. We have, however, established the mythical character of the baptismal phenomena, without presupposing the result of the previous chapter; and thus the two independently obtained conclusions may serve to strengthen each other.

Supposing all the immediate circumstances of the baptism of Jesus unhistorical, the question occurs, whether the baptism itself be also a mere mythus. Fritzsche seems not disinclined to the affirmative, for he leaves it undecided whether the first Christians knew historically, or only supposed, in conformity with their messianic expectations, that Jesus was consecrated to his messianic office by John, as his Forerunner. This view may be supported by the observation, that in the Jewish expectation, which originated in the history of David, combined with the prophecy of Malachi, there was

---

* Chagiga c. ii. : *Spiritus Dei ferebatur super aquas, sicut columba, quæ fertur super pullos suos nec tangit illos.* Ir Gibborim ad Genes. 1, 2, ap. Schöttgen, horæ, i. p. 9. † Torgum Koheleth, ii. 12, *vox turturis* is interpreted as *vox spiritus sancti.* To regard this, with Lücke, as an arbitrary interpretation, seems itself like arbitrariness, in the face of the above data. ‡ Bereshith rabba, S. 2, f. 4, 4, ad Genes. T. 2 (ap. Schöttgen ut sup.): *intelligatur spiritus regis Messiæ, de quo dicitur Jes. xi. 2 : et quiescet super illum spiritus Domini.* § Sohar. Numer. f. 68. col. 271 f. (in Schöttgen, horæ, 2, p. 537 f.). The purport of this passage rests on the following cabalistic conclusion : If David, according to Ps. lii. 10, is the olive tree; the Messiah, a scion of David, is the olive leaf: and since it is said of Noah's dove, Gen. viii. 11, that it carried an olive leaf in its mouth ; the Messiah will be ushered into the world by a dove.—Even Christian interpreters have compared the dove at the baptism of Jesus to the Noachian one ; see Suicer, Thesaurus, 2. Art. περιστερὰ, p. 688. It has been customary to cite in this connexion, that the Samaritans paid divine honours to a dove under the name of Achima, on Mount Gerizim ; but this is a Jewish accusation, grounded on a wilful misconstruction. See Ständlin's and Tzschirner's Archiv. für K. G. 1, 3, S. 66. Lücke, 1, S. 367. ‖ See Fritzsche, Comm. in Matt. p. 148.

adequate inducement to assume such a consecration of Jesus by the
Baptist, even without historical warrant; and the mention of John's
baptism in relation to Jesus (Acts i. 22,) in a narrative, itself traditional, proves nothing to the contrary. Yet, on the other hand, it
is to be considered, that the baptism of Jesus by John furnishes the
most natural basis for an explanation of the messianic project of
Jesus. When we have two cotemporaries, one of whom announces
the proximity of the Messiah's kingdom, and the other subsequently
assumes the character of Messiah; the conjecture arises, even without positive information, that they stood in a relation to each other,—
that the latter owed his idea to the former. If Jesus had the messianic idea excited in him by John, yet, as is natural, only so far
that he also looked forward to the advent of the messianic individual, whom he did not, in the first instance, identify with himself;
he would most likely submit himself to the baptism of John. This
would probably take place without any striking occurrences; and
Jesus, in no way announced by it as the Baptist's superior, might,
as above remarked, continue for some time to demean himself as his
disciple.

If we take a comparative retrospect of our evangelical documents,
the pre-eminence which has of late been sought for the fourth Gospel, appears totally unmerited. The single historical fact, the baptism of Jesus by John, is not mentioned by the fourth evangelist,
who is solicitous about the mythical adjuncts alone, and these he in
reality gives no more simply than the synoptical writers, his omission of the opening heaven excepted; for the divine speech is not
wanting in his narrative, if we read it impartially. In the words,
i. 33: *He that sent me to baptize with water, the same said unto
me, Upon whom thou shalt see the Spirit descending, and remaining on him, the same is he which baptizeth with the Holy Ghost,*
we have not only substantially the same purport as that conveyed
by the heavenly voice in the synoptical gospels, but also a divine
declaration: the only difference being, that here John is addressed
exclusively, and prior to the baptism of Jesus. This difference originated partly in the importance, which the fourth evangelist attached
to the relation between the Baptist and Jesus, and which required
that the criteria of the messianic individual, as well as the proximity
of his kingdom, should have been revealed to John at his call to baptize; and it might be partly suggested by the narrative, in 1 Sam.
xvi., according to which Samuel, being sent by Jehovah to anoint
a king selected from the sons of Jesse, is thus admonished by Jehovah, on the entrance of David: *Arise and anoint him, for this
is he* (v. 12.). The descent of the Spirit, which in David's case follows his consecration, is, by the fourth evangelist, made an antecedent sign of the Messiahship of Jesus.

§ 52.   RELATION OF THE SUPERNATURAL AT THE BAPTISM OF JESUS TO THE SUPERNATURAL IN HIS CONCEPTION.

At the commencement of this chapter, we inquired into the subjective views of Jesus in his reception of John's baptism, or the idea which he entertained of its relation to his own character. We close this discussion with an inquiry into the objective purpose of the miracles at the baptism of Jesus, or the mode in which they were to subserve the manifestation of his messiahship.

The common answer to such an inquiry is, that Jesus was thereby inducted to his public office, and declared to be the Messiah,[*] i. e. that nothing was conferred on him, and that simply the character which he already possessed was manifested to others. But, it may be asked, is such an abstraction intended by our narrators? A consecration to an office, effected by divine co-operation, was ever considered by antiquity as a delegation of divine powers for its fulfilment; hence, in the Old Testament, the kings, as soon as they are anointed, are filled with the spirit of God (1 Sam. x. 6, 10, xvi. 13); and in the New Testament also, the apostles, before entering on their vocation, are furnished with supernatural gifts (Acts ii.). It may, therefore, be beforehand conjectured, that according to the original sense of the Gospels, the consecration of Jesus at his baptism was attended with a supply of higher powers; and this is confirmed by an examination of our narratives. For the synoptical writers all state, that after the baptism, the Spirit led Jesus into the wilderness, obviously marking this journey as the first effect of the higher principle infused at his baptism: and in John, the words μένειν ἐπ᾽ αὐτὸν, applied to the descending Spirit, seem to intimate, that from the time of the baptism there was a relation not previously subsisting, between the πνεῦμα ἅγιον and Jesus.

This interpretation of the marvels at the baptism of Jesus, seems in contradiction with the narratives of his conception. If Jesus, as Matthew and Luke state, was conceived by the Holy Ghost: or if, as John propounds, the divine λόγος, *the word*, was made flesh in him, from the beginning of his earthly existence; why did he yet need, at his baptism, a special intromission of the πνεῦμα ἅγιον? Several modern expositors have seen, and sought to solve, this difficulty. Olshausen's explanation consists in the distinction between the potential and the actual; but it is self-contradictory.[†] For if the character of the Χριστὸς which was manifested *actu*, with the ripened manhood of Jesus, at his baptism, was already present *potentia* in the child and youth; there must have also been an inward principle of development, by means of which his powers would gradually unfold themselves from within, instead of being first awakened by a sudden illapse of the Spirit from without. This, however, does not preclude the possibility that the divine principle, existing in Jesus, as supernaturally conceived, from the moment of his birth,

---

* Hess, Geschichte Jesu, 1, S. 120.   † Bibl. Comm. 1, S. 175 f.

might need, owing to the human form of its development, some impulse from without; and Lüke* has more justly proceeded on this contrast between external impulse and inward development. The λόγος, present in Jesus from his birth, needed, he thinks, however strong might be the inward bent, some external stimulus and vivification, in order to arrive at full activity and manifestation in the world; and that which awakens and guides the divine life-germ in the world is, on apostolic showing, the πνεῦμα ἅγιον. Allowing this, yet the inward disposition and the requisite force of the outward stimulus stand in an inverse relation to each other; so that the stronger the outward stimulus required, the weaker is the inward disposition; but in a case where the inward disposition is consummate,—as it must be supposed in Jesus, engendered by the Spirit, or animated by the λόγος,—the exterior impulse ought to be a *minimum*, that is, every circumstance, even the most common, might serve as a determination of the inward tendency. But at the baptism of Jesus we see the *maximum* of exterior impulse, in the visible descent of the divine Spirit; and although we allow for the special nature of the messianic task, for the fulfilment of which he must be qualified,† yet the maximum of inward disposition, which fitted him to be the υἱὸς Θεοῦ, cannot at the same time be supposed as existing in him from his birth: a consequence which Lücke only escapes, by reducing the baptismal scene to a mere inauguration, thus, as has been already shown, contradicting the evangelical records.

We must here give a similar decision to that at which we arrived concerning the genealogies; viz., that in that circle of the early Christian church, in which the narrative of the descent of the πνεῦμα on Jesus at his baptism was formed, the idea that Jesus was generated by the same πνεῦμα cannot have prevailed; and while, at the present day, the communication of the divine nature to Jesus is thought of as cotemporary with his conception, those Christians must have regarded his baptism as the epoch of such communication. In fact, those primitive Christians whom, in a former discussion, we found to have known nothing, or to have believed nothing, of the supernatural conception of Jesus, were also those who connected the first communication of divine powers to Jesus with his baptism in the Jordan. For no other doctrine did the orthodox fathers of the church more fiercely persecute the ancient Ebionites,‡ with their gnostic fellow-believer Cerinthus,§ than for this: that the Holy Spirit first united himself with Jesus at his baptism. In the gospel

* Comm. zum Evang. Joh. 1, S. 378 f.   † From the orthodox point of view, it cannot be consistently said, with Hoffmann (p. 301), that for the conviction of his messiahship and the maintenance of the right position, amid so many temptations and adverse circumstances, an internally wrought certainty did not suffice Jesus, and external confirmation by a fact was requisite.   ‡ Epiphan. hæres xxx. 11: ἐπειδὴ γὰρ βούλονται τὸν μὲν Ἰησοῦν ὄντως ἄνθρωπον εἶναι, Χριστὸν δὲ ἐν αὐτῷ γεγενῆσθαι τὸν ἐν εἴδει περιστερᾶς καταβεβηκότα κ. τ. λ.:— They maintain that Jesus was really a man, but that that which descended from heaven in the form of a dove became Christ in him.   § Epiphan. hæres. xxviii. 1.

of the Ebionites it was written that the πνεῦμα not only descended on Jesus in the form of a dove, but entered into him :* and according to Justin, it was the general expectation of the Jews, that higher powers would first be granted to the Messiah, when he should be anointed by his forerunner Elias.†

The development of these ideas seems to have been the following. When the messianic dignity of Jesus began to be acknowledged among the Jews, it was thought appropriate to connect his coming into possession of the requisite gifts, with the epoch from which he was in some degree known, and which, from the ceremony that marked it, was also best adapted to represent that anointing with the Holy Spirit, expected by the Jews for their Messiah : and from this point of view was formed the legend of the occurrences at the baptism. But as reverence for Jesus was heightened, and men appeared in the Christian church who were acquainted with more exalted messianic ideas, this tardy manifestation of messiahship was no longer sufficient; his relation with the Holy Spirit was referred to his conception: and from this point of view was formed the tradition of the supernatural conception of Jesus. Here too, perhaps, the words of the heavenly voice, which might originally be those of Ps. ii. 7, were altered after Isaiah xlii. 1. For the words, σήμερον γεγέννηκα σε, *This day have I begotten thee*, were consistent with the notion that Jesus was constituted the Son of God at his baptism; but they were no longer suitable to that occasion, when the opinion had arisen that the origin of his life was an immediate divine act. By this later representation, however, the earlier one was by no means supplanted, but on the contrary, tradition and her recorders being large-hearted, both narratives—that of the miracles at the baptism, and that of the supernatural conception, or the indwelling of the λόγος in Jesus from the commencement of his life, although, strictly, they exclude each other, went forth peaceably side by side, and so were depicted by our evangelists, not excepting even the fourth. Just as in the case of the genealogies : the narrative of the imparting of the Spirit at the baptism could not arise after the formation of the idea that Jesus was engendered by the Spirit; but it might be retained as a supplement, because tradition is ever unwilling to renounce any of its acquired treasures.

§. 53. PLACE AND TIME OF THE TEMPTATION OF JESUS—DIVERGENCIES OF THE EVANGELISTS ON THIS SUBJECT.

THE transition from the baptism to the temptation of Jesus, as it is made by the synoptical writers, is attended with difficulty in relation both to place and time.

With respect to the former, it strikes us at once, that according to all the synoptical gospels, Jesus after his baptism was led into

---

* Epiphan. hæres. xxx. 13 :—περιστερᾶς κατελθούσης καὶ εἰσελθούσης εἰς αὐτὸν :—*of a dove descending and entering into him.* † See the passage above, § 48.

the wilderness to be tempted, implying that he was not previously in the wilderness, although, according to Matt. iii. 1, John, by whom he was baptized, exercised his ministry there. This apparent contradiction has been exposed by the most recent critic of Matthew's gospel, for the sake of proving the statement that John baptized in the wilderness to be erroneous.* But they who cannot resolve to reject this statement on grounds previously laid down, may here avail themselves of the supposition, that John delivered his preliminary discourses in the wilderness of Judea, but resorted to the Jordan for the purpose of baptizing; or, if the banks of the Jordan be reckoned part of that wilderness, of the presumption that the evangelists can only have intended that the Spirit led Jesus farther into the recesses of the wilderness, but have neglected to state this with precision, because their description of the scene at the baptism had obliterated from their imagination their former designation of the locality of John's agency.

But there is, besides, a chronological difficulty: namely that while, according to the synoptical writers, Jesus, in the plenitude of the Spirit, just communicated to him at the Jordan, betakes himself, in consequence of that communication, for forty days to the wilderness, where the temptation occurs, and then returns into Galilee; John, on the contrary, is silent concerning the temptation, and appears to suppose an interval of a few days only, between the baptism of Jesus and his journey into Galilee; thus allowing no space for a six weeks' residence in the wilderness. The fourth evangelist commences his narrative with the testimony which the Baptist delivers to the emissaries of the Sanhedrim (i. 19.); *the next day* (τῇ ἐπαύριον) he makes the Baptist recite the incident which in the synoptical gospels is followed by the baptism (v. 29.): again, *the next day* (τῇ ἐπαύριον) he causes two of his disciples to follow Jesus (v. 35); farther, *the next day* (τῇ ἐπαύριον, v. 44), as Jesus is on the point of journeying into Galilee, Philip and Nathanael join him; and lastly, *on the third day*, τῇ ἡμέρᾳ τῇ τρίτῃ (ii. 1.), Jesus is at the wedding in Cana of Galilee. The most natural inference is, that the baptism took place immediately before John's narrative of its attendant occurrences, and as according to the synoptical gospels the temptation followed close on the baptism, both these events must be inserted between v. 28 and 29, as Euthymius supposed. But between that which is narrated down to v. 28, and the sequel from v. 29 inclusive, there is only the interval of a *morrow*, ἐπαύριον, while the temptation requires a period of forty days; hence, expositors have thought it necessary to give ἐπαύριον the wider sense of ὕστερον *afterwards;* this however is inadmissible, because the expression τῇ ἡμέρᾳ τῇ τρίτῃ, *the third day*, follows in connexion with ἐπαύριον, and restricts its meaning to *the morrow*. We might therefore be inclined, with Kuinöl, to separate the baptism and the temptation, to place the baptism after v. 28, and to regard the next day's interview between

* Schneckenburger, uber den Ursprung des ersten kanonischen Evang. S. 39.

17

Jesus and John (v. 29) as a parting visit from the former to the latter: inserting after this the journey into the wilderness and the
temptation.   But without insisting that the first three evangelists
seem not to allow even of a day's interval between the baptism and
the departure of Jesus into the wilderness, yet even later we have
the same difficulty in finding space for the forty days.   For it is no
more possible to place the residence in the wilderness between the
supposed parting visit and the direction of the two disciples to Jesus,
that is, between v. 34 and 35, as Kuinöl attempts, than between
v. 28 and 29, since the former as well as the latter passages are connected by τῇ ἐπαύριον, *on the morrow*.   Hence we must descend
to v. 43 and 44; but here also there is only the interval of a *morrow*, and even chap. ii. 1, we are shut out by an ἡμέρα τρίτη, *third
day*, so that, proceeding in this way, the temptation would at last
be carried to the residence of Jesus in Galilee, in direct opposition
to the statement of the synoptical writers; while, in further contradiction to them, the temptation is placed at a farther and farther
distance from the baptism.   Thus neither at v. 29, nor below it,
can the forty days' residence of Jesus in the wilderness with the
temptation be intercalated; and it must therefore be referred, according to the plan of Lücke and others,* to the period before v. 19,
which seems to allow of as large an interpolation as can be desired,
inasmuch as the fourth evangelist there commences his history.
Now it is true that what follows from v. 19 to 28 is not of a kind
absolutely to exclude the baptism and temptation of Jesus as earlier
occurences; but from v. 29 to 34, the evangelist is far from making
the Baptist speak as if there had been an interval of six weeks between the baptism and his narrative of its circumstances.†   That
the fourth evangelist should have omitted, by chance merely, the
history of the temptation, important as it was in the view of the
other evangelists, seems improbable; it is rather to be concluded,
either that it was dogmatically offensive to him, so that he omitted
it designedly, or that it was not current in the circle of tradition from
which he drew his materials.

The period of forty days is assigned by all three of the synoptical writers for the residence of Jesus in the wilderness; but to this
agreement is annexed the not inconsiderable discrepancy, that, according to Matthew, the temptation by the devil commences after
the lapse of the forty days, while, according to the others, it appears
to have been going forward during this time; for the words of Mark
(i. 13), *he was in the wilderness forty days tempted of Satan*, ἦν
ἐν τῇ ἐρήμῳ ἡμέρας τεσσαράκοντα πειραζόμενος ὑπο τοῦ Σατανᾶ and the
similar ones of Luke i. 2, can have no other meaning.   Added to
this, there is a difference between the two latter evangelists: Mark
only placing the temptation generally within the duration of forty
days, without naming the particular acts of the tempter, which according to Matthew, were subsequent to the forty days; while Luke

mentions both the prolonged temptation (πειράζεσθαι) of the forty days, and the three special temptations (πειρασμοὶ) which followed.* It has been thought possible to make the three accounts tally by supposing that the devil tempted Jesus during the forty days, as Mark states; that after the lapse of that time he approached him with the three temptations given by Matthew; and that Luke's narrative includes the whole.† Further, the temptations have been distinguished into two kinds; that which is only generally mentioned, as continued through the forty days being considered invisible, like the ordinary attempts of Satan against men; and the three particularized temptations being regarded as personal and visible assaults, resorted to on the failure of the first.‡ But this distinction is evidently built on the air; moreover, it is inconceivable why Luke should not specify one of the temptations of the forty days, and should only mention the three subsequent ones detailed by Matthew. We might conjecture that the three temptations narrated by Luke did not occur after the six weeks, but were given by way of specimen from among the many that took place during that time; and that Matthew misunderstood them to be a sequel to the forty days' temptation.§ But the challenge to make stones bread must in any case be placed at the end of that period, for it appealed to the hunger of Jesus, arising from a forty days' fast (a cause omitted by Mark alone.) Now in Luke also this is the first temptation, and if this occurred at the close of the forty days, the others could not have been earlier. For it is not to be admitted that the separate temptations being united in Luke merely by καί, and not by τότε and πάλιν as in Matthew, we are not bound to preserve the order of them, and that without violating the intention of the third evangelist we may place the second and third temptation before the first. Thus Luke is convicted of a want of historical tact; for after representing Jesus as tempted by the devil forty days, he has no details to give concerning this long period, but narrates later temptations; hence we are not inclined, with the most recent critic of Matthew's Gospel to regard Luke's as the original, and Matthew's as the traditional and adulterated narrative.‖ Rather, as in Mark the temptation is noticed without farther details than that it lasted forty days, and in Matthew the particular cases of temptation are narrated, the hunger which induced the first rendering it necessary to place them after the forty days; Luke has evidently the secondary statement, for he unites the two previous ones in a manner scarcely tolerable, giving the forty days' process of temptation, and then superfluously bringing forward particular instances as additional facts. It is not on this account to be concluded that Luke wrote after Mark, and in dependence on him; but supposing, on the contrary, that Mark here borrowed from Luke, he extracted only the first and general part of

---

* Compare Fritzsche, Comm. in Marc., S. 23 ; De Wette exeg. Handb., 1, 2, S. 33.
† Kuinöl, Comm. in Luc., S. 379. ‡ Ligthfoot, horæ, p. 243. § Schneckenburger, über den Ursprung des ersten kanonischen Evangeliums, S. 46. ‖ Ibid.

the latter evangelist's narrative, having ready, in lieu of the farther
detail of single temptations, an addition peculiar to himself; namely,
that Jesus, during his residence in the wilderness was μετὰ τῶν θη-
ρίων, *with the wild beasts.*

What was Mark's object in introducing the wild beasts, it is
difficult to say. The majority of expositors are of opinion that he
intended to complete the terrible picture of the wilderness ;* but to
this it is not without reason objected, that the clause would then
have been in closer connection with the words ἦν ἐν τῇ ἐρήμῳ, *he
was in the wilderness,* instead of being placed after πειραζόμενος,
tempted.† Usteri has hazarded the conjecture that this particularity
may be designed to mark Christ as the antitype of Adam, who, in
paradise, also stood in a peculiar relation to the animals,‡ and Olshausen has eagerly laid hold on this mystical notion; but it is an
interpretation which finds little support in the context. Schleiermacher, in pronouncing this feature of Mark's narrative extravagant,§ doubtless means that this evangelist here, as in other instances of exaggeration, borders on the style of the apocryphal
gospels, for whose capricious fictions we are not seldom unable to
suggest a cause or an object, and thus we must rest contented, for
the present, to penetrate no farther into the sense of his statement.

With respect to the difference between Matthew and Luke in the
arrangement of the several temptations, we must equally abide by
Schleiermacher's criticism and verdict, namely, that Matthew's order
seems to be the original, because it is founded on the relative importance of the temptations, which is the main consideration,—the
invitation to worship Satan, which is the strongest temptation, being
made the final one; whereas the arrangement of Luke looks like a
later and not very happy transposition, proceeding from the consideration—alien to the original spirit of the narrative,—that Jesus
could more readily go with the devil from the wilderness to the ad-
jacent mountain and from thence to Jerusalem, than out of the wilderness to the city and from thence back again to the mountain.‖
While the first two evangelists close their narrative of the temptation with the ministering of angels to Jesus, Luke has a conclusion
peculiar to himself, namely, that the devil left Jesus *for a season,*
ἄχρι καιροῦ (v. 13.), apparently intimating that the sufferings of Jesus were a farther assault of the devil; an idea not resumed by
Luke, but alluded to in John xiv. 30.

§ 54. THE HISTORY OF THE TEMPTATION CONCEIVED IN THE SENSE OF THE EVANGELISTS.

FEW evangelical passages have undergone a more industrious
criticism, or more completely run through the circle of all possible

---

* Thus Euthymius, Kuinöl, and others.   † Fritzsche, in loc.   ‡ Beitrag zur Erklärung der Versuchungsgeschichte, in Ullmann's and Umbreit's Studien, 1834, 4, S. 789.
§ Ueber den Lukas.   ‖ Compare Schneckenburger, ut sup. S. 47 f.

interpretations, than the history in question. For the personal appearance of the devil, which it seems to contain, was a thorn which would not allow commentators to repose on the most obvious interpretation, but incessantly urged them to new efforts. The series of explanations hence resulting, led to critical comparisons, among which those of Schmidt,* Fritzsche,† and Usteri,‡ seem to have carried the inquiry to its utmost limits.

The first interpretation that suggests itself on an unprejudiced consideration of the text is this ; that Jesus was led by the Divine Spirit received at his baptism, into the wilderness, there to undergo a temptation by the devil, who accordingly appeared to him visibly and personally, and in various ways, and at various places to which he was the conductor. prosecuted his purpose of temptation ; but meeting with a victorious resistance, he withdrew from Jesus, and angels appeared to minister to him. Such is the simple exegesis of the narrative, but viewed as a history it is encumbered with difficulties.

To take the portions of the narrative in their proper order: if the Divine Spirit led Jesus into the wilderness with the design of exposing him to temptation, as Matthew expressly says, ἀνήχθη εἰς τὴν ἔρημον ὑπό τοῦ Πνεύματός πειρασθῆναι (iv. 1), of what use was this temptation? That it had a vicarious and redeeming value will hardly be maintained, or that it was necessary for God to put Jesus to a trial; neither can it be consistently shown that by this temptation Jesus was to be made like us, and, according to Heb. iv. 15, tempted in all things like as we are ; for the fullest measure of trial fell to his share in after life, and a temptation, effected by the devil in person, would rather make him *unlike* us, who are spared such appearances.

The forty day's fast, too, is singular. One does not understand how Jesus could hunger after six weeks of abstinence from all food, without having hungered long before ; since in ordinary cases the human frame cannot sustain a week's deprivation of nourishment. It is true, expositors§ console themselves by calling the forty days a round number, and by supposing that the expression of Matthew νηστεύσας, and even that of Luke, οὐκ ἔφαγεν οὐδὲν, are not to be taken strictly, and do not denote abstinence from all food, but only from that which is customary, so that the use of roots and herbs is not excluded. On no supposition, however, can so much be subtracted from the forty days as to leave only the duration of a conceivable fast ; and that nothing short of entire abstinence from all nourishment was intended by the evangelists, Fritzsche has clearly shown, by pointing out the parallel between the fast of Jesus and that of Moses and Elias, the former of whom is said to have eaten no bread and drunk no water for forty days (Exod. xxxiv. 28 ; Deut. ix. 9,

18), and the latter, to have gone for the same period in the strength of a meal taken before his journey (1 Kings xix. 8). But such a fast wants the credentials of utility, as well as of possibility. From the context it appears, that the fast of Jesus was prompted by the same Spirit which occasioned his journey to the wilderness, and which now moved him to a holy self-discipline, whereby men of God, under the old dispensation, purified themselves, and became worthy of divine visions. But it could not be hidden from that Spirit, that Satan, in attacking Jesus, would avail himself of this very fast, and make the hunger thence arising an accomplice in his temptation. And was not the fast, in this case, a kind of challenge to Satan, an act of presumption, ill becoming even the best warranted self-confidence?*

But the personal appearance of the devil is the great stumbling-block in the present narrative. If, it is said, there be a personal devil, he cannot take a visible form; and if that were possible, he would hardly demean himself as he is represented to have done in the gospels. It is with the existence of the devil as with that of angels—even the believers in a revelation are perplexed by it, because the idea did not spring up among the recipients of revelation, but was transplanted by them, during exile, from a profane soil.† Moreover, to those who have not quite shut out the lights of the present age, the existence of a devil is become in the highest degree doubtful.

On this subject, as well as on that of angels, Schleiermacher may serve as an interpreter of modern opinion. He shows that the idea of a being, such as the devil, is an assemblage of contradictions: that as the idea of angels originated in a limited observation of nature, so that of the devil originated in a limited observation of self, and as our knowledge of human nature progresses, must recede farther into the background, and the appeal to the devil be henceforth regarded as the resource of ignorance and sloth.‡ Even admitting the existence of a devil, a visible and personal appearance on his part, such as is here supposed, has its peculiar difficulties. Olshausen himself observes, that there is no parallel to it either in the Old or New Testament. Farther, if the devil, that he might have some hope of deceiving Jesus, abandoned his own form, and took that of a man, or of a good angel; it may be reasonably asked whether the passage, 2 Cor. xi. 14, *Satan is transformed into an angel of light*, be intended literally, and if so, whether this fantastic conception can be substantially true ?§

As to the temptations, it was early asked by Julian, how the devil could hope to deceive Jesus, knowing, as he must, his higher

* Usteri, über den Täufer Johannes, die Taufe und Versuchung Christi. In den theol. Studien und Kritiken, zweiten Jahrgangs (1829) drittes Heft, S. 450. De Wette, exeg. Handb., 1, 1, S. 38.   † De Wette, bibl. Dogmatik, §171.   Gramberg, Grundzüge einer Engellehre des A. T., §5, in Winer's Zeitschrift f. wissenschaftliche Theologie, I Bd. S. 182 f.   ‡ Glaubenslehre, 1, S. 44, 45, der zweiten Ausg.   § Schmidt, exeg. Beiträge. Kuinöl, in Matt.

nature ?* And Theodore's answer that the divinity of Jesus was then unknown to the devil, is contradicted by the observation, that had he not then beheld a higher nature in Jesus, he would scarcely have taken the trouble to appear specially to him in person. In relation to the particular temptations, an assent cannot be withheld from the canon, that, to be credible, the narrative must ascribe nothing to the devil inconsistent with his established cunning.† Now the first temptation, appealing to hunger, we grant, is not ill-conceived; if this were ineffectual, the devil, as an artful tactician, should have had a yet more alluring temptation at hand ; but instead of this, we find him, in Matthew, proposing to Jesus the neck-breaking feat of casting himself down from the pinnacle of the temple—a far less inviting experiment than the metamorphosis of the stones. This proposition finding no acceptance, there follows, as a crowning effort, a suggestion which, whatever might be the bribe, every true Israelite would instantly reject with abhorrence—to fall down and worship the devil. So indiscreet a choice and arrangement of temptations has thrown most modern commentators into perplexity.‡ As the three temptations took place in three different and distant places, the question occurs : how did Jesus pass with the devil from one to the other? Even the orthodox hold that this change of place was effected quite naturally, for they suppose that Jesus set out on a journey, and that the devil followed him.§ But the expressions, the devil *takes him—sets him*, παραλαμβάνει—ἵστησιν αὐτὸν ὁ διάβολος, in Matthew : *taking, ἀναγαγὼν, brought, ἤγαγεν, set, ἔστησεν,* in Luke, obviously imply that the transportation was effected by the devil, and moreover, the particular given in Luke, that the devil showed Jesus all the kingdoms of the world in a moment of time, points to something magical ; so that without doubt the evangelists intended to convey the idea of magical transportations, as in Acts viii. 29, a power of *carrying away, ἁρπάζειν,* is attributed to the *Spirit of the Lord.* But it was early found irreconcileable with the dignity of Jesus that the devil should thus exercise a magical power over him, and carry him about in the air :‖ an idea which seemed extravagant even to those who tolerated the personal appearance of the devil. The incredibility is augmented, when we consider the sensation which the appearance of Jesus on the roof of the temple must have excited, even supposing it to be the roof of Solomon's Porch only, in which case the gilded spears on the Holy Place, and the prohibition to laymen to tread its roof, would not be an obstacle.* The well-known question suggested by the last

---

* In a fragment of Theodore of Mopsuestia in Munter's Fragm. Patr. Graec. Fasc. 1, p. 99 f.   † Paulus.   ‡ Hoffmann thinks that the devil, in his second temptation, designedly chose so startling an example as the leap from the temple roof, the essential aim of the temptation being to induce Jesus to a false use of his miraculous power and consciousness of a divine nature. But this evasion leaves the matter where it was, for there is the same absurdity in choosing unfit examples as unfit temptations.   § Hess, Geschichte Jesu, 1, S. 124.   ¦ See the author of the discourse *de jejunio et tentationibus Christi,* among Cyprian's works.   ● Compare Joseph, b. j. v. v. 6, vi. v. 1. Fritzsche, in Matth., S. 164. De Wette, exeg. Handb., 1, 1, S. 40.

temptation, as to the situation of the mountain, from whose summit
may be seen all the kingdoms of the world, has been met by the information that κόσμος here means no more than Palestine, and βασι-
λείας, its several kingdoms and tetrarchies;* but this is a scarcely less
ludicrous explanation than the one that the devil showed Jesus all
the kingdoms of the world on a map! No answer remains but that
such a mountain existed only in the ancient idea of the earth as a
plain, and in the popular imagination, which can easily stretch a
mountain up to heaven, and sharpen an eye to penetrate infinity.

Lastly, the incident with which our narrative closes, namely,
that angels came and ministered to Jesus, is not without difficulty,
apart from the above-mentioned doubts as to the existence of such
beings. For the expression διηκόνουν can signify no other kind of
ministering than that of presenting food; and this is proved not only
by the context, according to which Jesus had need of such tendance,
but by a comparison of the circumstances with 1 Kings xix. 5, where
an angel brings food to Elijah. But of the only two possible suppositions, both are equally incongruous : that ethereal beings like
angels should convey earthly material food, or that the human body
of Jesus should be nourished with heavenly substances, if any such
exist.

§ 55. THE TEMPTATION CONSIDERED AS A NATURAL OCCURRENCE EITHER INTERNAL OR EXTERNAL; AND ALSO AS A PARABLE.

THE impossibility of conceiving the sudden removals of Jesus to
the temple and the mountain, led some even of the ancient commentators to the opinion, that at least the locality of the second and third
temptations was not present to Jesus corporeally and externally, but
merely in a vision ;† while some modern ones, to whom the personal
appearance of the devil was especially offensive, have supposed that
the whole transaction with him passed from beginning to end within
the recesses of the soul of Jesus. Herewith they have regarded the
forty day's fast either as a mere internal representation‡ (which, however, is a most inadmissible perversion of the plainly historic text :
νηστεύσας ἡμέρας τεσσαράκοντα ὕστερον ἐπείνασε, Matt. iv. 2), or as a
real fact, in which case the formidable difficulties mentioned in the
preceding section remain valid. The internal representation of the
temptations is by some made to accompany a state of ecstatic vision,
for which they retain a supernatural cause, deriving it either from
God, or from the kingdom of darkness :§ others ascribe to the vision

---

* The one proposed by Kuinöl, in Matth., p. 60; the other by Fritzsche, p. 168.
† Theodore of Mopsuestia, ut sup. p. 107, maintained against Julian that the devil had
made the image of a mountain, φαντασίαν ὄρους τὸν διάβολον πεποιηκέναι, and according
to the author of the discourse already cited, de j·junio et tentationibus Christi, the first
temptation it is true passed localiter in deserto, but Jesus only went to the temple and the
mountain as Ezekiel did from Chaboras to Jerusalem—that is, in spiritu.   ‡ Paulus, S.
379.   § See for the former, H. Farmer, Gratz, Comm. zum Ev. Matth. 1, S. 217; for
the latter, Olshausen in loc., and Hoffmann (S. 327 f.) if I rightly apprehend him.

more of the nature of a dream, and accordingly seek a natural cause for it, in the reflections with which Jesus was occupied during his waking moments.* According to this theory, Jesus, in the solemn mood which the baptismal scene was calculated to produce, reviews his messianic plan, and together with the true means for its execution, he recals their possible abuses; an excessive use of miracles and a love of domination, by which man, in the Jewish mode of thinking, became, instead of an instrument of God, a promoter of the plans of the devil. While surrendering himself to such meditations, his finely organized body is overcome by their exciting influence; he sinks for some time into deep exhaustion, and then into a dream-like state, in which his mind unconsciously embodies his previous thoughts in speaking and acting forms.

To support this transference of the whole scene to the inward nature of Jesus, commentators think that they can produce some features of the evangelical narrative itself. The expression of Matthew (iv. 1), ἀνήχθη εἰς τὴν ἔρημον ὑπὸ τοῦ Πνεύματος, and still more that of Luke (iv. 1), ἤγετο ἐν τῷ Πνεύματι, correspond fully to the forms : ἐγενόμην ἐν πνεύματι, Rev. i. 10, ἀπήνεγκέ με εἰς ἔρημον ἐν πνεύματι, xvii. 3, and to similar ones in Ezekiel ; and as in these passages inward intuition is alone referred to, neither in the evangelical ones, it is said, can any external occurrence be intended. But it has been with reason objected,† that the above forms may be adapted either to a real external abduction by the Divine Spirit (as in Acts viii. 39, 2 Kings ii. 16), or to one merely internal and visionary, as in the quotation from the Apocalypse, so that between these two possible significations the context must decide ; that in works replete with visions, as are the Apocalypse and Ezekiel, the context indeed pronounces in favour of a merely spiritual occurrence; but in an historical work such as our gospels, of an external one. Dreams, and especially visions, are always expressly announced as such in the historical books of the New Testament: supposing, therefore, that the temptation was a vision, it should have been introduced by the words, εἶδεν ἐν ὁράματι, ἐν ἐκστάσει, as in Acts ix. 12 ; x. 10 ; or ἐφάνη αὐτῷ κατ ὄναρ, as in Matt. i. 20 ; ii. 13. Besides, if a dream had been narrated, the transition to a continuation of the real history must have been marked by a διεγερθεὶς, *being awaked*, as in Matt. i. 24 ; ii, 14, 21 ; whereby, as Paulus truly says, much labour would have been spared to expositors.

It is further alleged against the above explanations, that Jesus does not seem to have been at any other time subject to ecstacies, and that he nowhere else attaches importance to a dream, or even recapitulates one.‡ To what end God should have excited such a vision in Jesus, it is difficult to conceive, or how the devil should have had power and permission to produce it ; especially in Christ.

The orthodox, too, should not forget that, admitting the temptation to be a dream, resulting from the thoughts of Jesus, the false messianic ideas which were a part of those thoughts, are supposed to have had a strong influence on his mind.[*]

If, then, the history of the temptation is not to be understood as confined to the soul of Jesus, and if we have before shown that it cannot be regarded as supernatural; nothing seems to remain but to view it as a real, yet thoroughly natural, event, and to reduce the tempter to a mere man. After John had drawn attention to Jesus as the Messiah, (thinks the author of the Natural History of the Prophet of Nazareth,[†]) the ruling party in Jerusalem commissioned an artful Pharisee to put Jesus to the test, and to ascertain whether he really possessed miraculous powers, or whether he might not be drawn into the interest of the priesthood, and be induced to give his countenance to an enterprize against the Romans. This conception of the διάβολος is in dignified consistency with that of the ἄγγελοι, who appeared after his departure to refresh Jesus, as an approaching caravan with provisions, or as soft reviving breezes.[‡] But this view, as Usteri says, has so long completed its phases in the theological world, that to refute it would be to waste words.

If the foregoing discussions have proved that the temptation, as narrated by the synoptical evangelists, cannot be conceived either as an external or internal, a supernatural or natural occurrence, the conclusion is inevitable, that it cannot have taken place in the manner represented.

The least invidious expedient is to suppose that the source of our histories of the temptation was some real event in the life of Jesus, so narrated by him to his disciples as to convey no accurate impression of the fact. Tempting thoughts, which intruded themselves into his soul during his residence in the wilderness, or at various seasons, and under various circumstances, but which were immediately quelled by the unimpaired force of his will, were, according to the oriental mode of thought and expression, represented by him as a temptation of the devil; and this figurative narrative was understood literally.[§] The most prominent objection to this view, that it compromises the impeccability of Jesus,[‖] being founded on a dogma, has no existence for the critic: we can, however, gather from the tenor of the evangelical history, that the practical sense of Jesus was thoroughly clear and just; but this becomes questionable, if he could ever feel an inclination corresponding to the second temptation in Matthew, or even if he merely chose such a form for communicating a more reasonable temptation to his disciples. Further, in such a narrative Jesus would have presented a confused mixture of fiction and truth out of his life, not to be expected from an in-

* Usteri, S. 776. † 1 Bd. S. 512 ff. ‡ The former in Henke's n. Magazin 4, 2, S. 352; the latter in the natürlichen Geschichte, 1, S. 591 ff. § This view is held by Ullmann, Hase, and Neander. ‖ Schleiermacher, über den Lukas, S. 54. Usteri, ut sup. S. 777.

genuous teacher, as he otherwise appears to be, especially if it be supposed that the tempting thoughts did not really occur to him after his forty days' sojourn in the wilderness, and that this particular is only a portion of the fictitious investiture; while if it be assumed, on the contrary, that the date is historical, there remains the forty day's fast, one of the most insurmountable difficulties of the narrative. If Jesus wished simply to describe a mental exercise in the manner of the Jews, who, tracing the effect to the cause, ascribed evil thoughts to diabolical agency, nothing more was requisite than to say that Satan suggested such and such thoughts to his mind; and it was quite superfluous to depict a personal devil and a journey with him, unless, together with the purpose of narration, or in its stead, there existed a poetical and didactic intention.

Such an intention, indeed, is attributed to Jesus by those who hold that the history of the temptation was narrated by him as a parable, but understood literally by his disciples. This opinion is not encumbered with the difficulty of making some real inward experience of Jesus the basis of the history:* it does not suppose that Jesus himself underwent such temptations, but only that he sought to secure his disciples from them, by impressing on them, as a compendium of messianic and apostolic wisdom, the three following maxims: first, to perform no miracle for their own advantage even in the greatest exigency; secondly, never to venture on a chimerical undertaking in the hope of extraordinary divine aid; thirdly, never to enter into fellowship with the wicked, however strong the enticement.† It was long ago observed, in opposition to this interpretation, that the narrative is not easily recognized as a parable, and that its moral is hard to discern.‡ With respect to the latter objection, it is true that the second temptation would be an ill-chosen image; but the former remark is the more important one. To prove that this narrative has not the characteristics of a parable, the following definition has been recently given: a parable, being essentially historical in its form, is only distinguishable from real history when its agents are of an obviously fictitious character.§ This is the case where the subjects are mere generalizations, as in the parables of the sower, the king, and others of a like kind; or when they are, indeed, individualized, but so as to be at once recognized as unhistorical persons, as mere supports for the drapery of fiction, of which even Lazarus, in the parable of the rich man, is an example, though distinguished by a name. In neither species of parable is it admissible to introduce as a subject a person corporeally present, and necessarily determinate and historical. Thus Jesus could not make Peter or any other of his disciples the subject of a parable,

* If something really experienced by Jesus is supposed as the germ of the parable, this opinion is virtually the same as the preceding.   † J. E. C. Schmidt, in seiner Biblio-thek, 1, 1, S. 60 f   Schleiermacher, über den Lukas, S. 51 f.   Usteri, über den Täufer Johannes, die Taufe und Versuchung Christi, in den theolog. Studien, 2, 3, S. 156 ff.   ‡ K. Ch. L. Schmidt, exeg. Beiträge, 1, S. 339.   § Hasert, Bemerkungen über die Ansichten Ullmann's and Usteri's von der Versuchungsgesch., Studien, 3, 1, S. 71 f

still less himself, for the reciter of a parable is pre-eminently present
to his auditors; and hence he cannot have delivered the history of
the temptation, of which he is the subject, to his disciples as a
parable. To assume that the history had originally another subject,
for whom oral tradition substituted Jesus, is inadmissible, because
the narrative, even as a parable, has no definite significance unless
the Messiah be its subject.[*]

If such a parable concerning himself or any other person, could
not have been delivered by Jesus, yet it is possible that it was made
by some other individual concerning Jesus; and this is the view
taken by Theile, who has recently explained the history of the temptation as a parabolic admonition, directed by some partisan of Jesus
against the main features of the worldly messianic hope, with the
purpose of establishing the spiritual and moral view of the new
economy.[†] Here is the transition to the mythical point of view,
which the above theologian shuns, partly because the narrative is
not sufficiently picturesque (though it is so in a high degree); partly
because it is too pure (though he thus imputes false ideas to the primitive Christians); and partly because the formation of the mythus
was too near the time of Jesus (an objection which must be equally
valid against the early misconstruction of the parable). If it can
be shown, on the contrary, that the narrative in question is formed
less out of instructive thoughts and their poetical clothing, as is the
case with a parable, than out of Old Testament passages and types,
we shall not hesitate to designate it a mythus.

§ 56.   THE HISTORY OF THE TEMPTATION AS A MYTHUS.

SATAN, the evil being and enemy of mankind, borrowed from
the Persian religion, was by the Jews, whose exclusiveness limited
all that was good and truly human to the Israelitish people, viewed
as the special adversary of their nation, and hence as the lord of the
heathen states with whom they were in hostility.[‡] The interests of
the Jewish people being centred in the Messiah, it followed that Satan was emphatically his adversary; and thus throughout the New
Testament we find the idea of Jesus as the Messiah associated with
that of Satan as the enemy of his person and cause. Christ having
appeared to destroy the works of the devil (1 John iii. 8), the latter
seizes every opportunity of sowing tares among the good seed (Matt.
xiii. 39), and not only aims, though unsuccessfully, at obtaining the
mastery over Jesus himself (John xiv. 30), but continually assails
the faithful (Eph. vi. 11; 1 Pet. 5. 8). As these attacks of the
devil on the pious are nothing else than attempts to get them into

---

* Hasert, ut sup. S. 76.   † Zur Biographie Jesu, § 23.   ‡ See Zechar. iii. 1, where
Satan resists the high priest standing before the angel of the Lord; farther Vajikra rabba,
f. cli. (in Bertholdt, Christol. Jud. p. 183), where, according to Rabbi Jochanan, Jehovah
said to הרוחה אלבמ (i. e. to Satan, comp. Heb. ii. 14 and Lightfoot, horæ, p. 1088):
Feci quidem te κοσμοκρατορα, at vero cum populo fœderis negotium nulla in re tibi est.

his power, that is, to entice them to sin ; and as this can only be done by the indirect suggestion or immediate insinuation of evil, seductive thoughts, Satan had the appellation of ὁ πειράζων, *the tempter.* In the prologue to the book of Job, he seeks to seduce the pious man from God, by the instrumentality of a succession of plagues and misfortunes : while the ensnaring counsel which the serpent gave to the woman was early considered an immediate diabolical suggestion. (Wisdom ii. 24; John viii. 44; Rev. xii. 9.)

In the more ancient Hebrew theology, the idea was current that temptation (נִסָּה, LXX. πειράζειν) was an act of God himself, who thus put his favourites, as Abraham (Gen. xxii. 1), and the people of Israel (Exod. xvi. 4, and elsewhere), to the test, or in just anger even instigated men to pernicious deeds. But as soon as the idea of Satan was formed, the office of temptation was transferred to him, and withdrawn from God, with whose absolute goodness it began to be viewed as incompatible (James i. 13). Hence it is Satan, who by his importunity obtains the divine permission to put Job to the severest trial through suffering; hence David's culpable project of numbering the people, which in the second book of Samuel was traced to the anger of God, is in the later chronicles (1 Chron. xxii. 1) put directly to the account of the devil ; and even the well-meant temptation with which, according to Genesis, God visited Abraham, in requiring from him the sacrifice of his son, was in the opinion of the later Jews, undertaken by God at the instigation of Satan.* Nor was this enough—scenes were imagined in which the devil personally encountered Abraham on his way to the place of sacrifice, and in which he tempted the people of Israel during the absence of Moses.†

If the most eminent men of piety in Hebrew antiquity were thus tempted, in the earlier view, by God, in the later one, by Satan, what was more natural than to suppose that the Messiah, the Head of all the righteous, the representative and champion of God's people, would be the primary object of the assaults of Satan ?‡ And we find this actually recorded as a rabbinical opinion,§ in the material mode

* See the passages quoted by Fabricius in Cod. pseudepigr. V. T. p. 395., from Gemara Sanhedrin. † The same, p. 396. As Abraham went out to sacrifice his son in obedience to Jehovah, *antevertit eum Satanas in via, et tali colloquio cum ipso habito a proposito avertere cum conatus est,* etc.. Schemoth, R. 41 (ap. Wetstein in loc. Matth.): *Cum Moses in altum adscenderet, dixit Israeli : post dies XL hora sexta redibo. Cum autem XL illi dies elapsi essent, venit Satanas, et turbavit mundum, dixitque : ubi est Moses, magister vester ? mortuus est.* It is worthy of remark that here also the temptation takes place after the lapse of 40 days. ‡ Thus Fritzsche, in Matt. p. 173. His very title is striking, p. 154 : *Quod in vulgari Judæorum opinione erat, fore, ut Satanas salutaribus Messiæ consiliis omni modo, sed sine effectu, tamen, nocere studeret, id ipsum Jesu Messiæ accidit. Nam quum is ad exemplum illustrium majorum quadraginta dierum in deserto loco egisset jejunium, Satanas cum convenit, proterviisque atque impiis — — consiliis ad impietatem deducere frustra conatus est.* § Schöttgen, horæ, ii. 538, adduces from Fini Flagellum Judæorum, iii. 35, a passage of Pesikta : *Ait Satan : Domine, permitte me tentare Messiam et ejus generationem ? Cui inquit Deus : Non haberes ullam adversus eum potestatem. Satanas iterum ait : Sine me, quia potestatem habeo. Respondit Deus : Si in hoc diutius perseverabis, Satan, potius (te) de mundo perdam quam aliquam animam generationis Messiæ perdi permittam.* This passage at least proves that a temptation of the Messiah undertaken by

of representation of the later Judaism, under the form of a bodily appearance and a personal dialogue.

If a place were demanded where Satan might probably undertake such a temptation of the Messiah, the wilderness would present itself from more than one quarter. Not only had it been from Azazel (Lev. xvi. 8—10), and Asmodeus (Tobit viii. 3), to the demons ejected by Jesus (Matt. xii. 43), the fearful dwelling-place of the infernal powers: it was also the scene of temptation for the people of Israel, that *filius Dei collectivus.** Added to this, it was the habit of Jesus to retire to solitary places for still meditation and prayer (Matt. xiv. 13; Mark i. 35; Luke vi. 12; John vi. 15): to which after his consecration to the messianic office he would feel more than usually disposed. It is hence possible that, as some theologians† have supposed, a residence of Jesus in the wilderness after his baptism (though not one of precisely forty days' duration) served as the historical foundation of our narrative; but even without this connecting thread, both the already noticed choice of place and that of time are to be explained by the consideration, that it seemed consonant with the destiny of the Messiah that, like a second Hercules, he should undergo such a trial on his entrance into mature age and the messianic office.

But what had the Messiah to do in the wilderness? That the Messiah, the second Saviour, should like his typical predecessor, Moses, on Mount Sinai, submit himself to the holy discipline of fasting, was an idea the more inviting, because it furnished a suitable introduction to the first temptation which presupposed extreme hunger. The type of Moses and that of Elias (1 Kings xix. 8.), determined also the duration of this fast in the wilderness, for they too had fasted forty days; moreover, the number forty was held sacred in Hebrew antiquity.‡ Above all, the forty days of the temptation of Jesus seem, as Olshausen justly observes, a miniature image of the forty years' trial in the wilderness, endured by the Israelitish people as a penal emblem of the forty days spent by the spies in the land of Canaan (Numb. xiv. 34). For, that in the temptations of Jesus there was a special reference to the temptation of Israel in the wilderness, is shown by the circumstance that all the passages cited by Jesus in opposition to Satan are drawn from the recapitulatory description of the journeyings of the Israelites in Deut. vi. and viii. The apostle Paul too, 1 Cor. x. 6, enumerates a series of particulars from the behaviour of the Israelites in the wilderness, with the consequent judgments of God, and warns Christians against similar

the devil, was not foreign to the circle of Jewish ideas. Although the author of the above quotation represents the demand of Satan to have been denied, others, so soon as the imagination was once excited, would be sure to allow its completion.

   * Deut. viii. 2 (LXX.) the poeple are thus addressed: μνησθήσῃ πᾶσαν τὴν ὁδόν, ἣν ἤγαγέ σε Κύριος ὁ Θεός σου τοῦτο τεσσαρακοστὸν ἔτος ἐν τῇ ἐρήμῳ, ὅπως κακώσῃ σε καὶ πειράσῃ σε, καὶ διαγνωσθῇ τὰ ἐν τῇ καρδίᾳ σου, εἰ φυλάξῃ τὰς ἐντολὰς αἰτοῦ. ἢ οὔ.　† Ziegler, in Gabler's n. theol. Journ., 5, S. 201. Theile, zur Biogr. J., § 23.　‡ See Wetstein, S. 270; De Wette, Kritik der mos. Geschichte, S 246; the same in Daub's and Creuzer's Studien, 3, S. 245; v. Bohlen, Genesis, S. 63 f.

conduct, pronouncing, v. 6 and 11, the punishments inflicted on the ancients to be types for the admonition of the living, his cotemporaries, on whom the *ends of the world* were come; *wherefore*, he adds, *let him that thinketh he standeth take heed lest he fall*. It is not probable that this was merely the private opinion of the apostle—it seems rather to have been a current notion that the hard trials of the people led by Moses, as well as of Moses individually, were types of those which awaited the followers of the Messiah in the catastrophe which he was to usher in, and still more emphatically the Messiah himself, who here appears as the antitype of the people, gloriously overcoming all the temptations under which they had fallen.

The Israelites were principally tempted by hunger during their wandering in the wilderness;* hence the first temptation of the Messiah was determined beforehand. The rabbins, too, among the various temptations of Abraham which they recount, generally reckon hunger.† That Satan, when prompting Jesus to seek relief from his hunger by an exertion of his own will instead of awaiting it in faith from God, should make use of the terms given in our Evangelists, cannot be matter of surprise if we consider, not only that the wilderness was stony, but that to produce a thing from stones was a proverbial expression, denoting the supply of an object altogether wanting (Matt. iii. 9; Luke xix. 40.), and that stone and bread formed a common contrast (Matt. vii. 9). The reply of Jesus to this suggestion is in the same train of ideas on which the entire first act of temptation is constructed; for he quotes the lesson which, according to Deuteronomy viii. 3, the people of Israel tardily learned from the temptation of hunger (a temptation, however, under which they were not resigned, but were provoked to murmur): namely, that man shall not live by bread alone, &c.

But one temptation would not suffice. Of Abraham the rabbins enumerated ten: but this number was too large for a dramatic narrative like that in the Gospels, and among lower numbers the sacred three must have the preference. Thrice during his spiritual contest in Gethsemane Jesus severed himself from his disciples (Matt. xxvi.): thrice Peter denied his Lord, and thrice Jesus subsequently questioned his love (John xxi.). In that rabbinical passage which represents Abraham as tempted by the devil in person, the patriarch parries three thrusts from him; in which particular, as well as in the manner in which Old Testament texts are bandied by the parties, the scene is allied to the evangelical one.‡

The second temptation (in Matthew) was not determined by its relation to the preceding; hence its presentation seems abrupt, and the choice fortuitous or capricious. This may be true with respect to its form, but its substantial meaning is in close connection with the foregoing temptation, since it also has reference to the conduct of the Jewish people in the wilderness. To them the warning was given in Deut. vi. 16. to tempt God no more as they had tempted him at Massah; a warning which was reiterated 1 Cor. x. 9. to the members of the new covenant, though more in allusion to Numb. xxi. 4. To this crying sin, therefore, under which the ancient people of God had fallen, must the Messiah be incited, that by resisting the incitement he might compensate, as it were, for the transgression of the people. Now the conduct which was condemned in them as a *tempting of the Lord*, ἐκπειράζειν Κύριον, was occasioned by a dearth of water, and consisted in their murmurs at this deprivation. This, to later tradition, did not seem fully to correspond to the terms; something more suitable was sought for, and from this point of view there could hardly be a more eligible choice than the one we actually find in our history of the temptation, for nothing can be more properly called a tempting of God than so audacious an appeal to his extraordinary succour, as that suggested by Satan in his second temptation. The reason why a leap from the pinnacle of the temple was named as an example of such presumption, is put into the mouth of Satan himself.

It occurred to the originator of this feature in the narrative, that the passage Ps. xci. 11. was capable of perversion into a motive for a rash act. It is there promised to one dwelling under the protection of Jehovah, (a designation under which the Messiah was preeminently understood,) that *angels should bear him up in their hands, lest at any time he should dash his foot against a stone.* Bearing up in their hands to prevent a fall, seemed to imply a precipitation from some eminence, and this might induce the idea that the divinely-protected Messiah might hurl himself from a height with impunity. But from what height? There could be no hesitation on this point. To the pious man, and therefore to the head of all the pious, is appropriated, according to Ps. xv. 1; xxiv. 3, the distinction of going up to Jehovah's holy hill, and standing within his holy place: hence the pinnacle of the temple, in the presump-

---

2. *Satanas: Annon timor tuus, spes tua* (Job. iv. 6.)?
Abraham: Recordare quæso, quis est insons, qui perierit (v. 7.)?
3. *Quare, quum videret Satanas, se nihil proficere, nec Abrahamum sibi obedire, dixit ad illum: et ad me verbum furtim ablatum est* (v. 12.), *audivi—pecus futurum esse pro holocausto* (Gen. xxii. 7.), *non autem Isaacum.*
Cui resp. Abraham: Hæc est pœna mendacis, ut etiam cum vera loquitur, fides ei non habeatur.
I am far from maintaining that this rabbinical passage was the model of our history of the temptation; but since it is impossible to prove, on the other side, that such narratives were only imitations of the New Testament ones, the supposed independent formation of stories so similar shows plainly enough the ease with which they sprang out of the given premises.

tuous mode of inference supposed, might be regarded as the height whence the Messiah could precipitate himself unhurt.

The third temptation which Jesus underwent—to worship the devil—is not apparent among the temptations of God's ancient people. But one of the most fatal seductions by which the Israelites were led astray in the wilderness was that of idolatry; and the apostle Paul adduces it as admonitory to Christians. Not only is this sin derived immediately from the devil in a passage above quoted;* but in the later Jewish idea, idolatry was identical with the worship of the devil (Baruch iv. 7; 1 Cor. x. 20). How, then, could the worship of the devil be suggested to the Messiah in the form of a temptation? The notion of the Messiah as he who, being the King of the Jewish people, was destined to be lord of all other nations, and that of Satan as the ruler of the heathen world† to be conquered by the Messiah, were here combined. That dominion over the world which, in the christianized imagination of the period, the Messiah was to obtain by a long and painful struggle, was offered him as an easy bargain if he would only pay Satan the tribute of worship. This temptation Jesus meets with the maxim inculcated on the Israelites, Deut. vi. 13, that God alone is to be worshipped, and thus gives the enemy a final dismissal.

Matthew and Mark crown their history of the temptation with the appearance of angels to Jesus, and their refreshing him with nourishment after his long fast and the fatigues of temptation. This incident was prefigured by a similar ministration to Elijah after his forty days' fast, and was brought nearer to the imagination by the circumstance that the manna which appeased the hunger of the people in the wilderness was named, ἄρτος ἀγγέλων, *angels' food.* (Ps. lxxviii. 25. LXX.; Wisdom xvi. 20).‡

CHAPTER III.

LOCALITY AND CHRONOLOGY OF THE PUBLIC LIFE OF JESUS.

§ 57. DIFFERENCE BETWEEN THE SYNOPTICAL WRITERS AND JOHN, AS TO THE CUSTOMARY SCENE OF THE MINISTRY OF JESUS.

ACCORDING to the synoptical writers, Jesus, born indeed at Bethlehem in Judea, but brought up at Nazareth in Galilee, only absented himself from Galilee during the short interval between his

---

* Note 1. † Bertholdt, Christolog. Judæorum Jesu ætate, § 36. not. 1, and 2; Fritzsche, Comm. in Matth. S. 169 f. ‡ Compare with the above statement the deductions of Schmidt, Fritzsche, and Usteri, as given § 54, notes 1—3, and of De Wette, exeg. Handbuch, 1, 1. S. 41 ff.

baptism and the imprisonment of the Baptist; immediately after
which, he returned thither and began his ministry, teaching, healing,
calling disciples, so as to traverse all Galilee; using as the centre
of his agency, his previous dwelling-place, Nazareth, alternately
with Capernaum, on the north-west border of the lake of Tiberias
(Matt. iv. 12—25. parall.). Mark and Luke have many particulars
concerning this ministry in Galilee which are not found in Matthew,
and those which they have in common with him are arranged in a
different order; but as they all agree in the geographical circuit
which they assign to Jesus, the account of the first evangelist may
serve as the basis of our criticism. According to him the incidents
narrated took place in Galilee, and partly in Capernaum down to
viii. 18, where Jesus crosses the Galilean sea, but is scarcely landed
on the east side when he returns to Capernaum. Here follows a
series of scenes connected by short transitions, such as παράγων
ἐκεῖθεν (ix. 9, 27), passing from thence, τότε (v. 14.), then, ταῦτα
αὐτοῦ λαλοῦντος (v. 18), while he spake these things; expressions
which can imply no important change of place, that is, of one province for another, which it is the habit of the writer to mark much
more carefully. The passage, ix. 35, περιῆγεν ὁ Ἰησοῦς τὰς πόλεις
πάσας—διδάσκων ἐν ταῖς συναγωγαῖς αὐτῶν, is evidently only a repetition of iv. 23, and is therefore to be understood merely of excursions
in Galilee. The message of the Baptist (chap. xi.) is also received
by Jesus in Galilee, at least such appears to be the opinion of the
narrator, from his placing in immediate connexion the complaints
of Jesus against the Galilean cities. When delivering the parable
in chap. xiii. Jesus is by the sea, doubtless that of Galilee, and, as
there is mention of his *house*, οἰκία (v. 1.), probably in the vicinity
of Capernaum. Next, after having visited his native city Nazareth
(xiii. 53.) he passes over the sea (xiv. 13.), according to Luke (ix.
10.), into the country of Bethsaida (Julias); whence, however, after
the miracle of the loaves, he speedily returns to the western border
xiv. 34.). Jesus then proceeds to the northern extremity of Palestine, on the frontiers of Phœnicia (xv. 21.); soon, however, returned to the sea of Galilee (v. 29), he takes ship to the eastern
side, in the coast of Magdala (v. 39), but again departs northward
into the country of Cesarea Philippi (xvi. 13.), in the vicinity of
Lebanon, among the lower ridges of which is to be sought the
mount of the transfiguration (xvii. 1.). After journeying in Galilee
for some time longer with his disciples (xvii. 22.), and once more
visiting Capernaum (v. 24.), he leaves Galilee (xix. 1) to travel (as
it is most probably explained[*]) through Perea into Judea, (a journey
which, according to Luke ix. 52, he seems to have made through
Samaria); xx. 17, he is on his way to Jerusalem; v. 29, he comes
through Jericho; and xxi. 1, is in the neighbourhood of Jerusalem,
which, v. 10, he enters.

Thus, according to the synoptical writers, Jesus, from his return

* Fritzsche, p. 591.

after being baptized by John, to his final journey to Jerusalem, never goes beyond the limits of North Palestine, but traverses the countries west and east of the Galilean sea and the upper Jordan, in the dominions of Herod Antipas and Philip, without touching on Samaria to the south, still less Judea, or the country under the immediate administration of the Romans. And within those limits, to be still more precise, it is the land west of the Jordan, and the sea of Tiberias, and therefore Galilee, the province of Antipas, in which Jesus is especially active ; only three short excursions on the eastern border of the sea, and two scarcely longer on the northern frontiers of the country, being recorded.

Quite otherwise is the theatre of the ministry of Jesus marked out in the fourth Gospel. It is true that here also he goes after his baptism by John into Galilee, to the wedding at Cana (ii. 1.), and from thence to Capernaum (v. 12); but in a few days the approaching passover calls him to Jerusalem (v. 13.). From Jerusalem he proceeds into the country of Judea (iii. 22.), and after some time exercising his ministry there (iv. 1.), he returns through Samaria into Galilee (v. 43). Nothing is reported of his agency in this province but a single cure, and immediately on this a new feast summons him to Jerusalem (v. 1.), where he is represented as performing a cure, being persecuted, and delivering long discourses, until he betakes himself (vi. 1.) to the eastern shore of the sea of Tiberias, and from thence to Capernaum (v. 17, 59). He then itinerates for some time in Galilee (vii. 1), but again leaves it, on occasion of the feast of tabernacles, for Jerusalem (v. 2, 10). To this visit the evangelist refers many discourses and vicissitudes of Jesus (vii. 10; x. 21.), and moreover connects with it the commencement of his public ministry at the feast of dedication, without noticing any intermediate journey out of Jerusalem and Judea (x. 22.). After this Jesus again retires into the country of Perea, where he had first been with the Baptist (x. 40.), and there remains until the death of Lazarus recalls him to Bethany, near Jerusalem (xi. 1.), whence he withdraws to Ephraim, in the vicinity of the wilderness of Judea, until the approach of the passover, which he visited as his last (xii. 1 ff.).

Thus, according to John, Jesus was present at four feasts in Jerusalem, before the final one : was besides once in Bethany, and had been active for a considerable time in Judea and on his journey through Samaria.

Why, it must be asked, have the synoptical writers been silent on this frequent presence of Jesus in Judea and Jerusalem ? Why have they represented the matter, as if Jesus, before his last fatal journey to Jerusalem, had not overstepped the limits of Galilee and Perea ? This discrepancy between the synoptical writers and John was long overlooked in the church, and of late it has been thought feasible to deny its existence. It has been said, that Matthew, at the commencement, lays the scene in Galilee and Capernaum, and

pursues his narrative without noticing any journey into Judea until
the last; but that we are not hence to conclude that Matthew was
unacquainted with the earlier ministry of Jesus in Judea, for as with
this evangelist the local interest is subordinate to the effort at an
appropriate arrangement of his events, many particulars in the former part of his history, which he narrates without indicating any
place, may have been known, though not stated by him, to have
occurred in the earlier journeys and residences in Judea.* But this
alleged subordination of the local interest in Matthew, is nothing
more than a fiction of the harmonist, as Schneckenburger has recently proved.† Matthew very carefully marks (chap. iv.) the beginning and (chap. xix.) the end of the almost exclusive residence
of Jesus in Galilee; all the intervening narration must therefore be
regarded as belonging to that residence, unless the contrary be expressed; and since the evangelist is on the alert to notice the short
excursions of Jesus across the lake and into the north of Galilee,
he would hardly pass over in silence the more important, and sometimes prolonged visits to Judea, had they been known or credited
by him. Thus much only is to be allowed, that Matthew frequently
neglects the more precise statement of localities, as the designation
of the spot or neighbourhood in which Jesus laboured from time to
time : but in his more general biographical statements, such as the
designation of the territories and provinces of Palestine, within the
boundaries of which Jesus exercised his ministry, he is as accurate
as any other evangelist.

   Expositors must therefore accommodate themselves to the admission of a difference between the synoptical writers and John,‡
and those who think it incumbent on them to harmonize the Gospels must take care lest this difference be found a contradiction;
which can only be prevented by deducing the discrepancy, not from
a disparity between the ideas of the evangelists as to the sphere of
the ministry of Jesus, but from the difference of mental bias under
which they severally wrote. Some suppose that Matthew, being a
Galilean, saw the most interest in Galilean occurrences, and hence
confined his narrative to them, though aware of the agency of Jesus
at Jerusalem.§ But what biographer, who had himself accompanied
his hero into various provinces, and beheld his labours there, would
confine his narration to what he had performed in his (the biographer's) native province? Such provincial exclusiveness would surely
be quite unexampled. Hence others have preferred the supposition
that Matthew, writing at Jerusalem, purposely selected from the
mass of discourses and actions of Jesus with which he was acquainted, those of which Galilee was the theatre, because they were
the least known at Jerusalem, and required narrating more than
what had happened within the hearing, and was fresh in the memo-

---

* Olshausen, bibl. Comm., 1, S. 189 f. † Schneckenburger, Beiträge, S. 38 f.; über
den Ursprung u. s. f. S. 7 f. ‡ De Wette, Einleitung in das N. T. § 98 u. 106. § Paulus, exeg. Handb., 1, a, S. 39.

ries of its inhabitants.* In opposition to this it has been already remarked,† that there is no proof of Matthew's Gospel being especially intended for the Christians of Judea and Jerusalem: that even assuming this, a reference to the events which had happened in the reader's own country could not be superfluous; and that, lastly, the like limitation of the ministry of Jesus to Galilee by Mark and Luke cannot be thus accounted for, since these evangelists obviously did not write for Judea, (neither were they Galileans, so that this objection is equally valid against the first explanation;) and were not in so servile a relation to Matthew as to have no access to independent information that might give them a more extended horizon. It is curious enough that these two attempts to solve the contradiction between the synoptical writers and John, are themselves in the same predicament of mutual contradiction. For if Matthew has been silent on the incidents in Judea, according to one, on account of his proximity, according to the other, on account of his remoteness, it follows that, two contrary hypotheses being made with equal ease to explain the same fact, both are alike inadequate.

No supposition founded on the local relations of the writers sufficing to explain the difference in question, higher ground must be taken, in a consideration of the spirit and tendency of the evangelical writings. From this point of view the following proposition has been given: The cause which determined the difference in the contents of the fourth Gospel and that of the synoptical ones, accounts also for their divergency as to the limits they assign to the ministry of Jesus; in other words, the discourses delivered by Jesus in Jerusalem, and recorded by John, required for their comprehension a more mature development of Christianity than that presented in the first apostolic period; hence they were not retained in the primitive evangelical tradition, of which the synoptical writers were the organs, and were first restored to the church by John, who wrote when Christianity was in a more advanced stage.‡ But neither is this attempt at an explanation satisfactory, though it is less superficial than the preceding. For how could the popular and the esoteric in the teaching of Jesus be separated with such nicety, that the former should be confined to Galilee, and the latter to Jerusalem (the harsh discourse in the synagogue at Capernaum alone excepted?) It may be said: in Jerusalem he had a more enlightened public around him, and could be more readily understood than in Galilee. But the Galileans could scarcely have misunderstood Jesus more lamentably than did the Jews from first to last, according to John's representation, and as in Galilee he had the most undisturbed communion with his disciples, we should rather have conjectured that here would be the scene of his more profound instruction. Besides, as the synoptical writers have given a plentiful gleaning of lucid and popular discourses from the final residence of Jesus in Jerusalem, there is no ground whatever for believing that his earlier visits were devoid of such, and that his converse on these occasions took throughout a higher tone. But even allowing that all the earlier discourses of Jesus in Judea and Jerusalem were beyond the range of the first apostolic tradition, *deeds* were performed there, such as the cure of the man who had had an infirmity thirty-eight years, the conferring of sight on the man born blind, and the raising of Lazarus, which, from their imposing rank among the evidences of Christianity, must almost have necessitated the mention of those early visits of Jesus to Judea during which they occurred.

Thus it is impossible to explain why the synoptical writers, if they knew of the earlier visits of Jesus to Jerusalem, should not have mentioned them, and it must be concluded that if John be right, the first three evangelists knew nothing of an essential part of the earlier ministry of Jesus; if, on the other hand, the latter be right, the author of the fourth Gospel, or of the tradition by which he was guided, fabricated a large portion of what he has narrated concerning the ministry of Jesus, or at least assigned to it a false locality.

On a closer examination, however, the relation between John and the synoptical writers is not simply such, that the latter might not know what the former records, but such, that they must have proceeded from positively opposite data. For example, the synoptical writers, Matthew especially, as often as Jesus leaves Galilee, from the time that he takes up his abode there after the Baptist's imprisonment, seldom neglect to give a particular reason; such as that he wished to escape from the crowd by a passage across the sea (Matt. viii. 18), or that he withdrew into the wilderness of Perea to avoid the snares of Herod (xiv. 13), or that he retired into the region of Tyre and Sidon on account of the offence taken by the scribes at his preaching (xv. 21.): John, on the contrary, generally alleges a special reason why Jesus leaves Judea and retires into Galilee. Not to contend that his very first journey thither appears to be occasioned solely by the invitation to Cana, his departure again into Galilee after the first passover attended by him in his public character, is expressly accounted for by the ominous attention which the increasing number of his disciples had excited among the Pharisees (iv. 1 ff.). His retirement after the second feast also, into the country east of the Sea of Tiberias (vi. 1.), must be viewed in relation to the ἐζήτουν αὐτὸν οἱ Ἰουδαῖοι ἀποκτεῖναι (v. 18.), since immediately after, the evangelist assigns as a reason for the continuance of Jesus in Galilee, the malignant designs of his enemies, which rendered his abode in Judea perilous to his life (vii. 1.). The interval between the Feast of Tabernacles and the Feast of the Dedication seems to have been spent by Jesus in the capital,* no unpro-

* Tholuck, Comm. zum Evang. Joh. p. 207.

pitious circumstances compelling him to absent himself (x. 22.); on the other hand his journey into Perea (x. 40.) and that into Ephraim (xi. 54.) are presented as effects of his persecution by the Jews.

Thus precisely the same relation as that which exists between Matthew and Luke, with respect to the original dwelling-place of the parents of Jesus, is found between the first three evangelists and the fourth, with respect to the principal theatre of his ministry. As, in the former instance, Matthew presupposes Bethlehem to be the original place of abode, and Nazareth the one subsequently adopted through fortuitous circumstances, while Luke gives the contrary representation; so in the latter, the entire statement of the synoptical writers turns on the idea that, until his last journey, Galilee was the chosen field of the labours of Jesus, and that he only left it occasionally, from particular motives and for a short time; while that of John, on the contrary, turns on the supposition, that Jesus would have taught solely in Judea and Jerusalem had not prudence sometimes counselled him to retire into the more remote provinces.[*]

Of these two representations one only can be true. Before they were perceived to be contradictory, the narrative of John was incorporated with that of the synoptical writers; since they have been allowed to be irreconcileable, the verdict has always been in favour of the fourth evangelist; and so prevalent is this custom, that even the author of the Probabilia does not use the difference to the disadvantage of the latter. De Wette numbers it among the objections to the authenticity of Matthew's Gospel, that it erroneously limits the ministry of Jesus to Galilee,[†] and Schneckenburger has no more important ground of doubt to produce against the apostolic origin of the first canonical Gospel, than the unacquaintance of its author with the extra-Galilean labours of Jesus.[‡] If this decision be well-founded, it must rest on a careful consideration of the question, which of the two incompatible narratives has the greater corroboration from external sources, and the more internal verisimilitude? We have shown in the introduction that the external evidence or testimony for the authenticity of the fourth Gospel and of the synoptical ones, that of Matthew emphatically, is of about equal value; that is, it determines nothing in either case, but leaves the decision to the internal evidence. In relation to this, the following question must be considered: is it more probable that, although Jesus was actually often in Judea and Jerusalem previous to his last journey, yet at the time and place whence the synoptical gospels arose, all traces of the fact had disappeared; or that, on the contrary, although Jesus never entered Judea for the exercise of his public ministry before his last journey thither, yet at the time and place of the composition of the fourth Gospel a tradition of several such visits had been formed?

* Comp. Lücke, ut sup. S. 516. † De Wette, Einl. in das N. T., § 98. ‡ Schneckenburger, uber den Ursprung u. s. f., S. 7., Beiträge u. s. f., S. 38 ff.

The above critics seek to show that the first might be the case, in the following manner. The first Gospel, they say[*] and more or less the two middle ones, contain the tradition concerning the life of Jesus as it was formed in Galilee, where the memory of what Jesus did and said in that province would be preserved with a natural partiality,—while, of that part of his life which was spent out of Galilee, only the most critical incidents, such as his birth, consecration, and especially his last journey, which issued in his death, would be retained; for the remainder, including his early journeys to the various feasts, being either unknown or forgotten, so that any fragments of information concerning one or other of the previous residences of Jesus at Jerusalem would be referred to the last, no other being known.

But John himself, in whom our theologians rest all their confidence, expressly mentions (iv. 45) that at the first passover visited by Jesus after his baptism (and probably at others also) the Galileans were present, and apparently in great numbers, since as a consequence of their having witnessed his works in Jerusalem, Jesus found a favourable reception in Galilee. If we add to this, that most of the disciples who accompanied Jesus in his early journeys to the feasts were Galileans (John iv. 22, ix. 2), it is inconceivable that tidings of the ministry of Jesus at Jerusalem should not from the first reach Galilee. Once there, could time extinguish them? We grant that it is in the nature of tradition to fuse and remodel its materials, and as the last journey of Jesus to Jerusalem was preeminently memorable, it might absorb the recollections of the previous ones. But tradition has also another impulse, and it is its strongest; namely to glorify. It may indeed be said that to circumscribe the early ministry of Jesus by the frontiers of Galilee would serve the purpose of glorifying that province, in which the synoptical tradition had its origin. But the aim of the synoptical legend was not to glorify Galilee, on which it pronounces severe judgments;— Jesus is the object round which it would cast a halo, and his greatness is proportionate to the sphere of his influence. Hence, to show that from the beginning of his ministry he made himself known beyond the Galilean *angulus terræ*, and that he often presented himself on the brilliant theatre of the capital, especially on occasions when it was crowded with spectators and hearers from all regions, was entirely according to the bent of the legend. If, therefore, there had historically been but one journey of Jesus to Jerusalem, tradition might be tempted to create more by degrees, since it would argue—how could so great a light as Jesus have remained so long under a bushel, and not rather have early and often placed himself on the lofty stand which Jerusalem presented? Opponents, too, might object, like the unbelieving brethren of Jesus, (John vii. 3. 4.) that he who is conscious of the power to perform something truly

---

[*] Schneckenburger, Beiträge S. 207. Comp. Gabler's Treatise on the Resurrection of Lazarus, in his Journal für auserlesene theol. Literatur, 3, 2.

great, does not conceal himself, but seeks publicity, in order that
his capabilities may be recognized; and to these opponents it was
thought the best answer to show that Jesus actually did seek such
publicity, and early obtained recognition in an extended sphere.
Out of this representation would easily grow the idea which lies at
the foundation of the fourth Gospel, that not Galilee, but Judea,
was the proper residence of Jesus.

Thus, viewed from the point of the possible formation of a legend,
the balance inclines in favour of the synoptical writers. But is the
result the same when we ascend to the relations and designs of Jesus, and from this point of view inquire, if it be more probable that
Jesus visited Jerusalem once only or several times during his public life?

The alleged difficulty, that the various journeys to the feasts offer
the principal means of accounting for the intellectual development
of Jesus, is easily removed. For those journeys alone would not
suffice to explain the mental pre-eminence of Jesus, and as the main
stress must still be placed on his internal gifts, we cannot pronounce
whether to a mind like his, even Galilee might not present enough
aliment for their maturing; besides, an adherence to the synoptical
writers would only oblige us to renounce those journeys to the feasts
which Jesus took after his public appearance, so that he might still
have been present at many feasts previous to his messianic career,
without assuming a conspicuous character. It has been held inconceivable that Jesus, so long after his assumption of the messianic
character, should confine himself to Galilee instead of taking his
stand in Judea and Jerusalem, which, from the higher culture and
more extensive foreign intercourse of their population, were a much
more suitable field for his labours; but it has been long remarked,
on the other hand, that Jesus could find easier access to the simple
and energetic minds of Galilee, less fettered by priestcraft and Phar-
isaism, and therefore acted judiciously in obtaining a firm footing
there by a protracted ministry, before he ventured to Jerusalem,
where, in the centre of priestly and Pharisaic domination, he must
expect stronger opposition.

There is a graver difficulty in the synoptical statement, considered in relation to the Mosaic law and Jewish custom. The law
rigorously required that every Israelite should appear before Jehovah
yearly at the three principal feasts (Exod. xxiii. 14 ff.), and the reverence of Jesus for the Mosaic institutes (Matt. v. 17 ff.) renders it
improbable that, during the whole course of his ministry, he should
have undertaken but one journey of observance.* The Gospel of
Matthew, however, be our judgment what it may as to the date and
place of its composition, did certainly arise in a community of Jewish Christians, who well knew what the law prescribed to the devout
Israelite, and must therefore be aware of the contradiction to the law
in which the practice of Jesus was involved, when, during a public

* Hug, Einl. in das N. T., 2, S. 210.

ministry of several years' duration, only one attendance at Jerusalem
was noticed, or (in case the synoptical writers supposed but a single
year's ministry, of which we shall speak below) when he was represented as neglecting two of the great annual feasts. If, then, a
circle in close proximity to Jewish usage found nothing offensive in
the opinion that Jesus attended but one feast, may not this authority
remove all hesitation on the subject from our minds? Besides, on
a more careful weighing of the historical and geographical relations,
the question suggests itself, whether between the distant, half Gentile
Galilee, and Jerusalem, the ecclesiastical bond was so close that the
observance of all the feasts could be expected from a Galilean?
Even according to the fourth Gospel, Jesus omitted attending one
Passover that occurred in the period of his public career (John vi. 4).

There is, however, one point unfavourable to the synoptical
writers. That Jesus in his last visit to Jerusalem should, within
the short space of the feast day, have brought himself into such decided hostility to the ruling party in the capital, that they contrived
his arrest and death, is inexplicable, if we reject the statement of
John, that this hostility originated and was gradually aggravated
during his frequent previous visits.* If it be rejoined, that even in
Galilean synagogues there were stationary scribes and pharisees
(Matt. ix. 3. xii. 14), that such as were resident in the capital often
visited the provinces (Matt. xv. 1), and that thus there existed a
hierarchical nexus by means of which a deadly enmity against Jesus
might be propagated in Jerusalem, before he had ever publicly appeared there: we then have precisely that ecclesiastical bond between
Galilee and Jerusalem which renders improbable on the part of Jesus the non-observance of a series of feasts. Moreover the synoptical writers have recorded an expression of Jesus which tells strongly
against their own view. The words: *Jerusalem, Jerusalem—how
often would I have gathered thy children together—and ye would
not*, have no meaning whatever in Luke, who puts them into the
mouth of Jesus before he had even seen Jerusalem during his public
ministry (xiii. 34); and even from the better arrangement of Matthew
(xxiii. 37) it is not be understood how Jesus, after a single residence
of a few days in Jerusalem, could found his reproaches on multiplied
efforts to win over its inhabitants to his cause. This whole apos-
trophe of Jesus has so original a character, that it is difficult to believe it incorrectly assigned to him; hence to explain its existence, we
must suppose a series of earlier residences in Jerusalem, such as those
recorded by the fourth evangelist. There is only one resource,—
to pronounce the statement of the synoptical writers unhistorical in
the particular of limiting the decisive visit of Jesus to Jerusalem to
the few days of the feast, and to suppose that he made a more protracted stay in the capital.†

It will be seen from the foregoing discussion, whether, when so
much is to be argued *pro* and *contra*, the unhesitating decision of

* Hug, ut supra, S. 211 f.   † Compare Weisse, die evang. Geschichte 1, S. 29 ff.

the critics in favour of the fourth evangelist's statement is a just one. For our own part, we are far from being equally hasty in declaring for the synoptical writers, and are content to have submitted the actual state of the controversy, as to the comparative merits of John and the synoptical writers, to farther consideration.

§ 58. THE RESIDENCE OF JESUS AT CAPERNAUM.

DURING the time spent by Jesus in Judea, the capital and its environs recommended themselves as the most eligible theatre for his agency; and we might have conjectured that in like manner when in Galilee, he would have chosen his native city, Nazareth, as the centre of his labours. Instead of this we find him, when not travelling, domesticated at Capernaum, as already mentioned : the synoptical writers designate this place the ἰδία πόλις of Jesus (Matt. ix. 1, comp. Mark. ii. 1); here, according to them, was the οἶκος, which Jesus was accustomed to inhabit, (Mark ii. 1; iii. 20; Matt. xiii. 1. 36,) probably that of Peter (Mark i. 29; Matt. viii. 14; xvii. 25; Luke iv. 38). In the fourth Gospel, which only mentions very transient visits of Jesus to Galilee, Capernaum is not given as his dwelling-place, and Cana is the place with which he is supposed to have the most connection. After his baptism he proceeds first to Cana, (ii. 1) on a special occasion, it is true: after this he makes a short stay at Capernaum (v. 12); and on his return from his first attendance at the passover, it is again Cana to which he resorts, and in which the fourth evangelist makes him effect a cure (iv. 46 ff.), according to the synoptical writers, performed at Capernaum, and after this we find him once again in the synagogue at Capernaum (vi. 59). The most eminent disciples, also, are said by the writer of the fourth Gospel, not, as by the synoptical writers, to come from Capernaum, but partly from Cana (xxi. 2) and partly from Beth-saida (i. 45). The latter place, even in the synoptical gospels, is mentioned, with Chorazin, as one in which Jesus had been pre-eminently active (Matt. xi. 21; Luke x. 13).

Why Jesus chose Capernaum as his central residence in Galilee, Mark does not attempt to show, but conducts him thither without comment after his return into Galilee, and the calling of the two pairs of fishermen (i. 21). Matthew (iv. 13 ff.) alleges as a motive, that an Old Testament prophecy, (Isai. viii. 23; ix. 1,) was thereby fulfilled; a dogmatical motive, and therefore of no historical value. Luke thinks he has found the reason in a fact, which is more worthy of notice. According to him, Jesus after his return from baptism does not immediately take up his residence in Capernaum, but makes an essay to teach in Nazareth, and after its failure first turns to Capernaum. This evangelist tells us in the most graphic style, how Jesus presented himself at the synagogue on the sabbath-day, and expounded a prophetic passage, so as to excite general admiration, but at the same time to provoke malicious reflections on the narrow

circumstances of his family. Jesus, in reply, is made to refer the
discontent of the Nazarenes, that he performed no miracles before
them as at Capernaum, to the contempt which every prophet meets
with in his own country, and to threaten them in Old Testament
allusions, that the divine benefits would be withdrawn from them
and conferred on strangers. Exasperated by this, they lead him to
the brow of the hill, intending to cast him down: he, however,
passes unhurt through the midst of them (iv. 16—30).

Both the other synoptical writers, are acquainted with a visit of
Jesus to Nazareth; but they transfer it to a much later period, when
Jesus had been long labouring in Galilee, and resident in Capernaum
(Matt. xiii. 54 ff.; Mark vi. 1 ff.). To reconcile their narrative with
that of Luke, it has been customary to suppose that Jesus, notwithstanding his first rough reception, as described by Luke, wished to
make one more experiment whether his long absence and subsequent fame might not have altered the opinion of the Nazarenes—
an opinion worthy of a petty town; but the result was equally unfavourable.* The two scenes, however, are too similar to be prevented from mingling with each other. In both instances the teaching of Jesus in the synagogue makes the same impression on the
Nazarenes,—that of amazement at the wisdom of the carpenter's
son (Luke only giving more details); in both instances there is a
lack of miracles on the part of Jesus, the first two evangelists presenting more prominently its cause, namely, the unbelief of the Nazarenes, and the third dwelling more on its unfavourable effect; lastly,
in both instances, Jesus delivers the maxim (the result of his experience), that a prophet is the least esteemed in his own country; and
to this Luke appends a more ample discourse, which irritates the
Nazarenes to attempt an act of violence, unnoticed by the other
evangelists. But the fact which most decisively shows that the two
narratives cannot exist in each other's presence, is that they both
claim to relate the first incident of the kind :† for in both, the Nazarenes express their astonishment at the suddenly revealed intellectual gifts of Jesus, which they could not at once reconcile with his
known condition.‡ The first supposition that presents itself is, that
the scene described by Luke preceded that of Matthew and Mark;
but if so, the Nazarenes could not wonder a second time and inquire,
whence hath this man this wisdom? since they must have had proof
on that point on the first occasion; if, on the contrary, we try to
give the later date to Luke's incident, it appears unnatural, for the
same reason that they should wonder at *the gracious words which
proceeded out of his mouth,* neither could Jesus well say, *This day
is this scripture fulfilled in your ears,* without severely reflecting
on their former insensibility, which had retarded that fulfilment.
These considerations have led the majority of modern commen-

* Paulus, exeg. Handb. 1, 6, S. 403.   † This Schleiermacher has made evident, über
den Lukas, S. 63.   ‡ Sieffert, über den Ursprung des ersten kanonischen Evangeliums,
S. 89.

tators to the opinion, that Luke and the other synoptical evangelists have here given the same history, merely differing in the date, and in the colouring of the facts ;* and the only question among them is, which of the two narrations deserves the preference. With respect to the date, that of Luke seems, at the first glance, to have the advantage ; it gives the desiderated motive for the change of residence, and the wonder of the Nazarenes appears most natural on the supposition that then he first assumed the function of a public teacher; hence Matthew's divergency from Luke has been recently made a serious reproach to him, as a chronological error.† But there is one particular in all the three narratives which is an obstacle to our referring the incident to so early a period. If Jesus presented himself thus at Nazareth before he had made Capernaum the principal theatre of his agency, the Nazarenes could not utter the words which Jesus imputes to them in Luke: *Whatsoever we have heard done in Capernaum, do also here in thy country;* nor could they, according to Matthew and Mark, be astonished at the *mighty works* of Jesus,‡ for as he performed few if any miracles at Nazareth, that expression, nothwithstanding its perplexing connection with the σοφία, *the wisdom*, manifested in that city, must refer to works performed elsewhere. If, then, the Nazarenes wondered at the deeds of Jesus at Capernaum, or were jealous of the distinction conferred on that city, Jesus must have previously resided there, and could not have proceeded thither for the first time in consequence of the scene at Nazareth. From this, it is plain that the later chronological position of the narrative is the original one, and that Luke, in placing it earlier, out of mere conjecture, was honest or careless enough to retain the mention of the wonders at Capernaum, though only consistent with the later position.§ If, with regard to the date of the incident, the advantage is thus on the side of Matthew and Mark, we are left in darkness as to the motive which led Jesus to alter his abode from Nazareth to Capernaum ; unless the circumstance that some of his most confidential disciples had their home there, and the more extensive traffic of the place, may be regarded as inducements to the measure.

The fullness and particularity of Luke's description of the scene, contrasted with the summary style in which it is given by the other two evangelists, has generally won for the former the praise of superior accuracy.‖ Let us look more closely, and we shall find that the greater particularity of Luke shows itself chiefly in this, that he is not satisfied with a merely general mention of the discourse delivered by Jesus in the synagogue, but cites the Old Testament passage on which he enlarged, and the commencement of its application. The passage is from Isai. lxi. 1, 2, where the prophet an-

* Olshausen, Fritzsche, in loc. Hase, Leben Jesu, § 62. Sieffert, ut supra.
† Sieffert, ut supra. ‡ What these, *mighty works* were can only be made clear when we come to the chapter on the Miracles.
§ Schleiermacher ut supra,. S. 61.
‖ Ibid. S. 63 f.

nounces the return from exile, with the exception of the words *to
set at liberty them that are bruised*, ἀποστεῖλαι τεθραυσμένους ἐν
ἀφέσει, which are from Isai. lviii. 6.   To this passage Jesus gives
a messianic interpretation, for he declares it to be fulfilled by his
appearance.   Why he selected this text from among all others has
been variously conjectured.   It is known that among the Jews at
a later period, certain extracts from the Thorah and the Prophets
were statedly read on particular sabbaths and feast days, and it has
hence been suggested that the above passage was the selection appointed for the occasion in question.   It is true that the chapter
from which the words ἀποστεῖλαι κ. τ. λ. are taken, used to be read
on the great day of atonement, and Bengel has made the supposition, that the scene we are considering occurred on that day, a main
pillar of his evangelical chronology.*   But if Jesus had adhered to
the regular course of reading, he would not merely have extracted
from the lesson appointed for this feast a few stray words, to insert
them in a totally disconnected passage; and after all, it is impossible to demonstrate that, so early as the time of Jesus, there were
prescribed readings, even from the prophets.†   If then Jesus was
not thus circumstantially directed to the passage cited, did he open
upon it designedly or fortuitously?   Many imagine him turning over
the leaves until he found the text which was in his mind:‡ but Olshausen is right in saying that the words ἀναπτύξας τό βιβλίον εὗρε
τὸν τόπον do not imply that he found the passage after searching for
it, but that he alighted on it under the guidance of the Divine Spirit.§
This, however, is but a poor contrivance, to hide the improbability,
that Jesus should fortuitously open on a passage so well adapted to
serve as a motto for his first messianic enterprize, behind an appeal
to the Spirit, as *deus ex machina*.   Jesus might very likely have
quoted this text with reference to himself, and thus it would remain
in the minds of the evangelists as a prophecy fulfilled in Jesus;
Matthew would probably have introduced it in his own person with
his usual form, ἵνα πληρωθῇ, and would have said that Jesus had
now begun his messianic annunciation, κήρυγμα, that the prophecy
Isai, lxi. 1 ff. might be fulfilled; but Luke, who is less partial to
this form, or the tradition whence he drew his materials, puts the
words into the mouth of Jesus on his first messianic appearance,
very judiciously, it is true, but, owing to the chances which it is
necessary to suppose, less probably; so that I am more inclined to
be satisfied with the indefinite statement of Matthew and Mark.
The other point in which the description of Luke merits the praise
of particularity, is his dramatic picture of the tumultuary closing
scene: but this scene perplexes even those who on the whole give
the preference to his narrative.   It is not to be concealed that the
extremely violent expulsion of Jesus by the Nazarenes, seems to
have had no adequate provocation;‖ and we cannot, with Schleier-

* Ordo temporum, p. 220 ff. ed. 2.   † Paulus, ut supra, 1, B. S. 407.   ‡ Paulus, ut
supra. Lightfoot, horæ, p. 765.   § Bibl. Comm. 1, 470.   ‖ Hase, Leben Jesu, § 62.

macher,* expunge the notion that the life of Jesus was threatened, without imputing to the writer a false addition of the words εἰς τὸ κατακρημνίσαι αὐτὸν (v. 29.), and thus materially affecting the credibility of his entire narration. But the still more remarkable clause, διελθὼν διὰ μέσου αὐτῶν ἐπορεύετο (v. 30), is the main difficulty. It is not to be explained (at least not in accordance with the evangelist's view) as an effect merely of the commanding glance of Jesus, as Hase supposes; and Olshausen is again right when he says, that the evangelist intended to signify that Jesus passed unharmed through the midst of his furious enemies, because his divine power fettered their senses and limbs, because his hour was not yet come (John viii. 20), and because no man could take his life from him until he himself laid it down (John x. 18).† Here again we have a display of the glorifying tendency of tradition, which loved to represent Jesus as one defended from his enemies, like Lot (Gen. xix. 11), or Elisha (2 Kings vi. 18), by a heavenly hand, or better still, by the power of his own superior nature; unless there be supposed in this case, as in the two examples from the Old Testament, a temporary infliction of blindness, an *illudere per caliginem*, the idea of which Tertullian reprobates.‡ Thus in this instance also, the less imposing account of the first two evangelists is to be preferred, namely that Jesus, impeded from further activity by the unbelief of the Nazarenes, voluntarily forsook his ungrateful paternal city.

§. 59. DIVERGENCIES OF THE EVANGELISTS AS TO THE CHRONOLOGY OF THE LIFE OF JESUS—DURATION OF HIS PUBLIC MINISTRY.

In considering the chronology of the public life of Jesus, we must distinguish the question of its total duration, from that of the arrangement of its particular events.

Not one of our evanglists expressly tells us how long the public ministry of Jesus lasted; but while the synoptical writers give us no clue to a decision on the subject, we find in John certain data, which seem to warrant one. In the synoptical gospels there is no intimation how long after the baptism of Jesus his imprisonment and death occurred; nowhere are months and years distinguished: and though it is once or twice said: μεθ᾽ ἡμέρας ἓξ or δύο (Matt. xvii. 1: xxvi. 2), these isolated fixed points furnish us with no guidance in a sea of general uncertainty. On the contrary, the many journeys to the feasts by which the narrative of the fourth evangelist is distinguished from that of his predecessors, furnishes us, so to speak, with chronological abutments, as for each appearance of Jesus, at one of these annual feasts, the Passover especially, we must, deducting the first, reckon a full year of his ministry. We have, in the fourth Gospel, after the baptism of Jesus, and apparently at a short interval (comp. i. 29, 35, 44; ii. 1, 12), a passover attended by him

* Ueber den Lukas, S. 93. † Ut supra, 479; comp. 2, p. 211. ‡ Adv. Marcion, iv. 8.

(ii. 13). But the next feast visited by Jesus (v. 1.) which is indefinitely designated *a feast of the Jews*, has been the perpetual *crux* of New Testament chronologists. It is only important in determining the duration of the public life of Jesus, on the supposition that it was a passover; for in this case it would mark the close of his first year's ministry. We grant that ἡ ἑορτὴ τῶν Ἰουδαίων, THE *feast of the Jews*, might very probably denote the passover, which was pre-eminent among their institutions;* but it happens that the best manuscripts have in the present passage no article, and without it, the above expression can only signify indefinitely one of the Jewish feasts, which the author thought it immaterial to specify.† Thus intrinsically it might mean either the feast of Pentecost,‡ Purim,§ the Passover,‖ or any other;¶ but in its actual connection it is evidently not intended by the narrator to imply the Passover, both because he would hardly have glanced thus slightly at the most important of all the feasts, and because, vi. 4, there comes another Passover, so that on the supposition we are contesting, he would have passed in silence over a whole year between v. 47, and vi. 1. For to give the words ἦν δὲ ἐγγὺς τὸ πάσχα (vi. 4), a retrospective meaning, is too artificial an expedient of Paulus, since, as he himself confesses,** this phrase, elsewhere in John, is invariably used with reference to the immediately approaching feast (ii. 13; vii. 2; xi. 55), and must from its nature have a prospective meaning, unless the context indicate the contrary. Thus not until John vi. 4, do we meet with the second passover, and to this it is not mentioned that Jesus resorted.†† Then follow the feast of Tabernacles and that of the Dedication, and afterwards, xi. 55. xii. 1, the last passover visited by Jesus. According to our view of John v. 1, and vi. 4, therefore, we obtain two years for the public ministry of Jesus, besides the interval between his baptism and the first Passover. The same result is found by those who, with Paulus, hold the feast mentioned, v. 1, to be a passover, but vi. 4, only a retrospective allusion; whereas the ancient Fathers of the Church, reckoning a separate passover to each of the passages in question, made out three years. Meanwhile, by this calculation, we only get the minimum duration of the public ministry of Jesus possible according to the fourth Gospel, for the writer nowhere intimates that he has been punctilious in naming every feast that fell within that ministry, including those not observed by Jesus, neither, unless we regard it as established that the writer was the apostle John, have we any guarantee that he knew the entire number.

It may be urged in opposition to the calculations, built on the representations of John, that the synoptical writers give no reasons

* Paulus, exeg. Handb. 1, B. S. 788 f.   † Lücke, Comm. zum Evang. Joh. 2, S. 6.
‡ Bengel, ordo temporum, p. 219 f.   § Hug, Einl. in das N. T. 2, S. 229 ff.   ‖ Paulus,
Comm. zum Ev. Joh. S. 279 f. Exeg. Handb. 1, B. 784 ff.   ¶ Summaries of the different
opinions are given by Hase, L. J. § 53; and by Lücke, Comm. zum Ev. Joh., 2, S. 2 ff.
** Exeg. Handb. 1, B. S. 785.   †† See Storr, über den Zweck der evang. Gesch. und
der Briefe Johannis, S. 330.

for limiting the term of the public ministry of Jesus to a single year:* but this objection rests on a supposition borrowed from John himself, namely, that Jesus, Galilean though he was, made it a rule to attend every Passover: a supposition, again, which is overturned by the same writer's own representation. According to him, Jesus left unobserved the passover mentioned vi. 4, for from vi. 1, where Jesus is on the east side of the sea of Tiberias, through vi. 17 and 59, where he goes to Capernaum, and vii. 1, where he frequents Galilee, in order to avoid the Jews, to vii. 2 and 10, where he proceeds to Jerusalem on occasion of the Feast of Tabernacles, the Evangelist's narrative is so closely consecutive that a journey to the Passover can nowhere be inserted. Out of the synoptical gospels, by themselves, we gather nothing as to the length of the public ministry of Jesus, for this representation admits of our assigning him either several years of activity, or only one: their restriction of his intercourse with Jerusalem to his final journey being the sole point in which they control our conclusion. It is true that several Fathers of the Church,† as well as some heretics,‡ speak of the ministry of Jesus as having lasted but a single year; but that the source of this opinion was not the absence of early journeys to the feasts in the synoptical gospels, but an entirely fortuitous association, we learn from those Fathers themselves, for they derive it from the prophetic passage Isai. lxi. 1 f. applied by Jesus (Luke iv.) to himself. In this passage there is mention of *the acceptable year of the Lord*, ἐνιαυτὸς Κυρίου δεκτὸς, which the prophet or, according to the evangelical interpretation, the Messiah is sent to announce. Understanding this phrase in its strict chronological sense, they adopted from it the notion of a single messianic year, which was more easily reconcileable with the synoptical gospels than with that of John, after whose statement the calculation of the church soon came to be regulated.

In striking contrast with this lowest computation of time, is the tradition, also very ancient, that Jesus was baptized in his thirtieth year, but at the time of his crucifixion was not far from his fiftieth.§ But this opinion is equally founded on a misunderstanding. *The elders who had conversations with John the disciple of the Lord, in Asia,* πρεσβύτεροι οἱ κατὰ τὴν Ἀσίαν Ἰωάννῃ τῷ τοῦ Κυρίου μαθητῇ συμβεβληκότες,—on whose testimony Irenaeus relies when he says, *such is the tradition of John,* παραδεδωκέναι ταῦτα τὸν Ἰωάννην,—had given no information further than that Christ taught, *ætatem seniorem habens.* That this *ætas senior* was the age of from forty to fifty years is merely the inference of Irenaeus, founded on what the Jews allege as an objection to the discourse of Jesus, John viii. 57: *Thou art not yet fifty years old, and hast thou seen*

* Winer, bibl. Realwörterbuch 1, S. 666. † Clem. Alex. Stromat. 1, p. 174 Würzb. ed., 340 Sylburg; Orig. de principp. iv. 5, comp. homil. in Luc. 32. ‡ Iren. adv. haer. i. 1, 5. ii. 35, 38, on the Valentinians. Clem. hom. xvii. 19. § Iren. ii. xxii. 5 f. Comp. Credner, Einl. in das N. T. 1, S. 215.

Abraham? language which according to Irenæus could only be addressed to one, *qui jam quadraginta annos excessit, quinquagesimum autem annum nondum attigit.* But the Jews might very well say to a man a little more than thirty, that he was much too young to have seen Abraham, since he had not reached his fiftieth year, which, in the Jewish idea, completed the term of manhood.*

Thus we can obtain no precise information from our Gospels as to how long the public labours of Jesus lasted; all we can gather is, that if we follow the fourth Gospel we must not reckon less than two years and something over. But the repeated journeys to the feasts on which this calculation is founded, are themselves not established beyond doubt.

Opposed to this minimum, we gain a maximum, if we understand from Luke iii. 1 ff. and 23, that the baptism of Jesus took place in the fifteenth year of Tiberius, and add to this that his crucifixion occurred under the procuratorship of Pontius Pilate. For as Pilate was recalled from his post in the year of Tiberius's death,† and as Tiberius reigned rather more than seven years after the fifteenth year of his reign,‡ it follows that seven years are the maximum of the possible duration of the ministry of Jesus after his baptism. But while one of these data, namely, that Jesus was crucified under Pilate, is well attested, the other is rendered suspicious by its association with a chronological error, so that in fact we cannot achieve here even a proximate, still less an accurate solution of our question.

§. 60. THE ATTEMPTS AT A CHRONOLOGICAL ARRANGEMENT OF THE PARTICULAR EVENTS IN THE PUBLIC LIFE OF JESUS.

In attempting a chronological arrangement of the particular events occurring in the interval between the baptism of Jesus and his crucifixion, the peculiar relation of the synoptical writers to John, renders it necessary to give them both a separate and a comparative examination. As to the latter, if its result be a reconciliation of the two accounts, the journeys to the feasts in John must form the panels between which the materials of the synoptical writers must be so inserted, that between each pair of journeys with the incidents at Jerusalem to which they gave rise, would fall a portion of the Galilean history. For this incorporation to be effected with any certainty, two things would be essential; first, a notice of the departure of Jesus from Galilee by the first three evangelists, as often as the fourth speaks of a residence in Jerusalem; and, secondly, on the part of John, an intimation, if not a narration, between his accounts of the several feasts, of the Galilean occurrences represented by the synoptical writers as an uninterrupted train. But we have seen that the synoptical writers fail in the required notice; while it is

---

* Lightfoot and Tholuck in loc.   † Joseph. Antiq. xviii. iv. 2.   ‡ Sueton Tiber. c lxxiii.   Joseph. Antiq. xviii. vi. 10,

notorious that John, from the baptism of Jesus to the closing scenes of his life, is only in two or three instances in coincidence with the other evangelists. John says (iii. 24) that when Jesus began his ministry, *John was not yet cast into prison;* Matthew makes the return of Jesus into Galilee subsequent to the imprisonment of the Baptist (iv. 12), hence it has been inferred that that return was from the first passover, and not from the baptism;* but it is undeniable that Matthew places the commencement of the public ministry of Jesus in Galilee, and presupposes no earlier ministry at the feast in Jerusalem, so that the two statements, instead of dovetailing, as has been imagined, are altogether incompatible. The next, but very dubious point of contact, occurs in the healing of the nobleman's son, according to John iv. 46 ff, or the centurion's servant, according to Matt. viii. 5 ff, and Luke vii. 1 ff, which John places (v. 47) immediately after the return of Jesus from his prolonged residence in Judea and Samaria, during and after the first passover. It was to be expected, then, that the corresponding narration of the synoptical writers would be preceded by some intimation of the first journey made by Jesus to a feast. Not only is such an intimation wanting—there is not a single aperture to be found for the insertion of this journey, since, according to the synoptical writers, the cure in question was an immediate sequel to the Sermon on the Mount, which Matthew and Luke represent as the culminating point, of an apparently uninterrupted course of teaching and miracles in Galilee. Thus neither at this point is the chronology of the first three evangelists to be eked out by that of the fourth, since they nowhere present a joint on to which the statements of the latter can be articulated. Another more decided coincidence between the two parties exists in the associated narratives of the miracle of the loaves, and that of walking on the sea, John vi. 1—21, Matt. xiv. 14—36 parall., which John places in the interval immediately preceding the second passover, unvisited by Jesus; but he differs so completely from the synoptical writers in his account of these miracles, both in their introduction and termination, that either he or they must inevitably be wrong. For while, according to Matthew, Jesus retires from Nazareth probably, at all events from some part of Galilee, to the opposite side of the sea, where he effects the multiplication of the loaves; according to John he sets out from Jerusalem. Further, in the first two gospels Jesus proceeds after the miracle of the loaves into a district where he was less known, (both Matt. v. 35 and Mark v. 54 expressly stating that the people knew him,) whereas in John he goes directly to Capernaum, with which of all places he was the most familiar. We know not here whether to tax the synoptical writers or John with a mistake; and as we cannot pronounce whether he or they have placed this incident too early or too late, we are equally ignorant how much of the synoptical narratives we are to place before, and how much after, the second passover, which John

makes nearly cotemporary with the feeding of the five thousand.
Here, however, the points of contact between this evangelist and
his predecessors are at an end, until we come to the last journey of
Jesus; and if they are too uncertain to promise even a simple division of the synoptical materials by the two passovers, how can we
hope, by the journeys of Jesus to the *feast of the Jews*, ἑορτῇ τῶν
Ἰουδαίων, to the Feast of Tabernacles, or to the Feast of Dedication,
if that be a separate journey, to classify chronologically the uninterrupted series of Galilean occurences in the first three gospels? Nevertheless this has been attempted by a succession of theologians down
to the present time, with an expenditure of acumen and erudition,
worthy of a more fertile subject;* but unprejudiced judges have decided, that as the narrative of the first three evangelists has scarcely
any elements that can give certitude to such a classification, not one
of the harmonies of the gospels yet written has any claim to be considered anything more than a tissue of historical conjectures.†

It remains to estimate the chronological value of the synoptical
writers, apart from John. They are so frequently at variance with
each other in the order of events, and it is so seldom that one has
all the probabilities on his side, that each of them may be convicted
of numerous chronological errors, which must undermine our confidence in his accuracy. It has been maintained that, in the composition of their books, they meditated no precise chronological order,‡
and this is partially confirmed by their mode of narration. Throughout the interval between the baptism of Jesus and the history of the
Passion, their narratives resemble a collection of anecdotes, strung
together mostly on a thread of mere analogy and association of ideas.
But there is a distinction to be made in reference to the above opinion. It is true that from the purport of their narratives, and the
indecisiveness and uniformity of their connecting phrases, *we* can
detect their want of insight into the more accurate chronological relations of what they record; but that *the authors* flattered themselves they were giving a chronological narration, is evident from
those very connecting phrases, which, however indecisive, have almost always a chronological character, such as καταβάντι ἀπὸ τοῦ
ὄρους, παράγων ἐκεῖθεν, ταῦτα αὐτοῦ λαλοῦντος, ἐν αὐτῇ τῇ ἡμέρᾳ, τότε,
καὶ ἰδού, &c.§

The incidents and discourses detailed by John are, for the most
part, peculiar to himself; he is therefore not liable to the same control in his chronology from independent authors, as are the synoptical writers from each other; neither is his narration wanting in
connectedness and sequence. Hence our decision on the merits of
his chronological order is dependent on the answer to the following

---

* See especially the labours of Paulus in the Chronological *Excursus* of his Commentary and his exegetical Manual; of Hug, in the Einl. z. N. T. 2. S. 2, 233 ff.; and others,
given by Winer in his bibl. Realwörterbuch 1, S. 667. † Winer, ut sup.; comp. Kaiser,
biblische Theologie, 1 S. 254. Anm; die Abhandlung über die verschiedenen Rücksichten
u. s. w., in Bertholdt's krit. Journal, 5, S. 239. ‡ Olshausen 1, S. 24 ff. § Schneckenburger's Beiträge, S. 25 ff.

question: Is the development and progress of the cause and plan of Jesus, as given by the fourth evangelist, credible in itself and on comparison with available data, drawn from the other Gospels? The solution to this question is involved in the succeeding inquiry.

CHAPTER IV.

JESUS AS THE MESSIAH.*

§ 61. JESUS, THE SON OF MAN.

In treating of the relation in which Jesus conceived himself to stand to the messianic idea, we can distinguish his dicta concerning his own person from those concerning the work he had undertaken.

The appellation which Jesus commonly gives himself in the gospels is, *the Son of man*, ὁ υἱὸς τοῦ ἀνθρώπου. The exactly corresponding Hebrew expression בֶּן־אָדָם is in the Old Testament a frequent designation of man in general, and thus we might be induced to understand it in the mouth of Jesus. This interpretation would suit some passages; for example, Matt. xii. 8, where Jesus says: *The Son of man is lord also of the Sabbath day*, κύριος γάρ ἐστι τοῦ σαββάτου ὁ υἱὸς τοῦ ἀνθρώπου,—words which will fitly enough take a general meaning, such as Grotius affixes to them, namely, that man is lord of the Sabbath, especially if we compare Mark (ii. 27), who introduces them by the proposition, *The Sabbath was made for man, and not man for the Sabbath*, τὸ σάββατον διὰ τὸν ἄνθρωπον ἐγένετο, οὐχ ὁ ἄνθρωπος διὰ τὸ σάββατον. But in the majority of cases, the phrase in question is evidently used as a special designation. Thus, Matt. viii. 20, a scribe volunteers to become a disciple of Jesus, and is admonished to count the cost in the words, *The Son of man hath not where to lay his head*, ὁ υἱὸς τοῦ ἀνθρώπου οὐκ ἔχει, ποῦ τὴν κεφαλὴν κλίνῃ: here some particular man must be intended, nay, the particular man into whose companionship the scribe wished to enter, that is, Jesus himself. As a reason for the self-application of this term by Jesus, it has been suggested that he used the third person after the oriental manner, to avoid the *I*.† But for a speaker to use the third person

* All that relates to the idea of the Messiah as suffering, dying, and rising again, is here omitted, and reserved for the history of the Passion.   † Paulus, exeg. Handb. 1, 6. S. 465; Fritzsche, in Matth. p. 320.

in reference to himself, is only admissible, if he would be understood, when the designation he employs is precise, and inapplicable to any other person present, as when a father or a king uses his appropriate title of himself; or when, if the designation be not precise, its relation is made clear by a demonstrative pronoun, which limitation is eminently indispensable if an individual speak of himself under the universal designation *man*. We grant that occasionally a gesture might supply the place of the demonstrative pronoun; but that Jesus in every instance of his using this habitual expression had recourse to some visible explanatory sign, or that the evangelists would not, in that case, have supplied its necessary absence from a written document by some demonstrative addition, is inconceivable. If both Jesus and the evangelists held such an elucidation superfluous, they must have seen in the expression itself the key to its precise application. Some are of opinion that Jesus intended by it to point himself out as the ideal man—man in the noblest sense of the word;[*] but this is a modern theory, not an historical inference, for there is no trace of such an interpretation of the expression in the time of Jesus,[†] and it would be more easy to show, as others have attempted, that the appellation, *Son of man*, so frequently used by Jesus, had reference to his lowly and despised condition.[‡] Apart however from the objection that this acceptation also would require the addition of the demonstrative pronoun, though it might be adapted to many passages, as Matt. viii. 20, John i. 51, there are others, (such as Matt. xvii. 22, where Jesus, foretelling his violent death, designates himself ὁ υἱὸς τοῦ ἀνθρώπου,) which demand the contrast of high dignity with an ignominious fate. So in Matt. x. 23. the assurance given to the commissioned disciples that before they had gone over the cities of Israel the Son of Man would come, could have no weight unless this expression denoted a person of importance; and that such was its significance is proved by a comparison of Matt. xvi. 28, where there is also a mention of an ερχεσ-θαι, a *coming* of the Son of man, but with the addition ἐν τῇ βασιλείᾳ αὐτοῦ. As this addition can only refer to the messianic kingdom, the υἱὸς τοῦ ἀνθρώπου must be the Messiah.

How so apparently vague an appellation came to be appropriated to the Messiah, we gather from Matt. xxvi. 64 parall., where the Son of Man is depicted as coming *in the clouds of heaven*. This is evidently an allusion to Dan. vii. 13 f. where after having treated of the fall of the four beasts, the writer says: *I saw in the night visions, and behold, one like the Son of Man* (אֱנָשׁ כְּבַר, ὡς υἱὸς ἀνθρώπου, LXX.) *came with the clouds of heaven, and came to the Ancient of days. And there was given him dominion, and glory, and a kingdom, that all people, nations and languages should serve him: his dominion is an everlasting dominion.* The four beasts (v. 17 ff.) were symbolical of the four great empires, the last of which was the Macedonian, with its offshoot, Syria. After their fall, the kingdom was to be given in perpetuity to the People of God, *the saints of the Most High:* hence, he who was to come with *clouds of heaven* could only be, either a personification of the holy people,[*] or a leader of heavenly origin under whom they were to achieve their destined triumph,—in a word, the Messiah; and this was the customary interpretation among the Jews.[†] Two things are predicated of this personage,—that he was like the Son of Man, and that he came with the clouds of heaven; but the *former* particular is his distinctive characteristic, and imports either that he had not a superhuman form, that of an angel for instance, though descending from heaven, or else that the kingdom about to be established presented in its humanity a contrast to the inhumanity of its predecessors, of which ferocious beasts were the fitting emblems.[‡] At a later period, it is true, the Jews regarded the coming with the clouds of heaven עֲנָנֵי שְׁמַיָּא as the more essential attribute of the Messiah, and hence gave him the name Anani, after the Jewish taste of making a merely accessory circumstance the permanent epithet of a person or thing.[§] If, then, the expression ὁ υἱὸς τοῦ ἀνθρώπου necessarily recalled the above passage in Daniel, generally believed to relate to the Messiah, it is impossible that Jesus could so often use it, and in connexion with declarations evidently referring to the Messiah, without intending it as the designation of that personage.

That by the expression in question Jesus meant himself, without relation to the messianic dignity, is less probable than the contrary supposition, that he might often mean the Messiah when he spoke of the *Son of Man,* without relation to his own person. When, Matt. x. 23, on the first mission of the twelve apostles to announce the kingdom of heaven, he comforts them under the prospect of their future persecutions by the assurance that they would not *have gone over all the cities of Israel before the coming of the Son of Man,* we should rather, taking this declaration alone, think of a third person, whose speedy messianic appearance Jesus was promising, than of the speaker himself, seeing that he was already come, and it would not be antecedently clear how he could represent his own coming as one still in anticipation. So also when Jesus (Matt. xiii. 37 ff.) interprets the Sower of the parable to be the Son of Man, who at the end of the world will have a harvest and a tribunal, he might be supposed to refer to the Messiah as a third person distinct from himself. This is equally the case, xvi. 27 f., where, to prove the proposition that the loss of the soul is not to be compensated by the gain of the whole world, he urges the speedy coming

* Abenesra, see Havernick, ut sup. Comm. zum Daniel, S. 211. † Schöttgen, horæ, ii. S. 63, 75; Havernick, ut sup. S. 213 f. ‡ See for the most important opinions, Havernick, ut sup. 212 f. § Let the reader bear in mind the designation of David's elegy, 2 Sam. i. 17 ff. as קֶשֶׁת and the denomination of the Messiah, as צֶמַח. Had Schleiermacher considered the nature of Jewish appellatives, he would not have called the reference of υἱὸς τοῦ ἀ. to the passage in Daniel, a strange idea. (Glauben-l. § 99. Anm.).

of the Son of Man, to administer retribution. Lastly, in the connected discourses, Matt. xxiv. xxv. parall., many particulars would be more easily conceived, if the υἱὸς τοῦ ἀνθρώπου whose παρουσία Jesus describes, were understood to mean another than himself.

But this explanation is far from being applicable to the majority of instances in which Jesus uses this expression. When he represents the Son of Man, not as one still to be expected, but as one already come and actually present, for example, in Matt. xviii, 11, where he says: *The Son of Man is come to save that which was lost;* when he justifies his own acts by the authority with which the Son of Man was invested, as in Matt. ix. 6; when, Mark viii. 31 ff. comp. Matt. xvi. 22, he speaks of the approaching sufferings and death of the Son of Man, so as to elicit from Peter the exclamation, οὐ μὴ ἔσται σοι τοῦτο, *this shall not be unto thee*; in these and similar cases he can only, by the υἱὸς τοῦ ανθρωπου, have intended himself. And even those passages, which, taken singly, we might have found capable of application to a messianic person, distinct from Jesus, lose this capability when considered in their entire connexion. It is possible, however, either that the writer may have misplaced certain expressions, or that the ultimately prevalent conviction that Jesus was *the Son of Man* caused what was originally said merely of the latter, to be viewed in immediate relation to the former.

Thus besides the fact that Jesus on many occasions called himself the Son of Man, there remains the possibility that on many others, he may have designed another person; and if so, the latter would in the order of time naturally precede the former. Whether this possibility can be heightened to a reality, must depend on the answer to the following question: Is there, in the period of the life of Jesus, from which all his recorded declarations are taken, any fragment which indicates that he had not yet conceived himself to be the Messiah?

§ 62. HOW SOON DID JESUS CONCEIVE HIMSELF TO BE THE MESSIAH, AND FIND RECOGNITION AS SUCH FROM OTHERS?

Jesus held and expressed the conviction that he was the Messiah; this is an indisputable fact. Not only did he, according to the evangelists, receive with satisfaction the confession of the disciples that he was the Χριστὸς (Matt. xvi. 16 f.) and the salutation of the people, *Hosanna to the Son of David* (xxi. 15 f.); not only did he before a public tribunal (Matt. xxvi. 64, comp. John xviii. 37,) as well as to private individuals (John iv. 26, ix. 37, x. 25,) repeatedly declare himself to be the Messiah: but the fact that his disciples after his death believed and proclaimed that he was the Messiah, is not to be comprehended, unless, when living, he had implanted the conviction in their minds.

To the more searching question, how soon Jesus began to declare himself the Messiah and to be regarded as such by others, the evangelists almost unanimously reply, that he assumed that character from the time of his baptism. All of them attach to his baptism circumstances which must have convinced himself, if yet uncertain, and all others who witnessed or credited them, that he was no less than the Messiah; John makes his earliest disciples recognise his right to that dignity on their first interview (i. 42 ff.), and Matthew attributes to him at the very beginning of his ministry, in the sermon on the mount, a representation of himself as the Judge of the world (vii. 21 ff,) and therefore the Messiah.

Nevertheless, on a closer examination, there appears a remarkable divergency on this subject between the synoptical statement and that of John. While, namely, in John, Jesus remains throughout true to his assertion, and the disciples and his followers among the populace to their conviction, that he is the Messiah; in the synoptical gospels there is a vacillation discernible—the previously expressed persuasion on the part of the disciples and people that Jesus was the Messiah, sometimes vanishes and gives place to a much lower view of him, and even Jesus himself becomes more reserved in his declarations. This is particularly striking when the synoptical statement is compared with that of John; but even when they are separately considered, the result is the same.

According to John (vi. 15), after the miracle of the loaves the people were inclined to constitute Jesus their (messianic) King: on the contrary, according to the other three evangelists, either about the same time (Luke ix. 18 f.) or still later (Matt. xvi. 13 f. Mark viii. 27 f.) the disciples could only report, on the opinions of the people respecting their master, that some said he was the resuscitated Baptist, some Elias, and others Jeremiah or one of the old prophets: in reference to that passage of John, however, as also to the synoptical one, Matt. xiv. 33, according to which, some time before Jesus elicited the above report of the popular opinion, the people who were with him in the ship* when he had allayed the storm, fell at his feet and worshipped him as the Son of God, it may be observed that when Jesus had spoken or acted with peculiar impressiveness, individuals, in the exaltation of the moment, might be penetrated with a conviction that he was the Messiah, while the general and calm voice of the people yet pronounced him to be merely a prophet.

But there is a more troublesome divergency relative to the disciples. In John, Andrew, after his first interview with Jesus, says to his brother, *we have found the Messiah*, εὑρήκαμεν τὸν Μεσσίαν (i. 42); and Philip describes him to Nathanael as the person foretold by Moses and the prophets (v. 46); Nathanael salutes him as the Son of God and King of Israel (v. 50): and the subsequent confession of Peter appears merely a renewed avowal of what had been long a familiar truth. In the synoptical evangelists it is only after

---

* That the expression οἱ ἐν τῷ πλοίῳ includes more than the disciples, vid. Fritzsche, in loc.

prolonged intercourse with Jesus, and shortly before his sufferings, that the ardent Peter arrives at the conclusion that Jesus is the Χριστος, ὁ υἱὸς τοῦ Θεοῦ τοῦ ζῶντος (Matt. xvi. 16, parall.). It is impossible that this confession should make so strong an impression on Jesus that, in consequence of it, he should pronounce Peter blessed, and his confession the fruit of immediate divine revelation, as Matthew narrates; or that, as all the three evangelists inform us, (xvi. 20, viii. 30, ix. 21,) he should, as if alarmed, forbid the disciples to promulgate their conviction, unless it represented not an opinion long cherished in the circle of his disciples, but a new light, which had just flashed on the mind of Peter, and through him was communitated to his associates.

There is a third equally serious discrepancy, relative to the declarations of Jesus concerning his Messiahship. According to John, he sanctions the homage which Nathanael renders to him as the Son of God and King of Israel, in the very commencement of his public career, and immediately proceeds to speak of himself under the messianic title, Son of Man (i. 51 f.): to the Samaritans also after his first visit to the passover (iv. 26, 39 ff.), and to the Jews on the second (v. 46), he makes himself known as the Messiah predicted by Moses. According to the synoptical writers, on the contrary, he prohibits, in the instance above cited and in many others, the dissemination of the doctrine of his Messiahship, beyond the circle of his adherents. Farther, when he asks his disciples, *Whom do men say that I am?* (Matt. xvi. 15) he seems to wish* that they should derive their conviction of his Messiahship from his discourses and actions, and when he ascribes the avowed faith of Peter to a revelation from his heavenly Father, he excludes the possibility of his having himself previously made this disclosure to his disciples, either in the manner described by John, or in the more indirect one attributed to him by Matthew in the Sermon on the Mount; unless we suppose that the disciples had not hitherto believed his assurance, and that hence Jesus referred the new-born faith of Peter to divine influence.

Thus, on the point under discussion the synoptical statement is

* There is a difficulty involved in the form of the question, put by Jesus to his disciples : τίνα με λέγουσιν οἱ ἄνθρωποι εἶναι τὸν υἱὸν τοῦ ἀνθρώπου ; i. e. what opinion have the people of me, the Messiah? This, when compared with the sequel, seems a premature disclosure ; hence expositors have variously endeavoured to explain away its primâ facie meaning. Some (e. g. Beza) understand the subordinate clause, not as a declaration of Jesus concerning his own person, but as a closer limitation of the question : For whom do the people take me? for the Messiah? But this would be a leading question, which, as Fritzsche well observes, would indicate an eagerness for the messianic title, not elsewhere discernible in Jesus. (Others, therefore, (as Paulus and Fritzsche,) give the expression υἱὸς τ. ἀ. a general signification, and interpret the question thus : Whom do men say that I, the individual addressing you, am? But this explanation has been already refuted in the foregoing section. If, then, we reject the opinion that the υἱὸς τ. ἀ. is an addition which the exuberant faith of the writer was apt to suggest even in an infelicitous connexion, we are restricted to De Wette's view, (exeg. Handb. 1, 1, S. 86 f.), namely, that the expression, ὁ υἱὸς τ. ἀ. was indeed an appellation of the Messiah, but an indirect one, so that it might convey that meaning, as an allusion to Daniel, to Jesus and those already aware of his messiahsip, while to others it was merely the equivalent of, *this man.*

contradictory, not only to that of John, but to itself; it appears therefore that it ought to be unconditionally surrendered before that of John, which is consistent with itself, and one of our critics has justly reproached it with deranging the messianic economy in the life of Jesus.* But here again we must not lose sight of our approved canon, that in glorifying narratives, such as our gospels, where various statements are confronted, that is the least probable which best subserves the object of glorification. Now this is the case with John's statement; according to which, from the commencement to the close of the public life of Jesus, his Messiahship shines forth in unchanging splendour, while, according to the synoptical writers, it is liable to a variation in its light. But though this criterion of probability is in favour of the first three evangelists, it is impossible that the order in which they make ignorance and concealment follow on plain declarations and recognitions of the Messiahship of Jesus can be correct: and we must suppose that they have mingled and confounded two separate periods of the life of Jesus, in the latter of which alone he presented himself as the Messiah. We find, in fact, that the watchword of Jesus on his first appearance differed not, even verbally, from that of John, who professed merely to be a forerunner; it is the same *Repent, for the kingdom of heaven is at hand* (Matt. iv. 17) with which John had roused the Jews (iii. 2); and indicates in neither the one nor the other an assumption of the character of Messiah, with whose coming the kingdom of heaven was actually to commence, but merely that of a teacher who points to it as yet future.† Hence the latest critic of the first gospel justly explains all those discourses and actions therein narrated, by which Jesus explicitly claims to be the Messiah, or, in consequence of which this dignity is attributed to him and accepted, if they occur before the manifestation of himself recorded in John v., or before the account of the apostolic confession (Matt. xvi.), as offences of the writer against chronology or literal truth.‡ We have only to premise, that as chronological confusion prevails throughout, the position of this confession shortly before the history of the Passion, in nowise obliges us to suppose that it was so late before Jesus was recognised as the Messiah among his disciples, since Peter's avowal may have occurred in a much earlier period of their intercourse. This, however, is incomprehensible— that the same reproach should not attach even more strongly to the fourth gospel than to the first, or to the synoptical writers in general. For it is surely more pardonable that the first three evangelists should give us the pre-messianic memoirs in the wrong place, than that the fourth should not give them at all; more endurable in the former, to mingle the two periods, than in the latter, quite to obliterate the earlier one.

---

* Schneckenburger, über den Ursprung u. s. f. S. 28 f. † This distinction of two periods in the public life of Jesus is also made by Fritzsche, Comm. in Matth. S. 213, 536, and Schneckenburger ut sup. ‡ Schneckenburger, ut sup. S. 29.

If then Jesus did not lay claim to the Messiahship from the beginning of his public career, was this omission the result of uncertainty in his own mind; or had he from the first a conviction that he was the Messiah, but concealed it for certain reasons? In order to decide this question, a point already mentioned must be more carefully weighed. In the first three evangelists, but not so exclusively that the fourth has nothing similar, when Jesus effects a miracle of healing he almost invariably forbids the person cured to promulgate the event, in these or similar words, ὅρα μηδενὶ εἴπῃς; e. g. the leper, Matt. viii. 4; parall.; the blind men, Matt. ix. 30; a multitude of the healed, Matt. xii. 16; the parents of the resuscitated damsel, Mark v. 43; above all he enjoins silence on the demoniacs, Mark i. 34. iii. 12.; and John v. 13, it is said, after the cure of the man at the pool of Bethesda, *Jesus had conveyed himself away, a multitude being in that place.* Thus also he forbade the three who were with him on the mount of the Transfiguration, to publish the scene they had witnessed, (Matt. xvii. 9); and after the confession of Peter, he charges the disciples to tell no man the conviction it expressed (Luke ix. 21). This prohibition of Jesus could hardly, as most commentators suppose,* be determined by various circumstantial motives, at one time having relation to the disposition of the person healed, at another to the humour of the people, at another to the situation of Jesus: rather, as there is an essential similarity in the conditions under which he lays this injunction on the people, if we discern a probable motive for it on any occasion, we are warranted in applying the same motive to the remaining cases. This motive is scarcely any other than the desire that the belief that he was the Messiah should not be too widely spread. When (Mark i. 34) Jesus would not allow the ejected demons to speak *because they knew him,* when he charged the multitudes *that they should not make him known* (Matt. xii. 16), he evidently intended that the former should not proclaim him in the character in which their more penetrative, demoniacal glance had viewed him, nor the latter in that revealed by the miraculous cure he had wrought on them—in short, they were not to betray their knowledge that he was the Messiah. As a reason for this wish on the part of Jesus, it has been alleged, on the strength of John vi. 15., that he sought to avoid awakening the political idea of the Messiah's kingdom in the popular mind, with the disturbance which would be its inevitable result.† This would be a valid reason; but the synoptical writers represent the wish, partly as the effect of humility:‡ Matthew, in connexion with a prohibition of the kind alluded to, applying to Jesus a passage in Isaiah (xlii. 1 f.) where the servant of God is said to be distinguished by his stillness and unobtrusiveness: partly, and in a greater degree, as the effect of an

* Fritzsche, in Matth. p. 309. comp. 352. Olshausen, S. 265.   † Fritzsche, p. 352.
Olshausen, ut sup.   ‡ The opposite view is held by the Fragmentist, who thinks the prohibition was intended to stimulate the popular eagerness.

apprehension that the Messiah, at least such an one as Jesus, would be at once proscribed by the Jewish hierarchy.

From all this it might appear that Jesus was restrained merely by external motives, from the open declaration of his messiahship, and that his own conviction of it existed from the first in equal strength; but this conclusion cannot be maintained in the face of the consideration above mentioned, that Jesus began his career with the same announcement as the Baptist, an announcement which can scarcely have more than one import—an exhortation to prepare for a coming Messiah. The most natural supposition is that Jesus, first the disciple of the Baptist, and afterwards his successor, in preaching repentance and the approach of the kingdom of heaven, took originally the same position as his former master in relation to the messianic kingdom, nothwithstanding the greater reach and liberality of his mind, and only gradually attained the elevation of thinking himself the Messiah. This supposition explains in the simplest manner the prohibition we have been considering, especially that annexed to the confession of Peter. For as often as the thought that he might be the Messiah suggested itself to others, and was presented to him from without, Jesus must have shrunk, as if appalled, to hear confidently uttered that which he scarcely ventured to surmise, or which had but recently become clear to himself. As, however, the evangelists often put such prohibitions into the mouth of Jesus unseasonably, (witness the occasion mentioned, Matt. viii. 4, when after a cure effected before a crowd of spectators, it was of little avail to enjoin secrecy on the cured,*) it is probable that evangelical tradition, enamoured of the mysteriousness that lay in this incognito of Jesus,† unhistorically multiplied the instances of its adoption.

§ 63. JESUS, THE SON OF GOD.

In Luke i. 35, we find the narrowest and most literal interpretation of the expression, ὁ υἱὸς τοῦ θεοῦ; namely, as derived from his conception by means of the Holy Ghost. On the contrary, the widest moral and metaphorical sense is given to the expression in Matt. v. 45, where those who imitate the love of God towards his enemies are called the sons of the Father in heaven. There is an intermediate sense which we may term the metaphysical, because while it includes more than mere conformity of will, it is distinct from the notion of actual paternity, and implies a spiritual community of being. In this sense it is profusely employed and referred to in the fourth gospel; as when Jesus says that he speaks and does nothing of himself, but only what as a son he has learned from the Father (v. 19; xii. 49, and elsewhere), who, moreover, is in him (xvii. 21), and nothwithstanding his exaltation over him (xiv. 28), is yet one with him (x. 30). There is yet a fourth sense in which

---

* Fritzsche, S. 309.   † Comp. Schleiermacher, über den Lukas, S. 74.

the expression is presented. When (Matt. iv. 3) the devil challenges
Jesus to change the stones into bread, making the supposition, *If
thou be the Son of God;* when Nathanael says to Jesus, *Thou art
the Son of God, the King of Israel* (John i. 49); when Peter confesses, *Thou art the Christ, the Son of the living God* (Matt. xvi.
16; comp. John vi. 69); when Martha thus expresses her faith in
Jesus, *I believe that thou art the Christ, the Son of God* (John xi.
27); when the high priest adjures Jesus to tell him if he be *the
Christ, the Son of God* (Matt. xxvi. 63): it is obvious that the devil
means nothing more than, If thou be the Messiah; and that in the
other passages the υἱὸς τοῦ θεοῦ, united as it is with Χριστὸς and
βασιλεὺς, is but an appellation of the Messiah.

In Hos. xi. 1, Exod. iv. 22, the people of Israel, and in 2 Sam.
vii. 14, Ps. ii. 7, (comp. lxxxix. 28) the king of that people, are
called the son and the first-born of God. The kings (as also the
people) of Israel had this appellation, in virtue of the love which
Jehovah bore them, and the tutelary care which he exercised over
them (2 Sam vii. 14); and from the second psalm we gather the
farther reason, that as earthly kings choose their sons to reign with
or under them, so the Israelitish kings were invested by Jehovah,
the supreme ruler, with the government of his favourite province.
Thus the designation was originally applicable to every Israelitish
king who adhered to the principle of the theocracy; but when the
messianic idea was developed, it was pre-eminently assigned to the
Messiah, as the best-beloved Son, and the most powerful vicegerent
of God on earth.*

If, then, such was the original historical signification of the epithet, *Son of God,* as applied to the Messiah, we have to ask: is it
possible that Jesus used it of himself in this signification only, or
did he use it also in either of the three senses previously adduced?
The narrowest, the merely physical import of the term is not put
into the mouth of Jesus, but into that of the annunciating angel,
Luke i. 35; and for this the evangelist alone is responsible. In the
intermediate, metaphysical sense, implying unity of essence and community of existence with God, it might possibly have been understood by Jesus, supposing him to have remodelled in his own conceptions the theocratic interpretation current among his compatriots.
It is true that the abundant expressions having this tendency in the
gospel of John, appear to contradict those of Jesus on an occasion
recorded by the synoptical writers (Mark x. 17 f.; Luke xviii. 18 f.),
when to a disciple who accosts him as *Good Master*, he replies:
*Why callest thou me good? there is none good but one, that is
God.* Here Jesus so tenaciously maintains the distinction between
himself and God, that he renounces the predicate of (perfect) goodness, and insists on its appropriation to God alone.† Olshausen

---

* Comp. the excellent treatise of Paulus on the following question in the Einl. zum
Leben Jesu, 1, a., 28 f.   † Even if a different reading be adopted for the parallel passage
in Matthew (xix. 16 f.), it must remain questionable whether his statement deserve the
preference to that of the two other evangelists.

supposes that this rejection related solely to the particular circumstances of the disciple addressed, who regarding Jesus as a merely human teacher, ought not from his point of view to have given him a divine epithet, and that it was not intended by Jesus as a denial that he was, according to a just estimate of his character, actually the ἀγαθὸς in whom the one good Being was reflected as in a mirror: but this is to take for granted what is first to be proved, namely, that the declarations of Jesus concerning himself in the fourth gospel are on a level as to credibility with those recorded by the synoptical writers. Two of these writers cite some words of Jesus which have an important bearing on our present subject: *All things are delivered to me of my Father: and no man knoweth the Son but the Father: neither knoweth any man the Father, but the Son, and he to whomsoever the Son will reveal him*, Matt. xi. 27. Taking this passage in connexion with the one before quoted, we must infer that Jesus had indeed an intimate communion of thought and will with God, but under such limitations, that the attribute of perfect goodness, as well as of absolute knowledge (e. g. of the day and hour of the last day, Mark xiii. 32 parall.) belonged exclusively to God, and hence the boundary line between divine and human was strictly preserved. Even in the fourth gospel Jesus declares, *My Father is greater than I*, ὁ πατήρ μου μείζων μου ἐστὶ, (xiv. 28), but this slight echo of the synoptical statement does not remove the difficulty of conciliating the numerous discourses of a totally different tenor in the former, with the rejection of the epithet ἀγαθὸς in the latter. It is surprising, too, that Jesus in the fourth gospel appears altogether ignorant of the theocratic sense of the expression υἱὸς τοῦ Θεοῦ, and can only vindicate his use of it in the metaphysical sense, by retreating to its vague and metaphorical application. When, namely, (John x. 34 ff.) to justify his assumption of this title, he adduces the scriptural application of the term Θεοὶ to other men, such as princes and magistrates, we are at a loss to understand why Jesus should resort to this remote and precarious argument, when close at hand lay the far more cogent one, that in the Old Testament, a theocratic king of Israel, or according to the customary interpretation of the most striking passages, the Messiah, is called the Son of Jehovah, and that therefore he, having declared himself to be the Messiah (v. 25), might consistently claim this appellation.

With respect to the light in which Jesus was viewed as the Son of God by others, we may remark that in the addresses of well-affected persons the title is often so associated as to be obviously a mere synonym of Χριστὸς, and this even in the fourth gospel: while on the other hand the contentious Ἰουδαῖοι of this gospel seem in their objections as ignorant as Jesus in his defence, of the theocratic, and only notice the metaphysical meaning of the expression. It is true that, even in the synoptical gospels, when Jesus answers affirmatively the question whether he is the Christ, the Son of the living God (Matt. xxvi. 65 par.), the high priest taxes him with blasphemy; but he refers merely to what he considers the unwarranted arrogation of the theocratic dignity of the Messiah, whereas in the fourth gospel, when Jesus represents himself as the Son of God (v. 17 f. x. 30 ff.) the Jews seek to kill him for the express reason that he thereby makes himself ἴσον τῷ Θεῷ, nay even ἑαυτὸν Θεὸν. According to the synoptical writers, the high priest so unhesitatingly considers the idea of the Son of God to pertain to that of the Messiah, that he associates the two titles as if they were interchangeable, in the question he addresses to Jesus : on the contrary the Jews in the Gospel of John regard the one idea as so far transcending the other, that they listen patiently to the declaration of Jesus that he is the Messiah (x. 25), but as soon as he begins to claim to be the Son of God, *they take up stones to stone him.* In the synoptical gospels the reproach cast on Jesus is, that being a *common* man, he gives himself out for the Messiah ; in the fourth gospel, that being a mere *man,* he gives himself out for a *divine* being. Hence Olshausen and others have justly insisted that in those passages of the latter gospel to which our remarks have reference, the υἱὸς τοῦ Θεοῦ is not synonymous with Messiah, but is a name far transcending the ordinary idea of the Messiah ;* they are not, however, warranted in concluding that therefore in the first three evangelists also† the same expression imports more than the Messiah. For the only legitimate interpretation of the high priest's question in Matthew makes ὁ υἱὸς τοῦ Θεοῦ a synonym of ὁ Χριστὸς, and though in the parallel passage of Luke, the judges first ask Jesus if he be the Christ (xx. 67.)? and when he declines a direct answer,—predicting that they will behold the Son of Man seated at the right hand of God,—hastily interrupt him with the question, *Art thou the Son of God?* (v. 70) ; yet, after receiving what they consider an affirmative answer, they accuse him before Pilate as one who pretends to be Christ, a king (xxiii. 2), thus clearly showing that Son of Man, Son of God, and Messiah, must have been regarded as interchangeable terms. It must therefore be conceded that there is a discrepancy on this point between the synoptical writers and John, and perhaps also an inconsistency of the latter with himself; for in several addresses to Jesus he retains the customary form, which associated *Son of God* with *Christ or King of Israel,* without being conscious of the distinction between the signification which υἱὸς τ. Θ. must have in such a connexion, and that in which he used it elsewhere—a want of perception which habitual forms of expression are calculated to induce. We have before cited examples of this oversight in the fourth evangelist (John i. 49. vi. 69. xii 27).

The author of the Probabilia reasonably considers it suspicious that, in the fourth gospel, Jesus and his opponents should appear entirely ignorant of the theocratic sense which is elsewhere attached to the expression ὁ υἱὸς τοῦ Θεοῦ, and which must have been more familiar to the Jews than any other, unless we suppose some of

* Bibl. Comm. 2, S. 130, 253.   † Olshausen ut sup. 1, S. 108 ff.

them to have partaken of Alexandrian culture. To such, we grant, as well as to the fourth evangelist, judging from his prologue, the metaphysical relation of the λόγος μονογενὴς to God would be the most cherished association.

§ 64. THE DIVINE MISSION AND AUTHORITY OF JESUS—HIS PRE-EXISTENCE.

The four evangelists are in unison as to the declaration of Jesus concerning his divine mission and authority. Like every prophet, he is sent by God (Matt. x. 40. John v. 23 f. 56 f.), acts and speaks by the authority, and under the immediate guidance of God (John v. 19 ff.), and exclusively possesses an adequate knowledge of God, which it is his office to impart to men (Matt. xi. 27. John iii. 13). To him, as the Messiah, all power is given (Matt. xi. 27); first, over the kingdom which he is appointed to found and to rule with all its members (John x. 29. xvii. 6); next, over mankind in general (John xvii. 2), and even external nature (Matt. xxviii. 18); consequently, should the interests of the messianic kingdom demand it, power to effect a thorough revolution in the whole world. At the future commencement of his reign, Jesus, as Messiah, is authorized to awake the dead (John v. 28.), and to sit as a judge, separating those worthy to partake of the heavenly kingdom from the unworthy (Matt. xxv. 31 ff. John v. 22. 29.): offices which Jewish opinion attributed to the Messiah,* and which Jesus, once convinced of his messiahship, would necessarily transfer to himself.

The evangelists are not equally unanimous on another point. According to the synoptical writers, Jesus claims, it is true, the highest human dignity, and the most exalted relation with God, for the present and future, but he never refers to an existence anterior to his earthly career: in the fourth gospel, on the contrary, we find several discourses of Jesus which contain the repeated assertion of such a pre-existence. We grant that when Jesus describes himself as coming down from heaven (John iii. 13. xvi. 28.), the expression, taken alone, may be understood as a merely figurative intimation of his superhuman origin. It is more difficult, but perhaps admissible, to interpret, with the Socinian Crell, the declaration of Jesus *Before Abraham was, I am,* πρὶν Ἀβραὰμ γενέσθαι, ἐγώ εἰμι (John viii. 58.), as referring to a purely ideal existence in the pre-determination of God; but scarcely possible to consider the prayer to the Father (John xvii. 5.) to confirm the δόξα (*glory*) which Jesus had with Him *before the world was,* πρὸ τοῦ τὸν κόσμον εἶναι, as an entreaty for the communication of a glory predestined for Jesus from eternity. But the language of Jesus, John vi. 62., where he speaks of the Son of Man *reascending* ἀναβαίνειν *where he was before* ὅπου ἦν τὸ πρότερον, is, in its intrinsic meaning, as well as in that which is re-

* Bertholdt, Christol. Judær. §§ 8, 35, 42.

flected on it from other passages, unequivocally significative of actual, not merely ideal, pre-existence.

It has been already conjectured* that these expressions, or at least the adaptation of them to a real pre-existence, are derived, not from Jesus, but from the author of the fourth gospel, with whose opinions, as propounded in his introduction, they specifically agree; for if *the Word was in the beginning with God* (ἐν ἀρχῇ πρὸς τὸν Θεόν), Jesus, in whom it was *made flesh*, might attribute to himself an existence before Abraham, and a participation of glory with the Father before the foundation of the world. Nevertheless, we are not warranted in adopting this view, unless it can be shown, that neither was the idea of the pre-existence of the Messiah extant among the Jews of Palestine before the time of Jesus, nor is it probable that Jesus attained such a notion, independently of the ideas peculiar to his age and nation.

The latter supposition, that Jesus spoke from his own memory of his pre-human and pre-mundane existence, is liable to comparison with dangerous parallels in the history of Pythagoras, Ennius, and Apollonius of Tyana, whose alleged reminiscenses of individual states which they had experienced prior to their birth,† are now generally regarded either as subsequent fables, or as enthusiastic self-delusions of those celebrated men. For the other alternative, that the idea in question was common to the Jewish nation, a presumption may be found in the description, already quoted from Daniel, of the Son of Man coming in the clouds of heaven, since the author, possibly, and, at all events, many readers, imagined that personage to be a superhuman being, dwelling beforehand with God, like the angels. But that every one who referred this passage to the Messiah, or that Jesus in particular, associated with it the notion of a pre-existence, is not to be proved; for, if we exclude the representation of John, Jesus depicts his coming in the clouds of heaven, not as if he had come as a visitant to earth from his home in heaven, but, according to Matt. xxvi. 65. (comp. xxiv. 25), as if he, the earth-born, after the completion of his earthly course, would be received into heaven, and from thence would return to establish his kingdom : thus making the coming from heaven not necessarily include the idea of pre-existence. We find in the Proverbs, in Sirach, and the Book of Wisdom, the idea of a personified and even hypostasized Wisdom of God, and in the Psalms and Prophets, strongly marked personifications of the Divine word :‡ and it is especially worthy of note, that the later Jews, in their horror of anthropomorphism in the idea of the Divine being, attributed his speech, appearance, and immediate agency, to the *Word* (מימרא) or the *dwelling place* (שכינתא) of Jehovah, as may be seen in the venerable§

---

* Bretschneider, Probab. p. 59. † Porphyr. Vita Pythag. 26 f. Jamblich. 14, 63 Diog. Laert. viii. 4 f. 14. Bauer, Apollonius von Tyana, p. 61 f. 98 f. 185 f. ‡ See a notification and exposition of the passages in Lucke, Comm. zum Ev. Joh. 1, S. 211 ff. § Winer, de Onkeloso, p. 10. Comp. De Wette, Einleit. in das A. T. §. 58.

Targum of Onkelos.* These expressions, at first mere paraphrases of the name of God, soon received the mystical signification of a veritable hypostasis, of a being, at once distinct from, and one with God. As most of the revelations and interpositions of God, whose organ this personified Word was considered to be, were designed in favour of the Israelitish people, it was natural for them to assign to the manifestation which was still awaited from Him, and which was to be the crowning benefit of Israel,—the manifestation, namely, of the Messiah,—a peculiar relation with the Word or Shechina.† From this germ sprang the opinion that with the Messiah the Shechina would appear, and that what was ascribed to the Shechina pertained equally to the Messiah: an opinion not confined to the Rabbins, but sanctioned by the Apostle Paul. According to it, the Messiah was, even in the wilderness, the invisible guide and benefactor of God's people (1 Cor. x. 4, 9.):‡ he was with our first parents in Paradise;§ he was the agent in creation (Col. i. 16.): he even existed before the creation,‖ and prior to his incarnation in Jesus, was in a glorious fellowship with God (Phil. ii. 6.).

As it is thus evident that, immediately after the time of Jesus, the idea of a pre-existence of the Messiah was incorporated in the higher Jewish theology, it is no far-fetched conjecture, that the same idea was afloat when the mind of Jesus was maturing, and that in his conception of himself as the Messiah, this attribute was included. But whether Jesus were as deeply initiated in the speculations of the Jewish schools as Paul, is yet a question, and as the author of the fourth gospel, versed in the Alexandrian doctrine of the λόγος, stands alone in ascribing to Jesus the assertion of a pre-existence, we are unable to decide whether we are to put the dogma to the account of Jesus, or of his biographer.

§ 65. THE MESSIANIC PLAN OF JESUS—INDICATIONS OF A POLITICAL ELEMENT.

THE Baptist pointed to a future individual, and Jesus to himself, as the founder of the kingdom of heaven. The idea of that messianic kingdom belonged to the Israelitish nation; did Jesus hold it in the form in which it existed among his cotemporaries, or under modifications of his own?

The idea of the Messiah grew up amongst the Jews in soil half religious, half political: it was nurtured by national adversity, and in the time of Jesus, according to the testimony of the gospels, it was

---

* Bertholdt, Christol. Judæor. §§ 23—25. Comp. Lücke ut sup. S. 211, note.
† Schöttgen, ii. S. 6 f. ‡ Targ. Jes. xvi. 1: *Iste (Messias) in deserto fuit rupes ecclesiæ Zionis.* In Bertholdt, ut sup. p. 115. § Sohar chadasch f. lxxxii. 4, ap. Schöttgen, ii. S. 140. ‖ Nezach Israel c. xxxv. f. xlviii. 1. Schmidt, Bibl. für Kritik u. Exegese, I, S. 38; מקדם מבת הדרו Sohar Levit. f. xiv. 56. Schöttgen, ii. S. 436: *Septem (lumina condita sunt, antequam mundus conderetur), nimirum . . . . . . et lumen Messiæ.* Here we have the preexistence of the Messiah represented as a real one: for a more ideal conception of it, see Bereschith Rabba, sect. 1, f. iii. 3 (Schöttgen).

embodied in the expectation that the Messiah would ascend the throne of his ancestor David, free the Jewish people from the Roman yoke, and found a kingdom which would last for ever (Luke i. 32 f. 68 ff. Acts i. 6.). Hence our first question must be this: Did Jesus include this political element in his messianic plan ?

That Jesus aspired to be a temporal ruler, has at all times been an allegation of the adversaries of Christianity, but has been maintained by none with so much exegetical acumen as by the author of the Wolfenbüttel Fragments,* who, be it observed, by no means denies to Jesus the praise of aiming at the moral reformation of his nation. According to this writer, the first indication of a political plan on the part of Jesus is, that he unambiguously announced the approaching messianic kingdom, and laid down the conditions on which it was to be entered, without explaining what this kingdom was, and wherein it consisted,* as if he supposed the current idea of its nature to be correct. Now the fact is, that the prevalent conception of the messianic reign had a strong political bias ; hence, when Jesus spoke of the Messiah's kingdom without a definition, the Jews could only think of an earthly dominion, and as Jesus could not have presupposed any other interpretation of his words, he must have wished to be so understood. But in opposition to this it may be remarked, that in the parables by which Jesus shadowed forth the kingdom of heaven ; in the Sermon on the Mount, in which he illustrates the duties of its citizens; and lastly, in his whole demeanour and course of action, we have sufficient evidence, that his idea of the messianic kingdom was peculiar to himself. There is not so ready a counterpoise for the difficulty, that Jesus sent the apostles, with whose conceptions he could not be unacquainted, to announce the Messiah's kingdom throughout the land (Matt. x.). These, who disputed which of them should be greatest in the kingdom of their master (Matt. xviii. 1, Luke xvii. 24); of whom two petitioned for the seats at the right and left of the messianic king (Mark x. 35 ff.); who, even after the death and resurrection of Jesus, expected a restoration of the kingdom to Israel (Acts i. 6:)—these had clearly from the beginning to the end of their intercourse with Jesus, no other than the popular notion of the Messiah ; when, therefore, Jesus despatched them as heralds of his kingdom, it seems necessarily a part of his design, that they should disseminate in all places their political messianic idea.

Among the discourses of Jesus there is one especially worthy of note in Matt. xix. 28. (comp. Luke xxii. 30.). In reply to the question of Peter, *We have left all and followed thee ; what shall we have therefore?* Jesus promises to his disciples that in the παλιγγενεσία, *when the Son of Man shall sit on his throne, they also shall sit on twelve thrones, judging the twelve tribes of Israel.* That the literal import of this promise formed part of the tissue of

* Von dem Zweck Jesu und seiner Jünger, S. 108—157.   † Comp. Fritzsche, in Matth. S. 114.

the messianic hopes cherished by the Jews of that period, is not to be controverted. It is argued, however, that Jesus spoke figuratively on this occasion, and only employed familiar Jewish images to convey to the apostles an assurance, that the sacrifices they had made here would be richly compensated in their future life by a participation in his glory.[*] But the disciples must have understood the promise literally, when, even after the resurrection of Jesus, they harboured anticipations of worldly greatness; and as Jesus had had many proofs of this propensity, he would hardly have adopted such language, had he not intended to nourish their temporal hopes. The supposition that he did so merely to animate the courage of his disciples, without himself sharing their views, imputes duplicity to Jesus;—a duplicity in this case quite gratuitous, since, as Olshausen justly observes, Peter's question would have been satisfactorily answered by any other laudatory acknowledgment of the devotion of the disciples. Hence it appears a fair inference, that Jesus himself shared the Jewish expectations which he here sanctions; but expositors have made the most desperate efforts to escape from this unwelcome conclusion. Some have resorted to an arbitrary alteration of the reading :[†] others to the detection of irony, directed against the disproportion between the pretensions of the disciples, and their trivial services :[‡] others to different expedients, but all more unnatural than the admission, that Jesus, in accordance with Jewish ideas, here promises his disciples the dignity of being his assessors in his visible messianic judgment, and that he thus indicates the existence of a national element in his notion of the Messiah's kingdom. It is observable, too, that in the Acts (i. 7.), Jesus, even after his resurrection, does not deny that he will restore the kingdom to Israel, but merely discourages curiosity as to the times and seasons of its restoration.

Among the actions of Jesus, his last entry into Jerusalem (Matt. xxi. 1 ff.) is especially appealed to as a proof that his plan was partly political. According to the Fragmentist, all the circumstances point to a political design: the time which Jesus chose,—after a sufficiently long preparation of the people in the provinces; the passover, which they visited in great numbers; the animal on which he rode, and by which, from a popular interpretation of a passage in Zachariah, he announced himself as the destined King of Jerusalem; the approval which he pronounces when the people receive him with a royal greeting: the violent procedure which he hazards in the temple: and finally, his severe philippic on the higher class of the Jews (Matt. xxiii.), at the close of which he seeks to awe them into a reception of him as their messianic king, by the threat that he will show himself to them no more in any other guise.

§ 66.   DATA FOR THE PURE SPIRITUALITY OF THE MESSIANIC PLAN
                    OF JESUS—BALANCE.

NOWHERE in our evangelical narratives is there a trace of Jesus
having sought to form a political party. On the contrary, he withdraws from the eagerness of the people to make him a king (John
vi. 15.); he declares that the messianic kingdom comes not with
observation, but is to be sought for in the recesses of the soul (Luke
xvii. 20 f.); it is his principle to unite obedience to God with obedience to temporal authority, even when heathen (Matt. xxii. 21.);
on his solemn entry into the capital, he chooses to ride the animal
of peace, and afterwards escapes from the multitude, instead of using
their excitement for the purposes of his ambition ; lastly, he maintains before his judge, that his kingdom is not *from hence* οὐκ ἐντεῦθεν, *is not of this world* οὐκ ἐκ τοῦ κόσμου τούτου (John xvi. 36.),
and we have no reason in this instance to question either his or the
evangelist's veracity.

Thus we have a series of indications to counterbalance those detailed in the preceding section. The adversaries of Christianity
have held exclusively to the arguments for a political, or rather a
revolutionary, project, on the part of Jesus, while the orthodox theologians adhere to those only which tell for the pure spirituality of
his plan ;* and each party has laboured to invalidate by hermeneu-
tical skill the passages unfavourable to its theory. It has of late
been acknowledged that both are equally partial, and that there is
need of arbitration between them.

This has been attempted chiefly by supposing an earlier and a
later form of the plan of Jesus.† Although, it has been said, the
moral improvement and religious elevation of his people were from
the first the primary object of Jesus, he nevertheless, in the beginning of his public life, cherished the hope of reviving, by means of
this internal regeneration, the external glories of the theocracy, when
he should be acknowledged by his nation as the Messiah, and thereby
be constituted the supreme authority in the state. But in the dis-
appointment of this hope, he recognized the Divine rejection of every
political element in his plan, and thenceforth refined it into pure
spirituality. It is held to be a presumption in favour of such a
change in the plan of Jesus, that there is a gladness diffused over
his first appearance, which gives place to melancholy in the latter
period of his ministry ; that instead of the acceptable year of the
Lord, announced in his initiative address at Nazareth, sorrow is the
burthen of his later discourses, and he explicitly says of Jerusalem,
that he had attempted to save it, but that now its fall, both religious

* So Reinhard, über den Plan, welchen der Stifter der christlichen Religion zum
Besten der Menschheit entwarf. S. 57 ff. (4te Aufl.)   † Paulus, Leben Jesu 1. B. S. 85,
94, 106 ff.; Venturini, 2, S. 310 f. Hase, Leben Jesu, 1 ed. § § 49, 50. (comp. theol.
Streitschrift, 1, S. 61 ff.), though with apparent reluctance, and he now maintains that
Jesus had risen above the political notion of the messianic kingdom before his public ap-
pearance.

and political, was inevitable. As, however, the evangelists do not keep the events and discourses proper to these distinct periods within their respective limits, but happen to give the two most important data for the imputation of a political design to Jesus (namely the promise of the twelve.thrones and the public entrance into the capital,) near the close of his life; we must attribute to these writers a chronological confusion, as in the case of the relation which the views of Jesus bore to the messianic idea in general: unless as an alternative it be conceivable, that Jesus uttered during the same period, the declarations which seem to indicate, and those which disclaim, a political design.

This, in our apprehension, is not inconceivable: for Jesus might anticipate a καθίζεσθαι ἐπὶ θρόνοις for himself and his disciples, not regarding the means of its attainment as a political revolution, but as a revolution to be effected by the immediate interposition of God. That such was his view may be inferred from his placing that judiciary appearance of his disciples in the παλιγγενεσία; for this was not a political revolution, any more than a spiritual regeneration,—it was a resurrection of the dead, which God was to effect through the agency of the Messiah, and which was to usher in the messianic times.[†] Jesus certainly expected to restore the throne of David, and with his disciples to govern a liberated people; in no degree, however, did he rest his hopes on the sword of human adherents (Luke xxii. 38. Matt. xxvi. 52.), but on the legions of angels, which his heavenly Father could send him (Matt. xxvi. 53). Wherever he speaks of coming in his messianic glory, he depicts himself surrounded by angels and heavenly powers (Matt. xvi. 27, xxiv. 30 f. xxv. 31; John i. 52.); before the majesty of the Son of Man, coming in the clouds of heaven, all nations are to bow without the coercion of the sword, and at the sound of the angel's trumpet, are to present themselves, with the awakened dead, before the judgment-seat of the Messiah and his twelve apostles. All this Jesus would not bring to pass of his own will, but he waited for a signal from his heavenly Father, who alone knew the appropriate time for this catastrophe (Mark xiii. 32.), and he apparently was not disconcerted when his end approached without his having received the expected intimation. They who shrink from this view, merely because they conceive that it makes Jesus an enthusiast,[†] will do well to reflect how closely such hopes corresponded with the long cherished messianic idea of the Jews,[‡] and how easily, in that day of supernaturalism, and in a nation segregated by the peculiarities of its faith, an idea, in itself extravagant, if only it were consistent, and had, in some of its aspects, truth and dignity, might allure even a reasonable man beneath its influence.

With respect to that which awaits the righteous after judgment,—everlasting life in the kingdom of the Father,—it is true

* Fritzsche, in Matth. p. 606 f.   † De Wette, Bibl. Dogm. § 216.   ‡ Bertholdt, Christol. Judæor. §§ 30 ff.

that Jesus, in accordance with Jewish notions,* compares it to a feast (Matt. viii. 11; xxii. 2 ff.), at which he hopes himself to taste the fruit of the vine (Matt. xxvi. 29.), and to celebrate the passover (Luke xxii. 16.): but his declaration that in the αἰὼν μέλλων the organic relation between the sexes will cease, and men will be *like the angels* (ἰσάγγελοι, Luke xx. 35 ff.), seems more or less to reduce the above discourses to a merely symbolical significance.

Thus we conclude that the messianic hope of Jesus was not political, nor even merely earthly, for he referred its fulfilment to supernatural means, and to a supermundane theatre (the regenerated earth) : as little was it a purely spiritual hope, in the modern sense of the term, for it included important and unprecedented changes in the external condition of things : but it was the national, theocratic hope, spiritualized and ennobled by his own peculiar moral and religious views.

§ 67. THE RELATION OF JESUS TO THE MOSAIC LAW.

THE mosaic institutions were actually extinguished in the church of which Jesus was the founder; hence it is natural to suppose that their abolition formed a part of his design :—a reach of vision, beyond the horizon of the ceremonial worship of his age and country, of which apologists have been ever anxious to prove that he was possessed.† Neither are there wanting speeches and actions of Jesus which seem to favour their effort. Whenever he details the conditions of participation in the kingdom of heaven, as in the sermon on the mount, he insists, not on the observance of the Mosaic ritual, but on the spirit of religion and morality ; he attaches no value to fasting, praying, and almsgiving, unless accompanied by a corresponding bent of mind (Matt. vi. 1—18) ; the two main elements of the Mosaic worship, sacrifice and the keeping of sabbaths and feasts, he not only nowhere enjoins, but puts a marked slight on the former, by commending the scribe who declared that the love of God and one's neighbour was *more than whole burnt-offerings and sacrifices*, as one *not far from the kingdom of God* (Mark xii. 23 f.),‡ and he ran counter in action as well as in speech to the customary mode of celebrating the Sabbath (Matt. xii. 1—13 ; Mark ii. 23—28 ; iii. 1—5 ; Luke vi. 1—10 ; xiii. 10. ff. ; xiv. 1. ff. ; John v. 5. ff. ; vii. 22 ; ix. 1. ff.), of which in his character of Son of Man he claimed to be Lord. The Jews, too, appear to have expected a revision of the Mosaic law by their Messiah.§ A somewhat analogous sense is couched in the declarations attributed by the fourth evangelist to Jesus (ii. 19) ; Matthew (xxvi. 61.) and Mark (xiv. 58.) represent him as being accused by false witnesses of saying, *I am able to destroy* (John, *destroy*)

* Berthold, Christ. Jud. § 39.   † E. g. Reinhard, Plan Jesu, S. 14 ff.   ‡ For an exaggeration in the Ebionite Gospel, vid. Epiphanius, hæres. xxx. 16.   § Bertholdt, ut sup. § 31.

the temple of God (Mark, *that is made with hands*), *and to build it in three days* (Mark, *I will build another made without hands*). The author of the Acts has something similar as an article of accusation against Stephen, but instead of the latter half of the sentence it is thus added, *and* (he i. e. Jesus) *shall change the customs which Moses delivered us ;* and perhaps this may be regarded as an authentic comment on the less explicit text. In general it may be said that to one who, like Jesus, is so far alive to the absolute value of the internal compared with the external, of the bent of the entire disposition compared with isolated acts, that he pronounces the love of God and our neighbour to be the essence of the law (Matt. xxii. 36 ff.),—to him it cannot be a secret, that all precepts of the law which do not bear on these two points are unessential. But the argument apparently most decisive of a design on the part of Jesus to abolish the Mosaic worship, is furnished by his prediction that the temple, the centre of Jewish worship (Matt. xxiv. 2. parall.), would be destroyed, and that the adoration of God would be freed from local fetters, and become purely spiritual (John iv. 21 ff.).

The above, however, presents only one aspect of the position assumed by Jesus towards the Mosaic law ; there are also data for the belief that he did not meditate the overthrow of the ancient constitution of his country. This side of the question has been, at a former period, and from easily-conceived reasons, the one which the enemies of Christianity in its ecclesiastical form, have chosen to exhibit ;* but it is only in recent times that, the theological horizon being extended, the unprejudiced expositors of the church† have acknowledged its existence. In the first place, during his life Jesus remains faithful to the paternal law ; he attends the synagogue on the sabbath, journeys to Jerusalem at the time of the feast, and eats of the paschal lamb with his disciples. It is true that he heals on the sabbath, allows his disciples to pluck ears of corn (Matt. xii. 1. ff.), and requires no fasting or washing before meat in his society (Matt. iv. 14 ; xv. 2). But the Mosaic law concerning the sabbath simply prescribed cessation from common labour, מְלָאכָה, (Exod. xx. 8. ff. ; xxxi. 12. ff. ; Deut. v. 12. ff.), including ploughing, reaping, (Ex. xxxiv. 21), gathering of sticks (Numb. xv. 32. ff.) and similar work, and it was only the spirit of petty observance, the growth of a later age, that made it an offence to perform cures, or pluck a few ears of corn.‡ The washing of hands before eating was but a rabbinical custom :§ in the law one general yearly fast was alone prescribed (Lev. xvi. 29 ff. ; xxiii. 27 ff.) and no private fasting required ; hence Jesus cannot be convicted of infringing the precepts of Moses.‖ In that very sermon on the mount in which Jesus exalts spiritual religion so far above all ritual, he clearly

* This is done the most concisely in the Wolfenbüttel Fragments, von dem Zweck u. s. f. S. 66 ff.   † Especially Fritzsche, in Matt. S. 211 ff.   ‡ Winer, bibl. Realwörterbuch, 2, S. 406 ff.   § Comp. Paulus, exeg. Handb. 2, S. 273.   ‖ Winer, bibl. Realw. 1. Bd. S. 426.

presupposes the continuation of sacrifices (Matt. v. 23 f.), and declares that he is not come to destroy the law and the prophets, but to fulfil (Matt. v. 17.). Even if κληρῶσαι, in all probability, refers chiefly to the accomplishment of the Old Testament prophecies, οὐκ ἦλθὸν καταλῦσαι must at the same time be understood of the conservation of the Mosaic law, since in the context, perpetuity is promised to its smallest letter, and he who represents its lightest precept as not obligatory, is threatened with the lowest rank in the kingdom of heaven.* In accordance with this, the apostles adhered strictly to the Mosaic law, even after the Feast of Pentecost; they went at the hour of prayer into the temple (Acts iii. 1.), clung to the synagogues and to the Mosaic injunctions respecting food (x. 14), and were unable to appeal to any express declaration of Jesus as a sanction for the procedure of Barnabas and Paul, when the judaizing party complained of their baptizing Gentiles without laying on them the burthen of the Mosaic law.

This apparent contradiction in the conduct and language of Jesus, has been apologetically explained by the supposition, that not only the personal obedience of Jesus to the law, but also his declarations in its favour, were a necessary concession to the views of his cotemporaries, who would at once have withdrawn their confidence from him, had he announced himself as the destroyer of their holy and venerated law.† We allow that the obedience of Jesus to the law in his own person, might be explained in the same way as that of Paul, which, on his own showing, was a measure of mere expediency (1 Cor. ix. 20. comp. Acts xvi. 3.). But the strong declarations of Jesus concerning the perpetuity of the law, and the guilt of him who dares to violate its lightest precept, cannot possibly be derived from the principle of concession; for to pronounce that indispensable, which one secretly holds superfluous, and which one even seeks to bring gradually into disuse, would, leaving honesty out of the question, be in the last degree injudicious.

Hence others have made a distinction between the moral and the ritual law, and referred the declaration of Jesus that he wished not to abrogate the law, to the former alone, which he extricated from a web of trivial ceremonies, and embodied in his own example.‡ But such a distinction is not found in those striking passages from the Sermon on the Mount; rather, in the νόμος and προφῆται, *the law and the prophets*, we have the most comprehensive designation of the whole religious constitution of the Old Testament,§ and under the most trivial commandment, and the smallest letter of the law, alike pronounced imperishable, we cannot well understand any thing else than the ceremonial precepts.‖

A happier distinction is that between really Mosaic institutes, and their traditional amplifications.¶ It is certain that the Sabbath

* Fritzsche, S. 214 ff. † Reinhard, S. 15 ff. Planck, Geschichte des Christenthums in der Periode seiner Einführung, 1, S. 175 ff. ‡ De Wette, bibl. Dogm. § 210. § Fritzsche, S. 214. ‖ Vid. the Fragmentist, S. 69. ¶ Paulus, exeg. Handb. 1, B. S. 600 f. Leben Jesu, 1, a, S. 296, 312.

cures of Jesus, his neglect of the pedantic ablutions before eating, and the like, ran counter, not to Moses, but to later rabbinical requirements, and several discourses of Jesus turn upon this distinction. Matt. xv. 3 ff., Jesus places the commandment of God in opposition to the tradition of the elders, and Matt. xxiii. 23, he declares that where they are compatible, the former may be observed without rejecting the latter, in which case he admonishes the people to do all that the Scribes and Pharisees enjoin; where on the contrary, either the one or the other only can be respected, he decides that it is better to transgress the tradition of the Elders, than the commandment of God as given by Moses (Matt. xv. 3 ff.). He describes the mass of traditional precepts, as a burthen grievous to be borne, which he would remove from the oppressed people, substituting his own light burthen and easy yoke: whence it may be seen, that with all his forbearance towards existing institutions, so far as they were not positively pernicious, it was his intention that all these *commandments of men*, as plants which his heavenly Father had not planted, should be rooted up (xv. 9. 13.). The majority of the Pharisaical precepts referred to externals, and had the effect of burying the noble morality of the Mosaic law under a heap of ceremonial observances; a gift to the temple sufficed to absolve the giver from his filial duties (xv. 5.), and the payment of tithe of anise and cummin superseded justice, mercy and faith (xxiii. 23.). Hence this distinction is in some degree identical with the former, since in the rabbinical institutes it was their merely ceremonial tendency that Jesus censured, while, in the Mosaic law, it was the kernel of religion and morality that he chiefly valued. It must only not be contended that he regarded the Mosaic law as permanent solely in its spiritual part, for the passages quoted, especially from the Sermon on the Mount, clearly show that he did not contemplate the abolition of the merely ritual precepts.

Jesus, supposing that he had discerned morality and the spiritual worship of God to be the sole essentials in religion, must have rejected all which, being merely ritual and formal, had usurped the importance of a religious obligation, and under this description must fall a large proportion of the Mosaic precepts; but it is well known how slowly such consequences are deduced, when they come into collision with usages consecrated by antiquity. Even Samuel, apparently, was aware that obedience is better than sacrifice (1 Sam. xv. 22), and Asaph, that an offering of thanksgiving is more acceptable to God than one of slain animals (Ps. l.); yet how long after were sacrifices retained together with true obedience, or in its stead! Jesus was more thoroughly penetrated with this conviction than those ancients; with him, the true commandments of God in the Mosaic law were simply, *Honour thy father and thy mother, Thou shalt not kill*, &c., and above all, *Thou shalt love the Lord thy God with all thy heart, and thy neighbour as thyself*. But his deep-rooted respect for the sacred book of the law, caused him, for the sake of these essential contents, to honour the unessential which was the more natural, as in comparison with the absurdly exaggerated pedantry of the traditional observances, the ritual of the Pentateuch must have appeared highly simple. To honour this latter part of the law as of Divine origin, but to declare it abrogated on the principle, that in the education of the human race, God finds necessary for an earlier period an arrangement which is superfluous for a later one, implies that idea of *the law as a schoolmaster*, νόμος παιδαγωγὸς (Gal. iii. 24.), which seems first to have been developed by the apostle Paul; nevertheless its germ lies in the declaration of Jesus, that God had permitted to the early Hebrews, *on account of the hardness of their hearts*, (Matt. xix. 8 f.) many things, which, in a more advanced stage of culture, were inadmissible.

A similar limitation of the duration of the law is involved in the predictions of Jesus, (if indeed they were uttered by Jesus, a point which we have to discuss,) that the temple would be destroyed at his approaching advent (Matt. xxiv. parall.), and that devotion would be freed from all local restrictions (John iv.); for with these must fall the entire Mosaic system of external worship. This is not contradicted by the declaration that the law would endure until heaven and earth should pass away (Matt. v. 18.), for the Hebrew associated the fall of his state and sanctuary with the end of the old world or dispensation, so that the expressions, so long as the temple stands, and so long as the world stands, were equivalent.* It is true that the words of Jesus, Luke xvi. 16., ὁ νόμος καὶ οἱ προφῆται ἑως 'Ιωάννου· seem to imply, that the appearance of the Baptist put an end to the validity of the law; but this passage loses its depreciatory sense when compared with its parallel, Matt. xi. 13. On the other hand, Luke xvi. 17. controls Matt. v. 18., and reduces it to a mere comparison between the stability of the law and that of heaven and earth. The only question then is, in which of the gospels are the two passages more correctly stated? As given in the first, they intimate that the law would retain its supremacy until, and not after, the close of the old dispensation. With this agrees the prediction, that the temple would be destroyed; for the spiritualization of religion, and, according to Stephen's interpretation, the abolition of the Mosaic law, which were to be the results of that event, were undoubtedly identified by Jesus with the commencement of the αἰὼν μέλλων of the Messiah. Hence it appears, that the only difference between the view of Paul and that of Jesus is this: that the latter anticipated the extinction of the Mosaic system as a concomitant of his glorious advent or return to the regenerated earth, while the former believed its abolition permissible on the old, unregenerated earth, in virtue of the Messiah's first advent.†

§ 68. SCOPE OF THE MESSIANIC PLAN OF JESUS—RELATIONS TO THE GENTILES.

ALTHOUGH the church founded by Jesus did, in fact, early extend itself beyond the limits of the Jewish people, there are yet indications which might induce a belief that he did not contemplate such an extension.* When he sends the twelve on their first mission, his command is, *Go not into the way of the Gentiles—Go rather to the lost sheep of the house of Israel* (Matt. x. 5 f.). That Matthew alone has this injunction and not the two other synoptists, is less probably explained by the supposition that the Hebrew author of the first gospel interpolated it, than by the opposite one, namely, that it was wilfully omitted by the Hellenistic authors of the second and third gospels. For, as the judaizing tendency of Matthew is not so marked that he assigns to Jesus the intention of limiting the messianic kingdom to the Jews; as, on the contrary, he makes Jesus unequivocally foretel the calling of the Gentiles (viii. 11 f. xxi. 33 ff. xxii. 1 ff. xxviii. 19 f.): he had no motive for fabricating this particularizing addition; but the two other evangelists had a strong one for its omission; in the offence which it would cause to the Gentiles already within the fold. Its presence in Matthew, however, demands an explanation, and expositors have thought to furnish one by supposing the injunction of Jesus to be a measure of prudence.† It is unquestionable that, even if the plan of Jesus comprehended the Gentiles as well as the Jews, he must at first, if he would not for ever ruin his cause with his fellow-countrymen, adopt, and prescribe to the disciples, a rule of national exclusiveness. This necessity on his part might account for his answer to the Canaanitish woman, whose daughter he refuses to heal, because he was only sent to the lost sheep of the house of Israel (Matt. xv. 24), were it not that the boon which he here denies is not a reception into the messianic kingdom, but a temporal benefit, such as even Elijah and Elisha had conferred on those who were not Israelites (1 Kings xvii. 9 ff. 2 Kings v. 1 ff.)—examples to which Jesus elsewhere appeals (Luke iv. 25 ff.). Hence the disciples thought it natural and unobjectionable to grant the woman's petition, and it could not be prudential considerations that withheld Jesus, for a time, from compliance. That an aversion to the Gentiles may not appear to be his motive, it has been conjectured‡ that Jesus, wishing to preserve an incognito in that country, avoided the performance of any messianic work. But such a design of concealment is only mentioned by Mark (vii. 25.), who represents it as being defeated by the entreaties of the woman, contrary to the inclinations of Jesus; and as this evangelist omits the declaration of Jesus, that he was not sent but to the lost sheep of the house of

* Thus the Wolfenbüttel Fragmentist, ut sup. S. 72 ff.   † Reinhard; Planck, Geschichte des Christenthums in der Per. seiner Einführung, 1, S. 179 ff.   ‡ Paulus, Leben Jesu, 1, a, S. 380 f.   Hase, L. J. § 102.

Israel, we must suspect that he was guided by the wish to supply a less offensive motive for the conduct of Jesus, rather than by historical accuracy. Had Jesus really been influenced by the motive which Mark assigns, he must at once have alleged it to his disciples instead of a merely ostensible one, calculated to strengthen their already rigid exclusiveness. We should therefore rather listen to the opinion that Jesus sought, by his repeated refusal, to prove the faith of the woman, and furnish an occasion for its exhibition,[*] if we could find in the text the slightest trace of mere dissimulation; and none of a real change of mind.[†] Even Mark, bent as he was on softening the features of the incident, cannot have thought of a dissimulation of this kind: otherwise, instead of omitting the harsh words and making the inadequate addition, *and would have no man know it*, he would have removed the offence in the most satisfactory manner, by an observation such as, *he said this to prove her* (comp. John vi. 6.). Thus it must be allowed that Jesus in this case seems to share the antipathy of his countrymen towards the Gentiles, nay, his antipathy seems to be of a deeper stamp than that of his disciples; unless their advocacy of the woman be a touch from the pencil of tradition, for the sake of contrast and grouping.

This narrative, however, is neutralized by another, in which Jesus is said to act in a directly opposite manner. The centurion of Capernaum, also a Gentile, (as we gather from the remarks of Jesus,) has scarcely complained of a distress similar to that of the Canaanitish woman, when Jesus himself volunteers to go and heal his servant (Matt. viii. 5.). If, then, Jesus has no hesitation, in this instance, to exercise his power of healing in favour of a heathen, how comes it that he refuses to do so in another quite analogous case? Truly if the relative position of the two narratives in the gospels have any weight, he must have shown himself more harsh and narrow at the later period than at the earlier one. Meanwhile, this single act of benevolence to a Gentile, standing as it does in inexplicable contradiction to the narrative above examined, cannot prove, in opposition to the command expressly given to the disciples, not to go to the Gentiles, that Jesus contemplated their admission as such into the messianic kingdom.

Even the prediction of Jesus that the kingdom of heaven would be taken from the Jews and given to the Gentiles, does not prove this. In the above interview with the centurion of Capernaum, Jesus declares that *many shall come from the east and the west*, and sit down with the patriarchs in *the kingdom of heaven*, while the *children of the kingdom*, (obviously the Jews,) for whom it was originally designed, will be cast out (Matt. viii. 11 f.). Yet more decidedly, when applying the parable of the husbandmen in the vineyard, he warns his countrymen that *the kingdom of God shall be taken from them, and given to a nation bringing forth the fruits thereof* (Matt. xxi. 43.). All this may be understood in the sense intended by the prophets, in their promises that the messianic kingdom would extend to all nations; namely, that the Gentiles would turn to the worship of Jehovah, embrace the Mosaic religion in its entire form, and afterwards be received into the Messiah's kingdom. It would accord very well with this expectation, that, prior to such a conversion, Jesus should forbid his disciples to direct their announcement of his kingdom to the Gentiles.

But in the discourses concerning, his re-appearance, Jesus regards the publication of the Gospel to all nations as one of the circumstances that must precede that event: (Matt. xxiv, 14. Mark xiii. 10.), and after his resurrection, according to the synoptists, he gave his disciples the command, *Go ye, and teach all nations, baptizing them,* &c. (Matt. xxviii. 19; Mark xvi. 15; Luke xxiv. 47.): i. e. go to them with the offer of the Messiah's kingdom, even though they may not beforehand have become Jews. Not only, however, do the disciples, after the first Pentecost, neglect to execute this command, but when a case is thrust on them which offers them an opportunity for compliance with it, they act as if they were altogether ignorant that such a direction had been given by Jesus (Acts x. xi.). The heathen centurion Cornelius, worthy, from his devout life, of a reception into the messianic community is pointed out by an angel to the apostle Peter. But because it was not hidden from God, with what difficulty the apostle would be induced to receive a heathen, without further preliminary, into the Messiah's kingdom, he saw it needful to prepare him for such a step by a symbolical vision. In consequence of such an admonition Peter goes to Cornelius; but to impel him to baptize him and his family, he needs a second sign, the pouring out of the Holy Ghost on these uncircumcised. When, subsequently, the Jewish Christians in Jerusalem call him to account for this reception of Gentiles, Peter appeals in his justification solely to the recent vision, and to the Holy Ghost given to the centurion's family. Whatever judgment we may form of the credibility of this history, it is a memorial of the many deliberations and contentions which it cost the apostles after the departure of Jesus, to convince themselves of the eligibility of Gentiles for a participation in the kingdom of their Christ, and the reasons which at last brought them to a decision. Now if Jesus had given so explicit a command as that above quoted, what need was there of a vision to encourage Peter to its fulfilment? or, supposing the vision to be a legendary investiture of the natural deliberations of the disciples, why did they go about in search of the reflection, that all men ought to be baptized, because before God all men and all animals, as his creatures, are clean, if they could have appealed to an express injunction of Jesus? Here, then, is the alternative: if Jesus himself gave this command, the disciples cannot have been led to the admission of the Gentiles by the means narrated in Acts x. xi.; if, on the other hand, that narrative is authentic, the alleged command of Jesus cannot be historical. Our canon decides for the latter proposition. For that the subsequent practice and pre-eminent distinction of the Christian Church, its accessibility to all nations, and its indifference to circumcision or uncircumcision, should have lain in the mind of its founder, is the view best adapted to exalt and adorn Jesus; while, that, first after his death, and through the gradual development of relations, the church, which its Founder had designed for the Gentiles only in so far as they became Jews, should break through these limits, is in the simple, natural, and therefore the probable course of things.

§ 69.   RELATION OF THE MESSIANIC PLAN OF JESUS TO THE SAMARI-
TANS—HIS INTERVIEW WITH THE WOMAN OF SAMARIA.

THERE is the same apparent contradiction in the position which Jesus took, and prescribed to his disciples, towards the inhabitants of Samaria. While in his instructions to his disciples, (Matt. x. 5,) he forbids them to visit any city of the Samaritans, we read in John (iv.) that Jesus himself in his journey through Samaria laboured as the Messiah with great effect, and ultimately stayed two days in a Samaritan town; and in the Acts (i. 8), that before his ascension he charged the disciples to be his witnesses, not only in Jerusalem and in all Judea, but also in Samaria. That Jesus did not entirely shun Samaria, as that prohibition might appear to intimate, is evident from Luke ix. 52. (comp. xvii. 11.), where his disciples bespeak lodgings for him in a Samaritan village, when he has determined to go to Jerusalem; a circumstance which accords with the information of Josephus, that those Galileans who journeyed to the feasts usually went through Samaria.* That Jesus was not unfavourable to the Samaritans, nay, that in many respects he acknowledged their su-periority to the Jews, is evident from his parable of the Good Sa-maritan (Luke x. 30 ff.); he also bestows a marked notice on the case of a Samaritan, who, among ten cleansed, was the only one that testified his gratitude (Luke xvii. 16): and, if we may venture on such a conclusion from John iv. 25, and subsequent records,† the inhabitants of Samaria themselves had some tincture of the messi-anic idea.

However natural it may appear that Jesus should avail himself of this susceptible side of the Samaritans, by opportunely announc-ing to them the messianic kingdom; the aspect which the four evangelists bear to each other on this subject must excite surprise. Matthew has no occasion on which Jesus comes in contact with the Samaritans, or even mentions them, except in the prohibition above quoted; Mark is more neutral than Matthew, and has not even that prohibition; Luke has two instances of contact, one of them unfa-vourable, the other favourable, together with the parable in which Jesus presents a Samaritan as a model, and his approving notice of

* Antiq. xx. vi. 1.   For some rabbinical rules not quite in accordance with this, see Lightfoot, p. 991.   † Bertholdt, Christol. Judær. ? 7.

the gratitude of one whom he had healed; John, finally, has a narrative in which Jesus appears in a very intimate and highly favourable relation to the Samaritans. Are all these various accounts well-founded? If so, how could Jesus at one time prohibit his disciples from including the Samaritans in the messianic plan, and at another time, himself receive them without hesitation? Moreover, if the chronological order of the evangelists deserve regard, the ministry of Jesus in Samaria must have preceded the prohibition contained in his instructions to his disciples on their first mission. For the scene of that mission being Galilee, and there being no space for its occurrence during the short stay which, according to the fourth evangelist, Jesus made in that province before the first passover (ii. 1—13.), it must be placed after that passover: and, as the visit to Samaria was made on his journey, after that visit also. How, then, could Jesus, after having with the most desirable issue, personally taught in Samaria, and presented himself as the Messiah, forbid his disciples to carry thither their messianic tidings? On the other hand, if the scenes narrated by John occured after the command recorded by Matthew, the disciples, instead of wondering that Jesus talked so earnestly with a *woman* (John iv, 27.), ought rather to have wondered that he held any converse with a *Samaritan.**

Since then of the two extreme narratives at least, in Matthew and John, neither presupposes the other, we must either doubt the authenticity of the exclusive command of Jesus, or of his connexion with the inhabitants of Samaria.

In this conflict between the gospels, we have again the advantage of appealing to the Book of Acts as an umpire. Before Peter, at the divine instigation, had received the first fruits of the Gentiles into the Messiah's kingdom, Philip the deacon, being driven from Jerusalem by the persecution of which Stephen's death was the commencement, journeyed to the city of Samaria, where he preached Christ, and by miracles of all kinds won the Samaritans to the faith, and to the reception of baptism (Acts viii. 5 ff.). This narrative is a complete contrast to that of the first admission of the Gentiles: while in the one there was need of a vision, and a special intimation from the Spirit, to bring Peter into communication with the heathens: in the other, Philip, without any precedent, unhesitatingly baptizes the Samaritans. And lest it should be said that the deacon was perhaps of a more liberal spirit than the apostle, we have Peter himself coming forthwith to Samaria in company with John,—an incident which forms another point of opposition between the two narratives: for, while the first admission of the Gentiles makes a highly unfavourable impression on the mother church at Jerusalem, the report that *Samaria had received the word of God* meets with so warm an approval there, that the two most distinguished apostles are commissioned to confirm and consummate the work begun by Philip. The tenor of this proceeding makes it

* Some erroneously attribute this meaning to their question; see in Lücke 1, S. 533.

not improbable that there was a precedent for it in the conduct of Jesus, or at least a sanction in his expressions.

The narrative in the fourth Gospel (iv.) would form a perfect precedent in the conduct of Jesus, but we have yet to examine whether it bear the stamp of historical credibility. We do not, with the author of the Probabilia, stumble at the designation of the locality, and the opening of the conversation between Jesus and the woman:* but from v. 16 inclusively, there are, as impartial expositors confess,† many grave difficulties. The woman had entreated Jesus to give her of the water which was for ever to extinguish thirst, and Jesus immediately says, *Go, call thy husband.* Why so? It has been said that Jesus, well knowing that the woman had no lawful husband, sought to shame her, and bring her to repentance.‡ Lücke, disapproving the imputation of dissimulation to Jesus, conjectures that, perceiving the woman's dulness, he hoped by summoning her husband, possibly her superior in intelligence, to create an opportunity for a more beneficial conversation. But if Jesus, as it presently appears, knew that the woman had not at the time any proper husband, he could not in earnest desire her to summon him: and if, as Lücke allows, he had that knowledge in a supernatural manner, it could not be hidden from him, who knew what was in man, that she would be little inclined to comply with his injunction. If however, he had a prescience that what he required would not be done, the injunction was a feint, and had some latent object. But that this object was the penitence of the woman there is no indication in the text, for the ultimate effect on her is not shame and penitence, but faith in the prophetic insight of Jesus (v. 19). And this was doubtless what Jesus wished, for the narrative proceeds as if he had attained his purpose with the woman, and the issue corresponded to the design. The difficulty here lies, not so much in what Lücke terms dissimulation,—since this comes under the category of blameless temptation (πειράζειν), elsewhere occurring,—as in the violence with which Jesus wrests an opportunity for the display of his prophetic gifts.

By a transition equally abrupt, the woman urges the conversation to a point at which the Messiahship of Jesus may become fully evident. As soon as she has recognized Jesus to be a prophet, she hastens to consult him on the controversy pending between the Jews and Samaritans, as to the place appropriated to the true worship of God (v. 20.). That so vivid an interest in this national and religious question is not consistent with the limited mental and circumstantial condition of the woman, the majority of modern commentators virtually confess, by their adoption of the opinion, that her drift in this remark was to turn away the conversation from her own affairs.‡ If then the implied query concerning the place for the true worship of God, had no serious interest for the woman, but was prompted by

* Bretschneider, ut sup. S. 47 ff. 97 f. † Lücke, I, S. 520 ff. ‡ Tholuck, in loc.
§ Lücke and Tholuck, in loc. Hase, L. J. 67.

a false shame calculated to hinder confession and repentance, those expositors should remember what they elsewhere repeat to satiety,[*] that in the gospel of John the answers of Jesus refer not so much to the ostensible meaning of questions, as to the under current of feeling of which they are the indications. In accordance with this method, Jesus should not have answered the artificial question of the woman as if it had been one of deep seriousness; he ought rather to have evaded it, and recurred to the already detected stain on her conscience, which she was now seeking to hide, in order if possible to bring her to a full conviction and open avowal of her guilt. But the fact is that the object of the evangelist was to show that Jesus had been recognized, not merely as a prophet, but as the Messiah, and he believed that to turn the conversation to the question of the legitimate place for the worship of God, the solution of which was expected from the Messiah,[†] would best conduce to that end.

Jesus evinces (v. 17.) an acquaintance with the past history and present position of the woman. The rationalists have endeavoured to explain this by the supposition, that while Jesus sat at the well, and the woman was advancing from the city, some passer-by hinted to him that he had better not engage in conversation with her, as she was on the watch to obtain a sixth husband.[‡] But not to insist on the improbability that a passer-by should hold a colloquy with Jesus on the character of an obscure woman, the friends as well as the enemies of the fourth gospel now agree, that every natural explanation of that knowledge on the part of Jesus, directly counteracts the design of the evangelist.[§] For according to him, the disclosure which Jesus makes of his privity to the woman's intimate concerns, is the immediate cause, not only for her own faith in him, but of that of many inhabitants of the city (v. 39.), and he obviously intends to imply that they were not too precipitate in receiving him as a prophet, on that ground alone. Thus in the view of the evangelist, the knowledge in question was an effluence of the higher nature of Jesus, and modern supranaturalists adhere to this explanation, adducing in its support the power which John attributes to him (ii. 24 f.), of discerning what is in man without the aid of external testimony.[‖] But this does not meet the case; for Jesus here not only knows what is in the woman,—her present equivocal state of mind towards him who is not her husband,—he has cognizance also of the extrinsic fact that she has had five husbands, of whom we cannot suppose that each had left a distinct image in her mind traceable by the observation of Jesus. That by means of the penetrative acumen with which he scrutinized the hearts of those with whom he had to do, Jesus should also have a prophetic insight into his own messianic destiny, and the fortunes of his kingdom, may under a certain view of his person appear probable, and in any case must be deemed in the highest degree dignified; but that he should be acquainted, even to the most trivial details, with the adventitious history of obscure individuals, is an idea that degrades him in proportion to the exaltation of his prophetic dignity. Such empirical *knowingness* (not omniscience) would moreover annihilate the human consciousness which the orthodox view supposes to co-exist in Jesus.* But the possession of this knowledge, however it may clash with our conception of dignity and wisdom, closely corresponds to the Jewish notion of a prophet, more especially of the Messiah; in the Old Testament, Daniel recites a dream of Nebuchadnezzar, which that monarch himself had forgotten (Dan. ii.); in the Clementine Homilies, the true prophet is ὁ πάντοτε πάντα εἰδώς· τὰ μὲν γεγονότα ὡς ἐγένετο, τὰ δὲ γινόμενα ὡς γίνεται, τὰ δὲ ἐσόμενα ὡς ἔσται;† and the rabbins number such a knowledge of personal secrets among the signs of the Messiah, and observe that from the want of it, Bar-Cocheba was detected to be a pseudo-Messiah.‡

Farther on (v. 23.) Jesus reveals to the woman what Hase terms the sublimest principle of his religion, namely, that the service of God consists in a life of piety: tells her that all ceremonial worship is about to be abolished; and that he is the personage who will effect this momentous change, that is, the Messiah. We have already shown it to be improbable that Jesus, who did not give his disciples to understand that he was the Messiah until a comparatively late period, should make an early and distinct disclosure on the subject to a Samaritan woman. In what respect was she worthy of a communication more explicit than ever fell to the lot of the disciples? What could induce Jesus to send roaming into the futurity of religious history, the contemplation of a woman, whom he should rather have induced to examine herself, and to ponder on the corruptions of her own heart? Nothing but the wish to elicit from her, at any cost, and without regard to her moral benefit, an acknowledgement, not only of his prophetic gifts, but of his Messiahship; to which end it was necessary to give the conversation the above direction. But so contracted a design can never be imputed to Jesus, who on other occasions, exemplifies a more suitable mode of dealing with mankind: it is the design of the glorifying legend, or of an idealizing biographer.

Meanwhile, continues the narrative (v. 27.), the disciples of Jesus returned from the city with provisions, and marvelled that he talked with a woman, contrary to rabbinical rule.§ While the woman, excited by the last disclosure of Jesus, hastens homeward to invite her fellow-citizens to come and behold the Messiah-like stranger, the disciples entreat him to partake of the food they have procured; he answers, *I have meat to eat that ye know not of* (v. 32). They, misunderstanding his words, imagine that some person has supplied him with food in their absence: one of those carnal interpretations

---

* Comp. Bretschneider, ut sup. S. 49 f.   † Homil. ii. 6. comp. iii. 12.   ‡ Schöttgen, horæ, ii. p. 3, 971 f.   § Lightfoot, p. 1002.

of expressions intended spiritually by Jesus, which are of perpetual recurrence in the fourth gospel, and are therefore suspicious. Then follows a discourse on sowing and reaping (v. 35 ff.), which, compared with v. 37., can only mean that what Jesus has sown, the disciples will reap.* We admit that this is susceptible of the general interpretation, that the germ of the kingdom of God, which blossomed and bore fruit under the cultivation of the apostles, was first deposited in the world by Jesus : but it cannot be denied that a special application is also intended. Jesus foresees that the woman, who is hastening towards the city, will procure him an opportunity of sowing the seed of the gospel in Samaria, and he promises the disciples that they at a future time shall reap the fruits of his labours. Who is not here reminded of the propagation of Christianity in Samaria by Philip and the apostles, as narrated in the Acts ?† That, even abstracting all supernaturalism from our idea of the person of Jesus, he might have foreseen this progress of his cause in Samaria from his knowledge of its inhabitants, is not to be denied : but as the above figurative prediction forms part of a whole more than improbable in an historical point of view, it is equally liable to suspicion, especially as it is easy to show how it might originate without any foundation in fact. According to the prevalent tradition of the early church, as recorded in the synoptical gospels, Jesus laboured personally in Galilee, Judea, and Perea only,—not in Samaria, which, however, as we learn from the Acts, embraced the gospel at no remote period from his death. How natural the tendency to perfect the agency of Jesus, by representing him to have sown the heavenly seed in Samaria, thus extending his ministry through all parts of Palestine ; to limit the glory of the apostles and other teachers to that of being the mere reapers of the harvest in Samaria ; and to put this distinction, on a suitable occasion, into the mouth of Jesus !

The result, then, of our examination of John's Samaritan narrative is, that we cannot receive it as a real history : and the impression which it leaves as a whole tends to the same conclusion. Since Heracleon and Origen,‡ the more ancient commentators have seldom refrained from giving the interview of Jesus with the woman of Samaria an allegorical interpretation, on the ground that the entire scene has a legendary and poetic colouring. Jesus is seated at a well,—that idyllic locality with which the old Hebrew legend associates so many critical incidents : at the identical well, moreover, which a tradition, founded on Gen. xxxiii. 19 ; xlviii. 22 ; Josh. xxiv. 32, reported to have been given by Jacob to his son Joseph : hence the spot, in addition to its idyllic interest, has the more decided consecration of national and patriarchal recollections, and is all the more worthy of being trodden by the Messiah. At the well Jesus meets with a woman who has come out to draw water, just

* Lücke, 1, S. 512.   † Lücke, S. 510, note. Bretschneider, S. 52.   ‡ Comm. in Joan, tom. 13.

as, in the Old Testament, the expectant Eliezer encounters Rebekah with her pitcher, and as Jacob meets with Rachel, the destined ancestress of Israel, or Moses with his future wife. Jesus begs of the woman to let him drink; so does Eliezer of Rebekah; after Jesus has made himself known to the woman as the Messiah, she runs back to the city, and fetches her neighbours: so Rebekah, after Eliezer has announced himself as Abraham's steward, and Rachel, after she has discovered that Jacob is her kinsman, hasten homeward to call their friends to welcome the honoured guest. It is, certainly, not one blameless as those early mothers in Israel, whom Jesus here encounters; for this woman came forth as the representative of an impure people, who had been faithless to their marriage bond with Jehovah, and were then living in the practice of a false worship; while her good-will, her deficient moral strength, and her obtuseness in spiritual things, perfectly typify the actual state of the Samaritans. Thus, the interview of Jesus with the woman of Samaria, is only a poetical representation of his ministry among the Samaritans narrated in the sequel; and this is itself a legendary prelude to the propagation of the gospel in Samaria after the death of Jesus.

Renouncing the event in question as unhistorical, we know nothing of any connexion formed by Jesus with the Samaritans, and there remain as indications of his views regarding them, only his favourable notice of an individual from among them, (Luke xvii. 16.); his unpropitious reception in one of their villages (Luke ix. 53.); the prohibition with respect to them, addressed to his disciples (Matt. x. 5.); the eulogistic parable, (Luke x. 30. ff.); and his valedictory command, that the gospel should be preached in Samaria (Acts i. 8). This express command being subsequent to the resurrection of Jesus, its reality must remain problematical for us until we have examined the evidence for that capital fact; and it is to be questioned whether without it, and notwithstanding the alleged prohibition, the unhesitating conduct of the apostles, Acts viii., can be explained. Are we then to suppose on the part of the apostolic history, a cancelling of hesitations and deliberations that really occurred; or on the part of Matthew, an unwarranted ascription of national bigotry to Jesus; or, finally, on the part of Jesus, a progressive enlargement of view?

CHAPTER V.

THE DISCIPLES OF JESUS.

---

§ 70. CALLING OF THE FIRST COMPANIONS OF JESUS—DIFFERENCE
BETWEEN THE EVANGELISTS AND THE FOURTH.

THE first two evangelists agree in stating that Jesus, when walking by the sea of Galilee, called, first, the two brothers Andrew and
Peter, and immediately after, James and John, to forsake their fishing nets, and to follow him (Matt. iv. 18—22; Mark i. 16—20).
The fourth evangelist also narrates (i. 35—51,) how the first disciples came to attach themselves to Jesus, and among them we find
Peter and Andrew, and, in all probability, John, for it is generally
agreed that the nameless companion of Andrew was that ultimately
favourite apostle. James is absent from this account, and instead
of his vocation, we have that of Philip and Nathanael. But even
when the persons are the same, all the particulars of their meeting
with Jesus are variously detailed. In the two synoptical gospels,
the scene is the coast of the Galilean sea: in the fourth, Andrew,
Peter, and their anonymous friend, unite themselves to Jesus in the
vicinity of the Jordan; Philip and Nathanael, on the way from
thence into Galilee. In the former, again, Jesus in two instances
calls a pair of brothers: in the latter, it is first Andrew and his companion, then Peter, and anon Philip and Nathanael, who meet with
Jesus. But the most important difference is this: while, in Matthew and Mark, the brethren are called from their fishing immediately by Jesus; in John, nothing more is said of the respective situations of those who were summoned, than that they *come*, and *are
found*, and Jesus himself calls only Philip; Andrew and his nameless companion being directed to him by the Baptist, Peter brought
by Andrew, and Nathanael by Philip.

Thus the two narratives appear to refer to separate events; and
if it be asked which of those events was prior to the other, we must
reply that John seems to assign the earlier date to his incidents, for
he represents them as taking place before the return of Jesus from
the scene of his baptism into Galilee; while the synoptists place
theirs after that journey, especially if, according to a calculation often adopted, we regard the return into Galilee, which they make so
important an epoch, as being that from the first passover, not from
the baptism. It is evident, too, from the intrinsic nature of the occurrences reported by the fourth evangelist, that they could not have

succeeded those in Matthew and Mark. For if, as these writers tell us, Andrew and John had already followed Jesus, they could not again be in the train of the Baptist, as we see them in the fourth gospel, nor would it have been necessary for that teacher to have directed their attention to Jesus; neither if Peter had already been called by Jesus himself to become a fisher of men, was there any need for his brother Andrew to bring him to his already elected master. Nevertheless, expositors with one voice declare that the two narratives are equally adapted to precede, or follow, each other. The fourth gospel, say they,* recounts merely the first introduction of these men to Jesus; they did not forthwith become his constant followers, but were first installed by Jesus in their proper discipleship on the occasion which the synoptists have preserved.

Let us test the justness of their view. In the synoptical narrative Jesus says to his future disciples, *Come after me*, δεῦτε ὀπίσω μου, and the result is that they follow him (ἠκολούθησαν αὐτῷ). If we understand from this that the disciples thenceforth constantly followed Jesus, how can we give a different interpretation to the similar expression in the fourth gospel, *Follow me*, ἀκολούθει μοι? It is therefore a laudable consistency in Paulus, to see, in both instances, merely an invitation to a temporary companionship during a walk in the immediate neighbourhood.† But this interpretation is incompatible with the synoptical history. How could Peter, at a later period, say so emphatically to Jesus, *We have left all, and followed thee: what shall we have therefore?*—how could Jesus promise to him and to every one who had forsaken houses, &c. a hundredfold recompense (Matt. xix. 27 ff.), if this forsaking and following had been so transient and interrupted? From these considerations alone it is probable that the ἀκολούθει μοι in John also denotes the commencement of a permanent connexion; but there are besides the plainest indications that this is the case in the context to the narrative. Precisely as in the synoptical gospels, Jesus appears alone before the scene of the vocation, but after this on every fit occasion the attendance of his disciples is mentioned: so in the fourth gospel, from the time of the occurrence in question, the previously solitary Jesus appears in the company of his disciples (ii. 2; xii. 17; iii. 22; iv. 8, 27, &c.). To say that these disciples, acquired in Peraea, again dispersed themselves after the return of Jesus into Galilee,‡ is to do violence to the gospels out of harmonistic zeal. But even supposing such a dispersion, they could not, in the short time which it is possible to allow for their separation from Jesus, have become so completely strangers to him, that he would have been obliged to re-open an acquaintance with them after the manner narrated by the synoptical writers. Still less probable is it that Jesus, after having distinguished Simon in the most individual

---

* Kuinöl, Comm. in Matth. S. 100; Lücke, Comm. zum Joh. 1, S. 388; Olshausen biblischer Comm., 1, S. 197; Hase, Leben Jesu, § 56, 61. † Leben Jesu, 1, a. S. 212.
‡ Paulus, Leben Jesu, 1, a, S. 213; Sieffert, über den Ursprung u. s. f., S. 72.

manner by the surname Cephas on their first interview, would on a later occasion address to him the summons to be a *fisher of men*—a destination which was common to all the disciples.

The rationalistic commentators perceive a special advantage in their position of the two narratives. It accounts, say they, for what must otherwise be in the highest degree surprising, namely, that Jesus merely in passing, and at the first glance, should choose four fishermen for his disciples, and that among them he should have alighted on the two most distinguished apostles; that, moreover, these four men, actively employed in their business, should leave it on the instant of their receiving an enigmatical summons from a man with whom they had no intimate acquaintance, and devote themselves to him as his followers. Now on comparing the fourth gospel, we see that Jesus had learned to know these men long before, and that they, too, had had demonstration of his excellence, whence it is easy to understand the felicity of his choice, and their readiness to follow him. But this apparent advantage is the condemning circumstance in the above position; for nothing can more directly counteract the intention of the first two evangelists, than to suppose a previous acquaintance between Jesus and the brethren whom he summons to follow him. In both gospels, great stress is laid on the fact that they *immediately εὐθέως* left their nets, resolved to follow Jesus: the writers must therefore have deemed this something extraordinary, which it certainly was not, if these men had previously been in his train. In relation to Jesus also, the point of the narrative lies in his having, with a prophetic spirit, and at the first glance, selected the right individuals, *not needing that any should testify of man, for he knew what was in man*, according to John ii. 25, and thus presenting one of the characteristics which the Jews expected in their Messiah.

If, then, each of these two diverse narratives professes to describe the first acquaintance of Jesus with his most distinguished disciples, it follows that one only can be correct, while the other is necessarily erroneous.* It is our task to inquire which has the more intrinsic proofs of veracity. With respect to the synoptical representation, we share the difficulty which is felt by Paulus, in regarding it as a true account of the first interview between the parties. A penetration into the character of men at the first glance, such as is here supposed to have been evinced by Jesus, transcends all that is naturally possible to the most fortunate and practised knowledge of mankind. The nature of man is only revealed by his words and actions: the gift of discerning it without these means, belongs to the visionary, or to that species of intuition for which the rabbinical designation of this messianic attribute, *odorando judicare*,† is not at all too monstrous. Scarcely less improbable is the unhesitating obedience of the disciples, for Jesus had not yet acquired his Galilean fame: and to account for this promptitude we must suppose

* See Fritzsche, in Matt. p. 189. † Schottgen, horæ, ii. p. 372.

that the voice and will of Jesus had a coercive influence over minds, independently of preparation and motives,* which would be to complete the incredibility of the narrative by adding a magical trait to the visionary one already exposed.

If these negative arguments are deemed strong enough to annul the pretensions of the narrative to an historical character, the alternative is to assign to it a mythical interpretation, if we can show on positive grounds that it might have been constructed in a traditional manner without historical foundation. As adequate inducements to the formation of such a legend, we may point, not only to the above cited Jewish notion of the Messiah as the searcher of hearts, but to a specific type of this vocation of the apostles, contained in the narrative (1 Kings xix. 19—21.) of the mode in which the prophet Elijah summoned Elisha to become his follower. Here Jesus calls the brethren from their nets and their fishing; there the prophet calls his future disciple from the oxen and the plough; in both cases there is a transition from simple, physical labour, to the highest spiritual office—a contrast which, as is exemplified in the Roman history, tradition is apt either to cherish or to create. Further, the fishermen, at the call of Jesus, forsake their nets and follow him; so Elisha, when Elijah cast his mantle over him, *left the oxen, and ran after Elijah.* This is one apparent divergency, which is a yet more striking proof of the relation between the two narratives, than is their general similarity. The prophet's disciple entreated that before he attached himself entirely to Elijah, he might be permitted to take leave of his father and mother; and the prophet does not hesitate to grant him this request, on the understood condition that Elisha should return to him. Similar petitions are offered to Jesus (Luke ix. 59 ff.; Matt. viii. 21 f.) by some whom he had called, or who had volunteered to follow him; but Jesus does not accede to these requests: on the contrary, he enjoins the one who wished previously to bury his father, to enter on his discipleship without delay; and the other, who had begged permission to bid farewell to his friends, he at once dismisses as unfit for the kingdom of God. In strong contrast with the divided spirit manifested by these feeble proselytes, it is said of the apostles, that they, without asking any delay, immediately forsook their occupation, and, in the case of James and John, their father. Could any thing betray more clearly than this one feature, that the narrative is an embellished imitation of that in the Old Testament, intended to show that Jesus, in his character of Messiah, exacted a more decided adhesion, accompanied with greater sacrifices, than Elijah, in his character of Prophet merely, required or was authorized to require?† The historical germ of the narrative may be this: several of the most eminent disciples of Jesus, particularly Peter, dwelling on the shores of the sea of Galilee, had been fishermen, whence Jesus during their subsequent apostolic agency may have sometimes styled them *fishers of men.* But without doubt, their relation with Jesus was formed gradually, like other human relations, and is only elevated into a marvel through the obliviousness of tradition.

By removing the synoptical narrative we make room for that of John; but whether we are to receive it as historical, can only be decided by an examination of its matter. At the very outset, it excites no favourable prejudice, that John the Baptist is the one who directs the first two disciples to Jesus; for if there be any truth in the representation given in a former chapter of the relation between Jesus and the Baptist, some disciples of the latter might, indeed, of their own accord attach themselves to Jesus, formerly their fellow-disciple, but nothing could be farther from the intention of the Baptist than to resign his own adherents to Jesus. This particular seems indebted for its existence to the apologetic interest of the fourth gospel, which seeks to strengthen the cause of Jesus by the testimony of the Baptist. Further, that Andrew, after one evening's intercourse with Jesus, should announce him to his brother with the words, *We have found the Messiah* (i. 42.); that Philip too, immediately after his call, should speak of him in a similar manner to Nathanael (v. 46); is an improbability which I know not how to put strongly enough. We gather from the synoptical statement, which we have above decided to be trustworthy, that some time was necessary for the disciples to recognize Jesus as the Messiah, and openly confess their belief through their spokesman Peter, whose tardy discernment Jesus would have been incorrect in panegyrizing as a divine revelation, if it amounted to no more than what was communicated to him by his brother Andrew at the commencement of his discipleship. Equally unnatural is the manner in which Jesus is said to have received Simon. He accosts him with the words, *Thou art Simon, the son of Jona,*—a mode of salutation which seems, as Bengel has well remarked, to imply that Jesus had a supernatural acquaintance with the name and origin of a man previously unknown to him, analogous to his cognizance of the number of the Samaritan woman's husbands, and of Nathanael's presence under the fig-tree. Jesus then proceeds to bestow on Simon the significant surname of Cephas or Peter. If we are not inclined to degrade the speech of Jesus into buffoonery, by referring this appellation to the bodily organization of the disciple,[*] we must suppose that Jesus at the first glance, with the eye of him who knew hearts, penetrated into the inmost nature of Simon, and discovered not only his general fitness for the apostleship, but also the special, individual qualities which rendered him comparable to a rock. According to Matthew, it was not until after long intercourse with Jesus, and after he had given many manifestations of his peculiar character, that this surname was conferred on Simon, accompanied by an explanation of its meaning (xvi. 18.): evidently

* Paulus, Leben Jesu, 1, a, S. 168.

a much more natural account of the matter than that of the fourth evangelist, who makes Jesus discern at the first glance the future value of Simon to his cause, an *odorando judicare* which transcends the synoptical representation in the same ratio as the declaration. *Thou shalt be called Cephas*, presupposes a more intimate knowledge, than the proposal, *I will make you fishers of men.* Even after a more lengthened conversation with Peter, such as Lücke supposes, Jesus could not pronounce so decidedly on his character, without being a searcher of hearts, or falling under the imputation of forming too precipitate a judgment. It is indeed possible that the Christian legend, attracted by the significance of the name, may have represented Jesus as its author, while, in fact, Simon had borne it from his birth.

The entire narrative concerning Nathanael is a tissue of improbabilities. When Philip speaks to him of a Messiah from Nazareth, he makes the celebrated answer, *Can any good thing come out of Nazareth* (v. 47.)? There is no historical datum for supposing that Nazareth, when Jesus began his ministry, was the object of particular odium or contempt,* and there is every probability that the adversaries of Christianity were the first to cast an aspersion on the native city of the Messiah whom they rejected. In the time of Jesus, Nazareth was only depreciated by the Jews, as being a Galilean city— a stigma which it bore in common with many others: but in this sense it could not be despised by Nathanael, for he was himself a Galilean (xxi. 2.). The only probable explanation is that a derisive question, which, at the time of the composition of the fourth gospel, the Christians had often to hear from their opponents, was put into the mouth of a cotemporary of Jesus, that by the manner in which he was divested of his doubt, others might be induced to comply with the invitation, *to come and see.* As Nathanael approaches Jesus, the latter pronounces this judgment on his character, *Behold an Israelite indeed, in whom is no guile* (v. 48.)! Paulus is of opinion that Jesus might have previously gathered some intimations concerning Nathanael at Cana, where he had just been attending a marriage of some relations.† But if Jesus had become acquainted with Nathanael's character in a natural way, he must, in answer to the question *Whence knowest thou me?* either have reminded him of the occasion on which they had had an earlier interview, or referred to the favourable report of others. Instead of this he speaks of his knowledge that Nathanael had been tarrying under a figtree : a knowledge which from its result is evidently intended to appear supernatural. Now to use information, obtained by ordinary means, so as to induce a belief that it has been communicated supernaturally, is charlatanism, if anything deserve the name. As, however, the narrator certainly did not mean to impute such artifice to Jesus, it is undeniably his intention to ascribe to him a supernatural knowledge of Nathanael's character. As little are the words,

* Vid. Lücke, S. 389 f. † Ut sup.

When thou wast under the figtree, I saw thee, explained by the exclamation of Paulus, "How often one sees and observes a man who is unconscious of one's gaze!" Lücke and Tholuck are also of opinion, that Jesus observed Nathanael under the fig-tree in a natural manner; they add, however, the conjecture, that the latter was engaged in some occupation, such as prayer or the study of the law, which afforded Jesus a key to his character. But if Jesus meant to imply, "How can I fail to be convinced of thy virtue, having watched thee during thy earnest study of the law, and thy fervent prayer under the fig-tree?" he would not have omitted the word προσευχόμενον (*praying*), or ἀναγινώσκοντα (*reading*), for want of which we can extract no other sense from his declaration than this: "Thou mayest be assured of my power to penetrate into thy inmost soul, from the fact that I beheld thee when thou wast in a situation from which all merely human observers were excluded."

Here the whole stress is thrown not on any peculiarity in the situation of the person seen, but on the fact that Jesus saw him, whence it is necessarily inferred that he did so by no ordinary, natural, means. To imagine that Jesus possessed such a second sight, is, we grant, not a little extravagant; but for that very reason, it is the more accordant with the then existing notions of a prophet, and of the Messiah. A like power of seeing and hearing beyond the limits assigned to human organs, is attributed to Elisha in the Old Testament. When (2 Kings vi. 8, ff.) the king of Syria makes war against Israel, Elisha indicates to the king of Israel every position of the enemy's camp; and when the king of Syria expresses his suspicion that he is betrayed by deserters, he is told that the Israelitish prophet knows all the words that he, the king of Syria, speaks in his private chamber. Thus also (xxi. 32.) Elisha knows that Joram has sent out messengers to murder him. How could it be endured that the Messiah should fall short of the prophet in his powers of vision? This particular, too, enables our evangelist to form a climax, in which Jesus ascends from the penetration of one immediately present (v. 42), to that of one approaching for the first time (v. 48), and finally, to the perception of one out of the reach of human eyesight. That Jesus goes a step farther in the climax, and says, that this proof of his messianic second sight is a trifle compared with what Nathanael has yet to see,—that on him, the Son of man, the angels of God shall descend from the opened heavens (v. 51),—in nowise shows, as Paulus thinks, that there was nothing miraculous in that first proof, for there is a gradation even in miracles.

Thus in the narrative of John we stumble at every step on difficulties, in some instances greater than those with which the synoptical accounts are encumbered: hence we learn as little from the one as the other, concerning the manner in which the first disciples attached themselves to Jesus. I cannot agree with the author of the

Probabilia,* in deriving the divergency of the fourth evangelist from his predecessors, from the wish to avoid mentioning the derided fishing-trade of the most distinguished apostles ; since in chap. xxi., which Bretschneider allows to be by the same hand as the rest of the gospel, he unhesitatingly introduces the obnoxious employment. I rather surmise that the idea of their having received their decisive apostolic call while actually engaged with their fishing-nets, was not afloat in the tradition from which the fourth evangelist drew ; and that this writer formed his scenes, partly on the probably historical report that some disciples of Jesus had belonged to the school of the Baptist, and partly from the wish to represent in the most favourable light the relation between Jesus and the Baptist, and the supernatural gifts of the former.

§ 71. PETER'S DRAUGHT OF FISHES.

WE have hitherto examined only two accounts of the vocation of Peter and his companions ; there is a third given by Luke (v. 1—11.). I shall not dilate on the minor points of difference† between his narrative and that of the first two evangelists ; the essential distinction is, that in Luke the disciples do not, as in Matthew and Mark, unite themselves to Jesus on a simple invitation, but in consequence of a plentiful draught of fishes, to which Jesus has assisted Simon. If this feature be allowed to constitute Luke's narrative a separate one from that of his predecessors, we have next to inquire into its intrinsic credibility, and then to ascertain its relation to that of Matthew and Mark.

Jesus, oppressed by the throng of people on the shore of the Galilean sea, enters into a ship, that he may address them with more ease at a little distance from land. Having brought his discourse to a close, he desires Simon, the owner of the boat, to launch out into the deep, and let down his nets for a draught. Simon, although little encouraged by the poor result of the last night's fishing, declares himself willing, and is rewarded by so extraordinary a draught, that Peter and his partners, James and John (Andrew is not here mentioned), are struck with astonishment, the former even with awe, before Jesus, as a superior being. Jesus then says to Simon, *Fear not ; from henceforth thou shalt catch men*, and the issue is that the three fishermen forsake all, and follow him.

The rationalistic commentators take pains to show that what is above narrated might occur in a natural way. According to them, the astonishing consequence of letting down the net was the result of an accurate observation on the part of Jesus, assisted by a happy fortuity. Paulus‡ supposes that Jesus at first wished to launch out farther into the deep merely to escape from the crowd, and that it was not until after sailing to some distance, that, descrying a place

---

* P. 141.   † Storr, über den Zweck der evang. Gesch. und der Briefe Joh , S. 350.
‡ Exeg. Handb. 1. B. S. 449.

where the fish were abundant, he desired Peter to let down the net. But he has fallen into a twofold contradiction of the evangelical narrative. In close connexion with the command to launch out into the deep, Jesus adds, *Let down your nets for a draught* (ἐπανάγαγε εἰς τὸ βάθος, καὶ χαλάσατε τὰ δίκτυα, κ. τ. λ.), as if this were one of his objects in changing the locality ; and if he spoke thus when at a little distance only from the shore, his hope of a successful draught could not be the effect of his having observed a place abundant in fish on the main sea, which the vessel had not yet reached. Our rationalists must therefore take refuge in the opinion of the author of the Natural History of the Great Prophet of Nazareth, who says, Jesus conjectured on general grounds, that under existing circumstances (indicative probably of an approaching storm), fishing in the middle of the sea would succeed better than it had done in the night. But, proceeding from the natural point of view, how could Jesus be a better judge in this matter, than the men who had spent half their life on the sea in the employment of fishing? Certainly if the fishermen observed nothing which could give them hope of a plentiful draught, neither in a natural manner could Jesus ; and the agreement between his words and the result, must, adhering to the natural point of view, be put down wholly to the account of chance. But what senseless audacity, to promise at random a success, which, judging from the occurrences of the past night, was little likely to follow ! It is said, however, that Jesus only desires Peter to make another attempt, without giving any definite promise. But, we must rejoin, in the emphatic injunction, which Peter's remark on the inauspicious aspect of circumstances for fishing does not induce him to revoke, there is a latent promise, and the words, *Let down your nets*, &c., in the present passage, can hardly have any other meaning than that plainly expressed in the similar scene, John xxi. 6., *Cast the net on the right side of the ship, and ye shall find*. When, moreover, Peter retracts his objection in the words, *Nevertheless at thy word I will let down the net*, ἐπὶ δὲ τῷ ῥήματί σου χαλάσω τὸ δίκτυον, though ῥῆμα may be translated by *command* rather than by *promise*, in either case he implies a hope that what Jesus enjoins will not be without result. If Jesus had not intended to excite this hope, he must immediately have put an end to it, if he would not expose himself to disgrace in the event of failure : and on no account ought he to have accepted the attitude and expressions of Peter as his due, if he had only merited them by a piece of lucky advice given at a venture.

The drift of the narrative, then, obliges us to admit that the writer intended to signalize a miracle. This miracle may be viewed either as one of power, or of knowledge. If the former, we are to conceive that Jesus, by his supernatural power, caused the fish to congregate in that part of the sea where he commanded Peter to cast in his net. Now that Jesus should be able, by the immediate action of his will, to influence men, in the nature of whose minds his spir-

itual energy might find a fulcrum, may to a certain extent be conceived, without any wide deviation from psychological laws: but that
he could thus influence irrational beings, and those not isolated animals immediately present to him, but shoals of fish in the depths
of the sea, it is impossible to imagine out of the domain of magic.
Olshausen compares this operation of Jesus to that of the divine
omnipotence in the annual migrations of fish and birds:* but the
comparison is worse than lame,—it lacks all parallelism: for the
latter is an effect of the divine agency, linked in the closest manner
with all the other operations of God in external nature, with the
change of seasons, &c.: while the former, even presupposing Jesus
to be actually God, would be an isolated act, interrupting the chain
of natural phenomena: a distinction that removes any semblance of
parallelism between the two cases. Allowing the possibility of such
a miracle, (and from the supranaturalistic point of view, nothing is
in itself impossible,) did it subserve any apparent object, adequate
to determine Jesus to so extravagant a use of his miraculous powers?
Was it so important that Peter should be inspired by this incident
with a superstitious fear, not accordant with the spirit of the New
Testament? Was this the only preparation for engrafting the true
faith? or did Jesus believe that it was only by such signs that he
could win disciples? How little faith must he then have had in the
force of mind and of truth! how much too meanly must he have
estimated Peter, who, at a later period at least (John vi. 68), clung
to his society, not on account of the miracles which he beheld Jesus
perform, but for the sake of *the words of eternal life*, which came
from his lips!

Under the pressure of these difficulties, refuge may be sought in
the other supposition as the more facile one: namely, that Jesus, by
means of his superhuman knowledge, was merely aware that in a
certain place there was then to be found a multitude of fishes, and
that he communicated this information to Peter. If by this it be
meant that Jesus, through the possession of an omniscience such as
is commonly attributed to God, knew at all times, all the fish, in all
seas, rivers, and lakes; there is an end to his human consciousness.
If, however, it be merely meant that when he crossed any water he
became cognizant of its various tribes of fish, with their relative position; even this would be quite enough to encumber the space in
his mind that was due to more weighty thoughts. Lastly, if it be
meant that he knew this, not constantly and necessarily, but as
often as he wished; it is impossible to understand how, in a mind
like that of Jesus, a desire for such knowledge should arise,—how
he, whose vocation had reference to the depths of the human heart,
should be tempted to occupy himself with the fish-frequented depths
of the waters.

But before we pronounce on this narrative of Luke, we must
consider it in relation to the cognate histories in the first two synop-

* Bibl. Comm. 1, p. 283.

tical gospels. The chronological relation of the respective events is the first point. The supposition that the miraculous draught of fishes in Luke was prior to the vocation narrated by the two other evangelists, is excluded by the consideration, that the firm attachment which that miracle awakened in the disciples, would render a new call superfluous: or by the still stronger objection, that if an invitation, accompanied by a miracle, had not sufficed to ally the men to Jesus, he could hardly flatter himself that a subsequent bare summons, unsupported by any miracle, would have a better issue. The contrary chronological position presents a better climax: but why a second invitation, if the first had succeeded? For to suppose that the brethren who followed him on the first summons, again left him until the second, is to cut the knot, instead of untying it. Still more complicated is the difficulty, when we take in addition the narrative of the fourth evangelist: for what shall we think of the connexion between Jesus and his disciples, if it began in the manner described by John: if, after this, the disciples having from some unknown cause separated from their master, he again called them, as if nothing of the kind had before occurred, on the shore of the Galilean sea; and if, this invitation also producing no permanent adherence, he for the third time summoned them to follow him, fortifying this final experiment by a miracle? The entire drift of Luke's narrative is such as to exclude, rather than to imply, any earlier and more intimate relation between Jesus and his ultimate disciples. For the indifferent mention of two ships on the shore, whose owners were gone out of them to wash their nets, Simon being unnamed until Jesus chooses to avail himself of his boat, seems, as Schleiermacher has convincingly shewn,[*] to convey the idea that the two parties were entire strangers to each other, and that these incidents were preparatory to a relation yet to be formed, not indicative of one already existing: so that the healing of Peter's mother-in-law, previously recounted by Luke, either occurred, like many other cures of Jesus, without producing any intimate connexion, or has too early a date assigned to it by that evangelist. The latter conjecture is supported by the fact that Matthew places the miracle later.

Thus, it fares with the narrative of Luke, when viewed in relation to that of Matthew and Mark, as it did with that of John, when placed in the same light; neither will bear the other to precede, or to follow it,—in short, they exclude each other.[†] Which then is the correct narrative? Schleiermacher prefers that of the evangelist on whom he has commented, because it is more particular:[‡] and Sieffert[§] has recently asserted with great emphasis, that no one has ever yet doubted the superiority of Luke's narrative, as a faithful picture of the entire occurrence, the number of its special dramatic, and intrinsically authenticated details, advantageously

* Ueber den Lukas, S. 70.   † This with the legendary character of both narratives, is acknowledged by De Wette, exeg. Handb. 1, 1, S. 17, 1, 2, S. 38 f.   ‡ Neander is of the same opinion, L. J. S. 249 f.   § Ueber den Ursprung des ersten kan. Ev. S. 73.

distinguishing it from the account in the first (and second) gospel,
which by its omission of the critical incident, the turning point in
the narrative (the draught of fishes), is characterized as the recital
of one who was not an eye-witness. I have already presented myself elsewhere* to this critic, as one hardly enough to express the
doubt of which he denies the existence, and I here repeat the
question : supposing one only of the two narratives to have been
modified by oral tradition, which alternative is more in accordance
with the nature of that means of transmission,—that the tangible
fact of a draught of fishes should evaporate into a mere saying respecting fishers of men, or that this figurative expression should be
condensed into a literal history? The answer to this question cannot be dubious ; for when was it in the nature of the legend to
spiritualize ? to change the real, such as the story of a miracle, into
the ideal, such as a mere verbal image ? The stage of human culture to which the legend belongs, and the mental faculty in which
it originates, demand that it should give a stable body to fleeting
thought, that it should counteract the ambiguity and changeableness of words, by affixing them to the permanent and universally
understood symbol of action.

It is easy to show how, out of the expression preserved by the
first evangelist, the miraculous story of the third might be formed.
If Jesus, in allusion to the former occupation of some of his apostles,
had called them fishers of men ; if he had compared the kingdom
of heaven to a net cast into the sea, in which all kinds of fish were
taken (Matt. xiii. 47) ; it was but a following out of these ideas to
represent the apostles as those who, at the word of Jesus, cast out
the net, and gathered in the miraculous multitude of fishes.† If we
add to this, that the ancient legend was fond of occupying its won-
der-workers with affairs of fishing, as we see in the story related
of Pythagoras by Jamblichus and Porphyry ;‡ it will no longer appear improbable, that Peter's miraculous draught of fishes is but
the expression about the fishers of men, transmuted into the history of a miracle, and this view will at once set us free from all the
difficulties that attend the natural, as well as the supranatural, interpretation of the narrative.

A similar miraculous draught of fishes is recorded in the appendix to the fourth gospel, as having occurred after the resurrection
(ch. xxi.). Here again Peter is fishing on the Galilean sea, in company with the sons of Zebedee and some other disciples, and again
he has been toiling all night, and has taken nothing.§ Early in the

morning, Jesus comes to the shore, and asks, without their recognizing him, if they have any meat? On their answering in the negative, he directs them to cast the net on the right side of the ship, whereupon they have an extremely rich draught, and are led by this sign to recognize Jesus. That this history is distinct from the one given by Luke, is, from its great similarity, scarcely conceivable: the same narrative has doubtless been placed by tradition in different periods of the life of Jesus.*

Let us now compare these three fishing histories,—the two narrated of Jesus, and that narrated of Pythagoras,—and their mythical character will be obvious. That which, in Luke, is indubitably intended as a miracle of power, is, in the history of Jamblichus, a miracle of knowledge; for Pythagoras merely tells in a supernatural manner the number of fish already caught by natural means. The narrative of John holds a middle place, for in it also the number of the fish (153) plays a part: but instead of being predetermined by the worker of the miracle, it is simply stated by the narrator. One legendary feature common to all the three narratives, is the manner in which the multitude and weight of the fishes are described: especially as this sameness of manner accompanies a diversity in particulars. According to Luke, the multitude is so great that the net is broken, one ship will not hold them, and after they have been divided between the two vessels, both threaten to sink. In the view of the tradition given in the fourth gospel, it was not calculated to magnify the power of the miraculous agent, that the net which he had so marvellously filled should break; but as here also the aim is to exalt the miracle by celebrating the number and weight of the fishes, they are said to be μεγάλοι (*great*), and it is added that the men *were not able to draw the net for the multitude of fishes:* instead, however, of lapsing out of the miraculous into the common by the breaking of the net, a second miracle is ingeniously made,—that *for all there were so many, yet was not the net broken.* Jamblichus presents a further wonder (the only one he has, besides the knowledge of Pythagoras as to the number of the fish): namely, that while the fish were being counted, a process that must have required a considerable time, not one of them died. If there be a mind that, not perceiving in the narratives we have compared the finger-marks of tradition, and hence the legendary character of these evangelical anecdotes, still leans to the historical interpretation, whether natural or supernatural; that mind must be alike ignorant of the true character both of legend and of history, of the natural and the supernatural.

---

* Comp. d. Welte, exeg. Handb., 1, 3, S. 213.

§ 72. CALLING OF MATTHEW—CONNEXION OF JESUS WITH THE PUBLICANS.

THE first gospel (ix. 9 ff.) tells of *a man named Matthew*, to whom, when sitting at the receipt of custom, Jesus said, *Follow me*. Instead of Matthew, the second and third gospels have *Levi*, and Mark adds that he was *the son of Alpheus* (Mark ii. 14 ff. ; Luke v. 27 ff.). At the call of Jesus, Luke says that he left all ; Matthew merely states, that he followed Jesus and prepared a meal, of which many publicans and sinners partook, to the great scandal of the Pharisees.

From the difference of the names it has been conjectured that the evangelists refer to two different events ;* but this difference of the name is more than counterbalanced by the similarity of the circumstances. In all the three cases the call of the publican is preceded and followed by the same occurrences ; the subject of the narrative is in the same situation ; Jesus addresses him in the same words ; and the issue is the same.† Hence the opinion is pretty general, that the three synoptists have in this instance detailed only one event. But did they also understand only one person under different names, and was that person the apostle Matthew ?

This is commonly represented as conceivable on the supposition that Levi was the proper name of the individual, and Matthew merely a surname ;‡ or that after he had attached himself to Jesus, he exchanged the former for the latter.§ To substantiate such an opinion, there should be some indication that the evangelists who name the chosen publican Levi, intend under that designation no other than the Matthew mentioned in their catalogues of the apostles (Mark iii, 18 ; Luke vi. 15 ; Acts i. 13.). On the contrary, in these catalogues, where many surnames and double names occur, not only do they omit the name of Levi as the earlier or more proper appellation of Matthew, but they leave him undistinguished by the epithet, ὁ τελώνης (*the publican*), added by the first evangelist in his catalogue (x. 3.) ; thus proving that they do not consider the apostle Matthew to be identical with the Levi summoned from the receipt of custom.‖

If then the evangelists describe the vocation of two different men in a precisely similar way, it is improbable that there is accuracy on both sides, since an event could hardly be repeated in its minute particulars. One of the narratives, therefore, is in error ; and the burthen has been thrown on the first evangelist, because he places the calling of Matthew considerably after the sermon on the mount ; while according to Luke (vi. 13. ff.), all the twelve had been chosen before that discourse was delivered.¶ But this would only

---

* Vid. Kuinöl, in Matth. p. 255. † Sieffert, ut sup. p. 55. ‡ Kuinöl, ut sup. Paulus, exeg. Handb., I. B. S. 513. L. J., 1, a, 240. § Bertholdt, Einleitung 3, S. 1255 f. Fritzsche, S. 310. ‖ Sieffert, S. 56 ; De Wette, exeg. Handb., 1, 1, S. 91. ¶ Sieffert, S. 60.

prove, at the most, that the first gospel gives a wrong position to the history; not that it narrates that history incorrectly. It is therefore unjust to impute special difficulties to the narrative of the first evangelist: neither are such to be found in that of Mark and Luke, unless it be thought an inconsistency in the latter to attribute a *forsaking of all*, καταλιπὼν ἅπαντα, to one whom he does not include among the constant followers of Jesus.* The only question is, do they not labour under a common difficulty, sufficient to stamp both accounts as unhistorical?

The close analogy between this call and that of the two pairs of brethren, must excite attention. They were summoned from their nets; he from the custom-house; as in their case, so here, nothing further is needed than a simple *Follow me;* and this call of the Messiah has so irresistible a power over the mind of the called, that the publican, like the fishermen, *leaves all, and follows him.* It is not to be denied, that as Jesus had been for a considerable time exercising his ministry in that country, Matthew must have long known him; and this is the argument with which Fritzsche repels the accusation of Julian and Porphyry, who maintain that Matthew here shows himself rash and inconsiderate. But the longer Jesus had observed him, the more easily might he have found opportunity for drawing him gradually and quietly into his train, instead of hurrying him in so tumultuary a manner from the midst of his business. Paulus indeed thinks that no call to discipleship, no sudden forsaking of a previous occupation, is here intended, but that Jesus having brought his teaching to a close, merely signified to the friend who had given him an invitation to dinner, that he was now ready to go home with him, and sit down to table.† But the meal appears, especially in Luke, to be the consequence, and not the cause, of the summons; moreover, a modest guest would say to the host who had invited him, *I will follow thee,* ἀκολουθήσω σοι, not *Follow me,* ἀκολούθει μοι; and in fine, this interpretation renders the whole anecdote so trivial, that it would have been better omitted.‡ Hence the abruptness and impetuosity of the scene return upon us, and we are compelled to pronounce that such is not the course of real life, nor the procedure of a man who, like Jesus, respects the laws and formalities of human society; it is the procedure of legend and poetry, which love contrasts and effective scenes, which aim to give a graphic conception of a man's exit from an old sphere of life, and his entrance into a new one, by representing him as at once discarding the implements of his former trade, leaving the scene of his daily business, and straightway commencing a new life. The historical germ of the story may be, that Jesus actually had publicans among his disciples, and possibly that Matthew was one. These men had truly left the custom-house to fol-

* De Wette, ut sup.
† Exeg. Handb. 1. B. S. 510. L. J. 1, a, 210
‡ Schleiermacher, über den Lukas, S 76.

low Jesus; but only in the figurative sense of his concise expression, not in the literal one depicted by the legend.

It is not less astonishing that the publican should have a great feast in readiness for Jesus immediately after his call. For that this feast was not prepared until the following day,[*] is directly opposed to the narratives, the two first especially. But it is entirely in the tone of the legend to demonstrate the joy of the publican, and the condescension of Jesus, and to create an occasion for the reproaches cast on the latter on account of his intimacy with sinners, by inventing a great feast, given to the publicans at the house of their late associate immediately after his call.

Another circumstance connected with this narrative merits particular attention. According to the common opinion concerning the author of the first gospel, Matthew therein narrates his own call. We may consider it granted that there are no positive indications of this in the narrative; but it is not so clear that there are no negative indications which render it impossible or improbable. That the evangelist does not here speak in the first person, nor when describing events in which he had a share in the first person plural, like the author of the Acts of the Apostles, proves nothing; for Josephus and other historians not less classical, write of themselves in the third person, and the *we* of the pseudo-Matthew in the Ebionite gospel has a very suspicious sound. The use of the expression, ἄνθρωπον, Ματθαῖον λεγόμενον, which the Manicheans made an objection,[†] as they did the above-mentioned circumstance, is not without a precedent in the writings of Xenophon, who in his Anabasis introduces himself as *Xenophon, a certain Athenian*, Ξενοφῶν τις Ἀθηναῖος.[‡] The Greek, however, did not fall into this style from absorption in his subject, nor from unaffected freedom from egotism,—causes which Olshausen supposes in the evangelist; but either from a wish not to pass for the author, as an old tradition states,[§] or from considerations of taste, neither of which motives will be attributed to Matthew. Whether we are therefore to consider that expression as a sign that the author of the first gospel was not Matthew, may be difficult to decide:[‖] but it is certain that this history of the publican's call is throughout less clearly narrated in that gospel than in the third. In the former, we are at a loss to understand why it is abruptly said that Jesus sat at meat in the house, if the evangelist were himself the hospitable publican, since it would then seem most natural for him to let his joy on account of his call appear in the narrative, by telling as Luke does, that he immediately made a great feast in his house. To say that he withheld this from modesty, is to invest a rude Galilean of that age with the affectation belonging to the most refined self-consciousness of modern days.

To this feast at the publican's, of which many of the same ob-

* Gratz, Comm. zum Matth. 1, S. 470. † Augustin, c. Faust. Manich. xvii. 1.
‡ iii. i. 4. § Plutarch. de gloria Atheniens., at the beginning. ‖ Schulz, Ueber das Abendmahl, S. 308.

noxious class partook, the evangelists annex the reproaches cast at the disciples by the Pharisees and Scribes, because their master ate with publicans and sinners. Jesus, being within hearing of the censure, repelled it by the well-known text on the destination of the physician for the sick, and the Son of man for sinners (Matt. ix. 11 ff. parall.). That Jesus should be frequently taunted by his pharisaical enemies with his too great predilection for the despised class of publicans (comp. Matt. xi. 19), accords fully with the nature of his position, and is therefore historical, if anything be so : the answer, too, which is here put into the mouth of Jesus, is from its pithy and concise character well adapted for literal transmission. Further, it is not improbable that the reproach in question may have been especially called forth, by the circumstance that Jesus ate with publicans and sinners, and went under their roofs. But that the cavils of his opponents should have been accompaniments of the publican's dinner, as the evangelical account leads us to infer, especially that of Mark (v. 16), is not so easily conceivable.* For as the feast was *in the house* (εν τῇ οἰκίᾳ), and as the disciples also partook of it, how could the Pharisees utter their reproaches to them, while the meal was going forward, without defiling themselves by becoming the *guests of a man that was a sinner,*—the very act which they reprehended in Jesus? (Luke xix. 7.) It will hardly be supposed that they waited outside until the feast was ended. It is difficult for Schleiermacher to maintain, even on the representation of Luke taken singly, that the evangelical narrative only implies, that the publican's feast was the cause of the Pharisees' censure, and not that they were cotemporary.† Their immediate connexion might easily originate in a legendary manner : in fact, one scarcely knows how tradition, in its process of transmuting the abstract into the concrete, could represent the general idea that the Pharisees had taken offence at the friendly intercourse of Jesus with the publicans, otherwise than thus : Jesus once feasted in a publican's house, in company with many publicans ; the Pharisees saw this, went to the disciples and expressed their censure, which Jesus also heard, and parried by a laconic answer.

After the Pharisees, Matthew makes the disciples of John approach Jesus with the question, why his disciples did not fast, as they did (v. 14 f.) : in Luke (v. 33 ff.) : it is still the Pharisees who vaunt their own fasts and those of John's disciples, as contrasted with the eating and drinking of the disciples of Jesus : Mark's account is not clear (v. 18). According to Schleiermacher, every unprejudiced person must perceive in the statement of Matthew compared with that of Luke, the confusing emendations of a second editor, who could not explain to himself how the Pharisees came to appeal to the disciples of John ; whereas, thinks Schleiermacher, the question would have been puerile in the mouth of the latter ; but

* Comp. De Wette, exeg. Handb., 1, 2, p. 131.
† Ut sup. p. 77.

it is easy to imagine that the Pharisees might avail themselves of an external resemblance to the disciples of John when opposing Jesus, who had himself received baptism of that teacher. It is certainly surprising that after the Pharisees, who were offended because Jesus ate with publicans, some disciples of John should step forth as if they had been cited for the purpose, to censure generally the unrestricted eating and drinking of Jesus and his disciples. The probable explanation is, that evangelical tradition associated the two circumstances from their intrinsic similarity, and that the first evangelist erroneously gave them the additional connexion of time and place. But the manner in which the third evangelist fuses the two particulars, appears a yet more artificial combination, and is certainly not historical, because the reply of Jesus could only be directed to John's disciples, or to friendly inquirers: to Pharisees, he would have given another and a more severe answer.*

Another narrative, which is peculiar to Luke (xix. 1—10), treats of the same relation as that concerning Matthew or Levi. When Jesus, on his last journey to the feast, passes through Jericho, a *chief among the publicans* ἀρχιτελώνης, named Zacchæus, that he might, notwithstanding his short stature, get a sight of Jesus among the crowd, climbed a tree, where Jesus observed him, and immediately held him worthy to entertain the Messiah for the night. Here, again, the favour shown to a publican excites the discontent of the more rigid spectators; and when Zacchæus has made vows of atonement and beneficence, Jesus again justifies himself, on the ground that his office had reference to sinners. The whole scene is very dramatic, and this might be deemed by some an argument for its historical character; but there are certain internal obstacles to its reception. We are not led to infer that Jesus previously knew Zacchæus, or that some one pointed him out to Jesus by name;† but, as Olshausen truly says, the knowledge of Zacchæus that Jesus here suddenly evinced, is to be referred to his power of discerning what was in men without the aid of testimony. We have before decided that this power is a legendary attribute; hence the above particular, at least, cannot be historical, and the narrative is possibly a variation on the same theme as that treated of in connexion with the account of Matthew's call, namely, the friendly relation of Jesus to the publicans.

§ 73.   THE TWELVE APOSTLES.

THE men whose vocation we have been considering, namely, the sons of Jonas and of Zebedee, with Philip and Matthew (Nathanael alone being excepted), form the half of that narrow circle of disciples which appears throughout the New Testament under the name of *the twelve,* οἱ δώδεκα *the twelve disciples* or *apostles,* οἱ δώδεκα μαθή-ται or ἀπόστολοι. The fundamental idea of the New Testament writers concerning the twelve, is that Jesus himself chose them (Mark iii. 13 f.; Luke vi. 13; John vi. 70; xv. 16.). Matthew does not give us the history of the choice of all the twelve, but he tacitly presupposes it by introducing them as a college already instituted (x. i.). Luke, on the contrary, narrates how, after a night spent on the mountain in vigils and prayer, Jesus selected twelve from the more extensive circle of his adherents, and then descended with them to the plain, to deliver what is called the Sermon on the Mount (vi. 12.). Mark also tells us in the same connexion, that Jesus when on a mountain made a voluntary choice of twelve from the mass of his disciples (iii. 13.). According to Luke, Jesus chose the twelve immediately before he delivered the sermon on the mount, and apparently with reference to it: but there is no discoverable motive which can explain this mode of associating the two events, for the discourse was not specially addressed to the apostles,* neither had they any office to execute during its delivery. Mark's representation, with the exception of the vague tradition from which he sets out, that Jesus chose the twelve, seems to have been wrought out of his own imagination, and furnishes no distinct notion of the occasion and manner of the choice.† Matthew has adopted the best method in merely presupposing, without describing, the particular vocation of the apostles; and John pursues the same plan, beginning (vi. 67.) to speak of *the twelve,* without any previous notice of their appointment.

Strictly speaking, therefore, it is merely presupposed in the gospels, that Jesus himself fixed the number of the apostles. Is this presupposition correct? There certainly is little doubt that this number was fixed during the lifetime of Jesus; for not only does the author of the Acts represent the twelve as so compact a body immediately after the ascension of their master, that they think it incumbent on them to fill up the breach made by the apostacy of Judas by the election of a new member (i. 15 ff.); but the apostle Paul also notices an appearance of the risen Jesus, specially to *the twelve* (1 Cor. xv. 5.). Schleiermacher, however, doubts whether Jesus himself chose the twelve, and he thinks it more probable that the peculiar relation ultimately borne to him by twelve from amongst his disciples, gradually and spontaneously formed itself.‡ We have, indeed, no warrant for supposing that the appointment of the twelve was a single solemn act; on the contrary, the gospels explicitly narrate, that six of them were called singly, or by pairs, and on separate occasions; but it is still a question whether the number twelve was not determined by Jesus, and whether he did not willingly abide by it as an expedient for checking the multiplication of his familiar companions. The number is the less likely to have been fortuitous,

* Schleiermacher, über den Lukas, S. 85.
† Ib.   ‡ Ut sup. S. 88.

the more significant it is, and the more evident the inducements to its choice by Jesus. He himself, in promising the disciples (Matt. xix. 28.) *that they shall sit on twelve thrones, judging the twelve tribes of Israel*, gives their number a relation to that of the tribes of his people; and it was the opinion of the highest Christian antiquity that this relation determined his choice.[*] If he and his disciples were primarily sent to the *lost sheep of the house of Israel* (Matt. x. 6; xv. 24), it might seem appropriate that the number of the shepherds should correspond to that of the shepherdless tribes (Matth. ix. 36.).

The destination of the twelve is only generally intimated in John (xv. 16.); in Mark, on the contrary, it is particularly, and without doubt accurately, stated. *He ordained twelve*, it is here said, *that they should be with him*, that is, that he might not be without companionship, aid, and attendance on his journeys; and accordingly we find them helpful to him in procuring lodgings (Luke ix. 52; Matt. xxvi. 17 f.), food (John iv. 8.), and other travelling requisites (Matt. xxi. 1 ff.); but above all they were in his society to become *scribes well instructed unto the kingdom of heaven* (Matt. xiii. 52.). To this end they had the opportunity of being present at most of the discourses of Jesus, and even of obtaining private elucidations of their meaning (Matt. xiii. 10 ff. 36 ff.); of purifying their minds by his severe but friendly discipline (Matt. viii. 26; xvi. 23; xviii. 1 ff. 21 ff.; Luke ix. 50, 55 f.; John xiii. 12 ff. &c.), and of elevating their souls by the contemplation of his example (John xiv. 19.). Another motive of Jesus in choosing the twelve, was according to Mark, *that he might send them forth to preach*, that is, to preach the kingdom of heaven during his life, according to the immediate meaning of Mark; but the promulgation of his cause after his death, must be supposed as an additional object on the part of Jesus. (Mark proceeds to enumerate the powers of healing and of casting out devils; but on these points we cannot dilate until we reach a future stage of our inquiry.)

It was this latter destination that won for them the distinguished name of *apostles*, ἀπόστολοι (Matt. x. 2; Mark vi. 30; Luke vii. 13. &c.). It has been doubted whether Jesus himself conferred this name on the twelve, according to Luke vi. 13, and it has been suggested that it was not given them until later, *ex eventu*.[†] But that Jesus should have called them his envoys cannot be improbable, if he really sent them on a journey to announce the approaching kingdom of the Messiah. We grant that it is possible to regard this journey as an event transposed from the period after the death of Jesus to his lifetime, in order that a sort of rehearsal of the subsequent mission of the apostles might pass under the eye of Jesus; but as it is not improbable that Jesus, perhaps even before he had a full conviction of his own Messiahship, sent out messengers to an-

[*] Ep. Barnab. 8, and the Gospel of the Ebionites ap. Epiphanius, hær. xxx. 13.
[†] Schleiermacher, ut sup. S. 87.

nounce the Messiah's kingdom, we are not warranted to urge such a doubt.

John knows nothing of this mission, recorded by the synoptists. On the other hand, they are ignorant of a circumstance alleged by John, namely, that the disciples baptized during the life of Jesus (iv. 2.). According to the synoptical evangelists, it was not until after the resurrection, that Jesus gave his disciples authority to baptize (Matt. xxviii. 19. parall.). As, however, the rite of baptism was introduced by John, and we have reason to believe that Jesus, for a time, made that teacher his model, it is highly probable that he and his disciples also practised baptism, and hence that the positive statement of the fourth gospel is correct. But the negative statement that *Jesus himself baptized not* (iv. 2.), has the appearance of an after-thought, intended to correct the import of the previous passages (iii. 22 ; iv. 1.), and is most probably to be accounted for by the tendency of the fourth gospel to exalt Jesus above the Baptist, and by a corresponding dread of making Jesus exercise the function of the mere forerunner. The question whether Jesus did not baptize at least the apostles, afterwards occasioned much demur in the church.

With the exception of the mission mentioned above, the gospels speak of no important separation between Jesus and his twelve disciples, for there is nothing certain to be gathered from the resumption of their business after his death (John xxi. 2 ff.). No one could detect in our gospels any indications of a repeated interruption to the intercourse of Jesus with his disciples, but theologians, whose harmonistic zeal wished to find room for a second and third vocation; or expositors, who, in their unwearied application to details, cast about for a means of subsistence for so many indigent men, and thought is necessary to suppose that they were occasionally provided for by a return to their secular labours. As to the subsistence of Jesus and his disciples, we have sufficient sources for it in the hospitality of the East, which, among the Jews, was especially available to the rabbins ; in the companionship of rich women *who ministered unto him of their substance* (Luke viii. 2 f.) : and finally in the γλωσσόκομον, mentioned, it is true, only by the fourth evangelist (xii. 6, xiii. 29), which was ample enough to furnish assistance to the poor, as well as to supply the wants of the society, and in which, it is probable, presents from wealthy friends of Jesus were deposited. They who do not hold these means adequate without the labour of the disciples, or who think, on more general grounds, that the total renunciation of their secular employment on the part of the twelve, is improbable, must not try to force their opinion on the evangelists, who by the stress which they lay on the expression of the apostles, *we have left all* (Matt. xix. 27 ff.), plainly intimate the opposite view.

We gather, as to the rank of the twelve disciples of Jesus, that they all belonged to the lower class: four, or perhaps more (John xxi. 2,) were fishermen, one a publican, and for the others, it is probable from the degree of cultivation they evince, and the preference always expressed by Jesus for the *poor* πτωχούς, and *the little ones,* νηπίους (Matt. v. 3; xi. 5. 25), that they were of a similar grade.

§ 74. THE TWELVE CONSIDERED INDIVIDUALLY—THE THREE OR FOUR MOST CONFIDENTIAL DISCIPLES OF JESUS.

WE have in the New Testament four catalogues of the apostles; one in each of the synoptical gospels, and one in the Acts (Matt. x. 2—4; Mark iii. 6—10; Luke vi. 14—16; Acts i. 13). Each of these four lists may be divided into three quaternions; in each corresponding quaternion the first member is the same; and in the last, the concluding member also, if we except Acts i. 13, where he is absent: but the intermediate members are differently arranged, and in the concluding quaternions there is a difference of names or of persons.)

At the head of the first quaternion in all the catalogues, and in Matthew with the prefix πρῶτος (*the first*), stands Simon Peter, the son of Jonas (Matt. xvi. 17): according to the fourth gospel, of Bethsaida (i. 45): according to the synoptists, resident in Capernaum* (Matt. viii. 14 parall.). We hear an echo of the old polemical dispute, when Protestant expositors ascribe this position to mere chance,—an assumption which is opposed by the fact that all four of the catalogues agree in giving the precedence to Peter, though they differ in other points of arrangement; or when those expositors allege, in explanation, that Peter was first called,† which, according to the fourth gospel, was not the case. That this invariable priority is indicative of a certain pre-eminence of Peter among the twelve, is evident from the part he plays elsewhere in the evangelical history. Ardent by nature, he is always beforehand with the rest of the apostles, whether in speech (Matt. xv. 15; xvi. 16. 22; xvii. 4; xviii. 21; xxvi. 33; John vi. 68), or in action (Matt. xiv. 28; xxvi. 58; John xviii 10); and if it is not seldom the case that the speech and action are faulty, and that his prompt courage quickly evaporates, as his denial shows, yet he is, according to the synoptical statement, the first who expresses a decided conviction of the Messiahship of Jesus (Matt. xvi. 16. parall.). It is true that of the eulogies and prerogatives bestowed on him on that occasion, that which is implied in his surname is the only one that remains peculiarly his; for the authority to *bind and to loose,* that is, to forbid and to permit,‡ in the newly-founded Messianic kingdom, is soon after extended to all the apostles (xviii. 18). Yet more decidedly does this pre-eminence of Peter among the original apostles appear in the Acts, and in the epistles of Paul.

---

* If ἡ πόλις Ἀνδρέου καὶ Πέτρου, John i. 45, mean the same as ἡ ἰδία πόλις, Matth. ix. 1, that is, the place where they were resident, there exists a contradiction on this point between John and the synoptists.   † Comp. Fritzsche, in Matth. p. 358.   ‡ Comp. Lightfoot, in loc.

Next to Peter, the catalogue of the first and third gospels places his brother Andrew; that of the second gospel and the Acts, James, and after him, John. The first and third evangelists are evidently guided by the propriety of uniting the couples of brethren; Mark, and the author of the Acts, by that of preferring the two apostles next in distinction to Peter to the less conspicuous Andrew, whom they accordingly put last in the quaternion. We have already considered the manner in which these four apostles are signalized in the Christian legend by a special history of their vocation. They appear together in other passages of Mark; first (i. 29,) where Jesus, in company with the sons of Zebedee, enters the house of Simon and Andrew: as, however, the other evangelists only mention Peter on this occasion, Mark may have added the other names inferentially, concluding that the four fishermen, so recently called, would not be apart from Jesus, and that Andrew had a share in his brother's house, a thing in itself probable.* Again, Mark xiii. 3, our four apostles concur in asking Jesus *privately* (κατ᾽ ἰδίαν) concerning the time of the destruction of the temple, and of his second advent. But the parallel passages in the other gospels do not thus particularize any of the disciples. Matthew says, *The disciples came to him privately* (xxiv. 3); hence it is probable that Mark's limitation is an erroneous one. Possibly the words κατ᾽ ἰδίαν, being used in the document to which he referred to denote the separation of the twelve from the multitude, appeared to him, from association, an introductory form, of which there are other examples (Matt. xvii. 1; Mark ix. 2), to a private conference of Jesus with Peter, James and John, to whom he might add Andrew on account of the fraternity. Luke, on the other hand, in his account of the miraculous draught of fishes, and the vocation of the fishermen (v. 10), omits Andrew, though he is included in corresponding narratives, probably because he does not elsewhere appear as one of the select apostles; for except on the occasions already noticed, he is only mentioned by John (vi. 9; xxi. 22), and that in no very important connexion.

The two sons of Zebedee are the only disciples whose distinction rivals that of Peter. Like him, they evince an ardent and somewhat rash zeal (Luke ix. 55; once John is named alone, Mark ix. 38: Luke ix. 49); and it was to this disposition, apparently, that they owed the surname *Sons of Thunder*, בְּנֵי רֶגֶשׁ υἱοὶ βροντῆς (Mark iii. 17),† conferred on them by Jesus. So high did they stand among the twelve, that either they (Mark xi. 35 ff.), or their mother for them (Matt. xx. 20 ff.), thought they might claim the first place in the Messiah's kingdom. It is worthy of notice that not only in the four catalogues, but elsewhere when the two brothers are named, as in Matt. iv. 21; xvii. 1; Mark i. 19, 29; v. 37; ix. 2; x. 35; xiii. 3; xiv. 33; Luke v. 10; ix. 54; with the exception of Luke viii. 51; ix. 28; James is always mentioned first, and John is appended

---

* Comp. Saunier, uber die Quellen des Markus, S. 55 f.   † Comp. de Wette, in loc.

to him as *his brother* (ὁ ἀδελφὸς αὐτοῦ). This is surprising; because, while we know nothing remarkable of James, John is memorable as the favourite disciple of Jesus. Hence it is supposed that this precedence cannot possibly denote a superiority of James to John, and an explanation has been sought in his seniority.* Nevertheless, it remains a doubt whether so constant a precedence do not intimate a pre-eminence on the part of James; at least, if, in the apprehension of the synoptists, John had been as decidedly preferred as he is re- presented to have been in the fourth gospel, we are inclined to think that they would have named him before his brother James, even allowing him to be the younger. This leads us to a difference be- tween the first three evangelists and the fourth which requires a closer examination.

In the synoptical gospels, as we have observed, Peter, James, and John, form the select circle of disciples whom Jesus admits to certain scenes, which the rest of the twelve were not spiritually mature enough to comprehend; as the transfiguration, the conflict in Gethsemane, and, according to Mark (v. 37), the raising of the daughter of Jairus.† After the death of Jesus, also, a James, Peter and John appear as the *pillars* of the church (Gal. ii. 9); this James, however, is not the son of Zebedee, who had been early put to death (Acts xii. 2), but James, the brother of the Lord (Gal. i. 19), who even in the first apostolic council appears to have possessed a predominant authority, and whom many hold to be the second James of the apostolic catalogue given in Acts i.‡ It is observable from the beginning of the Acts, that James the son of Zebedee, is eclipsed by Peter and John. As, then, this James the elder was not enough distinguished or even known in the primitive church, for his early martyrdom to have drawn much lustre on his name, tradition had no inducement from subsequent events, to reflect an unhistorical splendour on his relation to Jesus; there is therefore no reason to doubt the statement as to the prominent position held by James, in conjunction with Peter and John, among the twelve apostles.

So much the more must it excite surprise to find, in the fourth gospel the triumvirate almost converted into a monarchy: James, like another Lepidus, is wholly cast out, while Peter and John are in the position of Antony and Octavius, the latter having nearly stripped his rival of all pretensions to an equal rank with himself, to say nothing of a higher. James is not even named in the fourth gospel; only in the appendix (xxi. 2) is there any mention of the *sons of Zebedee;* while several narratives of the vocations of differ- ent apostles are given, apparently including that of John himself,

* Paulus, exeg. Handb. 1. B. S. 566. † This is probably a mere inference of Mark. Because Jesus excluded the multitude, and forbade the publication of the evangelist saw in it one of those secret scenes, to which Jesus was accustomed to admit only the three favoured apostles. ‡ In the ancient church is was thought that Jesus had communicated to these three individuals the γνῶσις, to be mysteriously transmitted. Vid. in Gieseler, K. G. 1, S. 234.

no James appears in them, neither is there any speech of his, as of many other apostles, throughout this gospel.

Quite differently does the fourth evangelist treat Peter. He makes him one of the first who enter the society of Jesus, and gives him a prominent importance not less often than the synoptists; he does not conceal that Jesus bestowed on him an honourable surname (i. 43); he puts in his mouth (vi. 68 f.) a confession which seems but a new version of the celebrated one in Matt. xvi. 16; according to him, Peter once throws himself into the sea that he may more quickly reach Jesus (xxi. 7); at the last supper, and in the garden of Gethsemane, he makes Peter more active than even the synoptists represent him (xiii. 6 ff.: xviii. 10 f.); he accords him the honour of following Jesus into the high priest's palace (xviii. 15), and of being one of the first to visit the grave of Jesus after the resurrection (xx. 3 ff.); nay, he even details a special conversation between the risen Jesus and Peter (xxi. 15 ff.). But these advantages of Peter are in the fourth gospel invalidated in a peculiar manner, and put into the shade, in favour of John. The synoptists tell us that Peter and John were called to the apostleship in the same way, and the former somewhat before the latter; the fourth evangelist prefers associating Andrew with the •nameless disciple who is taken for John, and makes Peter come to him through the instrumentality of his brother.* He also admits the honourable interpretation of the surname Peter, and the panegyric on Peter's confession; but this he does in common with Mark and Luke, while the speeches and the action attributed in the fourth gospel to Peter during the last supper and in the garden, are to be classed as only so many mistakes. The more we approach the catastrophe, the more marked is the subordination of Peter to John. At the last supper indeed, Peter is particularly anxious for the discovery of the traitor: he cannot, however, apply immediately to Jesus (xiii. 23 ff.), but is obliged to make John, *who was leaning on Jesus' bosom*, his medium of communication. While, according to the synoptists, Peter alone followed Jesus into the palace of the high priest; according to the fourth evangelist, John accompanied him, and under such circumstances, that without him Peter could not have entered,—John, as one known to the high priest, having to obtain admission for him (xviii. 15 f.). In the synoptical gospels, not one of the disciples is bold enough to venture to the cross: but in the fourth, John is placed under it, and is there established in a new relation to the mother of his dying master: a relation of which we elsewhere find no trace (xix. 26 f.). On the appearance of the risen Jesus at the Galilean sea (xxi.), Peter, as the θερμότερος, casts himself into the sea; but it is not until after John, as the διορατικότερος (Euthymius), has recognized the Lord in the person standing on the shore. In the ensuing conversation, Peter is indeed honoured with

* Even Paulus, L. J. 1, a. S. 167 f., remarks that the fourth evangelist seems to have a design in noticing this circumstance.

the commission, *Feed my sheep ;* but this honour is overshadowed by the dubitative question, *Lovest thou me ?* and while the prospect of martyrdom is held up to him, John is promised the distinction of tarrying till Jesus came again, an advantage which Peter is warned not to envy. Lastly, while, according to Luke (xxiv. 12), Peter, first among the apostles, and alone, comes to the vacant grave of his risen master, the fourth gospel (xx. 3), gives him a companion in John, who outruns Peter and arrives first at the grave. Peter goes into the grave before John, it is true; but it is the latter in whose honour it is recorded, that he *saw and believed*, almost in contradiction to the statement of Luke, that Peter went home *wondering in himself at that which was come to pass.* Thus in the fourth gospel, John, both literally and figuratively, *outruns Peter*, for the entire impression which the attentive reader must receive from the representation there given of the relative position of Peter and John, is that the writer wished a comparison to be drawn in favour of the latter.*

But John is moreover especially distinguished in the gospel which bears his name, by the constant epithet, *the beloved disciple, the disciple whom Jesus loved*, ὁ μαθητὴς ὅν ἠγάπα, or ἐφίλει ὁ Ἰησοῦς, (xiii. 23; xix. 26; xx. 2; xxi. 7, 20). It is true that we have no absolute proof from the contents of the fourth gospel, whether intrinsically or comparatively considered, that by the above formula, or the more indeterminate one, *the other* ὁ ἄλλος, or *another disciple*, ἄλλος μαθητής (x. 15 f.; xx. 3, 4, 8), which, as it appears from xx. 2 f., is its equivalent, we are to understand the apostle John. For neither is the designation in question anywhere used interchangeably with the name of the apostle, nor is there anything narrated in the fourth gospel of the favourite disciple, which in the three first is ascribed to John. Because in xxi. 2. the sons of Zebedee are named among the assistants, it does not follow that the disciple mentioned v. 7 as the one whom Jesus loved must be John; James, or one of the *two other disciples* mentioned in v. 2, might be meant. Nevertheless, it is the immemorial tradition of the church that the disciple whom Jesus loved was John, nor are all reasons for such a belief extinct even to us; for in the Greek circle from which the fourth gospel sprang, there could scarcely be among the apostles whom it leaves unnamed, one so well known as to be recognized under that description unless it were John, whose residence at Ephesus is hardly to be rejected as a mere fable.

It may appear more doubtful whether the author intended by

---

* This has not escaped the acumen of Dr. Paulus. In a review of the first volume of the second ed. of Lucke's Comm. zum Johannes, im Lit. Bl. zur allg. Kirchenzeitung, Febr. 1834, no. 18, S. 137 f., he says : "The gospel of John has only preserved the less advantageous circumstances connected with Peter (excepting vi. 68), *such as place him in marked subordination to John* [here the passages above considered are cited]. An adherent of Peter can hardly have had a hand in the gospel of John." We may add that it seems to have proceeded from an antagonist of Peter, for it is probable that he had such of the school of John, as well as of Paul.

this title to designate himself, and thus to announce himself as the apostle John. The conclusion of the twenty-first chapter, v. 24, does certainly make the favourite disciple the testifier and writer of the preceding history; but we may assume it as granted that this passage is an addition by a strange hand.* When, however, in the genuine text of the gospel, (xix. 35), the writer says of the effect produced by the piercing of the side of Jesus, *he that saw bare record*, ὁ ἑωρακὼς μεμαρτύρηκε; no other than the favourite disciple can be intended, because he alone among all the disciples (the only parties eligible as witnesses in the case), is supposed to be present at the cross. The probability that the author here speaks of himself is not at all affected by his use of the third person; but the preterite annexed to it may well excite a doubt whether an appeal be not here made to the testimony of John, as one distinct from the writer.† This mode of expression, however, may be explained also in accordance with the other supposition,‡ which is supported by the circumstance that the author in i. 14, 16, seems to announce himself as the eye-witness of the history he narrates.

Was that author, then, really the apostle John, as he apparently wishes us to surmise? This is another question, on which we can only pronounce when we shall have completed our investigation. We will merely allude to the difficulty of supposing that the apostle John could give so unhistorical a sketch of the Baptist as that in the fourth gospel. But we ask, is it at all probable that the real John would so unbecomingly neglect the well-founded claims of his brother James to a special notice? and is not such an omission rather indicative of a late Hellenistic author, who scarcely had heard the name of the brother so early martyred? The designation, *the disciple whom Jesus loved*, which in xxi. 20 has the prolix addition, *who also leaned on his breast at supper, and said, Lord, which is he that betrayeth thee?* is not to be considered as an offence against modesty.§ It is certainly far too laboured and embellished for one who, without any ulterior view, wishes to indicate himself, for such an one would, at least sometimes, have simply employed his name: but a venerator of John, issuing perhaps from one of his schools, might very naturally be induced to designate the revered apostle under whose name he wished to write, in this half honourable, half mysterious manner.‖

§ 75. THE REST OF THE TWELVE, AND THE SEVENTY DISCIPLES.

THE second quaternion in all the four catalogues begins with Philip. The three first gospels know nothing more of him than his name. The fourth alone gives his birth-place, Bethsaida, and narrates his vocation (i. 44 f.); in this gospel he is more than once

---

* Vid. Lücke, Comm. zum Joh. 2, S. 708.   † Paulus in his review of Bretschneider's Probabilien, in the Heidelberger Jahrbüchern, 1821, no. 9, S. 138.   ‡ Lücke, ut sup. S. 661.   § Bretschneider, Probabilia, p. 111 f.   ‖ Comp. Paulus ut sup. S. 137.

an interlocutor, but his observations are founded on mistakes (vi. 7; xiv. 8); and he perhaps appears with most dignity, when the Ἕλληνες, who wish to see Jesus, apply immediately to him (xii. 21).

The next in the three evangelical lists is Bartholomew; a name which is nowhere found out of the catalogues. In the synoptical gospels Bartholomew is coupled with Philip; in the history of the vocations given by the fourth evangelist (i. 46), Nathanael appears in company with the latter, and (xxi. 2) is again presented in the society of the apostles. Nathanael, however, finds no place among the twelve, unless he be identical with one otherwise named by the synoptists. If so, it is thought that Bartholomew is the most easily adapted to such an alias, as the three first gospels couple him with Philip, just as the fourth, which has no Bartholomew, does Nathanael; to which it may be added that בר תלמי is a mere patronymic, which must have been accompanied by a proper name, such as Nathanael.* But we have no adequate ground for such an identification, since the juxtaposition of Bartholomew and Philip is shown to be accidental, by our finding the former (Acts i. 13), as well as the latter (John xxi. 2), linked with different names; the absence of Bartholomew from the fourth gospel is not peculiar to him among the twelve; finally, second names as surnames were added to proper as well as to patronymic names, as Simon Peter, Joseph Caiaphas, John Mark, and the like; so that any other apostle not named by John might be equally well identified with Nathanael, and hence the supposed relation between the two appellations is altogether uncertain.

In the catalogue given in the Acts, Philip is followed, not by Bartholomew, but by Thomas, who in the list of the first gospel comes after Bartholomew, in that of the others, after Matthew. Thomas, in Greek Δίδυμος, appears in the fourth gospel, on one occassion, in the guise of mournful fidelity (xi. 16): on another, in the more noted one of incredulity (xx. 24. ff.); and once again in the appendix (xxi. 2). Matthew, the next in the series, is found nowhere else except in the history of his vocation.

The third quaternion is uniformly opened by James the son of Alpheus, of whom we have already spoken. After him comes in both Luke's lists, Simon, whom he calls Zelotes, or the zealot, but whom Matthew and Mark (in whose catalogues he is placed one degree lower) distinguish as the Canaanite ὁ κανανίτης (from קַנָא, to be zealous). This surname seems to mark him as a former adherent of the Jewish sect of zealots for religion,† a party which, it is true, did not attain consistence until the latest period of the Jewish state, but which was already in the process of formation. In all the lists that retain the name of Judas Iscariot, he occupies the last place, but of him we must not speak until we enter on the history of the passion. Luke, in his filling up of the remaining places of this quaternion, differs from the two other evangelists, and perhaps these also differ from each other; Luke has a second Judas, whom he styles the brother of James; Matthew, Lebbeus; and Mark, Thaddeus. It is true that we now commonly read in Matthew, *Lebbeus, whose surname was Thaddeus;* but the vacillation in the early readings seems to betray these words to be a later addition intended to reconcile the first two evangelists;* an attempt which others have made by pointing out a similarity of meaning between the two names, though such a similarity does not exist.† But allowing validity to one or other of these harmonizing efforts, there yet remains a discrepancy between Matthew and Mark with their Lebbeus-Thaddeus, and Luke with his Judas, the brother of James. Schleiermacher justly disapproves the expedients, almost all of them constrained and unnatural, which have been resorted to for the sake of proving that here also, we have but one person under two different names. He seeks to explain the divergency, by supposing, that during the lifetime of Jesus, one of the two men died or left the circle of the apostles, and the other took his place: so that one list gives the earlier, the other the later member.‡ But it is scarcely possible to admit that any one of our catalogues was drawn up during the life of Jesus; and after that period, no writer would think of including a member who had previously retired from the college of apostles; those only would be enumerated who were ultimately attached to Jesus. It is the most reasonable to allow that there is a discrepancy between the lists, since it is easy to account for it by the probability that while the number of the apostles, and the names of the most distinguished among them, were well known, varying traditions supplied the place of more positive data concerning the less conspicuous.

Luke makes us acquainted with a circle of disciples, intermediate to the twelve and the mass of the partisans of Jesus. He tells us (x. 1 ff.) that besides the twelve, Jesus chose *other seventy also,* and sent them two and two before him into all the districts which he intended to visit on his last journey, that they might proclaim the approach of the kingdom of heaven. As the other evangelists have no allusion to this event, the most recent critics have not hesitated to make their silence on this head a reproach to them, particularly to the first evangelist, in his supposed character of apostle.§ But the disfavour towards Matthew on this score ought to be moderated by the consideration, that neither in the other gospels, nor in the Acts, nor in any apostolic epistle, is there any trace of the seventy disciples, who could scarcely have passed thus unnoticed, had their mission been as fruitful in consequences, as it is commonly supposed. It is said, however, that the importance of this appointment lay in its significance, rather than in its effects. As the num-

---

* Comp. Credner, Einleit., 1, S. 64; De Wette, exeg. Handb. 1, 1, S. 98 f.   † De Wette, ut sup.   ‡ Ueber den Lukas, S. 88 f.   § Schulz, über das Abendmahl, S. 307. Schneckenburger, über den Ursprung, S. 13 f.

ber of the twelve apostles, by its relation to that of the tribes of Israel, shadowed forth the destination of Jesus for the Jewish people;
so the seventy, or as some authorities have it, the seventy-two disciples, were representatives of the seventy or seventy-two peoples,
with as many different tongues, which, according to the Jewish and
early Christian view, formed the sum of the earth's inhabitants,*
and hence they denoted the universal destination of Jesus and his
kingdom.† Moreover, seventy was a sacred number with the Jewish nation; Moses deputed seventy elders (Num. xi. 16, 25); the
Sanhedrim had seventy members;‡ the Old Testament, seventy
translators.

Had Jesus, then, under the pressing circumstances that mark
his public career, nothing more important to do than to cast about
for significant numbers, and to surround himself with inner and
outer circles of disciples, regulated by these mystic measures? or
rather, is not this constant preference for sacred numbers, this assiduous development of an idea to which the number of the apostles
furnished the suggestion, wholly in the spirit of the primitive Christian legend? This, supposing it imbued with Jewish prepossessions,
would infer, that as Jesus had respect to the twelve tribes in fixing
the number of his apostles, he would extend the parallel by appoint-
ing seventy subordinate disciples, corresponding to the seventy
elders; or, supposing the legend animated by the more universal
sentiments of Paul, it could not escape the persuasion that to the
symbol of the relation of his office to the Israelitish people, Jesus
would annex another, significative of its destination for all the kin-
dreds of the earth. However agreeable this class of seventy disciples may have always been to the church, as a series of niches for
the reception of men who, without belonging to the twelve, were yet
of importance to her, as Mark, Luke and Matthew; we are compelled to pronounce the decision of our most recent critic precipitate,
and to admit that the gospel of Luke, by its acceptance of such a
narrative, destitute as it is of all historical confirmation, and of any
other apparent source than dogmatical interests, is placed in disadvantageous comparison with that of Matthew. We gather, indeed,
from Acts i. 21 f. that Jesus had more than the twelve as his constant companions; but that these formed a body of exactly seventy,
or that that number was selected from them, does not seem adequately warranted.§

* Tuf haarez, f. xix. c. iii,; Clem. hom. xviii. 4; Recognit. Clement. ii. 42. Epiphan.
hær. i. 5.   † Schneckenburger, ut sup.; Gieseler, über Entstehung der schriftlichen
Evangelien, S. 127 f.   ‡ Lightfoot, p. 786.   § De Wette, exeg. Handb., 1, 1, S. 99 f. 1,
2, S. 61.   1, 3, S. 220; Theile, zur Biogr. J., § 24.   For the contrary opinion, see Neander, L. J. Chr., S. 498 f.

CHAPTER VI.

THE DISCOURSES OF JESUS IN THE THREE FIRST GOSPELS.*

§. 76. THE SERMON ON THE MOUNT.

In reviewing the public life of Jesus, we may separate from the events those discourses which were not merely incidental, but which stand independent and entire. This distinction, however, is not precise, for many discourses, owing to the occurrences that suggested them, may be classed as events; and many events, from the explanations annexed to them, seem to range themselves with the discourses. The discourses of Jesus given in the synoptical gospels, and those attributed to him in the fourth, differ widely both in form and matter, having only a few isolated sentences in common: they must, therefore, be subjected to a separate examination. Again, there is a dissimilitude between the three first evangelists: Matthew affects long discourses, and collects into one mass a number of sayings, which in Luke are distributed among various places and occasions; each of these two evangelists has also some discourses peculiar to himself. In Mark, the element of discourses exists in a very small proportion. Our purpose will, therefore, be best answered, if we make Matthew's comprehensive discourses our starting point; ascertain all the corresponding ones in the other gospels; inquire which amongst them has the best arrangement and representation of these discourses: and, finally, endeavour to form a judgment as to how far they really proceeded from the lips of Jesus.

The first long discourse in Matthew is that known as the sermon on the mount (v.—vii.). The evangelist, having recorded the return of Jesus after his baptism into Galilee, and the calling of the fishermen, informs us, that Jesus went through all Galilee, teaching and healing; that great multitudes followed him from all parts of Palestine: and that for their instruction he ascended a mountain, and delivered the sermon in question (iv. 23, ff). We seek in vain for its parallel in Mark, but Luke (vi. 20—49) gives a discourse which has the same introduction and conclusion, and presents in its whole tenor the most striking similarity with that of Matthew: moreover, in both cases, Jesus, at the termination of his discourse, goes to Capernaum, and heals the centurion's servant. It is true that Luke gives a later insertion to the discourse, for previous to it

---

* All that relates to the sufferings, death and resurrection of Jesus is here excluded.

he narrates many journeyings and cures of Jesus, which Matthew places after it; and while the latter represents Jesus as ascending a mountain, and being seated there during delivery of his discourse, Luke says, almost in contradiction to him, that Jesus *came down and stood in the plain.* Further, the sermon in Luke contains but a fourth part of that in Matthew, while it has some elements peculiarly its own.

To avoid the unpleasant admission that one of two inspired evangelists must be in error,—which is inevitable if in relation to the same discourse one of them makes Jesus deliver it on the mountain, the other in the plain; the one sitting, the other standing; the one earlier, the other later; if either the one has made important omissions, or the other as important additions;—the ancient harmonists pronounced these discourses to be distinct,* on the plea that Jesus must frequently have treated of the essential points of his doctrine, and may therefore have repeated word for word certain impressive enunciations. This may be positively denied with respect to long discourses, and even concise maxims will always be reproduced in a new guise and connexion by a gifted and inventive teacher; to say the least, it is impossible that any but a very barren mind should repeat the same formal exordium, and the same concluding illustration, on separate occasions.

The identity of the discourses being established, the first effort was to conciliate or to explain the divergencies between the two accounts so as to leave their credibility unimpeached. In reference to the different designation of the locality, Paulus insists on the ἐπὶ of Luke, which he interprets to imply that Jesus stood *over* the plain and therefore on a hill. Tholuck, more happily, distinguishes the *level space* τόπος πεδινὸς, from the plain properly so called, and regards it as a less abrupt part of the mountain. But as one evangelist makes Jesus ascend the mountain to deliver his discourse, while the other makes him descend for the same purpose, these conciliators ought to admit, with Olshausen, that if Jesus taught in the plain, according to Luke, Matthew has overlooked the descent that preceded the discourse; or if, as Matthew says, Jesus taught seated on the mountain, Luke has forgotten to mention that after he had descended, the pressure of the crowd induced him to reascend before he commenced his harangue. And without doubt each was ignorant of what he omits, but each knew that tradition associated this discourse with a sojourn of Jesus on a mountain. Matthew thought the mountain a convenient elevation for one addressing a multitude; Luke, on the contrary, imagined a descent necessary for the purpose; hence the double discrepancy, for he who teaches from a mountain is sufficiently elevated over his hearers to sit, but he who teaches in a plain will naturally stand. The chronological diver-

---

* Augustin, de consens. ev. ii. 19.; Storr, über den Zweck des Evang. und der Briefe Joh., S. 347 ff. For further references see Tholuck's Auslegung der Bergpredigt, Einl., § 1.

gencies, as well as the local, must be admitted, if we would abstain from fruitless efforts at conciliation.*

The difference as to the length and contents of the discourse is susceptible of three explanations: either the concise record of Luke is a mere extract from the entire discourse which Matthew gives without abridgment; or Matthew has incorporated many sayings belonging properly to other occasions; or lastly, both these causes of variety have concurred. He who, with Tholuck, wishes to preserve intact the *fides divina*, or with Paulus, the *fides humana* of the evangelists, will prefer the first supposition, because to withhold the true is more innocent than to add the false. The above theologians hold that the train of thought in the sermon on the mount as given by Matthew, is closely consecutive, and that this is a proof of its original unity. But any compiler not totally devoid of ability, can give a tolerable appearance of connectedness to sayings which did not originally belong to each other; and even these commentators are obliged to admit† that the alleged consecutiveness extends over no more than half the sermon, for from vi. 19, it is a string of more or less isolated sentences, some of them very unlikely to have been uttered on the occasion. More recent criticism has therefore decided that the shorter account of Luke presents the discourse of Jesus in its original form, and that Matthew has taken the license of incorporating with this much that was uttered by Jesus at various times, so as to retain the general sketch—the exordium, peroration, and essential train of thought; while between these compartments he inserted many sayings more or less analogous borrowed from elsewhere.‡ This view is especially supported by the fact that many of the sentences, which in Matthew make part of the sermon on the mount, are in Mark and Luke dispersed through a variety of scenes. Compelled to grant this, yet earnestly solicitous to avert from the evangelist an imputation that might invalidate his claim to be considered an eye-witness, other theologians maintain that Matthew did not compile the discourse under the idea that it was actually spoken on a single occasion, but with the clearest knowledge that such was not the case.§ It is with justice remarked in opposition to this, that when Matthew represents Jesus as ascending the mountain before he begins his discourse, and descending after its close, he obviously makes these two incidents the limits of a single address; and that when he speaks of the impression which the discourse produced on the multitude, whose presence he states as the inducement to its delivery, he could not but intend to convey the idea of a continuous harangue.‖ As to Luke's edition of the sermon, there are parts in which the interrupted connexion betrays deficiencies, and there are additions which do not look genuine;* it is also doubtful whether he assigns a more appropriate connexion to the passages in the position of which he differs from Matthew;† and hence, as we shall soon see more fully, he has in this instance no advantage over his predecessor.

The assemblage to whom the sermon on the mount was addressed, might from Luke's account be supposed a narrow circle, for he states that the choice of the apostles immediately preceded the discourse, and that at its commencement Jesus *lifted up his eyes on his disciples*, and he does not, like Matthew, note the multitude, ὄχλους, as part of the audience. On the other hand, Matthew also mentions that before the sermon the disciples gathered round Jesus and were taught by him; and Luke represents the discourse as being delivered *in the audience of the people* (vii. 1); it is therefore evident that Jesus spoke to the crowd in general, but with a particular view to the edification of his disciples.‡ We have no reason to doubt that a real harangue of Jesus, more than ordinarily solemn and public, was the foundation of the evangelical accounts before us.

Let us now proceed to an examination of particulars. In both editions, the sermon on the mount is opened by a series of beatitudes; in Luke, however, not only are several wanting which we find in Matthew, but most of those common to both are in the former taken in another sense than in the latter.§ The *poor*, πτωχοὶ, are not specified as in Matthew by the addition, *in spirit*, τῷ πνεύματι; they are therefore not those who have a deep consciousness of inward poverty and misery, but the literally poor; neither is the hunger of the πεινῶντες (*hungering*) referred to τὴν δικαιοσύνην (*righteousness*); it is therefore not spiritual hunger, but bodily; moreover, the adverb νῦν, now, definitively marks out *those who hunger* and *those who weep*, the πεινῶντες and κλαίοντες. Thus in Luke the antithesis is not, as in Matthew, between the present sorrows of pious souls, whose pure desires are yet unsatisfied, and their satisfaction about to come; but between present suffering and future well-being in general.‖ This mode of contrasting the αἰὼν οὗτος and the αἰὼν μέλλων, *the present age* and *the future*, is elsewhere observable in Luke, especially in the parable of the rich man; and without here inquiring which of the two representations is probably the original, I shall merely remark, that this of Luke is conceived entirely in the spirit of the Ebionites,—a spirit which has of late been supposed discernible in Matthew. It is a capital principle with the Ebionites, as they are depicted in the Clementine Homilies, that he who has his portion in the present age, will be destitute in the age to come; while he who renounces earthly pos-

---

* Schleiermacher, über den Lukas, S. 89 f.   † Tholuck, p. 11, and my Review of the writings of Sieffert and others in the Jahrbuch für wiss. Kritik, Nov. 1834; now in my Charakteristiken und Kritiken, S. 252 ff.   ‡ Comp. Tholuck, ut sup. S. 25 ff.; De Wette, exeg. Handbuch, 1, 1, S. 49.   § Storr, über den Zweck u. s. w., S. 348 f. Olshausen.   ‖ De Wette, exeg. Handb., 1, 2, S. 44 f.; Neander, L. J. Chr., S. 155 f. Anm.

sessions, thereby accumulates heavenly treasures.* The last beatitude relates to those who are persecuted for the sake of Jesus. Luke in the parallel passage has, *for the Son of man's sake;* hence the words *for my sake* in Matthew, must be understood to refer to Jesus solely in his character of Messiah.†

The beatitudes are followed in Luke by as many *woes οὐαὶ,* which are wanting in Matthew. In these the opposition established by the Ebionites between this world and the other, is yet more strongly marked; for woe is denounced on the rich, the full, and the joyous, simply as such, and they are threatened with the evils corresponding to their present advantages, under the new order of things to be introduced by the Messiah; a view that reminds us of the Epistle of James, v. 1 ff. The last woe is somewhat stiffly formed after the model of the last beatitude, for it is evidently for the sake of the contrast to the true prophets, so much calumniated, that the false prophets are said, without any historical foundation, to have been spoken well of by all men. We may therefore conjecture, with Schleiermacher,‡ that we are indebted for these maledictions to the inventive fertility of the author of the third gospel. He added this supplement to the beatitudes, less because, as Schleiermacher supposes, he perceived a chasm, which he knew not how to fill, than because he judged it consistent with the character of the Messiah, that, like Moses of old, he should couple curses with blessings. The sermon on the mount is regarded as the counterpart of the law, delivered on Mount Sinai; but the introduction, especially in Luke, reminds us more of a passage in Deuteronomy, in which Moses commands that on the entrance of the Israelitish people into the promised land, one half of them shall take their stand on Mount Gerizim, and pronounce a manifold blessing on the observers of the law, the other half on Mount Ebal, whence they were to fulminate as manifold a curse on its transgressors. We read in Josh. viii. 33 ff. that this injunction was fulfilled.§

With the beatitudes, Matthew suitably connects the representation of the disciples as *the salt of the earth,* and *the light of the world* (v. 13 ff.) In Luke, the discourse on the salt is, with a rather different opening, introduced in another place (xiv. 34 f.), where Jesus admonishes his hearers to ponder the sacrifices that must be made by those who would follow him, and rather to abstain from the profession of discipleship than to maintain it dishonourably; and to this succeeds aptly enough the comparison of such degenerate disciples to salt that has lost its savour. Thus the dictum accords

---

* Homil. xv. 7; comp. Credner in Winer's Zeitschrift f.wiss. Theologie, 1, S. 298 f.; Schneckenburger, uber das Evangelium der Aegyptier, § 6. † Schneckenburger, über den Ursprung, S. 29. ‡ Ut sup. S. 90. Neander agrees with him, ut sup. § The Rabbins also attached weight to these Mosaic blessings and curses, vid. Lightfoot, p 255. As here we have eight blessings, they held that Abraham had been blessed *benedictionibus septem* (Baal Turin, in Gen. xii. Lightfoot, p. 256); David, Daniel with his three companions, and the Messiah, *benedictionibus sex.* (Targ. Ruth. 3. ibid.) They also counted together with the twenty *beatitudines* in the Psalms, as many or in Isaiah. (Midrasch Tehillim in Ps. i. ib.)

with either context, and from its aphoristical conciseness would be likely to recur, so that it may have been really spoken in both discourses. On the contrary, it cannot have been spoken in the sequence in which it is placed by Mark (ix. 50): for the idea that every one shall be salted with fire (in allusion to hell), has no internal connexion with the comparison of the true disciples of Jesus to salt, denoting their superiority; the connexion is merely external, resulting from the verbal affinity of ἁλίζειν and ἅλας,—it is the connexion of the dictionary.* The altered sequel which Mark gives to the apothegm (*have salt in yourselves, and be at peace one with another*), might certainly be united to it without incongruity, but it would accord equally well with quite a different train of thought. The apothegm on the light which is not to be hidden, as the salt is not to be without savour, is also wanting in the sermon on the mount as given by Luke: who, however, omitting the special application to the disciples, has substantially the same doctrine in two different places. We find it first (viii. 16.) immediately after the interpretation of the parable of the sower, where it also occurs in Mark (iv. 21). It must be admitted that there is no incoherence in associating the shining of the light with the fructification of the seed; still, a judicious teacher will pause on the interpretation of a parable, and will not disturb its effect by a hasty transition to new images. At any rate there is no intrinsic connexion between the shining of the inward light, and the declaration appended to it by Luke, that all secrets shall be made manifest. We have here a case which is of frequent recurrence with this evangelist; that, namely, of a variety of isolated sayings being thrown confusedly together between two independent discourses or narratives. Thus between the parable of the sower and the narrative of the visit paid to Jesus by his mother and brethren, the apothegm on the light is inserted on account of its internal analogy with the parable; then, because in this apothegm there occurs the opposition between concealment and manifestation, it suggested to the writer the otherwise heterogeneous discourse on the revelation of all secrets; whereupon is added, quite irrelevantly to the context, but with some relation to the parable, the declaration, *Whosoever hath, to him shall be given.* In the second passage on the manifestation of the light (xi. 33), the subject has absolutely no connexion, unless we interpolate one,† with that of the context, which turns on the condemnation of the cotemporaries of Jesus by the Ninevites. The fact is, that here again, between the discourses against the demand for signs and those at the Pharisee's dinner, we have a chasm filled up with disjointed fragments of harangues.

At v. 17 ff. follows the transition to the main subject of the sermon; the assurance of Jesus that he came not to destroy the law and the prophets, but to fulfil, &c. Now as Jesus herein plainly

---

* Schneckenburger, Beiträge, S. 58. Neander tries to show, very artificially, a real connexion of thought, S. 157, Anm. † Olshausen in loc. The true reading is indicated by Schneckenburger, Beiträge, S. 58; Tholuck, ut sup. S. 11.

presupposes that he is himself the Messiah, to whom was ascribed authority to abolish a part of the law, this declaration cannot properly belong to a period in which, if Matt. xvi. 13 ff. be rightly placed, he had not yet declared himself to be the Messiah. Luke (xvi. 17) inserts this declaration together with the apparently contradictory one, that the law and the prophets were in force until the coming of John.   These are two propositions that we cannot suppose to have been uttered consecutively ; and the secret of their conjunction in Luke's gospel lies in the word νόμος, *law*, which happens to occur in both.* It is to be observed that between the parable of the steward and that of the rich man, we have another of those pauses in which Luke is fond of introducing his fragments.

So little, it appears from v. 20, is it the design of Jesus to inculcate a disregard of the Mosaic law, that he requires a far stricter observance of its precepts than the Scribes and Pharisees, and he makes the latter appear in contrast to himself as the underminers of the law.   Then follows a series of Mosaic commandments, on which Jesus comments so as to show that he penetrates into the spirit of the law, instead of cleaving to the mere letter, and especially discerns the worthlessness of the rabbinical glosses (48).   This section, in the order and completeness in which we find it in Matthew, is wanting in Luke's sermon on the mount ; a decisive proof that the latter has deficiencies.   For not only does this chapter contain the fundamental thought of the discourse as given by Matthew, but the desultory sayings which Luke gives, concerning the love of enemies, mercifulness and beneficence, only acquire a definite purpose and point of union in the contrast between the spiritual interpretation of the law given by Jesus, and the carnal one given by the doctors of the time.   The words, too, with which Luke makes Jesus proceed after the last woe : *But I say unto you*, and those at v. 39, *And he spake a parable unto them*, have been correctly pointed out as indicative of chasms.† As regards the isolated parallel passages, the admonition to a quick reconciliation with an adversary (v. 25 f.), is, to say the least, not so easily brought into connexion with the foregoing matter in Luke (xii. 58.) as in Matthew.‡ It is still worse with the passage in Luke which is parallel with Matt. v. 32 ; this text (relative to divorce), which in Matthew is linked in the general chain of ideas, is in Luke (xvi. 18.) thrust into one of the apertures we have noticed, between the assurance of the perpetuity of the law and the parable of the rich man.   Olshausen tries to find a thread of connexion between the passage and the one preceding it, by interpreting *adultery*, μοιχεύειν, allegorically, as faithlessness to the divine law ; and Schleiermacher§ attaches it to the succeeding parable by referring it to the adulterous Herod : but such interpretations are altogether visionary.‖ Probably tradition had apprized the evangelist that Jesus, after the foregoing declaration as to the perpetuity of the Mosaic law, had enunciated his severe principle on the subject of divorce, and hence he gave it this position, not knowing more of its original connexion. In Matt. xix. 9, we find a reiteration of this principle on an occasion very likely to call it forth. The exhortations to patience and submissiveness, form, in Matthew, the spiritual interpretation of the old rule, *an eye for an eye*, &c., and are therefore a following out of the previous train of thought. In Luke (vi. 29.), they are introduced with much less precision by the command concerning love to enemies: which command is also decidedly better given in Matthew as the rectification of the precept, *Thou shalt love thy neighbour, and hate thine enemy* (43 ff.). Again: the observation that to love friends is nothing more than bad men can do, is, in Matthew, made, in order to controvert the traditional perversion of the Mosaic injunction to love one's neighbour, into a permission to hate enemies: in Luke, the observation follows the rule, *Whatsoever ye would that men should do to you*, &c., which in Matthew occurs farther on (vii. 12.) without any connexion. On the whole, if the passage in Luke from vi. 2—36, be compared with the corresponding one in Matthew, there will be found in the latter an orderly course of thought; in the former, considerable confusion.*

The warnings against Pharisaic hypocrisy (vi. 1—6) are without a parallel in Luke; but he has one of the model prayer, which recent criticism has turned not a little to the disadvantage of Matthew. The ancient harmonists, it is true, had no hesitation in supposing that Jesus delivered this prayer twice,—in the connexion in which it is given by Matthew as well as under the circumstances narrated by Luke (xi. 1 ff.).† But if Jesus had already in the sermon on the mount given a model prayer, his disciples would scarcely have requested one afterwards, as if nothing of the kind had occured; and it is still more improbable that Jesus would repeat the same formulary, without any recollection that he had delivered it to these disciples long before. Hence our most recent critics have decided that Luke alone has preserved the natural and true occasion on which this prayer was communicated, and that like many other fragments, it was interpolated in Matthew's sermon on the mount by the writer.‡ But the vaunted naturalness of Luke's representation, I, for one, cannot discover. Apart from the improbability, admitted even by the above critics, that the disciples of Jesus should have remained without any direction to pray until the last journey, in which Luke places the scene; it is anything but natural that Jesus should abstain from giving his disciples the exemplar which was in his mind until they sought for it, and that then he should forthwith fall into prayer. He had, doubtless, often prayed in their circle from the

* De Wette, exeg. Handb., 1, 1, S. 48. † Orig. de. orat. xviii. and Hess, Gesch. Jesu, 2, S. 48 f. ‡ Schleiermacher ut sup. S. 173; Olshausen, 1, S. 235; Sieffert, S. 78 ff.; Neander, S. 235 f. note.

commencement of their intercourse; and if so, their request was superfluous, and must, as in John xiv. 9, have produced only an admonition to recollect what they had long seen and heard in his society. The account of Luke seems to have been framed on mere
conjecture: it was known that the above prayer proceeded from Jesus, and the further question as to the motive for its communication,
received the gratuitous answer: without doubt his disciples had
asked him for such an exemplar. Without, therefore, maintaining
that Matthew has preserved to us the connexion in which this prayer
was originally uttered by Jesus, we are not the less in doubt whether
it has a more accurate position in Luke.* With regard to the elements of the prayer, it is impossible to deny what Wetstein says:
tota hæc oratio ex formulis Hebræorum concinnata est;† but
Fritzsche's observation is also just, that desires of so general a nature
might be uttered in the prayers of various persons, even in similar
phraseology, without any other cause than the broad uniformity of
human feeling.‡ We may add that the selection and allocation of
the petitions in the prayer are entirely original, and bear the impress of that religious consciousness which Jesus possessed and
sought to impart to his followers.§ Matthew inserts after the conclusion of the prayer two propositions, which are properly the corol-
lary of the third petition, but which seem inaptly placed, not only
because they are severed by the concluding petition from the passage to which they have reference, but because they have no point
of coincidence with the succeeding censures and admonitions which
turn on the hypocrisy of the Pharisaic fasts. Mark, however, has
still more infelicitously appended these propositions to the discourse
of Jesus on the efficacy of believing prayer (xi. 25).‖

At vi. 19, the thread of strict connexion is broken, according to
the admission of Paulus, and so far all expositors are bound to
agree with him. But his position, that notwithstanding the admitted
lack of coherence in the succeeding collection of sentences, Jesus
spoke them consecutively, is not equally tenable; on the contrary,
our more recent critics have all the probabilities on their side when
they suppose, that in this latter half of the sermon on the mount
Matthew has incorporated a variety of sayings uttered by Jesus on
different occasions. First stands the apothegm on earthly and
heavenly treasures (19—21), which Luke, with more apparent correctness, inserts in a discourse of Jesus, the entire drift of which is
to warn his adherents against earthly cares (xii. 33 f.). It is otherwise with the next sentence, on the eye being the light of the body.
Luke annexes this to the apothegm already mentioned on the light
that is to be exhibited; now as the *light,* λύχνος, placed on a
candlestick, denotes something quite distinct from what is intended
by the comparison of the eye to a *light,* λύχνος, the only reason for

* Comp. De Wette, exeg. Handb. 1, 1, S. 69. 1, 2, S. 65. † N. T. 1, 323. The
parallels may be seen in Wetstein and Lightfoot. ‡ Comm. in Matth. p. 265. § Comp.
De Wette, 1, 1, S. 69 ff.; Neander, S. 237 ff. ‖ Comp. De Wette, 1, 2, S. 176.

combining the two apothegms lies in the bare word λύχνος: a rule of association which belongs properly to the dictionary, and which, beyond it, is worse than none. Then follows, also without any apparent connexion, the apothegm on the two masters, appended by Luke to the parable of the steward, with which it happens to have the word *Mammon*, μαμωνᾶς, in common. Next comes, in Matthew v. 25—34, a dissuasion from earthly solicitude, on the ground that natural objects flourish and are sustained without anxiety on their part; in Luke, this doctrine is consistently united with the parable (found only in the third gospel) of the man who, in the midst of amassing earthly treasures, is summoned away by death (xii. 22 ff.).* The warning not to be blind to our own faults while we are sharp-sighted and severe towards those of others (vii. 1—5), would, if we rejected the passage from v. 19, of chap. vi. to the end, form a suitable continuation to the previous admonition against Pharisaic sanctimoniousness (vi. 16—18), and might, therefore, have belonged to the original body of the discourse.† This is the more probable because Luke has the same warning in his sermon on the mount (37 f. 41 f.), where it happens to assort very well with the preceding exhortation to mercifulness; but at v. 39 and 40, and part of 38, it is interrupted by subjects altogether irrelevant. The text, *With what measure ye mete*, &c., is very inappropriately interposed by Mark (iv. 24), in a passage similar in kind to one of Luke's intermediate miscellanies. V. 6, in Matthew, is equally destitute of connexion and parallel; but the succeeding assurances and arguments as to the efficacy of prayer (v. 7—11), are found in Luke xi. 9, very fitly associated with another parable peculiar to that evangelist: that of the friend awaked at midnight. The apothegm, *What ye would that men should do unto you*, &c., is quite isolated in Matthew; in Luke, it has only an imperfect connexion.‡ The following passage (v. 13 f.) on the *straight gate*, στενὴ πύλη, is introduced in Luke (xiii. 23.) by the question, addressed to Jesus : *Are there few that be saved?* εἰ ὀλίγοι οἱ σωζόμενοι ; which seems likely enough to have been conceived by one who knew that Jesus had uttered such a saying as the above, but was at a loss for an occasion that might prompt the idea; moreover, the image is far less completely carried out in Luke than in Matthew, and is blended with parabolical elements.§ The apothegm on the tree being known by its fruits (v. 16—20), appears in Luke (vi. 43 ff.), and even in Matthew, farther on (xii. 33 ff.), to have a general explication but in Matthew's sermon on the mount, it has a special relation to the false prophets; in Luke, it is in the last degree misplaced. The denunciation of those who say to Jesus, *Lord, Lord,* but who, on account of their evil deeds will be rejected by him at the day of

---

* From vi. 19 to the end of the chapter, even Neander finds no orderly association, and conjectures that the editor of the Greek Gospel of Matthew was the compiler of this latter half of the discourse (p. 169, note).   † Neander, ut sup.; De Wette, in loc.   ‡ De Wette, 1, 2, S. 45.   § Ib. in loc. des Lukas.

judgment (21—23), decidedly presupposes the Messiahship of Jesus, and cannot, therefore, have well belonged to so early a period as that of the sermon on the mount; hence it is more appropriately placed by Luke (xiii. 25 ff.). The peroration of the discourse is, as we have mentioned, common to both evangelists.

The foregoing comparison shows us that the discourses of Jesus, like fragments of granite, could not be dissolved by the flood of oral tradition; but they were not seldom torn from their natural connexion, floated away from their original situation, and deposited in places to which they did not properly belong. Relative to this effect, there is this distinction between the three first evangelists; Matthew, like an able compiler, though far from being sufficiently informed to give each relic in its original connexion, has yet for the most part succeeded in judiciously associating analogous materials; while the two other evangelists have left many small fragments just where chance threw them, in the intervals between longer discourses. Luke has laboured in some instances to combine these fragments artificially, but he could not thus compensate for the absence of natural connexion.

§ 77. INSTRUCTIONS TO THE TWELVE—LAMENTATIONS OVER THE GALILEAN CITIES—JOY OVER THE CALLING OF THE SIMPLE.

THE first gospel (x.) reports another long discourse as having been delivered by Jesus, on the occasion of his sending out the twelve to preach the kingdom of heaven. Part of this discourse is peculiar to the first gospel; that portion of it which is common to the two other synoptists is only partially assigned by them to the same occasion, Luke introducing its substance in connexion with the mission of the seventy (x. 2 ff.), and in a subsequent conversation with the disciples (xii. 2 ff.). Some portion of the discourse is also found repeated both in Matthew and the other evangelists, in the prophetic description given by Jesus of his second advent.

In this instance again, while the older harmonists have no hesitation in supposing a repetition of the same discourse,* our more recent critics are of opinion that Luke only has the true occasions and the original arrangement of the materials, and that Matthew has assembled them according to his own discretion.† Those expositors who are apologetically inclined, maintain that Matthew was not only conscious of here associating sayings uttered at various times, but presumed that this would be obvious to his readers.‡ On the other hand, it is justly observed that the manner in which the discourse is introduced by the words: *These twelve Jesus sent forth, and commanded them* (v. 5); and closed by the words:

* E. g. Hess, Gesch. Jesu, 1, S. 515.   † Schulz, ut sup. S. 308, 314; Sieffert, S. 80 ff.   ‡ Olshausen, in loc. The latter bold assertion in Kern, über den Ursprung des Evang. Matth., S. 63.

when Jesus made an end of commanding his twelve disciples, &c.
(xi. 1.); proves clearly enough that it was the intention of the
evangelist to give his compilation the character of a continuous
harangue.*

Much that is peculiar to Matthew in this discourse, appears to
be merely an amplification on thoughts which are also found in the
corresponding passages of the two other synoptists; but there are
two particulars in the opening of the instructions as detailed by the
former, which differ specifically from anything presented by his fellow evangelists.   These are the limitation of the agency of the disciples to the Jews (v. 5, 6), and the commission (associated with
that to announce the kingdom of heaven and heal the sick, of which
Luke also speaks, ix. 2,) to raise the dead: a surprising commission,
since we know of no instances previous to the departure of Jesus, in
which the apostles raised the dead; and to suppose such when they
are not narrated, after the example of Olshausen, is an expedient to
which few will be inclined.

All that the synoptists have strictly in common in the instructions to the twelve, are the rules for their external conduct; how
they were to journey, and how to behave under a variety of circumstances (Matt. v. 9—11, 14; Mark vi. 8—11; Luke ix. 3—5). Here,
however, we find a discrepancy; according to Matthew and Luke,
Jesus forbids the disciples to take with them, not only gold, a scrip,
and the like, but even *shoes*, ὑποδήματα, and a *staff*, ῥάβδον; according to Mark, on the contrary, he merely forbids their taking more
than a *staff* and *sandals*, εἰ μὴ ῥάβδον μόνον and σανδάλια.   This
discrepancy is most easily accounted for by the admission, that tradition only preserved a reminiscence of Jesus having signified the
simplicity of the apostolic equipment by the mention of the staff and
shoes, and that hence one of the evangelists understood that Jesus
had interdicted all travelling requisites except these: the other, that
these also were included in his prohibition.   It was consistent with
Mark's love of the picturesque to imagine a wandering apostle furnished with a staff, and therefore to give the preference to the former view.

It is on the occasion of the mission of the seventy, that Luke
(x. 2) puts into the mouth of Jesus the words which Matthew gives
(ix. 37 f.) as the motive for sending forth the twelve, namely, the
apothegm, *The harvest truly is ready, but the labourers are few;*
also the declaration that the labourer is worthy of his hire (v. 7.
comp. Matt. x. 10); the discourse on the apostolic salutation and
its effect (Matt. v. 12 f. Luke v. 5 f.); the denunciation of those who
should reject the apostles and their message (Matt. v. 15; Luke v.
12); and finally, the words, *Behold, I send you forth as lambs,*
&c. (Matt. v. 16; Luke v. 3.)   The sequence of these propositions
is about equally natural in both cases.   Their completeness is alternately greater in the one than in the other; but Matthew's additions

* Schulz, S. 315.

generally turn on essentials, as in v. 16: those of Luke on externals, as in v. 7, 8, and in v. 4, where there is the singular injunction to salute no man by the way, which might appear an unhistorical exaggeration of the urgency of the apostolic errand, did we not know that the Jewish greetings of that period were not a little ceremonious.* Sieffert observes that the instructions which Jesus gave—according to Matthew, to the twelve, according to Luke, to the seventy—might, so far as their tenor is concerned, have been imparted with equal fitness on either occasion; but I doubt this, for it seems to me improbable that Jesus should, as Luke states, dismiss his more confidential disciples with scanty rules for their outward conduct, and that to the seventy he should make communications of much greater moment and pathos.† The above critic at length decides in favour of Luke, whose narrative appears to him more precise, because it distinguishes the seventy from the twelve. We have already discussed this point, and have found that a comparison is rather to the advantage of Matthew. The blessing pronounced on him who should give even a cup of cold water to the disciples of Jesus (v. 42), is at least more judiciously inserted by Matthew as the conclusion of the discourse of instructions, than in the endless confusion of the latter part of Mark ix. (v. 41), where ἐὰν, (*if*), and ὃς ἄν, (*whosoever*), seem to form the only tie between the successive propositions.

The case is otherwise when we regard those portions of the discourse which Luke places in his twelfth chapter, and even later, and which in Matthew are distinguishable as a second part of the same discourse. Such are the directions to the apostles as to their conduct before tribunals (Matt. x. 19 f.; Luke xii. 11): the exhortation not to fear those who can only kill the body (Matt. v. 28; Luke v. 4 f.); the warning against the denial of Jesus (Matt. v. 32 f.; Luke v. 8 f.); the discourse on the general disunion of which he would be the cause (Matt. v. 34 ff.; Luke v. 51 ff.); a passage to which Matthew, prompted apparently by the enumeration of the members of a family, attaches the declaration of Jesus that these are not to be valued above him, that his cross must be taken, &c., which he partly repeats on a subsequent occasion, and in a more suitable connexion (xvi. 24 f.): further, predictions which recur in the discourse on the Mount of Olives, relative to the universal persecution of the disciples of Jesus (v. 17 f. 22. comp. xxiv. 9, 13): the saying which Luke inserts in the sermon on the mount (vi. 40), and which also appears in John (xv. 20), that the disciple has no claim to a better lot than his master (v. 24 f.); lastly, the direction, which is peculiar to the discourse in Matthew, to flee from one city to another, with the accompanying consolation (v. 23). These commands and exhortations have been justly pronounced by critics† to be unsuitable to the first mission of the twelve, which, like the alleged mission of the seventy, had no other than happy results (Luke ix. 10; x. 17); they presuppose the troublous circumstances which supervened after the death of Jesus, or perhaps in the latter period of his life.   According to this, Luke is more correct than Matthew in assigning these discourses to the last journey of Jesus;[*] unless, indeed, such descriptions of the subsequent fate of the apostles and other adherents of Jesus were produced *ex eventu*, after his death, and put into his mouth in the form of prophecies; a conjecture which is strongly suggested by the words, *He who taketh not up his cross*, &c. (v. 38.).[†]

The next long discourse of Jesus in Matthew (chap. xi.) we have already considered, so far as it relates to the Baptist. From v. 20—24, there follow complaints and threatenings against the Galilean cities, in which *most of his mighty works were done*, and which, nevertheless, *believed not*.   Our modern critics are perhaps right in their opinion that these apostrophes are less suitable to the period of his Galilean ministry, in which Matthew places them, than to that in which they are introduced by Luke (x. 13 ff.); namely, when Jesus had left Galilee, and was on his way to Judea and Jerusalem, with a view to his final experiment.[‡]   But a consideration of the immediate context seems to reserve the probability.   In Matthew, the description of the ungracious reception which Jesus and John had alike met with, leads very naturally to the accusations against those places which had been the chief theatres of the ministry of the former; but it is difficult to suppose, according to Luke, that Jesus would speak of his past sad experience to the seventy, whose minds must have been entirely directed to the future, unless we conceive that he chose a subject so little adapted to the exigencies of those whom he was addressing, in order to unite the threatened judgment on the Galilean cities, with that which he had just denounced against the cities that should reject his messengers.   But it is more likely that this association proceeded solely from the writer, who, by the comparison of a city that should prove refractory to the disciples of Jesus, to Sodom, was reminded of the analogous comparison to Tyre and Sidon, of places that had been disobedient to Jesus himself, without perceiving the incongruity of the one with the circumstances which had dictated the other.[§]

The *joy*, ἀγαλλίασις, expressed by Jesus (v. 25—27) on account of the insight afforded to *babes*, νηπίοις, is but loosely attached by Matthew to the preceding maledictions.   As it supposes a change in the mental frame of Jesus, induced by pleasing circumstances, Luke (x. 17. 21 ff.) would have all the probabilities on his side, in making the return of the seventy with satisfactory tidings the cause

* The satisfactory connexion which modern criticism finds throughout the 12th chap. of Luke, I am as little able to discover as Tholuck, Auslegung der Bergpredigt, S. 13 f., who has strikingly exposed the partiality of Schleiermacher for Luke, to the prejudice of Matthew.   † Vid. De Wette, in loc.   ‡ Schleiermacher, über den Lukas, S. 169 f.; Schneckenburger, über den Ursprung u. s. f, S. 32 f.   § Comp. De Wette, exeg. Handb. 1, 1, S. 110. 1, 2, S. 62.

of the above expression: were it not that the appointment of the seventy, and consequently their return, are altogether problematical; besides it is possible to refer the passage in question to the return of the twelve from their mission.   Matthew connects with this rejoicing of Jesus his invitation to the *weary and heavy laden* (v. 28—30).   This is wanting in Luke, who, instead, makes Jesus turn to his disciples *privately*, and pronounce them blessed in being privileged to see and hear things which many prophets and kings yearned after in vain (23 f.): an observation which does not so specifically agree with the preceding train of thought, as the context assigned to it by Matthew, and which is moreover inserted by the latter evangelist in a connexion (xiii. 16 f.): that may be advantageously confronted with that of Luke.

§ 78.   THE PARABLES.

ACCORDING to Matthew (chap. xiii.), Jesus delivered seven parables, all relating to the βασιλεία τῶν οὐρανῶν.   Modern criticism, however, has doubted whether Jesus really uttered so many of these symbolical discourses on one occasion.*   The parable, it has been observed, is a kind of problem, to be solved by the reflection of the hearer; hence after every parable a pause is requisite, if it be the object of the teacher to convey real instruction, and not to distract by a multiplicity of ill-understood images.†   It will, at least, be admitted, with Neander, that parables on the same or closely-related subjects can only be spoken consecutively, when, under manifold forms, and from various points of view, they lead to the same result.‡ Among the seven parables in question, those of the mustard-seed and the leaven have a common fundamental idea, differently shadowed forth—the gradual growth and ultimate prevalence of the kingdom of God: those of the net and the tares represent the mingling of the good with the bad in the kingdom of God: those of the treasure and the pearl inculcate the inestimable and all-indemnifying value of the kingdom of God: and the parable of the sower depicts the unequal susceptibility of men to the preaching of the kingdom of God.   Thus there are no less than four separate fundamental ideas involved in this collection of parables—ideas which are indeed connected by their general relation to the kingdom of God, but which present this object under aspects so widely different, that for their thorough comprehension a pause after each was indispensable. Hence, it has been concluded, Jesus would not merit the praise of being a judicious teacher, if as Matthew represents, he had spoken all the above parables in rapid succession.§   If we suppose in this instance, again, an assemblage of discourses similar in kind, but delivered on different occasions, we are anew led to the discussion

    * Schulz, über das Abendmahl, S. 344.   † Olshausen, bibl. Comm. 1, S. 137.
‡ L. J. Chr., S. 175.   § Schneckenburger, über den Ursprung u. s. f., S. 33.

as to whether Matthew was aware of the latter circumstance, or
whether he believed that he was recording a continuous harangue.
The introductory form, *And he spake many things to them in parables*, (v. 3.): καὶ ἐλάλησεν αὐτοῖς πολλὰ ἐν παραβολαῖς, and the concluding one, *when Jesus had finished these parables* (v. 53): ὅτε
ἐτέλεσεν ὁ Ἰησοῦς τὰς παραβολὰς ταύτας, seem to be a clear proof that
he did not present the intermediate matter as a compilation. Mark,
indeed, narrates (iv. 10), that at the close of the first parable, the
disciples being again, καταμόνας, *in private*, with Jesus, asked him
for its interpretation; and hence it has been contended* that there
was an interruption of the discourse at this point; but this cannot
serve to explain the account of Matthew, for he represents the request of the disciples as being preferred on the spot, without any
previous retirement from the crowd; thus proving that he did not
suppose such an interruption. The concluding form which Matthew
inserts after the fourth parable (v. 34 f.), might, with better reason,
be adduced as intimating an interruption, for he there comprises all
the foregoing parables in one address by the words, *All these things
spake Jesus in parables, &c.*, ταῦτα πάντα ἐλάλησεν ὁ Ἰησοῦς ἐν
παραβολαῖς κ. τ. λ., and makes the pause still more complete by the
application of an Old Testament prophecy; moreover, Jesus is here
said (36) to change his locality, to dismiss the multitude to whom
he had hitherto been speaking on the shore of the Galilean sea, and
enter *the house*, εἰς τὴν οἰκίαν, where he gives three new parables,
in addition to the interpretation which his disciples had solicited of
the second. But that the delivery of the last three parables was
separated from that of the preceding ones by a change of place, and
consequently by a short interval of time, very little alters the state
of the case. For it is highly improbable that Jesus would without
intermission tax the memory of the populace, whose minds it was
so easy to overburthen, with four parables, two of which were highly
significant; and that he should forthwith overwhelm his disciples,
whose power of comprehension he had been obliged to aid in the
application of the first two parables, with three new ones, instead
of ascertaining if they were capable of independently expounding
the third and fourth. Further, we have only to look more closely
at Matthew's narrative, in order to observe that he has fallen quite
involuntarily on the interruption at v. 34 ff. If it were his intention to communicate a series of parables, with the explanations that
Jesus privately gave to his disciples of the two which were most
important, and were therefore to be placed at the head of the series,
there were only three methods on which he could proceed. First,
he might make Jesus, immediately after the enunciation of a parable,
give its interpretation to his disciples in the presence of the multitude, as he actually does in the case of the first parable (10—23). But
the representation is beset with the difficulty of conceiving how Jesus, surrounded by a crowd, whose expectation was on the stretch,

* Olshausen, S. 438.

could find leisure for a conversation aside with his disciples.* This inconvenience Mark perceived, and therefore chose the second resource that was open to him—that of making Jesus with his disciples withdraw after the first parable into *the house,* and there deliver its interpretation. But such a proceeding would be too great a hindrance to one who proposed publicly to deliver several parables one after the other: for if Jesus returned to the house immediately after the first parable, he had left the scene in which the succeeding ones could be conveniently imparted to the people. Consequently, the narrator in the first gospel cannot, with respect to the interpretation of the second parable, either repeat his first plan, or resort to the second; he therefore adopts a third, and proceeding uninterruptedly through two further parables, it is only at their close that he conducts Jesus to the house, and there makes him impart the arrear of interpretation. Herewith there arose in the mind of the narrator a sort of rivalry between the parables which he had yet in reserve, and the interpretation, the arrear of which embarrassed him; as soon as the former were absent from his recollection, the latter would be present with its inevitably associated form of conclusion and return homeward; and when any remaining parables recurred to him, he was obliged to make them the sequel of the interpretation. Thus it befel with the three last parables in Matthew's narration; so that he was reduced almost against his will to make the disciples their sole participants, though it does not appear to have been the custom of Jesus thus to clothe his private instructions; and Mark (v. 33 f.) plainly supposes the parables which follow the interpretation of the second, to be also addressed to the people.†

Mark, who (iv. 1) depicts the same scene by the sea-side, as Matthew, has in connexion with it only three parables, of which the first and third correspond to the first and third of Matthew, but the middle one is commonly deemed peculiar to Mark.‡ Matthew has in its place the parable wherein the kingdom of heaven is likened to a man who sowed good seed in his field; but while men slept, the enemy came and sowed tares among it, which grew up with the wheat. The servants know not from whence the tares come, and propose to root them up: but the master commands them to let both grow together until the harvest, when it will be time enough to separate them. In Mark, Jesus compares the kingdom of heaven to a man who casts seed into the ground, and while he sleeps and rises again, the seed passes, he knows not how, from one stage of development to another: *and when it is ripe, he puts in the sickle, because the harvest is come.* In this parable there is wanting what constitutes the dominant idea in that of Matthew, the tares, sown by the enemy; but as, nevertheless, the other ideas, of sowing,

* Schleiermacher, S. 120.   † Fritzsche, Comm. in Marc. S. 120, 128, 134; De Wette, in loc.   ‡ Comp. Saunier, über die Quellen des Markus, S. 74; Fritzsche, ut sup; De Wette, in loc.

sleeping, growing one knows not how, and harvest, wholly correspond, it may be questioned whether Mark does not here merely give the same parable in a different version, which he preferred to that of Matthew, because it seemed more intermediate between the first parable of the sower, and the third of the mustard-seed.

Luke, also, has only three of the seven parables given in Matt. xiii.; namely, those of the sower, the mustard-seed, and the leaven; so that the parables of the buried treasure, the pearl, and the net, as also that of the tares in the field, are peculiar to Matthew. The parable of the sower is placed by Luke (viii. 4 ff.) somewhat earlier, and in other circumstances, than by Matthew, and apart from the two other parables which he has in common with the first evangelist's series. These he introduces later, xiii. 18—21; a position which recent critics unanimously acknowledge as the correct one.* But this decision is one of the most remarkable to which the criticism of the present age has been led by its partiality to Luke. For if we examine the vaunted connectedness of this evangelist's passages, we find, that Jesus, having healed a woman *bowed down by a spirit of infirmity*, silences the punctilious ruler of the synagogue by the argument about the ox and ass, after which it is added (v. 17), *And when he had said these things, all his adversaries were ashamed; and all the people rejoiced for all the glorious things that were done by him.* Surely so complete and marked a form of conclusion is intended to wind up the previous narrative, and one cannot conceive that the sequel went forward in the same scene; on the contrary, the phrases, *then said he*, and *again he said*, by which the parables are connected, indicate that the writer had no longer any knowledge of the occasion on which Jesus uttered them, and hence inserted them at random in this indeterminate manner, far less judiciously than Matthew, who at least was careful to associate them with analogous materials.†

We proceed to notice the other evangelical parables,‡ and first among them, those which are peculiar to one evangelist. We come foremost in Matthew to the parable of the servant (xviii. 23 ff.) who, although his lord had forgiven him a debt of ten thousand talents, had no mercy on his fellow-servant who owed him a hundred; tolerably well introduced by an exhortation to placability (v. 15), and the question of Peter, *How oft shall my brother sin against me, and I forgive him?* Likewise peculiar to Matthew is the parable of the labourers in the vineyard (xx. 1 ff.), which suitably enough forms a counterpoise to the foregoing promise of a rich recompense to the disciples. Of the sentences which Matthew appends to this parable (v. 16), the first, *So the last shall be first, and the first last,* by which he had also prefaced it (xix. 30), is the only one with

---

* Schleiermacher, ut sup. S. 192; Olshausen, 1, S. 431; Schneckenburger, ut sup. S. 33. † Comp De Wette, exeg. Handb. 1, 2, S. 73 f. ‡ Analogies to these parables and apothegms, are given out of the rabbinical literature by Wetstein, Lightfoot, and Schöttgen, in loc.

which it has any internal connexion; the other, *for many are called, but few chosen*, rather gives the moral of the parable of the royal feast and the wedding garment, in connexion with which Matthew actually repeats it (xxii. 14). It was well adapted, however, even torn from this connexion, to circulate as an independent apothegm, and as it appeared fitting to the evangelist to annex one or more short sentences to the end of a parable, he might be induced, by some superficial similarity to the one already given, to place them in companionship. Farther, the parable of the two sons sent into the vineyard, is also peculiar to Matthew (xxi. 28 ff.), and is not ill-placed in connexion with the foregoing questions and retorts between Jesus and the Pharisees: its anti-Pharisaic significance is also well brought out by the sequel (31 f.).

Among the parables which are peculiar to Luke, that of the two debtors (vii, 41 ff.): that of the good Samaritan (x. 30 ff.); that of the man whose accumulation of earthly treasure is interrupted by death (xii. 16 ff. comp. Wis. xi. 17 ff.); and also the two which figure the efficacy of importunate prayer (xi. 5 ff. xviii. 2 ff.); have a definite, clear signification, and with the exception of the last, which is introduced abruptly, a tolerably consistent connexion. We may learn from the two last parables, that it is often necessary entirely to abstract particular features from the parables of Jesus, seeing that in one of them God is represented by a lukewarm friend, in the other by an unjust judge. To the latter is annexed the parable of the Pharisee and Publican (9—14), of which only Schleiermacher, on the strength of a connexion, fabricated by himself between it and the foregoing, can deny the antipharisaic tendency.[*] The parables of the lost sheep, the piece of silver, and the prodigal son (Luke xv. 3—32), have the same direction. Matthew also has the first of these (xviii. 12 ff.), but in a different connexion, which determines its import somewhat differently, and without doubt, as will presently be shown, less correctly. It is easy to imagine that these three parables were spoken in immediate succession, because the second is merely a variation of the first, and the third is an amplification and elucidation of them both. Whether, according to the opinion of modern criticism, the two succeeding parables also belong with the above to one continuous discourse,[†] must be determined by a closer examination of their contents, which are in themselves noteworthy.

The parable of the unjust steward, notoriously the *crux interpretum*, is yet without any intrinsic difficulty. If we read to the end of the parable, including the moral (v. 9), we gather the simple result, that the man who without precisely using unjust means to obtain riches, is yet in the sight of God an *unprofitable servant*, δοῦλος ἀχρεῖος (Luke xvii. 10), and, in the employment of the gifts intrusted to him by God, a *steward of injustice*, οἰκονόμος τῆς ἀδικίας, may best atone for this pervading unfaithfulness by lenity and bene-

* Ueber den Lukas, S. 220.   † Schleiermacher, ut sup. S. 202 ff.   Olshausen, in loc.

ficence towards his fellow-men, and may by their intervention procure a place in heaven. It is true that the beneficence of the fictitious steward is a fraud; but we must abstract this particular, as, in the case of two previous parables, we have to abstract the lukewarmness of the friend, and the injustice of the judge: nay, the necessity for such an abstraction is intimated in the narrative itself, for from v. 8. we gather that what the steward did in a worldly spirit is, in the application, to be understood in a more exalted sense of the *children of light*. Certainly, if we suppose the words, *He that is faithful in that which is least*, &c. (10—12) to have been uttered in their present connexion, it appears as if the steward were set forth as a model, deserving in some sense or other the praise of faithfulness; and when (v. 13) it is said that no servant can serve two masters, the intended inference seems to be that this steward had held to the rightful one. Hence we have expositions such as that of Schleier-macher, who under the master understands the Romans; under the debtors, the Jewish people; under the steward, the publicans, who were generous to the latter at the expense of the former; thus, in the most arbitrary manner, transforming the master into a violent man, and justifying the steward.* Olshausen carries the perversion of the parable to the extreme, for he degrades the master, who, by his judicial position evidently announces himself as the representative of God, into ἄρχων τοῦ κόσμου τούτου, *the prince of this world*, while he exalts the steward into the image of a man who applies the riches of this world to spiritual objects. But as in the moral (v. 9) the parable has a consistent ending; and as inaccurate association is by no means unexampled in Luke; it is not admissible to concede to the following verses any influence over the interpretation of the parable, unless a close relation of idea can be made manifest. Now the fact is, that the very opposite, namely, the most perplexing diversity, exists. Moreover, it is not difficult to show what might have seduced Luke into a false association. In the parable there was mention of the *mammon of unrighteousness*, μαμωνᾶς τῆς ἀδικίας; this suggested to him the saying of Jesus, that he who proves faithful in the ἀδίκῳ μαμωνᾷ, *the unrighteous mammon*, as that which is least, may also have the true riches committed to his trust. But the word *mammon* having once taken possession of the writer's mind, how could he avoid recollecting the well known aphorism of Jesus on God and Mammon, as two incompatible masters, and adding it (v. 13), however superfluously, to the preceding texts?†

* Ut sup.

† Schneckenburger has decided, Beiträge, No. V, where he refutes Olshausen's interpretation of the parable, that this verse does not really belong to its present position, while with respect to the preceding verses from v. 9, he finds it possible to hold the contrary opinion. De Wette also considers that v. 13 is the only one decidedly out of place. He thinks it possible, by supplying an intermediate proposition, which he supposes the writer to have omitted, and which led from the *prudent* use of riches to faithfulness in preserving those entrusted to us, to give a sufficient connexion to v. 9 and 10—12, without necessarily referring the idea of faithfulness to the conduct of the steward. The numerous attempts, both ancient and modern, to explain the parable of the steward without a critical

That by this addition the previous parable was placed in a thoroughly false light, gave the writer little concern, perhaps because he had not seized its real meaning, or because, in the endeavour completely to disburthen his evangelical meaning, he lost all solicitude about the sequence of his passages. It ought, in general, to be more considered, that those of our evangelists who, according to the now prevalent opinion, noted down oral traditions, must, in the composition of their writings have exerted their memory to an extent that would repress the activity of reflection; consequently the arrangement of the materials in their narratives is governed by the association of ideas, the laws of which are partly dependent on external relations: and we need not be surprised to find many passages, especially from the discourses of Jesus, ranged together for the sole cause that they happen to have in common certain striking consonant words.

If from hence we glance back on the position, that the parable of the unjust steward must have been spoken in connexion with the foregoing one of the prodigal son, we perceive that it rests merely on a false interpretation. According to Schleiermacher, it is the defence of the publicans against the Pharisees, that forms the bond; but there is no trace of publicans and Pharisees in the latter parable. According to Olshausen, the compassionate love of God, represented in the foregoing parable, is placed in juxtaposition with the compassionate love of man, represented in the succeeding one: but simple beneficence is the sole idea on which the latter turns, and a parallel between this and the manner in which God meets the lost with pardon, is equally remote from the intention of the teacher and the nature of the subject. The remark (v. 14) that the Pharisees heard all these things, and, being covetous, derided Jesus, does not necessarily refer to the individuals mentioned xv. 2, so as to imply that they had listened to the intermediate matter as one continuous discourse; and even if that were the case, it would only show the view of the writer with respect to the connectedness of the parables: a view which, in the face of the foregoing investigation, cannot possibly be binding on us.*

We have already discussed the passage from v. 15 to 18; it consists of disconnected sayings, and to the last, on adultery, is annexed the parable of the rich man, in a manner which, as we have already noticed, it is attempted in vain to show as a real connexion. It must, however, be conceded to Schleiermacher, that if we separate them, the alternative, namely, the common application of the parable to the penal justice of God, is attended with great difficulties.† For there is no indication throughout the parable, of any actions on the part of the rich man and Lazarus, that could, according to our notions, justify the exaltation of the one to a place in Abraham's

dislocation of the associated passages, are only so many proofs that it is absolutely requisite to a satisfactory interpretation.
* Comp. De Wette, exeg. Handbuch I, 2, S. 80.   † Ut sup. S. 208.

bosom, and the condemnation of the other to torment; the guilt of the one appears to lie in his wealth, the merit of the other in his poverty. It is indeed generally supposed of the rich man, that he was immoderate in his indulgence, and that he had treated Lazarus unkindly.* But the latter is nowhere intimated; for the picture of the beggar lying at the door of the rich man, is not intended in the light of a reproach to the latter, because he might easily have tendered his aid, and yet neglected to do so; it is designed to exhibit the contrast, not only between the earthly condition of the two parties, but between their proximity in this life, and their wide separation in another. So the other particular, that the beggar was eager for the crumbs that fell from the rich man's table, does not imply that the rich man denied him this pittance, or that he ought to have given him more than the mere crumbs; it denotes the deep degradation of the earthly lot of Lazarus compared with that of the rich man, in opposition to their reversed position after death, when the rich man is fain to entreat for a drop of water from the hand of Lazarus. On the supposition that the rich man had been wanting in compassion towards Lazarus, the Abraham of the parable could only reply in the following manner: "Thou hadst once easy access to Lazarus, and yet thou didst not relieve him; how then canst thou expect him to traverse a long distance to give thee alleviation?" The sumptuous life of the rich man, likewise, is only depicted as a contrast to the misery of the beggar; for if he had been supposed guilty of excess, Abraham must have reminded him that he had taken too much of the good things of this life, not merely that he had received his share of them. Equally groundless is it, on the other hand, to suppose high moral excellencies in Lazarus, since there is no intimation of such in the description of him, which merely regards his outward condition,—neither are such ascribed to him by Abraham: his sole merit is, the having received evil in this life. Thus, in this parable the measure of future recompense is not the amount of good done, or wickedness perpetrated, but of evil endured, and fortune enjoyed,† and the aptest motto for this discourse is to be found in the sermon on the mount, according to Luke's edition: *Blessed be ye poor, for yours is the kingdom of God! Woe to you that are rich! for ye have received your consolation;* a passage concerning which we have already remarked, that it accords fully with the Ebionite view of the world. A similar estimation of external poverty is ascribed to Jesus by the other synoptists, in the narrative of the rich young man, and in the aphorisms on the camel and the needle's eye (Matt. xix. 16 ff.; Mark x. 17 ff.; comp. Luke xviii. 18 ff.). Whether this estimation belong to Jesus himself, or only to the synoptical tradition concerning him, it was probably generated by the notions of the Essenes.‡ We have hitherto con-

---

* Vid. Kuinöl, in loc.   † Comp. De Wette, 1, 2, S. 86 f.   ‡ On the Essenes as *contemners of riches* (καταφρονητὰς πλούτου), comp. Joseph. b. j. ii. viii. 3; Credner, über Essener und Ebioniten, in Winer's Zeitschrift, 1, S. 217; Gfrörer, Philo, 2, S. 311.

sidered the contents of the parable down to v. 27: from whence to the conclusion the subject is, the writings of the Old Testament as the adequate and only means of grace.

In conclusion, we turn to a group of parables, among which some, as relating to the death and return of Christ, ought, according to our plan, to be excepted from the present review; but so far as they are connected with the rest, it is necessary to include them. They are the three parables of the rebellious husbandmen in the vineyard (Matt. xxi. 33 ff. parall.), of the talents or minæ (Matt. xxv. 14 ff.; Luke xix. 12 ff.), and the marriage feast (Matt. xxii. 3 ff.; Luke xiv. 16 ff.). Of these the parable of the husbandmen in all the accounts, that of the talents in Matthew, and that of the marriage feast in Luke, are simple parables, unattended with difficulty. Not so the parable of the minæ in Luke, and of the marriage feast in Matthew. That the former is fundamentally the same with that of the talents in Matthew, is undeniable, notwithstanding the many divergencies. In both are found the journey of a master; the assembling of the servants to entrust them with a capital, to be put into circulation; after the return of the master, a reckoning in which three servants are signalized, two of them as active, the third as inactive, whence the latter is punished, and the former rewarded; and in the annunciation of this issue the words of the master are nearly identical in the two statements. The principal divergency is, that besides the relation between the master who journeys into a far country and his servants, in Luke there is a second relation between the former and certain rebellious citizens: and accordingly, while in Matthew the master is simply designated ἄνθρωπος, *a man*, in Luke he is styled ἄνθρωπος εὐγενής, a *nobleman*, and a *kingdom* is assigned to him, the object of his journey being to *receive for himself a kingdom:* an object of which there is no mention in Matthew. The subjects of this personage, it is farther said, hated him, and after his departure renounced their allegiance. Hence at the return of the lord, the rebellious citizens, as well as the slothful servant, are punished; but in their case the retribution is that of death: the faithful servants, on the other hand, are not only rewarded generally by an entrance into the joy of their Lord, but royally, by the gift of a number of cities. There are other divergencies of less moment between Luke and Matthew; such as, that the number of servants is undetermined by the one, and limited to ten by the other; that in Matthew they receive talents, in Luke minæ; in the one unequal sums, in the other equal: in the one, they obtain unequal profits from unequal sums by an equal expenditure of effort, and are therefore equally rewarded: in the other, they obtain unequal profits from equal sums by an unequal expenditure of effort, and are therefore unequally rewarded.

Supposing this parable to have proceeded from the lips of Jesus on two separate occasions, and that Matthew and Luke are right in their respective arrangements, he must have delivered it first in the more complex form given by Luke, and then in the simple one given by Matthew ;* since the former places it before, the latter after the entrance into Jerusalem. But this would be contrary to all analogy. The first presentation of an idea is, according to the laws of thought, the most simple : with the second new relations may be perceived, the subject may be viewed under various aspects, and brought into manifold combinations. There is, therefore, a foundation for Schleiermacher's opinion, that contrary to the arrangement in the Gospels, Jesus first delivered the parable in the more simple form, and amplified it on a subsequent occasion.† But for our particular case this order is not less inconceivable than the other. The author of a composition such as a parable, especially when it exists only in his mind and on his lips, and is not yet fixed in writing, remains the perfect master of his materials even on their second and more elaborate presentation ; the form which he had previously given to them is not rigid and inflexible, but pliant, so that he can adapt the original thoughts and images to the additional ones, and thus give unity to his production. Hence, had he who gave the above parable the form which it has in Luke, been its real author, he would, after having transformed the master into a king, and inserted the particulars respecting the rebellious citizens, have entrusted arms to the servants instead of money (comp. Luke xxii. 36.),‡ and would have made them show their fidelity rather by conflict with the rebels, than by increasing their capital ; or in general would have introduced some relation between the two classes of persons in the parable, the servants and the citizens : instead of which, they are totally unconnected throughout, and form two ill-cemented divisions.§

This shows very decisively that the parable was not enriched with these additional particulars by the imagination of its author, but that it was thus amplified by another in the process of transmission. This cannot have been effected in a legendary manner, by the gradual filling up of the original sketch, or the development of the primitive germ; for the idea of rebellious citizens could never be evolved from that of servants and talents, but must have been added from without, and therefore have previously existed as part of an independent whole. This amounts to the position that we have here an example of two originally distinct parables, the one treating of servants and talents, the other of rebellious citizens, flowing together in consequence of their mutually possessing the images of a ruler's departure and return.‖ The proof of our proposition must depend on our being able easily to disentangle the two parables : and this we can effect in the most satisfactory manner, for by extracting v. 12, 14, 15, and 27, and slightly modifying them, we get in a rather curtailed but consistent form, the

---

* Thus Kuinöl, Comm. in Luc. p. 635. † Ueber den Lukas, 239 f. Neander agrees with him, L. J. Chr. p. 188.   ‡ This is a reply to Neander's objection, p. 191 note. § How Paulus, exeg. Handb. 3, a, p. 76, can pronounce the more complex form of the parable in Luke as not only the most fully developed but the best wound up, I am at a loss to understand. ‖ Comp. De Wette, 1, 1, S. 208 f.

parable of the rebellious citizens, and we then recognise the similarity of its tendency with that of the rebellious husbandmen in the vineyard.*

A similar relation subsists between the form in which the parable of the marriage feast is given by Luke (xiv. 16 ff.), and that in which it is given by Matthew (xxii. 2 ff.) ; only that in this case Luke, as in the other, Matthew, has the merit of having preserved the simple original version. On both sides, the particulars of the feast, the invitation, its rejection and the consequent bidding of other guests, testify the identity of the two parables ; but, on the other hand, the host who in Luke is merely *a certain man*, ἄνθρωπός τις, is in Matthew *a king*, βασιλεὺς, whose feast is occasioned by the marriage of his son ; the invited guests, who in Luke excuse themselves on various pleas to the messenger only once sent out to them, in Matthew refuse to come on the first invitation, and on the second more urgent one, some go to their occupations, while others maltreat and kill the servants of the king, who immediately sends forth his armies to destroy those murderers, and burn up their city. Nothing of this is to be found in Luke : according to him, the host merely causes the poor and afflicted to be assembled in place of the guests first invited, a particular which Matthew also appends to his fore-mentioned incidents. Luke closes the parable with the declaration of the host, that none of the first bidden guests shall partake of his supper; but Matthew proceeds to narrate how, when the house was full, and the king had assembled his guests, one was discovered to be without a wedding garment, and was forthwith carried away into outer darkness.

The maltreatment and murder of the king's messengers are features in the narrative of Matthew which at once strike us as inconsistent—as a departure from the original design. Disregard of an invitation is sufficiently demonstrated by the rejection of it on empty pretexts such as Luke mentions ; the maltreatment and even the murder of those who deliver the invitation, is an exaggeration which it is less easy to attribute to Jesus than to the Evangelist. The latter had immediately before communicated the parable of the rebellious husbandmen; hence there hovered in his recollection the manner in which they were said to have used the messengers of their lord, beating one, killing and stoning others, (λαβόντες τοὺς δούλοις αὐτοῦ ὃν μὲν ἔδειραν, ὃν δὲ ἀπέκτειναν, ὃν δὲ ἐλιθοβόλησαν,) and he was thus led to incorporate similar particulars into the present parable (κρατήσαντες τοὺς δούλους αὐτοῦ ὕβρισαν καὶ ἀπέκτειναν,) overlooking the circumstance that what might have been perpetrated with sufficient motive against servants who appeared with demands

---

* V. 12. Ἄνθρωπός τις εὐγενὴς ἐπορεύθη εἰς χώραν μακρὰν, λαβεῖν ἑαυτῷ βασιλείαν, καὶ ὑποστρέψαι. 14 οἱ δὲ πολῖται αὐτοῦ ἐμίσουν αὐτόν, καὶ ἀπέστειλαν πρεσβείαν ὀπίσω αὐτοῦ, λέγοντες· οὐ θέλομεν τοῦτον βασιλεῦσαι ἐφ' ἡμᾶς. 15. καὶ ἐγένετο ἐν τῷ ἐπανελθεῖν αὐτὸν λαβόντα τὴν βασιλείαν, καὶ εἶπε φωνηθῆναι αὐτῷ τοὺς δούλους—(καὶ εἶπεν αὐτοῖς) 27. —τοὺς ἐχθρούς μου ἐκείνους, τοὺς μὴ θελήσαντάς με βασιλεῦσαι ἐπ' αὐτοὺς, ἀγάγετε ὧδε καὶ κατασφάξατε ἔμπροσθέν μου.

and authority to enforce them, had in the latter case no motive whatever. That hereupon, the king, not satisfied with excluding them from this feast, sends out his armies to destroy them and burn up their city, necessarily follows from the preceding incidents, but appears, like them, to be the echo of a parable which presented the relation between the master and the dependents, not in the milder form of a rejected invitation, but in the more severe one of an insurrection: as in the parable of the husbandmen in the vineyard, and that of the rebellious citizens, which we have above separated from the parable of the minæ. Yet more decidedly does the drift of the last particular in Matthew's parable, that of the wedding garment, betray that it was not originally associated with the rest. For if the king had commanded that all, *both bad and good*, who were to be found in the highways, should be bidden to the feast, he could not wonder that they had not all wedding attire. To assume that those thus suddenly summoned went home to wash, and adjust their dress, is an arbitrary emendation of the text.* Little preferable is the supposition that, according to oriental manners, the king had ordered a caftan to be presented to each guest, and might therefore justly reproach the meanest for not availing himself of the gift;† for it is not to be proved that such a custom existed at the period,‡ and it is not admissible to presuppose it merely because the anger of the king appears otherwise unfounded. But the addition in question is not only out of harmony with the imagery, but with the tendency of this parable. For while hitherto its aim had been to exhibit the national contrast between the perversity of the Jews, and the willingness of the gentiles: it all at once passes to the moral one, to distinguish between the worthy and the unworthy. That after the Jews had contemned the invitation to partake of the kingdom of God, the heathens would be called into it, is one complete idea, with which Luke very properly concludes his parable; that he who does not prove himself worthy of the vocation by a corresponding disposition, will be again cast out of the kingdom, is another idea, which appears to demand a separate parable for its exhibition. Here again it may be conjectured that the conclusion of Matthew's parable is the fragment of another, which, from its also referring to a feast, might in tradition, or in the memory of an individual, be easily mingled with the former, preserved in its purity by Luke.§ This other parable must have simply set forth, that a king had invited various guests to a wedding feast, with the tacit condition that they should provide themselves with a suitable dress, and that he delivered an individual who had neglected this observance to his merited punishment. Supposing our conjectures correct,

---

* Fritzsche, p. 656. This remark serves to refute De Wette's vindication of the above particular in his exeg. Handb.   † Paulus, exeg. Handb. 3, a, S. 210; Olshausen, bibl. Comm. 1, S. 811.   ‡ Vid. Fritzsche, ut sup.   § From the appendix to Schnecken-burger's Beiträgen, I see that a reviewer in the Theol. Literaturblatt, 1831, No. 83, has also conjectured that we have here a blending of two originally distinct parables.

we have here a still more compound parable than in the former case: a parable in which, 1stly, the narrative of the ungrateful invited parties (Luke xiv.) forms the main tissue, but so that, 2ndly, a thread from the parable of the rebellious husbandmen is interwoven; while, 3rdly, a conclusion is stitched on, gathered apparently from an unknown parable on the wedding garment.

This analysis gives us an insight into the procedure of evangelical tradition with its materials, which must be pregnant with results.

§ 79. MISCELLANEOUS INSTRUCTIONS AND CONTROVERSIES OF JESUS.

As the discourses in Matt. xv. 1—20 have been already considered, we must pass on to xviii. 1 ff., Mark ix. 33 ff., Luke ix. 46 ff., where various discourses are connected with the exhibition of a little child, occasioned by a contention for pre-eminence among the disciples. The admonition to become as a little child, and to humble one's self as a little child, in Matthew forms a perfectly suitable comment on the symbolical reproof (v. 3, 4.); but the connexion between this and the following declaration of Jesus, that whosoever receives one such little child in his name, receives him, is not so obvious. For the child was set up to teach the disciples in what they were to imitate it, not how they were to behave towards it, and how Jesus could all at once lose sight of his original object, it is difficult to conceive. But yet more glaring is the irrelevance of the declaration in Mark and Luke; for they make it follow immediately on the exhibition of the child, so that, according to this, Jesus must, in the very act, have forgotten its object, namely, to present the child to his ambitious disciples as worthy of imitation, not as in want of reception.* Jesus was accustomed to say of his disciples, that whosoever received them, received him, and in him, the Father who had sent him (Matt. x. 40 ff.; Luke x. 16; John xiii. 20). Of children he elsewhere says merely, that whosoever does not receive the kingdom of heaven as a little child cannot enter therein (Mark x. 15. Luke xviii. 17.) This declaration would be perfectly adapted to the occasion in question, and we may almost venture to conjecture that ὃς ἐὰν μὴ δέξηται τὴν βασιλείαν τῶν οὐρανῶν ὡς παιδίον, was the original passage, and that the actual one is the result of its confusion with Matt. x. 40, ὃς ἐὰν δέξηται παιδίον τοιοῦτον ἓν ἐπὶ τῷ ὀνόματί μου.

Closely connected by the word ἀποκριθείς, answering, with the sentences just considered, Mark (ix. 38 f.) and Luke (ix. 49 f.) introduce the information which John is said to give to Jesus, that the disciples having seen one casting out devils in the name of Jesus, without attaching himself to their society, had forbidden him. Schleiermacher explains the connexion thus: because Jesus had commanded the reception of children in his name, John was led to

---

* Comp. De Wette, 1, 1, S. 152.

the confession, that he and his associates had hitherto been so far from regarding the performing of an act in the name of Jesus as the point of chief importance, that they had interdicted the use of his name to one who followed not with them.* Allowing this explanation to be correct, we must believe that John, arrested by the phrase, *in my name* (which yet is not prominent in the declaration of Jesus, and which must have been thrown still farther into the background, by the sight of the child set up in the midst), drew from it the general inference, that in all actions the essential point is to perform them *in the name of Jesus;* and with equal rapidity, leaped to the remote reflection, that the conduct of the disciples towards the exorcist was in contradiction with this rule. But all this supposes the facility of combination which belongs to a Schleiermacher, not the dulness which still characterized the disciples. Nevertheless, the above critic has unquestionably opened on the true vein of connexion between the preceding apothegm and this ἀπόκρισις of John; he has only failed to perceive that this connexion is not intrinsic and original, but extrinsic and secondary. It was quite beyond the reach of the disciples to apply the words *in my name,* by a train of deductions, to an obliquely connected case in their own experience; but, according to our previous observations, nothing could be more consistent with the habit of association that characterizes the writer of the evangelical tradition in the third Gospel, whence the second evangelist seems to have borrowed, than that he should be reminded by the striking phrase, *in my name,* in the preceding discourse of Jesus, of an anecdote containing the same expression, and should unite the two for the sake of that point of external similarity alone.†

To the exhortation to receive such little children, Matthew annexes the warning against *offending one of these little ones,* σκανδαλίζειν ἕνα τῶν μικρῶν τούτων, an epithet which, in x. 42, is applied to the disciples of Jesus, but in this passage, apparently, to children.‡ Mark (v. 42) has the same continuation, notwithstanding the interruption above noticed, probably because he forsook Luke (who here breaks off the discourse, and does not introduce the admonition against offences until later, xvii. 1. f., and apart from any occasion that might prompt it), and appealed to Matthew.§ Then follows in Matthew (v. 8 f.) and Mark (v. 43 f.) a passage which alone ought to open the eyes of commentators to the mode in which the synoptists arrange the sayings of Jesus. To the warning against the *offending,* σκανδαλίζειν, of the little ones, and the woe pronounced on those by whom *offences come,* το σκάνδαλον ἔρχεται, they annex the apothegm on the *offending* σκανδαλίζειν, of the hand, eye, &c. Jesus could not proceed thus,—for the injunctions: Mislead not the little ones! and, Let not your sensuality mislead you! have nothing in common but the word *mislead.* It is easy, however, to account

* Ueber den Lukas, S. 153 f.
† Comp. De Wette, in loc.
‡ Vid. Fritzsche and De Wette, in loc.
§ Saunier, über die Quellen des Markus, S. 111.

for their association by the writer of the first Gospel.* The word σκανδαλίζειν recalled to his mind all the discourses of Jesus containing a similar expression that had come to his knowledge, and also he had previously presented the admonitions concerning seduction by the members, in a better connexion, as part of the sermon on the mount, he could not resist the temptation of reproducing them here, for the sake of this slight verbal affinity with the foregoing text. But at v. 10 he resumes the thread which he had dropped at v. 7, and adds a further discourse on the *little ones*, μικροῖς. Matthew makes Jesus confirm the value of the little ones by the declaration, that the Son of Man was come to seek the lost, and by the parable of the lost sheep, (v. 11—14). It is not, however, evident why Jesus should class the μικροῖς with the ἀπολωλὸς (*lost*): and both the declaration and the parable seem to be better placed by Luke, who introduces the former in the narrative of the calling of Zaccheus (xix. 10.), and the latter, in a reply to the objections of the Pharisees against the amity of Jesus with the publicans (xv. 3 ff.). Matthew seems to have placed them here, merely because the discourse on the little ones reminded him of that on the lost,—both exemplifying the mildness and humility of Jesus.

Between the moral of the above parable (v. 14) and the following rules for the conduct of Christians under injuries (v. 15 ff.), there is again only a verbal connexion, which may be traced by means of the words, ἀπόληται, should perish, and ἐκέρδησας, *thou hast gained;* for the proposition: God wills not that one of these little ones should perish, might recall the proposition: We should endeavour to win over our brother, by showing a readiness to forgive. The direction to bring the offender before the *church*, ἐκκλησία, is generally adduced as a proof that Jesus intended to found a church. But he here speaks of the ἐκκλησία as an institution already existing: hence we must either refer the expression to the Jewish synagogue, an interpretation which is favoured by the analogy of this direction with Jewish precepts; or if, according to the strict meaning of the word and its connexion, ἐκκλησία must be understood as the designation of the Christian community, which did not then exist, it must be admitted that we have here, at least in the form of expression, an anticipation of a subsequent state of things.† The writer certainly had in view the new church, eventually to be founded in the name of Jesus, when, in continuation, he represented the latter as imparting to the body of the disciples the authority to bind and to loose, previously given to Peter, and thus to form a messianic religious constitution. The declarations concerning the success of unanimous prayer, and the presence of Jesus among two or three gathered together in his name, accord with this prospective idea.‡

The next discourse that presents itself (Matt. xix. 3—12, Mark,

---

* Comp. De Wette, in loc. Matt.   † Vid. De Wette, exeg. Handbuch 1, 1, p. 155.
‡ Analogous passages from Jewish writings are given in Wetstein, Lightfoot, Schottgen, in loc.

25

x. 2—12), though belonging, according to the evangelists, to the last journey of Jesus, is of the same stamp with the disputations which they, for the most part, assign to the last residence of Jesus in Jerusalem. Some Pharisees propose to Jesus the question, at that time much discussed in the Jewish schools,[*] whether it be lawful for a man to put away his wife for every cause. To avoid a contradiction between modern practice and the dictum of Jesus, it has been alleged that he here censures the species of divorce, which was the only one known at that period, namely, the arbitrary dismissal of a wife; but not the judicial separation resorted to in the present day.[†] But this very argument involves the admission, that Jesus denounced all the forms of divorce known to him; hence the question still remains whether, if he could have had cognizance of the modern procedure in disolving matrimony, he would have held it right to limit his general censure. Of the succeeding declaration, prompted by a question of the disciples,[‡] namely, that celibacy may be practised for the kingdom of heaven's sake, Jesus himself says, that it cannot be understood by all, but only by those *to whom it is given* (v. 11). That the doctrine of Jesus may not run counter to modern opinion, it has been eagerly suggested, that his panegyric on celibacy had relation solely to the circumstances of the coming time, or to the nature of the apostolic mission, which would be impeded by family ties.[§] But there is even less intimation of this special bearing in the text, than in the analogous passage 1 Cor. vii. 25 ff.,[||] and, adhering to a simple interpretation, it must be granted that we have here one of the instances in which ascetic principles, such as were then prevalent, especially among the Essenes,[¶] manifest themselves in the teaching of Jesus, as represented in the synoptical gospels.

The controversial discourses which Matthew, almost throughout in agreement with the other synoptists, places after the entrance of Jesus into Jerusalem (xxi. 23—27; xxii. 15—46),[**] are certainly pre-eminently genuine fragments, having precisely the spirit and tone of the rabbinical dialectics in the time of Jesus. The third and fifth among them are particularly worthy of note, because they exhibit Jesus as an interpreter of Scripture. With respect to the former, wherein Jesus endeavours to convince the Sadducees that there will be a resurrection of the dead, from the Mosaic designation of God as the God of Abraham, of Isaac, and of Jacob, maintaining that he is not the God of the dead, but of the living (Matt. xxii. 31—33

---

* Bemidbar R. ad. Num. v. 30, in Wetstein, p. 303.   † E. g. Paulus, L. J. 1. B. S. 46.   ‡ For probable doubts as to the correctness of the position given to this discourse of Jesus, vid. Neander, L. J. Chr. S. 525, Anm.   § Paulus, ib. S. 50, exeg. Handb. 2, S. 569. || In this passage, it is true that celibacy is at first recommended as good for *the present distress*: but the Apostle does not rest there; for at v. 32 ff. he adds, *He that is unmarried careth for the things of the Lord—he that is married for the things of the world*: —a motive to celibacy which must be equally valid under all circumstances, and which affords us a glimpse into the fundamental asceticism of Paul's views. Comp. Rückert's Commentary in loc.   ¶ Vid. Gfrörer, Philo. 2, S. 310 f.   ** A concise elucidation of them may be found in Hase, L. J. § 129.

parall.): Paulus admits that Jesus here argues subtilly, while he contends that the conclusion is really involved in the premises. But in the expression אֱלֹהֵי־אַבְרָהָם *the God of Abraham* &c., which had become a mere formula, nothing more is implied than that Jehovah, as he had been the protecting Deity of these men, would for ever continue such to their posterity. An individual relation subsisting between Jehovah and the patriarchs after their death, is nowhere else alluded to in the Old Testament, and could only be discovered in the above form by rabbinical interpreters, at a time when it was thought desirable, at any cost, to show that the idea of immortality, which had become prevalent, was contained in the law; where, however, it is not to be met with by unprejudiced eyes. We find the relation of God to Abraham, Isaac, and Jacob, adduced as a guarantee of immortality elsewhere in rabbinical argumentations, all of which could hardly have been modelled on this one of Jesus.[*] If we look into the most recent commentaries, we nowhere find a candid confession as to the real character of the argumentation in question. Olshausen has wonders to tell of the deep truth contained in it, and thinks that he can deduce from it, in the shortest way, the authenticity and divinity of the Pentateuch. Paulus sees the validity of the proof between the lines of the text; Fritzsche is silent. Wherefore these evasions? Why is the praise of having seen clearly, and spoken openly, in this matter, abandoned to the Wolfenbüttel Fragmentist?[†] What spectres and doublesighted beings, must Moses and Jesus have been, if they mixed with their cotemporaries without any real participation in their opinions and weaknesses, their joys and griefs; if, mentally dwelling apart from their age and nation, they conformed to these relations only externally and by accommodation, while, internally and according to their nature, they stood among the foremost ranks of the enlightened in modern times! Far more noble were these men, nay, they would then only engage our sympathy and reverence, if, in a genuinely human manner, struggling with the limitations and prejudices of their age, they succumbed to them in a hundred secondary matters, and only attained perfect freedom, in relation to the one point by which each was destined to contribute to the advancement of mankind.

A controversial question concerning the Messiah is proposed (v. 51—46) to the Pharisees by Jesus, namely, How can the same personage be at once the Lord and the son of David? Paulus maintains that this is a model of interpretation in conformity with the text:[‡] an assertion which is no good augury that his own possesses that qualification. According to him, Jesus, in asking how David could call the Messiah, *Lord*, when in the general opinion he was his son, intended to apprise the Pharisees, that in this Psalm it is not David who is speaking of the Messiah, but another poet who is speaking

* Vid. Gemara Hieros. Berac. f. v. 4, in Lightfoot, p. 423, and R. Manasse Ben Isr. in Schöttgen, i. p. 180.   † See his 4th Fragment, Lessing's Item Beitrag, S. 431 ff. ‡ L. J. I. B. S. 115 ff.

of David as his lord, so that to suppose this warlike psalm a messianic one, is a mistake. Why, asks Paulus, should not Jesus have found out this interpretation, since it is the true one? But this is the grand error of his entire scheme of interpretation—to suppose that what is truth in itself, or more correctly, for us, must, even to the minutest details, have been truth for Jesus and the apostles. The majority of ancient Jewish interpreters apply this psalm to the Messiah;[*] the apostles use it as a prophecy concerning Christ (Acts ii. 34 f. ; 1 Cor. xv. 25); Jesus himself, according to Matthew and Mark, adds ἐν πνεύματι to Δαβίδ καλεῖ αὐτὸν Κύριον, thus plainly giving his approval to the notion that it is David who there speaks, and that the Messiah is his subject: how then can it be thought that he held the contrary opinion? It is far more probable, as Olshausen has well shown, that Jesus believed the psalm to be a messianic one: while, on the other hand, Paulus is equally correct in maintaining that it originally referred, not to the Messiah, but to some Jewish ruler, whether David or another. Thus we find that Jesus here gives a model of interpretation, in conformity, not with the text, but with the spirit of his time; a discovery which, if the above observations be just, ought to excite no surprise. The solution of the enigma which Jesus here proposes to the Pharisees, lay without doubt, according to his idea, in the doctrine of the higher nature of the Messiah; whether he held that, in virtue of this, he might be styled the Lord of David, while, in virtue of his human nature, he might also be regarded as his son : or whether he wished to remove the latter notion as erroneous.[†] The result, however, and perhaps also the intention of Jesus with respect to the Pharisees, was merely to convince them that he was capable of retaliating on them, in their own way, by embarassing them with captious questions, and that with better success than they had obtained in their attempts to entrap him. Hence the evangelists place this passage at the close of the disputations prompted by the Pharisees, and Matthew adds, *Neither durst any man from that day forth ask him any more questions:* a concluding form which is more suitable here than after the lesson administered to the Sadducees, where it is placed by Luke (xx. 40), or than after the discussion on the greatest commandment, where it is introduced by Mark (xii. 34.).

Immediately before this question of Jesus, the first two evangelists narrate a conversation with a *lawyer*, νομικὸς, or *scribe*, γραμματεὺς, concerning the greatest commandment. (Matt. xxii. 34 ff. ; Mark xii. 28 ff.) Matthew annexes this conversation to the dispute with the Sadducees, as if the Pharisees wished, by their question as to the greatest commandment, to avenge the defeat of the Sadducees. It is well known, however, that these sects were not thus friendly; on the contrary, we read in the Acts (xxiii. 7), that the Pharisees were inclined to go over to the side of one whom they had

---

* Vid. Wetstein, in loc. Hengstenberg, Christol. 1, a, S. 140 f.; also Paulus himself, exeg. Handb. 3, a, S. 283 f.   † Comp. De Wette, in loc.

previously persecuted, solely because he had had the address to take the position of an opponent towards the Sadducees. We may here quote Schneckenburger's observation,* that Matthew not seldom (iii. 7 ; xvi. 1) places the Pharisees and Sadducees side by side in a way that represents, not their real hostility, but their association in the memory of tradition, in which one opposite suggested another. In this respect, Mark's mode of annexing this conversation to the foregoing, is more consistent ; but all the synoptists seem to labour under a common mistake in supposing that these discussions, grouped together in tradition on account of their analogy, followed each other so closely in time, that one colloquy elicited another. Luke does not give the question concerning the greatest commandment in connexion with the controversies on the resurrection and on the Messiah ; but he has a similar incident earlier, in his narrative of the journey to Jerusalem (x. 25 ff.). The general opinion is that the first two evangelists recount the same occurrence, and the third, a distinct one.† It is true that the narrative of Luke differs from that of Matthew and Mark, in several not immaterial points. The first difference, which we have already noticed, relates to chronological position, and this has been the chief inducement to the supposition of two events. The next difference lies in the nature of the question, which, in Luke, turns on the rule of life calculated to insure the inheritance of eternal life, but, in the other evangelists, on the greatest commandment. The third difference is in the subject who pronounces this commandment. the first two synoptists representing it to be Jesus, the third, the lawyer. Lastly, there is a difference as to the issue, the lawyer in Luke putting a second, self-vindicatory, question, which calls forth the parable of the good Samaritan ; while in the two other evangelists, he retires either satisfied, or silenced by the answer to the first. Meanwhile, even between the narrative of Matthew and that of Mark, there are important divergencies. The principal relates to the character of the querist, who in Matthew proposes his question with a view to *tempt* Jesus ($\pi\epsilon\iota\rho\acute{\alpha}\zeta\omega\nu$); in Mark, with good intentions, because he had perceived that Jesus had answered the Sadducees well. Paulus, indeed, although he elsewhere (Luke x. 25) considers the act of tempting ($\dot{\epsilon}\kappa\pi\epsilon\iota\rho\acute{\alpha}\zeta\omega\nu$) as the putting a person to the proof to subserve interested views, pronounces that the word $\pi\epsilon\iota\rho\acute{\alpha}\zeta\omega\nu$ in this instance can only be intended in a good sense. But the sole ground for this interpretation lies, not in Matthew, but in Mark, and in the unfounded supposition that the two writers could not have a different idea of the character and intention of the inquiring doctor of the law. Fritzsche has correctly pointed out the difficulty of conciliating Matthew and Mark as lying, partly in the meaning of the word $\pi\epsilon\iota\rho\acute{\alpha}\zeta\omega\nu$, and partly in the context, it being inadmissible to suppose one among a series of malevolent questions friendly, without any intimation of the distinction on the part of the writer. With this important diversity is connected the minor one, that while in Matthew, the scribe, after Jesus has recited the two commandments, is silent, apparently from shame, which is no sign of a friendly disposition on his part towards Jesus: in Mark, he not only bestows on Jesus the approving expression, *Well, Master, thou hast said the truth*, but enlarges on his doctrine so as to draw from Jesus the declaration that he has *answered discreetly*, and is *not far from the kingdom of God*. It may be also noticed that while in Matthew Jesus simply repeats the commandment of love, in Mark he prefaces it by the words, *Hear, O Israel, the Lord thy God is one Lord*. Thus, if it be held that the differences between the narrative of Luke, and that of the two other evangelists, entail a necessity for supposing that they are founded on two separate events; the no slighter differences between Mark and Matthew, must in all consistency be made a reason for supposing a third. But it is so difficult to credit the reality of three occurrences essentially alike, that the other alternative, of reducing them to one, must, prejudice apart, be always preferred. The narratives of Matthew and Mark are the most easily identified; but there are not wanting points of contact between Matthew and Luke, for in both the *lawyer* νομικὸς appears as a tempter (πειράζων), and is not impressed in favour of Jesus by his answer; nor even between Luke and Mark, for these agree in appending explanatory remarks to the greatest commandment, as well as in the insertion of forms of assent, such as *Thou hast answered right, Thou hast said the truth*. Hence it is evident that to fuse only two of their narratives is a half measure, and that we must either regard all three as independent, or all three as identical: whence again we may observe the freedom which was used by the early Christian legend, in giving various forms to a single fact or idea,— the fundamental fact in the present case being, that, out of the whole Mosaic code, Jesus had selected the two commandments concerning the love of God and our neighbour as the most excellent.*

We come now to the great anti-pharisaic discourse, which Matthew gives (xxiii.) as a sort of pitched battle after the skirmishing of the preceding disputations. Mark (xii. 38 ff.) and Luke (xx. 45 ff.) have also a discourse of Jesus against the *scribes* γραμματεῖς, but extending no farther than a few verses. It is however highly probable, as our modern critics allow,† that Jesus should launch out into fuller invectives against that body of men under the circumstances in which Matthew places that discourse, and it is almost certain that such sharp enunciations must have preceded the catastrophe; so that it is not admissible to control the account of the first evangelist by the meagre one of the two other synoptists,‡ especially as the former is distinguished by connectedness and unity. It is true that much of what Matthew here presents as a continuous address, is assigned by Luke to various scenes and occasions, and

---

* Comp. De Wette, exeg. Handb., 1, 1, S. 186.   † Sieffert, über den Ursprung des ersten Ev., S. 117 f.   ‡ Comp. De Wette, 1, 1, S. 189.

it would hence follow that the former has, in this case again, blended the original elements of the discourse with kindred matter, belonging to the discourses of various periods,* if it could be shown that the arrangement of Luke is the correct one: a position which must therefore be examined. Those parts of the anti-pharisaic harangue which Luke has in common with Matthew, are, excepting the couple of verses which he places in the same connexion as Matthew, introduced by him as concomitant with two entertainments to which he represents Jesus as being invited by Pharisees (xi. 37 ff. ; xiv. 1 ff.)—a politeness on their part which appears in no other Gospel. The expositors of the present day, almost with one voice, concur in admiring the naturalness and faithfulness with which Luke has preserved to us the original occasions of these discourses.† It is certainly natural enough that, in the second entertainment, Jesus, observing the efforts of the guests to obtain the highest places for themselves. should take occasion to admonish them against assuming the precedence at feasts, even on the low ground of prudential considerations ; and this admonition appears in a curtailed form, and without any special cause in the final anti-pharisaic discourse in Matthew, Mark, and even in Luke again (xx. 46). But is it otherwise with the discourse which Luke attaches to the earlier entertainment in the Pharisee's house. In the very commencement of this repast, Jesus not only speaks of the *ravening*, ἁρπαγὴ, and *wickedness*, πονηρία, with which the Pharisees fill the cup and platter, and honours them with the title of *fools*, ἄφρονες, but breaks forth into a denunciation of *woe* οὐαί, against them and the scribes and doctors of the law, threatening them with retribution for all the blood that had been shed by their fathers, whose deeds they approved. We grant that Attic urbanity is not to be expected in a Jewish teacher, but even according to the oriental standard, such invectives uttered at table against the host and his guests, would be the grossest dereliction of what is due to hospitality. This was obvious to Schleiermacher's acute perception ; and he therefore supposes that the meal passed off amicably, and that it was not until its close, when Jesus was again out of the house, that the host expressed his surprise at the neglect of the usual ablutions by Jesus and his disciples, and that Jesus answered with so much asperity.‡ But to assume that the writer has not described the meal itself and the incidents that accompanied it, and that he has noticed it merely for the sake of its connexion with the subsequent discourse, is an arbitrary mode of overcoming the difficulty. For the text runs thus : *And he went in and sat down to meat. And when the Pharisee saw it, he marvelled that he had not first washed before dinner. And the Lord said unto him,* εἰσελθὼν δὲ ἀνέπεσεν ὁ δὲ Φαρισαῖος ἰδὼν ἐθαύμασεν, ὅτι οὐ πρῶτον ἐβαπτίσθη—· εἶπε δὲ ὁ Κύριος πρὸς αὐτὸν. It is mani-

---

* Schulz, über das Abendmahl, S. 313 f. ; Schneckenburger, über den Ursprung, S. 54. † Schleiermacher, über den Lukas, S. 182, 196, f.; Olshausen, in loc., and the writers mentioned in the foregoing note. ‡ Ut sup. S. 180.

festly impossible to thrust in between these sentences the duration of the meal, and it must have been the intention of the writer to attach *he marvelled ἐθαύμασεν* to *he sat down to meat ἀνέπεσεν*, and *he said εἶπεν* to *he marvelled ἐθαύμασεν*. But if this could not really have been the case, unless Jesus violated in the grossest manner the simplest dictates of civility, there is an end to the vaunted accuracy of Luke in his allocation of this discourse: and we have only to inquire how he could be led to give it so false a position. This is to be discovered by comparing the manner in which the two other synoptists mention the offence of the Pharisees, at the omission of the ablutions before meals by Jesus and his disciples: a circumstance to which they annex discourses different from those given by Luke. In Matthew (xv. 1 ff.), scribes and Pharisees from Jerusalem ask Jesus why his disciples do not observe the custom of washing before meat? It is thus implied that they knew of this omission, as may easily be supposed, by report. In Mark (vii. 1 ff.), they look on (ἰδόντες), while some disciples of Jesus eat with unwashen hands, and call them to account for this irregularity. Lastly, in Luke, Jesus himself dines with a Pharisee, and on this occasion it is observed, that he neglects the usual washings. This is an evident climax: hearing, witnessing taking food together. Was it formed, in the descending gradation, from Luke to Matthew, or, in the ascending one, from Matthew to Luke? From the point of view adopted by the recent critics of the first Gospel, the former mode will be held the most probable, namely, that the memory of the original scene, the repast in the Pharisee's house, was lost in the process of tradition, and is therefore wanting in the first Gospel. But, apart from the difficulty of conceiving that this discourse was uttered under the circumstances with which it is invested by Luke, it is by no means in accordance with the course of tradition, when once in possession of so dramatic a particular as a feast, to let it fall again, but rather to supply it, if lacking. The general tendency of the legend is to transform the abstract into the concrete, the mediate into the immediate, hearsay into vision, the spectator into the participator; and as the offence taken against Jesus by the Pharisees referred, among other things, to the usages of the table, nothing was more natural than for legend to associate the origin of the offence with a particular place and occasion, and for this purpose to imagine invitations given to Jesus by Pharisees—invitations which would be historically suspicious, if for no other reason than that Luke alone knows anything of them. Here, then, we again find Luke in his favourite employment of furnishing a frame to the discourses of Jesus which tradition had delivered to him; a procedure much farther removed from historic faithfulness, than the effort of Matthew to give unity to discourses gathered from different periods, without adding matter of his own. The formation of the climax above displayed, can only be conceived, in accordance with the general relation between the synoptists, in the following manner: Mark, who in this instance evidently had Matthew before him, enriched his account with the dramatic expression ἰδόντες; while Luke, independent of both, has added a repast, δεῖπνον, whether presented to him by a more developed tradition, or invented by his own more fertile imagination. Together with this unhistorical position, the proportions themselves seem to be disfigured in Luke (xi. 39—41, 49.), and the observation of the lawyer, *Master, thus saying thou reproachest us also* (xi. 45), too much resembles an artificial transition from the philippic against the Pharisees, to that against the doctors of the law.*

Another passage in this discourse has been the subject of much discussion. It is that (v. 35) in which Jesus threatens his cotemporaries, that all the innocent blood shed from that of Abel to that of Zacharias, the son of Barachias, slain in the temple, will be required of their generation. The Zacharias of whom such an end is narrated 2 Chron. xxiv. 20 ff. was a son, not of Barachias, but of Jehoiada. On the other hand, there was a Zacharias, the son of Baruch, who came to a similar end in the Jewish war.† Moreover, it appears unlikely that Jesus would refer to a murder which took place 850 B. C. as the last. Hence it was at first supposed that we have in v. 35 a prophecy, and afterwards, a confusion of the earlier with the later event; and the latter notion has been used as an accessory proof that the first gospel is a posterior compilation.‡ It is, however, equally probable, that the Zacharias, son of Jehoiada, whose death is narrated in the Chronicles, has been confounded with the prophet Zachariah, who was a son of Barachias (Zach. i. 1; LXX.; Baruch, in Josephus, is not the same name);§ especially as a Targum, evidently in consequence of a like confusion with the prophet who was a grandson of Iddo, calls the murdered Zachariah a son of Iddo.‖ The murder of a prophet, mentioned by Jeremiah (xxvi. 23.), was doubtless subsequent to that of Zachariah, but in the Jewish order of the canonical books, Jeremiah precedes the Chronicles; and to oppose a murder revealed in the first canonical book, to one recorded in the last, was entirely in the style of Jewish parlance.¶

After having considered all the discourses of Jesus given by Matthew, and compared them with their parallels, with the exception of those which had come before us in previous discussions, or which have yet to come before us in our examination of single incidents in the public ministry, or of the history of the passion: it might appear requisite to the completeness of our criticism, that we should also give a separate investigation to the connexion in which the two other synoptists give the discourses of Jesus, and from this point review the parallels in Matthew. But we have already cast a comparative glance over the most remarkable discourses in Luke and Mark, and

* Comp. De Wette, exeg. Handb. 1, 1, S. 189. 1, 2, S. 67, 76.   † Joseph b. j. iv. v. 4   ‡ Eichhorn, Einleitung in das N. T., 1, S. 510 ff.; Hug, Einl. in das N. T., 2, S. 10 ff.; Credner, Einl., 1, S. 207.   § Vid. Theile, über Zacharias Barachias Sohn, in Winer's und Engelhardt's neuem krit. Journ., 2, S. 101 ff.; De Wette, in loc.   ‖ Targum Thren. ii. 20, in Wetstein, S. 494.   ¶ Comp. De Wette, in loc.

gone through the parables which are peculiar to each; and as to the remainder of what they offer in the form of discourses, it will either come under our future consideration, or if not, the point of view from which it is to be criticised, has been sufficiently indicated in the foregoing investigations.

CHAPTER VII.

DISCOURSES OF JESUS IN THE FOURTH GOSPEL.

§ 80. CONVERSATION OF JESUS WITH NICODEMUS.

The first considerable specimen which the fourth Gospel gives of the teaching of Jesus, is his conversation with Nicodemus (iii. 1—21.). In the previous chapter (23—25.) it is narrated, that during the first passover attended by Jesus after his entrance on his public ministry, he had won many to faith in him by the *miracles*, σημεῖα, which he performed, but that he did not commit himself to them because he saw through them: he was aware, that is, of the uncertainty and impurity of their faith. Then follows in our present chapter, as an example, not only of the adherents whom Jesus had found even thus early, but also of the wariness with which he tested and received them, a more detailed account how Nicodemus, a ruler of the Jews and a Pharisee, applied to him, and how he was treated by Jesus.

It is through the Gospel of John alone that we learn anything of this Nicodemus, who in vii. 50 f. appears as the advocate of Jesus, so far as to protest against his being condemned without a hearing, and in xix. 39, as the partaker with Joseph of Arimathea of the care of interring Jesus. Modern criticism, with reason, considers it surprising that Matthew (with the other synoptists) does not even mention the name of this remarkable adherent of Jesus, and that we have to gather all our knowledge of him from the fourth Gospel; since the peculiar relation in which Nicodemus stood to Jesus, and his participation in the care of his interment, must have been as well known to Matthew as to John. This difficulty has been numbered among the arguments which are thought to prove that the first Gospel was not written by the apostle Matthew, but was the product of a tradition considerably more remote from the time and locality of Jesus.* But the fact is that the common fund of tradition on which

---

* Schulz, über das Abendmahl.

all the synoptists drew had preserved no notice of this Nicodemus. With touching piety the Christian legend has recorded in the tablets of her memory, the names of all the others who helped to render the last honours to their murdered master—of Joseph of Arimathea and the two Marys (Matt. xxvii. 56—61 parall.): why then was Nicodemus the only neglected one—he who was especially distinguished among those who tended the remains of Jesus, by his nocturnal interview with the teacher sent from God, and by his advocacy of him among the chief priests and Pharisees? It is so difficult to conceive that the name of this man, if he had really assumed such a position, would have vanished from the popular evangelical tradition, without leaving a single trace, that one is induced to inquire whether the contrary supposition be not more capable of explanation : namely, that such a relation between Nicodemus and Jesus might have been fabricated by tradition, and adopted by the author of the fourth Gospel without having really subsisted.

John xii. 42, it is expressly said that *many among the chief rulers* believed on Jesus, but concealed their faith from dread of excommunication by the Pharisees, because *they loved the praise of men more than the praise of God.** That towards the end of his career *many* people of rank believed in Jesus, even in secret only, is not very probable, since no indication of it appears in the Acts of the Apostles : for that the advice of Gamaliel (Acts v. 34 ff.) did not originate in a positively favourable disposition towards the cause of Jesus, seems to be sufficiently demonstrated by the spirit of his disciple Saul. Moreover the synoptists make Jesus declare in plain terms that the secret of his Messiahship had been revealed only to *babes*, and hidden from the *wise* and *prudent* (Matt. xi. 25; Luke x. 21.), and Joseph of Arimathea is the only individual of the ruling class whom they mention as an adherent of Jesus. How, then, if Jesus did not really attach to himself any from the upper ranks, came the case to be represented differently at a later period? In John vii. 48 f. we read that the Pharisees sought to disparage Jesus by the remark that none of the rulers or of the Pharisees, but only the ignorant populace, believed on him : and even later adversaries of Christianity, for example, Celsus, laid great stress on the circumstance that Jesus had had as his disciples ἐπιρρήτους ἀνθρώπους, τελώνας καὶ ναύτας τοὺς πονηροτάτους.† This reproach was a thorn in the side of the early church, and though as long as her members were drawn only from the people, she might reflect with satisfaction on the declarations of Jesus, in which he had pronounced the *poor*, πτωχούς, and *simple*, νηπίους, blessed: yet so soon as she was joined by men of rank and education, these would lean to the idea that con-

<hr/>

* This "secret information" is very welcome to Dr. Paulus, because it gives a useful hint "as to many occurrences in the life of Jesus, the causes of which are not obvious" (L. J. I. B. S. 111); that is, Paulus, like Bahrdt and Venturini, though less openly, is fond of using such secret and influential allies as *deus ex machina*, for the explanation of much that is miraculous in the life of Jesus (the transfiguration, residence after the resurrection, &c.).   † Orig. c. Cels. i. 62.

verts like themselves had not been wanting to Jesus during his life. But, it would be objected, nothing had been hitherto known of such converts. Naturally enough, it might be answered; since fear of their equals would induce them to conceal their relations with Jesus. Thus a door was opened for the admission of any number of secret adherents among the higher class (John xii. 42 f.). But, it would be farther urged, how could they have intercourse with Jesus, unobserved? Under the veil of the night, would be the answer: and thus the scene was laid for the interviews of such men with Jesus (xix. 39.). This, however, would not suffice: a representative of this class must actually appear on the scene: Joseph of Arimathea might have been chosen, his name being still extant in the synoptical tradition; but the idea of him was too definite, and it was the interest of the legend to name more than one eminent friend of Jesus. Hence a new personage was devised, whose Greek name Νικόδημος seems to point him out significantly as the representative of the dominant class.* That this development of the legend is confined to the fourth Gospel, is to be explained, partly by the generally admitted lateness of its origin, and partly on the ground that in the evidently more cultivated circle in which it arose, the limitation of the adherents of Jesus to the common people would be more offensive, than in the circle in which the synoptical tradition was formed. Thus the reproach which modern criticism has cast on the first Gospel, on the score of its silence respecting Nicodemus, is turned upon the fourth, on the score of its information on the same subject.

These considerations, however, should not create any prejudice against the ensuing conversation, which is the proper object of our investigations. This may still be in the main genuine; Jesus may have held such a conversation with one of his adherents, and our evangelist may have embellished it no further than by making this interlocutor a man of rank. Neither will we, with the author of the Probabilia, take umbrage at the opening address of Nicodemus, nor complain, with him, that there is a want of connexion between that address and the answer of Jesus.† The requisition of a *new birth* (γεννηθῆναι ἄνωθεν), as a condition of entrance into the kingdom of heaven, does not differ essentially from the summons with which Jesus opens his ministry in the synoptical gospels, *Repent ye, for the kingdom of heaven is at hand.* New birth, or new creation, was a current image among the Jews, especially as denoting the conversion of an idolater into a worshipper of Jehovah. It was

___

* Let the reader bear in mind the kindred names Nicolaus and Nicolaitans.

† Prob. p. 44. Bretschneider is right, however, in declaring against Kuinöl's method of supplying a connexion between the discourses in John, by the insertion of propositions and intermediate discourses supposed to have been omitted. Lücke judiciously admits (1, p. 446) that if, in John, something appears to be wanting between two consecutive expressions of Jesus, we are yet to suppose that there was an immediate connexion between them in the mind of the evangelist, and it is this connexion which it is the task of exegesis to ascertain. In truth the discourses in the 4th Gospel are never entirely wanting in connexion (apart from the exceptions to be noticed § 81), though that connexion is sometimes very latent.

customary to say of Abraham, that when, according to the Jewish supposition, he renounced idolatry for the worship of the true God, he became a new creature (בריה הדשה).[*] The proselyte, too, in allusion to his relinquishing all his previous associations, was compared to a new-born child.[†] That such phraseology was common among the Jews at that period, is shown by the confidence with which Paul applies, as if it required no explanation, the term *new creation*, καινὴ κτίσις, to those truly converted to Christ. Now, if Jesus required, even from the Jews, as a condition of entrance into the messianic kingdom, the *new birth* which they ascribed to their heathen proselytes, Nicodemus might naturally wonder at the requisition, since the Israelite thought himself, as such, unconditionally entitled to that kingdom: and this is the construction which has been put upon his question v. 4.[‡] But Nicodemus does not ask, How canst thou say that a Jew, or a child of Abraham, must be born again? His ground of wonder is that Jesus appears to suppose it possible for a *man* to be born again, and that *when he is old*. It does not, therefore, astonish him that spiritual new birth should be expected in a Jew, but corporeal new birth in a man. How an oriental, to whom figurative speech in general—how a Jew, to whom the image of the new birth in particular must have been familiar— how especially a *master of Israel*, in whom the misconstruction of figurative phrases cannot, as in the Apostles (e. g. Matt. xv. 15 f. ; xvi. 7.), be ascribed to want of education—could understand this expression literally, has been matter of extreme surprise to expositors of all parties, as well as to Jesus (v. 10). Hence some have supposed that the Pharisee really understood Jesus, and only intended by his question to test the ability of Jesus to interpret his figurative expression into a simple proposition:[§] but Jesus does not treat him as a hypocrite, as in that case he must have done—he continues to instruct him, as one really *ignorant* οὐ γινώσκοντα (v. 10). Others give the question the following turn: This cannot be meant in a physical sense, how then otherwise?[‖] But the true drift of the question is rather the contrary: By these words I can only understand physical new birth, but how is this possible? Our wonder at the ignorance of the Jewish doctor, therefore, returns upon us; and it is heightened when, after the copious explanation of Jesus (v. 5—8.), that the new birth which he required was a *spiritual birth*, γεννηθῆναι ἐκ τοῦ πνεύματος, Nicodemus has made no advance in comprehension, but asks with the same obtuseness as before (v. 9.), *How can these things be?* By this last difficulty Lucke is so straitened, that, contrary to his ordinary exegetical tact, he refers the continued amazement of Nicodemus, (as other expositors had referred his original question,) to the circumstance that Jesus maintained the necessity of new birth even for Israelites. But, in that case, Nicodemus would have inquired concerning the necessity, not the possibility, of that birth : instead of asking, *How can these things be ?* he would have asked, *Why must* these things be ? This inconceivable mistake in a Jewish doctor is not then to be explained away, and our surprise must become strong suspicion so soon as it can be shown, that legend or the evangelist had inducements to represent this individual as more simple than he really was. First, then, it must occur to us, that in all descriptions and recitals, contrasts are eagerly exhibited ; hence in the representation of a colloquy in which one party is the teacher, the other the taught, there is a strong temptation to create a contrast to the wisdom of the former, by exaggerating the simplicity of the latter. Further, we must remember the satisfaction it must give to a Christian mind of that age, to place a master of Israel in the position of an unintelligent person, by the side of the Master of the Christians. Lastly it is, as we shall presently see more clearly, the constant method of the fourth evangelist in detailing the conversations of Jesus, to form the knot and the progress of the discussion, by making the interlocutors understand literally what Jesus intended figuratively.

In reply to the second query of Nicodemus, Jesus takes entirely the tone of the fourth evangelist's prologue (v. 11—13*). The question hence arises, whether the evangelist borrowed from Jesus, or lent to him his own style. A previous investigation has decided in favour of the latter alternative.† But this inquiry referred merely to the form of the discourses ; in relation to their matter, its analogy with the ideas of Philo, does not authorize us at once to conclude that the writer here puts his Alexandrian doctrine of the Logos into the mouth of Jesus :‡ because the expressions, *We speak that we do know*, &c. ὃ οἴδαμεν λαλοῦμεν κ. τ λ., and, *No man hath ascended up to heaven*, &c. οὐδεὶς ἀναβέβηκεν κ. τ. λ., have an analogy with Matt. xi. 27.; and the idea of the pre-existence of the Messiah which is here propounded, is, as we have seen, not foreign to the apostle Paul.

V. 14 and 15 Jesus proceeds from the more simple things of the earth, ἐπιγείοις, the communications concerning the new birth, to the more difficult things of heaven, ἐπουρανίοις, the announcement of the destination of the Messiah to a vicarious death. The Son of Man, he says, must *be lifted up* (ὑψωθῆναι, which, in John's phraseology, signifies crucifixion, with an allusion to a glorifying exaltation), in the same way, and with the same effect, as the brazen serpent Numb. xxi. 8, 9. Here many questions press upon us. Is it credible, that Jesus already, at the very commencement of his

---

* III. 11: ὁ ἑωράκαμεν μαρτυροῦμεν καὶ τὴν μαρτυρίαν ἡμῶν οὐ λαμβάνετε. 13: καὶ οὐδεὶς ἀναβέβηκεν εἰς τὸν οὐρανὸν, εἰ μὴ ὁ ἐκ τοῦ οὐρανοῦ καταβὰς, ὁ υἱὸς τοῦ ἀνθρώπου ὁ ὢν ἐν τῷ οὐρανῷ.

I. 18: θεὸν οὐδεὶς ἑώρακε πώποτε ὁ μονογενὴς υἱὸς, ὁ ὢν εἰς τὸν κόλπον τοῦ πατρὸς, ἐκεῖνος ἐξηγήσατο. 11: —καὶ οἱ ἴδιοι αὐτὸν οὐ παρέλαβον.

† Sup. § 46.   ‡ This is inferred in the Probabilia, p. 46.

public ministry, foresaw his death, and in the specific form of crucifixion? and that long before he instructed his disciples on this point, he made a communication on the subject to a Pharisee? Can it be held consistent with the wisdom of Jesus as a teacher, that he should impart such knowledge to Nicodemus? Even Lücke* puts the question why, when Nicodemus had not understood the more obvious doctrine, Jesus tormented him with the more recondite, and especially with the secret of the Messiah's death, which was then so remote? He answers: it accords perfectly with the wisdom of Jesus as a teacher, that he should reveal the sufferings appointed for him by God as early as possible, because no instruction was better adapted to cast down false worldly hopes. But the more remote the idea of the Messiah's death from the conceptions of his cotemporaries, owing to the worldliness of their expectations, the more impressively and unequivocally must Jesus express that idea, if he wished to promulgate it; not in an enigmatical form which he could not be sure that Nicodemus would understand. Lücke continues: Nicodemus was a man open to instruction; one of whom good might be expected. But in this very conversation, his dulness of comprehension in *earthly things*, ἐπίγεια, had evinced that he must have still less capacity for *heavenly things*, ἐπουράνια; and, according to v. 12, Jesus himself despaired of enlightening him with respect to them. Lücke, however, observes, that it was a practice with Jesus to follow up easy doctrine which had not been comprehended, by difficult doctrine which was of course less comprehensible; that he purposed thus to give a spur to the minds of his hearers, and by straining their attention, engage them to reflect. But the examples which Lücke adduces of such proceeding on the part of Jesus, are all drawn from the fourth gospel. Now the very point in question is, whether that gospel correctly represents the teaching of Jesus; consequently Lücke argues in a circle. We have seen a similar procedure ascribed to Jesus in his conversation with the woman of Samaria, and we have already declared our opinion that such an overburthening of weak faculties with enigma on enigma, does not accord with the wise rule as to the communication of doctrine, which the same gospel puts into the mouth of Jesus, xvi. 12. It would not stimulate, but confuse, the mind of the hearer, who persisted in a misapprehension of the well-known figure of the new birth, to present to him the novel comparison of the Messiah and his death, to the brazen serpent and its effects: a comparison quite incongruous with his Jewish ideas.† In the first three gospels Jesus pursues an entirely different course. In these, where a misconstruction betrays itself on the part of the disciples, Jesus (except where he breaks off altogether, or where it is evident that the evangelist unhistorically associates a number of metaphorical discourses) applies himself with the assiduity of an earnest teacher to the thorough explanation of the difficulty, and not until

---

* Ut sup. p. 476.   † Comp. Bretschneider, ut sup.

he has effected this does he proceed, step by step, to convey further instruction (e. g. Matt. xiii. 10 ff. 36 ff.; xv. 16; xvi. 8 ff.)* This is the method of a wise teacher; on the contrary, to leap from one subject to another, to overburthen and strain the mind of the hearer, a mode of instruction which the fourth evangelist attributes to Jesus, is wholly inconsistent with that character. To explain this inconsistency, we must suppose that the writer of the fourth gospel thought to heighten in the most effective manner the contrast which appears from the first, between the wisdom of the one party and the incapacity of the other, by representing the teacher as overwhelming the pupil who put unintelligent questions on the most elementary doctrine, with lofty and difficult themes, beneath which his faculties are laid prostrate.

From v. 16, even those commentators who pretend to some ability in this department, lose all hope of showing that the remainder of the discourse may have been spoken by Jesus. Not only does Paulus make this confession, but even Olshausen, with a concise statement of his reasons.† At the above verse, any special reference to Nicodemus vanishes, and there is commenced an entirely general discourse on the destination of the Son of God, to confer a blessing on the world, and on the manner in which unbelief forfeits this blessing. Moreover, these ideas are expressed in a form, which at one moment appears to be a reminiscence of the evangelist's introduction, and at another has a striking similarity with passages in the first epistle of John.‡ In particular, the expression *the only begotten Son, ὁ μονογενὴς υἱὸς*, which is repeatedly (v. 16 and 18.) attributed to Jesus as a designation of his own person, is nowhere else found in his mouth, even in the fourth gospel; this circumstance, however, marks it still more positively as a favourite phrase of the evangelist (i. 14—18.), and of the writer of the Epistles (1 John iv. 9). Further, many things are spoken of as past, which at the supposed period of this conversation with Nicodemus were yet future. For even if the words, *he gave, ἔδωκεν*, refer not to the giving over

---

* De Wette adduces as examples of a similar procedure on the part of Jesus in the synoptical gospels, Matth. xix. 21; xx. 22 f. But these two cases are of a totally different kind from the one under consideration in John. We have here to treat of a want of comprehension, in the face of which it is surprising that Jesus instead of descending to its level, chooses to elevate himself to a still less attainable altitude. In the passages quoted from the synoptists, on the other hand, we have examples of an excessive self-valuation, too high an estimate of their ability to promote the cause of Jesus, on the part of the rich young man and of the sons of Zebedee, and Jesus with perfect propriety checks their egotistic ardour by the abrupt presentation of a higher demand. These instances could only be parallel with that of Nicodemus, if the latter had piqued himself on his enlightenment, and Jesus, by a sudden flight into a higher region, had sought to convince him of his ignorance.   † Bibl. Comm. 2, S. 96.

‡ III. 19: αὕτη δέ ἐστιν ἡ κρίσις, ὅτι τὸ φῶς ἐλήλυθεν εἰς τὸν κόσμον, καὶ ἠγάπησαν οἱ ἄνθρωποι μᾶλλον τὸ σκότος ἢ τὸ φῶς.
III. 16: οὕτω γὰρ ἠγάπησεν ὁ θεὸς τὸν κόσμον, ὥστε τὸν υἱὸν αὑτοῦ τὸν μονογενῆ ἔδωκεν, ἵνα πᾶς ὁ πιστεύων εἰς αὑτὸν, μὴ ἀπόληται, ἀλλ' ἔχῃ ζωὴν αἰώνιον.

I. 9: ἦν τὸ φῶς τὸ ἀληθινὸν, τὸ φωτίζον πάντα ἄνθρωπον, ἐρχόμενον εἰς τὸν κόσμον. 5: καὶ τὸ φῶς ἐν τῇ σκοτίᾳ φαίνει, καὶ ἡ σκοτία αὐτὸ οὐ κατέλαβεν.
1 John iv. 9: ἐν τούτῳ ἐφανερώθη ἡ ἀγάπη τοῦ θεοῦ ἐν ἡμῖν, ὅτι τὸν υἱὸν αὐτοῦ τὸν μονογενῆ ἀπέστειλεν ὁ θεὸς εἰς τὸν κόσμον, ἵνα ζήσωμεν δι' αὐτοῦ.

to death, but to the sending of the Messiah into the world; the expressions, *men loved darkness* ἠγάπησαν οἱ ἄνθρωποι τὸ σκότος, and, *their deeds were evil,* ἦν πονηρὰ αὐτῶν τὰ ἔργα (v. 19.), as Lücke also remarks, could only be used after the triumph of darkness had been achieved in the rejection and execution of Jesus: they belong then to the evangelist's point of view at the time when he wrote, not to that of Jesus when on the threshold of his public ministry. In general the whole of this discourse attributed to Jesus, with its constant use of the third person to designate the supposed speaker: with its dogmatical terms *only begotten, light,* and the like, applied to Jesus: with its comprehensive view of the crisis and its results, which the appearance of Jesus produced, is far too objective for us to believe that it came from the lips of Jesus. Jesus could not speak thus of himself, but the evangelist might speak thus of Jesus. Hence the same expedient has been adopted, as in the case of the Baptist's discourse already considered, and it has been supposed that Jesus is the speaker down to v. 16, but that from that point the evangelist appends his own dogmatic reflections.* But there is again here no intimation of such a transition in the text; rather, the connecting word *for,* γὰρ (v. 16.), seems to indicate a continuation of the same discourse. No writer, and least of all the fourth evangelist (comp. vii. 39; xi. 51 f.; xii. 16: xxxiii. 37 ff.), would scatter his own observations thus undistinguishingly, unless he wished to create a misapprehension.†

If then it be established that the evangelist, from v. 16. to the end of the discourse, means to represent Jesus as the speaker, while Jesus can never have so spoken: we cannot rest satisfied with the half measure adopted by Luke, when he maintains that it is really Jesus who continues to speak from the above passage, but that the evangelist has interwoven his own explanations and amplifications more liberally than before. For this admission undermines all certainty as to how far the discourse belongs to Jesus, and how far to the evangelist: besides, as the discourse is distinguished by the closest uniformity of thought and style, it must be ascribed either wholly to Jesus or wholly to the evangelist. Of these two alternatives the former is, according to the above considerations, impossible; we are

---

* Paulus and Olshausen, in loc. † Tholuck (Glaubwürdigkeit, S. 335.) adduces as examples of a similar unobserved fusion of a discourse quoted from a foreign source, with the writer's own matter, Gal. ii. 14 ff. Euseb. H. E. iii. 1, 39. Hieron. Comm. in Jes. 53. But such instances in an epistle, a commentary or an historical work interspersed with reasoning and criticism, are not parallel with those in an historical narrative of the nature of our fourth gospel. In works of the former kind, the reader expects the author to reason, and hence, when the discourse of another party has been introduced, he is prepared at the slightest pause to see the author again take up the argument. It is quite different with a work like our fourth gospel. The introduction, it is true, is put forth as the author's own reasoning, and it is there quite natural that after a brief quotation from the discourse of another, v. 15, he should, at v. 16, resume the character of speaker without any express intimation. But when once he has entered on his narrative, which is strictly a recital of what has been done, and what has been said, all that he annexes without any mark of distinction (as e. g. xii. 37.) to a discourse explicitly ascribed to another, must be considered as a continuation of that discourse.

therefore restricted to the latter, which we have observed to be entirely consistent with the manner of the fourth evangelist.

But not only on the passage v. 16—21 must we pass this judgment : v. 14 has appeared to us out of keeping with the position of
Jesus ; and the behaviour of Nicodemus, v. 4 and 9, altogether inconceivable. Thus in the very first sample, when compared with
the observations which we have already made on John iii. 22 ff. ;
iv. 1 ff., the fourth gospel presents to us all the peculiarities which
characterize its mode of reporting the discourses of Jesus. They
are usually commenced in the form of dialogue, and so far as this
extends, the lever that propels the conversation is the striking contrast between the spiritual sense and the carnal interpretation of the
language of Jesus ; generally, however, the dialogue is merged into
an uninterrupted discourse, in which the writer blends the person
of Jesus with his own, and makes the former use concerning himself, language which could only be used by John concerning Jesus.

§ 81.   THE DISCOURSES OF JESUS, JOHN V—XII.

In the fifth chapter of John, a long discourse of Jesus is connected with a cure wrought by him on the sabbath (19—47). The
mode in which Jesus at v. 17 defends his activity on the sabbath,
is worthy of notice, as distinguished from that adopted by him in
the earlier Gospels. These ascribe to him, in such cases, three arguments : the example of David, who ate the shew-bread : the precedent of the sabbatical labours of the priest's in the temple, quoted
also in John vii. 23 (Matt. xii. 3 ff. parall.) : and the course pursued
with respect to an ox, sheep, or ass, that falls into the pit (Matt. xii.
11 parall.), or is let out to watering on the sabbath (Luke xiii. 18.):
all which arguments are entirely in the practical spirit that characterizes the popular teaching of Jesus. The fourth evangelist, on the
contrary, makes him argue from the uninterrupted activity of God,
and reminds us by the expression which he puts into the mouth of
Jesus, *My Father worketh hitherto, ὁ πατήρ ἕως ἄρτι ἐργάζεται*, of
a principle in the Alexandrian metaphysics, viz. *God never ceases
to act, ποιῶν ὁ Θεὸς οὐδέποτε παύεται :** a metaphysical proposition
more likely to be familiar to the author of the fourth gospel than to
Jesus. In the synoptical gospels, miracles of healing on the sabbath
are followed up by declarations respecting the nature and design of
the sabbatical institution, a species of instruction of which the people
were greatly in need : but in the present passage, a digression is immediately made to the main theme of the gospel, the person of Christ
and his relation to the Father. The perpetual recurrence of this
theme in the fourth gospel has led its adversaries, not without reason, to accuse it of a tendency purely theoretic, and directed to the
glorification of Jesus. In the matter of the succeeding discourse

* Philo. Opp. ed. Mang. i. 44. apud Gfrörer, i. p. 122.

there is nothing to create a difficulty, nothing that Jesus might not have spoken, for it treats, with the strictest coherence, of things which the Jews expected of the Messiah, or which Jesus attributed to himself, according to the synoptists also: as, for instance, the raising of the dead, and the office of judging the world. But this consistency in the matter, only heightens the difficulty connected with the form and phraseology in which it is expressed. For the discourse, especially its latter half (from v. 31), is full of the closest analogies with the first epistle of John, and with passages in the gospel in which either the author speaks, or John the Baptist.* One means of explaining the former resemblance is to suppose, that the evangelist formed his style by closely imitating that of Jesus. That this is possible, is not to be disputed; but it is equally certain that it could proceed only from a mind destitute of originality and self-confidence,—a character which the fourth evangelist in nowise exhibits. Farther, as in the other gospels Jesus speaks in a thoroughly different tone and style, it would follow, if he really spoke as he is represented to have done by John, that the manner attributed to him by the synoptists is fictitious. Now, that this manner did not originate with the evangelists is plain from the fact, that each of them is so little master of his matter. Neither could the bulk of the discourses have been the work of tradition, not only because they have a highly original cast, but because they bear the impress of the alleged time and locality. On the contrary, the fourth evangelist, by the ease with which he disposes his materials, awakens the suspicion that they are of his own production; and some of his favourite ideas and phrases, such as, *The Father showeth the Son all that himself doeth,*† and those already quoted, seem to have

---

* John. v. 20: ὁ γὰρ πατὴρ φιλεῖ τὸν υἱὸν καὶ πάντα δείκνυσιν αὐτῷ ἃ αὐτὸς ποιεῖ.

21: ὁ τὸν λόγον μου ἀκούων—μεταβέβηκεν ἐκ τοῦ θανάτου εἰς τὴν ζωήν.

32: καὶ οἶδα, ὅτι ἀληθής ἐστιν ἡ μαρτυρία, ἣν μαρτυρεῖ περὶ ἐμοῦ.

34: ἐγὼ δὲ οὐ παρὰ ἀνθρώπου τὴν μαρτυρίαν λαμβάνω.

36: ἐγὼ δὲ ἔχω μαρτυρίον μεῖζον τοῦ Ἰωάννου.

37: καὶ ὁ πέμψας με πατὴρ αὐτὸς μεμαρτύρηκε περὶ ἐμοῦ.

Ib.: οὔτε τὴν φωνὴν αὐτοῦ ἀκηκόατε πώποτε, οὔτε τὸ εἶδος αὐτοῦ ἑωράκατε.

38: καὶ τὸν λόγον αὐτοῦ οὐκ ἔχετε μένοντα ἐν ὑμῖν.

40: καὶ οὐ θέλετε ἐλθεῖν πρός με, ἵνα ζωὴν ἔχητε.

42: ὅτι τὴν ἀγάπην τοῦ θεοῦ οὐκ ἔχετε ἐν ἑαυτοῖς.

44: πῶς δύνασθε ὑμεῖς πιστεῦσαι, δόξαν παρὰ ἀλλήλων λαμβάνοντες, καὶ τὴν δόξαν τὴν παρὰ τοῦ μόνου θεοῦ οὐ ζητεῖτε;

John iii. 35 (the Baptist): ὁ γὰρ πατὴρ ἀγαπᾷ τὸν υἱὸν καὶ πάντα δέδωκεν ἐν τῇ χειρὶ αὐτοῦ.

1 Joh. iii. 14: ἡμεῖς οἴδαμεν, ὅτι μεταβεβήκαμεν ἐκ τοῦ θανάτου εἰς τὴν ζωήν.

Joh. xix. 35: καὶ ἀληθινὴ ἐστιν αὐτοῦ ἡ μαρτυρία, κἀκεῖνος οἶδεν, ὅτι ἀληθῆ λέγει. Comp. xxi. 24. 1 Joh. 3, 12.

1 John. v. 9: εἰ τὴν μαρτυρίαν τῶν ἀνθρώπων λαμβάνομεν, ἡ μαρτυρία τοῦ θεοῦ μείζων ἐστίν· ὅτι αὕτη ἐστιν ἡ μαρτυρία τοῦ θεοῦ, ἣν μεμαρτύρηκε περὶ τοῦ υἱοῦ αὐτοῦ.

Joh. i. 18: θεὸν οὐδεὶς ἑώρακε πώποτε. Comp. 1, Joh. iv. 12.

1 Joh. i. 10: καὶ ὁ λόγος αὐτοῦ οὐκ ἔστιν ἐν ὑμῖν.

1 Joh. v. 12: ὁ μὴ ἔχων τὸν υἱὸν τοῦ θεοῦ ζωὴν οὐκ ἔχει.

1 Joh. ii. 15: οὐκ ἔστιν ἡ ἀγάπη τοῦ πατρὸς ἐν αὐτῷ.

Joh. xi. 43: ἠγάπησαν γὰρ τὴν δόξαν τῶν ἀνθρώπων μᾶλλον, ἤπερ τὴν δόξαν τοῦ θεοῦ.

† Vid. the passages compared by Gfrörer, 1, S. 191, from Philo, de linguarum confusione.

sprung from an Hellenistic source, rather than from Palestine. But the chief point in the argument is, that in this gospel John the Baptist speaks, as we have seen, in precisely the same strain as the author of the gospels, and his Jesus. It cannot be supposed, that not only the evangelist, but the Baptist, whose public career was prior to that of Jesus, and whose character was strongly marked, modelled his expressions with verbal minuteness on those of Jesus. Hence only two cases are possible: either the Baptist determined the style of Jesus and the evangelist (who indeed appears to have been the Baptist's disciple); or the evangelist determined the style of the Baptist and Jesus. The former alternative will be rejected by the orthodox, on the ground of the higher nature that dwelt in Christ; and we are equally disinclined to adopt it, for the reason that Jesus, even though he may have been excited to activity by the Baptist, yet appears as a character essentially distinct from him, and original; and for the still more weighty consideration, that the style of the evangelist is much too feeble for the rude Baptist,—too mystical for his practical mind. There remains, then, but the latter alternative, namely, that the evangelist has given his own style both to Jesus and to the Baptist: an explanation in itself more natural than the former, and supported by a multitude of examples from all kinds of historical writers. If however the evangelist is thus responsible for the form of this discourse, it is still possible that the matter may have belonged to Jesus, but we cannot pronounce to what extent this is the case, and we have already had proof that the evangelist, on suitable opportunities, very freely presents his own reflections in the form of a discourse from Jesus.

In chap. vi., Jesus represents himself, or rather his Father, v. 27 ff., as the giver of the spiritual manna. This is analogous to the Jewish idea above quoted, that the second Goël, like the first, would provide manna;[*] and to the invitation of Wisdom in the Proverbs, ix. 5, *Come, eat of my bread:* ἔλθετε, φάγετε τῶν ἐμῶν ἄρτων. But the succeeding declaration, that he is himself *the bread of life that cometh down from heaven,* ἄρτος ὁ ζῶν ὁ ἐκ τοῦ οὐρανοῦ καταβὰς (v. 33 and 35) appears to find its true analogy only in the idea of Philo, that the *divine word,* λόγος θεῖος, is *that which nourishes the soul,* τὸ τρέφον τὴν ψυχήν.[†] From v. 51, the difficulty becomes still greater. Jesus proceeds to represent his flesh as the bread from heaven, which he will give for the life of the world, and *to eat the flesh of the Son of Man, and to drink his blood,* he pronounces to be the only means of attaining *eternal life.* The similarity of these expressions to the words which the synoptists and Paul attribute to Jesus, at the institution of the Lord's Supper, led the older commentators generally to understand this passage as having refer-

---

[*] Sup. § 14.

[†] De profugis, Opp. Mang., i. S. 566 Gfrörer, 1, S. 202. What is farther said of the λόγος : ἀφ' οὗ πᾶσαι παιδεία καὶ σοφίαι ῥέουσιν ἀένναοι may be compared with John iv. 14; vii. 38.

ence to the Sacramental supper, ultimately to be appointed by Jesus.[*] The chief objection to this interpretation is, that before the institution of the supper, such an allusion would be totally unintelligible. Still the discourse might have some sense, however erroneous, for the hearers, as indeed it had, according to the narrator's statement: and the impossibility of being understood is not, in the fourth gospel, so shunned by Jesus, that that circumstance alone would suffice to render this interpretation improbable. It is certainly supported by the analogy between the expressions in the discourse, and the words associated with the institution of the supper, and this analogy has wrung from one of our recent critics the admission, that even if Jesus himself, in uttering the above expressions, did not refer to the supper, the evangelist, in choosing and conveying this discourse of Jesus, might have had that institution in his mind, and might have supposed that Jesus here gave a premonition of its import.[†] In that case, however, he could scarcely have abstained from modifying the language of Jesus ; so that, if the choice of the expression *eat the flesh*, &c., can only be adequately explained on the supposition of a reference to the Lord's Supper, we owe it, without doubt, to the evangelist alone. Having once said, apparently in accordance with Alexandrian ideas, that Jesus had described himself as *the bread of life*, how could he fail to be reminded of the *bread*, which in the Christian community was partaken of as the body of Christ, together with a beverage, as his blood? He would the more gladly seize the opportunity of making Jesus institute the supper prophetically, as it were; because, as we shall hereafter see, he knew nothing definite of its historical institution by Jesus.[‡]

The discourse above considered, also bears the form of a dialogue, and it exhibits strikingly the type of dialogue which especially belongs to the fourth gospel: that, namely, in which language intended spiritually, is understood carnally. In the first place (v. 34), the Jews (as the woman of Samaria in relation to the water) suppose that by *the bread which cometh down from heaven*, Jesus means some material food, and entreat him evermore to supply them with such. Such a misapprehension was certainly natural; but one would have thought that the Jews, before they carried the subject farther, would have indignantly protested against the assertion of Jesus (v. 32), that Moses had not given them heavenly bread. When Jesus proceeds to call himself *the bread from heaven*, the Jews in the synagogue at Capernaum murmur that he, the son of Joseph, whose father and mother they knew, should arrogate to himself a descent from heaven (v. 41): a reflection which the synoptists with more probability attribute to the people of Nazareth, the native city of Jesus, and to which they assign a more natural cause. That the Jews should not understand (v. 53) how Jesus could give them his flesh to eat is very conceivable; and for that reason, as we have observed, it is the less so that Jesus should express himself thus unintelligibly. Neither is it surprising that this *hard saying* σκληρὸς λόγος should cause many disciples to fall away from him, nor easy to perceive how Jesus could, in the first instance, himself give reason for the secession, and then, on its occurrence, feel so much displeasure as is implied in v. 61 and 67. It is indeed said, that Jesus wished to sift his disciples, to remove from his society the superficial believers, the earthly-minded, whom he could not trust; but the measure which he here adopted was one calculated to alienate from him even his best and most intelligent followers. For it is certain that the twelve, who on other occasions knew not what was meant by the leaven of the Pharisees (Matt. xvi. 7), or by the opposition between what goes into the mouth, and what comes out of it (Matt. xv. 15), would not understand the present discourse; and the *words of eternal life*, for the sake of which they remained with him (v. 68), were assuredly not the words of this sixth chapter.*

The farther we read in the fourth gospel, the more striking is the repetition of the same ideas and expressions. The discourses of Jesus during the Feast of Tabernacles, ch. vii. and viii. are, as Lücke has remarked, mere repetitions and amplifications of the oppositions previously presented (especially in ch. v.), of the coming, speaking, and acting, of Jesus, and of God (vii. 17, 28 f.; viii. 28 f., 38, 40, 42. compare with v. 30, 43; vi. 38.); of being *from above*, εἶναι ἐκ τῶν ἄνω, and *from beneath*, ἐκ τῶν κάτω (viii. 23 comp. iii. 31.); of bearing witness of one's self, and receiving witness from God (viii. 13—19. comp. v. 31—37.); of light and darkness (viii. 12. comp. iii. 10 ff., also xii. 35 f.); of true and false judgment (viii. 15 f., comp. v. 30.). All that is new in these chapters, is quickly repeated, as the mention of the departure of Jesus whither the Jews cannot follow him (vii. 33 f., viii. 21.; comp. xiii. 33., xiv. 2 ff., xvi. 16 ff.); a declaration, to which are attached, in the first two instances, very improbable misapprehensions or perversions on the part of the Jews, who, although Jesus had said, *I go unto him that sent me*, are represented as imagining, at one time, that he purposed journeying to the *dispersed among the Gentiles*, at another, that he meditated suicide. How often, again, in this chapter are repeated the asseverations, that he seeks not his own honour, but the honour of the Father (vii. 17 f., viii. 50, 54): that the Jews neither know whence he came, nor the father who sent him (vii. 28; viii. 14, 19, 54); that whosoever believeth in him shall have eternal life, shall not see death, while whosoever believeth not must die in his sins, having no share in eternal life (viii. 21, 24, 51; comp. iii. 36, vi. 40.).—The ninth chapter, consisting chiefly of the deliberations of the Sanhedrim with the man born blind, whom Jesus had restored

---

* In relation to this chapter, I entirely approve the following remark in the Probabilia (p. 56): *videretur—Jesus ipse studuisse, ut verbis illuderet Judæis, nec ab iis intelligeretur. Ita vero nec egit, nec agere potuit, neque si ita docuisset, tanta effecisset, quanta illum effecisse historia testatur.* Comp. De Wette, exeg. Handb. 1, 3, S. 6.

to sight, has of course the form of conversation, but as Jesus is less on the scene than heretofore, there is not the usual amount of artificial contrast; in its stead, however, there is, as we shall presently find, another evidence of artistic design in the narrator.

The tenth chapter commences with the well-known discourse on the Good Shepherd; a discourse which has been incorrectly called a parable.* Even the briefest among the other parables of Jesus, such as that of the leaven and of the mustard-seed, contain the outline of a history that developes itself, having a commencement, progress, and conclusion. Here, on the contrary, there is no historical development; even the particulars that have an historical character are stated generally, as things that are wont to happen, not as things that once happened, and they are left without farther limitation; moreover, the *door* usurps the place of the Shepherd, which is at first the principal image : so that we have here, not a parable, but an allegory. Therefore this passage at least—(and we shall find no other, for the similitude of the vine, ch. xv., comes, as Lücke confesses, under the same category as the one in question)—furnishes no argument against the allegation by which recent critics have justified their suspicions as to the authenticity of the fourth gospel; namely, that its author seems ignorant of the parabolic mode of teaching which, according to the other evangelists, was habitual with Jesus. It does not however appear totally unknown to the fourth evangelist that Jesus was fond of teaching by parables, for he attempts to give examples of this method, both in ch. x. and xv., the first of which he expressly styles a *parable*, παροιμία. But it is obvious that the parabolic form was not accordant with his taste, and that he was too deficient in the faculty of depicting external things, to abstain from the intermixture of reflections, whence the parable in his hand became an allegory.

The discourses of Jesus at the Feast of Tabernacles extend to x. 18. From v. 25, the evangelist professes to record sayings which were uttered by Jesus three months later, at the Feast of Dedication. When, on this occasion, the Jews desire from him a distinct declaration whether he be the Messiah, his immediate reply is, that he has already told them this sufficiently, and he repeats his appeal to the testimony of the Father, as given in the *works*, ἔργα, done by Jesus in his name (as in v. 36.). Hereupon, by reason of the incidental remark that his unbelieving questioners were not of his sheep, the evangelist reverts to the allegory which he had recently abandoned, and repeats part of it word for word.† But not recently

---

* E. g. by Tholuck and Lücke. The latter, however, allows that it is rather an incipient than a complete parable. Olshausen also remarks, that the discourses of the Shepherd and the Vine are rather comparisons than parables; and Neander shows himself willing to distinguish the parable presented by the synoptists as a species, under the genus similitude, to which the παροιμίαι of John belong.

† x. 27: τα πρόβατα τα ἐμὰ τῆς φωνῆς x. 3: καὶ τὰ πρόβατα τῆς φωνῆς αὐτου
μου ἀκούει, ἀκούει·
κἀγω γινώσκω αὐτα 11: καὶ γινώσκω τα ἐμα,
28 : καὶ ἀκολουθοῦσι μοι. 4: καὶ τα πρόβατα αὐτῳ ἀκολουθεῖ.

had Jesus abandoned this allegory; for since its delivery three months are supposed to have elapsed, and it is certain that in the interim much must have been spoken, done, and experienced by Jesus, that would thrust this figurative discourse into the background of his memory, so that he would be very unlikely to recur to it, and in no case would he be able to repeat it, word for word. He who had just quitted the allegory was the evangelist, to whom three months had not intervened between the inditing of the first half of this chapter, and that of the second. He wrote at once what, according to his statement, was chronologically separated by a wide interval; and hence the allegory of the shepherd might well leave so distinct an echo in his memory, though not in that of Jesus. If any think that they can solve this difficulty by putting only the *verbal* similarity of the later discourse to the earlier one to the account of the evangelist, such an opinion cannot be interdicted to them. For others, this instance, in connexion with the rest, will be a positive proof that the discourses of Jesus in the fourth gospel are to a great extent the free compositions of the evangelist.

The same conclusion is to be drawn from the discourse with which the fourth evangelist represents Jesus as closing his public ministry (xii. 44—50). This discourse is entirely composed of reminiscences out of previous chapters,* and, as Paulus expresses it,† is a mere echo of some of the principal apophthegms of Jesus occurring in the former part of the gospel. One cannot easily consent to let the ministry of Jesus close with a discourse so little original, and the majority of recent commentators are of opinion that it is the intention of the evangelist here to give us a mere epitome of the teaching of Jesus.‡ According to our view also, the evangelist is the real speaker; but we must contend that his introductory words, *Jesus cried and said*, 'Ισοῦς δέ ἔκραξε καὶ εἶπεν, are intended to imply that what follows is an actual harangue, from the lips of Jesus. This commentators will not admit, and they can appeal, not without a show of reason, to the statement of the evangelist, v. 36, that Jesus withdrew himself from the public eye, and to his ensuing observations on the obstinate unbelief of the Jews, in which he seems to put a period to the public carreer of Jesus; whence it would be contrary to his plan to make Jesus again step forward to deliver a valedictory discourse. I will not, with the older expositors, oppose to these arguments the supposition that Jesus, after his withdrawal, returned to pronounce these words in the ears of the Jews; but I hold fast to the proposition, that by the introduction above quoted, the evangelist can only have intended to announce an actual harangue. It is said, indeed, that the aorist in ἔκραξε and εἶπε has the

---

Also κἀγὼ ζωὴν αἰώνιον δίδωμι αὐτοῖς corresponds to ἐγὼ ἦλθον, ἵνα ζωὴν ἔχωσι, v. 10, and καὶ οὐχ ἁρπάσει τις αὐτὰ ἐκ τῆς χειρός μου is the counterpart of what is said v. 12 of the hireling who allows the sheep to be scattered.
* Comp. v. 44 with vii. 17; v. 46 with viii. 12; v. 47 with iii. 17; v. 48 with iii. 28; v. 50 with vi. 40; vii. 17; viii. 28. † L. J. b. S. 142. ‡ Lücke, Tholuck, Paulus, in loc.

signification of the pluperfect, and that we have here a recapitulation of the previous discourses of Jesus, notwithstanding which the Jews had not given him credence. But to give this retrospective signification there ought to be a corresponding indication in the words themselves, or in the context, whereas this is far less the case than e. g. in John xviii. 24. Hence the most probable view of the question is this: John had indeed intended to close the narrative of the public ministry of Jesus at v. 36, but his concluding observations, v. 37 ff., with the categories of *faith*, πίστις, and *unbelief*, ἀπιστία, reminded him of discourses which he had already recorded, and he could not resist the temptation of making Jesus recapitulate them with additional emphasis in a parting harangue.

§ 82. ISOLATED MAXIMS OF JESUS, COMMON TO THE FOURTH GOSPEL AND THE SYNOPTICAL ONES.

THE long discourses of Jesus above examined are peculiar to the fourth gospel; it has only a few brief maxims to which the synoptists present parallels. Among the latter, we need not give a special examination to those which are placed by John in an equally suitable connexion, with that assigned to them by the other evangelists (as xii. 25. comp. with Matt. x. 39; xvi. 25; and xiii. 16. comp. with Matt. x. 24.); and as the passage ii. 19 compared with Matt. xxvi. 61, must be reserved until we treat of the history of the Passion, there remain to us only three passages for our present consideration.

The first of these is iv. 44, where the evangelist, after having mentioned that Jesus departed from Samaria into Galilee, adds, *For Jesus himself testified that a prophet has no honour in his own country*, αὐτὸς γὰρ ὁ Ἰ. ἐμαρτύρησεν, ὅτι προφήτης ἐν τῇ ἰδίᾳ πατρίδι τιμὴν οὐκ ἔχει. We find the same idea in Matthew xiii. 57. (Mark vi. 4; Luke iv. 24.), *A prophet is not without honour, save in his own country and in his own house*, οὐκ ἔστι προφήτης ἄτιμος, εἰ μὴ ἐν τῇ πατρίδι αὐτοῦ καὶ ἐν τῇ οἰκίᾳ αὐτοῦ. But while in the latter case it stands in a highly appropriate connexion, as a remark prompted by the ungracious reception which Jesus met with in his native city, and which caused him to leave it again: in John, on the contrary, it is given as a motive for the return of Jesus into his own country, Galilee, where, moreover, he is immediately said to be warmly received. The experience stated in the above sentence, would rather have disinclined than induced Jesus to undertake a journey into Galilee: hence the expedient of translating γὰρ by *although*, is the best adapted to the necessity of the case, and has even been embraced by Kuinöl, except that, unhappily, it is an open defiance of the laws of language. Unquestionably, if Jesus knew that the prophet held this unfavourable position in his *native country*, πατρὶς, it is not probable that he would regard it as a reason for going thither. Some expositors,[*]

* Cyril, Erasmus, Tholuck's expedient, which Olshausen approves, is to give

therefore, have been induced to understand πατρὶς, not as the province, but in a narrower sense, as the native city, and to supply, after the statement that Jesus went into Galilee, the observation, which they assume the evangelist to have omitted, that he avoided his native city Nazareth, for the reason given in the ensuing verse. But an ellipsis such as this explanation requires us to suppose, belongs not less to the order of impossibilities than the transmutation of γὰρ into *though*. The attempt to introduce the desiderated statement that Jesus did not visit his own πατρὶς into the present passage has been therefore renounced ; but it has yet been thought possible to discover there an intimation that he did not soon return thither ; a delay for which the maxim, ὁτι προφήτης κ. τ. λ. might consistently be quoted as a reason.* But to render this interpretation admissible, the entire period of the absence of Jesus from Galilee must have been mentioned immediately before the notice of his return ; instead of this, however, only the short time that Jesus had tarried in Samaria is given (v. 45), so that in ludicrous disproportion of cause and effect, the fear of the contempt of his fellow countrymen would, on the above supposition, be made the reason for delaying his return into Galilee, not until after a residence of some months in Judea, but until after the lapse of two days spent in Samaria. So long, therefore, as Galilee and Nazareth are admitted to be the πατρὶς of Jesus, the passage in question cannot be vindicated from the absurdity of representing, that Jesus was instigated to return thither by the contempt which he knew to await him. Consequently, it becomes the interest of the expositor to recollect, that Matthew and Luke pronounce Bethlehem to be the birthplace of Jesus, whence it follows that Judea was his native country, which he now forsook on account of the contempt he had there experienced.† But according to iv. 1. comp. ii. 24, iii. 26 ff., Jesus had won a considerable number of adherents in Judea, and could not therefore complain of a lack of *honour*, τιμὴ ; moreover the enmity of the Pharisees, hinted at in iv. 1, was excited by the growing consequence of Jesus in Judea, and was not at all referrible to such a cause as that indicated in the maxim : ὁτι προφήτης κ. τ. λ. Further, the entrance into Galilee is not connected in our passage with a departure from Judea, but from Samaria ; and as, according to the import of the text, Jesus departed from Samaria and went into Galilee, because he had found that a prophet has no honour in his own country, Samaria might rather seem to be pointed out as his native country, in conformity with the reproach cast on him by the Jews, viii. 48 ; though even this supposition would not give consistency to the passage, for

ἐμαρτύρησεν the signification of the pluperfect, and to understand γὰρ as an explicative. But I do not see how this can be of any avail, for γὰρ and οὖν (v. 45,) would still form a relation of agreement between two propositions, which one would have expected to be opposed to each other by μὲν and δὲ.

* Paulus. Comm 4, S. 251, 56.   † This idea is so entirely in the spirit of the ancient harmonists, that I can scarcely believe Lücke to be the first to whom it had occurred (Comm. 1. S. 545 f.).

in Samaria also Jesus is said, iv. 39, to have had a favourable reception. Besides, we have already seen* that the fourth evangelist knows nothing of the birth of Jesus in Bethlehem, but on all occasions presupposes him to be a Galilean and a Nazarene. From the above considerations we obtain only the negative result, that it is impossible to discover any consistent relation between the maxim in question and the context. A positive result,—namely, how the maxim came to occupy its actual position, notwithstanding this want of relation, will perhaps be obtained when we have examined the two other passages belonging to the present head of our inquiry.

The declaration xiii. 20, *He that receiveth you receiveth me, and he that receiveth me receiveth him that sent me*, has an almost verbal parallel in Matt. x. 40. In John, it is preceded by the prediction of the betrayal of Jesus, and his explanation to his disciples that he had told them this before it came to pass, in order that when his prediction was fulfilled, they might believe in him as the Messiah. What is the connexion between these subjects and the above declaration, or between the latter and its ensuing context, where Jesus recurs to his betrayer? It is said that Jesus wished to impress on his disciples the high dignity of a messianic missionary, a dignity which the betrayer thought lightly of losing:† but the negative idea of loss, on which this supposition turns, is not intimated in the text. Others are of opinion that Jesus, observing the disciples to be disheartened by the mention of the betrayer, sought to inspire them with new courage by representing to them their high value:‡ but in that case he would hardly have reverted immediately after to the traitor. Others, again, conjecture that some intermediate sentences have been omitted by the writer;§ but this expedient is not much happier than that of Kuinöl, who supposes the passage to be a gloss taken from Matt. x. 40, united originally to v. 16 of chap. xiii. of John, but by some chance transposed to the end of the paragraph. Nevertheless, the indication of v. 16 is an useful way-mark. This verse, as well as v. 20, has a parallel in the discourse of instructions in Matthew (x. 24.); if a few fragments of this discourse had reached the author of the fourth gospel through the medium of tradition, it is very probable that one of them would bring the others to his recollection. In v. 16 there is mention of the *sent*, ἀπόστολος, and of *him who sent him*, πέμψας αὐτὸν ; so in v. 20, of those whom Jesus will send, and of Him who sent Jesus. It is true, that the one passage has a humiliating, the other an encouraging tendency, and their affinity lies therefore, not in the sense, but in the words: so that as soon as the fourth evangelist puts down, from memory, traditional sayings of Jesus, we see him subject to the same law of association as the synoptists. It would have been the most natural arrangement to place v. 20 immediately after v. 16; but the thought of the traitor was uppermost in the mind of the writer, and he could

---

* Vid. sup. § 39. † Paulus, L. J. 1. B. S. 158. ‡ Lücke, 2, S. 478. § Tholuck, in loc.

easily postpone the insertion of an apophthegm that had only a verbal connexion with his previous matter.

Our third passage, xiv. 31, lies yet farther within the domain of the history of the Passion than the one last examined, but as, like this, it can be viewed quite independently, we shall not be anticipating if we include it in our present chapter. In the above passage, the words *Arise, let us go hence*, ἐγείρεσθε, ἄγωμεν ἐντεῦθεν, remind us of those by which Jesus, Matt. xxvi. 46, Mark xiv. 42, summons his disciples to join him in encountering the traitor : *Rise, let us be going*, ἐγείρεσθε ἄγωμεν. The position of the words in John is perplexing, because the summons to depart has no effect; Jesus, as if he had said nothing of the kind, immediately continues (xv. 1.), *I am the true vine*, &c., and does not take his departure with his disciples until after he has considerably prolonged his discourse. Expositors of every hue have been singularly unanimous in explaining the above words by the supposition, that Jesus certainly intended at the moment to depart and betake himself to Gethsemane, but love for his disciples, and a strong desire to impart to them still farther admonition and comfort, detained him ; that hence, the first part of the summons, *Arise*, was executed, but that, standing in the room in which he had supped, he pursued his discourse, until, later, (xviii. 1.), he also put into effect the words, *let us go hence.** It is possible that the circumstances were such; it is also possible that the image of this last evening, with all its details, might be engraven so deeply and accurately in the memory of a disciple, that he might narrate how Jesus arose, and how touchingly he lingered. But one who wrote under the influence of a recollection thus lively, would note the particulars which were most apparent ; the rising to depart and the delay,—not the mere words, which without the addition of those circumstances are altogether unintelligible. Here again, then, the conjecture arises that a reminiscence of the evangelical tradition presented itself to the writer, and that he inserted it just where it occured to him, not, as it happened, in the best connexion ; and this conjecture assumes probability so soon as we discover what might have reminded him of the above expression. In the synoptical parallels the command, *Rise, let us be going*, is connected with the announcement, *Behold the hour is at hand, and the Son of man is betrayed into the hands of sinners—behold he is at hand that doth betray me ;* with the announcement, that is, of the hostile power which is approaching, before which, however, Jesus exhibits no fear, but goes to encounter the danger with the decision implied in that command. In John's gospel, also, Jesus, in the passage under our notice, had been speaking of a hostile power when he said, *The prince of this world cometh and hath nothing in me.* It makes little difference that in John it is the power that dwells in the betrayer, and in those led by him, while, in the synoptical gospels,

---

* Paulus, L. J. 1. B. S. 175 ; Lücke, Tholuck, Olshausen, in loc. ; Hug, Einleit. in das N. T. 2, S. 209.

it is the betrayer who is impelled by that power, that is said to approach. If the author of the fourth gospel knew by tradition that Jesus had united with the announcement of an approaching danger the words, *Rise, let us be going*, this expression would be likely to occur to him on the mention of the prince of this world; and as in that stage of his narrative he had placed Jesus and his disciples in the city and within doors, so that a considerable change of place was necessary before they could encounter the enemy, he added to ἄγωμεν (*let us go*), ἐντεῦθεν (*hence*). As, however, this traditional fragment had intruded itself unawares into the train of thought, which he designed to put as a farewell discourse into the mouth of Jesus, it was immediately lost sight of, and a free course was given to the stream of valedictory instruction, not yet exhausted.

If, from the point of view now attained, we glance back on our first passage, iv. 44, it is easy to see how the evangelist might be led to insert in so unsuitable a connexion the testimony of Jesus as to the treatment of a prophet in his own country. It was known to him traditionally, and he appears to have applied it to Galilee in general, being ignorant of any unfavourable contact of Jesus with the Nazarenes. As, therefore, he knew of no special scene by which this observation might have been prompted, he introduced it where the simple mention of Galilee suggested it, apparently without any definite idea of its bearing.

The result of the above investigation is this; the fourth evangelist succeeds in giving connectedness to his materials, when he presents his own thoughts in the form of discourses delivered by Jesus; but he often fails lamentably in that particular, when he has to deal with the real traditional sayings of Jesus. In the above instances, when he has the same problem before him as the synoptists, he is as unfortunate in its solution as they; nay, he is in a yet more evil case, for his narrative is not homogeneous with the common evangelical tradition, and presented few places where a genuine traditional relic could be inserted. Besides, he was accustomed to cast his metal, liquid from his own invention, and was little skilled in the art of adapting independent fragments to each other, so as to form an harmonious mosaic.

§ 83.   THE MODERN DISCUSSIONS ON THE AUTHENTICITY OF THE DISCOURSES IN THE GOSPEL OF JOHN—RESULT.

THE foregoing examination of the discourses of Jesus in the fourth gospel, has sufficiently prepared us to form a judgment on the controversy of which they have recently been the subject. Modern criticism views these discourses with suspicion, partly on account of their internal contexture, which is at variance with certain generally received rules of historical probability, and partly on account of their external relation to other discourses and narratives. On the other hand, this gospel has had numerous defenders.

With respect to the internal contexture of the above discourses, there arises a twofold question: Does it correspond to the laws, first, of verisimilitude, and secondly, of memory?

It is alleged by the friends of the fourth gospel that its discourses are distinguished by a peculiar stamp of truth and credibility; that the conversations which it represents Jesus as holding with men of the most diverse disposition and capacity, are faithful delineations of character, satisfying the strictest demands of psychological criticism.* In opposition to this, it is maintained to be in the highest degree improbable, that Jesus should have adopted precisely the same style of teaching to persons differing widely in their degrees of cultivation; that he should have spoken to the Galileans in the synagogue at Capernaum not more intelligibly than to a *master of Israel*; that the matter of his discourses should have turned almost entirely on one doctrine—the dignity of his person; and that their form should have been such, as to seem selected with a view to perplex and repel his hearers. Neither, it is further urged, do the interlocutors express themselves in conformity with their position and character. The most educated Pharisee has no advantage in intelligence over a Samaritan woman of the lowest grade; the one, as well as the other, can only put a carnal interpretation on the discourse which Jesus intends spiritually; their misconstructions, too, are frequently so glaring, as to transcend all belief, and so uniform that they seem to belong to a standing set of features with which the author of the fourth gospel has chosen, for the sake of contrast, to depict those whom he brings into conversation with Jesus.† Hence, I confess, I understand not what is the meaning of verisimilitude in the mind of those who ascribe it to the discourses of Jesus in the gospel of John.

As to the second point, regarding the powers of memory, it is pretty generally agreed that discourses of the kind peculiar to John's gospel,—in contradistinction to the apothegms and parables, either isolated or strung together, in the synoptical gospels,—namely, series of dependent propositions, or prolonged dialogues, are among the most difficult to retain and reproduce with accuracy.‡ Unless such discourses were reduced to writing at the moment of their delivery, all hope of their faithful reproduction must be abandoned. Hence Dr. Paulus once actually entertained the idea, that in the judgment-halls of the temple or the synagogues at Jerusalem, there were stationed a sort of shorthand writers, whose office it was to draw up verbal processes, and that from their records the Christians, after the death of Christ, made transcripts.§ In like manner, Bertholdt was of opinion, that our evangelist, during the lifetime of

---

* Wegscheider, Einl. in das Evang. Joh. S. 271; Tholuck, Comm. S. 37 f.   † Thus Eckermann, theol. Beitrage, 5, 2, S. 228; (Vogel) der Evangelist Johannes und seine Ausleger vor dem jüngsten Gericht, 1, S. 28 ff., Wegscheider, S. 281; Bretschneider, Probabil. 33, 45, apud Wegscheider, ut sup. S. 281; Bretschneider, Probab. p. 33, 45. ‡ De Wette, Einl. in das N. T. § 105; Tholuck, Comm. z. Joh. S. 38 f.; Glaubwürdigkeit. S. 314 ff.; Lücke, 1, S. 198 f.   § Commentar. 4, S. 275 f.

Jesus, took down most of the discourses of Jesus in the Aramæan language, and made these notes the foundation of his gospel, composed at a much later period.* These modern hypotheses are clearly unhistorical;† nevertheless, their propounders were able to adduce many reasons in their support. The prophetic declarations of Jesus relative to his death and resurrection, said Bertholdt, are more indefinite in John than in the synoptical gospels, a sure sign that they were recorded before their fulfilment, for otherwise the writer's experience of the event would have reflected more clearness on the predictions. To this we may add the kindred argument, by which Henke thought it possible to establish the genuineness of the discourses in John: namely, that the fourth Evangelist not seldom appends explanatory remarks, often indeed erroneous, to the obscure expression of Jesus, thus proving that he was scrupulously conscientious in reporting the discourses, for otherwise he would have mingled his comments with their original matter.‡ But it is with justice objected, that the obscurity of the predictions in the fourth gospel is in perfect harmony with the mystical spirit that pervades the work, and as, besides, the author, together with his fondness for the obscure and enigmatical, indisputably possessed taste, he must have been conscious that a prophecy would only be the more piquant and genuine-looking, the more darkly it was delivered: hence, though he put those predictions into the mouth of Jesus long after the events to which they refer, he might yet chose to give them an indefinite form. This observation helps to explain why the evangelist, when elucidating some obscure expressions of Jesus, adds that his disciples did not understand them until after his resurrection, or after the outpouring of the Holy Spirit (ii. 22; vii. 39); for the opposition of the darkness in which the disciples at one time groped, to the light which ultimately arose on them, belongs to that order of contrasts with which this gospel abounds. Another argument, adopted by Bertholdt and approved by Tholuck, is, that in the discourses of the fourth gospel there sometimes occur observations, which, having no precise meaning in themselves, nor any connexion with the rest of the discourse, must have been occasioned by some external circumstance, and can only be accounted for on the supposition of prompt, nay, of immediate reduction to writing: and among their examples the passage, *Arise, let us go hence* (xiv. 31), is one of the most important. But the origin of such digressive remarks has been above explained, in a manner that renders the hypothesis of instantaneous note-taking superfluous.

Thus commentators had to excogitate some other means of certifying the genuineness of the discourses of Jesus in the fourth gospel. The general argument, so often adduced, founded on what a

* Verosimilia de origine evangelii Joannis, opusc. p. 1 ff. Einl. in das N. T. S. 1302 ff. This opinion is approved by Wegscheider, ut sup. p. 270 ff. and also Hug. 2, 263 f. and Tholuck, Comm. p. 38, think the supposition of early notes not to be altogether rejected. † Lücke, 1, S. 192 f. ‡ Henke, programm. quo illustratur Johannes apostolus nonnullorum Jesu apophthegmatum et ipse interpres.

good memory might achieve, especially among men of simple lives, unused to writing, lies in the region of abstract possibility, where, as Lücke remarks,[*] there may always be nearly as much said against as for a theory. It has been thought more effectual to adopt an argument resting on a narrower basis, and to appeal to the individual distinctions of the apostle John,—to his intimate and peculiar relation to Jesus as the favourite disciple,—to his enthusiasm for his master, which must surely have strengthened his memory, and have enabled him to preserve in the most lively recollection all that came from the lips of his divine friend.[†] Although this peculiar relation of John to Jesus rests on the authority of John's gospel alone, we might, without reasoning in a circle, draw from it conclusions as to the credibility of the discourses communicated by him, were the faults of which his gospel is accused only such as proceed from the inevitable fading of the memory; because the positive notices of that relation could never flow from this negative cause. As, however, the suspicion which has arisen to the prejudice of the fourth evangelist has gone far beyond those limits, even to the extent of taxing him with free invention, no fact resting on the word of John can be used in support of the discourses which he communicates. But neither the above relation, if admitted, nor the remark that John apparently attached himself to Jesus in early youth, when impressions sink deepest, and from the time of his master's death lived in a circle where the memory of his words and deeds was cherished,[‡] suffices to render it probable that John could retain in his mind long series of ideas, and complicated dialogues, until the period in which the composition of his gospel must be placed. For critics are agreed that the tendency of the fourth gospel, its evident aim to spiritualize the common faith of Christians into the Gnosis, and thus to crush many errors which had sprung up, is a decisive attestation that it was composed at a period when the church had attained a degree of maturity, and consequently in the extreme old age of the apostle.[§]

Hence the champions of the discourses in question are fain to bring forward, as a forlorn hope, the supernatural assistance of the Paraclete, which was promised to the disciples, and which was to restore all that Jesus had said to their remembrance. This is done by Tholuck with great confidence,[||] by Lücke with some diffidence,[¶] which Tholuck's Anzeiger severely censures, but which we consider laudable, because it implies a latent consciousness of the circle that is made, in attempting to prove the truthfulness of the discourses in John, by a promise which appears nowhere but in those discourses;[**] and of the inadequacy of an appeal, in a scientific inquiry, to a popular notion, such as that of the aid of the Holy Spirit. The con-

---

[*] Ut sup. p. 199.   [†] Wegscheider, p. 286; Lücke, p. 195 f.   [‡] Wegscheider, p. 285; Lücke, ut sup.   [§] Lücke, S. 124 f. 175. Kern, über den Ursprung des Ev. Matthäi, in der Tüb. Zeitschrift, 1834, 2, S. 109.   [||] S. 39.   [¶] S. 197. "But lastly, why should we fear to adduce," &c.   [**] The aid promised to the disciples when brought before rulers and tribunals, Matt. x. 19 f., is quite distinct from a bringing to remembrance of the discourses of Jesus (John xiv. 26).

sciousness of this inadequacy shows itself indirectly in Tholuck, for he ekes out the assistance of the Paraclete by early notes; and in Lücke also, for he renounces the verbal authenticity of the discourses in John, and only contends for their substantial veracity on grounds chiefly connected with the relation which they bear to other discourses.

The external relation of the discourses of Jesus in John's gospel is also twofold; for they may be compared both with those discourses which the synoptists put into the mouth of Jesus, and with the manner in which the author of the fourth gospel expresses himself when he is avowedly the speaker.

As a result of the former comparison, critics have pointed out the important difference that exists between the respective discourses in their matter, as well as in their form. In the first three gospels, Jesus closely adapts his teaching to the necessities of his shepherd-less people, contrasting, at one time, the corrupt institutions of the Pharisees with the moral and religious precepts of the Mosaic law; at another, the carnal messianic hopes of the age with the purely spiritual nature of his kingdom, and the conditions of entrance therein. In the fourth gospel, on the contrary, he is perpetually dilating, and often in a barren, speculative manner, on the doctrine of his person and higher nature: so that in opposition to the diversified doctrinal and practical materials of the synoptical discourses, we have in John a one-sided dogmatism.* That this opposition does not hold invariably, and that in the discourses of the synoptical gospels there are passages which have more affinity with those of John, and vice versa, must be granted to judicious critics;† but the important preponderance of the dogmatical element on the one side, and of the practical on the other, is a difficulty that demands a thorough explanation. In answer to this requisition, it is common to adduce the end which John is supposed to have had in view in the composition of his gospel: namely, to furnish a supplement to the first three gospels, and to supply their omissions. But if Jesus taught first in one style, then in another, how was it that the synoptists selected almost exclusively the practical and popular, John, nearly without exception, the dogmatic and speculative portions of his discourse? This is accounted for in a manner intrinsically probable. In the oral tradition, it is observed, on which the first three gospels were founded, the simple and popular, the concise and sententious discourses of Jesus, being the most easy of retention, would alone be propagated, while his more profound, subtle and diffuse discourses would be lost.‡ But according to the above supposition, the fourth evangelist came as a gleaner after the synoptists: now it is certain that all the discourses of Jesus having a practical tendency had not been preserved by them; hence, that the former has almost invariably avoided giving any relic of such discourses, can only be

---

* Bretschneider, Probab. p. 2, 3, 31 ff.   † De Wette Einleit. in das N. T. § 103; Hase, L. J. § 7.   ‡ Lücke, ut sup. p. 100.   Kern ut sup.

explained by his preference for the dogmatic and speculative vein:
a preference which must have had both an objective and a subjective
source, the necessities of his time and circumstances, and the bent
of his own mind. This is admitted even by critics who are favourable to the authenticity of the fourth gospel,* with the reservation,
that that preference betrays itself only negatively, by omission, not
positively, by addition.

There is a further difference between the synoptical gospels and
the fourth, as to the form of teaching adopted by Jesus ; in the one,
it is aphoristic and parabolic, in the other, dialectic.† We have seen
that the parable is altogether wanting in the fourth gospel, and it is
natural to ask why, since Luke, as well as Matthew, has many admirable parables peculiar to himself, John has not been able to make
a rich gleaning, even after those two predecessors? It is true that
isolated apothegms and sentences, similar to the synoptical ones, are
not entirely absent from the fourth gospel : but, on the other hand,
it must be admitted that the prevailing aphoristic and parabolic form
of instruction, ascribed to Jesus by the synoptists, is more suited to
the character of a popular teacher of Palestine, than the dialectic
form which he is made to adopt by John.‡

But the relation of the discourses of Jesus in the gospel of John,
to the evangelist's own style of thinking and writing, is decisive.
Here we find a similarity,§ which, as it extends to the discourses
of a third party, namely, the Baptist, cannot be explained by supposing that the disciple had formed his style on that of the master,‖
but requires us to admit that the evangelist has lent his own style
to the principal characters in his narrative. The latest commentator on John has not only acknowledged this with regard to the colouring of the expression ; he even thinks that in the matter itself
he can here and there detect the explanatory amplifications of the
evangelist, who, to use his own phrase, has had a hand in the composition of the longer and more difficult discourses.¶ But since the
evangelist does not plainly indicate his additions, what is to assure
us that they are not throughout interwoven with the ideas of Jesus,
nay, that all the discourses which he communicates are not entirely
his own productions? The style furnishes no guidance, for this is
every where the same, and is admitted to be the evangelist's own ;
neither does the sense, for in it also there is no essential difference
whether the evangelist speaks in his own name, or in that of Jesus :
where then is the guarantee that the discourses of Jesus are not, as
the author of the Probabilia maintains, free inventions of the fourth
evangelist ?

Lücke adduces some particulars, which on this supposition would
be in his opinion inexplicable.** First, the almost verbal agreement

---

    * Tholuck, ut sup.   † Bretschneider, ut sup.   ‡ De Wette, ut sup. § 105.   § Comp.
Schulze, der schriftst. Charakter und Werth des Johannes. 1803.   ‖ Stronck—de doctrina
et dictione Johannis apostoli, ad Jesu magistri doctrinam dictionemque exacte composita.
1797   ¶ Lücke, Comm. z. Joh. 1, p. 200.   ** Ut sup. p. 199.

of John with the synoptists in isolated sayings of Jesus. But as the fourth evangelist was within the pale of the Christian community, he must have had at his command a tradition, from which, though drawing generally on his own resources, he might occasionally borrow isolated, marked expressions, nearly unmodified. Another argument of Lücke is yet more futile. If, he says, John had really had the inclination and ability to invent discourses for Jesus, he would have been more liberal in long discourses; and the alternation of brief remarks with prolonged addresses, is not to be explained on the above supposition. But this would follow only if the author of the fourth gospel appeared to be a tasteless writer, whose perception did not tell him, that to one occasion a short discourse was suitable, to another a long one, and that the alternation of diffuse harangues with concise sentences was adapted to produce the best impression. Of more weight is the observation of Paulus, that if the fourth evangelist had given the rein to his invention in attributing discourses to Jesus, he would have obtruded more of his own views, of which he has given an abstract in his prologue; whereas the scrupulousness with which he abstains from putting his doctrine of the Logos into the mouth of Jesus, is a proof of the faithfulness with which he confined himself to the materials presented by his memory or his authorities.* But the doctrine of the Logos is substantially contained in the succeeding discourse of Jesus; and that the form in which it is propounded by the evangelist in his preface, does not also reappear, is sufficiently explained by the consideration, that he must have known that form to be altogether foreign to the teaching of Jesus.

We therefore hold it to be established, that the discourses of Jesus in John's gospel are mainly free compositions of the evangelist; but we have admitted that he has culled several sayings of Jesus from an authentic tradition, and hence we do not extend this proposition to those passages which are countenanced by parallels in the synoptical gospels. In these compilations we have an example of the vicissitudes which befal discourses, that are preserved only in the memory of a second party. Severed from their original connexion, and broken up into smaller and smaller fragments, they present when reassembled the appearance of a mosaic, in which the connexion of the parts is a purely external one, and every transition an artificial juncture. The discourses of Jesus in John present just the opposite appearance. Their gradual transitions, only rendered occasionally obscure by the mystical depths of meaning in which they lie, — transitions in which one thought develops itself out of another, and a succeeding proposition is frequently but an explanatory amplification of the preceding,† — are indicative of a pliable,

* In his review of the 2nd Ed. of Lücke's Commentar., in the Lit. Blatt der allgem. Kirchenzeitung 1834, no. 18.   † This peculiarity of the discourses in John cannot be better described than by Erasmus in his Epist. ad Ferdinandum, prefatory to his Paraphrase: *habet Johannes suum quoddam dicendi genus, ita sermonem velut ansulis ex sese*

unresisting mass, such as is never presented to a writer by the traditional sayings of another, but such as proceeds from the stores of his own thought, which he moulds according to his will. For this reason the contributions of tradition to these stores of thought, (apart from the sayings which are also found in the earlier gospels,) were not so likely to have been particular, independent dicta of Jesus, as rather certain ideas which formed the basis of many of his discourses, and which were modified and developed according to the bent of a mind of Alexandrian or Greek culture. Such are the correlative ideas of πατήρ and υἱός (*father* and *son*), φῶς and σκότος (*light* and *darkness*), ζωή and θάνατος (*life* and *death*), ἄνω and κάτω (*above* and *beneath*), σάρξ and πνεῦμα (*flesh* and *spirit*); also some symbolical expressions, as ἄρτος τῆς ζωῆς (*bread of life*), ὕδωρ ζῶν (*water of life*). These and a few other ideas, variously combined by an ingenious author, compose the bulk of the discourses attributed to Jesus by John; a certain uniformity necessarily attending this elemental simplicity.

CHAPTER VIII.

EVENTS IN THE PUBLIC LIFE OF JESUS, EXCLUDING THE MIRACLES.

§ 84. GENERAL COMPARISON OF THE MANNER OF NARRATION THAT DISTINGUISHES THE SEVERAL EVANGELISTS.

If, before proceeding to the consideration of details, we compare the general character and tone of the historical narration in the various gospels, we find differences, first, between Matthew and the two other synoptists; secondly, between the three first evangelists collectively and the fourth.

Among the reproaches which modern criticism has heaped on the gospel of Matthew, a prominent place has been given to its want of individualized and dramatic life; a want which is thought to prove that the author was not an eye-witness, since an eye-witness is ordinarily distinguished by the precision and minuteness of his narration.* Certainly, when we read the indefinite designation

coharentibus contexens, nonnunquam ex contrariis, nonnunquam ex similibus, nonnunquam ex iisdem, subinde repetitis,——ut orationis quodque membrum semper excipiat prius, sic ut prioris finis sit intium sequentis, etc.

* Schulz, über das Abendmahl, S. 303 ff.; Sieffert, über den Ursprung des ersten kanon. Evang. S. 58, 73, u. s. f.; Schneckenburger, über den Ursprung, S. 73.

of times, places and persons, the perpetually recurring τυτε, *then*, παράγων ἐκεῖθεν, *departing from thence*, ἄνθρωπος, *a man*, which characterize this gospel; when we recollect its wholesale statements, such as that Jesus went through all the cities and villages (ix. 35; xi. 1; comp. iv. 23); that they brought to him all sick people, and that he healed them all (iv. 24 f.; xiv. 35 f.; comp. xv. 29 ff.): and finally, the bareness and brevity of many isolated narratives: we cannot disapprove the decision of this criticism, that Matthew's whole narrative resembles a record of events which, before they were committed to writing, had been long current in oral tradition, and had thus lost the impress of particularity and minuteness. But it must be admitted, that this proof, taken alone, is not absolutely convincing; for in most cases we may verify the remark, that even an eye-witness may be unable graphically to narrate what he has seen.*

But our modern critics have not only measured Matthew by the standard of what is to be expected from an eye-witness, in the abstract; they have also compared him with his fellow-evangelists. They are of opinion, not only that John decidedly surpasses Matthew in the power of delineation, both in their few parallel passages and in his entire narrative, but also that the two other synoptists, especially Mark, are generally far clearer and fuller in their style of narration.† This is the actual fact, and it ought not to be any longer evaded. With respect to the fourth evangelist, it is true that, as one would have anticipated, he is not devoid of general, wholesale statements, such as, that Jesus during the feast did many miracles, that hence many believed on him (ii. 23), with others of a similar kind (iii. 22; vii. 1): and he not seldom designates persons indecisively. Sometimes, however, he gives the names of individuals whom Matthew does not specify (xii. 3, 4; comp. with Matt. xxvi. 7, 8; and xviii. 10. with Matt. xxvi. 51; also vi. 5 ff. with Matt. xiv. 16 f.); and he generally lets us know the district or country in which an event happened. His careful chronology we have already noticed: but the point of chief importance is that his narratives, (e. g. that of the man born blind, and that of the resurrection of Lazarus,) have a dramatic and life-like character, which we seek in vain in the first gospel. The two intermediate evangelists are not free from indecisive designations of time (e. g. Mark viii. 1; Luke v. 17; viii. 22); of place (Mark iii. 13; Luke vi. 12); and of persons (Mark x. 17; Luke xiii. 23); nor from statements that Jesus went through all cities, and healed all the sick (Mark i. 32 ff.; 38 f.; Luke iv. 40 f.): but they often give us the details of what Matthew has only stated generally. Not only does Luke associate many discourses of Jesus with special occasions concerning which Matthew is silent, but both he and Mark notice the office or names of persons, to whom Matthew gives no precise

* Olshausen, b. Comm. 1, S. 15.   † See the above named critics, passim; and Hug, Einl. in das N. T. 2, S. 212.

designation (Matt. ix. 18; Mark v. 22; Luke viii. 41; Matth. xix.
16; Luke xviii. 18; Matt. xx. 30; Mark x. 46). But it is chiefly
in the lively description of particular incidents, that we perceive
the decided superiority of Luke, and still more of Mark, over
Matthew. Let the reader only compare the narrative of the execution of John the Baptist in Matthew and Mark (Matth. xiv. 3;
Mark vi. 17), and that of the demoniac or demoniacs of Gadara
(Matt. viii. 28 ff. parall.).

These facts are, in the opinion of our latest critics, a confirmation
of the fourth evangelist's claim to the character of an eye-witness,
and of the greater proximity of the second and third evangelists to
the scenes they describe, than can be attributed to the first. But,
even allowing that one who does not narrate graphically cannot be
an eye-witness, this does not involve the proposition that whoever
does narrate graphically must be an eye-witness. In all cases in
which there are extant two accounts of a single fact, the one full, the
other concise, opinions may be divided as to which of them is the
original.* When these accounts have been liable to the modifications of tradition, it is important to bear in mind that tradition has
two tendencies: the one, to sublimate the concrete into the abstract,
the individual into the general; the other, not less essential, to substitute arbitrary fictions for the historical reality which is lost.† If
then we put the want of precision in the narrative of the first evangelist to the account of the former function of the legend, ought we at
once to regard the precision and dramatic effect of the other gospels,
as a proof that their authors were eye-witnesses? Must we not rather
examine whether these qualities be not derived from the second
function of the legend?‡ The decision with which the other inference is drawn, is in fact merely an after-taste of the old orthodox
opinion, that all our gospels proceed immediately from eye-witnesses,
or at least through a medium incapable of error. Modern criticism
has limited this supposition, and admitted the possibility that one or
the other of our gospels may have been affected by oral tradition.
Accordingly it maintains, not without probability, that a gospel in
which the descriptions are throughout destitute of colouring and life,
cannot be the production of an eye-witness, and must have suffered
from the effacing fingers of tradition. But the counter proposition,
that the other gospels, in which the style of narration is more detailed and dramatic, rest on the testimony of eye-witnesses, would
only follow from the supposed necessity that this must be the case
with some of our gospels. For if such a supposition be made with
respect to several narratives of both the above kinds, there is no
question that the more graphic and vivid ones are with preponderant
probability to be referred to eye-witnesses. But this supposition has

---

* Comp. Saunier, über die Quellen des Markus, S. 42 ff. † Kern, über den Urspr.
des Ev. Matth. ut sup. S. 70 f.   ‡ I say, *examine whether*—not, *consider it decided that*
—so that the accusation of opponents, that I use both the particularity and the brevity of
narratives as proofs of their mythical character, falls to the ground of itself.

merely a subjective foundation.   It was an easier transition for commentators to make from the old notion that all the gospels were immediately or mediately autoptical narratives, to the limited admission
that perhaps one may fall short of this character, than to the general
admission that it may be equally wanting to all.   But, according to
the rigid rules of consequence, with the orthodox view of the scriptural canon, falls the assumption of pure ocular testimony, not only for
one or other of the gospels, but for all : the possibility of the contrary must be presupposed in relation to them all, and their pretensions must be estimated according to their internal character, compared with the external testimonies.   From this point of view—the
only one that criticism can consistently adopt—it is as probable, considering the nature of the external testimonies examined in our Introduction, that the three last evangelists owe the dramatic effect in
which they surpass Matthew, to the embellishments of a more mature
tradition, as that this quality is the result of a closer communication
with eye-witnesses.

That we may not anticipate, let us, in relation to this question,
refer to the results we have already obtained.   The greater particularity by which Luke is distinguished from Matthew in his account
of the occasions that suggested many discourses of Jesus, has appeared to us often to be the result of subsequent additions; and the
names of persons in Mark (xiii. 3. comp. v. 37; Luke viii. 51.) have
seemed to rest on a mere inference of the narrator.   Now, however,
that we are about to enter on an examination of particular narratives,
we will consider, from the point of view above indicated, the constant
forms of introduction, conclusion, and transition, already noticed, in
the several gospels.   Here we find the difference between Matthew
and the other synoptists, as to their more or less dramatic style, im-
printed in a manner that can best teach us how much this style is
worth.

Matthew (viii. 16 f.) states in general terms, that on the evening
after the cure of Peter's mother-in-law, many demoniacs were brought
to Jesus, all of whom, together with others that were sick, he healed.
Mark (i. 32.) in a highly dramatic manner, as if he himself had witnessed the scene, tells, that on the same occasion, the whole city was
gathered together at the door of the house in which Jesus was; at
another time, he makes the crowd block up the entrance (ii. 2.): in
two other instances, he describes the concourse as so great, that Jesus and his disciples could not take their food (iii. 20; vi. 31.); and
Luke on one occasion states, that the people even gathered together
in innumerable multitudes so that *they trode one upon another.*
(xii. 1.).   All highly vivid touches, certainly: but the want of them
can hardly be prejudicial to Matthew, for they look thoroughly like
strokes of imagination, such as abound in Mark's narrative, and often,
as Schleiermacher observes,[*] give it almost an apocryphal appearance.   In detailed narratives, of which we shall presently notice

* Ueber den Lukas, S. 74, and elsewhere.

many examples, while Matthew simply tells what Jesus said on a
certain occasion, the two other evangelists are able to describe the
glance with which his words were accompanied (Mark iii. 5; x. 21;
Luke vi. 10). On the mention of a blind beggar of Jericho, Mark
is careful to give us his name, and the name of his father (x. 46).
From these particulars we might already augur, what the examination of single narratives will prove: namely, that the copiousness of
Mark and Luke is the product of the second function of the legend,
which we may call the function of embellishment. Was this embellishment gradually wrought out by oral tradition, or was it the
arbitrary addition of our evangelists? Concerning this, there may
be a difference of opinion, and a degree of probability in relation to
particular passages is the nearest approach that can be made to a decision. In any case, not only must it be granted, that a narrative
adorned by the writer's own additions is more remote from primitive
truth than one free from such additions; but we may venture to
pronounce that the earlier efforts of the legend are rapid sketches,
tending to set off only the leading points whether of speech or action,
and that at a later period it aims rather to give a symmetrical effect
to the whole, including collateral incidents; so that, in either view,
the closest approximation to truth remains on the side of the first
gospel.

While the difference as to the more or less dramatic style of
concluding and connecting forms, lies chiefly between Matthew and
the other synoptists; another difference with respect to these forms
exists between all the synoptists and John. While most of the
synoptical anecdotes from the public life of Jesus are wound up by
a panegyric, those of John generally terminate, so to speak, polemi-
cally. It is true that the three first evangelists sometimes mention,
by way of conclusion, the offence that Jesus gave to the narrow-
hearted, and the machinations of his enemies against him (Matt. viii.
34; xii. 14; xxi. 46; xxvi. 3 f.; Luke iv. 28 f.; xi. 35 f.); and, on
the other hand, the fourth evangelist closes some discourses and
miracles by the remark, that in consequence of them, many believed
on Jesus (ii. 23; iv. 39. 53; vii. 31. 40 f.; viii 30; x. 42; xi. 45).
But in the synoptical gospels, throughout the period previous to the
residence of Jesus in Jerusalem, we find forms implying that the
fame of Jesus had extended far and wide (Matt. iv. 24; ix. 26. 31;
Mark i. 28. 45; v. 20; vii. 36; Luke iv. 37; v. 15; vii. 17; viii.
39); that the people were astonished at his doctrine (Matt. vii. 28;
Mark i. 22; xi. 18; Luke xix. 48), and miracles (Matt. viii. 27;
ix. 8; xiv. 33; xv. 31), and hence followed him from all parts
(Matt. iv. 25; viii. 1; ix, 36; xii. 15; xiii. 2; xiv. 13). In the
fourth gospel, on the contrary, we are continually told that the Jews
sought to kill Jesus (v. 18; vii. 1); the Pharisees wish to take him,
or send out officers to seize him (vii. 30. 32. 54; comp. viii. 20;
x. 39); stones are taken up to cast at him (viii. 59; x. 31); and
even in those passages where there is mention of a favourable dis-

position on the part of the people, the evangelist limits it to one portion of them, and represents the other as inimical to Jesus (vii. 11—13). He is especially fond of drawing attention to such circumstances, as that before the final catastrophe all the guile and power of the enemies of Jesus were exerted in vain, because his hour was not yet come (vii. 30; viii. 20): that the emissaries sent out against him, overcome by the force of his words, and the dignity of his person, retired without fulfilling their errand (vii. 32. 44 ff.); and that Jesus passed unharmed through the midst of an exasperated crowd (viii. 59; x. 39: comp. Luke iv. 30). The writer, as we have above remarked, certainly does not intend us in these instances to think of a natural escape, but of one in which the higher nature of Jesus, his invulnerability so long as he did not choose to lay down his life, was his protection. And this throws some light on the object which the fourth evangelist had in view, in giving prominence to such traits as those just enumerated: they helped him to add to the number of the contrasts, by which, throughout his works, he aims to exalt the person of Jesus. The profound wisdom of Jesus, as the divine Logos, appeared the more resplendent, from its opposition to the rude unapprehensiveness of the Jews; his goodness wore a more touching aspect, confronted with the inveterate malice of his enemies; his appearance gained in impressiveness, by the strife he excited among the people; and his power, as that of one who had life in himself, commanded the more reverence, the oftener his enemies and their instruments tried to seize him, and, as if restrained by a higher power, were not able to lay hands on him,— the more marvellously he passed through the ranks of adversaries prepared to take away his life. It has been made matter of praise to the fourth evangelist, that he alone presents the opposition of the pharisaic party to Jesus, in its rise and gradual progress: but there are reasons for questioning whether the course of events described by him, be not rather fictitious than real. Partially fictitious, it evidently is; for he appeals to the supernatural for a reason why the Pharisees so long effected nothing against Jesus: whereas the synoptists preserve the natural sequence of the facts by stating as a cause, that the Jewish hierarchy feared the people, who were attached to Jesus as a prophet (Matt. xxi. 46; Mark xii. 12; Luke xx. 19). If then the fourth evangelist was so far guided by his dogmatical interest, that for the escape of Jesus from the more early snares and assaults of his enemies, he invented such a reason as best suited his purpose; what shall assure us that he has not also, in consistency with the characteristics which we have already discerned in him, fabricated, for the sake of that interest, entire scenes of the kind above noticed? Not that we hold it improbable, that many futile plots and attacks of the enemies of Jesus preceded the final catastrophe of his fate:—we are only dubious whether these attempts were precisely such as the gospel of John describes.

§ 85.   ISOLATED GROUPS OF ANECDOTES—IMPUTATION OF A LEAGUE
WITH BEELZEBUB, AND DEMAND OF A SIGN.

In conformity with the aim of our criticism, we shall here confine
our attention to those narratives, in which the influence of the legend
may be demonstrated.   The strongest evidence of this influence is
found where one narrative is blended with another, or where the one
is a mere variation of the other: hence, chronology having refused
us its aid, we shall arrange the anecdotes about to be considered
according to their mutual affinity.

To begin with the more simple form of legendary influence:
Schulz has already complained, that Matthew mentions two instances, in which a league with Beelzebub was imputed to Jesus,
and a sign demanded from him; circumstances which in Mark and
Luke happen only once.*   The first time the imputation occurs
(Matt. ix. 32 ff.), Jesus has cured a dumb demoniac; at this the
people marvel, but the Pharisees observe, *He casts out demons
through the prince* (ἄρχων) *of the demons.*   Matthew does not here
say that Jesus returned any answer to this accusation.   On the second occasion (xii. 22. ff), it is a blind and dumb demoniac whom
Jesus cures; again the people are amazed, and again the Pharisees
declare that the cure is effected by the help of Beelzebub, the ἄρχων of
the demons, whereupon Jesus immediately exposes the absurdity of
the accusation.   That it should have been alleged against Jesus
more than once when he cast out demons, is in itself probable.   It
is however suspicious that the demoniac who gives occasion to the
assertion of the Pharisees, is in both instances dumb (in the second
only, blindness is added).   Demoniacs were of many kinds, every
variety of malady being ascribed to the influence of evil spirits; why,
then, should the above imputation be not once attached to the cure
of another kind of demoniac, but twice to that of a dumb one?   The
difficulty is heightened if we compare the narrative of Luke (xi.
14 f.), which, in its introductory description of the circumstances,
corresponds not to the second narrative in Matthew, but to the first;
for as there, so in Luke, the demoniac is only dumb, and his cure
and the astonishment of the people are told with precisely the same
form of expression:—in all which points, the second narrative of
Matthew is more remote from that of Luke.   But with this cure of
the dumb demoniac, which Matthew represents as passing off in
silence on the part of Jesus, Luke connects the very discourse which
Matthew appends to the cure of the one both blind and dumb; so
that Jesus must on both these successive occasions, have said the
same thing.   This is a very unlikely repetition, and united with the
improbability, that the same accusation should be twice made in
connexion with a dumb demoniac, it suggests the question, whether
legend may not here have doubled one and the same incident?   How
this can have taken place, Matthew himself shows us, by represent-

* Ut sup. S. 311.

ing the demoniac as, in the one case, simply dumb, in the other, blind also. Must it not have been a striking cure which excited, on the one hand, the astonishment of the people, on the other, this desperate attack of the enemies of Jesus? Dumbness alone might soon appear an insufficient malady for the subject of the cure, and the legend, ever, prone to enhance, might deprive him of sight also. If then, together with this new form of the legend, the old one too was handed down, what wonder that a compiler, more conscientious than critical, such as the author of the first gospel, adopted both as distinct histories, merely omitting on one occasion the discourse of Jesus, for the sake of avoiding repetition.*

Matthew, having omitted (ix. 34) the discourse of Jesus, was obliged also to defer the demand of a sign, which required a previous rejoinder on the part of Jesus, until his second narration of the charge concerning Belzebub; and in this point again the narrative of Luke, who also attaches the demand of a sign to the accusation, is parallel with the latter passage of Matthew.† But Matthew not only has, with Luke, a demand of a sign in connexion with the

* Schleiermacher (S. 175), does not perceive the connexion of the discourse on the blasphemy against the Holy Ghost, in Matthew (xii. 31 f.) though it links on excellently to the foregoing expression, ἐγὼ ἐν πνεύματι θεοῦ ἐκβάλλω τὰ δαιμόνια (v. 28). It is more easy, however, to understand this difficulty, than that he should think (S. 185 f.) that discourse better introduced in Luke (xii. 10). For here, between the preceding proposition, that whosoever denies the Son of man before men, shall be denied before the angels of God, and the one in question, the only connexion is that the expression ἀρνεῖσθαι τὸν υἱὸν τοῦ ἀνθρώπου brought to the writer's recollection the words εἰπεῖν εἰς λόγον τὸν υἱὸν τοῦ ἀνθρώπου. One proof of this is that between the latter passage and the succeeding declaration, that the necessary words would be given to the disciples, when before the tribunal, by the πνεῦμα ἅγιον, the connexion consists just as superficially in the expression πνεῦμα ἅγιον. What follows in Matthew (v. 33—37), had been partly given already in the sermon on the mount, but stands here in a better connexion than Schleiermacher is willing to admit.

† Luke makes the demand of a sign follow immediately on the accusation, and then gives in succession the answers of Jesus to both. This representation modern criticism holds to be far more probable than that of Matthew, who gives first the accusation and its answer, then the demand of a sign and its refusal; and this judgment is grounded on the difficulty of supposing, that after Jesus had given a sufficiently long answer to the accusation, the very same people who had urged it would still demand a sign (Schleiermacher, S. 175; Schneckenburger, über den Ursprung, S. 52 f.) But on the other hand, it is equally improbable that Jesus, after having some time ago delivered a forcible discourse on the more important point, the accusation concerning Beelzebub, and even after an interruption which had led him to a totally irrelevant declaration (Luke xi. 27 f.), should revert to the less important point, namely, the demand of a sign. The discourse on the departure and return of the unclean spirit, is in Matthew (v. 43—45) annexed to the reply of Jesus to this demand; but in Luke (xi. 24 ff.) it follows the answer to the imputation of a league with Beelzebub, and this may at first seem to be a more suitable arrangement. But on a closer examination, it will appear very improbable that Jesus should conclude a defence, exacted from him by his enemies, with so calm and purely theoretical a discourse, which supposes an audience, if not favourably prepossessed, at least open to instruction; and it will be found that here again there is no further connexion than that both discourses treat of the expulsion of demons. By this single feature of resemblance, the writer of the third gospel was led to sever the connexion between the answer to the oft-named accusation, and that to the demand of a sign, which accusation and demand, as the strongest proofs of the malevolent unbelief of the enemies of Jesus, seem to have been associated by tradition. The first evangelist refrained from this violence, and reserved the discourse on the return of the unclean spirit, which was suggested by the suspicion cast on the expulsion of demons by Jesus, until he had communicated the answer by which Jesus parries the demand of a sign.

above charge; he has also another, after the second feeding of the multitude (xvi. 1 ff.), and this second demand Mark also has (viii. 11 f.), while he omits the first. Here the Pharisees come to Jesus (according to Matthew, in the unlikely companionship of Sadducees), and tempt him by asking for *a sign from heaven*, σημεῖον ἐκ τοῦ οὐρανοῦ. To this Jesus gives an answer, of which the concluding proposition, *a wicked and adulterous generation seeketh after a sign; and there shall no sign be given unto it, but the sign of the prophet Jonas*, γενεὰ πονηρὰ καὶ μοιχαλὶς σημεῖον ἐπιζητεῖ, καὶ σημεῖον οὐ δοθήσεται αὐτῇ, εἰ μὴ τὸ σημεῖον Ἰωνᾶ τοῦ προφήτου, in Matthew, agrees word for word with the opening of the earlier refusal. It is already improbable enough, that Jesus should have twice responded to the above requisition with the same enigmatical reference to Jonah; but the words (v. 2, 3) which, in the second passage of Matthew, precede the sentence last quoted, are totally unintelligible. For why Jesus, in reply to the demand of his enemies that he would show them a sign from heaven, should tell them that they were indeed well versed in the natural signs of the heavens, but were so much the more glaringly ignorant of the spiritual signs of the messianic times, is so far from evident, that the otherwise unfounded omission of v. 2 and 3, seems to have arisen from despair of finding any connexion for them.* Luke, who also has, (xii. 44 f.), in words only partly varied, this reproach of Jesus that his cotemporaries understood better the signs of the weather than of the times, gives it another position, which might be regarded as the preferable one; since after speaking of the fire which he was to kindle, and the divisions which he was to cause, Jesus might very aptly say to the people: You take no notice of the unmistakeable prognostics of this great revolution which is being prepared by my means, so ill do you understand the signs of the times.† But on a closer examination, Luke's arrangement appears just as abrupt here, as in the case of the two parables (xiii. 18).‡ If from hence we turn again to Matthew, we easily see how he was led to his mode of representation. He may have been induced to double the demand of a sign, by the verbal variation which he met with, the required sign being at one time called simply a σημεῖον, at another a σημεῖον ἐκ τοῦ οὐρανοῦ. And if he knew that Jesus had exhorted the Jews to study the signs of the times, as they had hitherto studied the appearance of the heavens, the conjecture was not very remote, that the Jews had given occasion for this admonition by demanding a *sign from heaven*, σημεῖον ἐκ τοῦ οὐρανοῦ. Thus Matthew here presents us, as Luke often does elsewhere, with a fictitious introduction to a discourse of Jesus; a proof of the proposition, advanced indeed, but too little regarded by Sieffert :§ that it is in the nature of traditional records, such as the three first gospels, that one particular should be best preserved in this

---

* Vid. Griesbach, Comm. crit. in loc.
† Comp. Schleiermacher, S. 190 f.
‡ Wette, exeg. Handbuch, i. S. 139.
§ Ueber den Urspr. S. 115.

narrative, another in that; so that first one, and then the other, is at a disadvantage, in comparison with the rest.

§ 86. VISIT OF THE MOTHER AND BRETHREN OF JESUS—THE WOMAN WHO PRONOUNCES THE MOTHER OF JESUS BLESSED.

ALL the synoptists mention a visit of the mother and brethren of Jesus, on being apprised of which Jesus points to his disciples, and declares that they who do the will of God are his mother and his brethren (Matt. xii. 46 ff.; Mark iii. 31 ff.; Luke viii. 19 ff.). Matthew and Luke do not tell us the object of this visit, nor, consequently, whether this declaration of Jesus, which appears to imply a disowning of his relatives, was occasioned by any special circumstance. On this subject Mark gives us unexpected information: he tells us (v. 21) that while Jesus was teaching among a concourse of people, who even prevented him from taking food, his relatives, under the idea that he was beside himself, went out to seize him, and take him into the keeping of his family.* In describing this incident, the evangelist makes use of the expression, ἔλεγον ὅτι ἐξέστη, (they said, he is beside himself), and it was merely this expression, apparently, that suggested to him what he next proceeds to narrate: οἱ γραμματεῖς ἔλεγον, ὅτι Βεελζεβοὺλ ἔχει κ. τ. λ. (the scribes said, he hath Beelzebub, &c., comp. John x. 20). With this reproach, which however, he does not attach to an expulsion of demons, he connects the answer of Jesus; he then recurs to the relatives, whom he now particularizes as the mother and brethren of Jesus, supposing them to have arrived in the meantime; and he makes their announcement call forth from Jesus the answer of which we have above spoken.

These particulars imparted by Mark are very welcome to commentators, as a means of explaining and justifying the apparent harshness of the answer which Jesus returns to the announcement of his nearest relatives, on the ground of the perverted object of their visit. But, apart from the difficulty that, on the usual interpretation of the accounts of the childhood of Jesus, it is not to be explained how his mother could, after the events therein described, be thus mistaken in her son, it is very questionable whether we ought to accept this information of Mark's. In the first place, it is associated with the obvious exaggeration, that Jesus and his disciples were prevented even from taking food by the throng of people; and in the second place, it has in itself a strange appearance, from its want of relation to the context. If these points are considered, it will scarcely be possible to avoid agreeing with the opinion of Schleiermacher, that no explanation of the then existing relations of Jesus with his family is to be sought in this addition; that it rather belongs to those exaggerations to which Mark is so prone, as well in his introductions to isolated incidents, as in his general state-

* For the proof of this interpretation, see Fritzsche, comm. in Marc. p. 97 ff.

ments.* He wished to make it understood why Jesus returned an ungracious answer to the announcement of his relatives; for this purpose he thought it necessary to give their visit an object of which Jesus did not approve, and as he knew that the Pharisees had pronounced him to be under the influence of Beelzebub, he attributed a similar opinion to his relatives.

If we lay aside this addition of Mark's, the comparison of the three very similar narratives presents no result as it regards their matter;† but there is a striking difference between the connexions in which the evangelists place the event. Matthew and Mark insert it after the defence against the suspicion of diabolical aid, and before the parable of the sower, whereas Luke makes the visit considerably prior to that imputation, and places the parable even before the visit. It is worthy of notice, however, that Luke has, after the defence against the accusation of a league with Beelzebub, in the position which the two other evangelists give to the visit of the relatives of Jesus, an incident which issues in a declaration, precisely similar to that which the announcement calls forth. After the refutation of the Pharisaic reproach, and the discourse on the return of the unclean spirit, a woman in the crowd is filled with admiration, and pronounces the mother of Jesus blessed, on which Jesus, as before on the announcement of his mother, replies; *Yea, rather blessed are they who hear the word of God and keep it!*‡ Schleiermacher here again prefers the account of Luke: he thinks this little digression on the exclamation of the woman, especially evinces a fresh and lively recollection, which has inserted it in its real place and circumstances; whereas Matthew, confounding the answer of Jesus to the ejaculation of the woman, with the very similar one to the announcement of his relatives, gives to the latter the place of the former, and thus passes over the scene with the woman.§ But how the woman could feel herself hurried away into so enthusiastic an exclamation, precisely on hearing tho abstruse discourse on the return of the expelled demons, or even the foregoing reprehensive reply to the Pharisees, it is difficult to understand, and the contrary conjecture to that of Schleiermacher might rather be established: namely, that in the place of the announcement of the relatives, the writer of the third gospel inserted the scene with the

---

* Ueber den Lukas, S. 121. † Schneckenburger, (über den Urspr. S. 54), finds an attempt at dramatic effect in the εἶπέ τις, and the ἐκτείνας τὴν χεῖρα of Matthew, as compared with the εἶπον and περιβλεψάμενος κύκλῳ of Mark.   This is a remarkable proof of the partial acumen which plays so distinguished a part to the disadvantage of Matthew in modern criticism.   For who does not see that if Matthew had εἶπον, it would be numbered among the proofs that his narrative is wanting in dramatic life? As for the words ἐκτείνας τὴν χεῖρα, there is nothing to be discovered in them which could give to them more than to the πειιβλεψάμενος of mark, the stamp of artificiality : we might as well attribute the latter expression to Mark's already discovered fondness for describing the action of the eyes, and consequently regard it as an addition of his own.

‡ Answer to the annoucement, viii. 21 :   Answer to the woman, xi. 28 : μενοῦνγε μήτηρ μοῦ καὶ ἀδελφοὶ μοῦ οὗτοί εἰσιν οἱ τὸν μακάριοι (sc. οἱ χ ἡ μήτηρ μοῦ, ἀλλ') οἱ ἀκούον-λόγον τοῦ θεοῦ ἀκούοντες καὶ ποιοῦντες αὐτόν.   τες τὸν λόγον τοῦ θεοῦ καὶ φυλάσσοντες αὐτόν.

§ Ut sup. S. 177 f.

woman, from its having a like termination. The evangelical tradition, as we see from Matthew and Mark, whether from historical or merely accidental motives, had associated the above visit and the saying about the spiritual relatives, with the discourse of Jesus on the accusation of a league with Beelzebub, and on the return of the unclean spirit; and Luke also, when he came to the conclusion of that discourse, was reminded of the anecdote of the visit and its point—the extolling of a spiritual relationship to Jesus. But he had already mentioned the visit;* he therefore seized on the scene with the woman, which presented a similar termination. From the strong resemblance between the two anecdotes, I can scarcely believe that they are founded on two really distinct incidents; rather, it is more likely that the memorable declaration of Jesus, that he preferred his spiritual before his bodily relatives, had in the legend received two different settings or frames. According to one, it seemed the most natural that such a depreciation of his kindred should be united with an actual rejection of them; to another, that the exaltation of those who were spiritually near to him, should be called forth by a blessing pronounced on those who were nearest to him in the flesh. Of these two forms of the legend, Matthew and Mark give only the first: Luke, however, had already disposed of this on an earlier occasion; when, therefore, he came to the passage where, in the common evangelical tradition, that anecdote occurred, he was induced to supply its place by the second form.

§ 87. CONTENTIONS FOR PRE-EMINENCE AMONG THE DISCIPLES. THE LOVE OF JESUS FOR CHILDREN.

The three first evangelists narrate several contentions for pre-eminence which arose among the disciples, with the manner in which Jesus composed these differences. One such contention, which is said to have arisen among the disciples after the transfiguration, and the first prediction of the passion, is common to all the gospels (Matt. xviii. 1 ff.; Mark ix. 33 ff.; Luke ix. 46 ff.). There are indeed divergencies in the narratives, but the identity of the incident on which they are founded is attested by the fact, that in all of them, Jesus sets a little child before his disciples as an example; a scene which, as Schleiermacher remarks,† would hardly be repeated. Matthew and Mark concur in mentioning a dispute about pre-eminence, which was excited by the two sons of Zebedee. These disciples (according to Mark), or their mother for them (according to Matthew), petitioned for the two first places next to

* That which decided the evangelist to place the visit after the parable of the sower, was probably not, as Schleiermacher thinks, a real chronological connexion. On the contrary, we recognize the usual characteristic of his arrangement, in the transition from the concluding sentence in the explanation of the parable: *those are they who having heard the word, keep it, and bring forth fruit with patience*, to the similar expression of Jesus on the occasion of the visit: *those who hear the word of God and do it.*

† Ut sup. S. 152.

Jesus in the messianic kingdom (Matt. xx. 20 ff. ; Mark x. 35 ff.).*
Of such a request on the part of the sons of Zebedee, the third
evangelist knows nothing ; but apart from this occasion, there is a
further contention for pre-eminence, on which discourses are uttered,
similar to those which the two first evangelists have connected with
the above petition. At the last supper of which Jesus partook with
his disciples before his passion, Luke makes the latter fall into a
φιλονεικία (dispute) which among them shall be the greatest ; a
dispute which Jesus seeks to quell by the same reasons, and partly
with the same words, that Matthew and Mark give in connexion
with the ἀγανάκτησις (indignation), excited in the disciples generally
by the request of the sons of Zebedee. Luke here reproduces a
sentence which he, in common with Mark, had previously given
almost in the same form, as accompanying the presentation of the
child ; and which Matthew has, not only on the occasion of Salome's
prayer, but also in the great anti-pharisaic discourse (comp. Luke
xxii. 26 ; Mark ix. 35 ; Luke ix. 48 ; Matt. xx. 26 f., xxiii. 11).
However credible it may be that with the worldly messianic hopes
of the disciples, Jesus should often have to suppress disputes among
them on the subject of their future rank in the Messiah's kingdom,
it is by no means probable that, for example, the sentence, *Whosoever will be great among you, let him be the servant of all :*
should be spoken, 1st, on the presentation of the child ; 2ndly, in
connexion with the prayer of the sons of Zebedee ; 3rdly, in the
anti-pharisaic discourse, and 4thly, at the last supper. There is
here obviously a traditional confusion, whether it be (as Sieffert in
such cases is fond of supposing) that several originally distinct
occurrences have been assimilated by the legend, i. e. the same
discourse erroneously repeated on various occasions ; or that out of
one incident the legend has made many, i. e. has invented various
occasions for the same discourse. Our decision between these two
possibilities must depend on the answer to the following question :
Have the various facts, to which the analogous discourses on humility are attached, the dependent appearance of mere frames to the
discourses, or the independent one of occurrences that carry their
truth and significance in themselves.

It will not be denied that the petition of the sons of Zebedee,
is in itself too specific and remarkable to be a mere background to
the ensuing discourse ; and the same judgment must be passed on
the scene with the child : so that we have already two cases of con-

* Schulz, (über das Abendmahl S. 320) speaks consistently with the tone of the
recent criticism on Matthew when he asserts, that he does not doubt *for a moment* that
every *observant* reader will, *without hesitation*, prefer the representation of Mark, who
without mentioning the mother, confines the whole transaction to Jesus and the two apostles. But so far as historical probability is concerned, I would ask, why should not a
woman, who was one of the female companions of Jesus (Matt. xxvii. 56), have ventured
on such a petition? As regards psychological probability, the sentiment of the church,
in the choice of the passage for St. James's day, has usually decided in favour of Matthew ;
for so solemn a prayer, uttered on the spur of the moment, is just in character with a
woman, and more especially a mother devoted to her sons.

tention for pre-eminence subsisting in themselves. If we would assign to each of these occurrences its appropriate discourses, the declarations which Matthew connects with the presentation of the child: *Unless ye become as this child, &c.*, and, *Whosoever shall humble himself as this child, &c.*, evidently belong to this occasion. On the other hand, the sentences on ruling and serving in the world and in the kingdom of Jesus, seem to be a perfectly suitable comment on the petition of the sons of Zebedee, with which Matthew associates them: also the saying about the first and the last, the greatest and the least, which Mark and Luke give so early as at the scene with the child, Matthew seems rightly to have reserved for the scene with the sons of Zebedee. It is otherwise with the contention spoken of by Luke (xxii. 24 ff.). This contention originates in no particular occasion, nor does it issue in any strongly marked scene, (unless we choose to insert here the washing of the disciples' feet, described by John, who, for the rest, mentions no dispute;—of which scene, however, we cannot treat until we come to the history of the Passion.) On the contrary, this contention is ushered in merely by the words, ἐγένετο δὲ καὶ φιλονεικία ἐν αὐτοῖς,— nearly the same by which the first contention is introduced, ix. 46,— and leads to a discourse from Jesus, which, as we have already noticed, Matthew and Mark represent him to have delivered in connexion with the earlier instances of rivalry; so that this passage of Luke has nothing peculiarly its own, beyond its position, at the last supper. This position, however, is not very secure; for that immediately after the discourse on the betrayer, so humiliating to the disciples, pride should so strongly have taken possession of them, is as difficult to believe, as it is easy to discover, by a comparison of v. 23 and 24, how the writer might be led, without historical grounds, to insert here a contention for pre-eminence. It is clear that the words καὶ αὐτοὶ ἤρξαντο συζητεῖν πρὸς ἑαυτοὺς, τὸ, τίς ἄρα εἴη ἐξ αὐτῶν ὁ τοῦτο μέλλων πράσσειν: suggested to him the similar ones, ἐγένετο δὲ καὶ φιλονεικία ἐν αὐτοῖς, τὸ, τίς αὐτῶν δοκεῖ εἶναι μείζων ; that is, the disputes about the betrayer called to his remembrance the disputes about pre-eminence. One such dispute indeed, he had already mentioned, but had only connected with it, one sentence excepted, the discourses occasioned by the exhibition of the child; he had yet in reserve those which the two first evangelists attach to the petition of the sons of Zebedee, an occasion which seems not to have been present to the mind of the third evangelist, whence he introduces the discourses pertaining to it here, with the general statement that they originated in a contention for pre-eminence, which broke out among the disciples. Meanwhile the chronological position, also, of the two first-named disputes about rank, has very little probability; for in both instances, it is after a prediction of the passion, which, like the prediction of the betrayal, would seem calculated to suppress such thoughts of earthly ambition.[*] We therefore

---

welcome the indication which the evangelical narrative itself presents, of the manner in which the narrators were led unhistorically to such an arrangement. In the answer of Jesus to the prayer of Salome, the salient point was the suffering that awaited him and his disciples; hence by the most natural association of ideas, the ambition of the two disciples, the antidote to which was the announcement of approaching trial, was connected with the prediction of the passion. Again, on the first occasion of rivalry, the preceding prediction of the passion leads in Mark and Luke to the observation, that the disciples did not understand the words of Jesus, and yet feared to ask him concerning them, whence it may be inferred that they debated and disputed on the subject among themselves; here, then, the association of ideas caused the evangelists to introduce the contention for pre-eminence, also carried on in the absence of Jesus. This explanation is not applicable to the narrative of Matthew, for there, between the prediction of the passion and the dispute of the disciples, the anecdote of the coin angled for by Peter, intervenes.

With the above contentions for pre-eminence, another anecdote is indirectly connected by means of the child which is put forward on one of those occasions. Children are brought to Jesus that he may bless them; the disciples wish to prevent it, but Jesus speaks the encouraging words, *Suffer little children to come unto me*, and adds that only for children, and those who resemble children, is the kingdom of heaven destined (Matt. xix. 13 ff.; Mark x. 13 ff.; Luke xviii. 15 ff.). This narrative has many points of resemblance to that of the child placed in the midst of the disciples. 1stly, in both, Jesus presents children as a model, and declares that only those who resemble children can enter the kingdom of God; 2ndly, in both, the disciples appear in the light of opposition to children; and, 3rdly, in both, Mark says, that Jesus took the children in his arms (εναγκαλισάμενος.) If these points of resemblance be esteemed adequate ground for reducing the two narratives to one, the latter must, beyond all question, be retained as the nearest to truth, because the saying of Jesus, *Suffer little children* &c. which, from its retaining this original form in all the narratives, bears the stamp of genuineness, could scarcely have been uttered on the other occasion; whereas, the sentences on children as patterns of humility, given in connection with the contention about rank, might very well have been uttered under the circumstances above described, in retrospective allusion to previous contentions about rank. Nevertheless, this might rather be the place for supposing an assimilation of originally diverse occurrences, since it is at least evident, that Mark has inserted the expression εναγκαλισάμενος in both, simply on account of the resemblance between the two scenes.

§ 88. THE PURIFICATION OF THE TEMPLE.

JESUS, during his first residence in Jerusalem, according to John (ii. 14 ff.); according to the synoptists, during his last (Matt. xxi.

12 ff. parall.), undertook the purification of the temple. The ancient commentators thought, and many modern ones still think,* that these were separate events, especially as, besides the chronological difference, there is some divergency between the three first evange- lists and the fourth in their particulars. While, namely, the former, in relation to the conduct of Jesus, merely speak in general terms of an *expulsion* ἐκβάλλειν, John says that he made a *scourge of small cords* φραγέλλιον ἐκ σχοινίων, for this purpose: again, while according to the former, he treats all the sellers alike, he appears, according to John, to make some distinction, and to use the sellers of doves somewhat more mildly: moreover, John does not say that he drove out the buyers, as well as the sellers. There is also a dif- ference as to the language used by Jesus on the occasion; in the synoptical gospels, it is given in the form of an exact quotation from the Old Testament; in John, merely as a free allusion. But, above all, there is a difference as to the result: in the fourth gospel, Jesus is immediately called to account; in the synoptical gospels, we read nothing of this, and according to them, it is not until the following day that the Jewish authorities put to Jesus a question. which seems to have reference to the purification of the temple (Matt. xxi. 23 ff.), and to which Jesus replies quite otherwise than to the remonstrance in the fourth gospel. To explain the repetition of such a measure, it is remarked that the abuse was not likely to cease on the first expulsion, and that on every revival of it, Jesus would feel himself anew called on to interfere; that, moreover, the temple purification in John is indicated to be an earlier event than that in the synoptical gospels, by the circumstance, that the fourth evangelist represents Jesus as being immediately called to account, while his impunity in the other case appears a natural consequence of the heightened consideration which he had in the meantime won.

But allowing to these divergencies their full weight, the agree- ment between the two narratives preponderates. We have in both the same abuse, the same violent mode of checking it, by *casting out* (ἐκβάλλειν) the people, and *overthrowing* (ἀναστρέφειν) the tables: nay, virtually, the same language in justification of this procedure, for in John, as well as in the other gospels, the words of Jesus con- tain a reference, though not a verbally precise one, to Isai. lvi. 7: Jer. vii. 11. These important points of resemblance must at least extort such an admission as that of Sieffert,† namely, that the two occurrences, originally but little alike, were assimilated by tradition, the features of the one being transferred to the other. But thus much seems clear: the synoptists know as little of an earlier event of this kind, as in fact of an earlier visit of Jesus to Jerusalem: and the fourth evangelist seems to have passed over the purification of the temple after the last entrance of Jesus into the metropolis, not be- cause he presumed it to be already known from the other gospels,

* Paulus and Tholuck, in loc.; Neander, L. J. Chr., S. 388, Anm. · † Ueber der Ursprung, S. 108 ff.

but because he believed that he must give an early date to the sole act of the kind with which he was acquainted. If then each of the evangelists knew only of one purification of the temple, we are not warranted either by the slight divergencies in the description of the event, or by the important difference in its chronological position, to suppose that there were two; since chronological differences are by no means rare in the gospels, and are quite natural in writings of traditional origin. It is therefore with justice that our most modern interpreters have, after the example of some older ones, declared themselves in favour of the identity of the two histories.*

On which side lies the error? We may know beforehand how the criticism of the present day will decide on this question: namely, in favour of the fourth gospel. According to Lücke, the scourge, the diversified treatment of the different classes of traders, the more indirect allusion to the Old Testament passage, are so many indications that the writer was an eye and ear witness of the scene he describes; while as to chronology, it is well known that this is in no degree regarded by the synoptists, but only by John, whence, according to Sieffert,† to surrender the narrative of the latter to that of the former, would be to renounce the certain for the uncertain. As to John's dramatic details, we may match them by a particular peculiar to Mark, *And they would not suffer that any man should carry any vessel through the temple* (v. 16), which besides has a support in the Jewish custom which did not permit the court of the temple to be made a thoroughfare.‡ If, nevertheless, this particular is put to the account of Mark's otherwise ascertained predilection for arbitrary embellishment,§ what authorizes us to regard similar artistic touches from the fourth evangelist, as necessary proofs of his having been an eye witness? To appeal here to his character of eye witness as a recognized fact, ‖ is too glaring a *petitio principii*, at least in the point of view taken by a comparative criticism, in which the decision as to whether the artistic details of the fourth evangelist are mere embellishments, must depend solely on intrinsic probability. Although the different treatment of the different classes of men is in itself a probable feature, and the freer allusion to the Old Testament is at least an indifferent one; it is quite otherwise with the most striking feature in the narrative of John. Origen has set the example of objecting to the twisting and application of the scourge of small cords, as far too violent and disorderly a procedure.¶ Modern interpreters soften the picture by supposing that Jesus used the scourge merely against the cattle** (a supposition, however, opposed to the text, which represents *all* πάντας as being driven out by the scourge); yet still they cannot avoid perceiving the use of a scourge at all to be unseemly in a person of the dignity of Jesus, and only

* Lücke, 1, S. 435 ff.; De Wette, exeg. Handb. i. 1, S. 174 f.; i. 3, S. 40. † Ut sup. S. 109; Comp. Schneckenburger, S. 26 f. ‡ Lightfoot, S. 632, from Bab. Jevamoth, f. vi. 2. § Lücke, S. 438. ‖ Lücke, S. 437; Sieffert, S. 110. ¶ Comm. in Joh. tom. 10, § 17; Opp. 1, p. 322, ed. Lommatzsch. ** Kuinöl, in loc.

calculated to aggravate the already tumultuary character of the proceeding.* The feature peculiar to Mark is encumbered with no such difficulties, and while it is rejected, is this of John to be received? Certainly not, if we can only find an indication in what way the fourth evangelist might be led to the free invention of such a particular. Now it is evident from the quotation v. 17, which is peculiar to him, that he looked on the act of Jesus as a demonstration of holy zeal—a sufficient temptation to exaggerate the traits of zealousness in his conduct.

In relation to the chronological difference, we need only remember how the fourth evangelist antedates the acknowledgment of Jesus as the Messiah by the disciples, and the conferring of the name of Peter on Simon, to be freed from the common assumption of his pre-eminent chronological accuracy, which is alleged in favour of his position of the purification of the temple. For this particular case, however, it is impossible to show any reason why the occurrence in question would better suit the time of the first, than of the last passover visited by Jesus, whereas there are no slight grounds for the opposite opinion. It is true that nothing in relation to chronology is to be founded on the improbability that Jesus should so early have referred to his death and resurrection, as he must have done, according to John's interpretation of the saying about the destruction and rebuilding of the temple;† for we shall see, in the proper place, that this reference to the death and resurrection, owes its introduction into the declaration of Jesus to the evangelist alone. But it is no inconsiderable argument against John's position of the event, that Jesus, with his prudence and tact, would hardly have ventured thus early on so violent an exercise of his messianic authority.‡ For in that first period of his ministry he had not given himself out as the Messiah, and under any other than messianic authority, such a step could than scarcely have been hazarded; moreover, he in the beginning rather chose to meet his cotemporaries on friendly ground, and it is therefore hardly credible that he should at once, without trying milder means, have adopted an appearance so antagonistic. But to the last week of his life such a scene is perfectly suited. Then, after his messianic entrance into Jerusalem, it was his direct aim in all that he did and said, to assert his messiahship, in defiance of the contradiction of his enemies; then, all lay so entirely at stake, that nothing more was to be lost by such a step.

As regards the nature of the event, Origen long ago thought it incredible, that so great a multitude should have unresistingly submitted to a single man,—one, too, whose claims had ever been obsti-

nately contested : his only resource in this exigency is to appeal to
the superhuman power of Jesus, by virtue of which he was able suddenly to extinguish the wrath of his enemies, or to render it impo-
tent ; and hence Origen ranks this expulsion among the greatest
miracles of Jesus.* Modern expositors decline the miracle,† but
Paulus is the only one among them who has adequately weighed
Origen's remark, that in the ordinary course of things the multitude
would have opposed themselves to a single person. Whatever may
be said of the surprise caused by the suddenness of the appearance
of Jesus‡ (if, as John relates, he made himself a scourge of cords, he
would need some time for preparation), of the force of right on his
side§ (on the side of those whom he attacked, however, there was
established usage); or, finally, of the irresistible impression produced
by the personality of Jesus|| (on usurers and cattle-dealers—on brute-
men, as Paulus calls them ?) : still, such a multitude, certain as it
might be of the protection of the priesthood, would not have unresistingly allowed themselves to be driven out of the temple by a
single man. Hence Paulus is of opinion that a number of others,
equally scandalized by the sacrilegious traffic, made common cause
with Jesus, and that to their united strength the buyers and sellers
were compelled to yield.¶ But this supposition is fatal to the entire
incident, for it makes Jesus the cause of an open tumult ; and it is
not easy either to reconcile this conduct with his usual aversion to
every thing revolutionary, or to explain the omission of his enemies
to use it as an accusation against him. For that they held themselves bound in conscience to admit that the conduct of Jesus was
justifiable in this case, is the less credible, since, according to a rabbinical authority,** the Jews appear to have been so far from taking
umbrage at the market in the court of the Gentiles (and this is all
we are to understand by the word ἱερὸν),†† that the absence of it
seemed to them like a melancholy desolation of the temple. According to this, it is not surprising that Origen casts a doubt on the historical value of this narrative, by the expression, εἴγε καὶ αὐτὴ γεγέ-
νηται, (if it really happened), and at most admits that the evangelist, in order to present an idea allegorically, καὶ γεγενημένῳ συνέ-
χρήσατο πράγματι (also borrowed the form of an actual occurrence).‡‡

But in order to contest the reality of this history, in defiance of
the agreement of all the four evangelists, the negative grounds
hitherto adduced must be seconded by satisfactory positive ones,
from whence it might be seen how the primitive Christian legend
could be led to the invention of such a scene, apart from any historical foundation. But these appear to be wanting. For our only
positive data in relation to this occurrence are the passages cited by
the synoptists from Isaiah and Jeremiah, prohibiting that the temple

* Comm. in Joh. Tom. 10, 16, p. 321 f. ed. Lommatzsch.   † Lücke, in loc.   ‡ Lücke,
S. 413.   § Ib. and Tholuck, in loc. || Olshausen, 1, S. 785.   ¶ Comment. 4, S. 164.
** Hieros. Joh. tolth. f. lxi. 3, ap. Lightfoot, p. 411.   †† Lücke, Comment. 1, S. 410.
‡‡ Ut sup. comp. also Woolston, Disc. 1.

should be made a den of robbers; and the passage from Malachi, iii. 1—3, according to which it was expected that in the messianic times Jehovah would suddenly come to his temple, that no one would stand before his appearing, and that he would undertake a purification of the people and the worship. Certainly these passages seem to have some bearing on the irresistible reforming activity of Jesus in the temple, as described by our evangelists; but there is so little indication that they had reference in particular to the market in the outer court of the temple, that it seems necessary to suppose an actual opposition on the part of Jesus to this abuse, in order to account for the fulfilment of the above prophecies by him being represented under the form of an expulsion of buyers and sellers.

§ 89.   NARRATIVES OF THE ANOINTING OF JESUS BY A WOMAN.

AN occasion on which Jesus was anointed by a woman as he sat at meat, is mentioned by all the evangelists (Matt. xxvi. 6 ff.; Mark xiv. 3 ff.; Luke vii. 36 ff.; John xii. 1 ff.), but with some divergencies, the most important of which lie between Luke and the other three. First, as to the chronology; Luke places the incident in the earlier period of the life of Jesus, before his departure from Galilee, while the other three assign it to the last week of his life; secondly, as to the character of the woman who anoints Jesus: she is, according to Luke, a *woman who was a sinner*, γυνὴ ἁμαρτωλὸς; according to the two other synoptists, a person of unsullied reputation; according to John, who is more precise, Mary of Bethany. From the second point of difference it follows, that in Luke the objection of the spectators turns on the admission of so infamous a person, in the other gospels, on the wastefulness of the woman; from both, it follows, that Jesus in his defence dwells, in the former, on the grateful love of the woman, as contrasted with the haughty indifference of the Pharisees, in the latter, on his approaching departure, in opposition to the constant presence of the poor. There are yet the minor differences, that the place in which the entertainment and the anointing occur, is by the two first and the fourth evangelists called Bethany (which according to John xi. 1, was a κώμη *town*), by Luke a πόλις (*city*), without any more precise designation; further, that the objection, according to the three former, proceeds from the disciples, according to Luke, from the entertainer. Hence the majority of commentators distinguish two anointings, of which one is narrated by Luke, the other by the three remaining evangelists.*

But it must be asked, if the reconciliation of Luke with the other three evangelists is despaired of, whether the agreement of the latter amongst themselves is so decided, and whether we must not rather proceed, from the distinction of two anointings, to the distinction of

three, or even four ? To four certainly it will scarcely extend ; for
Mark does not depart from Matthew, except in a few touches of his
well-known dramatic manner; but between these two evangelists on
the one side, and John on the other, there are differences which may
fairly be compared with those between Luke and the rest. The first·
difference relates to the house in which the entertainment is said to
have been given ; according to the two first evangelists, it was the
house of Simon the leper, a person elsewhere unnoticed ; the fourth
does not, it is true, expressly name the host, but since he mentions
Martha as the person who waited on the guests, and her brother
Lazarus as one of those who sat at meat, there is no doubt that he
intended to indicate the house of the latter as the locality of the repast.* Neither is the time of the occurrence precisely the same, for
according to Matthew and Mark the scene takes place after the
solemn entrance of Jesus into Jerusalem, only two days at the utmost before the passover; according to John, on the other hand,
before the entrance, as early as six days prior to the passover.†
Further, the individual whom John states to be that Mary of Bethany so intimately united to Jesus, is only known to the two first
evangelists a *a woman*, γυνή;† neither do they represent her as being.
like Mary, in the house, and one of the host's family, but as coming,
one knows not whence, to Jesus, while he reclined at table. Moreover the act of anointing is in the fourth gospel another than in the
two first. In the latter, the woman pours her ointment of spikenard
on the head of Jesus; in John, on the contrary, she anoints his feet,
and dries them with her hair,‡ a difference which gives the whole
scene a new character. Lastly, the two synoptists are not aware
that it was Judas who gave utterance to the censure against the
woman ; Matthew attributing it to the disciples, Mark, to the spectators generally.§
    Thus between the narrative of John, and that of Matthew and
Mark, there is scarcely less difference than between the account of
these three collectively, and that of Luke: whoever supposes two distinct occurrences in the one case, must, to be consistent, do so in the
other ; and thus, with Origen hold, at least conditionally, that there
were three separate anointings. So soon, however, as this consequence is more closely examined, it must create a difficulty, for how
improbable is it that Jesus should have been expensively anointed
three times, each time at a feast, each time by a woman, that woman
being always a different one; that moreover Jesus should, in each
instance, have had to defend the act of the woman against the censures of the spectators!¶ Above all, how is it to be conceived that
after Jesus, on one and even on two earlier occasions, had so de-

* This difference struck Origen, who has given a critical comparison of these four
narratives, to which, in point of acumen, there is no parallel in more modern commenta-
ries. See his *in Matth. Commentarior. series*, Opp. ed. de la Rue, 3, S. 892 ff.
† Origenes, ut sup.
‡ Ib. § Ib. ‖ Ib.
¶ Comp. Schleiermacher, über den Lukas, S. 111.

cidedly given his sanction to the honour rendered to him, the disciples, or one of them, should have persisted in censuring it ?*

These considerations oblige us to think of reductions, and it is the most natural to commence with the narratives of the two first synoptists and of John, for these agree not only in the place, Bethany, but also, generally, in the time of the event, the last week of the life of Jesus: above all, the censure and the reply are nearly the same on both sides. In connexion with these similarities the differences lose their importance, partly from the improbability that an incident of this kind should be repeated ; partly from the probability, that in the traditional propagation of the anecdote such divergencies should have insinuated themselves. But if in this case the identity of the occurrences be admitted, in consideration of the similarities, and in spite of the dissimilarities; then, on the other hand, the divergencies peculiar to the narrative of Luke, can no longer hinder us from pronouncing it to be identical with that of the three other evangelists, provided that there appear to be only a few important points of resemblance between the two. And such really exist, for Luke now strikingly accords with Matthew and Mark, in opposition to John; now, with the latter, in opposition to the former. Luke gives the entertainer the same name as the two first synoptists, namely, Simon, the only difference being, that the former calls him *a pharisee*, while the latter style him *the leper*. Again, Luke agrees with the other synoptists in opposition to John, in representing the woman who anoints Jesus as a nameless individual, not belonging to the house; and further, in making her appear with a *box of ointment*, ἀλάβαστρον μύρον, while John speaks only of a *pound of ointment*, λίτρα μυρον, without specifying the vessel. On the other hand, Luke coincides in a remarkable manner with John, and differs from the two other evangelists, as to the mode of the anointing. While, namely, according to the latter, the ointment is poured on the head of Jesus, according to Luke, the woman, *who was a sinner*, as, according to John, Mary, anoints the feet of Jesus; and even the striking particular, that she dried them with her hair,† is given by both in nearly the same words: excepting that in Luke, where the woman is described as a sinner, it is added that she bathed the feet of Jesus with her tears, and kissed them. Thus, without doubt, we have here but one history under three various forms; and this seems to have been the real conclusion of Origen, as well as recently of Schleiermacher.

In this state of the case, the effort is to escape as cheaply as possible, and to save the divergencies of the several evangelists at least from the appearance of contradiction. First, with regard to the differences between the two first evangelists and the last, it has been attempted to reconcile the discrepant dates by the supposition,

* Origenes and Schleiermacher. Winer, N. T. Gramm S. 119.
† Luke vii. 38 : ταις ποδας αιτου—ταις John xii. 3 : ἐξ μιξε ταις θριξὶν αὐτῆς τοῖς θριξι τας κεφ. ἤ εμαξε της ίτ μασε. ποδας αιτου.

that the meal at Bethany was held really, as John informs us, six
days before Easter; but that Matthew, after whom Mark wrote, has
no contradictory date; that rather he has no date at all; for though
he inserts the narrative of the meal and the anointing after the declaration of Jesus, *that after two days is the feast of the Passover*,
ὅτι μετὰ δύο ἡμέρας τὸ πάσχα γίνεται, this does not prove that he intended to place it later as to time, for it is probable that he gave it
this position simply because he wished to note here, before coming
to the betrayal by Judas, the occasion on which the traitor first embraced his black resolve, namely, the repast at which he was incensed
by Mary's prodigality, and embittered by the rebuke of Jesus.*
But in opposition to this, modern criticism has shown that, on the
one hand, in the mild and altogether general reply of Jesus there
could lie nothing personally offensive to Judas; and that, on the
other hand, the two first gospels do not name Judas as the party
who censured the anointing, but the disciples or the bystanders
generally: whereas, if they had noted this scene purely because it was
the motive for the treachery of Judas, they must have especially pointed out the manifestation of his feeling.† There remains, consequently,
a chronological contradiction in this instance between the two first
synoptists and John: a contradiction which even Olshausen admits.‡

It has been attempted in a variety of ways to evade the farther difference as to the person of the host. As Matthew and Mark speak only
of the *house of Simon the leper*, οἰκία Σίμωνος τοῦ λεπροῦ some have
distinguished the owner of the house, Simon, from the giver of the
entertainment, who doubtless was Lazarus, and have supposed that
hence, in both cases without error, the fourth evangelist mentions
the latter, the two first synoptists the former.§ But who would
distinguish an entertainment by the name of the householder, if he
were not in any way the giver of the entertainment? Again, since
John does not expressly call Lazarus the host, but merely one of
the συνανακειμένων (*those sitting at the table*), and since the inference
that he was the host is drawn solely from the circumstance that his
sister Martha *served* διηκόνει; others have regarded Simon as the
husband of Martha, either separated on account of his leprosy, or
already deceased, and have supposed that Lazarus then resided with
his widowed sister:‖ an hypothesis which it is more easy to reconcile with the narratives than the former, but which is unsupported
by any certain information.

We come next to the divergency relative to the mode of anointing; according to the two first evangelists, the ointment was poured
on the head of Jesus; according to the fourth, on his feet. The old,
trivial mode of harmonizing the two statements, by supposing that
both the head and the feet were anointed, has recently been expanded
into the conjecture that Mary indeed intended only to anoint the feet

---

* Kuinöl, Comm. in Matth. p. 687.   † Sieffert, über den Urspr. S. 125 f.   ‡ Bibl.
Comm. 2, S. 277.   § Vid. Kuinöl, ut sup. p. 688; also Tholuck, S. 228.   ‖ Paulus,
exeg. Handb. 2, S. 582; 3, b. S. 466.

of Jesus (John), but that as she accidentally broke the vessel (συν-τρίψασα, Mark), the ointment flowed over his head also (Matt.).*
This attempt at reconciliation falls into the comic, for as we cannot imagine how a woman who was preparing to anoint the feet of Jesus could bring the vessel of ointment over his head, we must suppose that the ointment spirted upwards like an effervescing draught. So that here also the contradiction remains, and not only between Matthew and John, where it is admitted even by Schneckenburger, but also between the latter evangelist and Mark.

The two divergencies relative to the person of the woman who anoints Jesus, and to the party who blames her, were thought to be the most readily explained. That what John ascribes to Judas singly, Matthew and Mark refer to all the disciples or spectators, was believed to be simply accounted for by the supposition that while the rest manifested their disapprobation by gestures only, Judas vented his in words.† We grant that the word ἔλεγον, (*they said*) preceded as it is in Mark, by the words ἀγανακτοῦντες πρὸς ἑαυτοὺς (*having indignation within themselves*), and followed, as in Matthew, by the words γνοὺς δὲ ὁ Ἰησοῦς (*but Jesus knowing*) does not necessarily imply that all the disciples gave audible expression to their feelings; as, however, the two first evangelists immediately after this meal narrate the betrayal by Judas, they would certainly have named the traitor on the above occasion, had he, to their knowledge, made himself conspicuous in connexion with the covetous blame which the woman's liberality drew forth. That John particularizes the woman, whose name is not given by the synoptists, as Mary of Bethany, is, in the ordinary view, only an example how the fourth evangelist supplies the omissions of his predecessors.‡ But as the two first synoptists attach so much importance to the deed of the woman, that they make Jesus predict the perpetuation of her memory on account of it—a particular which John has not—they would assuredly have also given her name had they known it : so that in any case we may conclude thus much ; they knew not who the woman was, still less did they conceive her to be Mary of Bethany.

Thus if the identity only of the last evangelist's narrative with that of the two first be acknowledged, it must be confessed that we have, on the one side or the other, an account which is inaccurate,

* Schneckenburger, über den Ursprung, u. s. f. S. 60. There is no trace in Mark's account that the words συντρίψασα τὸ ἀλάβαστρον signify an accidental fracture ; nor, on the other hand can they, without the harshest ellipsis, be understood to imply merely the removal of that which stopped the opening of the vessel, as Paulus and Fritzsche maintain. Interpreted without violence, they can only mean a breaking of the vessel itself. It is asked with Paulus (ex. Handb. 3. B. S. 471): To what purpose destroy a costly vessel ? or with Fritzsche (in Marc. p. 602): To what purpose risk wounding her own hand, and possibly the head of Jesus also ? These are questions which have a bearing on the matter considered as the act of the woman, but not as a narrative of Mark ; for that to him, the destruction of a precious vessel should appear suited to the noble prodigality of the woman, is in perfect accordance with the exaggerating style which we have often observed in him.   † Kuinöl, in Matth. p. 689.   ‡ Paulus, exeg. Handb. 3. B. S. 166, and many others.

and disfigured by tradition. It is, however, not only between these, but also between Luke and his fellow evangelists collectively, that they who suppose only one incident to be the foundation of their narratives, seek to remove as far as possible the appearance of contradiction. Schleiermacher, whose highest authority is John, but who will on no account renounce Luke, comes in this instance, when the two so widely diverge, into a peculiar dilemma, from which he must have thought that he could extricate himself with singular dexterity, since he has not evaded it, as he does others of a similar kind, by the supposition of two fundamental occurrences. It is true that he finds himself constrained to concede, in favour of John, that Luke's informant could not in this case have been an eye witness; whence minor divergencies, as for instance those relative to the locality, are to be explained. On the other hand, the apparently important differences that, according to Luke, the woman is a sinner, according to John, Mary of Bethany; that according to the former, the host, according to the latter, the disciples, make objections; and that the reply of Jesus is in the respective narrations totally different—these, in Schleiermacher's opinion, have their foundation in the fact that the occurrence may be regarded from two points of view. The one aspect of the occurrence is the murmuring of the disciples, and this is given by Matthew; the other, namely, the relations of Jesus with the pharisaic host, is exhibited by Luke; and John confirms both representations. The most decided impediment to the reconciliation of Luke with the other evangelists, his designation of the woman as *a sinner*, ἁμαρτωλός, Schleiermacher invalidates, by calling it a false inference of the narrator from the address of Jesus to Mary, *Thy sins are forgiven thee*, ἀφέωνταί σοι αἱ ἁμαρτίαι. This Jesus might say to Mary in allusion to some error, unknown to us, but such as the purest are liable to, without compromising her reputation with the spectators, who were well acquainted with her character; and it was only the narrator who erroneously concluded from the above words of Jesus, and from his further discourse, that the woman concerned was a sinner in the ordinary sense of the word, whence he has incorrectly amplified the thoughts of the host, v. 39.[*] It is not, however, simply of *sins*, ἁμαρτίαι, but of *many sins*, πολλαὶ ἁμαρτίαι, that Jesus speaks in relation to the woman; and if this also be an addition of the narrator, to be rejected as such because it is inconsistent with the character of Mary of Bethany, then has the entire speech of Jesus from v. 40—48, which turns on the opposition between forgiving and loving little and much, been falsified or misrepresented by the evangelist: and on the side of Luke especially, it is in vain to attempt to harmonize the discordant narratives.

If, then, the four narratives can be reconciled only by the supposition that several of them have undergone important traditional modifications: the question is, which of them is the nearest to the

---

[*] Ueber den Lukas, S. 111 ff.

original fact? That modern critics should unanimously decide in favour of John, cannot surprise us after our previous observations: and as little can the nature of the reasoning by which their judgment is supported. The narrative of John, say they, (reasoning in a circle,) being that of an eye witness, must be at once supposed the true one,[*] and this conclusion is sometimes rested for greater security on the false premiss, that the more circumstantial and dramatic narrator is the more accurate reporter—the eye witness.[†] The breaking of the box of ointment, in Mark, although a dramatic particular, is readily rejected as a mere embellishment; but does not John's statement of the quantity of spikenard as a pound, border on exaggeration? and ought not the extravagance which Olshausen, in relation to this disproportionate consumption of ointment, attributes to Mary's love, to be rather referred to the evangelist's imagination, which would then also have the entire credit of the circumstance, that *the house was filled with the odour of the ointment?* It is worthy of notice, that the estimate of the value of the perfume at 300 denarii, is given by John and Mark alone; as also at the miraculous feeding of the multitude, it is these two evangelists who rate the necessary food at 200 denarii. If Mark only had this close estimate, how quickly would it be pronounced, at least by Schleiermacher, a gratuitous addition of the narrator! What then is it that, in the actual state of the case, prevents the utterance of this opinion, even as a conjecture, but the prejudice in favour of the fourth gospel? Even the anointing of the head, which is attested by two of the synoptists, is, because John mentions the feet instead of the head, rejected as unusual, and incompatible with the position of Jesus at a meal:[‡] whereas the anointing of the feet with precious oil was far less usual; and this the most recent commentator on the fourth gospel admits.[§]

But peculiar gratitude is rendered to the eye witness John, because he has rescued from oblivion the names, both of the anointing woman, and of the censorious disciple.[‖] It has been supposed that the synoptists did in fact know the name of the woman, but withheld it from the apprehension that danger might possibly accrue to the family of Lazarus, while John, writing later, was under no such restraint:[¶] but this expedient rests on mere assumptions. Our former conclusion therefore subsists, namely, that the earlier evangelists knew nothing of the name of the woman; and the question arises, how was this possible? Jesus having expressly promised immortal renown to the deed of the woman, the tendency must arise to perpetuate her name also, and if this were identical with the known and oft repeated name of Mary of Bethany, it is not easy to understand how the association of the deed and the name could be lost in

---

* Sieffert, ut sup. S. 123 f.   † Schulz, ut sup. S. 320 f.   ‡ Schneckenburger, ut sup. S. 60.
§ Lücke, 2, S. 117; comp. Lightfoot, horæ, p. 168, 1081.
‖ Schulz, ut sup.
¶ Thus Grotius and Herder.

tradition, and the woman who anointed Jesus become nameless. It is perhaps still more incomprehensible, supposing the covetous blame cast upon the woman to have been really uttered by him who proved the betrayer, that this should be forgotten in tradition, and the expression of blame attributed to the disciples generally. When a fact is narrated of a person otherwise unknown, or even when the person being known, the fact does not obviously accord with his general character, it is natural that the name should be lost in tradition; but when the narrated word or work of a person agrees so entirely with his known character, as does the covetous and hypocritical blame in question with the character of the traitor, it is difficult to suppose that the legend would sever it from his name. Moreover, the history in which this blame occurs, verges so nearly on the moment of the betrayal, (especially according to the position given to it by the two first evangelists,) that had the blame really proceeded from Judas, the two facts would have been almost inevitably associated. Nay, even if that expression of latent cupidity had not really belonged to Judas, there must have been a temptation eventually to ascribe it to him, as a help to the delineation of his character, and to the explanation of his subsequent treachery. Thus the case is reversed, and the question is whether, instead of praising John that he has preserved to us this precise information, we ought not rather to give our approbation to the synoptists, that they have abstained from so natural but unhistorical a combination. We can arrive at no other conclusion with respect to the designation of the woman who anoints Jesus as Mary of Bethany. On the one hand, it is inconceivable that the deed, if originally hers, should be separated from her celebrated name; on the other, the legend, in the course of its development, might naturally come to attribute to one whose spiritual relations with Jesus had, according to the third and fourth gospels, early obtained great celebrity in the primitive church, an act of devoted love towards him, which originally belonged to another and less known person.

But from another side also we find ourselves induced to regard the narratives of Matthew and Mark, who give no name to the woman, rather than that of John, who distinguishes her as Mary of Bethany, as the parent stem of the group of anecdotes before us. Our position of the identity of all the four narratives must, to be tenable, enable us also to explain how Luke's representation of the facts could arise. Now, supposing the narrative of John to be the nearest to the truth, it is not a little surprising that in the legend, the anointing woman should doubly descend from the highly honoured Mary, sister of Lazarus, to an unknown, nameless individual, and thence even to a notorious sinner: it appears far more natural to give the intermediate position to the indifferent statement of the synoptists, out of whose equivocal nameless woman might equally be made, either in an ascending scale, a Mary; or, in a descending one, a sinner.

The possibility of the first transformation has been already shown: it must next be asked, where could be an inducement, without historical grounds, gradually to invest the anointing woman with the character of a sinner? In the narrative itself our only clue is a feature which the two first synoptists have not, but which John has in common with Luke; namely that the woman anointed the feet of Jesus. To the fourth evangelist, this tribute of feeling appeared in accordance with the sensitive, devoted nature of Mary, whom he elsewhere also (xi. 32), represents as falling at the feet of Jesus; but by another it might be taken, as by Luke, for the gesture of contrition; an idea which might favour the conception of the woman as a sinner.—Might *favour*, we say, not *cause:* for a cause, we must search elsewhere.

§ 90. THE NARRATIVES OF THE WOMAN TAKEN IN ADULTERY, AND OF MARY AND MARTHA.

In the Gospel of John (viii. 1—11), the Pharisees and scribes bring a woman taken in adultery to Jesus, that they may obtain his opinion as to the procedure to be observed against her: whereupon Jesus, by appealing to the consciences of the accusers, liberates the woman, and dismisses her with an admonition. The genuineness of this passage has been strongly contested, nay, its spuriousness might be regarded as demonstrated, were is not that even the most thorough investigations of the subject* indirectly betray a design, which Paulus openly avows, of warding off the dangerous surmises as to the origin of the fourth gospel, which are occasioned by the supposition that this passage, encumbered as it is with improbabilities, is a genuine portion of that gospel. For in the first place, the scribes say to Jesus: *Moses in the law commanded us that such should be stoned:* now in no part of the Pentateuch is this punishment prescribed for adultery, but simply death, the mode of inflicting it being left undetermined (Lev. xx. 10: Deut. xxii. 22); nor was stoning for adultery a later intsitution of the Talmud, for according to the canon: *omne mortis supplicium, in scriptura absolute positum, esse strangulationem.†* the punishment appointed for this offence in the Talmud is strangulation.‡ Further, it is difficult to discover what there was to ensnare Jesus in the question proposed to him:§ the scribes quoted to him the commandment of the law, as if they would warn him, rather than tempt him, for they could not expect that he would decide otherwise than agreeably to the law. Again, the decision of Jesus is open to the stricture, that if only he who is conscious of perfect purity were authorized to judge and punish, all social order would be at an end. The circumstance of Jesus writing on the ground has a legendary and mystical air, for even if it be

<hr/>

* Ap. Wetstein, Paulus, Lücke, in loc. † Maimonides on Sanhedr. 7, 1.
‡ Mischna, tr. c. 10. § For a thorough discussion of this and the following points, vid. Paulus and Lücke, in loc.

not correctly explained by the gloss of Jerome: *eorum videlicet, qui accusabant, et omnium mortalium peccata,* it yet seems to imply something more mysterious than a mere manifestation of contempt for the accusers. Lastly, it is scarcely conceivable that every one of those men who dragged the woman before Jesus, zealous for the law, and adverse to his cause as they are supposed to be, should have had so tender a conscience, as on the appeal of Jesus to retire without prosecuting their design, and leave the woman behind them uninjured; this rather appears to belong merely to the legendary or poetical embellishment of the scene. Yet however improbable it may appear, from these observations, that the occurrence happened precisely as it is here narrated, this, as Bretschneider justly maintains,[*] proves nothing against the genuineness of the passage, since it is arguing in a circle to assume the apostolic composition of the fourth gospel, and the consequent impossibility that a narrative containing contradictions should form a portion of it, prior to an examination of its several parts. Nevertheless, on the other hand, the absence of the passage in the oldest authorities is so suspicious, that a decision on the subject cannot be hazarded.

In any case, the narrative of an interview between Jesus and a woman of the above character must be very ancient, since, according to Eusebius, it was found in the gospel of the Hebrews, and in the writings of Papias.[†] It was long thought that the woman mentioned in the Hebrew gospel and by Papias was identical with the adulteress in John; but against this it has been justly observed, that one who had the reproach of *many* sins, must be distinct from her who was detected in the *one* act of adultery.[‡] I wonder, however, that no one has, to my knowledge, thought, in connexion with the passage of Eusebius, of the woman in Luke of whom Jesus says that her *many sins, ἁμαρτίαι πολλαί,* are forgiven. It is true that the word διαβληθείσης does not fully agree with this idea, for Luke does not speak of actual expressions of the Pharisee in disparagement of the woman, but merely of the unfavourable thoughts which he had concerning her; and in this respect the passage in Eusebius would agree better with the narrative of John, which has an express denunciation, a διαβάλλειν.

Thus we are led on external grounds, by the doubt whether an ancient notice refer to the one or the other of the two narratives, to a perception of their affinity,[§] which is besides evident from internal reasons. In both we have a woman, a sinner, before Jesus; in both, this woman is regarded with an evil eye by Pharisaic sanctimoniousness, but is taken into protection by Jesus, and dismissed with a friendly πορεύου, *go.* These were precisely the features, the origin of which we could not understand in the narrative of Luke, viewed

---

* Probab. p. 72 ff.

† Euseb. H. E. iii. 39 : ἐκτέθειται δὲ (ὁ Παπίας) καὶ ἄλλην ἱστορίαν περὶ γυναικὸς ἐπὶ πολλαῖς ἁμαρτίαις διαβληθείσης ἐπὶ τοῦ Κυρίου, ἣν τὸ καθ᾽ Ἑβραίους εὐαγγέλιον περιέχει.

‡ Lücke, 2, S. 217. Paulus, Comm. 4, S. 410.　§ Elsewhere also the two were confounded, vid. Fabricii Cod. apocryph. N. T. 1, S. 357, not.

as a mere variation of the history of the anointing given by the other evangelists. Now, what is more natural than to suppose that they were transferred into Luke's history of the anointing, from that of the forgiven sinner? If the Christian legend possessed, on the one side, a woman who had anointed Jesus, who was on this account reproached, but was defended by Jesus: and on the other side, a woman who was accused before him of many sins, but whom he pardoned; how easily, aided by the idea of an anointing of the feet of Jesus, which bears the interpretation of an act of penitence, might the two histories flow together—the anointing woman become also a sinner, and the sinner also an anointer? Then, that the scene of the pardon was an entertainment, was a feature also drawn from the history of the anointing: the entertainer must be a Pharisee, because the accusation of the woman ought to proceed from a Pharisaic party, and because, as we have seen, Luke has a predilection for Pharisaic entertainments. Lastly, the discourse of Jesus may have been borrowed, partly from the original narrative of the woman who was a sinner, partly from analogous occasions. If these conjectures be correct, the narratives are preserved unmixed, on the one hand, by the two first evangelists; on the other, by the fourth, or whoever was the author of the passage on the adulteress; for if the latter contains much that is legendary, it is at least free from any admixture of the history of the anointing.

Having thus accounted for one modification of the narrative concerning the anointing woman, namely, her degradation into a sinner, by the influence of another and somewhat similar anecdote, which was current in the first age of Christianity, we may proceed to consider experimentally, whether a like external influence may not have helped to produce the opposite modification of the unknown into Mary of Bethany: a modification which, for the rest, we have already seen to be easy of explanation. Such an influence could only proceed from the sole notice of Mary (with the exception of her appearance at the resurrection of Lazarus) which has been preserved to us, and which is rendered memorable by the declaration of Jesus, *One thing is needful, and Mary hath chosen*, &c. (Luke x. 38 ff.). We have, in fact, here as well as there, Martha occupied in serving (John xii. 2, καὶ ἡ Μάρθα διηκόνει; Luke x. 40, ἡ δὲ Μάρθα περιεσπᾶτο περὶ πολλὴν διακονίαν); here, Mary sitting at the feet of Jesus, there, anointing his feet; here, blamed by her sister, there by Judas, for her useless conduct, and in both cases, defended by Jesus. It is surely unavoidable to say: if once the narrative of the anointing of Jesus by a woman were current together with that of Mary and Martha, it was very natural, from the numerous points of resemblance between them, that they should be blended in the legend, or by some individual, into one story; that the unknown woman who anointed the feet of Jesus, who was blamed by the spectators, and vindicated by Jesus, should be changed into Mary, whom tradition had depicted in a similar situation; the task

of serving at the meal with which the anointing was connected
attributed to Mary's sister, Martha; and finally, her brother Lazarus
made a partaker of the meal:—so that here the narrative of Luke
on the one side, and that of the two synoptists on the other, appear
to be pure anecdotes, that of John a mixed one.

Further, in Luke's narrative of the visit of Jesus to the two
sisters, there is no mention of Lazarus, with whom, however,
according to John (xi. and xii.), Mary and Martha appear to have
dwelt; nay, Luke speaks precisely as if the presence or existence
of this brother, whom indeed neither he nor either of the other synoptists anywhere notices, were entirely unknown to him. For had
he known anything of Lazarus, or had he thought of him as present,
he could not have said: *A certain woman, named Martha, received him into her house;* he must at least have named her brother
also, especially as, according to John, the latter was an intimate
friend of Jesus. This silence is remarkable, and commentators
have not succeeded in finding a better explanation of it than that
given in the natural history of the prophet of Nazareth, where the
shortly subsequent death of Lazarus is made available for the supposition that he was, about the time of that visit of Jesus, on a
journey for the benefit of his health.[*] Not less striking is another
point relative to the locality of this scene. According to John,
Mary and Martha dwelt in Bethany, a small town in the immediate
vicinity of Jerusalem; whereas Luke, when speaking of the visit
of Jesus to these sisters, only mentions a *certain town,* κώμην τινὰ,
which is thought, however, to be easily reconciled with the statement
of John, by the observation, that Luke assigns the visit to the
journey of Jesus to Jerusalem, and to one travelling thither out of
Galilee, Bethany would lie in the way. But it would lie quite at
the end of this way, so that the visit of Jesus must fall at the close
of his journey, whereas Luke places it soon after the departure out
of Galilee, and separates it from the entrance into Jerusalem by a
multitude of incidents filling eight entire chapters. Thus much
then is clear: the author or editor of the third Gospel was ignorant
that that visit was paid in Bethany, or that Mary and Martha dwelt
there, and it is only that evangelist who represents Mary as the
anointing woman, who also names Bethany as the home of Mary:
the same place where, according to the two first synoptists, the
anointing occurred. If Mary were once made identical with the
anointing woman, and if the anointing were known to have happened
in Bethany, it would naturally follow that this town would be represented as Mary's home. Hence it is probable that the anointing
woman owes her name to the current narrative of the visit of Jesus
to Martha and Mary, and that Mary owes her home to the narrative
of the meal at Bethany.

We should thus have a group of five histories, among which
the narrative given by the two first synoptists of the anointing of

Jesus by a woman, would form the centre, that in John of the adulteress, and that in Luke of Mary and Martha, the extremes, while the anointing by the sinner in Luke, and that by Mary in John, would fill the intermediate places.   It is true that all the five narratives might with some plausibility be regarded as varied editions of one historical incident; but from the essential dissimilarity between the three to which I have assigned the middle and extreme places, I am rather of opinion that these are each founded on a special incident, but that the two intermediate narratives are secondary formations which owe their existence to the intermixture of the primary ones by tradition.